READINGS IN
AMERICAN
POLITICS

Fifth Edition

READINGS IN AMERICAN POLITICS

Analysis and Perspectives

Fifth Edition

Ken Kollman

UNIVERSITY OF MICHIGAN

W. W. Norton & Company ■ **New York** ■ **London**

W. W. Norton & Company has been independent since its founding in 1923, when William Warder Norton and Mary D. Herter Norton first published lectures delivered at the People's Institute, the adult education division of New York City's Cooper Union. The firm soon expanded its program beyond the Institute, publishing books by celebrated academics from America and abroad. By mid-century, the two major pillars of Norton's publishing program—trade books and college texts—were firmly established. In the 1950s, the Norton family transferred control of the company to its employees, and today—with a staff of four hundred and a comparable number of trade, college, and professional titles published each year—W. W. Norton & Company stands as the largest and oldest publishing house owned wholly by its employees.

Editor: Peter Lesser
Assistant Editor: Anna Olcott
Project Editor: Laura Dragonette
Production Supervisor: Stephen Sajdak
Permissions Manager: Bethany Salminen
Composition by Westchester Publishing Services
Manufacturing by LSC Communications, Crawfordsville

Library of Congress Cataloging-in-Publication Data

Names: Kollman, Ken, 1966- editor.
Title: Readings in American politics : analysis and perspectives / [edited by]
    Ken Kollman.
Description: Fifth edition. | New York : W.W. Norton & Company, [2019] |
    Includes bibliographical references.
Identifiers: LCCN 2019004284 | ISBN 9780393679168 (pbk.)
Subjects: LCSH: United States—Politics and government.
Classification: LCC JK21 .R387 2019 | DDC 320.473—dc23 LC record available at
https://lccn.loc.gov/2019004284

W. W. Norton & Company, Inc., 500 Fifth Avenue, New York, N.Y. 10110-0017

wwnorton.com

W. W. Norton & Company Ltd., 15 Carlisle Street, London W1D 3BS

1 2 3 4 5 6 7 8 9 0

To my amazing staff at CPS,
Lori and Dave especially.

CONTENTS

Preface   xiii
About the Editor   xix

1 FUNDAMENTALS

1.1   MANCUR OLSON JR., from *The Logic of Collective Action: Public Goods and the Theory of Groups*   1

1.2   GARRETT HARDIN, "The Tragedy of the Commons," *Science*   20

1.3   JANE MANSBRIDGE, "What Is Political Science For?" *Perspectives on Politics*   34

1.4   ROBERT A. DAHL, from *Polyarchy: Participation and Opposition*   45

1.5   HANNA FENICHEL PITKIN, from *The Concept of Representation*   51

2 THE CONSTITUTION AND THE FOUNDING

2.1   BRUTUS, *The Antifederalist*, No. 1   57

2.2   ROBERT A. DAHL, from *How Democratic Is the American Constitution?*   66

2.3   MILA VERSTEEG and EMILY ZACKIN, "Constitutions Un-entrenched: Toward an Alternative Theory of Constitutional Design," *American Political Science Review*   71

3 FEDERALISM

3.1   CHRISTOPHER HAMMONS, from "State Constitutions, Religious Protection, and Federalism," *University of St. Thomas Journal of Law and Public Policy*   85

3.2 WILLIAM H. RIKER, from *Federalism: Origin, Operation, Significance* 92

3.3 PAMELA J. CLOUSER McCANN, CHARLES R. SHIPAN, and CRAIG VOLDEN, from "Top-Down Federalism: State Policy Responses to National Government Discussions," *The Journal of Federalism* 106

4 CIVIL RIGHTS AND CIVIL LIBERTIES

4.1 MICHAEL TESLER, from *Post-Racial or Most-Racial? Race and Politics in the Obama Era* 113

4.2 *Brown v. Board of Education* (1954) 129

4.3 *District of Columbia v. Heller* (2008) 134

4.4 ANDREW R. LEWIS, from *The Rights Turn in Conservative Christian Politics: How Abortion Transformed the Culture Wars* 149

5 CONGRESS

5.1 DAVID R. MAYHEW, from *Congress: The Electoral Connection* 159

5.2 RICHARD F. FENNO JR., from *Home Style: House Members in Their Districts* 172

5.3 GARY W. COX and MATHEW D. McCUBBINS, from *Setting the Agenda: Responsible Party Government in the U.S. House of Representatives* 177

5.4 WILLIAM BERNHARD and TRACY SULKIN, from *Legislative Style* 197

5.5 FRANCES E. LEE, from *Insecure Majorities: Congress and the Perpetual Campaign* 206

6 THE PRESIDENCY

6.1 RICHARD E. NEUSTADT, from *Presidential Power and the Modern Presidents: The Politics of Leadership from Roosevelt to Reagan* 213

6.2 CHARLES M. CAMERON, from *Veto Bargaining: Presidents and the Politics of Negative Power* 222

6.3 BRANDICE CANES-WRONE, from *Who Leads Whom? Presidents, Policy, and the Public* 228

6.4 WILLIAM G. HOWELL, from *Power without Persuasion: The Politics of Direct Presidential Action* 249

6.5 COREY ROBIN, from *The Reactionary Mind: Conservatism from Edmund Burke to Donald Trump* 263

7 THE BUREAUCRACY

7.1 JAMES Q. WILSON, from *Bureaucracy: What Government Agencies Do and Why They Do It* 273

7.2 MATHEW D. McCUBBINS and THOMAS SCHWARTZ, "Congressional Oversight Overlooked: Police Patrols versus Fire Alarms," *American Journal of Political Science* 287

7.3 SUSAN L. MOFFITT, from *Making Public Policy: Participatory Bureaucracy in American Democracy* 302

8 THE JUDICIARY

8.1 GERALD N. ROSENBERG, from *The Hollow Hope: Can Courts Bring about Social Change?* 323

8.2 *Marbury v. Madison* (1803) 330

8.3 *Lawrence v. Texas* (2003) 339

8.4 *National Federation of Independent Business v. Sebelius* (2012) 350

8.5 TRACEY E. GEORGE and LEE EPSTEIN, "On the Nature of Supreme Court Decision Making," *American Political Science Review* 380

9 PUBLIC OPINION

9.1 ARTHUR LUPIA and MATHEW D. McCUBBINS, from *The Democratic Dilemma: Can Citizens Learn What They Need to Know?* 387

9.2 JOHN R. ZALLER, from *The Nature and Origins of Mass Opinion* 400

9.3 DONALD R. KINDER and CINDY D. KAM, from *Us Against Them: Ethnocentric Foundations of American Opinion* 405

9.4 KATHERINE J. CRAMER, from *The Politics of Resentment: Rural Consciousness in Wisconsin and the Rise of Scott Walker* 412

9.5 JAMES CAMPBELL, from *Polarized: Making Sense of a Divided America* 439

9.6 LILLIANA MASON, from *Uncivil Agreement: How Politics Became Our Identity* 451

10 PARTICIPATION

10.1 JANELLE WONG, S. KARTHICK RAMAKRISHNAN, TAEKU LEE, and JANE JUNN, from *Asian American Political Participation: Emerging Constituents and Their Political Identities* 465

10.2 JAN E. LEIGHLEY and JONATHAN NAGLER, from *Who Votes Now? Demographics, Issues, Inequality, and Turnout in the United States* 473

10.3 EITAN D. HERSH, from *Hacking the Electorate: How Campaigns Perceive Voters* 479

11 INTEREST GROUPS

11.1 KEN KOLLMAN, from *Outside Lobbying: Public Opinion and Interest Group Strategies* 489

11.2 LARRY M. BARTELS, from *Unequal Democracy: The Political Economy of the New Gilded Age* 504

11.3 BENJAMIN I. PAGE and MARTIN GILENS, from *Democracy in America? What Has Gone Wrong and What We Can Do About It* 513

12 POLITICAL PARTIES

12.1 JOHN H. ALDRICH, from *Why Parties? A Second Look* 521

12.2 ANGUS CAMPBELL, PHILIP E. CONVERSE, WARREN E. MILLER, and DONALD E. STOKES, from *The American Voter: An Abridgement* 537

12.3 MARTY COHEN, DAVID KAROL, HANS NOEL, and JOHN ZALLER, from *The Party Decides: Presidential Nominations Before and After Reform* 544

12.4 KEN KOLLMAN, "Who Drives the Party Bus?" 554

12.5   ERIC SCHICKLER, from *Racial Realignment: The Transformation of American Liberalism, 1932–1965*   557

13 ELECTIONS

13.1   *Citizens United v. Federal Election Commission* (2010)   567

13.2   *Shelby County, Alabama v. Holder* (2013)   579

13.3   RICHARD L. FOX and JENNIFER L. LAWLESS, from "Gendered Perceptions and Political Candidacies: A Central Barrier to Women's Equality in Electoral Politics," *American Journal of Political Science*   586

13.4   CHRISTOPHER ACHEN and LARRY M. BARTELS, from *Democracy for Realists: Why Elections Do Not Produce Responsive Government*   601

13.5   JAMES A. STIMSON, from *Tides of Consent: How Public Opinion Shapes American Politics*   612

14 THE MEDIA

14.1   MATTHEW A. BAUM, from *Soft News Goes to War: Public Opinion and American Foreign Policy in the New Media Age*   629

14.2   MARISA A. ABRAJANO, from *Campaigning to the New American Electorate: Advertising to Latino Voters*   633

14.3   HUNT ALLCOTT and MATTHEW GENTZKOW, from "Social Media and Fake News in the 2016 Election," *Journal of Economic Perspectives*   644

15 POLICY

15.1   SUZANNE METTLER, from *The Submerged State: How Invisible Government Policies Undermine American Democracy*   657

15.2   ANDREA LOUISE CAMPBELL, from *How Policies Make Citizens: Senior Political Activism and the American Welfare State*   672

15.3   MATT GUARDINO and DANNY HAYES, from "Foreign Voices, Party Cues, and U.S. Public Opinion about Military Action," *International Journal of Public Opinion Research*   678

Acknowledgments   685

[2.5] ERIC SCHLUTER, Inmigration, Integration, The Immigration...
of Integration (Segment 2), 2009. 535

13 ELECTIONS

13.1 Campaign Finance Reform, Election Reform... 1990-2004. 547

13.2 Stacia Gilliam, Alternative Voter... 559

13.3 RICHARD R. FOX and JENNIFER LAWLESS, Gendered...
Perceptions and Political Candidacy: A Central Barrier
to Women's Equality in Electoral Politics, Women and Social
of Political Science. 562

13.4 CHRISTOPHER ALBERT and ALBERT ANDREW LAWRENCE Q. the party
in Politics: How Americans Vote Presidential Deliberating. 581
conventions. 591

13.5 PAUL A. STRATOS, Uncertainty Governed Non-Partisan...
Supreme American Voice. 588

14 THE MEDIA

14.1 MATTHEW A. BAUM and Yuri Siva Guo, Media, Public Opinion,
and Foreign Policy, ROLE in the Arab uprising... 602

14.2 MARKUS PRIOR, News Consumption... in the Digital Age,
Education Advances in Democracy. 625

14.3 HUNT ALLCOTT and MATTHEW GENTZKOW, Fake Social Media,
and Politics, with The 2016 Election... Journal of Expectations... 641

15 POLICY

15.1 SUZANNE METTLER, How The Strength and State of American...
Understand Policies for Income Assistance. Princeton. 663

15.2 KATHRYN J. EDIN, Absolute Poverty, How Families Live in...
Social Mobility Journal and The Life Children Save. 672

15.3 MARTIN GILENS and BENJAMIN... from Theory, Media, and...
Test and FROG, Public... Military Affairs. 682

Acknowledgements. 687

PREFACE

This reader makes some of the most important work in political science and the subfield of American politics easily accessible to students in introductory courses. The selections included in this fifth edition were chosen to help accomplish several things: introduce students to fundamental concepts in political science and the study of American politics, such as collective-action problems, agenda-setting power, ideologies, and the median voter; provide specific insights into the workings of the major institutions and processes of American government; spur discussions on controversial topics, such as immigration, gay rights, campaign finance, and contemporary American foreign policy; and improve students' abilities to digest official government documents, such as Supreme Court cases.

The opening Fundamentals section introduces students to four crucial problems in politics:

1. *collective-action problems* among groups of people and how organizers and leaders of institutions can try to overcome such problems;
2. *common-resource problems,* which are variants of the standard collective-action problem but specifically refer to allocating scarce resources;
3. *legitimate government* protecting liberty under any form of government based on laws that constrain behavior; and
4. *representation and delegation problems*, which are ubiquitous in modern, democratic government, and require contract-like arrangements to solve.

The material in the Fundamentals section is a good foundation for students approaching the rest of the readings. With the above "problems" in mind, students will not only have a fresh perspective on classic selections, but will be able to analyze and make sense of more contemporary research. One can read Brutus's *Anti-Federalist* No. 1, for instance, with an eye toward common-resource problems. Brutus was concerned that an overpowering national government would oppress the states, and favored having a weak central government as it was under the Articles of Confederation. It is worth discussing the question: Was Brutus naïve about collective-action and common-resource problems inherent when the states compete for common resources? Did Brutus underestimate the potential role for centralized government to manage such problems? The selection from Robert Dahl offers criticisms of the solutions and compromises Madison and his fellow founders made when crafting the Constitution.

Many of the contemporary selections also have one or more of the "problems" from Chapter 1 as their backdrop. To take an example from Chapter 5 on Congress, the delegation problem is at the root of the arguments made by Cox and McCubbins on how (and why) partisan majorities grant agenda control to party leaders in Congress. And Wong et al's arguments in Chapter 10 focus on the ways Asian Americans have forged a collective identity across ethnicities to help solve internal collective-action problems. Students benefit greatly from seeing these theoretical threads in contemporary political science scholarship.

Quite a few of the readings provide grist for lively discussions on current events and policy controversies. Students will gain knowledge of legal arguments about gay marriage, health care reform, elections, education, and immigration, and they will confront arguments about the sustainability of recent trends in American foreign policy.

I use these readings when I teach. In preparing this fifth edition, I paid close attention to the suggestions from my students and other professors who assigned the previous edition. I hope you find these readings as useful as I do in understanding politics and, specifically, the American political system.

I owe special thanks to several people. For their wonderful feedback on previous editions, I thank:

Emily Acevedo, California State University, Los Angeles
E. Scott Adler, University of Colorado, Boulder
Tama Andrews, University of New Hampshire
John Aughenbaugh, Virginia Commonwealth University
Leslie Baker, Mississippi State University
Lauren Balasco, Pittsburg State University
Vilma Balmaceda, Nyack College
Paul Bellinger, Stephen F. Austin State University
Michael Berkman, Pennsylvania State University
Michael Berry, University of Colorado, Denver
Michael M. Binder, University of North Florida
Sarah Binder, George Washington University
Stephen Borrelli, University of Alabama
Matt Bosworth, Winona State University
Nicholas Boushee, San Diego City College
Dan Cassino, Fairleigh Dickinson University
Devin Caughey, Massachusetts Institute of Technology
Helen Chang, Lehman College
Neil Chaturvedi, Seattle University

Jangsup Choi, Texas A&M University, Commerce
Mary Ann Clarke, Bryant University
Ann Cohen, CUNY, Hunter College
Martin Cohen, James Madison University
Jeff Colbert, Elon University
Richard S. Conley, University of Florida
Mark Croatti, American University
Paul R. DeHart, Texas State University
David Dulio, Oakland University
Justin Dyer, University of Missouri
Matthew Eshbaugh-Soha, University of North Texas
Andrew M. Essig, DeSales University
Emily Farris, Texas Christian University
Kathleen Ferraiolo, James Madison University
Perri Gardner, College of Southern Idaho
Emily R. Gill, Bradley University
Brad T. Gomez, Florida State University
Craig Goodman, Texas Tech University
Paul N. Goren, University of Minnesota
Lou Graziano, St. John's University
Andrew Green, Central College
Steven Greene, North Carolina State University
Richard Haesly, California State University, Long Beach
Thomas Halper, Baruch College
Danny Hayes, George Washington University
Audrey A. Haynes, University of Georgia
Diane J. Heith, St. John's University
Roberta Herzberg, Utah State University
Marc Hetherington, Vanderbilt University
Leif Hoffmann, Lewis-Clark State College
Ronald J. Hrebenar, University of Utah
Ryan Hurl, University of Toronto Scarborough
Richard Jankowski, SUNY Fredonia
Dorothy James, Connecticut College
Marc James, Brock University
Kevin Jefferies, Alvin Community College
Jeff Jenkins, University of Virginia
Joel Johnson, Colorado State University, Pueblo
Timothy R. Johnson, University of Minnesota
Jennifer Jung-Kim, University of California, Los Angeles
Mary Kroeger, University of Rochester
David Lassen, University of Wisconsin, Madison
Serena Laws, Trinity College
Christine Lipsmeyer, Texas A&M University

Alyx Mark, North Central College
Kenneth R. Mayer, University of Wisconsin, Madison
Corrine McConnaughy, Ohio State University
Ian McDonald, Duke University
Mary McGrath, Northwestern University
Mark McKenzie, Texas Tech University
Bryan McQuide, Grand View University
Benjamin Melusky, Gettysburg College
Kristina Miler, University of Maryland
Fiona Miller, University of Toronto Mississauga
Nathan Mitchell, Prairie View A&M University
Ken Mulligan, Southern Illinois University
James Newman, Southeast Missouri State University
Sarah Niebler, Dickinson College
Timothy Nokken, Texas Tech University
Paul Nolette, Marquette University
Mikel Norris, Coastal Carolina University
Julie Pacheco, University of Iowa
Justin Phillips, Columbia University
Richard M. Pious, Barnard College
Taylor Price, University of Wisconsin, Madison
Nicholas Pyeatt, Pennsylvania State University, Altoona
Megan Remmel, Norwich University
Tim Reynolds, Alvin Community College
Kimberly Rice, Western Illinois University
Jason Roberts, University of North Carolina at Chapel Hill
Gregory Robinson, Binghamton University
Martin Saiz, California State University, Northridge
Dante Scala, University of New Hampshire
James Sheffield, University of Oklahoma
Sean M. Theriault, University of Texas at Austin
J. Alejandro Tirado, Texas Tech University
Terri Towner, Oakland University
Jessica Trounstine, University of California, Merced
Bob Turner, Skidmore College
Joseph Ura, Texas A&M University
Nicholas Valentino, University of Michigan
Justin Vaughn, Boise State University
Greg Vonnahme, University of Missouri, Kansas City
Charles Walcott, Virginia Tech
Harold M. Waller, McGill University
Patrick Wohlfarth, University of Maryland
Kent Worcester, Marymount Manhattan College
Jeffrey S. Worsham, West Virginia University

Erin Ackerman and Ann Shin made possible the first edition, and Hannah Bozian helped with the second edition. Erica Mirabitur's dedicated work made the process smooth for the third edition, and she also helped with this latest version. Samantha Held was also instrumental in helping me pull together the fourth edition. The fifth edition was made possible by the hard work of Max Housner and Anna Olcott, and many thanks to them.

Ken Kollman

ABOUT THE EDITOR

KEN KOLLMAN is the Director of the Center for Political Studies, the Frederick G. L. Huetwell Professor, and Professor of Political Science and Research Professor in the Institute for Social Research at the University of Michigan. His research and teaching focus on political parties, elections, lobbying, and federal systems. He also regularly teaches the introductory American politics course at the University of Michigan. In addition to numerous articles, he has written *Perils of Centralization: Lessons from Church, State, and Corporation* (2013), *The Formation of National Party Systems: Federalism and Party Competition in Canada, Great Britain, India, and the United States* (with Pradeep Chhibber, 2004) and *Outside Lobbying: Public Opinion and Interest Group Strategies* (1998). Professor Kollman is also the author of an American government textbook published by W. W. Norton, *The American Political System*, now in its third edition.

READINGS IN
AMERICAN
POLITICS

Fifth Edition

1

FUNDAMENTALS

1.1

MANCUR OLSON Jr.

From *The Logic of Collective Action: Public Goods and the Theory of Groups*

Olson introduces us to the concept of the collective action problem. This "problem" arises when individuals have incentives to free-ride off the contributions of others, reaping the benefits of some action without paying any of the costs. In describing the collective action problem and how groups or organizations can overcome it, Olson strongly challenges the widely held notion that having common interests is a sufficient condition for a political group to form.

I. A THEORY OF GROUPS AND ORGANIZATIONS

A. The Purpose of Organization

Since most (though by no means all) of the action taken by or on behalf of groups of individuals is taken through organizations, it will be helpful to consider organizations in a general or theoretical way.[1] The logical place to begin any systematic study of organizations is with their purpose. But there are all types and shapes and sizes of organizations, even of economic organizations, and there is then some question [of] whether there is any single purpose that would be characteristic of organizations generally. One purpose that is nonetheless characteristic of most organizations, and surely of practically all

From Mancur Olson Jr., *The Logic of Collective Action: Public Goods and the Theory of Groups* (Cambridge, MA: Harvard University Press, 1971).

organizations with an important economic aspect, is the furtherance of the interests of their members. That would seem obvious, at least from the economist's perspective. To be sure, some organizations may, out of ignorance, fail to further their members' interests, and others may be enticed into serving only the ends of the leadership.[2] But organizations often perish if they do nothing to further the interests of their members, and this factor must severely limit the number of organizations that fail to serve their members.

The idea that organizations or associations exist to further the interests of their members is hardly novel, nor peculiar to economics; it goes back at least to Aristotle, who wrote, "Men journey together with a view to particular advantage, and by way of providing some particular thing needed for the purposes of life, and similarly the political association seems to have come together originally, and to continue in existence, for the sake of the *general* advantages it brings."[3] More recently, Professor Leon Festinger, a social psychologist, pointed out that "the attraction of group membership is not so much in sheer belonging, but rather in attaining something by means of this membership."[4] The late Harold Laski, a political scientist, took it for granted that "associations exist to fulfill purposes which a group of men have in common."[5]

The kinds of organizations that are the focus of this study are *expected* to further the interests of their members.[6] Labor unions are expected to strive for higher wages and better working conditions for their members; farm organizations are expected to strive for favorable legislation for their members; cartels are expected to strive for higher prices for participating firms; the corporation is expected to further the interests of its stockholders;[7] and the state is expected to further the common interests of its citizens (though in this nationalistic age the state often has interests and ambitions apart from those of its citizens).

Notice that the interests that all of these diverse types of organizations are expected to further are, for the most part, *common* interests: the union members' common interest in higher wages, the farmers' common interest in favorable legislation, the cartel members' common interest in higher prices, the stockholders' common interest in higher dividends and stock prices, the citizens' common interest in good government. It is not an accident that the diverse types of organizations listed are all supposed to work primarily for the *common* interests of their members. Purely personal or individual interests can be advanced, and usually advanced most efficiently, by individual, unorganized action. There is obviously no purpose in having an organization when individual, unorganized action can serve the interests of the individual as well as or better than an organization; there would, for example, be no point in forming an organization simply to play solitaire. But when a number of individuals have a common or collective interest—when they share a single purpose or objective—individual, unorganized action (as we shall soon see) will either not be able to advance that common interest at all, or will not be able to advance that interest adequately. Organizations can therefore perform a function when there are common or group interests, and though organizations often also serve purely personal, individual interests, their characteristic and primary function is to advance the common interests of groups of individuals.

The assumption that organizations typically exist to further the common interests of groups of people is implicit in most of the literature about organizations, and two of the writers already cited make this assumption explicit: Harold Laski emphasized that organizations exist to achieve purposes or interests which "a group of men have in common," and Aristotle apparently had a similar notion in mind when he argued that political associations are created and maintained because of the "general advantages" they bring. R. M. MacIver also made this point explicitly when he said that "every organization presupposes an interest which its members all share."[8]

Even when unorganized groups are discussed, at least in treatments of "pressure groups" and "group theory," the word "group" is used in such a way that it means "a number of individuals with a common interest." It would of course be reasonable to label even a number of people selected at random (and thus without any common interest or unifying characteristic) as a "group"; but most discussions of group behavior seem to deal mainly with groups that do have common interests. As Arthur Bentley, the founder of the "group theory" of modern political science, put it, "there is no group without its interest."[9] The social psychologist Raymond Cattell was equally explicit, and stated that "every group has its interest."[10] This is also the way the word "group" will be used here.

Just as those who belong to an organization or a group can be presumed to have a common interest,[11] so they obviously also have purely individual interests, different from those of the others in the organization or group. All of the members of a labor union, for example, have a common interest in higher wages, but at the same time each worker has a unique interest in his personal income, which depends not only on the rate of wages but also on the length of time that he works.

B. Public Goods and Large Groups

The combination of individual interests and common interests in an organization suggests an analogy with a competitive market. The firms in a perfectly competitive industry, for example, have a common interest in a higher price for the industry's product. Since a uniform price must prevail in such a market, a firm cannot expect a higher price for itself unless all of the other firms in the industry also have this higher price. But a firm in a competitive market also has an interest in selling as much as it can, until the cost of producing another unit exceeds the price of that unit. In this there is no common interest; each firm's interest is directly opposed to that of every other firm, for the more other firms sell, the lower the price and income for any given firm. In short, while all firms have a common interest in a higher price, they have antagonistic interests where output is concerned. This can be illustrated with a simple supply-and-demand model. For the sake of a simple argument, assume that a perfectly competitive industry is momentarily in a disequilibrium position, with price exceeding marginal cost for all firms at their present output. Suppose, too, that all of the adjustments will be made by the firms already in the industry rather than by new entrants, and that the industry is on an inelastic portion of its demand curve. Since price exceeds marginal cost for all firms, output will increase. But as all firms increase production, the price falls; indeed, since the industry demand curve is by assumption inelastic, the total revenue of the industry will decline. Apparently, each firm finds that with price exceeding marginal cost, it pays to increase its output, but the result is that each firm gets a smaller profit. Some economists in an earlier day may have questioned this result,[12] but the fact that profit-maximizing firms in a perfectly competitive industry can act contrary to their interests as a group is now widely understood and accepted.[13] A group of profit-maximizing firms can act to reduce their aggregate profits because in perfect competition, each firm is, by definition, so small that it can ignore the effect of its output on price. Each firm finds it to its advantage to increase output to the point where marginal cost equals price and to ignore the effects of its extra output on the position of the industry. It is true that the net result is that all firms are worse off, but this does not mean that every firm has not maximized its profits. If a firm, foreseeing the fall in price resulting from the increase in industry output, were to restrict its own output, it would lose more than ever, for its price would fall quite as much in any case and it would have a smaller output as well. A firm in a perfectly competitive market gets only a small part of the benefit (of a small share of the industry's extra revenue) resulting from a reduction in that firm's output.

For these reasons it is now generally understood that if the firms in an industry are maximizing profits, the profits for the industry as a whole will be less than they might otherwise be.[14] And almost everyone would agree that this theoretical conclusion fits the facts for markets characterized by pure competition. The important point is that this is true because, though all the firms have a common interest in a higher price for the industry's product, it is in the interest of each firm that the other firms pay the cost—in terms of the necessary reduction in output—needed to obtain a higher price.

About the only thing that keeps prices from falling in accordance with the process just described in perfectly competitive markets is outside intervention. Government price supports, tariffs, cartel agreements, and the like may keep the firms in a competitive market from acting contrary to their interests. Such aid or intervention is quite common. It is then important to ask how it comes about. How does a competitive industry obtain government assistance in maintaining the price of its product?

Consider a hypothetical, competitive industry, and suppose that most of the producers in that industry desire a tariff, a price-support program, or some other government intervention to increase the price for their product. To obtain any such assistance from the government, the producers in this industry will presumably have to organize a lobbying organization; they will have to become an active pressure group.[15] This lobbying organization may have to conduct a considerable campaign. If significant resistance is encountered, a great amount of money will be required.[16] Public relations experts will be needed to influence the newspapers, and some advertising may be necessary. Professional organizers will probably be needed to organize "spontaneous grass roots" meetings among the distressed producers in the industry, and to get those in the industry to write letters to their congressmen.[17] The campaign for the government assistance will take the time of some of the producers in the industry, as well as their money.

There is a striking parallel between the problem the perfectly competitive industry faces as it strives to obtain government assistance, and the problem it faces in the marketplace when the firms increase output and bring about a fall in price. *Just as it was not rational for a particular producer to restrict his output in order that there might be a higher price for the product of his industry, so it would not be rational for him to sacrifice his time and money to support a lobbying organization to obtain government assistance for the industry. In neither case would it be in the interest of the individual producer to assume any of the costs himself. A lobbying organization, or indeed a labor union or any other organization, working in the interest of a large group of firms or workers in some industry, would get no assistance from the rational, self-interested individuals in that industry.* This would be true even if everyone in the industry were absolutely convinced that the proposed program was in their interest (though in fact some might think otherwise and make the organization's task yet more difficult).[18]

Although the lobbying organization is only one example of the logical analogy between the organization and the market, it is of some practical importance. There are many powerful and well-financed lobbies with mass support in existence now, but these lobbying organizations do not get that support because of their legislative achievements. The most powerful lobbying organizations now obtain their funds and their following for other reasons.

Some critics may argue that the rational person will indeed support a large organization, like a lobbying organization, that works in his interest, because he knows that if he does not, others will not do so either, and then the organization will fail, and he will be without the benefit that the organization could have provided. This argument shows the need for the analogy with the perfectly competitive market. For it would be quite as reasonable to argue that prices will never fall below the levels a monopoly would have charged in a perfectly competitive market, because if one firm increased its output, other firms would also, and the price would fall; but each firm could foresee this, so it would not start a chain of price-destroying increases in output. In fact, it does not work out this way in a competitive market; nor in a large organization. When the number of firms involved is large, no one will notice the effect on price if one firm increases its output, and so no one will change his plans because of it. Similarly, in a large organization, the loss of one dues payer will not noticeably increase the burden for any other one dues payer, and so a rational person would not believe that if he were to withdraw from an organization he would drive others to do so.

The foregoing argument must at the least have some relevance to economic organizations that are mainly means through which individuals attempt to obtain the same things they obtain through their activities in the market. Labor unions, for example, are organizations through which workers strive to get the same things they get with their individual efforts in the market—higher wages, better working conditions, and the like. It would be strange indeed if the workers did not confront some of the same problems in the union that they meet in the market, since their efforts in both places have some of the same purposes.

However similar the purposes may be, critics may object that attitudes in organizations are not at all like those in markets. In organizations, an emotional or ideological element is often also involved. Does this make the argument offered here practically irrelevant?

A most important type of organization—the national state—will serve to test this objection. Patriotism is probably the strongest non-economic motive for organizational allegiance in modern times. This age is sometimes called the age of nationalism. Many nations draw additional strength and unity from some powerful ideology, such as democracy or communism, as well as from a common religion, language, or cultural inheritance. The state not only has many such powerful sources of support; it also is very important economically. Almost any government is economically beneficial to its citizens, in that the law and order it provides is a prerequisite of all civilized economic activity. But despite the force of patriotism, the appeal of the national ideology, the bond of a common culture, and the indispensability of the system of law and order, no major state in modern history has been able to support itself through voluntary dues or contributions. Philanthropic contributions are not even a significant source of revenue for most countries. Taxes, *compulsory* payments by definition, are needed. Indeed, as the old saying indicates, their necessity is as certain as death itself.

If the state, with all of the emotional resources at its command, cannot finance its most basic and vital activities without resort[ing] to compulsion, it would seem that large private organizations might also have difficulty in getting the individuals in the groups whose interests they attempt to advance to make the necessary contributions voluntarily.[19]

The reason the state cannot survive on voluntary dues or payments, but must rely on taxation, is that the most fundamental services a nation-state provides are, in one important respect, like the higher price in a competitive market: they must be available to everyone if they are available to anyone. The basic and most elementary goods or services provided by government, like defense and police protection, and the system of law and order generally, are such that they go to everyone or practically everyone in the nation. It would obviously not be feasible, if indeed it were possible, to deny the protection provided by the military services, the police, and the courts to those who did not voluntarily pay their share of the costs of government, and taxation is accordingly necessary. The common or collective benefits provided by governments are usually called "public goods" by economists, and the concept of public goods is one of the oldest and most important ideas in the study of public finance. A common, collective, or public good is here defined as any good such that, if any person X_i in a group $X_1, \ldots, X_i, \ldots, X_n$ consumes it, it cannot feasibly be withheld from the others in that group.[20] In other words, those who do not purchase or pay for any of the public or collective good cannot be excluded or kept from sharing in the consumption of the good, as they can where noncollective goods are concerned.

Students of public finance have, however, neglected the fact that *the achievement of any common goal or the satisfaction of any common interest means that a public or collective good has been provided for that group.*[21] The very fact that a goal or purpose is *common* to a group means that no one in the group is excluded from the benefit or satisfaction brought about by its achievement. As the opening paragraphs of this chapter indicated, almost all groups and organizations have the purpose of serving the common interests of their members. As R. M. MacIver puts it, "Persons . . . have common interests in the degree to which they participate in a cause . . . which indivisibly embraces them all."[22] It is of the essence of an organization that it provides an inseparable, generalized benefit. It follows that the provision of public or collective goods is the fundamental function of organizations generally. A state is first of all an organization that provides public goods for its members, the citizens; and other types of organizations similarly provide collective goods for their members.

And just as a state cannot support itself by voluntary contributions, or by selling its basic services on the market, neither can other large organizations support themselves without providing some sanction, or some attraction distinct from the public good itself, that will lead individuals to help bear the burdens of maintaining the organization. The individual member of the typical large organization is in a position analogous to that of the firm in a perfectly competitive market, or the taxpayer in the state: his own efforts will not have a noticeable effect on the situation of his organization, and he can enjoy any improvements brought about by others whether or not he has worked in support of his organization.

There is no suggestion here that states or other organizations provide *only* public or collective goods. Governments often provide noncollective goods like electric power, for example, and they usually sell such goods on the market much as private firms would do. Moreover, as later parts of this study will argue, large organizations that are not able to make membership compulsory *must also* provide some noncollective goods in order to give potential members an incentive to join. Still, collective goods are the characteristic organizational goods, for ordinary noncollective goods can always be provided by individual action, and only where common purposes of collective goods are concerned is organization or group action ever indispensable.[23]

▪   ▪   ▪

Nontechnical Summary of Section D

The technical part of this section has shown that certain small groups can provide themselves with collective goods without relying on coercion or any positive inducements apart from the collective good itself.[24] This is because in some small groups each of the members, or at least one of them, will find that his personal gain from having the collective good exceeds the total cost of providing some amount of that collective good; there are members who would be better off if the collective good were provided, even if they had to pay the entire cost of providing it themselves, than they would be if it were not provided. In such situations there is a presumption that the collective good will be provided. Such a situation will exist only when the benefit to the group from having the collective good exceeds the total cost by more than it exceeds the gain to one or more individuals in the group. Thus, in a very small group, where each member gets a substantial proportion of the total gain simply because there are few others in the group, a collective good can often be provided by the voluntary, self-interested action of the members of the group. In smaller groups marked by considerable degrees of inequality— that is, in groups of members of unequal "size" or extent of interest in the collective good—there is the greatest likelihood that a collective good will be provided; for the greater the interest in the collective good of any single member, the greater the likelihood that that member will get such a signifi- cant proportion of the total benefit from the collective good that he will gain from seeing that the good is provided, even if he has to pay all of the cost himself.

Even in the smallest groups, however, the collective good will not ordinarily be provided on an optimal scale. That is to say, the members of the group will not provide as much of the good as it would be in their common interest to provide. Only certain special institutional arrangements will give the individ- ual members an incentive to purchase the amounts of the collective good that would add up to the amount that would be in the best interest of the group as a whole. This tendency toward suboptimality is due to the fact that a collective good is, by definition, such that other individuals in the group cannot be kept from consuming it once any individual in the group has provided it for him- self. Since an individual member thus gets only part of the benefit of any expenditure he makes to obtain more of the collective good, he will discon- tinue his purchase of the collective good before the optimal amount for the group as a whole has been obtained. In addition, the amounts of the collective good that a member of the group receives free from other members will fur- ther reduce his incentive to provide more of that good at his own expense.

Accordingly, *the larger the group, the farther it will fall short of providing an optimal amount of a collective good.*

This suboptimality or inefficiency will be somewhat less serious in groups composed of members of greatly different size or interest in the collective good. In such unequal groups, on the other hand, there is a tendency toward an arbitrary sharing of the burden of providing the collective good. The largest member, the member who would on his own provide the largest amount of the collective good, bears a disproportionate share of the burden of providing the collective good. The smaller member by definition gets a smaller fraction of the benefit of any amount of the collective good he provides than a larger member, and therefore has less incentive to provide additional amounts of the collective good. Once a smaller member has the amount of the collective good he gets free from the largest member, he has more than he would have purchased for himself, and has no incentive to obtain any of the collective good at his own expense. In small groups with common interests there is accordingly *a surprising tendency for the "exploitation" of the great by the small.*

The argument that small groups providing themselves with collective goods tend to provide suboptimal quantities of these goods, and that the burdens of providing them are borne in an arbitrary and disproportionate way, does not hold in all logically possible situations. Certain institutional or procedural arrangements can lead to different outcomes. The subject cannot be analyzed adequately in any brief discussion. For this reason, and because the main focus of this reading is on large groups, many of the complexities of small-group behavior have been neglected in this study. An argument of the kind just outlined could, however, fit some important practical situations rather well, and may serve the purpose of suggesting that a more detailed analysis of the kind outlined above could help to explain the apparent tendency for large countries to bear disproportionate shares of the burdens of multinational organizations, like the United Nations and NATO, and could help to explain some of the popularity of neutralism among smaller countries. Such an analysis would also tend to explain the continual complaints that international organizations and alliances are not given adequate (optimal) amounts of resources.[25] It would also suggest that neighboring local governments in metropolitan areas that provide collective goods (like commuter roads and education) that benefit individuals in two or more local government jurisdictions would tend to provide inadequate amounts of these services, and that the largest local government (e.g., the one representing the central city) would bear disproportionate shares of the burdens of providing them.[26] An analysis of the foregoing type might, finally, provide some additional insight into the phenomenon of price leadership, and particularly the possible disadvantages involved in being the largest firm in an industry.

The most important single point about small groups in the present context, however, is that they may very well be able to provide themselves with a collective good simply because of the attraction of the collective good to the individual members. In this, small groups differ from larger ones. The larger a group is, the f[u]rther it will fall short of obtaining an optimal supply of any collective good, and the less likely that it will act to obtain even a minimal amount of such a good. In short, the larger the group, the less it will further its common interests.

■ · ■ · ■

F. A Taxonomy of Groups

To be sure, there can also be many instances in inclusive or non-market groups in which individual members do take into account the reactions of other members to their actions when they decide what action to take—that is, instances in which there is the strategic interaction among members characteristic of oligopolistic industries in which mutual dependence is recognized. In groups of one size range at least, such strategic interaction must be relatively important. That is the size range where the group is not so small that one individual would find it profitable to purchase some of the collective good himself, but where the number in the group is nonetheless sufficiently small that each member's attempts or lack of attempts to obtain the collective good would bring about noticeable differences in the welfare of some, or all, of the others in the group. This can best be understood by assuming for a moment that an inclusive collective good is already being provided in such a group through a formal organization, and then asking what would happen if one member of the group were to cease paying his share of the cost of the good. If, in a reasonably small organization, a particular person stops paying for the collective good he enjoys, the costs will rise noticeably for each of the others in the group; accordingly, they may then refuse to continue making their contributions, and the collective good may no longer be provided. However, the first person could realize that this might be the result of his refusal to pay anything for the collective good, and that he would be worse off when the collective good is not provided than when it was provided and he met part of the cost. Accordingly he might continue making a contribution toward the purchase of the collective good. He might; or he might not. As in oligopoly in a market situation, the result is indeterminate. The rational member of such a group faces a strategic problem and while the Theory of Games and other types of analyses might prove very helpful, there seems to be no way at present of getting a general, valid, and determinate solution at the level of abstraction of this chapter.[27]

What is the range of this indeterminateness? In a small group in which a member gets such a large fraction of the total benefit that he would be better off if he paid the entire cost himself, rather than go without the good, there is some presumption that the collective good will be provided. In a group in which no one member got such a large benefit from the collective good that he had an interest in providing it even if he had to pay all of the cost, but in which the individual was still so important in terms of the whole group that his contribution or lack of contribution to the group objective had a noticeable effect on the costs or benefits of others in the group, the result is indeterminate.[28] By contrast, in a large group in which no single individual's contribution makes a perceptible difference to the group as a whole, or the burden or benefit of any single member of the group, it is certain that a collective good will *not* be provided unless there is coercion or some outside inducements that will lead the members of the large group to act in their common interest.[29]

The last distinction, between the group so large it definitely cannot provide itself with a collective good, and the oligopoly-sized group which may provide itself with a collective good, is particularly important. It depends upon whether any two or more members of the group have a perceptible interdependence, that is, on whether the contribution or lack of contribution of any one individual in the group will have a perceptible effect on the burden or benefit of any other individual or individuals in the group. Whether a group will have the possibility of providing itself with a collective good without coercion or outside inducements therefore depends to a striking degree upon the number of individuals in the group, since the larger the group, the less the likelihood that the contribution of any one will be perceptible. It is not, however, strictly accurate to say that it depends solely on the number of individuals in the group. The relation between the size of the group and the significance of an individual member cannot be defined quite that simply. A group which has members with highly unequal degrees of interest in a collective good, and which wants a collective good that is (at some level of provision) extremely valuable in relation to its cost, will be more apt to provide itself with a collective good than other groups with the same number of members. The same situation prevails in the study of market structure, where again the number of firms an industry can have and still remain oligopolistic (and have the possibility of supracompetitive returns) varies somewhat from case to case. The standard for determining whether a group will have the capacity to act, without coercion or outside inducements, in its group interest is (as it should be) the same for market and non-market groups: it depends on whether the individual actions of any one or more members in a group are noticeable to any other individuals in the group.[30] This is most obviously, but not exclusively, a function of the number in the group.

It is now possible to specify when either informal coordination or formal organization will be necessary to obtain a collective good. The smallest type of group—the group in which one or more members get such a large fraction of the total benefit that they find it worthwhile to see that the collective good is provided, even if they have to pay the entire cost—may get along without any group agreement or organization. A group agreement might be set up to spread the costs more widely or to step up the level of provision of the collective good. But since there is an incentive for unilateral and individual action to obtain the collective good, neither a formal organization nor even an informal group agreement is indispensable to obtain a collective good. In any group larger than this, on the other hand, no collective good can be obtained without some group agreement, coordination, or organization. In the intermediate or oligopoly-sized group, where two or more members must act simultaneously before a collective good can be obtained, there must be at least tacit coordination or organization. Moreover, the larger a group is, the more agreement and organization it will need. The larger the group, the greater the number that will usually have to be included in the group agreement or organization. It may not be necessary that the entire group be organized, since some subset of the whole group may be able to provide the collective good. But to establish a group agreement or organization will nonetheless always tend to be more difficult the larger the size of the group, for the larger the group the more difficult it will be to locate and organize even a subset of the group, and those in the subset will have an incentive to continue bargaining with the others in the group until the burden is widely shared, thereby adding to the expense of bargaining. In short, costs of organization are an increasing function of the number of individuals in the group. (Though the more members in the group the greater the total costs of organization, the costs of organization per person need not rise, for there are surely economies of scale in organization.) In certain cases a group will already be organized for some other purpose, and then these costs of organization are already being met. In such a case a group's capacity to provide itself with a collective good will be explained in part by whatever it was that originally enabled it to organize and maintain itself. This brings attention back again to the costs of organization and shows that these costs cannot be left out of the model, except for the smallest type of group in which unilateral action can provide a collective good. The costs of organization must be clearly distinguished from the type of cost that has previously been considered. The cost functions considered before involved only the direct resource costs of obtaining various levels of provision of a collective good. When there is no pre-existing organization of a group, and when the direct resource costs of a collective good it wants are more than any single individual could profitably bear, additional costs must be incurred to obtain an agreement about how the burden will be shared and to coordinate or organize the effort to obtain the collective good. These are the costs of communication among group members, the costs of any bargaining among them, and the costs of creating, staffing, and maintaining any formal group organization.

A group cannot get infinitesimally small quantities of a formal organization, or even of an informal group agreement; a group with a given number of members must have a certain minimal amount of organization or agreement if it is to have any at all. Thus there are significant initial or minimal costs of organization for each group. Any group that must organize to obtain a collective good, then, will find that it has a certain minimum organization cost that must be met, however little of the collective good it obtains. The greater the number in the group, the greater these minimal costs will be. When this minimal organizational cost is added to the other initial or minimal costs of a collective good, which arise from its previously mentioned technical characteristics, it is evident that the cost of the first unit of a collective good will be quite high in relation to the cost of some subsequent units. However immense the benefits of a collective good, the higher the absolute total costs of getting any amount of that good, the less likely it is that even a minimal amount of that good could be obtained without coercion or separate, outside incentives.

This means that there are now three separate but cumulative factors that keep larger groups from furthering their own interest. First, the larger the group, the smaller the fraction of the total group benefit any person acting in the group interest receives, and the less adequate the reward for any group-oriented action, and the f[u]rther the group falls short of getting an optimal supply of the collective good, even if it should get some. Second, since the larger the group, the smaller the share of the total benefit going to any individual, or to any (absolutely) small subset of members of the group, the less the likelihood that any small subset of the group, much less any single individual, will gain enough from getting the collective good to bear the burden of providing even a small amount of it; in other words, the larger the group the smaller the likelihood of oligopolistic interaction that might help obtain the good. Third, the larger the number of members in the group the greater the organization costs, and thus the higher the hurdle that must be jumped before any of the collective good at all can be obtained. For these reasons, the larger the group the f[u]rther it will fall short of providing an optimal supply of a collective good, and very large groups normally will not, in the absence of coercion or separate, outside incentives, provide themselves with even minimal amounts of a collective good.[31]

NOTES

1. Economists have, for the most part, neglected to develop theories of organizations, but there are a few works from an economic point of view on the subject. See, for example, three papers by Jacob Marschak, "Elements for a Theory of Teams," *Management Science*, I (January 1955), 127–137, "Towards an Economic Theory of Organization and Information," in *Decision Processes*, ed. R. M. Thrall, C. H. Combs, and R. L. Davis (New York: John Wiley, 1954), pp. 187–220, and "Efficient and Viable Organization Forms," in *Modern Organization Theory*, ed. Mason Haire (New York: John Wiley, 1959), pp. 307–320; two papers by R. Radner, "Application of Linear Programming to Team Decision Problems," *Management Science*, V (January 1959), 143–150, and "Team Decision Problems," *Annals of Mathematical Statistics*, XXXIII (September 1962), 857–881; C. B. McGuire, "Some Team Models of a Sales Organization," *Management Science*, VII (January 1961), 101–130; Oskar Morgenstern, *Prolegomena to a Theory of Organization* (Santa Monica, Calif.: RAND Research Memorandum 734, 1951); James G. March and Herbert A. Simon, *Organizations* (New York: John Wiley, 1958); Kenneth Boulding, *The Organizational Revolution* (New York: Harper, 1953).

2. Max Weber called attention to the case where an organization continues to exist for some time after it has become meaningless because some official is making a living out of it. See his *Theory of Social and Economic Organization*, trans. Talcott Parsons and A. M. Henderson (New York: Oxford University Press, 1947), p. 318.

3. Aristotle, *Ethics* viii.9.1160a.

4. Leon Festinger, "Group Attraction and Membership," in *Group Dynamics*, ed. Dorwin Cartwright and Alvin Zander (Evanston, Ill.: Row, Peterson, 1953), p. 93.

5. *A Grammar of Politics*, 4th ed. (London: George Allen & Unwin, 1939), p. 67.

6. Philanthropic and religious organizations are not necessarily expected to serve only the interests of their members; such organizations have other purposes that are considered more important, however much their members "need" to belong, or are improved or helped by belonging. But the complexity of such organizations need not be debated at length here, because this study will focus on organizations with a significant economic aspect. The emphasis here will have something in common with what Max Weber called the "associative group"; he called a group associative if "the orientation of social action with it rests on a rationally motivated agreement." Weber contrasted his "associative group" with the "communal group," which was centered on personal affection, erotic relationships, etc., like the family. (See Weber, pp. 136–139, and Grace Coyle, *Social Process in Organized Groups*, New York: Richard Smith, Inc., 1930, pp. 7–9.) The logic of the theory developed here can be extended to cover communal, religious, and philanthropic organizations, but the theory is not particularly useful in studying such groups.

7. That is, its members. This study does not follow the terminological usage of those organization theorists who describe employees as "members" of the organization for which they work. Here it is more convenient to follow the language of everyday usage instead, and to distinguish the members of, say, a union from the employees of that union. Similarly, the members of the union will be considered employees of the corporation for which they work, whereas the members of the corporation are the common stockholders.

8. R. M. MacIver, "Interests," *Encyclopaedia of the Social Sciences*, VII (New York: Macmillan, 1932), p. 147.

9. Arthur Bentley, *The Process of Government* (Evanston, Ill.: Principia Press, 1949), p. 211. David B. Truman takes a similar approach; see his *The Governmental Process* (New York: Alfred A. Knopf, 1958), pp. 33–35. See also Sidney Verba, *Small Groups and Political Behavior* (Princeton, N.J.: Princeton University Press, 1961), pp. 12–13.

10. Raymond Cattell, "Concepts and Methods in the Measurement of Group Syntality," in *Small Groups*, ed. A. Paul Hare, Edgard F. Borgatta, and Robert F. Bales (New York: Alfred A. Knopf, 1955), p. 115.

11. Any organization or group will of course usually be divided into subgroups or factions that are opposed to one another. This fact does not weaken the assumption made here that organizations exist to serve the common interests of members, for the assumption does not imply that intragroup conflict is neglected. The opposing groups within an organization ordinarily have some interest in common (if not, why would they maintain the organization?), and the members of any subgroup or faction also have a separate common interest of their own. They will indeed often have a common purpose in defeating some other subgroup or faction. The approach used here does not neglect the conflict within groups and organizations, then, because it considers each organization as a unit only to the extent that it does, in fact, attempt to serve a common interest, and considers the various subgroups as the relevant units with common interests to analyze the factional strife.

12. See J. M. Clark, *The Economics of Overhead Costs* (Chicago: University of Chicago Press, 1923), p. 417, and Frank H. Knight, *Risk, Uncertainty and Profit* (Boston: Houghton Mifflin, 1921), p. 193.

13. Edward H. Chamberlin, *Monopolistic Competition*, 6th ed. (Cambridge, Mass.: Harvard University Press, 1950), p. 4.

14. For a fuller discussion of this question, see Mancur Olson, Jr., and David McFarland, "The Restoration of Pure Monopoly and the Concept of the Industry, *Quarterly Journal of Economics*, LXXVI (November 1962), 613–31.

15. Robert Michels contends in his classic study that "democracy is inconceivable without organization," and that "the principle of organization is an absolutely essential condition for the political struggle of the masses." See his *Political Parties*, trans. Eden and Cedar Paul (New York: Dover Publications, 1959), pp. 21–22. See also Robert A. Brady, *Business as a System of Power* (New York: Columbia University Press, 1943), p. 193.

16. Alexander Heard, *The Costs of Democracy* (Chapel Hill: University of North Carolina Press, 1960), especially note 1, pp. 95–96. For example, in 1947 the National Association of Manufacturers spent over $4.6 million, and over a somewhat longer period the American Medical Association spent as much on a campaign against compulsory health insurance.

17. "If the full truth were ever known . . . lobbying, in all its ramifications, would prove to be a billion dollar industry." U.S. Congress, House, Select Committee on Lobbying Activities, *Report*, 81st Cong., 2nd Sess. (1950), as quoted in the *Congressional Quarterly Almanac*, 81st Cong., 2nd Sess., VI, 764–65.

18. For a logically possible but practically meaningless exception to the conclusion of this paragraph.

19. Sociologists as well as economists have observed that ideological motives alone are not sufficient to bring forth the continuing effort of large masses of people. Max Weber provides a notable example:

"All economic activity in a market economy is undertaken and carried through by individuals for their own ideal or material interests. This is naturally just as true when economic activity is oriented to the patterns of order of corporate groups . . .

"Even if an economic system were organized on a socialistic basis, there would be no fundamental difference in this respect . . . The structure of interests and the relevant situation might change; there would be other means of pursuing interests, but this fundamental factor would remain just as relevant as before. It is of course true that economic action which is oriented on purely ideological grounds to the interest of others does exist. But it is even more certain that the mass of men do not act in this way, and it is an induction from experience that they cannot do so and never will . . .

"In a market economy the interest in the maximization of income is necessarily the driving force of all economic activity." (Weber, pp. 319–20.)

Talcott Parsons and Neil Smelser go even further in postulating that "performance" throughout society is proportional to the "rewards" and "sanctions" involved. See their *Economy and Society* (Glencoe, Ill.: Free Press, 1954), pp. 50–69.

20. This simple definition focuses upon two points that are important in the present context. The first point is that most collective goods can only be defined with respect to some specific group. One collective good goes to one group of people, another collective good to another group; one may benefit the whole world, another only two specific people. Moreover, some goods are collective goods to those in one group and at the same time private goods to those in another, because some individuals can be kept from consuming them and others can't. Take, for example, the parade that is a collective good to all those who live in tall buildings overlooking the parade route, but which appears to be a private good to those who can see it only by buying a ticket for a seat in

the stands along the way. The second point is that once the relevant group has been defined, the definition used here, like Musgrave's, distinguishes collective good in terms of infeasibility of excluding potential consumers of the good. This approach is used because collective goods produced by organizations of all kinds seem to be such that exclusion is normally not feasible. To be sure, for some collective goods it is physically possible to practice exclusion. But, as Head has shown, it is not necessary that exclusion be technically impossible; it is only necessary that it be infeasible or uneconomic. Head has also shown most clearly that nonexcludability is only one of two basic elements in the traditional understanding of public goods. The other, he points out, is "jointness of supply." A good has "jointness" if making it available to one individual means that it can be easily or freely supplied to others as well. The polar case of jointness would be Samuelson's pure public good, which is a good such that additional consumption of it by one individual does not diminish the amount available to others. By the definition used here, jointness is not a necessary attribute of a public good. At least one type of collective good considered here exhibits no jointness whatever, and few, if any, would have the degree of jointness needed to qualify as pure public goods. Nonetheless, most of the collective goods to be studied here do display a large measure of jointness. On the definition and importance of public goods, see John G. Head, "Public Goods and Public Policy," *Public Finance*, vol. XVII, no. 3 (1962), 197–219; Richard Musgrave, *The Theory of Public Finance* (New York: McGraw-Hill, 1959); Paul A. Samuelson, "The Pure Theory of Public Expenditure," "Diagrammatic Exposition of a Theory of Public Expenditure," and "Aspects of Public Expenditure Theories," in *Review of Economics and Statistics*, XXXVI (November 1954), 387–390, XXXVII (November 1955), 350–56, and XL (November 1958), 332–38. For somewhat different opinions about the usefulness of the concept of public goods, see Julius Margolis, "A Comment on the Pure Theory of Public Expenditure," *Review of Economics and Statistics*, XXXVII (November 1955), 347–49, and Gerhard Colm, "Theory of Public Expenditures," *Annals of the American Academy of Political and Social Science*, CLXXXIII (January 1936), 1–11.

21. There is no necessity that a public good to one group in a society is necessarily in the interest of the society as a whole. Just as a tariff could be a public good to the industry that sought it, so the removal of the tariff could be a public good to those who consumed the industry's product. This is equally true when the public-good concept is applied only to governments; for a military expenditure, or a tariff, or an immigration restriction that is a public good to one country could be a "public bad" to another country, and harmful to world society as a whole.

22. R. M. MacIver in *Encyclopaedia of the Social Sciences*, VII, 147.

23. It does not, however, follow that organized or coordinated group action is *always* necessary to obtain a collective good.

24. I am indebted to Professor John Rawls of the Department of Philosophy at Harvard University for reminding me of the fact that the philosopher David Hume sensed that small groups could achieve common purposes but large groups could not. Hume's argument is, however, somewhat different from my own. In *A Treatise of Human Nature*, Everyman edition (London: J. M. Dent, 1952), II, 239, Hume wrote: "There is no quality in human nature, which causes more fatal errors in our conduct, than that which leads us to prefer whatever is present to the distant and remote, and makes us desire objects more according to their situation than their intrinsic value. Two neighbours may agree to drain a meadow, which they possess in common; because it is easy for them to know each other's mind; and each must perceive, that the immediate consequence of his failing in his part, is the abandoning of the whole project. But it is very difficult, and indeed

impossible, that a thousand persons should agree in any such action; it being difficult for them to concert so complicated a design, and still more difficult for them to execute it; while each seeks a pretext to free himself of the trouble and expense, and would lay the whole burden on others. Political society easily remedies both these inconveniences. Magistrates find an immediate interest in the interest of any considerable part of their subjects. They need consult nobody but themselves to form any scheme for promoting that interest. And as the failure of any one piece in the execution is connected, though not immediately, with the failure of the whole, they prevent that failure, because they find no interest in it, either immediate or remote. Thus, bridges are built, harbours opened, ramparts raised, canals formed, fleets equipped, and armies disciplined everywhere, by the care of government, which, though composed of men subject to all human infirmities, becomes, by one of the finest and most subtle inventions imaginable, a composition which is in some measure exempted from all these infirmities."

25. Some of the complexities of behavior in small groups are treated in Mancur Olson, Jr., and Richard Zeckhauser, "An Economic Theory of Alliances," *Review of Economics and Statistics*, XLVIII (August 1966), 266–79, and in "Collective Goods, Comparative Advantage, and Alliance Efficiency," in *Issues of Defense Economics* (A Conference of the Universities-National Bureau-Committee for Economics Research), ed. Roland McKean (New York: National Bureau of Economic Research, 1967), pp. 25–48. [Footnote added in 1970.]

26. I am indebted to Alan Williams of York University in England, whose study of local government brought the importance of these sorts of spillovers among local govenments to my attention.

27. It is of incidental interest here to note also that oligopoly in the marketplace is in some respects akin to logrolling in the organization. If the "majority" that various interests in a legislature need is viewed as a collective good—something that a particular interest cannot obtain unless other interests also share it—then the parallel is quite close. The cost each special-interest legislator would like to avoid is the passage of the legislation desired by the other special-interest legislators, for if these interests gain from their legislation, often others, including his own constituents, may lose. But unless he is willing to vote for the legislation desired by the others, the particular special-interest legislator in question will not be able to get his own legislation passed. So his goal would be to work out a coalition with other special-interest legislators in which they would vote for exactly the legislation he wanted, and he in turn would give them as little in return as possible, by insisting that they moderate their legislative demands. But since every potential logroller has this same strategy, the result is indeterminate: the logs may be rolled or they may not. Every one of the interests will be better off if the logrolling is done than if it is not, but as individual interests strive for better legislative bargains the result of the competing strategies may be that no agreement is reached. This is quite similar to the situation oligopolistic groups are in, as they all desire a higher price and will all gain if they restrict output to get it, but they may not be able to agree on market shares.

28. The result is clearly indeterminate when F_4 is less than C/V_g at every point and it is also true that the group is not so large that no one member's actions have a noticeable effect.

29. One friendly critic has suggested that even a large pre-existing organization could continue providing a collective good simply by conducting a kind of plebiscite among its members, with the understanding that if there were not a unanimous or nearly unanimous pledge to contribute toward providing the collective good, this good would no

longer be provided. This argument, if I understand it correctly, is mistaken. In such a situation, an individual would know that if others provided the collective good he would get the benefits whether he made any contribution or not. He would therefore have no incentive to make a pledge unless a completely unanimous set of pledges was required, or for some other reason his one pledge would decide whether or not the good would be provided. But if a pledge were required of every single member, or if for any other reason any one member could decide whether or not the group would get a collective good, this one member could deprive all of the others in the group of great gains. He would therefore be in a position to bargain for bribes. But since any other members of the group might gain just as much from the same holdout strategy, there is no likelihood that the collective good would be provided. See Buchanan and Tullock, pp. 96–116.

30. The noticeability of the actions of a single member of a group may be influenced by the arrangements the group itself sets up. A previously organized group, for example, might ensure that the contributions or lack of contributions of any member of the group, and the effect of each such member's course on the burden and benefit for others, would be advertised, thus ensuring that the group effort would not collapse from imperfect knowledge. I therefore define "noticeability" in terms of the degree of knowledge, and the institutional arrangements, that actually exist in any given group, instead of assuming a "natural noticeability" unaffected by any group advertising or other arrangements. This point, along with many other valuable comments, has been brought to my attention by Professor Jerome Rothenberg, who does, however, make much more of a group's assumed capacity to create "artificial noticeability" than I would want to do. I know of no practical example of a group or organization that has done much of anything, apart from improve information, to enhance the noticeability of an individual's actions in striving for a collective good.

31. There is one logically conceivable, but surely empirically trivial, case in which a large group could be provided with a very small amount of a collective good without coercion or outside incentives. If some very small group enjoyed a collective good so inexpensive that any one of the members would benefit by making sure that it was provided, even if he had to pay all of the cost, and if millions of people then entered the group, with the cost of the good nonetheless remaining constant, the large group could be provided with a little of this collective good. This is because by hypothesis in this example, the costs have remained unchanged, so that one person still has an incentive to see that the good is provided. Even in such a case as this, however, it would still not be quite right to say that the large group was acting in its group interest, since the output of the collective good would be incredibly suboptimal. The optimal level of provision of the public good would increase each time an individual entered the group, since the unit cost of the collective good by hypothesis is constant, while the benefit from an additional unit of it increases with every entrant. Yet the original provider would have no incentive to provide more as the group expanded, unless he formed an organization to share costs with the others in this (now large) group. But that would entail incurring the considerable costs of a large organization, and there would be no way these costs could be covered through the voluntary and rational action of the individuals in the group. Thus, if the total benefit from a collective good exceeded its costs by the thousandfold or millionfold, it is logically possible that a large group could provide itself with some amount of that collective good, but the level of provision of the collective good in such a case would be only a minute fraction of the optimal level. It is not easy to think of practical examples of groups that would fit this description. . . . It would be easy to rule out even any such exceptional cases, however, simply by defining *all* groups

that could provide themselves with some amount of a collective good as "small groups" (or by giving them other names), while putting all groups that could not provide themselves with a collective good in another class. But this easy route must be rejected, for that would make this part of the theory tautologous and thus incapable of refutation. Therefore the approach here has been to make the (surely reasonable) empirical hypothesis that the total costs of the collective goods wanted by large groups are large enough to exceed the value of the small fraction of the total benefit that an individual in a large group would get, so that he will not provide the good. There may be exceptions to this, as to any other empirical statement, and thus there may be instances in which large groups could provide themselves with (at most minute amounts of) collective goods through the voluntary and rational action of one of their members.

1.2

GARRETT HARDIN

"The Tragedy of the Commons"

In this powerful reading, Hardin builds on Olson's ideas to show the negative consequences that may ensue when people are not constrained in their acquisition of food, energy, land, water, minerals, and other natural resources. People pursuing their own interests can overdraw publicly owned resources, leading to a depletion of those resources. This argument is significant in the study of politics because many governmental institutions not only prevent the overdrawing of fixed resources, but also determine who has access to those resources.

The population problem has no technical solution; it requires a fundamental extension in morality.

At the end of a thoughtful article on the future of nuclear war, Wiesner and York[1] concluded that: "Both sides in the arms race are . . . confronted by the dilemma of steadily increasing military power and steadily decreasing national security. *It is our considered professional judgment that this dilemma has no technical solution.* If the great powers continue to look for solutions in the area of science and technology only, the result will be to worsen the situation."

I would like to focus your attention not on the subject of the article (national security in a nuclear world) but on the kind of conclusion they reached, namely that there is no technical solution to the problem. An implicit and almost universal assumption of discussions published in professional and semipopular scientific journals is that the problem under discussion has a technical solution. A technical solution may be defined as one that requires a change only in the techniques of the natural sciences, demanding little or nothing in the way of change in human values or ideas of morality.

In our day (though not in earlier times) technical solutions are always welcome. Because of previous failures in prophecy, it takes courage to assert that a desired technical solution is not possible. Wiesner and York exhibited this courage; publishing in a science journal, they insisted that the solution to the problem was not to be found in the natural sciences. They cautiously qualified

From Garrett Hardin, "The Tragedy of the Commons," *Science* 162, no. 3859 (December 1968): 1243–48.

their statement with the phrase, "It is our considered professional judgment. . . ." Whether they were right or not is not the concern of the present article. Rather, the concern here is with the important concept of a class of human problems which can be called "no technical solution problems," and, more specifically, with the identification and discussion of one of these.

It is easy to show that the class is not a null class. Recall the game of tick-tack-toe. Consider the problem, "How can I win the game of tick-tack-toe?" It is well known that I cannot, if I assume (in keeping with the conventions of game theory) that my opponent understands the game perfectly. Put another way, there is no "technical solution" to the problem. I can win only by giving a radical meaning to the word "win." I can hit my opponent over the head; or I can drug him; or I can falsify the records. Every way in which I "win" involves, in some sense, an abandonment of the game, as we intuitively understand it. (I can also, of course, openly abandon the game—refuse to play it. This is what most adults do.)

The class of "No technical solution problems" has members. My thesis is that the "population problem," as conventionally conceived, is a member of this class. How it is conventionally conceived needs some comment. It is fair to say that most people who anguish over the population problem are trying to find a way to avoid the evils of overpopulation without relinquishing any of the privileges they now enjoy. They think that farming the seas or developing new strains of wheat will solve the problem—technologically. I try to show here that the solution they seek cannot be found. The population problem cannot be solved in a technical way, any more than can the problem of winning the game of tick-tack-toe.

WHAT SHALL WE MAXIMIZE?

Population, as Malthus said, naturally tends to grow "geometrically," or, as we would now say, exponentially. In a finite world this means that the per capita share of the world's goods must steadily decrease. Is ours a finite world?

A fair defense can be put forward for the view that the world is infinite; or that we do not know that it is not. But, in terms of the practical problems that we must face in the next few generations with the foreseeable technology, it is clear that we will greatly increase human misery if we do not, during the immediate future, assume that the world available to the terrestrial human population is finite. "Space" is no escape.[2]

A finite world can support only a finite population; therefore, population growth must eventually equal zero. (The case of perpetual wide fluctuations above and below zero is a trivial variant that need not be discussed.) When this condition is met, what will be the situation of mankind? Specifically, can Bentham's goal of "the greatest good for the greatest number" be realized?

No—for two reasons, each sufficient by itself. The first is a theoretical one. It is not mathematically possible to maximize for two (or more) variables at the same time. This was clearly stated by von Neumann and Morgenstern,[3] but the principle is implicit in the theory of partial differential equations, dating back at least to D'Alembert (1717–1783).

The second reason springs directly from biological facts. To live, any organism must have a source of energy (for example, food). This energy is utilized for two purposes: mere maintenance and work. For man, maintenance of life requires about 1,600 kilocalories a day ("maintenance calories"). Anything that he does over and above merely staying alive will be defined as work, and is supported by "work calories" which he takes in. Work calories are used not only for what we call work in common speech; they are also required for all forms of enjoyment, from swimming and automobile racing to playing music and writing poetry. If our goal is to maximize population it is obvious what we must do: We must make the work calories per person approach as close to zero as possible. No gourmet meals, no vacations, no sports, no music, no literature, no art. . . . I think that everyone will grant, without argument or proof, that maximizing population does not maximize goods. Bentham's goal is impossible.

In reaching this conclusion I have made the usual assumption that it is the acquisition of energy that is the problem. The appearance of atomic energy has led some to question this assumption. However, given an infinite source of energy, population growth still produces an inescapable problem. The problem of the acquisition of energy is replaced by the problem of its dissipation, as J. H. Fremlin has so wittily shown.[4] The arithmetic signs in the analysis are, as it were, reversed; but Bentham's goal is still unobtainable.

The optimum population is, then, less than the maximum. The difficulty of defining the optimum is enormous; so far as I know, no one has seriously tackled this problem. Reaching an acceptable and stable solution will surely require more than one generation of hard analytical work—and much persuasion.

We want the maximum good per person; but what is good? To one person it is wilderness, to another it is ski lodges for thousands. To one it is estuaries to nourish ducks for hunters to shoot; to another it is factory land. Comparing one good with another is, we usually say, impossible because goods are incommensurable. Incommensurables cannot be compared.

Theoretically this may be true; but in real life incommensurables *are* commensurable. Only a criterion of judgment and a system of weighting are needed. In nature the criterion is survival. Is it better for a species to be small and hideable, or large and powerful? Natural selection commensurates the incommensurables. The compromise achieved depends on a natural weighting of the values of the variables.

Man must imitate this process. There is no doubt that in fact he already does, but unconsciously. It is when the hidden decisions are made explicit that the arguments begin. The problem for the years ahead is to work out an acceptable theory of weighting. Synergistic effects, nonlinear variation, and difficulties in discounting the future make the intellectual problem difficult, but not (in principle) insoluble.

Has any cultural group solved this practical problem at the present time, even on an intuitive level? One simple fact proves that none has: there is no prosperous population in the world today that has, and has had for some time, a growth rate of zero. Any people that has intuitively identified its optimum point will soon reach it, after which its growth rate becomes and remains zero.

Of course, a positive growth rate might be taken as evidence that a population is below its optimum. However, by any reasonable standards, the most rapidly growing populations on earth today are (in general) the most miserable. This association (which need not be invariable) casts doubt on the optimistic assumption that the positive growth rate of a population is evidence that it has yet to reach its optimum.

We can make little progress in working toward optimum population size until we explicitly exorcize the spirit of Adam Smith in the field of practical demography. In economic affairs, *The Wealth of Nations* (1776) popularized the "invisible hand," the idea that an individual who "intends only his own gain," is, as it were, "led by an invisible hand to promote . . . the public interest."[5] Adam Smith did not assert that this was invariably true, and perhaps neither did any of his followers. But he contributed to a dominant tendency of thought that has ever since interfered with positive action based on rational analysis, namely, the tendency to assume that decisions reached individually will, in fact, be the best decisions for an entire society. If this assumption is correct, it justifies the continuance of our present policy of laissez-faire in reproduction. If it is correct we can assume that men will control their individual fecundity so as to produce the optimum population. If the assumption is not correct, we need to reexamine our individual freedoms to see which ones are defensible.

TRAGEDY OF FREEDOM IN A COMMONS

The rebuttal to the invisible hand in population control is to be found in a scenario first sketched in a little-known pamphlet[6] in 1833 by a mathematical amateur named William Forster Lloyd (1794–1852). We may well call it "the tragedy of the commons," using the word "tragedy" as the philosopher Whitehead used it:[7] "The essence of dramatic tragedy is not unhappiness. It resides in the solemnity of the remorseless working of things." He then goes on to say, "This inevitableness of destiny can only be illustrated in terms of human life by incidents which in fact involve unhappiness. For it is only by them that the futility of escape can be made evident in the drama."

The tragedy of the commons develops in this way. Picture a pasture open to all. It is to be expected that each herdsman will try to keep as many cattle as possible on the commons. Such an arrangement may work reasonably satisfactorily for centuries because tribal wars, poaching, and disease keep the numbers of both man and beast well below the carrying capacity of the land. Finally, however, comes the day of reckoning; that is, the day when the long-desired goal of social stability becomes a reality. At this point, the inherent logic of the commons remorselessly generates tragedy.

As a rational being, each herdsman seeks to maximize his gain. Explicitly or implicitly, more or less consciously, he asks, "What is the utility *to me* of adding one more animal to my herd?" This utility has one negative and one positive component.

1. The positive component is a function of the increment of one animal. Since the herdsman receives all the proceeds from the sale of the additional animal, the positive utility is nearly +1.
2. The negative component is a function of the additional overgrazing created by one more animal. Since, however, the effects of overgrazing are shared by all the herdsmen, the negative utility for any particular decision-making herdsman is only a fraction of –1.

Adding together the component partial utilities, the rational herdsman concludes that the only sensible course for him to pursue is to add another animal to his herd. And another; and another. . . . But this is the conclusion reached by each and every rational herdsman sharing a commons. Therein is the tragedy. Each man is locked into a system that compels him to increase his herd without limit—in a world that is limited. Ruin is the destination toward which all men rush, each pursuing his own best interest in a society that believes in the freedom of the commons. Freedom in a commons brings ruin to all.

Some would say that this is a platitude. Would that it were! In a sense, it was learned thousands of years ago, but natural selection favors the forces of psychological denial.[8] The individual benefits as an individual from his ability to deny the truth even though society as a whole, of which he is a part, suffers. Education can counteract the natural tendency to do the wrong thing, but the inexorable succession of generations requires that the basis for this knowledge be constantly refreshed.

A simple incident that occurred a few years ago in Leominster, Massachusetts, shows how perishable the knowledge is. During the Christmas shopping season the parking meters downtown were covered with plastic bags that bore tags reading: "Do not open until after Christmas. Free parking courtesy of the mayor and city council." In other words, facing the prospect of an increased demand for already scarce space, the city fathers reinstituted the system of the commons. (Cynically, we suspect that they gained more votes than they lost by this retrogressive act.)

In an approximate way, the logic of the commons has been understood for a long time, perhaps since the discovery of agriculture or the invention of private property in real estate. But it is understood mostly only in special cases which are not sufficiently generalized. Even at this late date, cattlemen leasing national land on the western ranges demonstrate no more than an ambivalent understanding, in constantly pressuring federal authorities to increase the head count to the point where overgrazing produces erosion and weed-dominance. Likewise, the oceans of the world continue to suffer from the survival of the philosophy of the commons. Maritime nations still respond automatically to the shibboleth of the "freedom of the seas." Professing to believe in the "inexhaustible resources of the oceans," they bring species after species of fish and whales closer to extinction.[9]

The National Parks present another instance of the working out of the tragedy of the commons. At present, they are open to all, without limit. The parks themselves are limited in extent—there is only one Yosemite Valley—whereas population seems to grow without limit. The values that visitors seek in the parks are steadily eroded. Plainly, we must soon cease to treat the parks as commons or they will be of no value to anyone.

What shall we do? We have several options. We might sell them off as private property. We might keep them as public property, but allocate the right to enter them. The allocation might be on the basis of wealth, by the use of an auction system. It might be on the basis of merit, as defined by some agreed-upon standards. It might be by lottery. Or it might be on a first-come, first-served basis, administered to long queues. These, I think, are all the reasonable possibilities. They are all objectionable. But we must choose—or acquiesce in the destruction of the commons that we call our National Parks.

POLLUTION

In a reverse way, the tragedy of the commons reappears in problems of pollution. Here it is not a question of taking something out of the commons, but of putting something in—sewage, or chemical, radioactive, and heat wastes into water; noxious and dangerous fumes into the air; and distracting and unpleasant advertising signs into the line of sight. The calculations of utility are much the same as before. The rational man finds that his share of the cost of the wastes he discharges into the commons is less than the cost of purifying his wastes before releasing them. Since this is true for everyone, we are locked into a system of "fouling our own nest," so long as we behave only as independent, rational, free-enterprisers.

The tragedy of the commons as a food basket is averted by private property, or something formally like it. But the air and waters surrounding us cannot readily be fenced, and so the tragedy of the commons as a cesspool must be prevented by different means, by coercive laws or taxing devices that make it cheaper for the polluter to treat his pollutants than to discharge them untreated. We have not progressed as far with the solution of this problem as we have with the first. Indeed, our particular concept of private property, which deters us from exhausting the positive resources of the earth, favors pollution. The owner of a factory on the bank of a stream—whose property extends to the middle of the stream—often has difficulty seeing why it is not his natural right to muddy the waters flowing past his door. The law, always behind the times, requires elaborate stitching and fitting to adapt it to this newly perceived aspect of the commons.

The pollution problem is a consequence of population. It did not much matter how a lonely American frontiersman disposed of his waste. "Flowing water purifies itself every 10 miles," my grandfather used to say, and the myth was near enough to the truth when he was a boy, for there were not too many people. But as population became denser, the natural chemical and biological recycling processes became overloaded, calling for a redefinition of property rights.

HOW TO LEGISLATE TEMPERANCE?

Analysis of the pollution problem as a function of population density uncovers a not generally recognized principle of morality, namely: *the morality of an act is a function of the state of the system at the time it is performed.*[10] Using the commons as a cesspool does not harm the general public under frontier conditions, because there is no public; the same behavior in a metropolis is unbearable. A hundred and fifty years ago a plainsman could kill an American bison, cut out only the tongue for his dinner, and discard the rest of the animal. He was not in any important sense being wasteful. Today, with only a few thousand bison left, we would be appalled at such behavior.

In passing, it is worth noting that the morality of an act cannot be determined from a photograph. One does not know whether a man killing an elephant or setting fire to the grassland is harming others until one knows the total system in which his act appears. "One picture is worth a thousand words," said an ancient Chinese; but it may take 10,000 words to validate it. It is as tempting to ecologists as it is to reformers in general to try to persuade others by way of the photographic shortcut. But the essense of an argument cannot be photographed: it must be presented rationally—in words.

That morality is system-sensitive escaped the attention of most codifiers of ethics in the past. "Thou shalt not . . ." is the form of traditional ethical directives which make no allowance for particular circumstances. The laws of our society follow the pattern of ancient ethics, and therefore are poorly suited to governing a complex, crowded, changeable world. Our epicyclic solution is to augment statutory law with administrative law. Since it is practically impossible to spell out all the conditions under which it is safe to burn trash in the backyard or to run an automobile without smog-control, by law we delegate the details to bureaus. The result is administrative law, which is rightly feared for an ancient reason—*Quis custodiet ipsos custodes?*—"Who shall watch the watchers themselves?" John Adams said that we must have "a government of laws and not men." Bureau administrators, trying to evaluate the morality of acts in the total system, are singularly liable to corruption, producing a government by men, not laws.

Prohibition is easy to legislate (though not necessarily to enforce); but how do we legislate temperance? Experience indicates that it can be accomplished best through the mediation of administrative law. We limit possibilities unnecessarily if we suppose that the sentiment of *Quis custodiet* denies us the use of administrative law. We should rather retain the phrase as a perpetual reminder of fearful dangers we cannot avoid. The great challenge facing us now is to invent the corrective feedbacks that are needed to keep custodians honest. We must find ways to legitimate the needed authority of both the custodians and the corrective feedbacks.

FREEDOM TO BREED IS INTOLERABLE

The tragedy of the commons is involved in population problems in another way. In a world governed solely by the principle of "dog eat dog"—if indeed there ever was such a world—how many children a family had would not be a matter of public concern. Parents who bred too exuberantly would leave fewer descendants, not more, because they would be unable to care adequately for their children. David Lack and others have found that such a negative feedback demonstrably controls the fecundity of birds.[11] But men are not birds, and have not acted like them for millenniums, at least.

If each human family were dependent only on its own resources; *if* the children of improvident parents starved to death; *if*, thus, overbreeding brought its own "punishment" to the germ line—*then* there would be no public interest in controlling the breeding of families. But our society is deeply committed to the welfare state,[12] and hence is confronted with another aspect of the tragedy of the commons.

In a welfare state, how shall we deal with the family, the religion, the race, or the class (or indeed any distinguishable and cohesive group) that adopts overbreeding as a policy to secure its own aggrandizement?[13] To couple the concept of freedom to breed with the belief that everyone born has an equal right to the commons is to lock the world into a tragic course of action.

Unfortunately this is just the course of action that is being pursued by the United Nations. In late 1967, some 30 nations agreed to the following:[14]

> The Universal Declaration of Human Rights describes the family as the natural and fundamental unit of society. It follows that any choice and decision with regard to the size of the family must irrevocably rest with the family itself, and cannot be made by anyone else.

It is painful to have to deny categorically the validity of this right; denying it, one feels as uncomfortable as a resident of Salem, Massachusetts, who denied the reality of witches in the [seventeenth] century. At the present time, in liberal quarters, something like a taboo acts to inhibit criticism of the United Nations. There is a feeling that the United Nations is "our last and best hope," that we shouldn't find fault with it; we shouldn't play into the hands of the archconservatives. However, let us not forget what Robert Louis Stevenson said: "The truth that is suppressed by friends is the readiest weapon of the enemy." If we love the truth, we must openly deny the validity of the Universal Declaration of Human Rights, even though it is promoted by the United Nations. We should also join with Kingsley Davis[15] in attempting to get Planned Parenthood-World Population to see the error of its ways in embracing the same tragic ideal.

CONSCIENCE IS SELF-ELIMINATING

It is a mistake to think that we can control the breeding of mankind in the long run by an appeal to conscience. Charles Galton Darwin made this point when he spoke on the centennial of the publication of his grandfather's great book. The argument is straightforward and Darwinian.

People vary. Confronted with appeals to limit breeding, some people will undoubtedly respond to the plea more than others. Those who have more children will produce a larger fraction of the next generation than those with more susceptible consciences. The difference will be accentuated, generation by generation.

In C. G. Darwin's words: "It may well be that it would take hundreds of generations for the progenitive instinct to develop in this way, but if it should do so, nature would have taken her revenge, and the variety *Homo contracipiens* would become extinct and would be replaced by the variety *Homo progenitivus*."[16]

The argument assumes that conscience or the desire for children (no matter which) is hereditary—but hereditary only in the most general formal sense. The result will be the same whether the attitude is transmitted through germ cells, or exosomatically, to use A. J. Lotka's term. (If one denies the latter possibility as well as the former, then what's the point of education?) The argument has here been stated in the context of the population problem, but it applies equally well to any instance in which society appeals to an individual exploiting a commons to restrain himself for the general good—by means of his conscience. To make such an appeal is to set up a selective system that works toward the elimination of conscience from the race.

PATHOGENIC EFFECTS OF CONSCIENCE

The long-term disadvantage of an appeal to conscience should be enough to condemn it; but [it] has serious short-term disadvantages as well. If we ask a man who is exploiting a commons to desist "in the name of conscience," what are we saying to him? What does he hear?—not only at the moment but also in the wee small hours of the night when, half asleep, he remembers not merely the words we used but also the nonverbal communication cues we gave him unawares? Sooner or later, consciously or subconsciously, he senses that he has received two communications, and that they are contradictory: (i) (intended communication) "If you don't do as we ask, we will openly condemn you for not acting like a responsible citizen"; (ii) (the unintended communication) "If you *do* behave as we ask, we will secretly condemn you for a simpleton who can be shamed into standing aside while the rest of us exploit the commons."

Everyman then is caught in what Bateson has called a "double bind." Bateson and his co-workers have made a plausible case for viewing the double bind as an important causative factor in the genesis of schizophrenia.[17] The double bind may not always be so damaging, but it always endangers the mental health of anyone to whom it is applied. "A bad conscience," said Nietzsche, "is a kind of illness."

To conjure up a conscience in others is tempting to anyone who wishes to extend his control beyond the legal limits. Leaders at the highest level succumb to this temptation. Has any President during the past generation failed to call on labor unions to moderate voluntarily their demands for higher wages, or to steel companies to honor voluntary guidelines on prices? I can recall none. The rhetoric used on such occasions is designed to produce feelings of guilt in non-cooperators.

For centuries it was assumed without proof that guilt was a valuable, perhaps even an indispensable, ingredient of the civilized life. Now, in this post-Freudian world, we doubt it.

Paul Goodman speaks from the modern point of view when he says: "No good has ever come from feeling guilty, neither intelligence, policy, nor compassion. The guilty do not pay attention to the object but only to themselves, and not even to their own interests, which might make sense, but to their anxieties."[18]

One does not have to be a professional psychiatrist to see the consequences of anxiety. We in the Western world are just emerging from a dreadful two-centuries-long Dark Ages of Eros that was sustained partly by prohibition laws, but perhaps more effectively by the anxiety-generating mechanisms of education. Alex Comfort has told the story well in *The Anxiety Makers*;[19] it is not a pretty one.

Since proof is difficult, we may even concede that the results of anxiety may sometimes, from certain points of view, be desirable. The larger question we should ask is whether, as a matter of policy, we should ever encourage the use of a technique the tendency (if not the intention) of which is psychologically pathogenic. We hear much talk these days of responsible parenthood; the coupled words are incorporated into the titles of some organizations devoted to birth control. Some people have proposed massive propaganda campaigns to instill responsibility into the nation's (or the world's) breeders. But what is the meaning of the word responsibility in this context? Is it not merely a synonym for the word conscience? When we use the word responsibility in the absence of substantial sanctions are we not trying to browbeat a free man in a commons into acting against his own interest? Responsibility is a verbal counterfeit for a substantial *quid pro quo*. It is an attempt to get something for nothing.

If the word responsibility is to be used at all, I suggest that it be in the sense Charles Frankel uses it.[20] "Responsibility," says this philosopher, "is the product of definite social arrangements." Notice that Frankel calls for social arrangements—not propaganda.

MUTUAL COERCION MUTUALLY AGREED UPON

The social arrangements that produce responsibility are arrangements that create coercion, of some sort. Consider bank-robbing. The man who takes money from a bank acts as if the bank were a commons. How do we prevent such action? Certainly not by trying to control his behavior solely by a verbal appeal to his sense of responsibility. Rather than rely on propaganda we follow Frankel's lead and insist that a bank is not a commons; we seek the definite social arrangements that will keep it from becoming a commons. That we thereby infringe on the freedom of would-be robbers we neither deny nor regret.

The morality of bank-robbing is particularly easy to understand because we accept complete prohibition of this activity. We are willing to say, "Thou shalt not rob banks," without providing for exceptions. But temperance also can be created by coercion. Taxing is a good coercive device. To keep downtown shoppers temperate in their use of parking space we introduce parking meters for short periods, and traffic fines for longer ones. We need not actually forbid a citizen to park as long as he wants to; we need merely make it increasingly expensive for him to do so. Not prohibition, but carefully biased options are what we offer him. A Madison Avenue man might call this persuasion; I prefer the greater candor of the word coercion.

Coercion is a dirty word to most liberals now, but it need not forever be so. As with the four-letter words, its dirtiness can be cleansed away by exposure to the light, by saying it over and over without apology or embarrassment. To many, the word coercion implies arbitrary decisions of distant and irresponsible bureaucrats; but this is not a necessary part of its meaning. The only kind of coercion I recommend is mutual coercion, mutually agreed upon by the majority of the people affected.

To say that we mutually agree to coercion is not to say that we are required to enjoy it, or even to pretend we enjoy it. Who enjoys taxes? We all grumble about them. But we accept compulsory taxes because we recognize that voluntary taxes would favor the conscienceless. We institute and (grumblingly) support taxes and other coercive devices to escape the horror of the commons.

An alternative to the commons need not be perfectly just to be preferable. With real estate and other material goods, the alternative we have chosen is the institution of private property coupled with legal inheritance. Is this system perfectly just? As a genetically trained biologist I deny that it is. It seems to me that, if there are to be differences in individual inheritance, legal possession should be perfectly correlated with biological inheritance—that those who are biologically more fit to be the custodians of property and power should legally inherit more. But genetic recombination continually makes a mockery of the doctrine of "like father, like son" implicit in our laws of legal inheritance. An idiot can inherit millions, and a trust fund can keep his estate intact. We must admit that our legal system of private property plus inheritance is unjust—but we put up with it because we are not convinced, at the moment, that anyone has invented a better system. The alternative of the commons is too horrifying to contemplate. Injustice is preferable to total ruin.

It is one of the peculiarities of the warfare between reform and the status quo that it is thoughtlessly governed by a double standard. Whenever a reform measure is proposed it is often defeated when its opponents triumphantly discover a flaw in it. As Kingsley Davis has pointed out,[21] worshippers of the status quo sometimes imply that no reform is possible without unanimous agreement, an implication contrary to historical fact. As nearly as I can make out, automatic rejection of proposed reforms is based on one of two unconscious assumptions: (i) that the status quo is perfect; or (ii) that the choice we face is between reform and no action; if the proposed reform is imperfect, we presumably should take no action at all, while we wait for a perfect proposal.

But we can never do nothing. That which we have done for thousands of years is also action. It also produces evils. Once we are aware that the status quo is action, we can then compare its discoverable advantages and disadvantages with the predicted advantages and disadvantages of the proposed reform, discounting as best we can for our lack of experience. On the basis of such a comparison, we can make a rational decision which will not involve the unworkable assumption that only perfect systems are tolerable.

RECOGNITION OF NECESSITY

Perhaps the simplest summary of this analysis of man's population problems is this: the commons, if justifiable at all, is justifiable only under conditions of low-population density. As the human population has increased, the commons has had to be abandoned in one aspect after another.

First we abandoned the commons in food gathering, enclosing farm land and restricting pastures and hunting and fishing areas. These restrictions are still not complete throughout the world.

Somewhat later we saw that the commons as a place for waste disposal would also have to be abandoned. Restrictions on the disposal of domestic sewage are widely accepted in the Western world; we are still struggling to close the commons to pollution by automobiles, factories, insecticide sprayers, fertilizing operations, and atomic energy installations.

In a still more embryonic state is our recognition of the evils of the commons in matters of pleasure. There is almost no restriction on the propagation of sound waves in the public medium. The shopping public is assaulted with mindless music, without its consent. Our government is paying out billions of dollars to create supersonic transport which will disturb 50,000 people for every one person who is whisked from coast to coast 3 hours faster. Advertisers muddy the airwaves of radio and television and pollute the view[s] of travelers. We are a long way from outlawing the commons in matters of pleasure. Is this because our Puritan inheritance makes us view pleasure as something of a sin, and plain (that is, the pollution of advertising) as the sign of virtue?

Every new enclosure of the commons involves the infringement of somebody's personal liberty. Infringements made in the distant past are accepted because no contemporary complains of a loss. It is the newly proposed infringements that we vigorously oppose; cries of "rights" and "freedom" fill the air. But what does "freedom" mean? When men mutually agreed to pass laws against robbing, mankind became more free, not less so. Individuals locked into the logic of the commons are free only to bring on universal ruin; once they see the necessity of mutual coercion, they become free to pursue other goals. I believe it was Hegel who said, "Freedom is the recognition of necessity."

The most important aspect of necessity that we must now recognize is the necessity of abandoning the commons in breeding. No technical solution can rescue us from the misery of overpopulation. Freedom to breed will bring ruin to all. At the moment, to avoid hard decisions many of us are tempted to propagandize for conscience and responsible parenthood. The temptation must be resisted, because an appeal to independently acting consciences selects for the disappearance of all conscience in the long run, and an increase in anxiety in the short.

The only way we can preserve and nurture other and more precious freedoms is by relinquishing the freedom to breed, and that very soon. "Freedom is the recognition of necessity"—and it is the role of education to reveal to all the necessity of abandoning the freedom to breed. Only so, can we put an end to this aspect of the tragedy of the commons.

NOTES

1. J. B. Wiesner and H. F. York. *Sci. Amer.* 211 (No. 4), 27 (1964).

2. G. Hardin, *J. Hered.* 50, 68 (1959); S. von Hoernor, *Science* 137, 18 (1962).

3. J. von Neumann and O. Morgenstern, *Theory of Games and Economic Behavior* (Princeton Univ. Press, Princeton, N.J., 1947), p. 11.

4. J. H. Fremlin, *New Sci.*, No. 415 (1964), p. 285.

5. A. Smith, *The Wealth of Nations* (Modern Library, New York, 1937), p. 423.

6. W. F. Lloyd, *Two Lectures on the Checks to Population* (Oxford Univ. Press, Oxford, England, 1833), reprinted (in part) in *Population, Evolution, and Birth Control*, G. Hardin, Ed. (Freeman, San Francisco, 1964), p. 37.

7. A. N. Whitehead, *Science and the Modern World* (Mentor, New York, 1948), p. 17.

8. G. Hardin, Ed. *Population, Evolution, and Birth Control* (Freeman, San Francisco, 1964), p. 56.

9. S. McVay, *Sci. Amer.* 216 (No. 8), 13 (1966).

10. J. Fletcher, *Situation Ethics* (Westminster, Philadelphia, 1966).

11. D. Lack, *The Natural Regulation of Animal Numbers* (Clarendon Press, Oxford, 1954).

12. H. Girvetz, *From Wealth to Welfare* (Stanford Univ. Press, Stanford, Calif., 1950).

13. G. Hardin, *Perspec. Biol. Med.* 6, 366 (1963).

14. U. Thant, *Int. Planned Parenthood News*, No. 168 (February 1968), p. 3.

15. K. Davis, *Science* 158, 730 (1967).

16. S. Tax, Ed., *Evolution after Darwin* (Univ. of Chicago Press, Chicago, 1960), vol. 2, p. 469.

17. G. Bateson, D. D. Jackson, J. Haley, J. Weakland, *Behav. Sci.* 1, 251 (1956).

18. P. Goodman, *New York Rev. Books* 10 (No. 8), 22 (23 May 1968).

19. A. Comfort, *The Anxiety Makers* (Nelson, London, 1967).

20. C. Frankel, *The Case for Modern Man* (Harper, New York, 1955), p. 203.

21. J. D. Roslansky, *Genetics and the Future of Man* (Appleton-Century-Crofts, New York, 1966), p. 177.

1.3

JANE MANSBRIDGE

"What Is Political Science For?"

Mansbridge, as president of the American Political Science Association in 2012–13, gave this address (excerpted here) to discuss the central questions in the discipline of political science. How can humans govern themselves effectively? And, since coercion is necessary in governing, how can we ensure "legitimate coercion"? She says that political scientists have a role to play in evaluating the quality of governing institutions, and helping countries and their people judge the truth about illegitimate and legitimate forms of government coercion. People disagree on standards, perhaps, but collective evaluations based on facts and logic are the best means we have to decide what actions of governments are legitimate.

THE MANDATE

■ ■ ■

[I]f political science is "for" anything, I think it is, and should be, for helping us to govern ourselves. Political science is the only academic discipline specifically organized to study this question. Other disciplines—law, psychology, sociology, economics—make valuable contributions to answering it. But we, as a discipline, are organized around the issue of governing. Because we have consciously created social structures that let us think together, and because of our specialized toolkits, we—of all the people in the world—are the best organized to help do this. The world certainly needs that help.

Compared to our needs, we know very little about how to govern ourselves. We don't know how to coerce ourselves into giving up what we need to give up in order to stop global warming. We don't know how to stop nuclear proliferation. We don't know how to transition from autocracy to democracy without descending into violence. Closer to home, we don't know how to tax ourselves sufficiently to keep our infrastructure from crumbling or how to pay for the rising medical costs of an aging population. We don't know how to produce laws in a polarized Congress or how to reduce that polarization. We don't know how to keep ourselves from drifting into greater and greater inequality. At this

From Jane Mansbridge, "What Is Political Science For?" *Perspectives on Politics* 12, no. 1 (March 2014): 8–17.

moment of great need and relative ignorance, political science is the one academic discipline explicitly organized to study how we make our collective decisions on these matters, and how we can make them legitimately.

CREATING LEGITIMATE COERCION

Legitimate coercion is the fundamental problem of governance. How can large, highly interdependent structures produce sufficient legitimate coercion to solve their collective action problems? Such structures are evolving everywhere—even internationally—although in the case of nuclear proliferation and global warming we seem to be losing the race against time. On the domestic front, large-scale representative democracy has evolved only relatively recently, in the last 300 years, and we are continuing to experiment with the form. In the [United States], innovations in the primary system, redistricting, and Congressional rules have recently affected the way our democracy works. Elsewhere in the world nations and regions are experimenting institutionally with a realistic sense of urgency.

■   ■   ■

My central argument regarding coercion has three parts. First, in a world of increasing interdependence we face an almost infinite number of collective action problems that are created when something we want or need is a "free access" good. Second, solving most of those collective action problems requires coercion, which is the basic reason for government. Third, the best coercion is legitimate coercion. Important as legitimate coercion is, we do not know how to do it very well. The fundamental job of political science, I believe, is to help societies create and properly use legitimate coercion.

What do I mean by legitimate coercion? Coercion is relatively easy to define. By coercion I mean the threat of sanction ("Leave this room or I'll shoot you") or the use of force (carrying you out of the room kicking and screaming).[1] A sanction can be as small and informal as a dirty look or as large and formal as life imprisonment. Defining legitimacy is harder, and I will return to that.

Now, let me begin to walk through my argument.

Free-Access Goods Create Collective Action Problems

First, as most people here know, collective action problems arise whenever a "free-access good" must be produced. By a "free-access" good I mean a good that, once produced, anyone can consume even if they did not contribute to producing it. If common defense against enemies is provided, anyone can benefit even if they did not contribute. So, too, with law and order, or a toll-free road. Once some group of people has provided such a good, anyone can use it. Everyone is therefore tempted to free-ride, using the good without helping to create or to maintain it by contributing effort or money.

I use the term "free-access good" instead of the economists' terms "non-excludable good" and "public good" both because free access is easier to remember and for technical reasons.[2] All that matters for this analysis is that when a good has the characteristic of being free access—that is, open to all potential users—it tends to be under-produced.

A collective action exercise. I would like to ask even those of you who are deeply familiar with the collective action problem to participate with me in a brief collective action exercise. Imagine that you have $100 in your pocket. Now please take out a real piece of paper and write on it either zero dollars or one hundred dollars, for the contribution you will make to the common pot. Just zero or 100, please, nothing in between, for simplicity. I will be a doubling machine. I will double everything in the pot, with no effort on your part, and return that amount to everyone equally. That doubled money is a free-access good. If you give me zero, you get to keep your $100 and also get an equal share of whatever others put in the pot. But if everyone keeps his or her $100, you will all lose the chance to double your money without effort. This is the "common pool" version of the collective action problem. The point is that no matter what the others do, if you do not contribute you will end up with more than if you do contribute. Now please write either zero or 100 on the paper, fold it over so that no one can see what you wrote, and pass it to the aisle and then to the front of the room. Thank you.

While the counters are tallying up the results, let me assume that 80 percent of you contributed, using imaginary dollars that cost you nothing. [In the event, 76 percent of the 472 attendees contributed to the common pool, a higher percentage than in most such situations, explained by self-selection.] The percentage you give will normally decrease rapidly when the money you are asked to give is real and as the amount you are asked to give grows larger. But the precise percentage is irrelevant to my point. We can learn two things from this exercise.

First, we learn that many of you contributed $100. Assuming that you were confident of your anonymity, your motives were some mixture of solidarity and duty, two separate motives on which polities can build.[3] You may also have looked around and quickly calculated that more than half of the people in the room would contribute, so that you would at least not lose your stake—and psychologists have provided ample evidence that human beings hate losses even more than we like gains.[4] That kind of trust in the others in your community is another significant base on which polities can build.

Second, we also learn that some of you, even though the dollars were imaginary, have contributed zero. Some of you may have gone along with the assumption that the dollars were real and not wanted to risk that stake. Others may have been making a political point that you should not be asked to give up your $100 for a collective cause. Whatever the reason, at least 20 percent of you probably did not contribute. If we repeated this exercise over time your refusal to contribute would begin to undermine the contributions of others.

As Margaret Levi has pointed out in developing her concept of "contingent consent," people who think that others are paying their taxes are themselves less likely to cheat. When they think that others are free-riding, they often begin to free-ride, too.[5]

We can conclude both that we ought not to undermine the solidarity and conscience that lead some to contribute and that we need to find some way of getting the non-contributors to contribute—unless they had a good reason for not contributing, in which case we want the contributors to hear, understand, and accept that reason. In a small setting, contributors can use some version of the informal coercion of a dirty look to punish the non-contributors. Sometimes even large groups can handle a collective action problem through a combination of critical mass, solidarity, conscience, social sanction, and reciprocity based on reputation, for example in the strategy that game theorists call "generous Tit for Tat."[6] But in a large and relatively anonymous setting, where many people do not know the others' reputations, we usually need more formal coercion to solve collective action problems. Government is the set of institutions we create to develop and administer that coercion.[7]

Understanding the dynamics of the collective action problem is, in my view, a logical breakthrough comparable to understanding the implications of how supply and demand interact to determine price. But the collective action problem is a bit harder to understand than supply and demand. Until the last half of the twentieth century, no human being had access to this logic. Rousseau and Hume had developed partial formulations of one version of the problem, but only in the 1950s did scholars in the three separate fields of game theory, public finance, and fisheries management begin to work out its full logic.[8] The economist William Baumol was the first to stress that the problem must be solved with what Garrett Hardin later called "mutual coercion mutually arrived at."[9] For the next several decades the implications of the various forms of the collective action problem swept through the social sciences.[10] Yet the full implications have still not been assimilated into general knowledge. Even today I doubt that more than a small percentage of political science students understands the logic of collective action, its dependence on a free-access good, and its implications for coercion. Nor do they understand its corollary, that solving collective action problems is the most significant reason for government.

Nonetheless, collective action problems have become much more central to human life in the last hundred years. As we increase in number, free-access goods that were earlier supplied by nature (clean air, clean and sufficient water, fish in the sea) require more and more human action to maintain or produce them. As human beings also produce more complex goods and develop more refined demands (like blueberries in the winter), we become more and more interdependent. And as we become more interdependent, we require more free-access goods, such as contract enforcement and certain forms of reliable knowledge. To get these free-access goods, we need more legitimate coercion.[11]

Coercion Helps Solve Collective Action Problems

Take the looming catastrophe in climate change. Many people still do not see a reduction in global warming as a free-access good that we will have to coerce ourselves to produce. At the other end of a long spectrum, take the trivial case of blueberries in the winter. To get them on our tables, state coercion helps at every stage. In January, more than half of U.S. blueberries come from Chile.[12] Even before they are planted, the Chilean Agricultural Ministry gives farmers information about the crop, and the Chilean Plant and Animal Health Policy, which is one of the strictest in the world, helps keep dangerous organisms out of the agricultural system. Getting the berries to the table also takes a large number of free-access goods, each provided through some sort of state coercion, including the coercion needed to collect taxes. Highways, ports and airports, emissions and pollution regulations, safe seas, law and order, property rights protected by the courts—the list of free-access goods that we need to get those berries, accurately labeled and safe to eat, to our tables, runs on and on. The market depends on the coercion that makes those free access goods possible.

To keep this whole complex of free-access goods going smoothly, the necessary coercion must be relatively well designed, in recognition of its costs. For example, extrinsic motivation such as coercion tends to drive out intrinsic motivation.[13] Fining people if they pick up their children late from daycare increases rather than decreases the number of late pickups.[14] Paying Swiss communities to accept nuclear waste makes them less likely to accept it than asking them to do so for the nation's good.[15] So, on the implementation side, we often need more persuasion and less reliance on coercive power. As Elinor Ostrom and others have shown, even necessary coercion should be minimal, graduated, appropriately designed for the specific situation, and both formulated and applied by those who will have to live under it.[16] Yet Ostrom never confronted—I would say she avoided—the problem of legitimacy.

The Best Coercion Is Legitimate Coercion

Many studies have shown that people are more likely to obey a law they consider legitimate.[17] The more legitimate they think the coercion is, the less often sanctions need to be applied. Thus, the best coercion is legitimate coercion. Less legitimate coercion throws sand in the cogs, the system begins to grind more slowly and less well, and the product becomes more expensive— sometimes too expensive to compete.

■　　■　　■

Democracy is ideal based. In the advanced industrial democracies of the early twenty-first century, democratic systems are legitimated not by one ideal, but by a constellation of ideals. These include republican liberty (by which I mean autonomy or self-rule), "liberal" liberty (by which I mean the ideal of non-interference), a form of community grounded in equal respect, and various forms of equality based, among other things, on human dignity and formal justice.[18] These ideals derive from human experience, have evolved over time, and resonate among the marginalized as well as the powerful. They anchor the legitimacy of democratic systems. They also conflict with one another. Indeed, the ideals on which democracy is based are all what Kant called "regulative ideals"—ideals toward which we should strive, all other things equal, but which we can never expect to reach fully.[19] They are impossible to reach in all their fullness partly because of the nature of reality and partly because they do often conflict with one another. This means that no democracy is ever fully legitimate. Most people can tolerate this failure because they are practical. They don't expect things to be perfect. The feature that further legitimates democracy, when this is, in fact, the case, is that the institutions are designed to be likely to move, when possible, closer to these animating ideals.

■ ■ ■

NEGOTIATING TO AGREEMENT

■ ■ ■

One big lesson . . . is the importance of what negotiation theorists call "expanding the pie," which primarily means bringing in new issues on which the different parties have different priorities, allowing each side to trade its low priority items for higher priority items that matter less to the other side. However, the textbooks and courses in business, law, and policy schools aim primarily at teaching individuals how to be good negotiators, not at identifying institutions that facilitate successful negotiation. That is a task for political science.

Because negotiation is such a large part of politics, we need to identify institutions that help negotiators bring in new issues and make good trades. And because one function of institutions is to help correct individual mistakes, we need to figure out which institutions help participants combat the cognitive and emotional barriers to successful negotiation. Self-serving bias, for example, means that we tend to select our facts and even our conceptions of justice and the common good without noticing that we are selecting facts and concepts that benefit us more than others.[20] Well-designed institutions help participants agree on facts and see that their conceptions of justice are not shared by everyone else.

■ ■ ■

CONCLUSION

In a Venn diagram, the two concepts "collective action" and "need for formal government" have only a partial overlap. In the first place, as your recent voluntary donations to the common pool illustrate, we can largely solve some collective action problems without the formal coercion of government. In the second place, we need government for issues other than collective action problems. Government can act as a coordinator without coercion, as a model for right behavior, and as a voice for collective ideals. Government institutions can serve as deliberative arenas and focal points for [the] collective struggle over who we are. We may also need the formal coercion of government to accomplish other goals, such as justice, that are arguably not collective action problems.[21]

Yet, while I am not contending that the only function of government is coercion, I believe that coercion is government's most important and most controversial function. Most of that coercion is required to solve collective action problems. Surprisingly few people today understand the basic point that whenever you want to produce a free-access good—and they are all around us, everywhere, not least in our changing climate—you will often need some coercion to help make it happen. For large scale problems, you will very often need state coercion.

■   ■   ■

It would be astonishing if the use of coercion did not, as a general rule, favor the more powerful. It would be astonishing if even the most well-meaning bureaucracies did not want to advance their missions with ever more personnel and ever more access to coercive power. So coercion, whether state or private, will tend to be unequally applied and greater than necessary. Resistance to state coercion is therefore always an important part of governing ourselves. Even in relatively uncorrupt and just governments the threat of resistance plays an important role in keeping them relatively uncorrupt and just. Resistance has an especially important role when governments are corrupt, self-serving, unjust, or deeply misguided.

Viscerally and experientially I identify with resistance. Women, for example, have won most of our gains in the last two centuries by resisting the domination of men. My generation grew up with resistance and our political theory was largely about resistance. Nevertheless, I think the western democratic tradition, anchored in resistance to kings, has focused too much on the possibilities and actualities of tyranny and domination and not enough on the equally important problem of how to create legitimate coercion for collective action. In this talk I have focused on legitimate coercion because of its centrality to what political science should be about. I do not mean to exclude protest and resistance from the concept of governing ourselves; I just want to strike a better balance.

More broadly, on the mission of political science, I contend that political science has always organized itself at least in part to help human beings govern themselves. It is in our DNA. Aristotle, lecturing on politics, wanted his listeners not only to hear, but also, after hearing, to govern themselves well. So, too, Hobbes, Locke, Montesquieu, and Madison wrote to help their readers do better in this business of governing.

■   ■   ■

Democracy, as the pragmatists point out, lends itself particularly well to experimentation.[22] But experiments often need people to evaluate, sift, and pass on to others the results of the experiments. Political science performs this task.

All of the subfields in political science are involved in the process of trying to improve the processes by which we govern ourselves. We need to explore the ideals we have—or think we have—about how we should govern ourselves. We need to explore the polity we know most intimately, whether it be the United States of America or another polity, to understand it in greater depth. We need to compare existing governments to one another, to ferret out their greatest strengths and weaknesses. We need to understand better how states and other entities relate to one another and how they can do so more productively.

We also need to use all of the methodologies we have developed—from the close reading of thinkers whose subtleties have often been forgotten or never understood as the intellectual wave of the moment swept past them, to the stringent analysis through formal models of the possible interactions of individuals motivated only by self-interest, to experiments in labs and in the field, to interpretive immersion in the processes of governing and being governed, to the quantitative analysis of large data sets.

What we have in common, I believe, is that we can all try to help the human race figure out how to institute sufficient legitimate mutual coercion to stave off the catastrophes toward which we are heading—as well as to move toward goals that would be good, by and large, for us all.

NOTES

1. For a definition of coercion, i.e., "coercive power," see Mansbridge et al. 2010.

2. I do not use the term "public good" because in addition to being free access (or "non-excludable"), a "public good" must also be "jointly supplied" (or "non-rival"), meaning that one person using it does not reduce the quality or quantity available for others. When Samuelson 1954 first developed the concept of what are now called public goods, he made joint supply or non-rivalry its central criterion. Yet this characteristic is irrelevant for the logic I explore here.

3. Mansbridge 1990.

4. Kahneman and Tversky 1979, 1984; Bentham [1789] 1996.

5. Levi 1988; people also want to know that the taxes are being used well. See also Scholz et al. 1995, 1998.

6. E.g., Wu and Axelrod 1995; Oliver, Marwell, and Teixeira 1985.

7. "The theory of collective action is the central subject of political science. It is the core of the justification for the state"; Ostrom 1998, 1.

8. On the basis of the game theory developed in the 1940s by John von Neumann and Oskar Morgenstern, around 1950 the two mathematicians Merrill Flood and Melvin Drescher at RAND worked out the basic structure of the Prisoner's Dilemma (or "Prisoners' Dilemma," as in Taylor 1987). Independently, in the field of public finance, in 1952 William Baumol made the case for the necessity of coercion in the case of resources held in common, while in 1954 Paul Samuelson laid out his first ideas on "collective

consumption goods." Independently of both other fields, in the realm of fishery management the economists Scott Gordon in 1954 and, building on Gordon's work, Anthony Scott in 1955 made the case that because the seas were "no one's property," fishermen could enter and deplete the common supply. For early formulations of part of the problem see Rousseau [1754] 1997 on the stag hunt and Hume [1739–40] 1960 on draining a meadow. See Hardin 1982 for part of this history.

9. Hardin 1968; cf. Baumol 1952; also Barry and Hardin 1982. The formulation "coerce ourselves" blurs the distinction between the individual and the collective. I can, of course, coerce myself by setting up a system at Time 1 that creates sanctions at Time 2 if I do what my Time 1 self wanted to discourage, but by the phrase "coerce ourselves" I mean that we participate in a collective endeavor in which I coerce others as well as myself and they coerce me as well as themselves.

10. E.g., Stinchecombe 1980.

11. Since this talk was delivered, Offe 2013 has extended my point by terming legitimate state coercion a "'meta' collective good" and arguing that as the "demand" for this good has increased because of growing interdependence, its "supply" has decreased because of a justified horror of the state-sponsored murders of the twentieth century, the flight of capital from states that try to regulate it, and an increase in public distrust of elites.

12. Agricultural Marketing Resource Center 2013.

13. Deci, Koestner, and Ryan 1999.

14. Gneezy and Rustichini 2000.

15. Frey 1997.

16. Ostrom 1990; Ayres and Braithwaite 1992.

17. Tyler 1990.

18. On republican liberty, Pettit 2001; on non-interference, Berlin [1958] 1969; on relationships, Nedelsky 2001; on dignity and respect, Kant [1785] 2012, Kateb 2011, Rosen 2012, Waldron 2009; on formal equality, Berlin 1955–56; on equal respect in friendship, Brain 1979; and on the ideal of friendship for the polity, Aristotle [c. 347–325 B.C.] 1944.

19. Kant [1781] 1998, 552.

20. Foster, Mansbridge, and Martin 2013 on "negotiation myopia."

21. If most people want to live in a just society or benefit from the community of willing cooperation that a "nearly" just society tends to produce, justice could be considered a collective action problem; see Rawls 1971.

22. Other systems, particularly the contemporary Chinese, also stress experimentation, but the open-ended, fallibilistic quality of democracy seems particularly suited to it. See Ricci 1984, 104–6 on Dewey; Knight and Johnson 2011.

REFERENCES

Agricultural Marketing Resource Center. 2013. "Blueberries Profile." www.agmrc.org /commodities_products/fruits/blueberries-profile/ (accessed October 25, 2013).

Aristotle. 1944. [c. 347–325 B.C.] *Politics*. Trans. Harris Rackham. Cambridge, MA.: Harvard University Press/Loeb Classical Library.

Ayres, Ian, and John Braithwaite. 1992. *Responsive Regulation: Transcending the Deregulation Debate*. New York: Oxford University Press.

Barry, Brian, and Russell Hardin. 1982. "Individual Actions and Collective Consequences." In *Rational Man and Irrational Society?*, eds. Brian Barry and Russell Hardin. Beverly Hills: Sage.

Baumol, William J. 1952. *Welfare Economics and the Theory of the State.* New York: Longmans, Green.

Bentham, Jeremy. 1996 [1789]. *Introduction to the Principles of Morals and Legislation.* Oxford: Oxford University Press.

Berlin, Isaiah. 1955–56. "Equality." *Proceedings of the Aristotelian Society* 56: 301–26.

———. 1969 [1958]. "Two Concepts of Liberty." In *Four Essays on Liberty.* Oxford: Oxford University Press.

Brain, Robert. 1979. *Friends and Lovers.* New York: Basic Books.

Deci, Edward L., Richard Koestner, and Richard M. Ryan. 1999. "A Meta-Analytic Review of Experiments Examining the Effects of Extrinsic Rewards on Intrinsic Motivation." *Psychological Bulletin* 125(6): 627–68.

Foster, Chase, Jane Mansbridge, and Cathie Jo Martin. 2013. "Negotiation Myopia." In *Negotiating Agreement in Politics*, eds. Jane Mansbridge and Cathie Jo Martin. Washington DC: American Political Science Association.

Frey, Bruno S. 1997. "A Constitution for Knaves Crowds out Civic Virtues." *Economic Journal* 107(443): 1043–53.

Gordon, H. Scott. 1954. "The Economic Theory of a Common-Property Resource: The Fishery." *Journal of Political Economy* 62(2): 124–42.

Gneezy, Uri and Aldo Rustichini, 2000. "A Fine is a Price." *The Journal of Legal Studies* 29(1): 1–17.

Hardin, Garrett. 1968. "The Tragedy of the Commons." *Science* 162(3859): 1243–48.

Hardin, Russell. 1982. *Collective Action.* Baltimore, MD: Johns Hopkins University Press.

Hume, David. 1960 [1739–40]. *A Treatise of Human Nature.* Oxford: Oxford University Press.

Kahneman, Daniel, and Amos Tversky. 1979. "Prospect Theory: An Analysis of Decision under Risk." *Econometrica* 47(2): 263–92.

Kahneman, Daniel. 1984. "Choices, Values, and Frames." *American Psychologist* 39(4): 341–50.

Kant, Immanuel. 1998 [1781]. *Critique of Pure Reason*, eds. Paul Guyer and Allen W. Wood. Cambridge, UK: Cambridge University Press.

———. 2012 [1785]. *Groundwork of the Metaphysics of Morals.* Trans. Mary Gregor and Jens Timmermann. Cambridge, UK: Cambridge University Press.

Kateb, George. 2011. *Human Dignity.* Cambridge, MA: Harvard University Press.

Knight, Jack, and James Johnson. 2011. *The Priority of Democracy: Political Consequences of Pragmatism.* Princeton, NJ: Princeton University Press.

Levi, Margaret. 1988. *Of Rule and Revenue.* Berkeley: University of California Press.

Mansbridge, Jane. 1990. *Beyond Self-Interest.* Chicago: University of Chicago Press.

———. 2010. "Beyond the Tragedy of the Commons." Symposium on Elinor Ostrom's *Governing the Commons. Perspectives on Politics* 8(3): 590–93.

Mansbridge, Jane, with James Bohman, Simone Chambers, David Estlund, Andreas Follesdal, Archon Fung, Cristina Lafont, Bernard Manin, and José Luis Martí. 2010. "The Place of Self-Interest and the Role of Power in Deliberative Democracy." *Journal of Political Philosophy* 18(1): 64–100.

Nedelsky, Jennifer. 2001. *Law's Relations: A Relational Theory of Self, Autonomy, and Law.* New York: Oxford University Press.

Offe, Claus. 2013. "On the Normative Foundations of Public Policy." Unpublished manuscript, Berlin: Hertie School of Governance.

Oliver, Pamela, Gerald Marwell, and Ruy Teixeira. 1985. "A Theory of the Critical Mass. I. Interdependence, Group Heterogeneity, and the Production of Collective Action." *American Journal of Sociology* 91(3): 522–56.

Ostrom, Elinor. 1990. *Governing the Commons: The Evolution of Institutions for Collective Action*. Cambridge, UK: Cambridge University Press.

———. 1998. "A Behavioral Approach to the Rational Choice Theory of Collective Action." *American Political Science Review* 92(1): 1–22.

Pettit, Philip. 2001. *A Theory of Freedom: From the Psychology to the Politics of Agency*. Oxford: Blackwell.

Rawls, John. 1971. *A Theory of Justice*. Cambridge, MA: Harvard University Press.

Ricci, David M. 1984. *The Tragedy of Political Science: Politics, Scholarship, and Democracy*. New Haven, CT: Yale University Press.

Rosen, Michael. 2012. *Dignity: Its History and Meaning*. Cambridge, MA: Harvard University Press.

Rousseau, Jean-Jacques. 1997 [1754]. "Discourse on the Origin of Inequality." In *Rousseau: The Discourses and Other Early Political Writings*, ed.. Victor Gourevitch. Cambridge: Cambridge University Press.

Samuelson, Paul A. 1954. "The Pure Theory of Public Expenditure." *Review of Economics and Statistics* 3(4): 387–89.

Scholz, John T., and Mark Lubell. 1998. "Trust and Taxpaying: Testing the Heuristic Approach to Collective Action." *American Journal of Political Science* 42(2): 398–417.

Scholz, John T., and Neil Pinney. 1995. "Duty, Fear, and Tax Compliance: The Heuristic Basis of Citizenship Behavior." *American Journal of Political Science* 39(2): 490–512.

Scott, Anthony. 1955. "The Fishery: The Objectives of Sole Ownership." *Journal of Political Economy* 63(2): 116–24.

Stinchcombe, Arthur L. 1980. "Is the Prisoners' Dilemma all of Sociology?" *Inquiry* 23(2): 187–92.

Taylor, Michael. 1987. *The Possibility of Cooperation*. Cambridge, UK: Cambridge University Press.

Tyler, Tom R. 1990. *Why People Obey the Law*. New Haven, CT: Yale University Press.

Waldron, Jeremy. 2009. *Dignity, Rank and Rights*. New York: Oxford University Press.

Wu, Jianzhong, and Robert Axelrod. 1995. "How to Cope with Noise in the Iterated Prisoner's Dilemma." *The Journal of Conflict Resolution* 39(1): 183–89.

1.4

ROBERT A. DAHL

From *Polyarchy: Participation and Opposition*

Within the United States and around the world, increasingly people are worried about the stability of democratic regimes. In this passage from a famous book, Dahl defines democracy as having two core elements: open public contestation for power, and equal opportunity for all citizens to participate in civic life. Since no country approaches Dahl's ideal version of democracy, he refers to countries like the United States as polyarchies, *which, in his definition, means "relatively (but incompletely) democratized regimes." Preserving polyarchy, in his view, requires that government repression is punished by the people, and government toleration of opposition is rewarded.*

DEMOCRATIZATION AND PUBLIC OPPOSITION

■ ■ ■

I assume that a key characteristic of a democracy is the continuing responsiveness of the government to the preferences of its citizens, considered as political equals. What other characteristics might be required for a system to be strictly democratic, I do not intend to consider here. . . . I should like to reserve the term "democracy" for a political system one of the characteristics of which is the quality of being completely or almost completely responsive to all its citizens. Whether such a system actually exists, has existed, or can exist need not concern us for the moment. Surely one can conceive [of] a hypothetical system of this kind; such a conception has served as an ideal, or part of an ideal, for many people. As a hypothetical system, one end of a scale, or a limiting state of affairs, it can (like a perfect vacuum) serve as a basis for estimating the degree to which various systems approach this theoretical limit.

I assume further that in order for a government to continue over a period of time to be responsive to the preferences of its citizens, considered as political equals, all full citizens must have unimpaired opportunities:

From Robert A. Dahl, *Polyarchy: Participation and Opposition* (New Haven, CT: Yale University Press, 1971).

1. to formulate their preferences
2. to signify their preferences to their fellow citizens and the government by individual and collective action
3. to have their preferences weighed equally in the conduct of the government; that is, weighted with no discrimination because of the content or source of the preference

These, then, appear to me to be three necessary conditions for a democracy, though they are probably not sufficient. Next, I assume that for these three opportunities to exist among a large number of people, such as the number of people who comprise most nation-states at the present time, the institutions of the society must provide at least eight guarantees. These are indicated in Table [1].

TABLE [1] Some Requirements for a Democracy among a Large Number of People

For the opportunity to:	The following institutional guarantees are required:
I. Formulate preferences	1. Freedom to form and join organizations 2. Freedom of expression 3. Right to vote 4. Right of political leaders to compete for support 5. Alternative sources of information
II. Signify preferences	1. Freedom to form and join organizations 2. Freedom of expression 3. Right to vote 4. Eligibility for public office 5. Right of political leaders to compete for support 6. Alternative sources of information 7. Free and fair elections
III. Have preferences weighted equally in conduct of government	1. Freedom to form and join organizations 2. Freedom of expression 3. Right to vote 4. Eligibility for public office 5. Right of political leaders to compete for support 5a. Right of political leaders to compete for votes 6. Alternative sources of information 7. Free and fair elections 8. Institutions for making government policies depend on votes and other expressions of preference

I am going to make the further assumption that the connections between the guarantees and the three fundamental opportunities are sufficiently evident to need no further elaboration here.[1]

Now from examination of the list of eight institutional guarantees, it appears that they might provide us with a theoretical scale along which it would be possible to order different political systems. Upon closer examination, however, it appears that the eight guarantees might be fruitfully interpreted as constituting two somewhat different theoretical dimensions of democratization.

1. Both historically and at the present time, regimes vary enormously in the extent to which the eight institutional conditions are openly available, publicly employed, and fully guaranteed to at least some members of the political system who wish to contest the conduct of the government. Thus, a scale reflecting these eight conditions would enable us to compare different regimes according to the extent of permissible opposition, public contestation, or political competition.[2] However, since a regime might permit opposition to a very small or a very large proportion of the population, clearly we need a second dimension.

2. Both historically and contemporaneously, regimes also vary in the proportion of the population entitled to participate on a more or less equal plane in controlling and contesting the conduct of the government: to participate, so to speak, in the system of public contestation. A scale reflecting the breadth of the right to participate in public contestation would enable us to compare different regimes according to their inclusiveness.

The right to vote in free and fair elections, for example, partakes of both dimensions. When a regime grants this right to some of its citizens, it moves toward greater public contestation. But the larger the proportion of citizens who enjoy the right, the more inclusive the regime.

■   ■   ■

[O]ne of the most striking changes during [the twentieth] century [was] the virtual disappearance of an outright denial of the legitimacy of popular participation in government. Only a handful of countries have failed to grant at least a ritualistic vote to their citizens and to hold at least nominal elections; even the most repressive dictators usually pay some lip service today to the legitimate right of the people to participate in the government, that is, to participate in "governing," though not in public contestation.

Needless to say, in the absence of the right to oppose, the right to "participate" is stripped of a very large part of the significance it has in a country where public contestation exists. A country with universal suffrage and a completely repressive government would provide fewer opportunities for oppositions, surely, than a country with a narrow suffrage but a highly tolerant government. Consequently, when countries are ranked solely according to their inclusiveness, not taking into account the surrounding circumstances, the results are anomalous. Nonetheless, as long as we keep clearly in mind the

FIGURE [1]   Two Theoretical Dimensions of Democratization

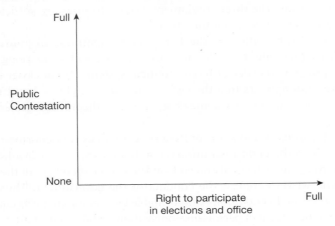

fact that the extent of the "suffrage" or, more generally, the right to partici-pate indicates only *one* characteristic of systems, a characteristic that cannot be interpreted except in the context of other characteristics, it is useful to dis-tinguish between regimes according to their inclusiveness.

Suppose, then, that we think of democratization as made up of at least two dimensions: public contestation and the right to participate (Figure [1]). Doubt-less most readers believe that democratization involves more than these two dimensions; in a moment I shall discuss a third dimension. But I propose to limit the discussion here to these two. For the point has already emerged, I think: developing a system of public contestation is not necessarily equivalent to full democratization.

To display the relationship between public contestation and democratization more clearly, let us now lay out the two dimensions as in Figure [1]. Since a regime may be located, theoretically, anywhere in the space bounded by the two dimensions, it is at once obvious that our terminology for regimes is almost hopelessly inadequate, for it is a terminology invariably based upon classify-ing rather than ranking. The space enclosed by our two dimensions could of course be cut up into any number of cells, each of which might be given a name. . . . Let me provide a small vocabulary—a reasonable one, I hope—that will enable me to speak precisely enough about the kinds of changes in regimes that I want to discuss.

Let me call a regime near the lower left corner of Figure [2] a closed hege-mony. If a hegemonic regime shifts upward, as along path I, then it is moving toward greater public contestation. Without stretching language too far, one could say that a change in this direction involves the liberalization of a regime; alternatively, one might say that the regime becomes more competitive. If a regime changes to provide greater participation, as along path II, it might be

FIGURE [2]   Liberalization, Inclusiveness, and Democratization

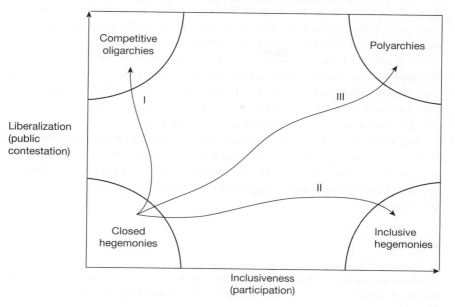

said to change toward greater popularization, or that it is becoming inclusive. A regime might change along one dimension and not the other. If we call a regime near the upper left corner a competitive oligarchy, then path I represents a change from a closed hegemony to a competitive oligarchy. But a closed hegemony might also become more inclusive without liberalizing, i.e., without increasing the opportunities for public contestation, as along path II. In this case the regime changes from a closed to an inclusive hegemony.

Democracy might be conceived of as lying at the upper right corner. But since democracy may involve more dimensions than the two in Figure [2], and since (in my view) no large system in the real world is fully democratized, I prefer to call real world systems that are closest to the upper right corner polyarchies. Any change in a regime that moves it upward and to the right, for example along path III, may be said to represent some degree of democratization. Polyarchies, then, may be thought of as relatively (but incompletely) democratized regimes, or, to put it in another way, polyarchies are regimes that have been substantially popularized and liberalized, that is, highly inclusive and extensively open to public contestation.

▪   ▪   ▪

When hegemonic regimes and competitive oligarchies move toward polyarchy they increase the opportunities for effective participation and contestation and hence the number of individuals, groups, and interests whose preferences have to be considered in policy making.

From the perspective of the incumbents who currently govern, such a transformation carries with it new possibilities of conflict as a result of which their goals (and they themselves) may be displaced by spokesmen for the newly incorporated individuals, groups, or interests.

The problem of their opponents is the mirror image of the problem of the incumbents. Any transformation that provides opponents of the government with greater opportunities to translate their goals into policies enforced by the state carries with it the possibility of conflict with spokesmen for the individuals, groups, or interests they displace in the government.

Thus, the greater the conflict between government and opposition, the more likely that each will seek to deny opportunities to the other to participate effectively in policy making. To put it another way, the greater the conflict between a government and its opponents, the more costly it is for each to tolerate the other.

NOTES

1. Some of the relationships are discussed in my *A Preface to Democratic Theory* (Chicago: University of Chicago Press, 1956), pp. 63–81, and in Robert A. Dahl and Charles E. Lindblom, *Politics, Economics and Welfare* (New York: Harper, 1953), chaps. 10 and 11.

2. The terms liberalization, political competition, competitive politics, public contestation, and public opposition are used interchangeably to refer to this dimension, and regimes relatively high on this dimension are frequently referred to as competitive regimes.

1.5

HANNA FENICHEL PITKIN

From *The Concept of Representation*

To represent means "to act for" or "to act on behalf of" others. The United States and other modern democracies are representative in form, meaning that elected people (either in assemblies or as executives) make most government policy decisions on behalf of their constituents. Pitkin, in this excerpt from her famous book, discusses the many facets of political representation. She describes the tensions in representation, for instance between following what constituents say they want and what a representative believes are the best actions. Her important contribution is to highlight the role of stable, credible democratic institutions—such as regular free and fair elections, and a free press—in leading to effective representation where representatives genuinely try to act for the public good.

POLITICAL REPRESENTATION

■   ■   ■

[R]epresenting here means acting in the interest of the represented, in a manner responsive to them. The representative must act independently; his action must involve discretion and judgment; he must be the one who acts. The represented must also be (conceived as) capable of independent action and judgment, not merely being taken care of. And, despite the resulting potential for conflict between representative and represented about what is to be done, that conflict must not normally take place. The representative must act in such a way that there is no conflict, or, if it occurs, an explanation is called for. He must not be found persistently at odds with the wishes of the represented without good reason in terms of their interest, without a good explanation of why their wishes are not in accord with their interest.

This rather complex view only sets the outer limits of what will be acceptable as representing in the substantive sense. Within those limits a wide range of positions is possible, depending on the writer's views about what is represented; about the nature of interests, welfare, or wishes; about the relative capacities of representative and constituents; and about the nature of the issues with

From Hanna F. Pitkin, *The Concept of Representation* (Berkeley, CA: University of California Press, 1967).

which the representative must deal. The first of these criteria is also the simplest. Where representation is conceived as being of unattached abstractions, the consultation of anyone's wishes or opinions is least likely to seem a significant part of representing.

■   ■   ■

We have said that the representative must pursue his constituents' interest, in a manner at least potentially responsive to their wishes, and that conflict between them must be justifiable in terms of that interest. But what becomes of terms like "interest" and "justifiable" if there can be lifelong, profound disagreement among men as to what their interest is—disagreement that remains despite deliberation and justification and argument? To the extent that this is so, the possibility of a substantive acting for others breaks down, and that view of the concept becomes irrelevant to politics. To the extent that this happens in practical political life, we seem then to fall back on descriptive representation; we choose a representative who shares our values and commitments and prevent the irresoluble conflict. Failing that, we can retreat to symbolic representation; we can let ourselves be influenced by emotional ties in spite of our doubts about whether our interests are being served. Or, failing even that, we can cling to our formal and institutional representative arrangements even when they seem devoid of substantive content. We can continue to obey, although we feel abused, or continue to remove a series of accountable representatives from office, although none of them serves our interest.

■   ■   ■

Does the representative frequently consult his constituents' wishes, or, if not, does he apply his expert knowledge to a dispassionate, rational evaluation of what is best for them and the nation? Again, if these are one's assumptions, the facts would seem very disillusioning. For the legislator's position is far more complex than such a model would suggest. The modern representative acts within an elaborate network of pressures, demands, and obligations; and there is considerable disagreement among legislators about the proper way to perform [his or her] role.[1]

In the first place, the political representative has a constituency and constituents, not a principal. He is chosen by a great number of people; and, while it may be difficult to determine the interests or wishes of a single individual, it is infinitely more difficult to do so for a constituency of thousands. On many issues a constituency may not have any interest, or its members may have several conflicting interests.[2] And the representative knows of the voters' ignorance and apathy and irrationality, the diversity of their views and interests. Further, he seldom has access to accurate information about what views and interests they do have.[3]

In the second place, he is a professional politician in a framework of political institutions,[4] a member of a political party who wants to get reëlected, and a member of legislature along with other representatives. He must be sensitive to his political party (both local and national) and to various public and private groups and interests. As a member of the legislature, he occupies an office to which certain obligations and expectations are attached.[5] He must comply with its traditions and work within the framework of the rules and mores of the legislative body. He must get along with his colleagues, especially certain important ones among them.[6] To act effectively he must keep in mind not only the formal and informal rules of his legislative body but also its place in the whole structure of government.

In the third place, he will also have views and opinions, at least on some issues. He will feel that some measures are intrinsically unsound, immoral, or undesirable. At the same time, his opinions may, in turn, be shaped by those around him and his sources of information. His own opinion on a measure may be shaped by party leaders or other colleagues, by friends or effective lobbyists, or even by the mail. He himself may not be a reliable source of information as to just what shapes his opinion on some issue or even what determines his vote.[7] And issues do not come before him in isolation; issues are interrelated, and he may wish to compromise on some in order to gain on others.[8] A particular measure may have many parts, to which he responds in varying ways.[9] He also may see measures as having a significance beyond their immediate content, for example as part of an overall party program.[10]

Thus, in legislative behavior a great complexity and plurality of determinants are at work, any number of which may enter into a legislative decision. The legislator represents neither by a simple response to constituency desires nor by detached. Olympian judgment on the merits of a proposal. None of the analogies of acting for others on the individual level seems satisfactory for explaining the relationship between a political representative and his constituents. He is neither agent nor trustee nor deputy nor commissioner; he acts for a group of people without a single interest, most of whom seem incapable of forming an explicit will on political questions.

Must we then abandon the idea of political representation in its most common sense of "acting for"? This possibility has sometimes been suggested; perhaps representation in politics is only a fiction, a myth forming part of the folklore of our society. Or perhaps representation must be redefined to fit our politics; perhaps we must simply accept the fact that what we have been calling representative government is in reality just party competition for office. Yet, to "redefine" representation to equate it with the empirical reality of representative government, even if that reality displays no elements of what we would ordinarily call representation, seems pointless and misleading.

But perhaps it is a mistake to approach political representation too directly from the various individual-representation analogies—agent and trustee and deputy. Perhaps that approach, like descriptive or symbolic representation, leads us to expect or demand features in the representative relationship which are not there and need not be there. Perhaps when we conventionally speak of political representation, representative government, and the like, we do not mean or require that the representative stand in the kind of one-to-one, person-to-person relationship to his constituency or to each constituent in which a private representative stands to his principal.[11] Perhaps when we call a governmental body or system "representative," we are saying something broader and more general about the way in which it operates as an institutionalized arrangement. And perhaps even the representing done by an individual legislator must be seen in such a context, as embodied in a whole political system.

Political representation is primarily a public, institutionalized arrangement involving many people and groups, and operating in the complex ways of large-scale social arrangements. What makes it representation is not any single action by any one participant, but the overall structure and functioning of the system, the patterns emerging from the multiple activities of many people. It is representation if the people (or a constituency) are present in governmental action, even though they do not literally act for themselves. Insofar as this is a matter of substantive acting for others, it requires independent action in the interest of the governed, in a manner at least potentially responsive to them, yet not normally in conflict with their wishes. And perhaps that can make sense and is possible even in politics, if we understand how and where to look for it.

Even if the representative does not examine his conscience as to the national interest on every issue, he may still be following a course of action designed to promote that interest. He may be playing his complicated role in the institutionalized political system in such a way that it strikes us as—that it *is*—representing. The mere fact that he is functioning within a representative system is, of course, no guarantee that he is truly representing; but it allows for more complex and long-range ways of representing than are possible for an isolated individual agent.

■   ■   ■

The voting behavior of people in a representative democracy can respond to issues and policies, even if many individual voters do not respond directly to them. The process may be complex, involving an interaction among organizations, news media, and personal relationships. Even if most people vote in an irrational and uninformed response to primary group pressures, this does not preclude the system as a whole from displaying a degree of "rational" response.

All this is only meant to sketch a framework on which one could maintain what seems to me, in fact, the case: that political representation is, in fact, representation, particularly in the sense of "acting for," and that this must be understood at the public level. The representative system must look after the public interest and be responsive to public opinion, except insofar as non-responsiveness can be justified in terms of the public interest. At both ends, the process is public and institutional. The individual legislator does not act alone, but as a member of a representative body. Hence his pursuit of the public interest and response to public opinion need not always be conscious and deliberate, any more than the individual voter's role. Representation may emerge from a political system in which many individuals, both voters and legislators, are pursuing quite other goals. I am not suggesting that it must emerge from any particular system; there is no guarantee that it will. But it may emerge, and to the extent that it does we consider that system as being a representative government.

∎   ∎   ∎

It seems to me that we show a government to be representative not by demonstrating its control over its subjects but just the reverse, by demonstrating that its subjects have control over what it does. Every government's actions are attributed to its subjects formally, legally. But in a representative government this attribution has substantive content: the people really do act through their government, and are not merely passive recipients of its actions. A representative government must not merely be in control, not merely promote the public interest, but must also be responsive to the people. The notion is closely related to the view of representing as a substantive activity. For in a representative government, the governed must be capable of action and judgment, capable of initiating government activity, so that the government may be conceived [of] as responding to them.

∎   ∎   ∎

Representative government is not defined by particular actions at a particular moment, but by long-term systematic arrangements—by institutions and the way in which they function.

NOTES

1. Dexter, "The Representative," p. 3; John C. Wahlke and Heinz Eulau, eds., *Legislative Behavior* (Glencoe, Ill., 1959), pp. 298–304; John C. Wahlke *et al.*, "American State Legislators' Role Orientation," *Journal of Politics*, XXII (May, 1960); Eulau, *op. cit.*; Charles O. Jones, "Representation in Congress," *American Political Science Review*, LV (December, 1961).

2. Sabine, "What Is the Matter?" in A. N. Christensen and E. M. Kirkpatrick, eds., *The People, Politics and the Politician* (New York, 1941); G. D. H. Cole, *Social Theory* (London, 1920), pp. 103–16; Dexter, "The Representative," pp. 4–5; Howard Lee McBain, *The Living Constitution* (New York, 1948), p. 233; Eulau, *op. cit.*, pp. 747, 751; Schumpeter, *op. cit.*, p. 261; Jones, *op. cit.*, pp. 358–59, 365.

3. Dexter, "The Representative"; and "What Do Congressmen Hear: The Mail," *Public Opinion Quarterly*, XX (Spring, 1956), 16–27; Eulau, *op. cit.*, p. 749; Frank Bonilla, "When Is Petition 'Pressure'?" *Public Opinion Quarterly*, XX (Spring, 1956), 39–48; David B. Truman, *The Governmental Process* (New York, 1959), chap. 11; Jones, *op. cit.*, pp. 366–67.

4. Henry B. Mayo, *An Introduction to Democratic Theory* (New York, 1960), p. 102; Wahlke and Eulau, *op. cit.*, p. 117; Jones, *op. cit.*, p. 359.

5. Robert M. MacIver, *The Modern State* (Oxford, 1926), p. 196; Joseph Tussman, *Obligation and the Body Politic* (New York, 1960), pp. 69, 75; Wahlke, *op. cit.*; Wahlke and Eulau, *op. cit.*, pp. 179–89, 284–93.

6. Dexter, "The Representative"; Wahlke and Eulau, *op. cit.*, pp. 204–17.

7. Gleeck, *op. cit.*, p. 7; Turner, *op. cit.*, p. 12; Dexter, "The Representative"; Truman, *op. cit.*, chap. 11.

8. Dexter, "The Representative," p. 5.

9. Jones, *op. cit.*, pp. 363–64.

10. Wahlke and Eulau, *op. cit.*, pp. 298–304.

11. Obviously important changes take place which make the substitute assembly far different from the direct meeting of the people." Alfred De Grazia, *Public and Republic* (New York, 1951), p. 126.

"When one person represents a group, and still more when a number of persons represent different groups, the problem becomes much more complicated." John A. Fairlie, "The Nature of Political Representation," *American Political Science Review*, XXXIV (June, 1940), 466.

"My conclusion from this discussion is that the concepts connected with representation of individual persons by individual persons have no simple application to representative government." A. Phillips Griffiths and Richard Wollheim, "How Can One Person Represent Another?" Aristotelian Society, Suppl. Vol. XXXIV (1960), 207.

See also Peter Laslett, "The Face to Face Society," *Philosophy, Politics and Society*, ed. Peter Laslett (New York, 1956).

DISCUSSION QUESTIONS

1. What implications does Olson's theory have for answering questions about who wields power and influence in American politics?
2. Describe several common pool resources in the United States and how government policy can lead to their sustainability or their depletion.
3. What are examples of coercion by local and state governments in the United States that you believe are illegitimate? Legitimate?
4. Which aspects of contemporary American politics lead us away from ideal forms of polyarchy? Devote some attention both to "open contestation for power" and to "equal opportunities for participation."
5. What characteristics make a good legislative representative in the American political system?
6. Describe as specifically as you can some of the ways governments in the United States solve collective action problems. Do they go too far, or not far enough?

2

THE CONSTITUTION
AND THE FOUNDING

2.1

BRUTUS

The Antifederalist, No. 1

Brutus (a pseudonym used by an anonymous Antifederalist author or authors) argues against the Constitution, saying that it will grant too much power to the central, national government. In this essay, Brutus warns that if the national government were granted the powers described in the Constitution, it would eventually come to dominate the states and oppress the people.

To the Citizens of the State of New York.

When the public is called to investigate and decide upon a question in which not only the present members of the community are deeply interested, but upon which the happiness and misery of generations yet unborn is in great measure suspended, the benevolent mind cannot help feeling itself peculiarly interested in the result.

In this situation, I trust the feeble efforts of an individual, to lead the minds of the people to a wise and prudent determination, cannot fail of being acceptable to the candid and dispassionate part of the community. Encouraged by this consideration, I have been induced to offer my thoughts upon the present important crisis of our public affairs.

From Brutus, *The Antifederalist*, No. 1 (1787).

Perhaps this country never saw so critical a period in their political concerns. We have felt the feebleness of the ties by which these United-States are held together, and the want of sufficient energy in our present confederation, to manage, in some instances, our general concerns. Various expedients have been proposed to remedy these evils, but none have succeeded. At length a Convention of the states has been assembled, they have formed a constitution which will now, probably, be submitted to the people to ratify or reject, who are the fountain of all power, to whom alone it of right belongs to make or unmake constitutions, or forms of government, at their pleasure. The most important question that was ever proposed to your decision, or to the decision of any people under heaven, is before you, and you are to decide upon it by men of your own election, chosen specially for this purpose. If the constitution, offered to your acceptance, be a wise one, calculated to preserve the invaluable blessings of liberty, to secure the inestimable rights of mankind, and promote human happiness, then, if you accept it, you will lay a lasting foundation of happiness for millions yet unborn; generations to come will rise up and call you blessed. You may rejoice in the prospects of this vast extended continent becoming filled with freemen, who will assert the dignity of human nature. You may solace yourselves with the idea, that society, in this favoured land, will fast advance to the highest point of perfection; the human mind will expand in knowledge and virtue, and the golden age be, in some measure, realised. But if, on the other hand, this form of government contains principles that will lead to the subversion of liberty—if it tends to establish a despotism, or, what is worse, a tyrannic aristocracy; then, if you adopt it, this only remaining assylum for liberty will be shut up, and posterity will execrate your memory.

Momentous then is the question you have to determine, and you are called upon by every motive which should influence a noble and virtuous mind, to examine it well, and to make up a wise judgment. It is insisted, indeed, that this constitution must be received, be it ever so imperfect. If it has its defects, it is said, they can be best amended when they are experienced. But remember, when the people once part with power, they can seldom or never resume it again but by force. Many instances can be produced in which the people have voluntarily increased the powers of their rulers; but few, if any, in which rulers have willingly abridged their authority. This is a sufficient reason to induce you to be careful, in the first instance, how you deposit the powers of government.

With these few introductory remarks, I shall proceed to a consideration of this constitution:

The first question that presents itself on the subject is, whether a confederated government be the best for the United States or not? Or in other words, whether the thirteen United States should be reduced to one great republic, governed by one legislature, and under the direction of one executive and judicial; or whether they should continue thirteen confederated republics, under the direction and controul of a supreme federal head for certain defined national purposes only?

This enquiry is important, because, although the government reported by the convention does not go to a perfect and entire consolidation, yet it approaches so near to it, that it must, if executed, certainly and infallibly terminate in it.

This government is to possess absolute and uncontroulable power, legislative, executive and judicial, with respect to every object to which it extends, for by the last clause of section 8th, article 1st, it is declared "that the Congress shall have power to make all laws which shall be necessary and proper for carrying into execution the foregoing powers, and all other powers vested by this constitution, in the government of the United States; or in any department or office thereof." And by the 6th article, it is declared "that this constitution, and the laws of the United States, which shall be made in pursuance thereof, and the treaties made, or which shall be made, under the authority of the United States, shall be the supreme law of the land; and the judges in every state shall be bound thereby, any thing in the constitution, or law of any state to the contrary notwithstanding." It appears from these articles that there is no need of any intervention of the state governments, between the Congress and the people, to execute any one power vested in the general government, and that the constitution and laws of every state are nullified and declared void, so far as they are or shall be inconsistent with this constitution, or the laws made in pursuance of it, or with treaties made under the authority of the United States.—The government then, so far as it extends, is a complete one, and not a confederation. It is as much one complete government as that of New-York or Massachusetts, has as absolute and perfect powers to make and execute all laws, to appoint officers, institute courts, declare offences, and annex penalties, with respect to every object to which it extends, as any other in the world. So far therefore as its powers reach, all ideas of confederation are given up and lost. It is true this government is limited to certain objects, or to speak more properly, some small degree of power is still left to the states, but a little attention to the powers vested in the general government, will convince every candid man, that if it is capable of being executed, all that is reserved for the individual states must very soon be annihilated, except so far as they are barely necessary to the organization of the general government. The powers of the general legislature extend to every case that is of the least importance—there is nothing valuable to human nature, nothing dear to freemen, but what is within its power. It has authority to make laws which will affect the lives, the liberty, and property of every man in the United States; nor can the constitution or laws of any state, in any way prevent or impede the full and complete execution of every power given. The legislative power is competent to lay taxes, duties, imposts, and excises;—there is no limitation to this power, unless it be said that the clause which directs the use to which those taxes, and duties shall be applied, may be said to be a limitation: but this is no restriction of the power at all, for by this clause they are to be applied to pay the debts and provide for the common defence and general welfare of the

United States; but the legislature have authority to contract debts at their discretion; they are the sole judges of what is necessary to provide for the common defence, and they only are to determine what is for the general welfare; this power therefore is neither more nor less, than a power to lay and collect taxes, imposts, and excises, at their pleasure; not only [is] the power to lay taxes unlimited, as to the amount they may require, but it is perfect and absolute to raise them in any mode they please. No state legislature, or any power in the state governments, have any more to do in carrying this into effect, than the authority of one state has to do with that of another. In the business therefore of laying and collecting taxes, the idea of confederation is totally lost, and that of one entire republic is embraced. It is proper here to remark, that the authority to lay and collect taxes is the most important of any power that can be granted; it connects with it almost all other powers, or at least will in process of time draw all other after it; it is the great mean of protection, security, and defence, in a good government, and the great engine of oppression and tyranny in a bad one. This cannot fail of being the case, if we consider the contracted limits which are set by this constitution, to the late [state?] governments, on this article of raising money. No state can emit paper money—lay any duties, or imposts, on imports, or exports, but by consent of the Congress; and then the net produce shall be for the benefit of the United States: the only mean therefore left, for any state to support its government and discharge its debts, is by direct taxation; and the United States have also power to lay and collect taxes, in any way they please. Every one who has thought on the subject, must be convinced that but small sums of money can be collected in any country, by direct taxe[s], when the foederal government begins to exercise the right of taxation in all its parts, the legislatures of the several states will find it impossible to raise monies to support their governments. Without money they cannot be supported, and they must dwindle away, and, as before observed, their powers absorbed in that of the general government.

It might be here shewn, that the power in the federal legislative, to raise and support armies at pleasure, as well in peace as in war, and their controul over the militia, tend, not only to a consolidation of the government, but the destruction of liberty.—I shall not, however, dwell upon these, as a few observations upon the judicial power of this government, in addition to the preceding, will fully evince the truth of the position.

The judicial power of the United States is to be vested in a supreme court, and in such inferior courts as Congress may from time to time ordain and establish. The powers of these courts are very extensive; their jurisdiction comprehends all civil causes, except such as arise between citizens of the same state; and it extends to all cases in law and equity arising under the constitution. One inferior court must be established, I presume, in each state, at least, with the necessary executive officers appendant thereto. It is easy to see, that in the common course of things, these courts will eclipse the dignity, and take away from the respectability, of the state courts. These courts will be, in themselves, totally independent of the states, deriving their authority from the United States, and receiving from them fixed salaries; and in the course of human events it is to be expected, that they will swallow up all the powers of the courts in the respective states.

How far the clause in the 8th section of the 1st article may operate to do away all idea of confederated states, and to effect an entire consolidation of the whole into one general government, it is impossible to say. The powers given by this article are very general and comprehensive, and it may receive a construction to justify the passing almost any law. A power to make all laws, which shall be *necessary and proper*, for carrying into execution, all powers vested by the constitution in the government of the United States, or any department or officer thereof, is a power very comprehensive and definite [indefinite?], and may, for ought I know, be exercised in a such manner as entirely to abolish the state legislatures. Suppose the legislature of a state should pass a law to raise money to support their government and pay the state debt, may the Congress repeal this law, because it may prevent the collection of a tax which they may think proper and necessary to lay, to provide for the general welfare of the United States? For all laws made, in pursuance of this constitution, are the supreme lay of the land, and the judges in every state shall be bound thereby, any thing in the constitution or laws of the different states to the contrary notwithstanding.—By such a law, the government of a particular state might be overturned at one stroke, and thereby be deprived of every means of its support.

It is not meant, by stating this case, to insinuate that the constitution would warrant a law of this kind; or unnecessarily to alarm the fears of the people, by suggesting, that the federal legislature would be more likely to pass the limits assigned them by the constitution, than that of an individual state, further than they are less responsible to the people. But what is meant is, that the legislature of the United States are vested with the great and uncontroulable powers, of laying and collecting taxes, duties, imposts, and excises; of regulating trade, raising and supporting armies, organizing, arming, and disciplining the militia, instituting courts, and other general powers. And are by this clause invested with the power of making all laws, *proper and necessary*, for carrying all these into execution; and they may so exercise this power as entirely to annihilate all the state governments, and reduce this country to one single government. And if they may do it, it is pretty certain they will; for it will be found that the power retained by individual states, small as it is, will be a clog upon the wheels of the government of the United States; the latter therefore will be naturally inclined to remove it out of the way. Besides, it is a truth confirmed by the unerring experience of ages, that every man, and every body of men, invested with power, are ever disposed to increase it, and to acquire a superiority over every thing that stands in their way. This disposition, which is implanted in human nature, will operate in the federal legislature to lessen and ultimately to subvert the state authority, and having such advantages, will most certainly succeed, if the federal government succeeds at all. It must be very evident then, that what this constitution wants of being a complete con-solidation of the several parts of the union into one complete government, possessed of perfect legislative, judicial, and executive powers, to all intents and purposes, it will necessarily acquire in its exercise and operation.

Let us now proceed to enquire, as I at first proposed, whether it be best the thirteen United States should be reduced to one great republic, or not? It is here taken for granted, that all agree in this, that whatever government we adopt, it ought to be a free one; that it should be so framed as to secure the liberty of the citizens of America, and such an one as to admit of a full, fair, and equal representation of the people. The question then will be, whether a government thus constituted, and founded on such principles, is practicable, and can be exercised over the whole United States, reduced into one state?

If respect is to be paid to the opinion of the greatest and wisest men who have ever thought or wrote on the science of government, we shall be con-strained to conclude, that a free republic cannot succeed over a country of such immense extent, containing such a number of inhabitants, and these encreasing in such rapid progression as that of the whole United States. Among the many illustrious authorities which might be produced to this point, I shall content myself with quoting only two. The one is the baron de Montesquieu, spirit of laws, chap. xvi. vol. I [book VIII]. "It is natural to a republic to have only a small territory, otherwise it cannot long subsist. In a large republic there are men of large fortunes, and consequently of less moderation; there are trusts too great to be placed in any single subject; he has interest of his own; he soon begins to think that he may be happy, great and glorious, by oppress-ing his fellow citizens; and that he may raise himself to grandeur on the ruins of his country. In a large republic, the public good is sacrificed to a thousand views; it is subordinate to exceptions, and depends on accidents. In a small one, the interest of the public is easier perceived, better understood, and more within the reach of every citizen; abuses are of less extent, and of course are less protected." Of the same opinion is the marquis Beccarari.

History furnishes no example of a free republic, any thing like the extent of the United States. The Grecian republics were of small extent; so also was that of the Romans. Both of these, it is true, in process of time, extended their con-quests over large territories of country; and the consequence was, that their governments were changed from that of free governments to those of the most tyrannical that ever existed in the world.

Not only the opinion of the greatest men, and the experience of mankind, are against the idea of an extensive republic, but a variety of reasons may be drawn from the reason and nature of things, against it. In every government, the will of the sovereign is the law. In despotic governments, the supreme authority being lodged in one, his will is law, and can be as easily expressed to a large extensive territory as to a small one. In a pure democracy the people are the sovereign, and their will is declared by themselves; for this purpose they must all come together to deliberate, and decide. This kind of government cannot be exercised, therefore, over a country of any considerable extent; it must be confined to a single city, or at least limited to such bounds as that the people can conveniently assemble, be able to debate, understand the subject submitted to them, and declare their opinion concerning it.

In a free republic, although all laws are derived from the consent of the people, yet the people do not declare their consent by themselves in person, but by representatives, chosen by them, who are supposed to know the minds of their constituents, and to be possessed of integrity to declare this mind.

In every free government, the people must give their assent to the laws by which they are governed. This is the true criterion between a free government and an arbitrary one. The former are ruled by the will of the whole, expressed in any manner they may agree upon; the latter by the will of one, or a few. If the people are to give their assent to the laws, by persons chosen and appointed by them, the manner of the choice and the number chosen, must be such, as to possess, be disposed, and consequently qualified to declare the sentiments of the people; for if they do not know, or are not disposed to speak the sentiments of the people, the people do not govern, but the sovereignty is in a few. Now, in a large extended country, it is impossible to have a representation, possessing the sentiments, and of integrity, to declare the minds of the people, without having it so numerous and unwieldly, as to be subject in great measure to the inconveniency of a democratic government.

The territory of the United States is of vast extent; it now contains near three millions of souls, and is capable of containing much more than ten times that number. Is it practicable for a country, so large and so numerous as they will soon become, to elect a representation, that will speak their sentiments, without their becoming so numerous as to be incapable of transacting public business? It certainly is not.

In a republic, the manners, sentiments, and interests of the people should be similar. If this be not the case, there will be a constant clashing of opinions; and the representatives of one part will be continually striving against those of the other. This will retard the operations of government, and prevent such conclusions as will promote the public good. If we apply this remark to the condition of the United States, we shall be convinced that it forbids that we should be one government. The United States includes a variety of climates. The productions of the different parts of the union are very variant, and their interests, of consequence, diverse. Their manners and habits differ as much as their climates and productions; and their sentiments are by no means coincident. The laws and customs of the several states are, in many respects, very diverse, and in some opposite; each would be in favor of its own interests and customs, and, of consequence, a legislature, formed of representatives from the respective parts, would not only be too numerous to act with any care or decision, but would be composed of such heterogenous and discordant principles, as would constantly be contending with each other.

The laws cannot be executed in a republic, of an extent equal to that of the United States, with promptitude.

The magistrates in every government must be supported in the execution of the laws, either by an armed force, maintained at the public expence for that purpose; or by the people turning out to aid the magistrate upon his command, in case of resistance.

In despotic governments, as well as in all the monarchies of Europe, standing armies are kept up to execute the commands of the prince or the magistrate, and are employed for this purpose when occasion requires: But they have always proved the destruction of liberty, and [are] abhorrent to the spirit of a free republic. In England, where they depend upon the parliament for their annual support, they have always been complained of as oppressive and unconstitutional, and are seldom employed in executing of the laws; never except on extraordinary occasions, and then under the direction of a civil magistrate.

A free republic will never keep a standing army to execute its laws. It must depend upon the support of its citizens. But when a government is to receive its support from the aid of the citizens, it must be so constructed as to have the confidence, respect, and affection of the people. Men who, upon the call of the magistrate, offer themselves to execute the laws, are influenced to do it either by affection to the government, or from fear; where a standing army is at hand to punish offenders, every man is actuated by the latter principle, and therefore, when the magistrate calls, will obey: but, where this is not the case, the government must rest for its support upon the confidence and respect which the people have for their government and laws. The body of the people being attached, the government will always be sufficient to support and execute its laws, and to operate upon the fears of any faction which may be opposed to it, not only to prevent an opposition to the execution of the laws themselves, but also to compel the most of them to aid the magistrate; but the people will not be likely to have such confidence in their rulers, in a republic so extensive as the United States, as necessary for these purposes. The confidence which the people have in their rulers, in a free republic, arises from their knowing them, from their being responsible to them for their conduct, and from the power they have of displacing them when they misbehave: but in a republic of the extent of this continent, the people in general would be acquainted with very few of their rulers: the people at large would know little of their proceedings, and it would be extremely difficult to change them. The people in Georgia and New-Hampshire would not know one another's mind, and therefore could not act in concert to enable them to effect a general change of representatives. The different parts of so extensive a country could not possibly be made acquainted with the conduct of their representatives, nor be informed of the reasons upon which measures were founded. The consequence will be, they will have no confidence in their legislature, suspect them of ambitious views, be jealous of every measure they adopt, and will not support the laws they pass. Hence the government will be nerveless and inefficient, and no way will be left to render it otherwise, but by establishing an armed force to execute the laws at the point of the bayonet—a government of all others the most to be dreaded.

In a republic of such vast extent as the United-States, the legislature cannot attend to the various concerns and wants of its different parts. It cannot be sufficiently numerous to be acquainted with the local condition and wants of the different districts, and if it could, it is impossible it should have sufficient time to attend to and provide for all the variety of cases of this nature, that would be continually arising.

In so extensive a republic, the great officers of government would soon become above the controul of the people, and abuse their power to the purpose of aggrandizing themselves, and oppressing them. The trust committed to the executive offices, in a country of the extent of the United-States, must be various and of magnitude. The command of all the troops and navy of the republic, the appointment of officers, the power of pardoning offences, the collecting of all the public revenues, and the power of expending them, with a number of other powers, must be lodged and exercised in every state, in the hands of a few. When these are attended with great honor and emolument, as they always will be in large states, so as greatly to interest men to pursue them, and to be proper objects for ambitious and designing men, such men will be ever restless in their pursuit after them. They will use the power, when they have acquired it, to the purposes of gratifying their own interest and ambition, and it is scarcely possible, in a very large republic, to call them to account for their misconduct, or to prevent their abuse of power.

These are some of the reasons by which it appears, that a free republic cannot long subsist over a country of the great extent of these states. If then this new constitution is calculated to consolidate the thirteen states into one, as it evidently is, it ought not to be adopted.

Though I am of opinion, that it is a sufficient objection to this government, to reject it, that it creates the whole union into one government, under the form of a republic, yet if this objection was obviated, there are exceptions to it, which are so material and fundamental, that they ought to determine every man, who is a friend to the liberty and happiness of mankind, not to adopt it. I beg the candid and dispassionate attention of my countrymen while I state these objections—they are such as have obtruded themselves upon my mind upon a careful attention to the matter, and such as I sincerely believe are well founded. There are many objections, of small moment, of which I shall take no notice—perfection is not to be expected in any thing that is the production of man—and if I did not in my conscience believe that this scheme was defective in the fundamental principles—in the foundation upon which a free and equal government must rest—I would hold my peace.

2.2

ROBERT A. DAHL

From *How Democratic Is the American Constitution?*

Dahl casts a critical eye on the American Constitution. He lists numerous problems with the document. Most important, it implicitly sanctioned slavery and set up two undemocratic institutions: the Supreme Court and the Senate. He concludes that it survived by allowing for mass elections to determine who controlled the national government, and thus was "democratic" enough to overcome its weaknesses.

UNDEMOCRATIC ELEMENTS IN THE FRAMERS' CONSTITUTION

. . . Judged from later, more democratic perspectives, the Constitution of the Framers contained at least seven important shortcomings.

Slavery

First, it neither forbade slavery nor empowered Congress to do so. In fact, the compromise on slavery not only denied Congress the effective power to prohibit the importation of slaves before 1808[1] but it gave constitutional sanction to one of the most morally objectionable byproducts of a morally repulsive institution: the Fugitive Slave laws, according to which a slave who managed to escape to a free state had to be returned to the slaveholder, whose property the slave remained.[2] That it took three-quarters of a century and a sanguinary civil war before slavery was abolished should at the least make us doubt whether the document of the Framers ought to be regarded as holy writ.

Suffrage

Second, the Constitution failed to guarantee the right of suffrage, leaving the qualifications of suffrage to the states.[3] It implicitly left in place the exclusion of half the population—women—as well as African Americans and Native Americans.[4] As we know, it took a century and a half before women were constitutionally guaranteed the right to vote, and nearly two centuries before a president and Congress could overcome the effective veto of a minority of

From Robert A. Dahl, *How Democratic Is the American Constitution?* (New Haven, CT: Yale University Press, 2001).

states in order to pass legislation intended to guarantee the voting rights of African Americans.

Election of the President

Third, the executive power was vested in a president whose selection, according to the intentions and design of the Framers, was to be insulated from both popular majorities and congressional control. As we'll see, the Framers' main design for achieving that purpose—a body of presidential electors composed of men of exceptional wisdom and virtue who would choose the chief executive unswayed by popular opinion—was almost immediately cast into the dustbin of history by leaders sympathetic with the growing democratic impulses of the American people, among them James Madison himself. Probably nothing the Framers did illustrates more sharply their inability to foresee the shape that politics would assume in a democratic republic. . . .

Choosing Senators

Fourth, senators were to be chosen not by the people but by the state legislatures, for a term of six years.[5] Although this arrangement fell short of the ambitions of delegates like Gouverneur Morris who wanted to construct an aristocratic upper house, it would help to ensure that senators would be less responsive to popular majorities and perhaps more sensitive to the needs of property holders. Members of the Senate would thus serve as a check on the Representatives, who were all subject to popular elections every two years.[6]

Equal Representation in the Senate

The attempt to create a Senate that would be a republican version of the aristocratic House of Lords was derailed, as we have seen, by a prolonged and bitter dispute over an entirely different question: Should the states be equally represented in Congress or should members of both houses be allocated according to population? This question not only gave rise to one of the most disruptive issues of the Convention, but it resulted in a fifth undemocratic feature of the Constitution. As a consequence of the famous—or from a democratic point of view, infamous—"Connecticut Compromise," each state was, as we have seen, awarded the same number of senators, without respect to population. Although this arrangement failed to protect the fundamental rights and interests of the most deprived minorities, some strategically placed and highly privileged minorities—slaveholders, for example—gained disproportionate power over government polices at the expense of less privileged minorities. . . .

Judicial Power

Sixth, the Constitution of the Framers failed to limit the powers of the judiciary to declare as unconstitutional laws that had been properly passed by Congress and signed by the president. What the delegates intended in the way of judicial review will remain forever unclear; probably many delegates were unclear in their own minds, and to the extent that they discussed the question at all, they were not in full agreement. But probably a majority accepted the view that the federal courts should rule on the constitutionality of state and federal laws in cases brought before them. Nevertheless, it is likely that a substantial majority intended that federal judges should not participate in making government laws and policies, a responsibility that clearly belonged not to the judiciary but to the legislative branch. Their opposition to any policy-making role for the judiciary is strongly indicated by their response to a proposal in the Virginia Plan that "the Executive and a convenient number of the National Judiciary, ought to compose a council of revision" empowered to veto acts of the National Legislature. Though this provision was vigorously defended by Madison and Mason, it was voted down, 6 states to 3.[7]

A judicial veto is one thing; judicial legislation is quite another. Whatever some of the delegates may have thought about the advisability of justices sharing with the executive the authority to veto laws passed by Congress, I am fairly certain that none would have given the slightest support to a proposal that judges should themselves have the power to legislate, to make national policy. However, the upshot of their work was that in the guise of reviewing the constitutionality of state and congressional actions or inactions, the federal judiciary would later engage in what in some instances could only be called judicial policy-making—or, if you like, judicial legislation.[8]

Congressional Power

Finally, the powers of Congress were limited in ways that could, and at times did, prevent the federal government from regulating or controlling the economy by means that all modern democratic governments have adopted. Without the power to tax incomes, for example, fiscal policy, not to say measures like Social Security, would be impossible. And regulatory actions—over railroad rates, air safety, food and drugs, banking, minimum wages, and many other policies—had no clear constitutional authorization. Although it would be anachronistic to charge the Framers with lack of foresight in these matters,[9] unless the Constitution could be altered by amendment or by heroic reinterpretation of its provisions—presumably by what I have just called judicial legislation—it would prevent representatives of later majorities from adopting the policies they believed were necessary to achieve efficiency, fairness, and security in a complex post-agrarian society.

Enlightened as the Framers' Constitution may have been by the standards of the eighteenth century, future generations with more democratic aspirations would find some of its undemocratic features objectionable—and even unacceptable. The public expression of these growing democratic aspirations was not long in coming.

Even Madison did not, and probably could not, predict the peaceful democratic revolution that was about to begin. For the American revolution was soon to enter into a new and unforeseen phase.

THE FRAMERS' CONSTITUTION MEETS EMERGENT DEMOCRATIC BELIEFS

We may tend to think of the American republic and its Constitution as solely the product of leaders inspired by extraordinary wisdom and virtue. Yet without a citizenry committed to republican principles of government and capable of governing themselves in accordance with those principles, the Constitution would soon have been little more than a piece of paper. As historical experience would reveal, in countries where democratic beliefs were fragile or absent, constitutions did indeed become little more than pieces of paper— soon violated, soon forgotten.

The American democratic republic was not created nor could it have been long maintained by leaders alone, gifted as they may have been. It was they, to be sure, who designed a framework suitable, as they thought, for a republic. But it was the American people, and the leaders responsive to them, who ensured that the new republic would rapidly become a *democratic* republic.

■　■　■

I have little doubt that if the American Constitutional Convention had been held in 1820, a very different constitution would have emerged from the deliberations—although, I hasten to add, we can never know what shape that constitution might have taken. We can be reasonably sure, however, that the delegates would have attempted to provide more support for, and fewer barriers to, a democratic republic.

As to the undemocratic features of the constitution created in 1787, let me suggest four conclusions.

First, the aspects of the Constitution that are most defective from a democratic point of view do not necessarily all reflect the intentions of the Framers, insofar as we may surmise them. Though the flaws are traceable to their handiwork, they are in some cases flaws resulting from the inability of these superbly talented craftsmen to foresee how their carefully crafted instrument of government would work under the changing conditions that were to follow—and most of all, under the impact of the democratic revolution in which Americans were, and I hope still are, engaged.

Second, some of the undemocratic aspects of the original design also resulted from the logrolling and compromises that were necessary to achieve agreement. The Framers were not philosophers searching for a description of an ideal system. Nor—and we may be forever grateful to them for this—were they philosopher kings entrusted with the power to rule. They were practical men, eager to achieve a stronger national government, and as practical men they made compromises. Would the country have been better off if they had refused to do so? I doubt it. But in any case, they did compromise, and even today the Constitution bears the results of some of their concessions.

Third, undemocratic aspects that were more or less deliberately built into the Constitution overestimated the dangers of popular majorities—American popular majorities, at any rate—and underestimated the strength of the developing democratic commitment among Americans. As a result, in order to adapt the original framework more closely to the requirements of the emerging democratic republic, with the passage of time some of these aspects of the original Constitution were changed, sometimes by amendment, sometimes, as with political parties, by new institutions and practices.

Finally, though the defects seem to me serious and may grow even more serious with time, Americans are not much predisposed to consider another Constitution, nor is it clear what alternative arrangements would serve them better.

As a result, the beliefs of Americans in the legitimacy of their Constitution will remain, I think, in constant tension with their beliefs in the legitimacy of democracy.

For my part, I believe that the legitimacy of the Constitution ought to derive solely from its utility as an instrument of democratic government—nothing more, nothing less.

NOTES

1. Article I, Section 9. For an excellent account of the only full public debate over the slavery issue, see Joseph J. Ellis, *Founding Brothers: The Revolutionary Generation* (New York: Alfred A. Knopf, 2000), 81–119. The debate took place in the House of Representatives in March 1790 in response to petitions from Quakers in New York and Philadelphia "calling for the federal government to put an immediate end to the African slave trade" (81).

2. Article IV, Section 2.

3. Article I, Sections 2, 3.

4. For a magisterial study of the evolution of American citizenship, see Rogers Smith, *Civic Ideals: Conflicting Visions of Citizenship in U.S. History* (New Haven: Yale University Press, 1997). On the constitution's omission of citizenship for women, Native Americans, and African Americans, see 130–34.

5. Article I, Section 3.

6. By the same electorate as that for "the most numerous branch of the state legislature" (Article I, Section 2).

7. *Records*, 2: 83.

8. For evidence that the Supreme Court sometimes plays such a role, see my "Decision-Making in a Democracy: The Supreme Court as a National Policy-Maker," *Journal of Public Law* 6, no. 2 (1957): 279–95.

9. It is only fair to point out that given the political opposition to any increase in federal powers, the Framers may well have gone as far as they could go. Their major opponents, the Anti-Federalists, who saw the constitution as a threat to popular government at the state level, objected that the powers of Congress to regulate interstate commerce were excessive. Richard L. Perry, ed., *The Sources of Our Liberties: Documentary Origins of Individual Liberties in the United States Constitution and Bill of Rights* (New York: American Bar Association, 1959), 240.

2.3

MILA VERSTEEG AND EMILY ZACKIN

"Constitutions Un-entrenched: Toward an Alternative Theory of Constitutional Design"

Versteeg and Zackin compare two ways of drafting constitutions. Entrenched constitutions are short, and describe broad principles intended to last for the long term across many generations. Unentrenched constitutions are long and specific, with the idea that they will be amended repeatedly as future generations decide on new constitutional means to solve contemporary problems. The U.S. Constitution is short and entrenched, while the American states differ among themselves on the length and entrenchment of their constitutions.

INTRODUCTION

One of the central problems of constitutionalism is how to establish and simultaneously control a government. As James Madison expressed in Federalist 51, "you must first enable the government to control the governed; and in the next place oblige it to control itself."[1] Many familiar constitutional features are tools to oblige government to control itself; frequent elections, separation of powers, explicit limitations on government's scope and authority are several of the most prominent examples. In order to maintain, not merely establish, a democratic polity, however, these institutional features alone are insufficient. If members of government, or the temporary majorities whom they represent, can subvert the very mechanisms designed to keep them in check, they can exceed the bounds on their authority without repercussions.

A dominant theme of the constitutional theory literature is that successful constitutions must not only constrain those in power, but must do so over long time horizons, establishing constraints durable enough to bind across generations. This "entrenchment function" (Young 2008) . . . is often described as a defining feature and central goal of constitutionalism (Waluchow 2012).

■　■　■

Constitutional entrenchment has also been described as a mechanism for permanently removing some questions from the political agenda, thereby

From Mila Versteeg and Emily Zackin, "Constitutions Un-entrenched: Toward an Alternative Theory of Constitutional Design," *American Political Science Review* 110, no. 4 (November 2016): 1–34.

creating a stable set of rules that allows people to conduct politics in the presence of disagreement (Holmes 1995; Sunstein 1991). . . .

Members of the U.S. Supreme Court (even those with very different political positions) have also expressed the view that entrenchment is the central purpose of constitutionalism. According to Justice Scalia (1997, 40) the "whole purpose [of a constitution] is to prevent change—to embed certain rights in such a manner that future generations cannot readily take them away." Justice Brennan (1991, 4) likewise notes: "[i]n my view, it is crucial to the durability and efficacy of a charter of personal liberties that it not be subject to easy alteration or suspension. . . . [R]obust entrenchment forbidding compromise or requiring supermajoritarian approval for amendments seems to me best."

▪   ▪   ▪

Entrenched constitutions are typically constructed as spare frameworks, rather than detailed policy directives, since highly specific documents are unlikely to remain relevant over long time horizons. As a result, along with rigidity, "generality and abstraction" are also widely considered to be defining features of written constitutions (Marmor 2007, 91–94). Highly specific constitutions, by contrast, are often dismissed as insufficiently majestic, or constitutional, in nature. As Justice Marshall famously remarked, "only [the Constitution's] great outlines should be marked, its important objects designated, and the minor ingredients which compose those objects be deduced from the nature of those objects themselves," since anything else would "partake a prolixity of a legal code."[2] Others have suggested that specificity indicates that constitution drafters were less concerned with constraining those in power (Ginsburg and Posner 2010) or that it actually imposes harm on majorities (Nardi and Tsebelis 2014).

The model of an entrenched and spare document, which changes meaning primarily through judicial interpretation, successfully describes the U.S. Constitution. However, it does a poor job of depicting most other national democratic constitutions, or even U.S. state constitutions.

▪   ▪   ▪

Entrenched/spare and un-entrenched/specific can be understood as two different solutions to the same problem: enabling people to control their government. Those who conceptualize constitutionalism as a form of contracting describe the people as a "principal," which, in creating a representative government, has employed "agents" to better realize its ends.[3] This formulation highlights the fact that agents are often in the position to pursue their own interests over that of the principal. Stable constitutional documents can be seen as attempts to solve this "principal-agent" problem by entrenching durable constraints on agents who, left unchecked, would amend the constitution to reflect their own interest. We argue here that specific constitutions are also attempts to solve this principal-agent problem, not by circumscribing the agent's actions through fixed constitutional boundaries (entrenchment), but by limiting the latitude within which agents operate (through specificity) and relaxing the rigidity of the constitutional boundaries (increasing flexibility) to accommodate constitutions' increased scope and detail. One might describe this design strategy as "constitutional micromanagement."

▪   ▪   ▪

[We will] demonstrate that constitutional drafters increasingly chose specificity over entrenchment as a means to constrain the exercise of political power. In doing so, they embarked on a developmental path that was very different from the course of federal constitutional development in the United States. Scholars of American constitutional development have documented the country's long journey toward judicial supremacy over federal constitutional meanings but in other democratic polities, both within and outside the United States, constitution-makers have attempted [to] restrict the latitude of judiciaries, and even legislatures, in interpreting and applying constitutional documents. The result has been a new model of constitutional design, one that has yet to be fully recognized in constitutional theory.

TWO MODELS OF CONSTITUTIONAL DESIGN

The Entrenched Constitution

Entrenchment, or rigidity, may allow constitutional texts to establish enduring authority over governmental activities. As people come to believe that these constitutional boundaries will remain in place, they may then establish political and economic arrangements premised upon them, creating incentives for the actors involved to continue to preserve these original boundaries (Hardin 1999; Levinson 2011). Constitutional courts may then emerge from these larger political and economic structures and participate in the enforcement (and further entrenchment) of the constitutional commitments upon which these institutions were founded (Hardin 1999; Hirschl 2004; Law 2009).

Importantly, entrenchment discourages the inclusion of highly specific policy choices in constitutional documents, since specific policies are unlikely to remain appropriate or popular in the face of changing economic and social conditions. Another reason that entrenchment works against constitutional specificity is that it is generally easier for diverse groups to agree on broad standards or principles than on specific policies (Lerner 2011). We might expect this difficulty to be heightened if those agreements will be difficult to revise (Hardin 1999, 84). Entrenched constitutions, therefore, tend to be narrow in scope, describing only the basic structures of government, the powers entrusted to it, and the rights it cannot violate. They also tend to exclude detailed or technical instructions, employing broad statements of principle in lieu of comprehensive policies.

▪   ▪   ▪

The Specific Constitution

. . . [M]any real-world constitution-makers have found a different solution to some of the agency problems in constitutional design: specificity. By placing a broad range of detailed policies directly in a constitutional text, constitution-makers can attempt to constrain the exercise of political power. In other words, the principal can use a constitutional text to tell its agents exactly what to do and not do. The resulting constitutions tend to emphasize rules over standards, attempting to define much of the content of law *ex ante* rather than allowing it to be defined by its interpreters *ex post* (Kaplow 1992). Since these specific rules leave less room for interpretative disagreement, they can facilitate political coordination to support their own enforcement (Weingast 1997; Hadfield and Weingast 2013). It is relatively easy to agree when a government has violated a detailed instruction and to mobilize opposition around that blatant violation.

A high degree of specificity requires constitutional texts to become un-entrenched. While specific provisions might seem attractive at the time of founding, they can quickly grow outdated. Thus, highly specific constitutions typically require frequent updating. Furthermore, if constitutions are updated frequently, this flexibility may encourage people [to] pursue constitutional change in their efforts to advance particular policy goals (Elkins, Ginsburg, and Melton 2009, 89). Perhaps more fundamentally, some degree of flexibility is a central part of a constitutional strategy that envisions continuous control over constitutional agents, since flexibility is required for contemporary majorities to correct governmental policies through textual constitutional instructions.

■ ■ ■

There are . . . potential downsides of specific and flexible constitutions. First, because these constitutions envision an ongoing constitutional micro-management, they impose significant costs associated with the monitoring of office holders. There are also costs associated with the frequent revisions necessary to ensure that the constitution's highly specific text will remain relevant, especially when those revisions require legislative action or referenda. Second, it is not clear that the strategy is actually successful in practice (Dixon 2014). Specificity is certainly no guarantee of compliance with drafters' intentions. In fact, since the early twentieth century, legal realists have emphasized the indeterminacy of legal rules (Llewellyn 1930), and some scholars believe that judiciaries are unlikely to enforce positive rights against the government (Cross 2001). While specificity often represents an attempt to curb judicial discretion, some have suggested that constitutions that are too specific may enhance discretion by requiring judges to balance the competing values that these constitutions contain (Posner 2013).

■ ■ ■

EMPIRICAL EXPLORATION OF CONSTITUTIONAL MODELS

■ ■ ■

Measuring Entrenchment and Specificity

There are different ways to measure a constitution's degree of entrenchment. Individual constitutions lie somewhere along a continuum from highly entrenched and unchangeable to extremely flexible, and within a single constitution, some provisions may be more entrenched than others. It is not entirely clear how best to determine a constitution's place along this axis. Some studies assess flexibility according to the formal amendment rules of the constitutions (Lutz 1994; Lijphart 1999; La Porta et al. 2004; Lorenz 2005), others count the number of times the constitution has been amended (Ginsburg and Posner 2010), or the frequency with which a single polity adopts entirely new constitutions (Elkins, Ginsburg, and Melton 2009).

To describe the level of entrenchment of constitutional texts, we calculate each constitution's *entrenchment score*, which we define as the total number of years a democratic polity has existed, divided by the total number of years in which it witnessed constitutional change (either through replacement or amendment). The resulting measure captures the average number of years that a polity has gone between constitutional revisions. In constructing this entrenchment score, we do not distinguish between amendment and replacement because this distinction is often not a meaningful one: some polities have employed the formal amendment process to overhaul their entire constitutions, while the promulgation of a "new" constitution sometimes reflects no significant differences in content (Arato 2014).[4] Thus, we consider both types of textual changes evidence of flexibility. The measure does not rely on formal amendment rules because these rules are mediated so dramatically by political norms. For instance, the Japanese constitution, which is widely considered one of the world's most entrenched, contains the same formal amendment rule as most U.S. state constitutions, which are generally understood to be highly flexible. Finally, since our purpose is to reveal how readily those living under a democratic constitution modify its text, our measure excludes non-textual change.

To describe constitutions' *specificity,* we simply calculate the number of words they contain. Specificity, however, comes in different forms. A constitution may be specific because it describes many different topics. Many democratic constitutions cover a wide range of topics, including matters such as fiscal policy and economic development, the management of natural resources, animals, matters of cultural significance, and citizen character. This type of specificity is often described as *scope* (Ginsburg 2010). To capture the scope of democratic constitutions, we calculate the number of unique words in each constitutional text, on the premise that a larger number of unique words reflects the constitution's inclusion of a larger number of unique issues.[5]

A second form of specificity is [the] extent to which each topic is discussed. We refer to this form of specificity as *detail*. To measure a constitution's detail, we divide the total word count of the constitution by its number of unique words, thus creating a proxy for how many words are spent on each unique topic.[6] It is important to note that scope and detail are closely related concepts. For instance, imagine a constitution that grants all citizens a right to education, but subsequently adds provisions on teachers' pay or the content of the curriculum. These provisions could be regarded as a larger number of topics covered in the constitution (increasing its scope), but could also be viewed as a more exhaustive treatment of the general topic of education (increasing its detail). Because we have measured constitutional scope according to the number of unique words in a constitution, we treat all of these additional policies as an expansion of scope, rather than detail.

Historical Trajectory

The historical data we have collected suggest that, over the past two centuries, democratic constitutions have become less entrenched, while their specificity has increased. Figure [1] shows the historical trajectory of all democratic constitutions, including both democratic national constitutions and state constitutions. Panel 1 demonstrates that constitutions of democratic polities have become less entrenched over time as witnessed by their declining entrenchment scores.[7] Panel 2 depicts the average word count of these constitutions (as measured at the time of their adoption) and reveals that democratic

FIGURE [1]   Democratic Countries and U.S. States

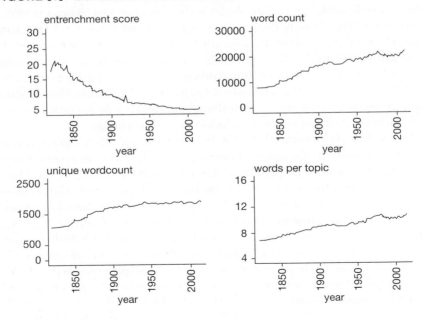

FIGURE [2]   Democratic Countries Only

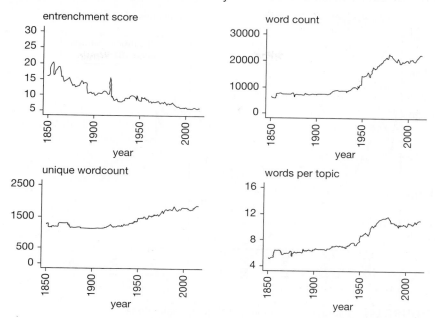

constitutions have grown in specificity.[8] Panel 3 depicts the growth in the scope of these constitutions as captured by their unique word count over time.[9] Panel 4 depicts their increase in their detail as captured by the number of words they spend on each topic. Overall, Figure [1] depicts a large-scale shift away from sparseness and entrenchment, towards flexibility and specificity. For comparison, Figure [2] depicts the same information for democratic countries only (excluding state constitution) and reveals the same trends.

∎   ∎   ∎

U.S. State Constitutions

In the U.S. states, the shift away from entrenched, spare constitutions to flexible and detailed documents began in the mid-nineteenth century. Figure [3] depicts the historical development of U.S. state constitutions' average entrenchment score, while Figure [4] depicts the average word count. The left-hand panels of both figures are based on all states for which we have data, while the right-hand panels are based on those states that have continuously been in our sample since 1815 for each of these measures. Shifts depicted in the right-hand panels do not result from new states entering the sample. Figure [4] shows that the increase in state constitutions' flexibility first occurs in the 1830s, while the increase in specificity occurs around the same time. Our specificity data depicted by the solid lines in Figure [4] understate the growth of states' constitutions, since subsequent constitutional amendments are

FIGURE [3]   Average Entrenchment Scores of State Constitutions

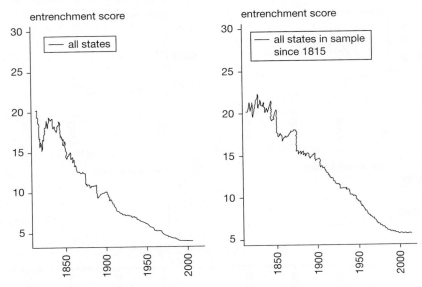

FIGURE [4]   Average Word Count of State Constitutions*

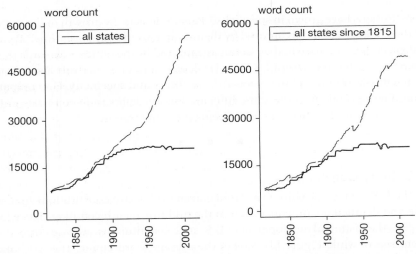

*Solid lines denote constitutional texts as adopted; dotted lines take account of subsequent amendments.

excluded from our analysis. To give a fuller sense of the dramatic increase in specificity, the dotted lines in Figure [4] show the average word count for state constitutions when including subsequent amendments.[10]

As many scholars of U.S. state constitutions have noted, detailed instructions were constitutionalized as part of a nationwide, nineteenth-century movement to enhance popular control over policymaking. Over the course of the nineteenth century, the drafters of U.S. state constitutions also adopted increasingly flexible constitutions. In part, this increased flexibility may have been necessitated by the documents' mounting detail, but state constitutional drafters also redesigned constitutions to be more flexible so that they could better serve as vehicles of democratic control over courts and legislatures (Dinan 2006, 62–63; Fritz 1994).

The original impetus to include detailed policy instructions in state constitutions is often traced to the economic crisis of 1839, which revealed the fiscal blunders that many state legislatures had made, and motivated a wave of constitutional change designed to prevent legislatures from repeating these mistakes (Tarr 1998, 112). Earlier in the decade, state legislatures had invested heavily in canals, railroads, and banks, and had financed these investments not through taxation, but through indebtedness. When the economic boom of the 1830s ended with an equally dramatic bust, these schemes proved disastrous. Many heavily indebted states were forced to default on their interest payments, while others only narrowly avoided default. These crises triggered widespread calls to ensure that legislatures would be barred from this type of boom-time policymaking. Between 1842 and 1852, ten of the eleven states that held constitutional conventions wrote procedural restrictions on the way that states could issue debt directly into their constitutions (Wallis 2005, 219).

Throughout the second half of the nineteenth century and into the twentieth, agrarian reformers and advocates of organized labor pursued constitutional specificity for a similar purpose: to preempt particular policy choices and to force state governments into enacting new slates of popular policies. Agrarian populists, for instance, used constitutions to establish state oversight and regulation of railroad operations, increasing the scope of these documents (Buck 1913, 195–98). In many states, labor unions employed a similar strategy, pursuing the insertion of specific labor regulations directly into constitutional documents (Zackin 2013, 106–45). In its endorsement of a constitutional provision establishing an eight-hour workday, for instance, the *Montana Labor News* explained that the state had already regulated the working hours in a number of industries, but that to ensure democratic control over these policies, it was also necessary to add an eight-hour provision to the state constitution: "[a]ll of these 8-hour laws may be destroyed by the corporations unless you pass this 8-hour amendment. Usually, the courts function in the interests of the corporations; so does the legislature."[11] This embrace of constitutional specificity reflected the recognition that judges and legislatures can exert enormous influence over public policy and that highly specific constitutions can curtail the discretion of these agents.

As the twentieth century dawned, it became increasingly apparent that judges were not neutral monitors, overseeing government officials on behalf of the people, but were themselves consequential policymakers. Progressive reformers realized that specific constitutional provisions could check judicial power over the policymaking process by explicitly identifying particular policies as constitutionally permissible. This insight generated a wave of court-constraining constitutional provisions, designed to prevent state courts from invalidating legislation on subjects related to maximum working hours, minimum wages, collective bargaining, workers' compensation, and other social welfare programs (Dinan 2007).

Contemporaneous observers described enhanced constitutional detail a reflection of drafters' desires to exert control over those who would later interpret and apply their constitutions. An 1892 article in the *Harvard Law Review* described newly written state constitutions as products of the pervasive belief that "the agents of the people, whether legislative, executive, or judicial, are not to be trusted; so that it is necessary to enter into the most minute particulars as to what they shall not do" (Eaton 1892, 121). Critics of this new form of constitutionalism recognized that greater specificity reflected a distrust of office holders, and admonished constitutional drafters to avoid constitutionalizing detailed policies. One famous jurist, for instance, addressed North Dakota's constitutional convention with this advice: "[d]on't in your Constitution-making legislate too much . . . You have got to trust somebody in the future and it is right and proper that each department of government should be trusted to perform its legitimate function" (cited in Leahy 2003). As we have seen, however, these calls to preserve spare constitutional documents went largely unheeded.

▪ ▪ ▪

CONCLUSION

▪ ▪ ▪

[A]ll constitutional drafters face the paradox that majority rule both defines and threatens democracy. Entrenched constitutional texts may be robust to attempts to undermine constitutional constraints through formal revision, but such documents often allow for markedly anti-democratic governance. Specific constitutions grew out of a desire for tighter democratic control over policymaking, but as a result, they are likely to be far worse at hindering officeholders or tyrannical majorities who attempt to revise them. It is perhaps fortunate, therefore, that the actual practice of constitutional drafting does not require a dichotomous choice between the two models we have described. In fact, many national constitution-makers have inserted eternity clauses, declaring certain basic constitutional principles un-amendable, while leaving the rest of the constitution more flexible.

NOTES

1. "The Structure of the Government Must Furnish the Proper Checks and Balances Between the Different Departments." *The Federalist 51*, 1788 (James Madison).

2. *McCulloch v. Maryland*, 17 U.S. (4 Wheat) 316 (1819).

3. Of course, "the principal" and "the people" are abstractions. The extent to which different democratic constitutions reflect a genuine consensus among the citizenry remains an open question.

4. To illustrate, Chile's 1980 constitution has never been replaced since the fall of the Pinochet regime, and yet, has been changed radically through amendment (Arato 2014). Conversely, Louisiana's 1861 constitution was exactly the same as the 1852 constitution, except for its replacing the words "United States" with "Confederate States" throughout.

5. Elkins, Ginsburg, and Melton (2009, 104) capture specificity by counting how many of a predetermined list of topics are covered in a constitution. The downside of this measure is that it is limited to a set of fairly common set of topics (92 topics), and thus does not capture those constitutions widest in scope because they cover topics not on the list. The correlation between our unique word count measure and the existing scope measure is 0.59.

6. Elkins, Ginsburg and Melton (2009) measure detail as the constitution's total word count divided by the number of topics (out of 92) it deals with. The correlation between their measure and ours is 0.92.

7. The amendment and replacement data for state constitutions comes from Dixon and Holden (2012), and is available for 44 states. The data is current as of 2005. We expanded the coverage of their dataset by using the NBER State Constitutions database. The same data for national constitutions comes from the Comparative Constitutions Project (CCP) and is current as of 2014. To capture the historical changes in entrenchment, we calculate the number of years a polity has been in existence and divide it by the total number of revisions (either amendment or replacement) it has undergone at that point in time.

8. The historical texts of national constitutions at the time of their adoption were provided by Comparative Constitutions Project; the state constitutional texts were collected by the UVA Law Library. We calculate the number of words in each constitution at the time of adoption using the "tm" package in R and assign this to all subsequent years, until a new constitution is adopted. We do so because constitutional texts that incorporate all subsequent amendments are not systematically available.

9. We first "stem" our data to remove common stop words, after which we estimate the number of unique words using the "tm" package in R. We thank Adam Chilton for sharing R-code for this.

10. We obtained state constitutional texts with their amendments from the NBER State Constitutions Project. This database includes all the subsequent amendments for 38 state constitutions. The dotted lines are thus based on a smaller sample of states than the solid lines.

11. "All These Laws Will Be in Danger If the Eight Hour Amendment is Defeated by the People November 3." *Montana Labor News*, Butte: October 29, 1936, 1.

REFERENCES

Aghion, Phillipe and Bolton, Patrick. 2003 "Incomplete Social Contracts." *Journal of the European Economic Association*. 1(1): 38–67.

Arato, Andrew. 2014. "Beyond the Alternative Reform or Revolution: Post Sovereign Constitution Making and Latin America." Working paper.

Brennan Jr., William J. 1991. "Why Have a Bill of Rights?" *Valparaiso University Law Review* 26 (1): 1–19.

Buck, Solon Justus. 1913. *The Granger Movement: A Study of Agricultural Organization and its Political, Economic and Social Manifestations, 1870–1880*. Cambridge: Harvard University Press.

Buchanan, James and Tullock, Gordon. 1962. *The Calculus of Consent: The Logical Foundations of Constitutional Democracy*.

Cross, Frank B. 2001. "The Error of Positive Rights." *UCLA Law Review*, 48(4), 857–924.

Dinan, John J. 2006. *The American State Constitutional Tradition*. Lawrence: University of Kansas Press.

Dinan, John J. 2007. "Foreword: Court-Constraining Amendments and the State Constitutional Tradition." *Rutgers Law Journal* 38 (Summer): 983–1040.

Dixon, Rosalind. 2014. "Partial Constitutional Codes." UNSW Law Research Paper No. 2014–37. University of New South Wales, New South Wales, Australia.

Dixon, Rosalind, and Richard Holden. 2012. "Constitutional Amendment Rules: The Denominator Problem." In *Comparative Constitutional Design*, ed. Tom Ginsburg. New York: Cambridge University Press.

Eaton, Amasa M. 1892. "Recent State Constitutions." *Harvard Law Review* 6 (3): 109–24.

Elkins, Zachary, Tom Ginsburg, and James Melton. 2009. *The Endurace of National Constitutions*. Cambridge; New York: Cambridge University Press.

Fritz, Christian. 1994. "Rethinking the American Constitutional Tradition: National Dimensions in the Formation of State Constitutions." *California Supreme Court Historical Society Yearbook* 1:103–22.

Gardner, James A. 1992. "The Failed Discourse of State Constitutionalism." *Michigan Law Review* 90 (February): 761–837.

Gillman, Howard. 2002. "How Political Parties Can Use the Courts to Advance Their Agendas: Federal Courts in the United States, 1875–91." *American Political Science Review* 96 (September): 511–24.

Ginsburg, Tom, and James Melton. 2014. "Does the Constitutional Amendment Rule Matter at All? Amendment Cultures and the Challenges of Measuring Amendment Difficulty." University of Chicago Coase-Sandor Institute for Law and Economics Working Paper No. 682 (2D Series).

Ginsburg, Tom, and Eric A. Posner. 2010. "Subconstitutionalism." *Stanford Law Review* 62(6): 1584–1628.

Graber, Mark A. 1993. "The Nonmajoritarian Difficulty: Legislative Deference to the Judiciary." *Studies in American Political Development* 7 (Spring): 35–73.

Hardin, Russell. 1999. *Liberalism, Constitutionalism and Democracy*. Oxford: Oxford University Press.

Hadfield, Gillian K., and Barry R. Weingast. 2013. Constitutions as Coordination Devices in *Institutions, Property Rights, and Economic Growth: The Legacy of Douglass North*, edited by S. Galiani and I. Sened. Cambridge: Cambridge University Press. Forthcoming.

Hammons, Christopher W. 1999. "Was James Madison Wrong? Rethinking the American Preference for Short, Framework-Oriented Constitutions." *American Political Science Review* 93 (July): 837–49.

Hirschl, Ran. 2004. *Towards Juristocracy: The Origins and Consequences of the New Constitutionalism*. Cambridge: Harvard University Press.

Holmes, Stephen. 1995. *Passions and Constraints: On the Theory of Liberal Democracy*. Chicago: University of Chicago Press.

Howard, A.E. Dick. 1968. "'For the Common Benefit:' Constitutional History in Virginia as a Casebook for the Modern Constitution-Maker." *Virginia Law Review* 54 (June): 816.

Kahana, Tsvi. 2013. "Majestic Constitutionalism: The Notwithstanding Mechanism in Israel", *Israeli Constitutionalism from a Comparative Perspective*. Eds. in Aaron Barak, Daphne Barak-Erez & Gideon Spair, eds. Hart Publishing.

Kaplow, Louis. 1992. "Rules Versus Standards: An Economic Analysis." *Duke Law Journal* 42: 557–629.

Klug, Heinz. 2015. "Constitutional Amendments." *Annual Review of Law and Social Science*. 11:95–110.

La Porta, Raphael, et al. 2004. "Judicial Checks and Balances." *Journal of Political Economy* 112(2): 445–70.

Law, David S. 2009. "A Theory of Judicial Power and Judicial Review." *Georgetown Law Journal* 97: 723–801.

Leahy, James E., and North Dakota. 2003. *The North Dakota State Constitution: A Reference Guide*. Westport, CT: Praeger Publishers.

Lerner, Hannah. 2011. *Making Constitutions in Deeply Divided Societies*. Cambridge: Cambridge University Press.

Levinson, Daryl J. 2011. "Parchment and Politics: The Positive Puzzle of Constitutional Commitment." *Harvard Law Review* 124 (January): 657–746.

Lijphardt, Arend. 1999. *Patterns of Democracy: Government Forms and Performance in Thirty-Six Democracies*. New Haven: Yale University Press.

Llewellyn, Karl N. 1930. *The Bramble Bush: Some Lectures on Law and Its Study*. New York: Columbia University Press.

Lorenz, Astrid. 2005. "How to Measure Constitutional Rigidity: Four Concepts and Two Alternatives." *Journal of Theoretical Politics* 17 (July): 339–61.

Lutz, Donald S. 1994. "Toward a Theory of Constitutional Amendment." *American Political Science Review* 88 (June): 355–70.

Marmor, Andrei. 2007. *Law in the Age of Pluralism*. New York: Oxford University Press.

Nardi, Dominic and George Tsebelis. 2014. "A Long Constitution is a (Positively) Bad Constitution: Evidence from OECD Countries." *British Journal of Political Science*. 1–22.

Persson, Thorsten, et al. 1997. "Separation of Powers and Political Accountability." *Quarterly Journal of Economics* 112(4): 1163–1202.

Posner, Eric. 2013. *The Twilight of Human Rights*. New York: Oxford University Press.

Scalia, Antonin, & Gutmann, Amy. 1997. *A Matter of Interpretation: Federal Courts and the Law: An Essay*. Princeton, N.J.: Princeton University Press.

Sunstein, Cass R. 1991. "Constitutionalism and Secession." *The University of Chicago Law Review* 58 (2): 633–70.

Tarr, G. Alan. 1998. *Understanding State Constitutions*. Princeton: Princeton University Press.

Versteeg, Mila, and Emily Zackin. 2014. "American Constitutional Exceptionalism Revisited." *The University of Chicago Law Review*.

Wallis, John Joseph. 2005. "Constitutions, Corporations, and Corruption: American States and Constitutional Change, 1842 to 1852." *The Journal of Economic History* 65(1): 211–56.

Waluchow, Will. 2012. "Constitutionalism." *The Stanford Encyclopedia of Philosophy*. http://plato.stanford.edu/archives/win2012/entries/constitutionalism/ (Sept. 11, 2012).

Weingast, Barry. 1997. Political Foundations of Democracy and the Rule of Law. *American Political Science Review* 91(2): 245–63.

Whittington, Keith E. 2007. *Political Foundations of Judicial Supremacy: The Presidency, the Supreme Court, and Constitutional Leadership in U.S. History*. Princeton: Princeton University Press.

Young, Ernest. 2008. "Constitutive and Entrenchment Functions of Constitutions: A Research Agenda." *University of Pennsylvania Journal of Constitutional Law* 10 (2): 399–411.

Zackin, Emily. 2013. *Looking for Rights in all the Wrong Places: Why State Constitutions Contain America's Positive Rights.* Princeton: Princeton University Press.

DISCUSSION QUESTIONS

1. Do you agree with any of the complaints by Brutus about the U.S. Constitution? Which ones, and why?

2. Assume for the moment that you agree with all or most of Dahl's critiques of the U.S. Constitution. How might the problems be fixed?

3. Would you rather that the state you live in have an entrenched constitution, or an unentrenched constitution? Why?

4. Constitutions both constrain (limit) and enable (give authority to) governments. Discuss two ways that the U.S. Constitution constrains government, and two ways that it enables government.

3

FEDERALISM

3.1

CHRISTOPHER HAMMONS

From "State Constitutions, Religious Protection, and Federalism"

Interpretation of the "Establishment Clause" of the U.S. Constitution, which has to do with religious liberty and state intrusion, has been controversial. Aside from this passage, the Constitution is silent on religion. Hammons points out that state constitutions in the United States invoke religion and God much more frequently, and that constitution-making at the state level, even in contemporary times, has had a strong religious flavor. He makes the argument that the Founders of the U.S. Constitution likely considered religion to be mostly a state-level issue and thus favored keeping the national government out of decisions over regulation of religious institutions and practices.

Advocates of a strict separation of church and state make a compelling case that the agnostic and neutral language of the First Amendment is meant to shield people from public support of religion. These "separationists" contend that the United States Constitution does not provide any validation for religious belief in the public sphere. Traditional focus and interpretation of the First Amendment of the U.S. Constitution has resulted in a jurisprudence that interprets the religious clauses primarily as ensuring "freedom *from* religion" rather than protecting "freedom *for* religion." This has become the dominant mode of legal thought regarding religious liberty in the United States.

From Christopher Hammons, "State Constitutions, Religious Protection, and Federalism," *University of St. Thomas Journal of Law and Public Policy* 7, no. 22 (2013): 226–39.

Religious liberty clauses at the state level offer a different perspective. An analysis of early and current state constitutions reveals that our federal political system has a long tradition of accommodating religious liberty. Furthermore, these state constitutions often validate religion by invoking God as the foundation of order, liberty, and good government. Advocates of religious liberty might do better to focus their attention on state constitutions rather than their national counterpart. State constitutions avoid the agnostic and neutral language found in the U.S. Bill of Rights and typically offer stronger protection for religious liberty as well.

■　■　■

To this end, advocates of religious liberty might consider pursuing a "federal" approach to religious freedom as a means of achieving a higher level of protection than is found in the U.S. Constitution. An examination of state constitutions provides compelling evidence that religious freedom, like many aspects of the Constitution, was meant to be dealt with largely at the state level.

. . . The U.S. Constitution depends heavily on state constitutions. The Constitution itself is a product of the state constitutional tradition and makes use of state constitutions to complete those issues where the U.S. Constitution is largely silent. Religion is one of these issues.

Religion is addressed most frequently, but not exclusively, in the preamble of most state constitutions. The purpose of a preamble at the beginning of a written constitution is largely philosophical. Preambles are not legally binding. Nor do they establish political institutions or policies. The main purpose of a constitutional preamble is to provide a statement of values and beliefs about the origin, operation, and purpose of government. In essence, constitutional preambles provide the basic beliefs of the constitutional framers.[1] The preamble to the United States Constitution is probably the best example of this:

> We the People of the United States, in Order to form a more perfect Union, establish Justice, insure domestic Tranquility, provide for the common defence, promote the general Welfare, and secure the Blessings of Liberty to ourselves and our Posterity, do ordain and establish this Constitution for the United States of America.[2]

In essence, the preamble addresses some of the most fundamental questions of political theory. In the case of the U.S. Constitution, the preamble provides the function of government (order, justice, peace, prosperity), the philosophical justification of government (preservation of liberty), and the source of governmental authority (the people of the United States).

A similar pattern is seen in state constitutions, although there are some striking differences. Since 1776, there have been 145 state constitutions used by the American states. The number is a product of a greater replacement rate among state constitutions and unique historical circumstances such as southern secession.[3] Almost all of the 145 state constitutions have a preamble. Only two current constitutions, New Hampshire and Virginia, do not. These two constitutions start with a Bill of Rights, which in many ways provides the same philosophical underpinnings of government but has the added impact of legal enforceability. Putting a Bill of Rights at the beginning of the document, rather than at the end, is a common pattern in state constitutions.[4]

State constitutional preambles frequently invoke God as the source of good government. The reference to God usually takes one of several forms—the Almighty, the Supreme Being, the Supreme Ruler, Divine Providence, or simply God. Perhaps more poetically, the South Carolina Constitution of 1868 professes its gratitude to the "Great Legislator of the Universe," while the Vermont Constitution of 1777 acknowledges the goodness of the "Great Governor of the Universe."[5]

Of the 145 constitutions used by the American states since 1776, eighty-nine constitutions, or sixty-one percent, contain references to God in their preambles. In most cases these preambles invoke God as the source of good government, appeal to God for help with good governance, or give thanks to God for the blessings of good government. The aforementioned Vermont Constitution of 1777, for example, gives thanks to the "Great Governor of the Universe" for the blessings of democratic government, noting that He alone "knows to what degree of earthly happiness mankind may attain by perfecting the arts of government."[6] The preamble to the Connecticut Constitution of 1818 acknowledges "with gratitude, the good providence of God, in having permitted [the people of Connecticut] to enjoy free government. . . ."[7] The North Carolina Constitution of 1868 states that the people of North Carolina are "grateful to Almighty God . . . for our civil, political, and religious liberties. . . ."[8]

While it is tempting to say that such references merely reflect the literary style of early American people or the unique colonial experience of the states formed during the Revolution, the pattern is not restricted to those constitutions drafted during the days of the early Republic. Of the fifty constitutions currently in use by the American states today, an astounding ninety percent mention God in their preamble. To this end, invocations of God in state constitutions are not just an artifact of the past.

For example, God is mentioned prominently in the preamble to the Wyoming Constitution, which gives thanks to "Almighty God for our civil, political, and religious liberties. . . ."[9] The current constitution of Wisconsin is "grateful to Almighty God for freedom. . . ."[10] Washington's Constitution gives thanks to the "Supreme Ruler of the Universe for our liberties. . . ."[11] While establishing their constitution, the people of Texas "humbly [invoke] the blessings of Almighty God. . . ."[12] Utah is "[g]rateful to Almighty God for life and liberty. . . ."[13] New York professes thanks to "Almighty God for our freedom. . . ."[14] Even California operates under a state constitution that invokes

God.[15] In total, forty-five of fifty current state constitutions mention God in the preamble. The distribution of the five states that do not mention God in their preambles—New Hampshire, Oregon, Vermont, Tennessee, and Virginia—indicate that there is no geographical or regional pattern for the references to God, or lack thereof, in state constitutions.

What state constitutions reveal is that unlike the national constitution, which is devoid of religious reference, previous and modern state constitutions explicitly invoke God in the preambles as the basis of good government, order, and liberty. This is part of a long constitutional tradition in the United States—a tradition that starts well over 150 years before the U.S. Constitution was drafted.[16]

■　　■　　■

The Founding Generation . . . believed that religion was an important force for the preservation of the fledgling United States. This generation's argument went something like this: democratic government is based on the people; the people need virtue and morality to maintain self-government; religion provides the necessary moral compass and virtue for self-government; therefore, religion and good government are inherently linked. John Adams supported this argument through his comment that constitutional government would only work for "a moral and religious people." In connection, Benjamin Rush said that while all religions promote virtue, Christianity was most suited to virtuous government. Even those men that remained suspicious of organized religion, like Benjamin Franklin and Thomas Jefferson, still considered the teachings of Christ as valuable to a virtuous democratic system. Apparently to them the tenets of "love thy neighbor" and "thy brother's keeper" complemented the democratic ideal.

Because religion was viewed as a complementary part of good government, the fifty-five men who met in Philadelphia in 1787 harbored no opposition to religion as a positive social force. Instead, their disagreements centered on the extent to which government should sanction or endorse religion. This is why state constitutions play such an important role in our constitutional system. Well aware of the long religious traditions and stark denominational differences of each state, the Founders realized there was very little consensus on the degree, form, or doctrine of worship at the national level. This awareness led to there being minimal discussion of religion at the Constitutional Convention since most delegates recognized that any effort to centralize religious authority was not only unlikely, but contrary to the purpose of designing a *limited* national government.

As a result, the U.S. Constitution only references religion in three places. The first mention of religion is in the No Religious Test Clause found in Article VI, clause 3 of the U.S. Constitution.[17] This provision prohibits the requirement that officeholders adhere to or participate in a certain religion. However, it does not prohibit a person from holding office *because* they are religious.

The latter formulation would have been foreign to the Founding Fathers. This provision simply protects people from religious discrimination without being anti-religious in intent.

The second reference is found in Article II, § 1, which specifies the wording of the oath of office for the President of the United States. This oath, which takes into consideration that presidents may be religious, is required before the President begins execution of the office.[18] By its wording, it allows a president-elect to *affirm* rather than *swear* his duty to uphold the Constitution. This often overlooked provision is a nod toward Pennsylvania Quakers who were influential in Pennsylvania politics. It is designed to accommodate men whose religion would prevent them from swearing allegiance to anything other than God. Atheists and proponents of a strict separation of church and state incorrectly read the word "affirm" as providing a way of avoiding swearing an oath. Thus, they believe that it allows for a non-reliance on religion in upholding the Constitution. The fact that the alternative to "affirm" was originally included in the oath to *accommodate* religious people has been lost.

The third and most famous reference to religion in the U.S. Constitution is the Free Exercise Clause of the First Amendment. This clause states that "Congress shall make no law respecting an establishment of religion, or prohibiting the free exercise thereof. . . ."[19] The prohibition is telling to the extent that the restrictions are clearly directed toward the actions of the *national* government, with no mention of the states. This is because religion, like many other constitutional issues, was left to the jurisdiction of the states.

The wording of the First Amendment to the U.S. Constitution when contrasted with similar religious liberty amendments at the state level helps make the case that religion has a special status in American state constitutions that is absent in the national constitution. While the national constitution uses agnostic language which implies no government interference or endorsement of religion, most state constitutions take a markedly different approach to protecting religious liberty. Many state constitutions openly use the word "God" or make direct reference to the "Almighty" in their religious liberty clauses. For example, the New Hampshire Constitution states "[e]very individual has a natural and unalienable right to worship God according to the dictates of his own conscience, and reason; and no subject shall be hurt, molested, or restrained, in his [personal] liberty, or estate, for worshipping God in the manner and season most agreeable to the dictates of his own conscience. . . ."[20] The Virginia Constitution reads:

> [t]hat religion or the duty which we owe to our Creator, and the manner of discharging it, can be directed only by reason and conviction, not by force or violence; and, therefore, all men are equally entitled to the free exercise of religion, according to the dictates of conscience; and that it is the mutual duty of all to practice Christian forbearance, love, and charity towards each other.[21]

The Nebraska Constitution reads, "[a]ll persons have a natural and indefensible right to worship Almighty God according to the dictates of their own consciences."[22] The Oregon Constitution similarly declares, "[a]ll men shall be secure in their Natural right, to worship Almighty God according to the dictates of their own conscience."[23]

All of the above provisions are still in effect today. It is interesting to think how different the legal debate over religious freedom in the United States would be if the First Amendment to the U.S. Constitution stated, "Congress shall make no law respecting an establishment of religion, or prohibiting the free worship of Almighty God." Such a statement would be an endorsement of religion. The specific reference to God in the provision would prevent the agnostic or atheistic interpretations that often accompany First Amendment legal cases today.

The frequent invocations of God in the preambles and in the religious liberty clauses of state constitutions indicate that religion, far from vanquished in American constitutionalism, is merely another aspect of our federal government intended for state jurisdiction. The fact that the references to God found in state constitutional preambles and religious liberty clauses are absent in the national constitution indicates that the state language is more than mere stylistic prose or eighteenth-century tradition. If it were perfunctory language—merely stylistic window dressing for state constitutions—there would have been little resistance to including similar language at the national level as well. The absence of such language at the national level, and near ubiquity at the state level, means the religious invocations found in state constitutions had significant meaning that the Framers of the national constitution wished to avoid. In short, religion was one of the issues that was largely meant to be punted back to the states in our federal system.

■　■　■

While the Free Exercise Clause can be incorporated and applied to the states, the Establishment Clause should be interpreted as jurisdictional with the intent to shield state religious practices from national interference. . . .

. . . It seems unlikely that the Court will adopt a "federal" perspective on the Establishment Clause anytime soon. Though there is a compelling case for such an interpretation, [researchers] contend that there are too many forces pushing against a change in the way the Court looks at the First Amendment. Many of the constituencies that are most interested in church-state issues—interest groups, local government, churches—benefit from the current interpretation of the First Amendment either through protection of their immediate interests or from the opportunity to foist controversial issues on the national government and hence avoid the ire of unhappy supporters. . . .

NOTES

1. Allan G. Tarr, *Understanding State Constitutions* 90 (2000).
2. U.S. Const. pmbl.
3. Christopher Hammons, "Was James Madison Wrong? Rethinking the American Preference for Short, Framework-Oriented Constitutions," 93 *Am. Pol. Sci. Rev.* 837 (1999).
4. Tarr, *supra* note 1, at 11.
5. S.C. Const. (1868); Vt. Const. (1777).
6. Vt. Const. pmbl. (1777).
7. Conn. Const. pmbl. (1818).
8. N.C. Const. pmbl. (1868).
9. Wyo. Const. pmbl. (1889).
10. Wis. Const. pmbl. (1848).
11. Wash. Const. pmbl. (1889).
12. Tex. Const. pmbl. (1876).
13. Utah Const. pmbl. (1895).
14. N.Y. Const. pmbl. (1777).
15. Cal. Const. pmbl. (1879).
16. Donald Lutz, *A Preface to American Political Theory* 113–40 (1992).
17. U.S. Const. art. VI, cl. 3.
18. U.S. Const. art. II, § 1.
19. U.S. Const. amend. 1.
20. N.H. Const. art. V.
21. Va. Const. art. I, § 16.
22. Neb. Const. art. I, § 4.
23. Or. Const. art. I, § 2.

3.2

WILLIAM H. RIKER

From *Federalism: Origin, Operation, Significance*

In this selection from his classic book on federalism, Riker offers a largely nega-
tive view of American federalism. While the benefits of federalism can be identi-
fied in theory, the costs have been steep in actual practice: through the 1960s the
protection of privileged, wealthy minorities by state governments resulted in the
oppression of poor, previously enslaved minorities.

IS THE FEDERAL BARGAIN WORTH KEEPING?

Up to this point this interpretation of federalism has been as simply descriptive as I have been able to keep it. The questions of whether or not federalism
is superior to its contemporary alternative, unitary government, or its previous alternative, imperialism; of whether or not federalism makes for good
government or the good life; of whether or not federalism is an effective
instrument of political integration—all these I have tried to keep out of the
discussion in order to concentrate on the descriptive questions: What occasions federalism and what maintains it?

But most of the interest in federalism, both academic and popular, is about
the further question: Is federalism worth keeping? [We] shall consider this
moral question, not attempting to answer it but rather attempting to indicate some of the considerations that may properly enter into the answer.

Please note that I put the question "Is federalism worth keeping?" not "Is
federalism worth starting?" If the argument has any validity at all, the latter
question is trivial. In the drive for territorial expansion at the breakup of
empire, one either needs to use the federal device to expand or one does not.
Normative considerations presumably do not enter into calculation, once the
decision to expand has been made. (Of course, that decision is itself normative;
but, once it is made, the decision on the procedure of expansion is purely technical. Since the normative question is usually settled by unconscious consensus, the salient question at the beginning of federalisms is typically the technical
one.) But even if the original question of adopting federalism is purely technical,
still, once federalism has been established and once a federalism has reached

From William H. Riker, *Federalism: Origin, Operation, Significance* (Boston: Little, Brown, 1964).

that degree of centralization previously described as category B, the question of whether or not it ought to be maintained is open. Presumably a society with a federal government in category B has attained sufficient unity that it is no longer necessary to use the federal device to keep the expanded society viable. So at that point a normative judgment can be made about whether or not to keep the institutions that originally permitted the expansion.

Of course, the question of whether or not federalism is worth keeping seldom arises as a matter of complete constitutional revision (e.g., in Austria and Germany after each of the world wars). More frequently, the question arises in a partial form; i.e., "What attitude ought one to adopt on this measure that will tend to reinforce (or break down) the guarantees of federalism?" In mature and stable federalisms such as the United States or Australia, where complete constitutional revision seems unlikely in the foreseeable future, there is nevertheless a frequent opportunity to decide constitutional questions on the basis of an attitude toward federalism and this is where the partial form of the question arises.[1] Whether the question arises in its partial form or in a proposal for full-scale constitutional revision is, however, irrelevant to the considerations involved in the answer. Hence, the evaluation of whether or not federalism is worth keeping need not be restrained by the infrequency of constitutional conventions. Rather it is a question that politicians in a mature federalism, especially politicians in a category B federalism, must think about almost every day.

The considerations that commonly enter into decisions on these questions are the arguments advanced in favor of maintaining (or abrogating) the guarantees to constituent units. In the following sections, we shall therefore examine these arguments and some of the evidence adduced in support of them.

I. Federalism and Freedom—The Theoretical Argument for Retention

Probably the commonest argument in public debate for support of the guarantees to constituent units is the assertion that federalism is a guarantee of freedom, followed by the prescription that, in order to preserve freedom, one must preserve federalism. Assuming, as most of us would, that freedom (whatever it is) is worth preserving, the prescription nevertheless depends on a purportedly descriptive assertion, which may or may not be true. In what way is federalism related to freedom?

The political traditions of most federally governed societies predispose most of their citizens to believe that their constitutional form (i.e., federalism) encourages a state of affairs (i.e., freedom) that is almost universally approved. And in the traditions of both Anglo-American and Latin-American federalisms this predisposition has been reinforced by the identification of the spirit of federalism with the notion of local self-government, which in turn is often identified with freedom.

But despite these predispositions of the tradition, there are also some *a priori* reasons to be skeptical about the truth of the assertion that federalism encourages freedom. There are, for example, a number of societies that keep a high degree of freedom without the use of federalism and, on the other hand, a number of federalisms simultaneously have been dictatorships. Local self-government and personal freedom both coexist with a highly centralized unitary government in Great Britain, and the Vargas dictatorship in Brazil managed to coexist with federalism.

In the United States, moreover, we have even more reasons to be skeptical about the truth of the assertion when we observe that the most persistent exponents of "states' rights"—a doctrine that makes much of the freedom-encouraging features of federalism—have been those who use the doctrine as a veiled defense first of slavery, then of civil tyranny. Here it seems that federalism may have more to do with destroying freedom than with encouraging it.

Clearly the relationship, if any, between federalism and freedom is not immediately clear and deserves further investigation.

The traditional argument, which derives from *The Federalist* papers and which has been reiterated continually by advocates of states' rights in all federal systems, is the assertion that concentrated power is dangerous, a position best expressed in Acton's aphorism that power tends to corrupt and absolute power corrupts absolutely. Federalism is said to be a device to prevent absolute power and therefore to prevent tyranny. I do not think we need to take this argument very seriously. It is based on a wise saw that has the same standing in the study of politics that weather wisdom has in the study of meteorology. The aphorism is not true—indeed, sometimes its opposite is.[2] And indeed, even if it were true, there is no assurance that separating power is the appropriate way to prevent tyranny. The separation may actually promote tyranny by its constant frustration of majorities which, in their frustration, come to behave tyrannically.[3] So let us leave aside the traditional argument, which is at best folk wisdom, and examine the relationship between federalism and freedom *de novo*.

Of course, though we know fairly well what "federalism" means, we have at best a confused notion of what "freedom" means. So before we can go further, the word "freedom" must be defined. And many volumes have been written on this subject without conspicuous success in reaching agreement. Owing to the tradition of controversy over the meaning of this word, we do know, however, that one of the variables involved in the notion is the specific reference to persons. That is, one elementary question about freedom is: "freedom for whom?"

The question arises in this way: given a society with a multiplicity of goals (and surely all societies with federal governments satisfy this assumption) and given the possibility that the achievement of goal A renders the achievement of another goal, B, unlikely or impossible. Then, when one speaks of freedom, one must specify whether one means freedom for the supporters of goal A or for those of goal B. If political life were conveniently arranged so that all feasible goals were compatible with one another, then this question could not arise. But usually we do not find such neat dovetailing of aspirations. And so in the presence of conflicting goals, a definition of freedom must always specify freedom for whom.

One convenient answer that some theories of freedom have offered is "the majority," which is unfortunately a highly artificial creation of rules of voting. Owing to this artificiality, therefore, other theories of freedom have suggested that freedom involves liberty for minorities to achieve their goals. The first kind of answer solves the problem in a somewhat arbitrary fashion, whereas the second kind begs the question completely.

But since this reading has no space to pursue the problem of the meaning of freedom, we shall merely assume the existence of two kinds, majoritarian and minoritarian, and then inquire whether or not it is theoretically true that federalism is a guarantee of either kind.

Considering, first, majoritarian freedom, it seems fairly obvious that federalism cannot at all be a guarantee of this kind of freedom; but rather can actually be an impediment. The effect of allowing ultimate decision at two different levels of government (which is the essence of the federal relationship) is that the losers at the national level may reverse the decision at the constituent level. Thus, the losers nationally may become the winners locally which of course negates the national decision in at least portions of the federal nation. Thereby, of course, the freedom of the national majority is infringed upon by local majorities.

A notorious example of such negation is the reversal of decision on civil rights for Negroes in the Southern and border states. The original national decision, taken by a narrow majority in the Civil War era, was soon reversed by local decisions in the South and along the border—where, of course, most Negroes lived. As a consequence, the Civil War decisions were thoroughly negated for most Negroes until sufficient numbers migrated northward and reawakened interest in again enforcing the old and, in recent years, frequently reaffirmed national decision.

To one who believes in the majoritarian notion of freedom, it is impossible to interpret federalism as other than a device for minority tyranny. At the present time in the United States (i.e., from roughly 1954 to that future time, if it ever comes, when most Negroes have full citizen rights) the chief question of public morals is whether or not the national decision will be enforced. To those who wish to enforce it, the plea for states' rights or for maintaining the guarantees of federalism is simply a hypocritical plea for the special privilege to disregard the national majority and, of course, to permit one minority, segregationist Southern whites, to tyrannize over another minority, the Southern Negroes. When freedom is defined as the right of self-direction for majorities, then the assertion that federalism promotes freedom is simply a hypocritical falsehood.

Considering, in the second place, minoritarian freedom, which is usually presented as the freedom of a minority to preserve its civil rights against a tyrannical majority, it is apparent, I shall argue, that for this kind of freedom federalism is, if not an impediment, still quite irrelevant.

Minoritarian freedom can be interpreted either as (1) the right of minorities to have a chance to become majorities and thus to make policy or (2) the right of minorities to make policy without becoming majorities. The first interpretation, i.e., the right to the chance to make policy, is in practice the maintenance of civil liberties so that prospective majorities will not be destroyed before they become such. The latter interpretation, though often set forth as the abstract ideal of freedom, is of course simply a rationale of confusion. Given, as previously, the existence of conflicting social goals, then the guarantee of the right of minorities to make policy merely assures the simultaneous existence of contradictory policies.

If minoritarian freedom is the right to have a chance to make policy, then federalism is undoubtedly an impediment to freedom in many circumstances and irrelevant to it in others. Federalism is a guarantee to constituent units of the *right* to make policy, not of the *chance* to make policy. Thus it grants far more than is necessary for freedom. The analysis works out as follows: suppose the constituent unit granted the right to make policy agrees for the most part with the kind of policy that would be made by the national officials. Then the right to make policy means relatively little and in general federalism is irrelevant to the maintenance of freedom. Suppose, however, that the constituent unit does not so agree; then the right to make policy allows it to impinge on the right of local minorities to become majorities. This is exactly what has happened in the American South where, under its freedom to make policy, the local majority (which is a minority nationally) has deprived the local minority of its civil rights (even though that local minority has close links with the national majority). In short, federalism that grants *more* local autonomy than is necessary for freedom and civil liberty encourages local tyranny, even when freedom is narrowly interpreted as the grant of the right to minorities to have a chance to become majorities.

If, on the other hand, minoritarian freedom is the right to make policy, i.e., to allow minorities to create confusion, then federalism is again irrelevant to freedom in some circumstances and a positive hindrance to freedom in others. One may distinguish the circumstances according to whether or not it costs the society more to obtain uniformity than uniformity is worth. Consider an instance in which the cost of uniformity is greater than the reward: women's clothing. At numerous times in many societies sumptuary laws and laws against nudity have been passed and frequently they have been enforced only briefly. Presumably in such instances of laxity the cost of enforcement against numerous minorities of one is greater than the reward of uniformity. When enforcement costs more than the reward, federalism is irrelevant to freedom. If freedom is the grant to minorities of one of the right to decide, e.g., on physical decoration, then the right of constituent units to make policy they probably will not care to enforce against minorities is a meaningless grant. In such an instance, federalism has nothing to do with freedom, although it may guarantee tyranny.

But when national uniformity is worth more than confusion, then federalism is an impediment to freedom because it deprives the national majority of the chance to eliminate the excess costs of confusion. Consider, for example, the matter of civil rights for Negroes in the United States. The grant to constituent units to make policy on this question has meant at least the following consequences: for the last century approximately 10 percent of the people have been denied civil rights. Those so denied have been a kind of *lumpenproletariat* and hence a drain on the whole society. In short, the grant of autonomy to local majorities to create confused policies has resulted in a cost to the whole society that is probably greater than the cost of uniformity. At least, so the present restiveness of the national majority toward Southern whites' practices of tyranny so indicates. In such an instance, we may infer that, when the costs of the consequences of federalism are greater than the costs of enforcing uniformity, local tyrannies are also national tyrannies because they prevent national majorities from reducing costs. For example, the national costs of putting up with the consequences of Southern bigotry are so great that the permission to enforce bigotry locally constitutes a cost on the whole nation, a cost which is presumably greater than the cost of enforcing desegregation. In this instance, therefore, federalism is an impediment to the freedom of everybody except segregationist whites in the South.

In summary, the abstract assertion that federalism is a guarantee of freedom is undoubtedly false. If this assertion is intended as a description of nature, then it is manifestly false, as shown by counterinstances of the coexistence of federalism and dictatorship. If it is, however, intended as a theoretical assertion about an abstract relationship undisturbed by other institutional arrangements, then it is still false. If freedom is interpreted in a majoritarian way, then the assertion is invariably false, for federalism is an impediment to freedom. If freedom is interpreted in a minoritarian way, then either federalism has nothing to do with freedom or federalism is again an impediment to freedom.

II. The High Cost of Uniformity—The Practical Argument for Retention

The most frequently presented practical argument for the maintenance of the federal guarantees to the constituent units is that the cost of national decision making is greater than the reward that might be obtained from it. This argument is usually presented as a defense of expediency (e.g., that it would cost more in prospective civil disturbance to integrate the schools of Mississippi than can presently be gained from this action). But sometimes it is also presented as a moral good (e.g., that a positive value is obtained from diversity of culture). (The latter was a favorite argument of Justice Holmes, who interpreted the states as laboratories for solving public problems.) In either form, however, this argument is essentially an economic one involving a kind of cost analysis of constitutional forms.[4]

National decision making is in the abstract more efficient than local decision making on every issue. That is, assuming uniformity is itself costless, it is cheaper on any subject of legislation to have a uniform rule, which is made by a majority, than not to have uniformity. There are at least two strong theoretical reasons for this circumstance. For one thing there is some saving in uniformity; and for another, there is less likelihood of a minority imposing high external costs on the majority. Considering the first and lesser reason, it is apparent that there is some saving in personal learning to have something like nationally uniform rules of the road. If a red light meant different things in different localities it is highly likely that the cost of enforcement of road rules would increase enormously. But the more important saving through uniformity is the minimization of the external costs imposed on individuals when minorities are allowed to legislate a minority policy. These costs are, of course, very high when two minority policies are in direct conflict. But even when they do not seem to be in direct conflict, external costs may still be inordinately high. Consider the sum of the costs to individuals when there are different minimum wages in different localities. There is then much likelihood of capital flow from the high-wage localities to the low-wage localities for all those industries in which labor represents a high proportion of the cost. Aside from the imposition of a nationally uniform minimum wage, the only way that high-wage localities may counter this capital flow is by reducing the minimum wage level. Thus the localities with the low minimum wage are permitted to set this wage nationally. For all the localities that would like to have the high wage, the imposition of the low wage is, of course, a high external cost. Since only the lowest-wage locality will be satisfied, all other localities will suffer these external costs. The obvious way to reduce this cost is to impose a national policy. It is this possibility that accounts for the greater efficiency of uniform rules. The only circumstances in which the uniform policy would not reduce external costs over local policies would be when the low-wage locality constituted a national majority. But in this case, the supposedly local policy is in fact imposed by a national majority and is thus a uniform policy. Hence in all cases a uniform policy is cheaper from the point of view of external costs than a nonuniform policy.

Or consider the savings from uniformity in the regulation of morality rather than the regulation of the economy. Given the possibility of variation in divorce codes among constituent units, divorce may be easier to obtain in one jurisdiction than in another. Then, so long as some provision like the full faith and credit clause of the United States Constitution exists—and all federalisms have something like it—it follows that the code that will in fact regulate is the one with easiest divorce. We have an excellent example of this in the United States, where the national scandal of excessively large numbers of divorces and the concomitant scandal of ill-considered marriages are both the consequences of a variation in divorce codes. The existence of a few jurisdictions that grant divorces on the most trivial grounds and after only the briefest periods of residence are sufficient to render nugatory the more restrictive grounds and longer residence requirements of most other states. Thus the different moral standards of a few states, the codes of which seem to have been motivated more by a concern for tourist business than by any convictions one way or another about family stability, have the effect of imposing easy divorce on all jurisdictions. The external costs of the existence of what most citizens of most states regard as low moral standards are thus very high for the probably overwhelming majority that opposes easy divorce. Uniformity of divorce laws could materially lighten these costs for the majority, although it might raise costs for Nevada lawyers.

It seems clear on the basis of both theory and example that uniform national decision making is invariably more efficient, i.e., less costly in undesired impositions on other people, than is local decision making. This is simply to say that decisions made by a majority hurt fewer people than do decisions made by minorities. Since constituent governments are invariably minorities in the nation, the maintenance of federal guarantees to constituent units assures that the whole society must bear some extra and unnecessary external costs.

So far, however, we have considered the cost of decision making only in a vacuum. Even if national decision making is clearly more efficient in decreasing external costs, it still may be more expensive than local decision making because of (1) costs of decision making and (2) costs of enforcement.

Costs of decision making are those incurred in the process of assembling a coalition of the size necessary to make a decision. As the requirements increase from minorities (e.g., majorities in a constituent unit) to majorities (i.e., a national majority), the cost of making side payments to reluctant members (i.e., logrolling) and of negotiating with all prospective members increases greatly. The cost of national decision making may well be greater than the rewards obtained from eliminating anarchy. Consider, for example, standards of beach clothing for females. Possibly a majority of people in the United States are offended by the appearance of bikinis and, were the decision costless, they would be glad to prohibit them. But, in fact, the decision is not costless. Some effort must be expended on defining what is offensive and what is not; more effort must be expended on finding the people who make up this majority; and finally additional effort must be expended on bringing them together in a group for action. In this imaginary example, the cost of decision is clearly very high, whereas the sum of the rewards to the majority is probably relatively low. Quite possibly the decision costs exceed the rewards.

Costs of enforcement are those incurred in the process of enforcing a majority decision against a recalcitrant minority. These costs vary with (1) the relative size of the minority, (2) the intensity of feeling of the minority, and (3) the ability of the minority to resist enforcement. It makes a difference for the existence of a national policy of prohibition, for example, whether or not most of the people are convinced teetotalers. In the United States during the prohibition era, the minority of regular users of alcohol was almost as large as the group of teetotalers, if indeed not larger. Hence enforcement was exceptionally costly. In India, on the other hand, where a much larger proportion of the population consists of teetotalers and where the indigenous pharmaco-poeia includes a variety of drugs with physiological and social effects similar to those of alcohol, the enforcement of prohibition is relatively less costly. Again it makes a difference for the existence of a national policy of assessing an income tax whether or not the prosperous and the rich believe deeply that they should not be taxed. Thus, in the United States, the prosperous and the rich accept the basic notion of the tax and hence usually obey the exact letter of the law. The existence of this attitude means that enforcement officers are freed to pursue the minority of dishonest taxpayers. Hence the income tax works pretty well as the basic tax of the nation. In India, on the other hand, the justice of the tax is not as widely acknowledged by the prosperous and rich. Hence enforcement agents must spend most of their efforts on what would elsewhere be regarded as ordinary collection. As a consequence, enforcement is costly and the income tax cannot be used as the basic tax system. Finally, it makes a difference for the existence of a national policy of civil rights for depressed classes whether or not those who oppress them can successfully defend the oppression both practically and philosophically. Again compare India and the United States, in both of which national decisions have repeat-edly condemned the oppression of in one case the Scheduled Castes and in the other case Negroes. In both cases there are good practical devices to avoid enforcement; e.g., the relative unanimity of the rural upper classes on the desirability of resistance. In both cases there are also good philosophical grounds to resist enforcement; e.g., the doctrine of states' rights in the United States and the doctrines of Hinduism in India. But the outlook for enforce-ment of the national policy is much better in the United States than in India simply because (1) the unanimity of the rural upper classes is nationwide in India whereas in the United States it is breaking down and indeed is limited to two or three very recalcitrant states and (2) the doctrine of states' rights is increasingly regarded as a sham for oppression whereas, owing to the new nationalism, the doctrines of Hinduism are held to even more tenaciously than before. Negroes are likely to obtain civil rights sooner than untouch-ables simply because the ability of their oppressors to resist enforcement is less.

In this analysis of the costs of national decision making in relation to deci-sion making by constituent units, we have thus identified three kinds of charges:

1. the profits of uniformity, symbolized by "U"; which are invariably posi-tive in sign because majority decision is always better than anarchy;
2. the costs of making decisions, symbolized by "D," which are invari-ably negative in sign because it is more costly to assemble a majority than a minority; and
3. the costs of enforcement of decisions, symbolized by "E," which are also invariably negative in sign because the existence of a majority implies the existence of a minority that must be coerced.

The practical argument in favor of maintaining the federal guarantees to the constituent units is that $U+D+E\leq0$. Of course, this argument cannot be uttered generally for it would mean the desirability of the dissolution of federalism. Rather, it must be uttered in particular instances and where it is asserted after a rough assessment of the values of U, D, and E. Since the argument cannot be asserted generally except as a proposal for civil war, one wonders about what kind of instances it seems reasonable in. In short, what kinds of circumstances minimize the sum of U, D, and E?

It is impossible, of course, to offer an exhaustive list; but one can specify some typical circumstances. As for minimizing U, which of course increases the likelihood that the inequation $U+D+E\leq0$ will hold, the most important circumstance probably is that the policy field will be fairly low on the preference schedules of most of the members of the prospective majority. If most people don't care much whether or not policy in a specific area (e.g., women's beachwear) is anarchic, then the positive value of U will be low. The issue of whether or not to maintain the federal guarantee to constituent units does not, however, arise when U is low, for to say U is low is to say it concerns something to which most people are close to indifferent. So the problem is: In what circumstances, when U is high, is $(D+E)$ higher?

What minimizes D is the existence of numerous territorial minorities, each of whose schedules of preference is quite different from [the] others. The fact that these minorities are territorially based gives them some strength to insist on obtaining their preferences, and the fact that their preference schedules are different renders the bargaining process expensive. India is a federalism in which, *a priori*, one might expect D to be very low in many areas of public policy.

What minimizes E is the intensity of feeling of a minority, a defensive sense that their separateness is both under attack and worth preserving. Coupled with this sense of separateness must also be a large territorial and population base so that the minority actually has some strength to resist enforcement. Canada is a federalism in which, *a priori*, one might expect E to be very low in many areas of public policy.

The practical argument for the maintenance of the federal guarantees to the constituent units, *viz.*, that $U+D+E\leq0$, is clearly dependent upon the calculations of politicians and citizens about the magnitudes of U, D, and E in particular sets of circumstances. In general, if there are numerous areas *of importance* in which it is agreed that the inequation $U+D+E\leq0$ holds, then the argument in favor of maintaining the guarantees is good. If not, then the argument fails. For me, the argument is reasonable and impressive with respect to such federalisms as Canada and India, but it is specious and unreasonable with respect to such federalisms as the United States, Germany, Austria, and Australia.

III. Abrogating the Guarantees

The main theoretical argument in favor of abrogating the federal guarantees to constituent units has already been developed in connection with arguments for maintaining them: decisions made by constituent units are invariably minority decisions that impose high external costs on the national majority. This assertion is wholly irrefutable on the level of theory, although it may be shown, as I have also indicated, that in particular instances it may cost more to remove the external costs than is saved with uniformity. But even though the assertion is theoretically irrefutable some effort has been expended in showing that it is not necessarily true in all circumstances. Cohen and Grodzins, for example, have attempted to show that state fiscal policies in the United States do not always conflict with national policies.[5] And they did indeed show that the state policies are less sharply in conflict with national policy than had previously been believed.[6] But to show that the anarchy of numerous minority decisions does not impose external costs as high as Hansen and Perloff believed is also to admit that external costs do exist. Indeed, the chief significance of Cohen and Grodzins' work is that they found a way to measure them. The existence of external costs is an invitation to eliminate them, which is the chief theoretical argument in favor of abrogating the guarantees.

Unfortunately, the theoretical arguments, though theoretically decisive, are practically uncertain because of the uncertainty surrounding the magnitudes of U, D, and E. Hence, to decide in particular instances whether or not to abrogate the guarantees, it is necessary to examine the cultural and institutional setting of the constitution. The appropriate questions are: Who benefits by the imposition of external costs on others? or, What minority is allowed by the federal device to impose its rules on the majority? According as one disapproves or approves of the values and purposes of these minorities, one favors or opposes the abrogation of the guarantees. One does not decide on the merits of federalism by an examination of federalism in the abstract, but rather on its actual meaning for particular societies.

What minorities benefit from the grant to make policy in:

The United States?
The main beneficiary throughout American history has been the Southern whites, who have been given the freedom to oppress Negroes, first as slaves and later as a depressed caste. Other minorities have from time to time also managed to obtain some of these benefits; e.g., special business interests have been allowed to regulate themselves, especially in the era from about 1890 to 1936, by means of the judicial doctrine of dual federalism, which eliminated both state and national regulation of such matters as wage rates and hours of labor. But the significance of federal benefits to economic interests pales beside the significance of benefits to the Southern segregationist whites. The judgment to be passed on federalism in the United States is therefore a judgment on the values of segregation and racial oppression.

Canada?

The main beneficiary in Canada from the beginning has been the French-speaking minority, whose dissidence was the original occasion for adopting federalism and is the justification for retaining it today. Secondarily, as in the United States, commercial interests have also benefited by escaping regulation. But since the French Canadians have no particular alliance with business, economic conservatives have benefited less in Canada than in the United States (where Southern segregationists have a tacit alliance with economic conservatives). That is, the French speakers have seen less reason to rig the competitive market to the advantage of owners (as against workers or consumers) because very few French Canadians have been owners.

Brazil?

The most significant minority benefiting from Brazilian federalism is the class of large landowners, especially in the relatively underdeveloped north and east. Although Brazilian federalism lacks the tone of racism associated with federalism in the United States, the social consequences are the same: the maintenance of a class of poor and inefficient farm laborers for the presumed benefit of agrarian landlords.

India?

Indian federalism is probably too youthful to identify the main beneficiaries of the privilege of minority decision making. But two kinds of minorities have tended to emphasize states' rights: non-Hindi-speaking groups (who, together, are of course a majority) and landlords in the least-developed agricultural areas.

Australia?

Since no single minority has been able to exploit the advantages of minority decision exclusively or for long periods of time, it is difficult to identify the main beneficiary. Nevertheless, it seems that commercial interests have been granted freedom from regulation more than any other group.

Germany?

Originally, federalism was intended to grant the right of minority decision to the non-Prussian southwest. But the significance of this minority has declined in the successive transformations of German federalism so that today it is difficult to specify who, if anyone, benefits most.

The foregoing survey of several federal systems suggests the wide variety of [the] kinds of minorities that may benefit especially from the privilege to legislate. The kind of minorities that appears most frequently on this list is business and agricultural owners. It is not difficult to understand why. In capitalistic nations conflicting economic interests are engaged constantly

TABLE [1] Main Beneficiaries of Federalism

	Capitalists	Landlords	Linguistic Minorities	Racists
United States	X	X		X
Canada	X		X	
Mexico		X		
Brazil	X	X		
Argentina	X	X		
Australia	X			
India		X	X	
Switzerland	X		X	
Germany	X			
Yugoslavia			X	
Soviet Union			X	

in an effort to rig the competitive system in their favor. Those groups which constitute national majorities, e.g., workers, farm laborers, consumers, etc., are those which might be expected to benefit most from majoritarian decision processes. To allow minoritarian processes is, therefore, to deprive the very large groups of their chance to influence outcomes. Of course, the minority most likely to benefit from the chance to manipulate the market is that of the owners, business or agricultural according to whether the nation is primarily industrial or agrarian.

But it is not always or only the owners who benefit, for, as the brief survey indicates, linguistic or racist minorities may also thrive on federalism. One possible classification of federalism, especially appropriate for passing judgment on the desirability of retaining federalism, is by the main beneficiaries of the chance of minorities to legislate for the whole. A moral judgment must be passed in each instance and for comparative purposes I submit a list (Table [1]) of the main characteristics of the main federalisms. It is notable that the federalism of the United States is unique in fostering racism.

IV. Is Federalism Worth Keeping?

One seldom has the opportunity to rewrite whole constitutions so the question of keeping or abandoning federalism can seldom arise. But a related question does frequently arise: What ought to be one's posture toward federalism? Should one always attempt to maintain or abrogate the guarantees to the constituent units?

In pure theory, the answer is that what one ought to seek to abrogate for federalism is a system of minority decision that imposes high external costs on everybody other than the minority. But practically the answer is not so clear, for the costs of decision and enforcement may outweigh the advantages of majoritarianism when the minority favored by federalism is passionate in its convictions.

Since the actual calculation of rewards and costs from abrogating federal guarantees is simply a rough "more or less" necessarily calculated by interested parties, one probably cannot even use a cost analysis in judging actual federalisms. Rather one must look to what they do and determine what minorities they favor. If one approves the goals and values of the privileged minority, one should approve the federalism. Thus, if in the United States one approves of Southern white racists, then one should approve of American federalism. If, on the other hand, one disapproves of the values of the privileged minority, one should disapprove of federalism. Thus, if in the United States one disapproves of racism, one should disapprove of federalism.

NOTES

1. For a concrete example of such an occasion, consider the creation (in 1935) of the unemployment insurance system as an adjunct to the social security system. President Roosevelt, apparently out of a concern for federalism, personally decided to assign the unemployment insurance and employment service to the states, at least so his advisor Tugwell tells us. (Rexford Tugwell, "The Experimental Roosevelt," *The Political Quarterly*, Vol. 21 (1950) pp. 239–62, at p. 241.) In turning down the advice of experts, Roosevelt personally preserved, at least in a small way, the constitutional guarantees of federalism. Whether or not he was wise to do so is, of course, another matter. Since the federal part of this system has been quietly and selectively administered, whereas the state part has been the center of much political turbulence and has often been charged with inefficiency, the experts were probably right from an administrative point of view. But constitutional considerations may be more important than administrative ones. What concerns us here, however, is not the correctness or incorrectness of Roosevelt's action, but simply the opportunity he had to decide a policy question on the basis of an interpretation of federalism.

2. See Arnold Rogow and Harold Lasswell, *Power, Corruption and Rectitude* (New York: Prentice-Hall, 1963).

3. See William H. Riker, *Democracy in the United States* (New York: Macmillan, 1953) Chapter 4.

4. An earlier attempt to apply a quasi-economic analysis to the costs of federalism is J. Roland Pennock, "Federal and Unitary Government—Disharmony and Frustration," *Behavioral Science*, Vol. 4 (1959) pp. 147–57. This article contains an *ad hoc* and tendentious model from which calculations are made of the "harmony (or lessened frustration) which it is the peculiar genius of federalism to achieve." By conveniently ignoring what are here called external costs, e.g., those imposed on the majority when the minority is permitted to make rules, the author finds that federalism lessens the frustrations of a minority, which, of course, no one has ever denied. The unanswered question is: At whose expense is the frustration relieved?

5. Jacob Cohen and Morton Grodzins, "How Much Economic Sharing in American Federalism," *American Political Science Review*, Vol. 57 (1963) pp. 5–23.

6. Alvin Hansen and Harvey Perloff, *State and Local Finance in the National Economy* (New York: Norton, 1944).

3.3

PAMELA J. CLOUSER McCANN, CHARLES R. SHIPAN,
AND CRAIG VOLDEN

From "Top-Down Federalism: State Policy Responses to National Government Discussions"

The American state governments can learn how to address social problems by paying attention to policy debates at the federal level. In this excerpt, McCann, Shipan, and Vogel analyze data on when and how extensively states adopted laws banning smoking inside workplaces, linking the timing to when the federal government debated and enacted new restrictions. Their research shows that states with more professional legislatures and more active health care interest groups adopted anti-smoking laws more in sync with federal actions.

The federal system in the United States creates opportunities for both the national government and state governments to enact policies to address societal problems. Because these separate but interconnected governments can observe each other's actions, policies that are stymied or not practical at one level might flourish at another. Furthermore, each level of government can react to the other's actions. Due to the high visibility of national-level policy discussions, for example, states can observe and learn from these activities. In other words, consideration of policies at the national level can diffuse downward to the states and influence state level policy adoptions.

This sort of vertical diffusion . . . can occur in multiple ways. In some cases, vertical policy diffusion may take a bottom-up form, such as where local policies spread to the state level, where state policies may serve as experiments for the national government, or where countries' experiences provide the basis for international policy choices. Conversely, top-down vertical policy diffusion results when the actions of a higher governmental level influence those of lower levels. Sources of such top-down influence range from intergovernmental grant conditions to mandates to preemptive lawmaking.

■　■　■

Scholars of federalism are often interested in the question of which policy areas are handled by which level of government. By focusing only on the decisions that come after national laws are passed, scholars are joining the discussion only *after* that key question has already been answered.

From Pamela J. Clouser McCann, Charles R. Shipan, and Craig Volden, "Top-Down Federalism: State Policy Responses to National Government Discussions," *The Journal of Federalism* 45, no. 4 (April 2015): 495–525.

[T]op-down federalism is a *conditional* process, in that responses to national policy discussions will vary by state. In some states, national activity will yield an increase in the attention paid to the issue, whereas in other states the same increased national activity will lead states to step back from passing their own policies. . . . Key aspects of the states' political environments will help determine how state governments respond to national policy attention. Specifically, highly professionalized state legislatures will rise to the challenge issued by national government involvement. Ambitious politicians in such states will seize upon policy solutions entertained at the national level and advance them in their home states. In contrast, politicians in less-professionalized state legislatures will interpret national activity as a sign that the national government may well address the issue at hand, so they can turn to other pressing business. Moreover, states with active policy entrepreneurs and interest groups will see an opportunity in the heightened awareness promoted by national government policy discussions to push their policy agendas, while policymakers in states without such groups will view the lack of such entrepreneurs in the face of the formation of a nationwide agenda as evidence against acting hastily on the issue at hand.

We explore these expectations by examining the policy choices that states made in response to congressional hearings and sponsored bills in the area of antismoking restrictions between 1975 and 2000. During this time period, the state and national roles in smoking policies were still being formed, and each level of government was exploring its policy options. How states responded to both local initiatives and national debates would set the stage for the state-by-state patchwork of policies in effect today.

■　　■　　■

[N]ational political discussions provide a stage for the entrance of political entrepreneurs and pressure groups on the various sides of a debate. Because state legislators have limited amounts of time and expertise, especially compared to Congress, they may rely on interest groups that monitor national policy activities as a short-cut to gaining information about the policy environment. This learning process provides states with knowledge about policies they can experiment with in their own jurisdictions, thereby potentially facilitating action and increasing both the speed and likelihood of adoptions.

A clear argument thus emerges for why state legislators might be more likely to adopt laws in a policy area when they observe congressional hearings and bill introductions in that area. Legislators can take this increased activity as a signal that the issue is salient, indicating they should devote some of their scarce time to it. They may also learn about the popularity of the issue, and if they see that it is indeed popular they will choose to address it at the state level. Additionally, they can gain important information about the policy, learning both about the policy options available to them and the potential outcomes associated with those policies, as well as about the political support for those options. Taken together, then, national policymaking activity can increase the likelihood of state legislative adoptions.[1]

■   ■   ■

As is well known, state legislatures differ markedly in their level of *professionalism*. Some state legislatures, such as in Michigan or California, meet regularly, attract highly qualified members who earn relatively high salaries, and have large staffs, including staff members who help standing committees develop expertise on topics within their jurisdiction. Other states, such as New Hampshire or South Dakota, have "citizen legislatures" that meet less often, pay their members a much lower salary, and tend to have fewer personal and committee staffers. Overall, state legislatures that are more professionalized tend to have greater *capacity* to tackle policy issues.

■   ■   ■

DATA AND EMPIRICAL ANALYSES

[W]e focus on one specific policy area: antismoking policies, and in particular what are known as clean indoor air laws. . . .

■   ■   ■

We obtained data from the MayaTech Corporation, which updated and corrected the National Cancer Institute's State Cancer Legislative Database. Between 1975 and 2000, forty states enacted laws restricting or banning smoking in government buildings and thirty-two states enacted similar laws for restaurants.[2] Our analysis focuses on whether the timing of these adoptions was influenced by national government policy activities. . . . [W]e want to assess whether policy activity that stops short of legislation, and thus does not directly create mandates or financial incentives for states to act, nevertheless affects state-level policy adoptions.

■   ■   ■

RESULTS

FIGURES [1] and [2]   Effect of Lagged Federal Activities on State Adoptions, Contingent on Legislative Professionalism, for [1] Government Buildings and [2] Restaurants.

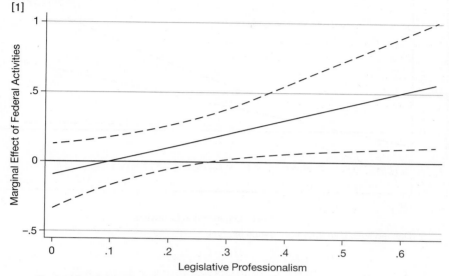

Dashed lines give 90% confidence interval.

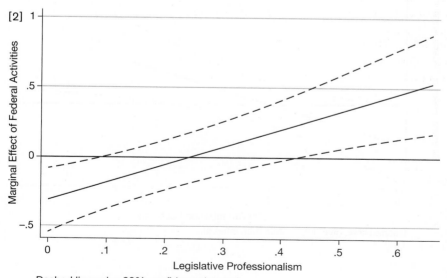

Dashed lines give 90% confidence interval.

FIGURES [3] AND [4] Effect of Lagged Federal Activities on State Adoptions, Contingent on Health Organization Lobbyists, for [3] Government Buildings and [4] Restaurants.

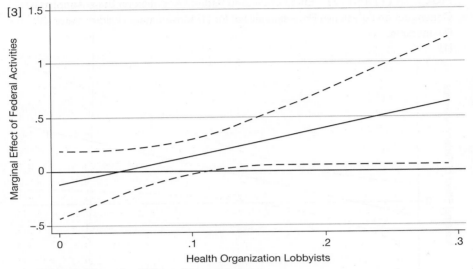

Dashed lines give 90% confidence interval.

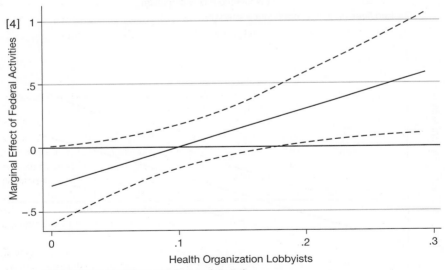

Dashed lines give 90% confidence interval.

DISCUSSION AND CONCLUSION

Our analysis . . . show[s] that policy *ideas* can diffuse in a top-down fashion, not just through grant conditions and mandates but also because national discussions may discussions may influence state policymakers' perceptions of the benefits of the policy, of the importance of the issue, and of their own need to act. Clearly it is important to understand the effects of mandates, grants, and other laws; but the analysis here shows a more nuanced way to capture national activity, one that potentially could be useful in a range of other studies.

[O]ur study provides additional insight into the ways in which Congress can influence other political actors, even when it does not pass laws (e.g., Ferejohn and Shipan 1990). In particular, we show that Congress can affect policy by engaging in various types of exploratory activities, such as hearings and bill introductions, as these ideas diffuse across levels of government in our federal system. In a system with a high degree of congressional gridlock, it is important to recognize that national policymakers can nevertheless stimulate the generation of policy solutions through the bills they sponsor and the hearings they hold.

Perhaps most importantly, we did not find that national activities affect all states equally. Indeed, we initially found no overall significant direct effect of federal activities. Instead, our results demonstrate that these activities mattered only under certain conditions, and that their effects were moderated by state-level characteristics. Thus, although top-down diffusion occurs, it does not occur unconditionally, but instead depends on the professionalism of a state's legislature and the degree of interest group activism. In other words, it is contingent on political and institutional factors within the state.

NOTES

1. We focus on policy adoptions in states because of their role in affecting the behavior of businesses and individuals. At the same time, we recognize that adoptions are the end result of a multistage process that takes place within each state. For national activities to affect state policy adoptions, they would first need to influence bill introductions in each state, the likelihood that introduced bills continue to move through the process, and so on. We abstract away from these complications, but here make two observations. First, in our tests we do account for some of the factors (e.g., legislative professionalism) that influence whether bills are likely to be introduced and whether, once introduced, they are likely to advance. Second, to the extent that there is any slippage between the factors that cause introductions and those that cause adoptions, it will be more difficult to find significant effects.

2. Other smoking restrictions, such as cigarette taxes or youth access restrictions, could form the basis of future studies replicating and extending the findings uncovered here.

REFERENCES

Ferejohn, John, and Charles R. Shipan. 1990. Congressional influence on bureaucracy. *Journal of Law, Economics, and Organization* 6: 1–20.

DISCUSSION QUESTIONS

1. What reasons does Hammons give for the federal courts to maintain the current interpretations of the Establishment Clause in the First Amendment?
2. Riker wrote this chapter of his book in the 1960s. What is the significance of the fact that he wrote this during social turmoil over civil rights for his conclusions about federalism? If he were writing on federalism in the United States today, would he come to the same conclusions?
3. What incentives do professional legislators at the state level have to pay attention to federal policy debates? How do those incentives differ from those of less professional state legislators?
4. Discuss several benefits and costs of having a federal system compared to a unified system of government, with a focus on religious liberties, civil rights, and smoking regulations (the topics in the three readings).

4

CIVIL RIGHTS AND CIVIL LIBERTIES

4.1

MICHAEL TESLER

From *Post-Racial or Most-Racial? Race and Politics in the Obama Era*

Using extensive survey data on political attitudes among African Americans, Latinos, Asian Americans, and whites, Tesler demonstrates that white Americans and members of several racial minority groups were deeply split in their attitudes toward Barack Obama and toward the two major political parties during the Obama presidency. The evidence shows striking gaps in support across racial groups and indicates that a substantial portion of the political polarization of American society stemmed from differences based on race.

BLACK-WHITE RACIAL DIVIDE IN OBAMA APPROVAL

. . . The black-white racial divide in 2012 presidential voting was about ten percentage points larger in 2012 than it was from 1988 to 2004. Merely looking at presidential voting understates the unique nature of the racial divide in public opinion about President Obama. Democratic presidential candidates received nearly 90 percent of the black vote in pre-Obama presidential elections from 1988 to 2004. That overwhelming black support created a ceiling

From Michael Tesler, *Post-Racial or Most-Racial? Race and Politics in the Obama Era* (Chicago: University of Chicago Press, 2016).

effect, which made it impossible for any Democratic presidential candidate to perform much better among this group. African Americans, however, have not been nearly as uniform in their approval of Democratic presidents' job performances. President Clinton, whose popularity among African Americans was considered at the time to be "exceptionally strong" (Tate 1994, 207), had an approval rating near 70 percent in three national surveys of black Americans commissioned during the first two years of his presidency. Consequently, the black-white racial divide in President Clinton's pooled approval ratings from the 1994–2000 ANES surveys (thirty percentage points) was considerably smaller than the forty-five-percentage-point divide in black and white Americans' support for Democratic presidential candidates between 1988 and 2004.

Barack Obama's approval ratings, however, were more divided by color than Bill Clinton's. Black Americans were about fifty percentage points more likely to approve of Barack Obama than whites in Gallup polls conducted throughout most of his presidency (see Figure [1]). The black-white racial divide in presidential approval was also more than fifty percentage points in the 2012 American National Election Study (ANES), with 92 percent of African Americans approving of Barack Obama's job performance in that survey compared to 40 percent of whites. Moreover, President Clinton's approval rating among blacks often increased and decreased in accordance with his white support. That is, when whites' opinions of Bill Clinton changed, so did those of blacks. President Obama's black approval rating, by contrast, was much more stable. Figure [1], which plots Obama's weekly Gallup approval rating by race, shows that President Obama's support from African Americans held pretty steady at around 90 percent approval throughout most of his first term in office. Meanwhile, white Americans fit the more usual pattern of presidential approval (Mueller 1973; Brody 1991; Green, Palmquist, and Schickler 2002; Sides and Vavreck 2013), whereby their support for Obama waned over time. With President Obama's white approval gradually declining during the course of his presidency, and his black support holding relatively constant, the racial divide in presidential approval increased from forty-two percentage points in 2009 to fifty points in 2010 and fifty-three points in 2014.

Kinder and Dale-Riddle (2012, 152) suggested that Barack Obama's unwavering support from African Americans was rooted in racial group consciousness: "Support for the president among African Americans," they wrote, "is perhaps, an affirmation of group solidarity; standing with the president an expression of racial pride." That contention seems hard to argue with, too. After all, group consciousness is one of the most important determinants of black public opinion and political behavior (Gurin, Hatchett, and Jackson 1989; Dawson 1994, 2001; Tate 1994; Kinder and Sanders 1996; Kinder and Winter 2001; Sears and Savalei 2006; Sniderman and Piazza 2002; Harris-Lacewell 2004; Kinder and Dale-Riddle 2012). Racial group identification was also a significant predictor of black support for presidential candidates like

FIGURE [1] President Obama's First-Term Weekly Approval Rating, by Race

SOURCE: Gallup's weekly tracking polls.

Jesse Jackson and Barack Obama (Dawson 1994; Tate 1994; Tesler and Sears 2010; Kinder and Dale-Riddle 2012). And, perhaps most important for our purposes, in-group consciousness shaped prior presidents' black approval ratings. As Michael Dawson (1994, 162) noted, "Historically, African Americans' perceptions of the relationship between racial group interests and the current administration have helped determine African American presidential approval."

We can also leverage the oversample of African Americans in the 2012 ANES survey to more directly determine whether Barack Obama's unusually strong black support was a byproduct of in-group solidarity. Racial group thermometers are one of many indicators of in-group favoritism (Sears and Savalei 2009), and Kinder and Dale-Riddle (2012, 188–89) used thermometer ratings of blacks to test the effects of "racial group solidarity" on African Americans' support for Jesse Jackson in 1988 and Barack Obama in 2008. . . .

. . . The results . . . suggest that Barack Obama's atypically strong support from African Americans was rooted in racial group consciousness. . . . The black thermometer was weakly related to African Americans' strong approval of Bill Clinton's job performance in pooled 1994–2000 ANES surveys. In the 2012 ANES, however, the black thermometer was a highly significant ($p < .001$) predictor of African Americans' strong support for Barack Obama. . . . Obama's greater popularity among African Americans (80 percent strongly approving compared to 66 percent strongly approving of Clinton) was most pronounced among racially conscious African Americans. Indeed, African Americans who rated their own group most favorably were about twenty percentage points more likely to strongly approve of President Obama than President Clinton. Consistent with that finding, there was a very similar pattern with black respondents' thermometer ratings of Bill Clinton and Barack Obama. That is, African Americans' warmer feelings toward President Obama than President Clinton were also most pronounced among blacks who rated their own group most favorably.

▪　▪　▪

All told, then, presidential assessments were increasingly divided by and over race during Barack Obama's presidency. The racial divide in Barack Obama's presidential approval ratings was about twenty to twenty-five percentage points greater than it had been for Bill Clinton. Moreover, this divide in support for President Obama was especially prominent between racially resentful whites, who, as shown . . . elsewhere (Tesler and Sears 2010), were more opposed to Obama than high-profile white Democrats and racially conscious blacks who had a stronger affinity for President Obama than they had for white Democrats like Bill Clinton.

▪　▪　▪

THE GROWING BLACK-WHITE RACIAL DIVIDE IN OBAMA-ERA MACROPARTISANSHIP

Barack Obama's presidency marked a potential turning point in the well-documented black-white racial divide in party identification. [T]he percentage of African Americans who identified with the Democratic Party gradually declined by roughly twenty percentage points from 1968 to 2004 (Hajnal and Lee 2011; Luks and Elms 2005). Luks and Elms (2005, 737) further argue that the increased willingness of young African Americans to identify as Republicans and Independents from 1973 to 1994 stemmed in part from the reluctance of recent Democratic administrations to intervene on behalf of racial progress the way that their presidential predecessors did during the civil rights era. This conclusion suggests that the ongoing generational replacement of older African Americans, who came of age when the party leadership was more active in support of racial equality, with younger blacks who came of age under a Democratic Party that generally heeded its electoral temptation of racial silence, would have further accelerated the black exodus from the Democratic Party in the years prior to Barack Obama's election.

Hajnal and Lee (2011, 141), however, wisely concluded their trend analysis of black partisanship by posing the question, "Does a black president mean the end of the decline in African American attachment to the Democratic Party?" There are reasons to believe that it might have. For starters, . . . health care results . . . indicate that Barack Obama's strong connection to the issue polarized public opinion by both racial attitudes *and* race. Moreover, . . . the changing effects of racial attitudes on white support for Hillary Clinton from

2008 to 2012 were very similar to the dynamic effects of race. We might, therefore, expect the spillover of racialization into partisan attachments to have also taken the form of a growing black-white racial divide in Obama-era party identification. Indeed, prior research showed that Jesse Jackson's 1984 primary campaign for the Democratic presidential nomination immediately polarized southern partisanship by both racial attitudes and race (Sears, Citrin, and Kosterman 1987).

We also saw that racial group consciousness undergirded African Americans' extraordinarily strong support for Barack Obama (see also Kinder and Dale-Riddle 2012). African Americans, especially those with high levels of in-group consciousness, may therefore have been increasingly drawn to the Democratic Party because a black president whom they overwhelmingly supported led it. That suspected movement of racially conscious African Americans to the Democratic Party in the Obama era would have inevitably caused a growing black-white racial divide in macropartisanship. The third major hypothesis, then, is that the large pre-Obama black-white racial divide in party identification grew even wider in the Age of Obama.

The huge pre-Obama racial divide in Democratic Party identification did, in fact, grow significantly wider during [and] after Barack Obama's rise to prominence. Figure [2] leverages the oversamples of African Americans in the 2008 and 2012 ANES surveys to show how the black-white divide in party identification changed in those two Obama-era surveys from its 1988–2004 baseline percentage. African Americans' identification with the Democratic Party was ten percentage points higher in 2012 than it was in the pooled pre-Obama ANES surveys. Meanwhile, white identification with the Democratic Party decreased by about four percentage points over that time period. As a result of those divergent trends, the black-white divide in macropartisanship expanded significantly in the Age of Obama.

Aside from the ANES results, a number of other commercial and academic surveys confirm that the black-white divide in party identification increased substantially during the Obama era. Figure [2] also uses Co-operative Congressional Election Study (CCES) data, which included at least two thousand black respondents in every one of its biennial election year surveys, to show that black identification with the Democratic Party increased by about nine percentage points from 2006 to 2012. At the same time, though, the percentage of white Democrats decreased by one to two percentage points from 2006 to 2012 in the CCES. Thus, the black-white divide in macropartisanship increased by double digits in CCES surveys. Survey data collected by Pew and Gallup throughout Barack Obama's presidency also suggested that the black-white divide in Democratic Party identification increased by as much as ten percentage points from before to after Barack Obama ran for president (Pew Research Center 2011, 2012; Newport 2013; Jones 2014; Hajnal and Lee 2011).

One likely reason African Americans became significantly more Democratic during this time period was that Barack Obama's rise to prominence

FIGURE [2]   Democratic Party Identification by Race

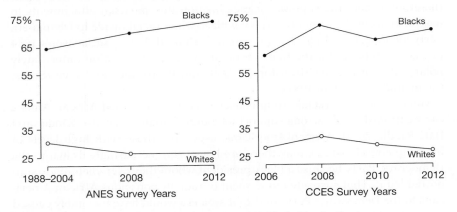

NOTE: Democratic-leaning Independents are not included in the figures.
SOURCES: American National Election Studies (ANES) cumulative file; 2012 ANES;
Cooperative Congressional Election Study (CCES) 2006; CCES 2008; and CCES 2012.

signaled his party might become more supportive of African American interests. Consistent with that expectation, African Americans saw a much larger
divide between Barack Obama and Mitt Romney in their support for "aid to
blacks" than they saw between prior Democratic and Republican presidential
candidates. That increase in perceived Democratic support for black interests could have been especially important for our purposes of explaining the
increase in black partisanship because racial identity measures like linked
fate—the notion that one's personal well-being is directly affected by the
well-being of the larger black community—were only "relatively small" pre-
dictors of Democratic partisanship in the National Black Election Studies
conducted during the 1980s and 1990s (Hajnal and Lee 2011, 134). In other
words, having an African American president from the Democratic Party in the
White House, who was perceived as more supportive of black interests than
his predecessors, could have made group consciousness a more important
determinant of African Americans' party identifications than it had been in
the pre-Obama era.

■   ■   ■

African Americans grew increasingly Democratic during the Obama era
in large part because of racial group solidarity. That is, African Americans
who rated blacks most favorably were most likely to migrate to Barack Obama's
Democratic Party. Those results . . . also suggest that attitudes about African
Americans drove the growing black-white divide in Obama-era party identification: white Americans who harbored out-group resentment toward blacks
became increasingly Republican, whereas African Americans who rated their

own racial group most favorably became more Democratic. The upshot was a growing polarization of mass partisanship by and over race.

THE GROWING WHITE-LATINO DIVIDE IN OBAMA-ERA PARTY IDENTIFICATION

This growing Obama-era divide in party identification by and over race was not too surprising. After all, the racial divide in approval of Barack Obama's presidency was exceptionally large, with that chasm greatest between racially conscious blacks and racially resentful whites. It makes perfect sense, according to the spillover of racialization hypothesis, for those same patterns to have reproduced themselves in the Obama-era partisan attachments of black and white Americans.

The growing partisan divide between whites and Latinos in the Age of Obama was more unexpected, though. As can be seen in Figure [3], the percentage of respondents who identified as Democrats in the Pew Hispanic Center's National Surveys of Latinos increased from 31 percent in both 2003 and 2007 all the way to 48 percent in 2012. In other words, Latinos were even more likely than African Americans to move to the Democratic Party in the Age of Obama. Given the trends in white partisanship shown in Figure [2], which revealed a slight decline in white Americans' Democratic Party identifications, the divide between whites and Latinos in macropartisanship increased by as much as twenty percentage points during Barack Obama's presidency.

Unlike African Americans' greater Democratic identification in the Obama era, it is difficult to make the case that Barack Obama, and the spillover of

FIGURE [3]   Percentage of Latinos Identifying as Democrats, 2003–12

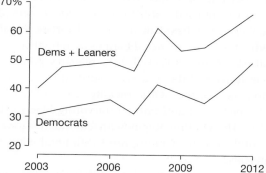

SOURCES: Pew Hispanic Center National Surveys; percentages accessed from Roper Center's iPOLL databank.

racialization from mass assessments of his presidency into related political opinions, was directly responsible for this growing white-Latino partisan divide. To be sure, Barack Obama was very popular with Latinos throughout most of his presidency. Yet, that popularity was not nearly as strong or stable as his black support. President Obama's Hispanic approval ratings in weekly Gallup polls eroded over the first three years of his presidency and dipped slightly below 50 percent in several 2011 surveys. Moreover, the exit polls suggest that Bill Clinton won an even larger share of the two-party Latino vote in his presidential elections than Barack Obama did in his victories. And Bill Clinton's longstanding support from Latinos was cited as a major reason why Hillary Clinton decisively won the Hispanic vote against Barack Obama in the 2008 presidential primaries (Barreto et al. 2008; Tesler and Sears 2010).

Rather than their affinity for President Obama, Latinos' growing identification with the Democratic Party was more likely rooted in the Republican Party's increasingly hostile rhetoric and policy positions toward minorities during Obama's presidency. Or as Stanford political scientist Gary Segura said in a 2012 PBS interview, "The president has widely disappointed Latino voters through the failure to pursue immigration reform through unprecedented deportations. But he can credibly claim to be better than the alternative when the alternative is saying horrible things." These "horrible things," perhaps most notably, included Republicans' and Tea Partiers' frequent portrayals of Latino immigrants and immigration as a threat to Americans and American culture (Parker and Barreto 2013, 166; Skocpol and Williamson 2012, 76).

Such sentiments were also prevalent in Republican-sponsored state and national policies. Arizona's SB 1070, which the Obama administration challenged in court because it allowed for the racial profiling of Latinos based on the suspicion that they could be undocumented immigrants, was passed into law in 2010 almost entirely with Republican votes. Barack Obama and the Republican Party also clashed over the DREAM Act—a policy supported by the president in 2011 and prevented from passing by House Republicans in 2012—which was to grant legal status to young undocumented immigrants if they attended college or enlisted in the armed forces. Finally, Republican presidential candidates surely alienated Latinos even further with their rhetoric and policy positions in the 2011 and 2012 primary debates. Collingwood, Barreto, and Garcia-Rios (2014, 4) aptly described these presidential candidates' strategy to appeal to the GOP's "racially resentful base" in 2012: "In an effort to attract a perceived anti-immigrant voting bloc in the conservative primary elections, the leading Republican candidates took very hardline stances against undocumented immigrants, bilingual education, and bilingual voting materials."

Those hardline policy positions and the anti-Latino rhetoric that accompanied them were likely to alter Hispanics' partisan attachments. In fact, prior research shows that Republicans' strong support for California's Proposition

187—a 1994 ballot initiative that rendered undocumented immigrants ineligible for such public services as health care and education—helped shift the partisan attachments of Latinos in the Golden State toward the Democrats (Bowler, Nicholson, and Segura 2006; Barreto and Ramirez 2013).

Polling data suggest that Latinos were paying attention to these partisan developments. Hispanics increasingly thought that the Democratic Party cared more about Latinos than Republicans did during Barack Obama's presidency. Figure [4], for example, shows that 55 percent of the Latino respondents surveyed by the Pew Hispanic Center in 2012 thought that the Democratic Party had more concern for Latinos than the Republican Party—an increase of more than twenty percentage points since 2007. Likewise, only 33 percent of respondents in a 2012 national survey of Latinos commissioned by CNN said that the Republican Party "is generally doing a good job these days of reaching out to blacks, Hispanics, and other minorities." That figure was down eighteen percentage points from the 51 percent of Latinos who thought Republicans were doing a good job of reaching out to minorities in a 2000 CNN Poll. Meanwhile, the percentage of Latinos who thought the Democratic Party was doing a good job with minorities slightly increased from 75 percent in 2000 to 77 percent in 2012. National surveys conducted in 2012 by the polling firm Latino Decisions also showed that Latinos were at least forty percentage points more likely to say that the Democratic Party was doing "a good job" in its outreach to Hispanic voters than they were to say the Republican Party was doing a good job of reaching out to their ethnic group.

FIGURE [4]　Percentage of Latinos Who Say the Democratic Party Has More Concern for Hispanics Than the Republican Party, 2004–12

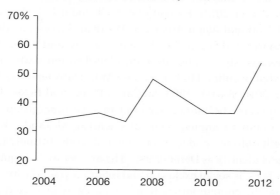

SOURCES: Pew Hispanic Center National Surveys; percentages accessed from Roper Center's iPOLL databank.

With the Democratic Party increasingly viewed as the party more support-ive of Latino interests in the Age of Obama, we might expect the relationship between Hispanic in-group consciousness and Democratic Party identifica-tion to have increased over time. After all, . . . the effect of black-thermometer ratings on African Americans' partisan attachments increased significantly after Barack Obama's ascendancy signaled that his party may be more support-ive of "aid to blacks." Moreover, and also like African Americans, in-group consciousness has long been an important predictor of Latinos' political atti-tudes and behavior (DeSipio 1996; Sanchez 2006; Barreto 2010; Hajnal and Lee 2011; Masuoka and Junn 2013). The fifth hypothesis, then, is that Latinos' in-group identifications may have been activated by the perceived growing distance between the parties in their concern for Hispanics.

▪ ▪ ▪

ASIAN AMERICANS AND REPUBLICANS AS THE PARTY OF WHITE PEOPLE

Asian Americans' support for the Democratic Party . . . has increased dramati-cally in the past two decades. In 1992, when the exit polls first reported Asian Americans' vote choices, this group decisively preferred George H. W. Bush to Bill Clinton (55 percent to 31 percent, respectively). Asian American support for Democratic presidential candidates, however, has increased in every subsequent election. So much so, that Barack Obama won 74 percent of the two-party Asian American vote in 2012. That growing Democratic support extended to party identification, as well. National surveys of Asian Americans conducted by the Pew Research Center in 2012 and 2013 found that 50 percent and 64 percent of Asians identified as Democrats or leaned Democratic in those respective polls (Pew Research Center 2013). By contrast, well under half the respondents in the 2000–2001 National Asian American Political Survey identified or leaned Democratic (Bowler and Segura 2012; Lien, Conway, and Wong 2004).

Asian Americans' strong and growing identification with the Democratic Party is somewhat peculiar. Higher-income Americans tend to support Repub-licans (Gelman 2010; Bartels 2008; McCarty, Poole, and Rosenthal 2006), and Asian Americans are the highest-earning racial/ethnic group in the United States. This paradox prompted political scientists Alexander Kuo, Neil Mal-hotra, and Cecilia Mo to conduct an important study, fittingly titled "Why Do Asian Americans Identify as Democrats?" The answer to their question, accord-ing to these authors, is social exclusion and intergroup solidarity. That is, "Asian Americans view the contemporary Republican Party as excluding them from society and perceiving them as foreign. . . . The second explanation [intergroup solidarity], which is not mutually exclusive, is that Asian Americans believe they have common interests with other ethnic minority groups that have been longstanding constituencies within the Democratic Party, and thus align themselves with these groups rather than whites" (Kuo, Malhotra, and Mo 2014, 3–4). Kuo, Malhotra, and Mo (2014) support those hypotheses with some ingenious experiments. Most notably, they found that priming social exclusion with the use of insensitive white lab administrators who questioned their participants' citizenship before entering the laboratory shifted Asian Americans' partisan preferences thirteen percentage points more Democratic.

Like our analyses of Latino partisanship above, those social exclusion findings suggest that Asian Americans largely viewed the contemporary Republican Party as the party of whites. We might, therefore, expect attitudes about white Americans to have also been important determinants of Asian Americans' partisan attachments. Unfortunately, the data for testing that hypothesis is not nearly as good as the data used to assess the changing impact on racial group thermometer ratings on the partisan attachments of whites, African Americans, and Latinos. The ANES, for example, includes only a tiny number of Asian Americans in their election-year surveys. Nevertheless, we can still glean some insights into how Asian Americans' thermometer ratings of various racial and ethnic groups impacted their partisan attachments in the 2011–12 CCAP survey because this massive survey of forty-four thousand respondents included more than eight hundred Asian Americans. At the same time, though, the CCAP's nationally representative Internet survey may not be representative of minority populations. Indeed, minority panelists who volunteer to take Internet surveys administered in English, such as the CCAP, are unlikely to reflect the full variation in these groups' political opinions. So, some caution is required in interpreting the results.

■ ■ ■

The large effects of antiwhite attitudes on Asian Americans' support for the Democratic Party seem to fit into that "party of whites" paradigm as well. Moreover, those strong effects of antiwhite affect are consistent with the contention by Kuo, Malhotra, and Mo (2014) that social exclusion of Asian Americans by whites drives support for the Democratic Party. . . . Intergroup solidarity also leads Asian Americans to identify with the Democratic Party. For, as can be seen, warmer thermometer ratings of blacks were also strongly linked to Asian Americans' identification with the Democratic Party. Finally, Asian Americans' thermometer ratings of their own group were not significantly related to their partisan attachments—a result similar to Hajnal and Lee's (2011) contention that racial identity has a weaker effect on Asian American partisanship than it does for Latinos.

There, unfortunately, has been very little work on the partisan attachments of Native Americans. So, we cannot similarly place the large effects of the white thermometer on their party identifications into a broader context. However, given the results for Asian Americans and Latinos, these findings suggest that Native Americans may have also viewed the modern Republican Party as the party of whites.

CONCLUDING REMARKS

The results . . . , in combination with the earlier findings . . . , suggest that the growing black-white divide in Obama-era political opinions was in large part about President Obama and attitudes toward African Americans. The exceptionally large black-white divide in Barack Obama's presidential approval ratings was most pronounced among racially resentful whites and racially conscious blacks. So, too, was the expanding racial divide in macropartisanship, as attitudes about African Americans became an increasingly important determinant of both black and white Americans' partisan identifications in the Age of Obama.

The growing number of Latinos and Asian Americans who identified as Democrats in the Obama era, however, seems to have been more about social exclusion and attitudes toward whites than it was about President Obama and feelings toward blacks. To be sure, Barack Obama's Democratic presidency and the hostile reaction to it from his partisan opponents likely contributed to minority groups' enhanced image of Republicans as the party of white people. A clear majority of Latinos, for example, thought that race was a factor in opposition to his presidency in a 2009 Pew poll (63 percent); and most of the Latinos (61 percent) in a 2010 ABC survey thought that the Tea Party Movement was based to some degree on racial prejudice toward the president. Barack Obama's ascendancy also helped give rise to the more ethnocentric elements of the Republican Party, such as the Tea Party (Parker and Barreto 2013), who were most opposed to immigration. Yet, unlike the growing black-white racial divide in Obama-era party identification, the partisan preferences of Latinos and Asian Americans would have most likely moved further away from white Americans even if Barack Obama had not been elected president in 2008. For, as mentioned earlier, Latinos preferred Hillary Clinton by a large margin to Barack Obama in the 2008 presidential primaries.

Minority voters' overwhelming support for Democrats could, therefore, continue into the foreseeable future. In fact, political commentators argued long before Barack Obama's presidential candidacy that the growing nonwhite electorate will inevitably lead to a longstanding Democratic majority in national politics (see for example, Judis and Teixeira 2004). Some astute academic commentators, however, have pushed back on this common "demographics as destiny" argument (Vavreck 2014; Bartels 2014; Piston 2014). Asian American and Latino voters, they point out, may not be as solidly Democratic as is often assumed. In keeping with that contention, Hajnal and Lee (2011) showed that these groups' party attachments are less crystallized than black and white partisanship. . . .

Conversely, Republicans could also stave off electoral defeat in the years ahead by turning out more whites and/or winning a larger share of their votes. Republican elites, in fact, regularly debated during Barack Obama's second term in office whether the party's best bet to retake the White House was to reach out to minorities or to pursue this white voter strategy (Edsall 2013; Trende 2013; Brownstein 2013). Republican strategist Sean Trende (2013) summarized the latter approach's potential: "It's entirely possible that as our nation becomes more diverse, our political coalitions will increasingly fracture along racial/ethnic lines rather than ideological ones. . . . I don't see any compelling reason why these trends can't continue, and why a Republican couldn't begin to approach Ronald Reagan's 30-point win with whites from 1984 in a more neutral environment than Reagan enjoyed."

There's some social scientific evidence to support that argument, too. Just drawing attention to the country's changing demographics in a survey experiment significantly increased the percentage of white Independents who expressed prejudiced attitudes, took conservative policy positions, and identified as Republicans (Craig and Richeson 2014a, 2014b). Ryan Enos's (2014, 2015) innovative work on racial threat similarly shows that increased contact with racial and ethnic minorities in Chicago and Boston, respectively, led whites to express more ethnocentric attitudes, turn out to vote in higher numbers, and support Republican candidates at greater rates. As a result of such studies, Larry Bartels (2014) concluded: "The changing American polity may come to look more like [Republican] Texas than like the multicultural Democratic stronghold of California. In an increasingly diverse America, identity politics will continue to cut both ways."

Finally, . . . Republicans could be quite constrained in their minority outreach after Barack Obama leaves office. . . . Rank-and-file Republicans were more racially conservative during his presidency than they had been in modern times. Consequently, it may be increasingly difficult for a Republican candidate to reach out to minorities and still win his or her party's presidential nomination. Mitt Romney, after all, had to take a very hard-line on immigration during the presidential primaries to curry favor with his party's base (Collingwood, Barreto, and Garcia-Rios 2014). . . . Internal divisions between congressional Republicans in the Obama era came down in large part to how racially resentful their constituents were. A majority of Republicans in the House of Representatives could, therefore, fear that reaching out to minorities will cost them their jobs. . . . The Republicans' most viable option going forward might be to try to mobilize and win more white votes. If so, then mass politics might grow even more divided by color in the post-Obama era.

REFERENCES

Barreto, Matt A. 2010. *Ethnic Cues: The Role of Shared Ethnicity in Latino Political Participation*. Ann Arbor: University of Michigan Press.

Barreto, Matt A., Luis R. Fraga, Sylvia Manzano, Valerie Martinez-Ebers, and Gary M. Segura. 2008. "'Should They Dance with the One Who Brung 'Em?' Latinos and the 2008 Presidential Election." *PS: Political Science and Politics* 61 (4): 753–61.

Barreto, Matt A., and Ricardo Ramirez. 2013. "Anti-Immigrant Politics and Lessons for the GOP from California." *Latino Decisions Blog*. www.latinodecisions.com /blog/2013/09/20/anti-immigrant-politics-and-lessons-for-the-gop-from -california.

Bartels, Larry. M. 2008. *Unequal Democracy: The Political Economy of the New Gilded Age*. New York: Russell Sage Foundation.

———. 2014. "Can the Republican Party Thrive on White Identity?" *Monkey Cage*. www .washingtonpost.com/blogs/monkey-cage/wp/2014/04/16/can-the-republican -party-thrive-on-white-identity.

Bowler, Shaun, Stephen P. Nicholson, and Gary M. Segura. 2006. "Earthquakes and Aftershocks: Race, Direct Democracy, and Partisan Change." *American Journal of Political Science* 50 (1): 146–59.

Bowler, Shaun, and Gary Segura. 2012. *The Future Is Ours: Minority Politics, Political Behavior, and the Multiracial Era of American Politics*. Washington, DC: CQ Press.

Brody, Richard A. 1991. *Assessing the President: The Media, Elite Opinion, and Public Support*. Stanford: Stanford University Press.

Brownstein, Ronald. 2013. "Bad Bet: Why the Republicans Can't Win with Whites Alone." *National Journal*, September 5. www.nationaljournal.com/magazine/bad -bet-why-republicans-can-t-win-with-whites-alone-20130905.

Collingwood, Loren, Matt A. Barreto, and Sergio I. Garcia-Rios. 2014. "Revisiting Latino Voting: Cross-Racial Mobilization in the 2012 Election." *Political Research Quarterly* 67 (3): 632–45. doi:10.117/1065912914532374.

Craig, Maureen A., and Jennifer A. Richeson. 2014a. "More Diverse Yet Less Toler-ant? How the Increasingly Diverse Racial Landscape Affects White Americans' Racial Attitudes." *Personality and Social Psychology Bulletin* 40: 750–61. doi:10.17177/0146167214524993.

Craig, Maureen A., and Jennifer A. Richeson. 2014b. "On the Precipice of a 'Majority-Minority' America Perceived Status Threat from the Racial Demographic Shift Affects White Americans' Political Ideology." *Psychological Science* 25 (6): 1189–97.

Dawson, Michael. 1994. *Behind the Mule: Race and Class in African American Politics*. Princeton, NJ: Princeton University Press.

———. 2001. Black Visions: *The Roots of Contemporary African American Political Ide-ologies*. Chicago: University of Chicago Press.

DeSipio, Louis. 1996. *Counting on the Latino Vote: Latinos as a New Electorate*. Charlot-tesville: University of Virginia Press.

Edsall, Thomas B. 2013. "Should the Republican Party Just Focus on White Voters?" *New York Times*, op-ed, July 3.

Enos, Ryan D. 2014. "Causal Effect of Intergroup Contact on Exclusionary Attitudes." *Proceedings of the National Academy of Sciences* III (10): 3699–704.

———. 2015. "What Tearing Down Public Housing Projects Teaches Us about the Effect of Racial Threat on Political Participation." *American Journal of Political Science* 59. doi:10.1111/ajps.12156.

Gelman, Andrew. 2010. *Red State, Blue State, Rich State, Poor State: Why Americans Vote the Way They Do*. Princeton, NJ: Princeton University Press.

Green, Donald, Bradley Palmquist, and Eric Schickler. 2002. *Partisan Hearts and Minds*. New Haven, CT: Yale University Press.

Gurin, Patricia, Shirley Hatchett, and James Jackson. 1989. *Hope and Independence: Blacks' Response to Electoral and Party Politics*. New York: Russell Sage Foundation.

Hajnal, Zoltan L., and Taeku Lee. 2011. *Why Americans Don't Join the Party: Race, Immigration, and the Failure (of Political Parties) to Engage the Electorate.* Princeton, NJ: Princeton University Press.

Harris-Lacewell, Melissa. 2004. *Barbershops, Bibles, and BET: Everyday Talk and Black Political Thought.* Princeton, NJ: Princeton University Press.

Jones, Jeffrey M. 2014. "U.S. Whites More Solidly Republican in Recent Years: Party Preferences More Polarized by Race and Ethnicity under Obama." www.gallup.com/poll/168059/whites-solidly-republican-recent-years.aspx.

Judis, John B., and Ruy Teixeira. 2004. *The Emerging Democratic Majority.* New York: Simon and Schuster.

Kinder, Donald R., and Allison Dale-Riddle. 2012. *The End of Race?* New Haven, CT: Yale University Press.

Kinder, Donald R., and Lynn M. Sanders. 1996. *Divided by Color: Racial Politics and Democratic Ideals.* Chicago: University of Chicago Press.

Kinder, Donald, and Nicholas Winter. 2001. "Exploring the Racial Divide: Blacks, Whites, and Opinion on National Policy." *American Journal of Political Science* 45: 439–56.

Kuo, Alexander, Neil A. Malhotra, and Cecilia Hyunjung Mo. 2014. "Why Do Asian Americans Identify as Democrats? Testing Theories of Social Exclusion and Intergroup Solidarity." Unpublished manuscript, Vanderbilt University.

Lien, Pei-Te, M. Margaret Conway, and Janelle Wong. 2004. *The Politics of Asian Americans.* New York: Routledge.

Luks, Samantha, and Laurel Elms. 2005. "African American Partisanship and the Legacy of the Civil Rights Movement: Generational, Regional, and Economic Influences on Democratic Identification, 1973–1994." *Political Psychology* 26: 735–54.

Masuoka, Natalie, and Jane Junn. 2013. *The Politics of Belonging: Race, Public Opinion, and Immigration.* Chicago: University of Chicago Press.

McCarty, Nolan, Keith T. Poole, and Howard Rosenthal. 2006. *Polarized America: The Dance of Ideology and Unequal Riches.* Cambridge, MA: MIT Press.

Mueller, John E. 1973. *War, Presidents and Public Opinion.* New York: Wiley.

Newport, Frank. 2013. "Democrats Racially Diverse; Republicans Mostly White: Democrats and Independents Grow More Diverse since 2008." www.gallup.com/poll/160373/democrats-racially-diverse-republicans-mostly-white.aspx.

Parker, Christopher S., and Matt A. Barreto. 2013. *Change They Can't Believe In: The Tea Party and Reactionary Politics in America.* Princeton, NJ: Princeton University Press.

Pew Research Center. 2011. "GOP Makes Big Gains among White Voters." July 22. www.people-press.org/2011/07/22/gop-makes-big-gains-among-white-voters.

———. 2012. "Partisan Polarization Surges in Bush and Obama Years." June 4. www.people-press.org/files/legacy-pdf/06-04-12%20Values%20Release.pdf.

———. 2013. "The Rise of Asian Americans." April 4. www.pewsocialtrends.org/files/2013/04/Asian-Americans-new-full-report-04-2013.pdf.

Piston, Spencer. 2014. "Lighter-Skinned Minorities Are More Likely to Support Republicans." *Monkey Cage.* www.washingtonpost.com/blogs/monkey-cage/wp/2014/09/17/lighter-skinned-minorities-are-more-likely-to-support-republicans.

Sanchez, Gabriel R. 2006. "The Role of Group Consciousness in Latino Public Opinion." *Political Research Quarterly* 59 (3): 435–46.

Sears, David O., Jack Citrin, and Richard Kosterman. 1987. "Jesse Jackson and the Southern White Electorate in 1984." In *Blacks in Southern Politics*, edited by Robert P. Steed, Laurence W. Moreland, and Tod A. Baker, 209–25. New York: Praeger.

Sears, David O., and Victoria Savalei. 2006. "The Political Color Line in America: Many Peoples of Color or Black Exceptionalism? *Political Psychology* 27: 895–924.

———. 2009. "Sharp or Blunt Instruments? Measuring Affect toward Ethnic and Racial Groups in Contemporary America." Paper presented at the annual meeting of the International Society for Political Psychology, Dublin, July 17.

Sides, John, and Lynn Vavreck 2013. *The Gamble: Choice and Chance in the 2012 Presidential Election*. Princeton, NJ: Princeton University Press.

Skocpol, Theda, and Vanessa Williamson. 2012. *The Tea Party and the Remaking of Republican Conservatism*. Oxford: Oxford University Press.

Sniderman, Paul M., and Thomas Piazza. 2002. *Black Pride and Black Prejudice*. Princeton, NJ: Princeton University Press.

Tate, Katherine. 1994. *From Protest to Politics: The New Black Voters in American Elections*. Cambridge, MA: Harvard University Press.

Tesler, Michael, and David O. Sears. 2010. *Obama's Race: The 2008 Election and the Dream of a Post-Racial America*. Chicago: University of Chicago Press.

Trende, Sean. 2013. "The Case of the Missing White Voters Revisited." June 21. *Real Clear Politics*. www.realclearpolitics.com/articles/2013/06/21/the_case_of_the_missing _white_voters_revisited_118893.html.

Vavreck, Lynn. 2014. "It's Not Too Late for Republicans to Win Latino Votes." *Upshot*. August 11. www.nytimes.com/2014/08/12/upshot/its-not-too-late-for-republicans -to-win-latino-votes.html?_r=0&abt=0002&abg=0.

4.2

Brown v. Board of Education (1954)

In one of the most important Supreme Court cases in American history, the justices unanimously and emphatically overturned the precedent from Plessy v. Ferguson (1896), which had upheld the right of local communities and states to maintain separate public facilities for the races. "[I]n the field of public education," the Court declared, "the doctrine of 'separate but equal' has no place." This 1954 decision started the American legal system down a new path of active intervention in the racial policies of government at all levels.

Mr. Chief Justice Warren delivered the opinion of the Court.

These cases come to us from the States of Kansas, South Carolina, Virginia, and Delaware. They are premised on different facts and different local conditions, but a common legal question justifies their consideration together in this consolidated opinion.

In each of the cases, minors of the Negro race, through their legal representatives, seek the aid of the courts in obtaining admission to the public schools of their community on a nonsegregated basis. In each instance, they had been denied admission to schools attended by white children under laws requiring or permitting segregation according to race. This segregation was alleged to deprive the plaintiffs of the equal protection of the laws under the Fourteenth Amendment. In each of the cases other than the Delaware case, a three-judge federal district court denied relief to the plaintiffs on the so-called "separate but equal" doctrine announced by this Court in *Plessy v. Ferguson*. Under that doctrine, equality of treatment is accorded when the races are provided substantially equal facilities, even though these facilities be separate. In the Delaware case, the Supreme Court of Delaware adhered to that doctrine, but ordered that the plaintiffs be admitted to the white schools because of their superiority to the Negro schools.

The plaintiffs contend that segregated public schools are not "equal" and cannot be made "equal," and that hence they are deprived of the equal protection of the laws. Because of the obvious importance of the question presented, the Court took jurisdiction. Argument was heard in the 1952 Term,

From *Brown v. Board of Education*, 347 U.S. 483 (1954).

and reargument was heard this Term on certain questions propounded by the Court.

Reargument was largely devoted to the circumstances surrounding the adoption of the Fourteenth Amendment in 1868. It covered exhaustively consideration of the Amendment in Congress, ratification by the states, then-existing practices in racial segregation, and the views of proponents and opponents of the Amendment. This discussion and our own investigation convince us that, although these sources cast some light, it is not enough to resolve the problem with which we are faced. At best, they are inconclusive. The most avid proponents of the post-War Amendments undoubtedly intended them to remove all legal distinctions among "all persons born or naturalized in the United States." Their opponents, just as certainly, were antagonistic to both the letter and the spirit of the Amendments and wished them to have the most limited effect. What others in Congress and the state legislatures had in mind cannot be determined with any degree of certainty.

An additional reason for the inconclusive nature of the Amendment's history with respect to segregated schools is the status of public education at that time. In the South, the movement toward free common schools, supported by general taxation, had not yet taken hold. Education of white children was largely in the hands of private groups. Education of Negroes was almost nonexistent, and practically all of the race were illiterate. In fact, any education of Negroes was forbidden by law in some states. Today, in contrast, many Negroes have achieved outstanding success in the arts and sciences, as well as in the business and professional world. It is true that public school education at the time of the Amendment had advanced further in the North, but the effect of the Amendment on Northern States was generally ignored in the congressional debates. Even in the North, the conditions of public education did not approximate those existing today. The curriculum was usually rudimentary; ungraded schools were common in rural areas; the school term was but three months a year in many states, and compulsory school attendance was virtually unknown. As a consequence, it is not surprising that there should be so little in the history of the Fourteenth Amendment relating to its intended effect on public education.

In the first cases in this Court construing the Fourteenth Amendment, decided shortly after its adoption, the Court interpreted it as proscribing all state-imposed discriminations against the Negro race.[1] The doctrine of "separate but equal" did not make its appearance in this Court until 1896 in the case of *Plessy v. Ferguson*, involving not education but transportation.[2] American courts have since labored with the doctrine for over half a century. In this Court, there have been six cases involving the "separate but equal" doctrine in the field of public education. In *Cumming v. County Board of Education*, and *Gong Lum v. Rice*, the validity of the doctrine itself was not challenged. In more recent cases, all on the graduate school level, inequality was found in that specific benefits enjoyed by white students were denied to Negro students of the same educational qualifications. *Missouri ex rel. Gaines v. Canada, Sipuel v. Okla-*

homa, Sweatt v. Painter, McLaurin v. Oklahoma State Regents. In none of these cases was it necessary to reexamine the doctrine to grant relief to the Negro plaintiff. And in *Sweatt v. Painter, supra,* the Court expressly reserved decision on the question whether *Plessy v. Ferguson* should be held inapplicable to public education.

In the instant cases, that question is directly presented. Here, unlike *Sweatt v. Painter,* there are findings below that the Negro and white schools involved have been equalized, or are being equalized, with respect to buildings, curricula, qualifications and salaries of teachers, and other "tangible" factors. Our decision, therefore, cannot turn on merely a comparison of these tangible factors in the Negro and white schools involved in each of the cases. We must look instead to the effect of segregation itself on public education.

In approaching this problem, we cannot turn the clock back to 1868, when the Amendment was adopted, or even to 1896, when *Plessy v. Ferguson* was written. We must consider public education in the light of its full development and its present place in American life throughout the Nation. Only in this way can it be determined if segregation in public schools deprives these plaintiffs of the equal protection of the laws.

Today, education is perhaps the most important function of state and local governments. Compulsory school attendance laws and the great expenditures for education both demonstrate our recognition of the importance of education to our democratic society. It is required in the performance of our most basic public responsibilities, even service in the armed forces. It is the very foundation of good citizenship. Today it is a principal instrument in awakening the child to cultural values, in preparing him for later professional training, and in helping him to adjust normally to his environment. In these days, it is doubtful that any child may reasonably be expected to succeed in life if he is denied the opportunity of an education. Such an opportunity, where the state has undertaken to provide it, is a right which must be made available to all on equal terms.

We come then to the question presented: Does segregation of children in public schools solely on the basis of race, even though the physical facilities and other "tangible" factors may be equal, deprive the children of the minority group of equal educational opportunities? We believe that it does.

In *Sweatt v. Painter,* in finding that a segregated law school for Negroes could not provide them equal educational opportunities, this Court relied in large part on "those qualities which are incapable of objective measurement but which make for greatness in a law school." In *McLaurin v. Oklahoma State Regents,* the Court, in requiring that a Negro admitted to a white graduate school be treated like all other students, again resorted to intangible considerations: ". . . his ability to study, to engage in discussions and exchange views with other students, and, in general, to learn his profession." Such considerations apply with added force to children in grade and high schools. To separate them from others of similar age and qualifications solely because of their race generates a feeling of inferiority as to their status in the community that may affect their hearts and minds in a way unlikely ever to be undone. The effect of this separation on their educational opportunities was well stated by a finding in the Kansas case by a court which nevertheless felt compelled to rule against the Negro plaintiffs: Segregation of white and colored children in public schools has a detrimental effect upon the colored children. The impact is greater when it has the sanction of the law, for the policy of separating the races is usually interpreted as denoting the inferiority of the negro group. A sense of inferiority affects the motivation of a child to learn. Segregation with the sanction of law, therefore, has a tendency to [retard] the educational and mental development of negro children and to deprive them of some of the benefits they would receive in a racial[ly] integrated school system.[3] Whatever may have been the extent of psychological knowledge at the time of *Plessy v. Ferguson*, this finding is amply supported by modern authority. Any language in *Plessy v. Ferguson* contrary to this finding is rejected.

We conclude that, in the field of public education, the doctrine of "separate but equal" has no place. Separate educational facilities are inherently unequal. Therefore, we hold that the plaintiffs and others similarly situated for whom the actions have been brought are, by reason of the segregation complained of, deprived of the equal protection of the laws guaranteed by the Fourteenth Amendment. This disposition makes unnecessary any discussion whether such segregation also violates the Due Process Clause of the Fourteenth Amendment.[4]

Because these are class actions, because of the wide applicability of this decision, and because of the great variety of local conditions, the formulation of decrees in these cases presents problems of considerable complexity. On reargument, the consideration of appropriate relief was necessarily subordinated to the primary question—the constitutionality of segregation in public education. We have now announced that such segregation is a denial of the equal protection of the laws. In order that we may have the full assistance of the parties in formulating decrees, the cases will be restored to the docket, and the parties are requested to present further argument on Questions 4 and 5 previously propounded by the Court for the reargument this Term.[5] The Attorney General of the United States is again invited to participate. The Attorneys General of the states requiring or permitting segregation in public education will also be permitted to appear as *amici curiae* upon request to do so by September 15, 1954, and submission of briefs by October 1, 1954.

It is so ordered.

NOTES

1. *Slaughter-House Cases*, 16 Wall. 36, 67–72 (1873); *Strauder v. West Virginia*, 100 U.S. 303, 307–8 (1880): It ordains that no State shall deprive any person of life, liberty, or property, without due process of law, or deny to any person within its jurisdiction the equal protection of the laws. What is this but declaring that the law in the States shall be

the same for the black as for the white; that all persons, whether colored or white, shall stand equal before the laws of the States, and, in regard to the colored race, for whose protection the amendment was primarily designed, that no discrimination shall be made against them by law because of their color? The words of the amendment, it is true, are prohibitory, but they contain a necessary implication of a positive immunity, or right, most valuable to the colored race—the right to exemption from unfriendly legislation against them distinctively as colored—exemption from legal discriminations, implying inferiority in civil society, lessening the security of their enjoyment of the rights which others enjoy, and discriminations which are steps towards reducing them to the condition of a subject race.

2. The doctrine apparently originated in *Roberts v. City of Boston*, 59 Mass.198, 206 (1850), upholding school segregation against attack as being violative of a state constitutional guarantee of equality. Segregation in Boston public schools was eliminated in 1855. Mass.Acts 1855, c. 256. But elsewhere in the North, segregation in public education has persisted in some communities until recent years. It is apparent that such segregation has long been a nationwide problem, not merely one of sectional concern.

3. A similar finding was made in the Delaware case: I conclude from the testimony that, in our Delaware society, State-imposed segregation in education itself results in the Negro children, as a class, receiving educational opportunities which are substantially inferior to those available to white children otherwise similarly situated. 87 A.2d 862, 865.

4. See *Bolling v. Sharpe*, post, p. 497, concerning the Due Process Clause of the Fifth Amendment.

5. Assuming it is decided that segregation in public schools violates the Fourteenth Amendment, (a) would a decree necessarily follow providing that, within the limits set by normal geographic school districting, Negro children should forthwith be admitted to schools of their choice, or (b) may this Court, in the exercise of its equity powers, permit an effective gradual adjustment to be brought about from existing segregated systems to a system not based on color distinctions?

4.3

District of Columbia v. Heller (2008)

In the majority opinion from this controversial Supreme Court decision, Justice Antonin Scalia offers a view of the Second Amendment that interprets the right to bear arms as applying to individuals. He argues against the notion that the amendment was written to apply to the rights of collectives, like states or communities, to bear arms. Instead, the writers of the amendment intended the right to bear arms to be an individual right. Applying this reasoning, the Court struck down the Washington, D.C., law banning handguns as unconstitutional.

ON WRIT OF CERTIORARI TO THE UNITED STATES COURT OF APPEALS FOR THE DISTRICT OF COLUMBIA CIRCUIT

JUSTICE SCALIA delivered the opinion of the Court.

We consider whether a District of Columbia prohibition on the possession of usable handguns in the home violates the Second Amendment to the Constitution.

I

The District of Columbia generally prohibits the possession of handguns. It is a crime to carry an unregistered firearm, and the registration of handguns is prohibited. Wholly apart from that prohibition, no person may carry a handgun without a license, but the chief of police may issue licenses for one-year periods. District of Columbia law also requires residents to keep their lawfully owned firearms, such as registered long guns, "unloaded and dissembled or bound by a trigger lock or similar device" unless they are located in a place of business or are being used for lawful recreational activities.

Respondent Dick Heller is a D.C. special police officer authorized to carry a handgun while on duty at the Federal Judicial Center. He applied for a registration certificate for a handgun that he wished to keep at home, but the District refused. He thereafter filed a lawsuit in the Federal District Court for

From *District of Columbia v. Heller*, 554 U.S. 570 (2008).

the District of Columbia seeking, on Second Amendment grounds, to enjoin the city from enforcing the bar on the registration of handguns, the licensing requirement insofar as it prohibits the carrying of a firearm in the home without a license, and the trigger-lock requirement insofar as it prohibits the use of "functional firearms within the home." The District Court dismissed respondent's complaint, The Court of Appeals for the District of Columbia Circuit, construing his complaint as seeking the right to render a firearm operable and carry it about his home in that condition only when necessary for self-defense. It held that the Second Amendment protects an individual right to possess firearms and that the city's total ban on handguns, as well as its requirement that firearms in the home be kept nonfunctional even when necessary for self-defense, violated that right. The Court of Appeals directed the District Court to enter summary judgment for respondent.

We granted certiorari.

II

We turn first to the meaning of the Second Amendment.

A

The Second Amendment provides: "A well regulated Militia, being necessary to the security of a free State, the right of the people to keep and bear Arms, shall not be infringed." In interpreting this text, we are guided by the principle that "[t]he Constitution was written to be understood by the voters; its words and phrases were used in their normal and ordinary as distinguished from technical meaning." *United States* v. *Sprague,* Normal meaning may of course include an idiomatic meaning, but it excludes secret or technical meanings that would not have been known to ordinary citizens in the founding generation.

The two sides in this case have set out very different interpretations of the Amendment. Petitioners and today's dissenting Justices believe that it protects only the right to possess and carry a firearm in connection with militia service. Respondent argues that it protects an individual right to possess a firearm unconnected with service in a militia, and to use that arm for traditionally lawful purposes, such as self-defense within the home.

The Second Amendment is naturally divided into two parts: its prefatory clause and its operative clause. The former does not limit the latter grammatically, but rather announces a purpose. The Amendment could be rephrased, "Because a well regulated Militia is necessary to the security of a free State, the right of the people to keep and bear Arms shall not be infringed." Although this structure of the Second Amendment is unique in our Constitution, other legal documents of the founding era, particularly individual-rights provisions of state constitutions, commonly included a prefatory statement of purpose.

Logic demands that there be a link between the stated purpose and the command. The Second Amendment would be nonsensical if it read, "A well regulated Militia, being necessary to the security of a free State, the right of the people to petition for redress of grievances shall not be infringed." That requirement of logical connection may cause a prefatory clause to resolve an ambiguity in the operative clause. But apart from that clarifying function, a prefatory clause does not limit or expand the scope of the operative clause. Therefore, while we will begin our textual analysis with the operative clause, we will return to the prefatory clause to ensure that our reading of the operative clause is consistent with the announced purpose.

1. Operative Clause

A. "RIGHT OF THE PEOPLE." The first salient feature of the operative clause is that it codifies a "right of the people." The unamended Constitution and the Bill of Rights use the phrase "right of the people" two other times, in the First Amendment 's Assembly-and-Petition Clause and in the Fourth Amendment 's Search-and-Seizure Clause. The Ninth Amendment uses very similar terminology ("The enumeration in the Constitution, of certain rights, shall not be construed to deny or disparage others retained by the people"). All three of these instances unambiguously refer to individual rights, not "collective" rights, or rights that may be exercised only through participation in some corporate body.

Three provisions of the Constitution refer to "the people" in a context other than "rights"—the famous preamble ("We the people"), §2 of Article I (providing that "the people" will choose members of the House), and the Tenth Amendment (providing that those powers not given the Federal Government remain with "the States" or "the people"). Those provisions arguably refer to "the people" acting collectively—but they deal with the exercise or reservation of powers, not rights. Nowhere else in the Constitution does a "right" attributed to "the people" refer to anything other than an individual right.

This contrasts markedly with the phrase "the militia" in the prefatory clause. As we will describe below, the "militia" in colonial America consisted of a subset of "the people"—those who were male, able bodied, and within a certain age range. Reading the Second Amendment as protecting only the right to "keep and bear Arms" in an organized militia therefore fits poorly with the operative clause's description of the holder of that right as "the people."

We start therefore with a strong presumption that the Second Amendment right is exercised individually and belongs to all Americans.

B. "KEEP AND BEAR ARMS." We move now from the holder of the right—"the people"—to the substance of the right: "to keep and bear Arms."

Before addressing the verbs "keep" and "bear," we interpret their object: "Arms." The eighteenth-century meaning is no different from the meaning today. The 1773 edition of Samuel Johnson's dictionary defined "arms" as "weapons of offence, or armour of defence." Timothy Cunningham's important 1771 legal dictionary defined "arms" as "any thing that a man wears for his defence, or takes into his hands, or useth in wrath to cast at or strike another."

We turn to the phrases "keep arms" and "bear arms." Johnson defined "keep" as, most relevantly, "[t]o retain; not to lose," and "[t]o have in custody." Webster defined it as "[t]o hold; to retain in one's power or possession." No party has apprised us of an idiomatic meaning of "keep Arms." Thus, the most natural reading of "keep Arms" in the Second Amendment is to "have weapons."

"Keep arms" was simply a common way of referring to possessing arms, for militiamen and everyone else.

At the time of the founding, as now, to "bear" meant to "carry." When used with "arms," however, the term has a meaning that refers to carrying for a particular purpose—confrontation. In *Muscarello* v. *United States*, in the course of analyzing the meaning of "carries a firearm" in a federal criminal statute, Justice Ginsburg wrote that "[s]urely a most familiar meaning is, as the Constitution's Second Amendment . . . indicate[s]: 'wear, bear, or carry . . . upon the person or in the clothing or in a pocket, for the purpose . . . of being armed and ready for offensive or defensive action in a case of conflict with another person.'" We think that Justice Ginsburg accurately captured the natural meaning of "bear arms." Although the phrase implies that the carrying of the weapon is for the purpose of "offensive or defensive action," it in no way connotes participation in a structured military organization.

From our review of founding-era sources, we conclude that this natural meaning was also the meaning that "bear arms" had in the eighteenth century. In numerous instances, "bear arms" was unambiguously used to refer to the carrying of weapons outside of an organized militia. The most prominent examples are those most relevant to the Second Amendment: Nine state constitutional provisions written in the eighteenth century or the first two decades of the nineteenth, which enshrined a right of citizens to "bear arms in defense of themselves and the state" or "bear arms in defense of himself and the state." It is clear from those formulations that "bear arms" did not refer only to carrying a weapon in an organized military unit.

The phrase "bear Arms" also had at the time of the founding an idiomatic meaning that was significantly different from its natural meaning: "to serve as a soldier, do military service, fight" or "to wage war." But it *unequivocally* bore that idiomatic meaning only when followed by the preposition "against," which was in turn followed by the target of the hostilities.

In any event, the meaning of "bear arms" that petitioners and Justice Stevens propose is *not even* the (sometimes) idiomatic meaning. Rather, they manufacture a hybrid definition, whereby "bear arms" connotes the actual carrying of arms (and therefore is not really an idiom) but only in the service of an organized militia. No dictionary has ever adopted that definition, and we have been apprised of no source that indicates that it carried that meaning at the time of the founding. But it is easy to see why petitioners and the dissent are driven to the hybrid definition. Giving "bear Arms" its idiomatic meaning would cause the protected right to consist of the right to be a soldier or to wage war—an absurdity that no commentator has ever endorsed.

Petitioners justify their limitation of "bear arms" to the military context by pointing out the unremarkable fact that it was often used in that context—the same mistake they made with respect to "keep arms." It is especially unremarkable that the phrase was often used in a military context in the federal legal sources (such as records of congressional debate) that have been the focus of petitioners' inquiry. Those sources would have had little occasion to use it *except* in discussions about the standing army and the militia. Other legal sources frequently used "bear arms" in nonmilitary contexts. If one looks beyond legal sources, "bear arms" was frequently used in nonmilitary contexts.

Justice Stevens points to a study by *amici* supposedly showing that the phrase "bear arms" was most frequently used in the military context. Of course, as we have said, the fact that the phrase was commonly used in a particular context does not show that it is limited to that context, and, in any event, we have given many sources where the phrase was used in nonmilitary contexts. Moreover, the study's collection appears to include (who knows how many times) the idiomatic phrase "bear arms against," which is irrelevant. The *amici* also dismiss examples such as "bear arms . . . for the purpose of killing game" because those uses are "expressly qualified." That analysis is faulty. If "bear arms" means, as we think, simply the carrying of arms, a modifier can limit the purpose of the carriage. But if "bear arms" means, as the petitioners and the dissent think, the carrying of arms only for military purposes, one simply cannot add "for the purpose of killing game." The right "to carry arms in the militia for the purpose of killing game" is worthy of the mad hatter. Thus, these purposive qualifying phrases positively establish that "to bear arms" is not limited to military use.

Justice Stevens places great weight on James Madison's inclusion of a conscientious-objector clause in his original draft of the Second Amendment: "but no person religiously scrupulous of bearing arms, shall be compelled to render military service in person." He argues that this clause establishes that the drafters of the Second Amendment intended "bear Arms" to refer only to military service. In any case, what Justice Stevens would conclude from the deleted provision does not follow. It was not meant to exempt from military service those who objected to going to war but had no scruples about personal gunfights.

Finally, Justice Stevens suggests that "keep and bear Arms" was some sort of term of art, presumably akin to "hue and cry" or "cease and desist." Justice Stevens believes that the unitary meaning of "keep and bear Arms" is established by the Second Amendment's calling it a "right" (singular) rather than "rights" (plural). There is nothing to this. State constitutions of the founding period routinely grouped multiple (related) guarantees under a singular "right," and the First Amendment protects the "right [singular] of the people peaceably to assemble, and to petition the Government for a redress of grievances."

C. MEANING OF THE OPERATIVE CLAUSE.   Putting all of these textual elements together, we find that they guarantee the individual right to possess and carry weapons in case of confrontation. This meaning is strongly confirmed by the historical background of the Second Amendment. We look to this because it has always been widely understood that the Second Amendment, like the First and Fourth Amendments, codified a *pre-existing* right. The very text of the Second Amendment implicitly recognizes the pre-existence of the right and declares only that it "shall not be infringed." As we said in *United States v. Cruikshank*, "[t]his is not a right granted by the Constitution. Neither is it in any manner dependent upon that instrument for its existence. The Second Amendment declares that it shall not be infringed. . . ."

Between the Restoration and the Glorious Revolution, the Stuart Kings Charles II and James II succeeded in using select militias loyal to them to suppress political dissidents, in part by disarming their opponents. Under the auspices of the 1671 Game Act, for example, the Catholic James II had ordered general disarmaments of regions home to his Protestant enemies. These experiences caused Englishmen to be extremely wary of concentrated military forces run by the state and to be jealous of their arms. They accordingly obtained an assurance from William and Mary, in the Declaration of Right (which was codified as the English Bill of Rights), that Protestants would never be disarmed: "That the subjects which are Protestants may have arms for their defense suitable to their conditions and as allowed by law." This right has long been understood to be the predecessor to our Second Amendment. It was secured to them as individuals, according to "libertarian political principles," not as members of a fighting force.

And, of course, what the Stuarts had tried to do to their political enemies, George III had tried to do to the colonists. In the tumultuous decades of the 1760s and 1770s, the Crown began to disarm the inhabitants of the most rebellious areas. That provoked polemical reactions by Americans invoking their rights as Englishmen to keep arms.

There seems to us no doubt, on the basis of both text and history, that the Second Amendment conferred an individual right to keep and bear arms. Of course the right was not unlimited, just as the First Amendment's right of free speech was not. Thus, we do not read the Second Amendment to protect the right of citizens to carry arms for *any sort* of confrontation, just as we do not read the First Amendment to protect the right of citizens to speak for *any purpose*. Before turning to limitations upon the individual right, however, we must determine whether the prefatory clause of the Second Amendment comports with our interpretation of the operative clause.

2. Prefatory Clause

The prefatory clause reads: "A well regulated Militia, being necessary to the security of a free State. . . ."

A. "WELL-REGULATED MILITIA." In *United States* v. *Miller* (1939), we explained that "the Militia comprised all males physically capable of acting in concert for the common defense."

Petitioners take a seemingly narrower view of the militia, stating that "[m]ilitias are the state- and congressionally-regulated military forces described in the Militia Clauses." Although we agree with petitioners' interpretive assumption that "militia" means the same thing in Article I and the Second Amendment, we believe that petitioners identify the wrong thing, namely, the organized militia. Unlike armies and navies, which Congress is given the power to create, the militia is assumed by Article I already to be *in existence*. Congress is given the power to "provide for calling forth the militia," §8, cl. 15; and the power not to create, but to "organiz[e]" it—and not to organize "a" militia, which is what one would expect if the militia were to be a federal creation, but to organize "the" militia, connoting a body already in existence. To be sure, Congress need not conscript every able-bodied man into the militia, because nothing in Article I suggests that in exercising its power to organize, discipline, and arm the militia, Congress must focus upon the entire body. Although the militia consists of all able-bodied men, the federally organized militia may consist of a subset of them.

Finally, the adjective "well-regulated" implies nothing more than the imposition of proper discipline and training.

B. "SECURITY OF A FREE STATE." The phrase "security of a free state" meant "security of a free polity," not security of each of the several States as the dissent below argued. Joseph Story wrote in his treatise on the Constitution that "the word 'state' is used in various senses [and in] its most enlarged sense, it means the people composing a particular nation or community." Moreover, the other instances of "state" in the Constitution are typically accompanied by modifiers making clear that the reference is to the several States—"each state," "several states," "any state," "that state," "particular states," "one state," "no state." And the presence of the term "foreign state" in Article I and Article III shows that the word "state" did not have a single meaning in the Constitution.

3. Relationship between Prefatory Clause and Operative Clause

Does the preface fit with an operative clause that creates an individual right to keep and bear arms? It fits perfectly, once one knows the history that the founding generation knew and that we have described above. That history showed that the way tyrants had eliminated a militia consisting of all the able-bodied men was not by banning the militia but simply by taking away the people's arms, enabling a select militia or standing army to suppress political opponents.

The debate with respect to the right to keep and bear arms, as with other guarantees in the Bill of Rights, was not over whether it was desirable (all agreed that it was) but over whether it needed to be codified in the Constitution.

During the 1788 ratification debates, the fear that the federal government would disarm the people in order to impose rule through a standing army or select militia was pervasive in Antifederalist rhetoric. Federalists responded that because Congress was given no power to abridge the ancient right of individuals to keep and bear arms, such a force could never oppress the people. It was understood across the political spectrum that the right helped to secure the ideal of a citizen militia, which might be necessary to oppose an oppressive military force if the constitutional order broke down.

It is therefore entirely sensible that the Second Amendment's prefatory clause announces the purpose for which the right was codified: to prevent elimination of the militia. The prefatory clause does not suggest that preserving the militia was the only reason Americans valued the ancient right; most undoubtedly thought it even more important for self-defense and hunting. But the threat that the new Federal Government would destroy the citizens' militia by taking away their arms was the reason that right—unlike some other English rights—was codified in a written Constitution. Justice Breyer's assertion that individual self-defense is merely a "subsidiary interest" of the right to keep and bear arms, is profoundly mistaken. He bases that assertion solely upon the prologue—but that can only show that self-defense had little to do with the right's *codification;* it was the *central component* of the right itself.

B

Our interpretation is confirmed by analogous arms-bearing rights in state constitutions that preceded and immediately followed adoption of the Second Amendment. Four States adopted analogues to the Federal Second Amendment in the period between independence and the ratification of the Bill of Rights. Two of them—Pennsylvania and Vermont—clearly adopted individual rights unconnected to militia service.

We therefore believe that the most likely reading of all of these pre-Second Amendment state constitutional provisions is that they secured an individual right to bear arms for defensive purposes.

> [A]t least seven [states] unequivocally protected an individual citizen's right to self-defense is strong evidence that that is how the founding generation conceived of the right.

The historical narrative that petitioners must endorse would thus treat the Federal Second Amendment as an odd outlier, protecting a right unknown in state constitutions or at English common law, based on little more than an overreading of the prefatory clause.

C

Justice Stevens relies on the drafting history of the Second Amendment—the various proposals in the state conventions and the debates in Congress. It is dubious to rely on such history to interpret a text that was widely understood to codify a pre-existing right, rather than to fashion a new one. But even assuming that this legislative history is relevant, Justice Stevens flatly misreads the historical record.

It is true, as Justice Stevens says, that there was concern that the Federal Government would abolish the institution of the state militia. That concern found expression, however, *not* in the various Second Amendment precursors proposed in the State conventions, but in separate structural provisions that would have given the States concurrent and seemingly nonpreemptible authority to organize, discipline, and arm the militia when the Federal Government failed to do so. The Second Amendment precursors, by contrast, referred to the individual English right already codified in two (and probably four) State constitutions. The Federalist-dominated first Congress chose to reject virtually all major structural revisions favored by the Antifederalists, including the proposed militia amendments. Rather, it adopted primarily the popular and uncontroversial (though, in the Federalists' view, unnecessary) individual-rights amendments. The Second Amendment right, protecting only individuals' liberty to keep and carry arms, did nothing to assuage Antifederalists' concerns about federal control of the militia.

Justice Stevens thinks it significant that the Virginia, New York, and North Carolina Second Amendment proposals were "embedded . . . within a group of principles that are distinctly military in meaning," such as statements about the danger of standing armies. But so was the highly influential minority proposal in Pennsylvania, yet that proposal, with its reference to hunting, plainly referred to an individual right. Other than that erroneous point, Justice Stevens has brought forward absolutely no evidence that those proposals conferred only a right to carry arms in a militia.

D

We now address how the Second Amendment was interpreted from immediately after its ratification through the end of the nineteenth century.

1. Post-Ratification Commentary

Three important founding-era legal scholars interpreted the Second Amendment in published writings. All three understood it to protect an individual right unconnected with militia service.

St. George Tucker's version conceived of the right as necessary for self-defense. He equated that right, absent the religious and class-based restrictions, with the Second Amendment. He grouped the right with some of the individual rights included in the First Amendment and said that if "a law be passed by congress, prohibiting" any of those rights, it would "be the province of the judiciary to pronounce whether any such act were constitutional, or not; and if not, to acquit the accused . . . ." It is unlikely that Tucker was referring to a person's being "accused" of violating a law making it a crime to bear arms in a state militia.

In 1825, William Rawle, a prominent lawyer who had been a member of the Pennsylvania Assembly that ratified the Bill of Rights, published an influential treatise.

Rawle clearly differentiated between the people's right to bear arms and their service in a militia. Rawle further said that the Second Amendment right ought not "be abused to the disturbance of the public peace," such as by assembling with other armed individuals "for an unlawful purpose"—statements that make no sense if the right does not extend to *any* individual purpose.

Joseph Story published his famous Commentaries on the Constitution of the United States in 1833. Justice Stevens suggests that "[t]here is not so much as a whisper" in Story's explanation of the Second Amendment that favors the individual-rights view. That is wrong. Story explained that the English Bill of Rights had also included a "right to bear arms," a right that, as we have discussed, had nothing to do with militia service.

Story's Commentaries also cite as support Tucker and Rawle, both of whom clearly viewed the right as unconnected to militia service. In addition, in a shorter 1840 work Story wrote: "One of the ordinary modes, by which tyrants accomplish their purposes without resistance, is, by disarming the people, and making it an offence to keep arms, and by substituting a regular army in the stead of a resort to the militia."

2. Pre–Civil War Case Law

The nineteenth-century cases that interpreted the Second Amendment universally support an individual right unconnected to militia service. In *Houston* v. *Moore*, this Court held that States have concurrent power over the militia, at least where not pre-empted by Congress. In the famous fugitive-slave case of *Johnson* v. *Tompkins*, Baldwin, sitting as a circuit judge, cited both the Second Amendment and the Pennsylvania analogue for his conclusion that a citizen has "a right to carry arms in defence of his property or person, and to use them, if either were assailed with such force, numbers or violence as made it necessary for the protection or safety of either."

Many early nineteenth-century state cases indicated that the Second Amendment right to bear arms was an individual right unconnected to militia service, though subject to certain restrictions.

An 1829 decision [*United States* v. *Sheldon*] by the Supreme Court of Michigan said:

> The constitution of the United States also grants to the citizen the right to keep and bear arms. But the grant of this privilege cannot be construed into the right in him who keeps a gun to destroy his neighbor. No rights are intended to be granted by the constitution for an unlawful or unjustifiable purpose.

In *Nunn* v. *State*, the Georgia Supreme Court construed the Second Amendment as protecting the "*natural* right of self-defence" and therefore struck down a ban on carrying pistols openly. Its opinion perfectly captured the way in which the operative clause of the Second Amendment furthers the purpose announced in the prefatory clause.

3. Post–Civil War Legislation

In the aftermath of the Civil War, there was an outpouring of discussion of the Second Amendment in Congress and in public discourse, as people debated whether and how to secure constitutional rights for newly free slaves. Since those discussions took place 75 years after the ratification of the Second Amendment, they do not provide as much insight into its original meaning as earlier sources. Yet those born and educated in the early nineteenth century faced a widespread effort to limit arms ownership by a large number of citizens; their understanding of the origins and continuing significance of the Amendment is instructive.

Blacks were routinely disarmed by Southern States after the Civil War. Those who opposed these injustices frequently stated that they infringed blacks' constitutional right to keep and bear arms. Needless to say, the claim was not that blacks were being prohibited from carrying arms in an organized state militia.

Congress enacted the Freedmen's Bureau Act on July 16, 1866. Section 14 stated:

> [T]he right . . . to have full and equal benefit of all laws and proceedings concerning personal liberty, personal security, and the acquisition, enjoyment, and disposition of estate, real and personal, including the constitutional right to bear arms, shall be secured to and enjoyed by all the citizens . . . without respect to race or color, or previous condition of slavery. . . .

The understanding that the Second Amendment gave freed blacks the right to keep and bear arms was reflected in congressional discussion of the bill, with even an opponent of it saying that the founding generation "were for every man bearing his arms about him and keeping them in his house, his castle, for his own defense."

It was plainly the understanding in the post–Civil War Congress that the Second Amendment protected an individual right to use arms for self-defense.

4. Post–Civil War Commentators

Every late-nineteenth-century legal scholar that we have read interpreted the Second Amendment to secure an individual right unconnected with militia service. The most famous was the judge and professor Thomas Cooley, who wrote a massively popular 1868 Treatise on Constitutional Limitations. Concerning the Second Amendment it said:

Among the other defences to personal liberty should be mentioned the right of the people to keep and bear arms . . . . The alternative to a standing army is 'a well-regulated militia,' but this cannot exist unless the people are trained to bearing arms. How far it is in the power of the legislature to regulate this right, we shall not undertake to say, as happily there has been very little occasion to discuss that subject by the courts.

All other post–Civil War nineteenth-century sources we have found concurred with Cooley.

E

We now ask whether any of our precedents forecloses the conclusions we have reached about the meaning of the Second Amendment.

United States v. *Cruikshank*, in the course of vacating the convictions of members of a white mob for depriving blacks of their right to keep and bear arms, held that the Second Amendment does not by its own force apply to anyone other than the Federal Government. The opinion explained that the right "is not a right granted by the Constitution [or] in any manner dependent upon that instrument for its existence. The second amendment . . . means no more than that it shall not be infringed by Congress." The limited discussion of the Second Amendment in *Cruikshank* supports, if anything, the individual-rights interpretation.

Presser v. *Illinois* (1886) held that the right to keep and bear arms was not violated by a law that forbade "bodies of men to associate together as military organizations, or to drill or parade with arms in cities and towns unless authorized by law." Justice Stevens presses *Presser* into service to support his view that the right to bear arms is limited to service in the militia by joining *Presser*'s brief discussion of the Second Amendment with a later portion of the opinion making the seemingly relevant (to the Second Amendment) point that the plaintiff was not a member of the state militia. Unfortunately for Justice Stevens' argument, that later portion deals with the *Fourteenth Amendment;* it was the *Fourteenth Amendment* to which the plaintiff's nonmembership in the militia was relevant. Thus, Justice Stevens' statement that *Presser* "suggested that . . . nothing in the Constitution protected the use of arms outside the context of a militia," is simply wrong. *Presser* said nothing about the Second Amendment's meaning or scope, beyond the fact that it does not prevent the prohibition of private paramilitary organizations.

Justice Stevens places overwhelming reliance upon this Court's decision in *United States* v. *Miller* (1939) . "[H]undreds of judges," we are told, "have relied on the view of the amendment we endorsed there," and "[e]ven if the textual and historical arguments on both sides of the issue were evenly balanced, respect for the well-settled views of all of our predecessors on this Court, and for the rule of law itself . . . would prevent most jurists from endorsing such a dramatic upheaval in the law," And what is, according to Justice Stevens, the holding of *Miller* that demands such obeisance? That the Second Amendment "protects the right to keep and bear arms for certain military purposes, but that it does not curtail the legislature's power to regulate the nonmilitary use and ownership of weapons."

Nothing so clearly demonstrates the weakness of Justice Stevens' case. *Miller* did not hold that and cannot possibly be read to have held that. The judgment in the case upheld against a Second Amendment challenge two men's federal convictions for transporting an unregistered short-barreled shotgun in interstate commerce, in violation of the National Firearms Act. It is entirely clear that the Court's basis for saying that the Second Amendment did not apply was *not* that the defendants were "bear[ing] arms" not "for . . . military purposes" but for "nonmilitary use." Rather, it was that the *type of weapon at issue* was not eligible for Second Amendment protection. Beyond that, the opinion provided no explanation of the content of the right.

Justice Stevens can say again and again that *Miller* did "not turn on the difference between muskets and sawed-off shotguns, it turned, rather, on the basic difference between the military and nonmilitary use and possession of guns," but the words of the opinion prove otherwise. The most Justice Stevens can plausibly claim for *Miller* is that it declined to decide the nature of the Second Amendment right.

It is particularly wrongheaded to read *Miller* for more than what it said, because the case did not even purport to be a thorough examination of the Second Amendment.

We conclude that nothing in our precedents forecloses our adoption of the original understanding of the Second Amendment. It should be unsurprising that such a significant matter has been for so long judicially unresolved. For most of our history, the Bill of Rights was not thought applicable to the States, and the Federal Government did not significantly regulate the possession of firearms by law-abiding citizens. Other provisions of the Bill of Rights have similarly remained unilluminated for lengthy periods. It is demonstrably not true that, as Justice Stevens claims, "for most of our history, the invalidity of Second-Amendment-based objections to firearms regulations has been well settled and uncontroversial." For most of our history the question did not present itself.

III

Like most rights, the right secured by the Second Amendment is not unlimited. Commentators and courts routinely explained that the right was not a right to keep and carry any weapon whatsoever in any manner whatsoever and for whatever purpose. Although we do not undertake an exhaustive historical analysis today of the full scope of the Second Amendment, nothing in our opinion should be taken to cast doubt on longstanding prohibitions on the possession of firearms by felons and the mentally ill, or laws forbidding the carrying of firearms in sensitive places such as schools and government buildings, or laws imposing conditions and qualifications on the commercial sale of arms.

IV

We turn finally to the law at issue here. As we have said, the law totally bans handgun possession in the home. It also requires that any lawful firearm in the home be disassembled or bound by a trigger lock at all times, rendering it inoperable.

As the quotations earlier in this opinion demonstrate, the inherent right of self-defense has been central to the Second Amendment right. The handgun ban amounts to a prohibition of an entire class of "arms" that is overwhelmingly chosen by American society for that lawful purpose. The prohibition extends, moreover, to the home, where the need for defense of self, family, and property is most acute. Under any of the standards of scrutiny that we have applied to enumerated constitutional rights, banning from the home "the most preferred firearm in the nation to 'keep' and use for protection of one's home and family," would fail constitutional muster.

Few laws in the history of our Nation have come close to the severe restriction of the District's handgun ban.

It is no answer to say, as petitioners do, that it is permissible to ban the possession of handguns so long as the possession of other firearms (i.e., long guns) is allowed. It is enough to note, as we have observed, that the American people have considered the handgun to be the quintessential self-defense weapon. There are many reasons that a citizen may prefer a handgun for home defense: It is easier to store in a location that is readily accessible in an emergency; it cannot easily be redirected or wrestled away by an attacker; it is easier to use for those without the upper-body strength to lift and aim a long gun; it can be pointed at a burglar with one hand while the other hand dials the police. Whatever the reason, handguns are the most popular weapon chosen by Americans for self-defense in the home, and a complete prohibition of their use is invalid.

We must also address the District's requirement (as applied to respondent's handgun) that firearms in the home be rendered and kept inoperable at all times. This makes it impossible for citizens to use them for the core lawful purpose of self-defense and is hence unconstitutional.

In sum, we hold that the District's ban on handgun possession in the home violates the Second Amendment, as does its prohibition against rendering any lawful firearm in the home operable for the purpose of immediate self-defense. Assuming that Heller is not disqualified from the exercise of Second Amendment rights, the District must permit him to register his handgun and must issue him a license to carry it in the home.

We are aware of the problem of handgun violence in this country, and we take seriously the concerns raised by the many *amici* who believe that prohibition of handgun ownership is a solution. The Constitution leaves the District of Columbia a variety of tools for combating that problem, including some measures regulating handguns. But the enshrinement of constitutional rights necessarily takes certain policy choices off the table. These include the absolute prohibition of handguns held and used for self-defense in the home. Undoubtedly some think that the Second Amendment is outmoded in a society where our standing army is the pride of our Nation, where well-trained police forces provide personal security, and where gun violence is a serious problem. That is perhaps debatable, but what is not debatable is that it is not the role of this Court to pronounce the Second Amendment extinct.

We affirm the judgment of the Court of Appeals.

It is so ordered.

4.4

ANDREW R. LEWIS

From *The Rights Turn in Conservative Christian Politics: How Abortion Transformed the Culture Wars*

Lewis describes a critical turning point in contemporary American politics, when conservative organizations and the Republican Party adopted ideas and language forcefully pressing for "rights" of speech and religion. In previous eras, promoting individual rights tended to be more common among liberal (left) organizations. Yet, recently, seeing themselves as having minority viewpoints in the areas of reproductive freedom (e.g., abortion) and gay rights, conservative groups, especially those promoting anti-abortion and Christian evangelical causes, have fought and won court and legislative battles to preserve their right to free speech. Two examples: whether state governments can regulate what doctors say to patients about abortion, and whether business owners must provide contraception coverage to employees. Conservative groups, and Republican voters in surveys, increasingly find themselves promoting legal interpretations promoting free speech against government intrusion.

RIGHTS ON THE RIGHT

In the spring of 2015, a diverse group of activists gathered to celebrate their victory in a hard-fought battle for the government protection of their rights. The achievement would fulfill essential constitutional guarantees and prevent this class of citizens from discrimination. Their victory was countered with prodigious backlash, resulting in a narrower protection than they desired, but the advocates prevailed. Those seeking the protection of their individual rights triumphed, which should come as no surprise. Rights are the currency of American politics, and rights-based arguments have been victorious for the better part of the past century.

What is surprising, however, is *who* was making this argument. This is not the story of gay marriage, with gay rights activists achieving the right for LGBT people to marry whom they wish via the Supreme Court's 5–4 decision in *Obergefell v. Hodges* (2015). Rather, this is the story of the 2015 Indiana Religious Freedom Restoration Act (RFRA), a measure passed by the Indiana

From Andrew R. Lewis, *The Rights Turn in Conservative Christian Politics: How Abortion Transformed the Culture Wars* (Cambridge, UK: Cambridge University Press, 2017).

legislature providing robust protections for religious freedom. This is the story of *conservatives*, not liberals.

More importantly, the battle over religious freedom in Indiana is emblematic of a seismic shift in American politics. Conservatives are now using typically liberal arguments, promoting *individual rights*. Conservatives are wielding these rights arguments with increasing frequency in judicial courts and courts of public opinion. And religious conservatives, such as evangelical Protestants and some Catholics, are at the helm, winning political victories and gaining legal protection. The result is a refashioning of the American "culture war." The political right has turned to rights. In the process, conservative Christians have shifted from protecting community morality to embracing certain liberties, particularly as free speech and religious liberty. Evangelicals, and their Christian Right allies, have been baptized into political liberalism. At least in *public* life, they have been converted; they now speak in the tongues of liberty, being filled with the rights spirit.

This change is monumental. Traditionally, as liberalism has been entrenched in rights,[1] conservatism, especially religious conservatism, has emphasized common morality, personal responsibility, and civic republicanism. In the process, religious conservatism has objected to liberalism's demand that religious and moral arguments be secularized.[2] These liberal and conservative viewpoints, while certainly not uniform, can be traced to variant perspectives on American democracy, with James Madison emphasizing pluralism and the respect for difference and Alexis de Tocqueville and John Adams emphasizing similarity. While liberals typically emphasized rights, conservatives typically promoted moral communities.

Building on this, Robert Bellah, the famed sociologist of culture, and his colleagues have identified different strands of American culture: biblical, republican, utilitarian individualist, and expressive individualist. The biblical and republican strands have been tied to political conservatism, while the individualist strands have been tied to liberalism.[3] The change for religious conservatives, then, is from a biblical conservatism to a utilitarian individualism, from communitarianism to pluralism, from morality to liberty.

Scholars are noticing this shift, with recent work identifying secular conservatives' transition toward libertarianism in free speech politics.[4] But scant attention has been given to religious conservatives in this process. Conservative Christians are now more supportive of political liberalism, though they continue to reject many items of expressive individualism, particularly individualist approaches to sexual morality. Rights then are more political, and less expressive in nature, for evangelicals and other religious conservatives.

The adoption of this form of liberalism is quite noteworthy. Only two decades ago some on the right argued that it was anathema to engage in liberal "rights talk." Harvard legal scholar Mary Ann Glendon, for example, in her 1991 book *Rights Talk*, delivered a sharp conservative critique of rights discourse. She argued:

Our rights talk, in its absoluteness, promotes unrealistic expectations, heightens social conflict, and inhibits dialogue that might lead toward consensus, accommodation, or at least discovery of common ground. In its silence concerning responsibilities, it seems to condone acceptance of the benefits of living in a democratic social welfare state, without accepting the corresponding personal and civic obligations. In its relentless individualism, it fosters a climate that is inhospitable to society's losers, and that systematically disadvantages caretakers and dependents, young and old.[5]

Despite this warning, religious conservatives, who were often seen as the last vestige of communitarianism as well as defenders [of] civic republicanism in American politics, have come to embrace rights and rights talk. Notwithstanding setbacks in the 2016 presidential campaign, political liberalism seems to be triumphing, as evangelicals and their allies increasingly turn to rights, particularly the utilitarian, political version of individualism. Due to the changing demographics in America, with white Christians increasingly becoming less of a numerical and cultural majority, this is likely to persist. Diversity will foster pluralism and rights politics.

▪   ▪   ▪

THE RIGHTS SHIFT

On some level, we should not be surprised that conservatives have come to utilize rights arguments. Individual rights are central to both American culture and American politics, profoundly affecting politics and law.[6] Though there has been some debate about the nature of rights and individualism in the American Founding,[7] the language of rights permeates American politics. While not exclusive values, individualism and liberty have also been prominent in American religious culture, influencing approaches to church-life, personal morality, and public policy.[8]

The American rights culture, however, has long been the domain of liberals, especially as the role of rights has increased in law and politics over the past century in what has been called the "rights revolution."[9] Liberal legal organizations developed sophisticated strategies to gain short- and long-term victories,[10] defeating conservatives with their rights-based arguments. These included victories in civil rights and civil liberties. In the area of civil rights, for example, African Americans gained access to the ballot box, black and white children were required to attend public school together, women and men were generally to receive equal legal treatment, and restaurants and hotels were required to serve all races. Extending civil liberties, women gained access to the birth control pill and abortions, the criminally accused received state-funded lawyers and the right-to-remain silent, gay sex was decriminalized and gay marriage was legalized, and Muslims were able to retain their beards in prison.

But even more, the secular and religious liberal successes in individual rights were largely responsible for activating the "culture wars" in American politics, pitting liberal individualists who were focused on rights against conservative traditionalists who were focused on morality.[11] Even after seeing their lost ground in the culture and before the Supreme Court in the latter half of the twentieth century, conservatives' initial push was not to pitch rights-based arguments, but to urge for limited government and law and order.[12] In fact, as discussed above, there was an aversion to doing so.[13]

I suggest that now the role of rights in American politics has been transformed; the paradox is that conservatives, particularly religious conservatives, have come to share the mantle of rights-based advocacy with liberals, though their focus on rights is centered more on political individualism than expressive individualism. These conservatives have shifted from defending cultural and biblical morality to cultivating a rights-based advocacy strategy, achieving considerable success in politics and especially law. In fact, some of this advocacy serves the dual purpose of expanding religious individualism while preserving elements of traditional morality.[14] Abortion politics are amenable to this opportunity.

Regarding morality, conservative rights talk has been used to counter other individual rights claims, seeking to reduce contraceptive coverage, fight nondiscrimination provisions, and protect the role of religion in public life. In addition, conservative rights claims are proffered to counter common good policies favored by liberals, such as limitations on campaign contributions, the separation of church and state, and national health insurance. At the same time, conservative rights claims are supporting political rights of radicals and minorities. These rights claims use individualism to preserve traditional morality, if not for the entire country at least for the religious sect. In the process, conservative Christian activists are making legal and political justifications that would have been controversial, if not untenable, only a generation ago. Some of their issue positions are quite different, too, though others are merely refashioned with the veneer of rights talk. In the process, the culture wars have been refashioned.

Free speech law is a notable example. . . . For much of the twentieth century, minority and radical political groups, such as the Ku Klux Klan and the Socialist Party, libertine social critics and so-called "smut peddlers" like comedian Lenny Bruce and Hustler founder Larry Flynt, respectively, were the frequent participants in free speech cases. Liberal mainstays such as the American Civil Liberties Union (ACLU) often defended these organizations and individuals. Conservatives, and particularly conservative evangelicals, were the supporters of the rule of law, order, and common morality. In the past two decades, this has changed for conservatives, with evangelical elites and organizations promoting an expansion of the individual rights approach to free speech, particularly in the areas of public protesting, campaign finance, and student speech.[15] Now those suing for their free speech rights include a school-aged religious group, the Good News Club, an anti-abortion organization, the Susan B. Anthony's List, and a religious wedding photographer from New Mexico, Elaine Huguenin.

HOW HAVE WE GOTTEN HERE?

Some prior research has identified this shift in conservative politics, highlighting conservatives' coopting the language of liberalism,[16] engaging in deliberative discourse,[17] and embracing libertarian approaches to free speech and other rights advocacy.[18] But what underlies the rights-based advocacy change? The previous studies suggest that political pragmatism, professionalization, and policy venue are causes, yet these works are largely silent on how religious conservatism cultivated rights arguments.[19] Scholars have underappreciated the breadth and underanalyzed the mechanisms that produced the religious conservative evolution in rights politics. In contrast, I tell the story of this rights evolution via its primary mechanism—abortion politics.

Following the Supreme Court's *Roe v. Wade* decision in 1973, anti-abortion activists became solidified as a political minority, and minority politics are often focused on rights and legal challenges. . . . Moreover, because it is an "easy issue," elites have utilized abortion to expand the domain of evangelical advocacy. As evangelicals have grown more accepting of their minority status, prompted by abortion politics and rising cultural diversity, they have turned toward rights.

There are two primary areas where individual rights have found a home in conservative Christian politics—religious liberty and abortion. Some religious groups were long-engaged on topics of rights and liberties, though most are newcomers. For much of American history, the Baptists were fervent defenders of the individual right to religious liberty,[20] though they often did so via the communitarian approach of church-state separation.[21] In the post–New Deal period, Catholic Christians, too, developed a commitment for a universal, individual right—the *right to life*—though it was wielded in service of their desire to protect common morality and sexual mores. . . .[22] Catholics increasingly framed their anti-abortion position in the language of human rights—the individual right to life—resulting in the creation of the National Right to Life Committee (NRLC) in 1968. Evangelicals were slow to adopt the Catholic position on abortion, and evangelicals and Catholics were often enemies in many public affairs battles.[23] Still, evangelicals increasingly opposed legalized abortion, though for a variety of reasons, including opposition to feminism and sexual freedom. Yet, in the mid-late 1970s evangelical thinker and apologist, Francis Schaeffer, helped bring the Catholic, rights-oriented opposition to abortion to evangelicalism, merging individual rights with cultural moral decline.[24] In short order, evangelicals joined Catholics to promote opposition to abortion, as the former enemies became allies.[25] By the second wave of the Christian Right activism in the 1990s, the right-to-life argument had come to the fore.[26] In due time, the Catholic human rights (or natural rights) approach to anti-abortion became the dominant public frame for evangelical activists. This prompted learning about the power of individual rights arguments and an application by activists to other policy areas.

▪   ▪   ▪

This has promoted an expansion of rights-based advocacy . . . as leaders found connections to these rights issues in abortion politics and other domains, and either expanded or altered their advocacy to support their pro-life and pro-religious freedom positions. The expanding rights sphere helped establish a minority politics perspective, often in service to protecting cultural morality. The activation of minority and rights politics among conservatives has also yielded secondary effects. The rights turn has yielded greater support for the rights to others, even disfavored groups.

▪   ▪   ▪

ABORTION AND CONTEMPORARY RFRA BATTLES

The link to abortion politics becomes quite clear as we consider the opening example from Indiana. In Indiana, one of the leading voices supporting the RFRA bill was the state's chapter of the National Right to Life Committee—a largely religious organization leading the anti-abortion movement.[27] [S]ome background regarding RFRA is illustrative. While many now consider opposition to abortion and religious freedom to be congruent ideological positions of American religious conservatives, this was not always the case. In fact, when the national RFRA legislation was debated in the early 1990s, many pro-life groups were concerned that the legislation might *promote* abortion. Some conservative anti-abortion groups, including the Southern Baptist Convention (SBC) and the U.S. Conference of Catholic Bishops (USCCB), were afraid that individuals might bring suits claiming that their religious beliefs necessitated their access to abortion coverage.[28] Such claims could override limitations on federal funding for abortion, commonly known as the Hyde Amendment. In the 1990s, liberal religious freedom advocates convinced conservatives that this was unlikely, and the legislation eventually passed with little opposition.

Nonetheless, a much different situation currently exists. Shortly after the passage of the Indiana RFRA, Mike Fichter, President of Indiana Right to Life, praised the bill for protecting anti-abortion advocates. "RFRA is an important bill to protect the religious freedom of Hoosiers who believe that the right to life comes from God, not government," he said.[29] While the RFRA coalition in Indiana was diverse, pro-life, pro-family conservatives dominated it. They sought to use rights politics to promote traditional morality and religious pluralism.

The connection between abortion politics and other rights claims, such as religious liberty, is an important shift in conservative politics. It helps explain the fundamental tension in American democracy between rights and morality, and it is an exemplar of the shifting role of religion in society.

Pro-life groups became especially interested in religious liberty concerns following the 2010 Affordable Care Act (ACA), which expanded health care coverage, and the following contraceptive coverage mandate. Religious individuals and groups sought protection from being required to provide insurance that covered contraceptives, a handful of which were said to cause abortions by ending a pregnancy shortly after conception (e.g., the "morning after" pill). These anti-abortion groups used the federal RFRA statute to gain greater protections from the courts, resulting in the 2014 Supreme Court case *Burwell v. Hobby Lobby*, in which the pro-life groups prevailed. Abortion politics triggered an emphasis on religious liberty advocacy, which has since been transferred to the domain of gay rights. As such, abortion politics has been instrumental to the expansion of conservative religious advocacy in the United States.

For most of the policy areas, abortion also contributed to evangelical Christians shifting their views over the past forty years. Abortion has been a prominent cause in evangelicals supporting a broader, more individual right to free speech, and it contributed to an increased focus on religious liberty as opposed to church-state separation. It has altered the considerations in debates regarding health care and the death penalty, and it is serving as an object lesson following the nationwide legalization of same-sex marriage. Consequently, the politics of abortion has transformed the landscape of conservative politics.

Certainly abortion is not the only thing affecting the conservative political views of the Christian Right. Still, the politics of abortion remains central. Abortion politics, especially as combined with evangelical minority politics, has taught evangelicals about rights and the political process, and it is often the substantive frame motivating other issue positions.

NOTES

1. See e.g., John Rawls, *Political Liberalism*, expanded ed. (New York: Columbia University Press, 2005). Ronald Dworkin, *Taking Rights Seriously* (Cambridge, MA: Harvard University Press, 1978).

2. See e.g., Stephen L. Carter, *The Culture of Disbelief* (New York: Anchor, 1991). Robert P. George, *Making Men Moral: Civil Liberties and Public Morals* (New York: Oxford University Press, 1995).

3. Robert N. Bellah et al., *Habits of the Heart: Individualism and Commitment in American Life* (Berkeley: University of California Press, 1985), 27–35.

4. Wayne Batchis, *The Right's First Amendment: The Politics of Free Speech and the Return of Conservative Libertarianism* (Stanford, CA: Stanford University Press, 2016).

5. Mary Ann Glendon, *Rights Talk: The Impoverishment of Political Discourse* (New York: Free Press, 1991), 14.

6. Louis Hartz, *The Liberal Tradition in America: An Interpretation of Political Thought* (New York: Harcourt, Brace, and World, 1955).

7. See e.g., John P. Diggins, *The Lost Soul of American Politics: Virtue, Self-Interest, and the Foundations of Liberalism* (Chicago: University of Chicago Press, 1984). Russell L. Hanson, *The Democratic Imagination in America: Conversations with Our Past* (Princeton, NJ: Princeton University Press, 1985). Barry Alan Shain, *The Myth of American Individualism: The Protestant Origins of American Political Thought* (Princeton, NJ: Princeton University Press, 1994). Rogers M. Smith, "Beyond Tocqueville, Myrdal, and Hartz: The Multiple Traditions in America," *American Political Science Review* 87, no. 3 (1993). Michael P. Zuckert, *The Natural Rights Republic: Studies in the Foundation of the American Political Tradition* (South Bend, IN: University of Notre Dame Press, 1996).

8. See e.g., William McLoughlin, *Soul Liberty: The Baptists' Struggle in New England, 1630–1833* (Hanover, NH: University Press of New England, 1991). Rhys H. Williams, "Visions of the Good Society and the Religious Roots of American Political Culture," *Sociology of Religion* 60, no. 1 (1999). John Witte, Jr., *The Reformation of Rights: Law, Religion, and Human Rights in Early Modern Calvinism* (New York: Cambridge University Press, 2007).

9. Richard L. Pacelle, Jr., *The Transformation of the Supreme Court's Agenda: From the New Deal to the Reagan Administration* (Boulder, CO: Westview Press, 1991).

10. See e.g., Charles R. Epp, *The Rights Revolution: Lawyers, Activists, and Supreme Courts in Comparative Perspective* (Chicago: University of Chicago Press, 1998). Jonathan Goldberg-Hiller, *The Limits to Union: Same-Sex Marriage and the Politics of Civil Rights* (Ann Arbor: University of Michigan Press, 2004). Michael W. McCann, *Rights at Work: Pay Equity Reform and the Politics of Legal Mobilization* (Chicago: University of Chicago Press, 1994). Mark V. Tushnet, *NAACP's Legal Strategy against Segregated Education, 1925–1950* (Chapel Hill: University of North Carolina Press, 2005).

11. James Davison Hunter, *Culture Wars: The Struggle to Define America* (New York: Basic Books, 1991).

12. Steven M. Teles, *The Rise of the Conservative Legal Movement: The Battle for Control of the Law* (Princeton, NJ: Princeton University Press, 2008).

13. Glendon, *Rights Talk*.

14. Ted G. Jelen, "Political Esperanto: Rhetorical Resources and Limitations of the Christian Right in the United States," *Sociology of Religion* 66, no. 3 (2005).

15. Batchis, *The Right's First Amendment*.

16. Matthew C. Moen, "From Revolution to Evolution: The Changing Nature of the Christian Right," *Sociology of Religion* 55, no. 3 (1994). Jelen, "Political Esperanto."

17. Jon A. Shields, *The Democratic Virtues of the Christian Right* (Princeton, NJ: Princeton University Press, 2009).

18. Steven P. Brown, *Trumping Religion: The New Christian Right, the Free Speech Clause, and the Courts* (Tuscaloosa: University of Alabama Press, 2002); Hans J. Hacker, *The Culture of Conservative Christian Litigation* (Lanham, MD: Rowman & Littlefield, 2005). Teles, *The Rise of the Conservative Legal Movement*. Joshua C. Wilson, *The Street Politics of Abortion: Speech, Violence, and America's Culture Wars* (Stanford, CA: Stanford University Press, 2013). Batchis, *The Right's First Amendment*.

19. Batchis's *The Right's First Amendment* is an exception here, as he identifies the reemergence of libertarian stream of American conservatism as the primary cause of the right's shift in free speech advocacy.

20. Barry Hankins, *Uneasy in Babylon: Southern Baptist Conservatives and American Culture* (Tuscaloosa: University of Alabama Press, 2002). William McLoughlin, *New England Dissent 1960–1833: The Baptists and the Separation of Church and State* (Cambridge, MA: Harvard University Press, 1971).

21. Philip Hamburger, *Separation of Church and State* (Cambridge, MA: Harvard University Press, 2002). Andrew R. Lewis, "Abortion Politics and the Decline of the Separation of Church and State: The Southern Baptist Case," *Politics & Religion* 7, no. 3 (2014).

22. Daniel K. Williams, *Defenders of the Unborn: The Pro-Life Movement before Roe v. Wade* (New York: Oxford University Press, 2016).

23. See Hamburger, *Separation of Church and State.*

24. Williams, *Defenders of the Unborn.*

25. Lewis, "Abortion Politics and the Decline of the Separation of Church and State." Carin Robinson, "Cross-Cutting Messages and Political Tolerance: An Experiment Using Evangelical Protestants," *Political Behavior* 32, no. 4 (2010).

26. For elites and pro-life rights, see: Moen, "From Revolution to Evolution." For the mass public and pro-life rights, see: Ted G. Jelen, "Changes in the Attitudinal Correlates of Opposition to Abortion," *Journal for the Scientific Study of Religion* 27, no. 2 (1988).

27. Chapter 2 will provide more detail about the history of National Right to Life Committee and its relationship between Catholics and evangelicals.

28. For the Southern Baptists, see: "Religious Liberty Bill before Congress Highlights Difference among Baptists," *SBC Today*, July 26, 1991; Brian Bolduc, "The Church and the RFRA," *National Review*, February 17, 2012.

29. Tony Cook, "Gov. Mike Pence Signs 'Religious Freedom' Bill in Private," *Indiana Star*, April 2, 2015.

DISCUSSION QUESTIONS

1. Can Republicans improve their standing among racial minorities in the United States, or is it a lost cause?

2. Which doctrine that came out of *Plessy v. Ferguson* was rejected by the Supreme Court in *Brown v. Board of Education*? Why did the Court claim that this earlier doctrine violated the Equal Protection Clause of the Fourteenth Amendment as applied to segregated schools?

3. Describe the two competing arguments over the Second Amendment at stake in *District of Columbia v. Heller*. Why did one argument win out over the other argument?

4. Discuss the ways in which free speech rights are not absolute. Which restrictions on speech rights are conservatives fighting against?

5. Take a controversial political issue from current events and discuss how it involves a trade-off of one right or liberty against another right or liberty. How are these controversies typically resolved in the American political system, if they are in fact resolved?

5

CONGRESS

5.1

DAVID R. MAYHEW

From *Congress: The Electoral Connection*

In this classic work on Congress, Mayhew asks: What would Congress look like and how would members of Congress behave if they were solely interested in one thing: getting reelected? Mayhew says they would posture and preen, but also occasionally produce valuable legislation. In other words, it would look like the Congress we actually observe in the United States.

Mostly through personal experience on Capitol Hill, I have become convinced that scrutiny of purposive behavior offers the best route to an understanding of legislatures—or at least of the United States Congress. In the fashion of economics, I shall make a simple abstract assumption about human motivation and then speculate about the consequences of behavior based on that motivation. Specifically, I shall conjure up a vision of United States congressmen as single-minded seekers of reelection, see what kinds of activity that goal implies, and then speculate about how congressmen so motivated are likely to go about building and sustaining legislative institutions and making policy. At all points I shall try to match the abstract with the factual.

I find an emphasis on the reelection goal attractive for a number of reasons. First, I think it fits political reality rather well. Second, it puts the spotlight directly on men rather than on parties and pressure groups, which in the past have often entered discussions of American politics as analytic phantoms.

From David R. Mayhew, *Congress: The Electoral Connection* (New Haven, CT: Yale University Press, 1974).

Third, I think politics is best studied as a struggle among men to gain and maintain power and the consequences of that struggle. Fourth—and perhaps most important—the reelection quest establishes an accountability relationship with an electorate, and any serious thinking about democratic theory has to give a central place to the question of accountability. The abstract assumption notwithstanding, I regard this venture as an exercise in political science rather than economics. Leaving aside the fact that I have no economics expertise to display, I find that economists who study legislatures bring to bear interests different from those of political scientists. Not surprisingly, the public finance scholars tend to look upon government as a device for spending money. I shall give some attention to spending, but also to other governmental activities such as the production of binding rules. And I shall touch upon such traditional subjects of political science as elections, parties, governmental structure, and regime stability. Another distinction here is that economics research tends to be infused with the normative assumption that policy decisions should be judged by how well they meet the standard of Pareto optimality. This is an assumption that I do not share and that I do not think most political scientists share. There will be no need here to set forth any alternative assumption. . . .

My subject of concern here is a single legislative institution, the United States Congress. In many ways, of course, the Congress is a unique or unusual body. It is probably the most highly "professionalized" of legislatures, in the sense that it promotes careerism among its members and gives them the salaries, staff, and other resources to sustain careers. Its parties are exceptionally diffuse. It is widely thought to be especially "strong" among legislatures as a checker of executive power. Like most Latin American legislatures but unlike most European ones, it labors in the shadow of a separately elected executive. My decision to focus on the Congress flows from a belief that there is something to be gained in an intensive analysis of a particular and important institution. But there is something general to be gained as well, for the exceptionalist argument should not be carried too far. In a good many ways the Congress is just one in a large family of legislative bodies. I shall find it useful at various points in the analysis to invoke comparisons with European parliaments and with American state legislatures and city councils. I shall ponder the question of what "functions" the Congress performs or is capable of performing—a question that can be answered only with the records of other legislatures in mind. Functions to be given special attention are those of legislating, overseeing the executive, expressing public opinion, and servicing constituents. No functional capabilities can be automatically assumed.[1] Indeed the very term *legislature* is an unfortunate one because it confuses structure and function. Accordingly, I shall here on use the more awkward but more neutral term *representative assembly* to refer to members of the class of entities inhabited by the United States House and Senate. Whatever the noun, the identifying characteristics of institutions in the class have been well stated by Loewenberg: it is true of all such entities that (1) "their members are formally equal to each other in status, distinguishing parliaments from hierarchically ordered organizations," and (2) "the authority of their members depends on their claim to representing the rest of the community, in some sense of that protean concept, representation."[2]

The following discussion will take the form of an extended theoretical essay. Perforce it will raise more questions than it answers. As is the custom in mono-causal ventures, it will no doubt carry arguments to the point of exaggeration; finally, of course, I shall be satisfied to explain a significant part of the variance rather than all of it. What the discussion will yield, I hope, is a picture of what the United States Congress looks like if the reelection quest is examined seriously.

■ ■ ■

The ultimate concern here is not how probable it is that legislators will lose their seats but whether there is a connection between what they do in office and their need to be reelected. It is possible to conceive of an assembly in which no member ever comes close to losing a seat but in which the need to be reelected is what inspires members' behavior. It would be an assembly with no saints or fools in it, an assembly packed with skilled politicians going about their business. When we say "Congressman Smith is unbeatable," we do not mean that there is nothing he could do that would lose him his seat. Rather we mean, "Congressman Smith is unbeatable as long as he continues to do the things he is doing." If he stopped answering his mail, or stopped visiting his district, or began voting randomly on roll calls, or shifted his vote record eighty points on the ADA scale, he would bring on primary or November election troubles in a hurry. It is difficult to offer conclusive proof that this last statement is true, for there is no congressman willing to make the experiment. But normal political activity among politicians with healthy electoral margins should not be confused with inactivity. What characterizes "safe" congressmen is not that they are beyond electoral reach, but that their efforts are very likely to bring them uninterrupted electoral success.

Whether congressmen think their activities have electoral impact, and whether in fact they have impact, are of course two separate questions. Of the former there can be little doubt that the answer is yes. In fact, in their own minds successful politicians probably overestimate the impact they are having. Kingdon found in his Wisconsin candidates a "congratulation-rationalization effect," a tendency for winners to take personal credit for their victories and for losers to assign their losses to forces beyond their control. The actual impact of politicians' activities is more difficult to assess. The evidence on the point is soft and scattered. It is hard to find variance in activities undertaken, for there are no politicians who consciously try to lose. There is no doubt that the electorate's general awareness of what is going on in Congress is something less than robust. Yet the argument here will be that congressmen's activities in fact do have electoral impact. Pieces of evidence will be brought in as the discussion proceeds.

The next step here is to offer a brief conceptual treatment of the relation between congressmen and their electorates. In the Downsian analysis, what national party leaders must worry about is voters' "expected party differential." But to congressmen this is in practice irrelevant, for reasons specified earlier. A congressman's attention must rather be devoted to what can be called an "expected incumbent differential." Let us define this "expected incumbent differential" as any difference perceived by a relevant political actor between what an incumbent congressman is likely to do if returned to office and what any possible challenger (in primary or general election) would be likely to do. And let us define "relevant political actor" here as anyone who has a resource that might be used in the election in question. At the ballot box the only usable resources are votes, but there are resources that can be translated into votes: money, the ability to make persuasive endorsements, organizational skills, and so on. By this definition a "relevant political actor" need not be a constituent; one of the most important resources, money, flows all over the country in congressional campaign years.

It must be emphasized that the average voter has only the haziest awareness of what an incumbent congressman is actually doing in office. But an incumbent has to be concerned about actors who do form impressions about him, and especially about actors who can marshal resources other than their own votes. Senator Robert C. Byrd (D.-W.Va.) has a "little list" of 2,545 West Virginians he regularly keeps in touch with. A congressman's assistant interviewed for a Nader profile in 1972 refers to the "thought leadership" back in the district. Of campaign resources, one of the most vital is money. An incumbent not only has to assure that his own election funds are adequate, he has to try to minimize the probability that actors will bankroll an expensive campaign against him. There is the story that during the first Nixon term, Senator James B. Pearson (R.-Kans.) was told he would face a well-financed opponent in his 1972 primary if he did not display more party regularity in his voting. Availability of money can affect strength of opposition candidacy in both primary and general elections.

Another resource of significance is organizational expertise, probably more important than money among labor union offerings. Simple ability to do electioneering footwork is a resource the invoking of which may give campaigns an interesting twist. Leut-hold found in studying ten 1962 House elections in the San Francisco area that 50 percent of campaign workers held college degrees (as against 12 percent of the Bay area population), and that the workers were more issue oriented than the general population. The need to attract workers may induce candidates to traffic in issues more than they otherwise would. Former Congressman Allard K. Lowenstein (D.-N.Y.) has as his key invokable resource a corps of student volunteers who will follow him from district to district, making him an unusually mobile candidate.

Still another highly important resource is the ability to make persuasive endorsements. Manhattan candidates angle for the imprimatur of the *New York Times*. New Hampshire politics rotates around endorsements of the *Manchester Union Leader*. Labor union committees circulate their approved lists.

Chicago Democratic politicians seek the endorsement of the mayor. In the San Francisco area and elsewhere, House candidates try to score points by winning endorsements from officials of the opposite party. As Neustadt argues, the influence of the president over congressmen (of both parties) varies with his public prestige and with his perceived ability to punish and reward. One presidential tool is the endorsement, which can be carefully calibrated according to level of fervor, and which can be given to congressmen or to challengers running against congressmen. In the 1970 election, Senator Charles Goodell (R.-N.Y.), who had achieved public salience by attacking the Nixon administration, was apparently done in by the resources called forth by that attack; the vice president implicitly endorsed his Conservative opponent, and the administration acted to channel normally Republican money away from Goodell.

What a congressman has to try to do is to insure that in primary and general elections the resource balance (with all other deployed resources finally translated into votes) favors himself rather than somebody else. To maneuver successfully he must remain constantly aware of what political actors' incumbent differential readings are, and he must act in a fashion to inspire readings that favor himself. Complicating his task is the problem of slack resources. That is, only a very small proportion of the resources (other than votes) that are conceivably deployable in congressional campaigns are ever, in fact, deployed. But there is no sure way of telling who will suddenly become aroused and with what consequence. For example, just after the 1948 election the American Medical Association, unnerved by the medical program of the Attlee Government in Britain and by Democratic campaign promises here to institute national health insurance, decided to venture into politics. By 1950, congressmen on record as supporters of health insurance found themselves confronted by a million-dollar AMA advertising drive, local "healing arts committees" making candidate endorsements, and even doctors sending out campaign literature with their monthly bills. By 1952, it was widely believed that the AMA had decided some elections, and few congressmen were still mentioning health insurance.

In all his calculations the congressman must keep in mind that he is serving two electorates rather than one—a November electorate and a primary electorate nested inside it but not a representative sample of it. From the standpoint of the politician, a primary is just another election to be survived. A typical scientific poll of a constituency yields a congressman information on the public standing of possible challengers in the other party but also in his own party. A threat is a threat. For an incumbent with a firm "supporting coalition" of elite groups in his party, the primary electorate is normally quiescent. But there can be sudden turbulence. And it sometimes happens that the median views of primary and November electorates are so divergent on salient issues that a congressman finds it difficult to hold both electorates at once. This has been a recurrent problem among California Republicans.

A final conceptual point has to do with whether congressmen's behavior should be characterized as "maximizing" behavior. Does it make sense to visualize the congressman as a maximizer of vote percentage in elections—November or primary or, with some complex trade-off, both? For two reasons the answer is probably no. The first has to do with his goal itself, which is to stay in office rather than to win all the popular vote. More precisely his goal is to stay in office over a number of future elections, which does mean that "winning comfortably" in any one of them (except the last) is more desirable than winning by a narrow plurality. The logic here is that a narrow victory (in primary or general election) is a sign of weakness that can inspire hostile political actors to deploy resources intensively the next time around. By this reasoning the higher the election percentages the better. No doubt any congressman would engage in an act to raise his November figure from 80 percent to 90 percent if he could be absolutely sure that the act would accomplish the end (without affecting his primary percentage) and if it could be undertaken at low personal cost. But still, trying to "win comfortably" is not the same as trying to win all the popular vote. As the personal cost (e.g., expenditure of personal energy) of a hypothetical "sure gain" rises, the congressman at the 55 percent November level is more likely to be willing to pay it than his colleague at the 80 percent level.

■   ■   ■

Whether they are safe or marginal, cautious or audacious, congressmen must constantly engage in activities related to reelection. There will be differences in emphasis, but all members share the root need to do things—indeed, to do things day in and day out during their terms. The next step here is to present a typology, a short list of the *kinds* of activities congressmen find it electorally useful to engage in. The case will be that there are three basic kinds of activities. . . .

One activity is *advertising,* defined here as any effort to disseminate one's name among constituents in such a fashion as to create a favorable image but in messages having little or no issue content. A successful congressman builds what amounts to a brand name, which may have a generalized electoral value for other politicians in the same family. The personal qualities to emphasize are experience, knowledge, responsiveness, concern, sincerity, independence, and the like. Just getting one's name across is difficult enough; only about half the electorate, if asked, can supply their House members' names. It helps a congressman to be known. "In the main, recognition carries a positive valence; to be perceived at all is to be perceived favorably." A vital advantage enjoyed by House incumbents is that they are much better known among voters than their November challengers. They are better known because they spend a great deal of time, energy, and money trying to make themselves better known. There are standard routines—frequent visits to the constituency, nonpolitical speeches to home audiences, the sending out of infant care booklets and letters of condolence and congratulation. Of 158 House members questioned in the mid-1960s, 121 said that they regularly sent newsletters to their constituents; 48 wrote separate news or opinion columns for newspapers; 82 regularly reported to their constituencies by radio or television; 89 regularly sent out mail questionnaires. Some routines are less standard. Congressman George E. Shipley (D.-Ill.) claims to have met personally about half his constituents (i.e., some 200,000 people). For over twenty years, Congressman Charles C. Diggs, Jr. (D.-Mich.) has run a radio program featuring himself as a "combination disc jockey-commentator and minister." Congressman Daniel J. Flood (D.-Pa.) is "famous for appearing unannounced and often uninvited at wedding anniversaries and other events." Anniversaries and other events aside, congressional advertising is done largely at public expense. Use of the franking privilege has mushroomed in recent years; in early 1973, one estimate predicted that House and Senate members would send out about 476 million pieces of mail in the year 1974, at a public cost of $38.1 million—or about 900,000 pieces per member with a subsidy of $70,000 per member. By far the heaviest mailroom traffic comes in Octobers of even-numbered years. There are some differences between House and Senate members in the ways they go about getting their names across. House members are free to blanket their constituencies with mailings for all boxholders; senators are not. But senators find it easier to appear on national television—for example, in short reaction statements on the nightly news shows. Advertising is a staple congressional activity, and there is no end to it. For each member there are always new voters to be apprised of his worthiness and old voters to be reminded of it.

A second activity may be called *credit claiming*, defined here as acting so as to generate a belief in a relevant political actor (or actors) that one is personally responsible for causing the government, or some unit thereof, to do something that the actor (or actors) considers desirable. The political logic of this, from the congressman's point of view, is that an actor who believes that a member can make pleasing things happen will no doubt wish to keep him in office so that he can make pleasing things happen in the future. The emphasis here is on individual accomplishment (rather than, say, party or governmental accomplishment) and on the congressman as doer (rather than as, say, expounder of constituency views). Credit claiming is highly important to congressmen, with the consequence that much of congressional life is a relentless search for opportunities to engage in it.

Where can credit be found? If there were only one congressman rather than 535, the answer would in principle be simple enough. Credit (or blame) would attach in Downsian fashion to the doings of the government as a whole. But there are 535. Hence it becomes necessary for each congressman to try to peel off pieces of governmental accomplishment for which he can believably generate a sense of responsibility. For the average congressman, the staple way of doing this is to traffic in what may be called "particularized benefits." Particularized governmental benefits, as the term will be used here, have two properties: (1) Each benefit is given out to a specific individual, group, or geographical constituency, the recipient unit being of a scale that allows a single congressman to be recognized (by relevant political actors and other congressmen) as the claimant for the benefit (other congressmen being perceived as indifferent or hostile); (2) Each benefit is given out in apparently ad hoc fashion (unlike, say, social security checks) with a congressman apparently having a hand in the allocation. A particularized benefit can normally be regarded as a member of a class. That is, a benefit given out to an individual, group, or constituency can normally be looked upon by congressmen as one of a class of similar benefits given out to sizable numbers of individuals, groups, or constituencies. Hence the impression can arise that a congressman is getting "his share" of whatever it is the government is offering. (The classes may be vaguely defined. Some state legislatures deal in what their members call "local legislation.")

In sheer volume, the bulk of particularized benefits come under the heading of "casework"—the thousands of favors congressional offices perform for supplicants in ways that normally do not require legislative action. High school students ask for essay materials, soldiers for emergency leaves, pensioners for location of missing checks, local governments for grant information, and on and on. Each office has skilled professionals who can play the bureaucracy like an organ—pushing the right pedals to produce the desired effects. But many benefits require new legislation, or at least they require important allocative decisions on matters covered by existent legislation. Here the congressman fills the traditional role of supplier of goods to the home district. It is a believable role; when a member claims credit for a benefit on the order of a dam, he may well receive it. Shiny construction projects seem especially useful. In the decades before 1934, tariff duties for local industries were a major commodity. In recent years, awards given under grant-in-aid programs have become more useful as they have become more numerous. Some quests for credit are ingenious; in 1971 the story broke that congressmen had been earmarking foreign aid money for specific projects in Israel in order to win favor with home constituents. It should be said of constituency benefits that congressmen are quite capable of taking the initiative in drumming them up; that is, there can be no automatic assumption that a congressman's activity is the result of pressures brought to bear by organized interests. Fenno shows the importance of member initiative in his discussion of the House Interior Committee.

A final point here has to do with geography. The examples given so far are all of benefits conferred upon home constituencies or recipients therein (the latter including the home residents who applauded the Israeli projects). But the properties of particularized benefits were carefully specified so as not to exclude the possibility that some benefits may be given to recipients outside the home constituencies. Some probably are. Narrowly drawn tax loopholes qualify as particularized benefits, and some of them are probably conferred upon recipients outside the home districts. (It is difficult to find solid evidence on the point.) Campaign contributions flow into districts from the outside, so it would not be surprising to find that benefits go where the resources are.

How much particularized benefits count for at the polls is extraordinarily difficult to say. But it would be hard to find a congressman who thinks he can afford to wait around until precise information is available. The lore is that they count—furthermore, given home expectations, that they must be supplied in regular quantities for a member to stay electorally even with the board. Awareness of favors may spread beyond their recipients, building for a member a general reputation as a good provider. "Rivers Delivers." "He Can Do More For Massachusetts." A good example of Capitol Hill lore on electoral impact is given in this account of the activities of Congressman Frank Thompson, Jr. (D.-N.J., 4th district):

> In 1966, the 4th was altered drastically by redistricting; it lost Burlington County and gained Hunterdon, Warren, and Sussex. Thompson's performance at the polls since 1966 is a case study of how an incumbent congressman, out of line with his district's ideological persuasions, can become unbeatable. In 1966, Thompson carried Mercer by 23,000 votes and lost the three new counties by 4,600, winning reelection with 56% of the votes. He then survived a district-wide drop in his vote two years later. In 1970, the Congressman carried Mercer County by 20,000 votes and the rest of the district by 6,000, finishing with 58%. The drop in Mercer resulted from the attempt of his hard-line conservative opponent to exploit the racial unrest which had developed in Trenton. But for four years Thompson had been making friends in Hunterdon, Warren, and Sussex, busy doing the kind of chores that congressmen do. In this case, Thompson concerned himself with the interests of dairy farmers at the Department of Agriculture. The results of his efforts were clear when the results came in from the 4th's northern counties.

So much for particularized benefits. But is credit available elsewhere? For governmental accomplishments beyond the scale of those already discussed? The general answer is that the prime mover role is a hard one to play on larger matters—at least before broad electorates. A claim, after all, has to be credible. If a congressman goes before an audience and says, "I am responsible for passing a bill to curb inflation," or "I am responsible for the highway program," hardly anyone will believe him. There are two reasons why people may be skeptical of such claims. First, there is a numbers problem. On an accomplishment of a sort that probably engaged the supportive interest of more than one member, it is reasonable to suppose that credit should be apportioned among them. But second, there is an overwhelming problem of information costs. For typical voters, Capitol Hill is a distant and mysterious place; few have anything like a working knowledge of its maneuverings. Hence there is no easy way of knowing whether a congressman is staking a valid claim or not. The odds are that the information problem cuts in different ways on different kinds of issues. On particularized benefits it may work in a congressman's favor; he may get credit for the dam he had nothing to do with building. Sprinkling a district with dams, after all, is something a congressman is supposed to be able to do. But on larger matters it may work against him. For a voter lacking an easy way to sort out valid from invalid claims, the sensible recourse is skepticism. Hence it is unlikely that congressmen get much mileage out of credit claiming on larger matters before broad electorates.

Yet there is an obvious and important qualification here. For many congressmen, credit claiming on non-particularized matters is possible in specialized subject areas because of the congressional division of labor. The term "governmental unit" in the original definition of credit claiming is broad enough to include committees, subcommittees, and the two houses of Congress itself. Thus many congressmen can believably claim credit for blocking bills in subcommittee, adding on amendments in committee, and so on. The audience for transactions of this sort is usually small. But it may include important political actors (e.g., an interest group, the president, the *New York Times*, Ralph Nader) who are capable of both paying Capitol Hill information costs and deploying electoral resources. There is a well-documented example of this in Fenno's treatment of post office politics in the 1960s. The postal employee unions used to watch very closely the activities of the House and Senate Post Office Committees, and supply valuable electoral resources (money, volunteer work) to members who did their bidding on salary bills. Of course, there are many examples of this kind of undertaking, and there is more to be said about it.

The third activity congressmen engage in may be called *position taking*, defined here as the public enunciation of a judgmental statement on anything likely to be of interest to political actors. The statement may take the form of a roll call vote. The most important classes of judgmental statements are those prescribing American governmental ends (a vote cast against the war; a statement that "the war should be ended immediately") or governmental means (a statement that "the way to end the war is to take it to the United Nations"). The judgments may be implicit rather than explicit, as in: "I will support the president on this matter." But judgments may range far beyond these classes to take in implicit or explicit statements on what almost anybody should do or how he should do it: "The great Polish scientist Copernicus has been unjustly neglected"; "The way for Israel to achieve peace is to give up the Sinai." The congressman as position taker is a speaker rather than a doer. The electoral requirement is not that he make pleasing things happen but that he make pleasing judgmental statements. The position itself is the political commodity. Especially on matters where governmental responsibility is widely diffused, it is not surprising that political actors should fall back on positions as tests of incumbent virtue. For voters ignorant of congressional processes, the recourse is an easy one. The following comment by one of Clapp's House interviewees is highly revealing: "Recently, I went home and began to talk about the ———— act. I was pleased to have sponsored that bill, but it soon dawned on me that the point wasn't getting through at all. What was getting through was that the act might be a help to people. I changed the emphasis: I didn't mention my role particularly, but stressed my support of the legislation."

The ways in which positions can be registered are numerous and often imaginative. There are floor addresses ranging from weighty orations to mass-produced "nationality day statements." There are speeches before home groups, television appearances, letters, newsletters, press releases, ghostwritten books, *Playboy* articles, even interviews with political scientists. On occasion, congressmen generate what amount to petitions; whether or not to sign the 1956 Southern Manifesto defying school desegregation rulings was an important decision for southern members. Outside the roll call process the congressman is usually able to tailor his positions to suit his audiences. A solid consensus in the constituency calls for ringing declarations; for years the late Senator James K. Vardaman (D.-Miss.) campaigned on a proposal to repeal the Fifteenth Amendment. Division or uncertainty in the constituency calls for waffling; in the late 1960s, a congressman had to be a poor politician indeed not to be able to come up with an inoffensive statement on Vietnam ("We must have peace with honor at the earliest possible moment consistent with the national interest"). On a controversial issue, a Capitol Hill office normally prepares two form letters to send out to constituent letter writers—one for the pros and one (not directly contradictory) for the antis. Handling discrete audiences in person requires simple agility, a talent well demonstrated in this selection from a Nader profile:

> "You may find this difficult to understand," said Democrat Edward R. Roybal, the Mexican-American representative from California's thirtieth district, "but sometimes I wind up making a patriotic speech one afternoon and later on that same day an anti-war speech. In the patriotic speech I speak of past wars but I also speak of the need to prevent more wars. My positions are not inconsistent; I just approach different people differently." Roybal went on to depict the diversity of crowds he speaks to: one afternoon he is surrounded by balding men wearing Veterans' caps and holding American flags; a few hours later he speaks to a crowd of Chicano youths, angry over American involvement in Vietnam. Such a diverse constituency, Roybal believes, calls for different methods of expressing one's convictions.

Indeed it does. Versatility of this sort is occasionally possible in roll call voting. For example a congressman may vote one way on recommittal and the other on final passage, leaving it unclear just how he stands on a bill. Members who cast identical votes on a measure may give different reasons for having done so. Yet it is on roll calls that the crunch comes; there is no way for a member to avoid making a record on hundreds of issues, some of which are controversial in the home constituencies. Of course, most roll call positions considered in isolation are not likely to cause much of a ripple at home. But broad voting patterns can and do; member "ratings" calculated by the Americans for Democratic Action, Americans for Constitutional Action, and other outfits are used as guidelines in the deploying of electoral resources. And particular issues often have their alert publics. Some national interest groups watch the votes of all congressmen on single issues and ostentatiously try to reward or punish members for their positions; over the years some notable examples of such interest groups have been the Anti-Saloon League, the early Farm Bureau, the American Legion, the American Medical Association, and the National Rifle Association. On rare occasions, single roll calls achieve a rather high salience among the public generally. This seems especially true of the Senate, which every now and then winds up for what might be called a "showdown vote," with pressures on all sides, presidential involvement, media attention given to individual senators' positions, and suspense about the outcome. Examples are the votes on the nuclear test-ban treaty in 1963, civil rights cloture in 1964, civil rights cloture again in 1965, the Haynsworth appointment in 1969, the Carswell appointment in 1970, and the ABM in 1970. Controversies on roll calls like these are often relived in subsequent campaigns, the southern Senate elections of 1970 with their Haynsworth and Carswell issues being cases in point.

Probably the best position-taking strategy for most congressmen at most times is to be conservative—to cling to their own positions of the past where possible and to reach for new ones with great caution where necessary. Yet in an earlier discussion of strategy, the suggestion was made that it might be rational for members in electoral danger to resort to innovation. The form of innovation available is entrepreneurial position taking, its logic being that for a member facing defeat with his old array of positions it makes good sense to gamble on some new ones. It may be that congressional marginals fulfill an important function here as issue pioneers—experimenters who test out new issues and thereby show other politicians which ones are usable. An example of such a pioneer is Senator Warren Magnuson (D.-Wash.), who responded to a surprisingly narrow victory in 1962 by reaching for a reputation in the area of consumer affairs. Another example is Senator Ernest Hollings (D.-S.C.), a servant of a shaky and racially heterogeneous southern constituency who launched "hunger" as an issue in 1969—at once pointing to a problem and giving it a useful nonracial definition. One of the most successful issue entrepreneurs of recent decades was the late Senator Joseph McCarthy (R.-Wis.); it was all there—the close primary in 1946, the fear of defeat in 1952, the desperate casting about for an issue, the famous 1950 dinner at the Colony Restaurant where suggestions were tendered, the decision that "Communism" might just do the trick.

NOTES

1. "But it is equally true, though only of late and slowly beginning to be acknowledged, that a numerous assembly is as little fitted for the direct business of legislation as for that of administration." John Stuart Mill, *Considerations on Representative Government* (Chicago: Regency, 1962), p. 104.

2. Gerhard Loewenberg, "The Role of Parliaments in Modern Political Systems," in Loewenberg (ed.), *Modern Parliaments: Change or Decline?* (Chicago: Aldine-Atherton, 1971), p. 3.

5.2

RICHARD F. FENNO JR.

From *Home Style: House Members in Their Districts*

*Fenno's study of members of Congress leads him to consider four groups of peo-
ple that a typical representative considers subsets of his or her constituency: (1)
all people in the district, (2) those who tend to vote for the representative in general elections, (3) those who ardently support and vote for the representative in
primary elections, and (4) those who contribute money and time to the representative's reelection. These groups are like concentric circles surrounding the representative, and he or she has to pay careful attention to all four of these groups.*

What does a House member see when looking at his or her constituency?
Kaleidoscopic variety, no doubt. That is why there can be no one "correct"
way of slicing up and classifying member perceptions—only "helpful" ways.
Most helpful to me has been the member's view of a constituency as a nest
of concentric circles. In one form or another, in one expression or another, in
one degree or another, this bull's-eye perception is shared by all House members. It is helpful to us for the same reason it is common to them. It is a perception constructed out of the necessities of political life.

THE GEOGRAPHICAL CONSTITUENCY:
THE DISTRICT

The largest of the concentric circles represents the House member's most
encompassing view of his or her constituency. It is "the district," the entity to
which, from which, and within which the member travels. It is the entity whose
boundaries have been fixed by state legislative enactment or by court decision.
It includes the entire population within those boundaries. Because it is a legal
entity, we could refer to it as the legal constituency. We capture more of what
the member has in mind when conjuring up "my district," however, if we think
of it as the *geographical constituency*. We then retain the idea that the district is
a legally bounded space, and emphasize that it is located in a particular place.

The Washington community is often described as a group of people all of
whom come from somewhere else. The House of Representatives, by design,

From Richard F. Fenno Jr., *Home Style: House Members in Their Districts* (New York: Pearson
Longman, 2003).

epitomizes this characteristic; and its members function with a heightened sense of their ties to another place. There are, of course, constant reminders. The member's district is, after all, "the Tenth District of *California*." Inside the chamber, he is "the gentleman from *California*." In the media, he is "Representative Smith (D. *California*)." So it is not surprising that when you ask a member, "What kind of district do you have?" the answer often begins with, and nearly always includes, a geographical, space-and-place perception. Thus, the district is seen as "the largest in the state, twenty-eight counties in the southeastern corner," or "three layers of suburbs to the west of the city, a square with the northwest corner cut out," or "a core district, the core of the city." If the boundaries have been changed by a recent redistricting, the geography of "the new district" will be compared to that of "the old district": "I picked up five northern counties and lost two on the eastern edge. The new district is a lot more spread out."

If one essential aspect of "the geographical constituency" is seen as its location and boundaries, another is its internal makeup. And House members describe their districts' internal makeup using political science's most familiar demographic and political variables: socioeconomic structure, ideology, ethnicity, residential patterns, religion, partisanship, stability, diversity, etc. Every congressman, in his mind's eye, sees his geographical constituency in terms of some special configuration of such variables.

■ ■ ■

THE REELECTION CONSTITUENCY: THE SUPPORTERS

Each congressman does perceive an explicitly political constituency nested within his geographical constituency. It is composed of those people in the district who he thinks vote for him. We shall call it his *reelection constituency*. But, because all members do not perceive their support in coalitional terms and because all members do see support in reelection terms, we shall use the more universal language.[1] As they move about "the district," House members continually draw the distinction between those people who vote for them and those who do not: "I do well here"; "I run poorly here"; "This group supports me"; "This group does not." By distinguishing supporters from nonsupporters, they articulate their fundamental political perception.

House members use two reference points—one cross-sectional, the other longitudinal—in shaping this perception. First, by a process of inclusion and exclusion, they come to a rough approximation of the upper and lower ranges of the reelection constituency. That is to say, there are some votes a member believes he nearly always gets. There are other votes he believes he almost never gets. Among those he thinks he usually gets, the perceived partisan component of the electorate is always a basic element. Every member begins with a perception of his partisan support—estimated by registration figures or poll data, and by political demography.

It's a good Democratic district now—59 percent registered Democrats. And for the first time I feel safe. . . . I used to brag that my old district was the wealthiest, best-educated district in the country represented by a Democrat. But I wasn't a bit sad to give up the wealthy part of the district and pick up all those poor, ill-educated good Democrats in the new part of the district.

When the partisan composition of the district is clearly insufficient for reelection, members express ideas about the nature of their cross-party supporters.

My district registers only 37 percent Republican. And they have no place else to go. My problem is, how can I get enough Democratic votes to win the general election. . . . Civil servants, bank clerks, insurance salesmen, bricklayers, carpenters, the craft unions; these have been the mainstream of my Democratic support—middle class and working class. . . . The hard hats are the people most likely to vote for me. That's my lucrative territory—not the liberal, intellectual wing [of the Democratic party].

Every member has some idea of the people most likely to join his reelection constituency, his "lucrative territory." During a campaign, these people will often be "targeted" and subjected to special recruiting or activating efforts.

A congressman's sense of the people least likely to join his reelection constituency is usually as well developed as his sense for his "lucrative territory." Comments like "I'll never carry this town"; "This part of the district is hopeless"; "I've never been able to crack these space industry guys"; "I'd love to get the pickup truck vote, but I never do" punctuate his travels in the district. If a member chooses to attack "the special interests" in his district, it is from these perceived never-supporters that the objects of his attacks will come.

■　■　■

Thinking about "last time's" electoral margin, if it was an apparently safe one, should assuage a good deal of a representative's uncertainty about his reelection constituency. And it does. But it does not produce certainty. Far from it. Most House members will have experienced, at some point in their careers, "the fight of my life"—a testing election they felt especially hard-pressed to win. When members recall their testing elections, they dwell on the immense organizational and personal efforts required to win.

THE PRIMARY CONSTITUENCY: THE STRONGEST SUPPORTERS

In thinking about their political condition, House members make distinctions *within* their reelection constituency, thus giving us a third, still smaller perceptual circle. Having distinguished between their nonsupporters and their supporters, they further distinguish between their weak supporters and their strong supporters. Weak supporters come in both the routine and the temporary varieties. Routine supporters do no more than vote for the member, often simply following party identification. Temporary supporters back the member as the best available alternative "this time," as "the lesser of two evils." Strong supporters display an intensity capable of producing additional political activity, and they tender their support "through thick and thin," regardless of who the challenger may be. Within each reelection constituency, then, nests a smaller constituency perceived as "my strongest supporters," "my loyalists," "my true believers," "my political base," "my hard core," "my nucleus," "my tough nut," "my bread basket." We shall think of these people as the ones each congressman believes would provide his last line of electoral defense in a primary contest, and label them the *primary constituency*.[2] We do not mean this label to include all the people who vote for him in a primary, only those from whom he expects a special solidity of support in a primary election.

A protected congressional seat is one protected as much from primary defeat as from general election defeat. And a primary constituency is something every congressman must have one of.

▪   ▪   ▪

THE PERSONAL CONSTITUENCY: THE INTIMATES

Within the primary constituency, House members perceive still a fourth, and final, concentric circle. These are the few individuals whose relationship with the member is so personal and so intimate that their relevance cannot be captured by any description of "very strongest supporters." Some of them are his closest political advisers and confidants. Others are people from whom he draws emotional sustenance for his political work. They are all people with whom the congressman has shared some crucial experience—usually early in his career, and often the "testing election." Times of relaxation are thick with reminiscence. Fellow feeling is heavily "we few, we happy few, we band of brothers." Sometimes a staff assistant is among these intimates; sometimes not. Sometimes the member's spouse is involved, but not always. These are the people, if any, to whom he has entrusted his political career. He can meet with all of them in one place, face to face, as he cannot with any of his other constituencies. He knows them by name, as individuals. He thinks of them as his friends. "A guy is lucky in politics," said one congressman. "He's carried here by his friends and he is kept here by his friends. That gives you a nice feeling." We shall think of these politically and emotionally supportive friends as the member's *personal constituency*.

▪   ▪   ▪

CONCLUSION

Each member of Congress perceives four concentric constituencies: geographic, reelection, primary, and personal. This is not the only way a member sees his or her "constituency"; but it is one way. It is a set of perceptions that emphasizes the context in which, and the strategies by which, the House member seeks electoral support. It is a complicated context, one featuring varying scopes of support and varying intensities of support. The strategies developed for getting and keeping electoral support involve the manipulation of these scopes and intensities. . . .

A perceptual analysis of congressional constituencies both complicates and clarifies efforts of political science to understand the relationship between congressman and constituency. It complicates matters both conceptually and statistically. For example, political scientists have a heavy investment in role conceptions that distinguish between the "trustee" who follows his independent judgment and the "delegate" who follows the wishes of his constituency. But we now must ask, which constituency? And we cannot be content with a conceptual scheme that provides only two answers to this question: "the district" and "the nation."[3] More frequent, we think, than this kind of choice is one in which the congressman must choose among constituencies *within* the district. Also, when studies of party voting conclude that a member of Congress can vote independently because he or she "knows the constituency isn't looking,"[4] we need to ask again, which constituency? One of the several constituencies may very well be looking.

NOTES

1. John Kingdon, *Candidates for Office: Beliefs and Strategies* (New York: Random House, 1966), chap. 3. In her study of congressional challengers in New York, Linda Fowler finds that some did not perceive or think in terms of an electoral "coalition." Linda Fowler, "The Cycle of Defeat: Recruitment of Congressional Challengers," unpublished manuscript, University of Rochester, 1977. When asked to describe his "supporters," one congressman in my group answered, "That's very hard to evaluate. I never thought in terms of groups. . . . I never thought of my support as coming from groups. The middle group, I guess, homeowners. It's very hard to say." The importance of the reelection constituency is well argued (though not subsequently employed) in Aage Clausen, *How Congressmen Decide: A Policy Focus* (New York: St. Martin's, 1973), p. 126.

2. The term is from Leo Snowiss, "Congressional Recruitment and Representation," *American Political Science Review* 60 (September 1966): 629–39.

3. For example, see Roger Davidson, *The Role of the Congressman* (New York: Pegasus, 1973).

4. David Stokes and Warren Miller, "Party Government and the Saliency of Congress," *Public Opinion Quarterly* 26 (Winter 1962): 531–46.

5.3

GARY W. COX AND MATHEW D. McCUBBINS

From *Setting the Agenda: Responsible Party Government in the U.S. House of Representatives*

The majority party in the House of Representatives closely controls legislative business, but to do so the party needs the cooperation of its members. How do majority political parties in Congress keep their coalitions together to pass legislation? Cox and McCubbins argue that party leaders, first, offer plum committee assignments and pork barrel benefits to rank-and-file members, and second, keep tight control over the agenda to ensure that no bills are voted upon that would potentially divide the party.

PROCEDURAL CARTEL THEORY

> The job of speaker is not to expedite legislation that runs counter to the wishes of the majority of his majority.
>
> —Speaker Dennis Hastert (R-II.)[1]

In this chapter, we present and discuss the assumptions that undergird procedural cartel theory. To provide a context for comparison, however, we first briefly survey the literature on partisan legislative organization.

Theories of Partisan Legislative Organization

Much of the literature on legislative organization focuses on why political parties are created within legislatures in the first place. We divide extant explanations into those that hinge primarily on the internal legislative payoffs to forming parties and those that hinge primarily on the external electoral payoffs. We then turn to survey the literature on how parties are organized and what parties do.

Why Are There Parties in Legislatures?

PARTIES ARE CREATED TO SOLVE INTERNAL COLLECTIVE ACTION PROBLEMS. One line of theorizing about why parties exist is similar to the distributive line of argument regarding committees. Absent any organization (other than a voting

From Gary W. Cox and Mathew D. McCubbins, *Setting the Agenda: Responsible Party Government in the U.S. House of Representatives* (New York: Cambridge University Press, 2005).

rule for floor decisions), legislators face a chaotic and unpredictable agenda. They cannot be sure that the legislature will not vote tomorrow to strip them of benefits conferred today. Nor is it clear how to ensure that the benefits are conferred to begin with, given a world where any legislator can move any amendment at any time.

In order to deal with the unpredictability—and unprofitability—of the unorganized legislature, legislators form political parties to bind themselves together in durable coalitions. Gains from legislative trade that could not be accrued without parties are thus accrued.

PARTIES ARE CREATED TO SOLVE EXTERNAL COLLECTIVE ACTION PROBLEMS. An alternative theory views legislative parties as being formed primarily to accrue electoral gains. Modern political parties facing mass electorates, similar to modern corporations facing mass markets, have a strong incentive to fashion and maintain a brand name. Such brand names are, however, public goods to all politicians running under the party's label. Thus, parties arise in order to ensure that the usual problems of providing and maintaining public goods are overcome—and in particular to internalize electoral externalities that would otherwise arise.

How Are Parties Organized?

If parties exist to solve collective action problems, as seems the main tenet in the literature, then how do they organize to solve these problems? The literature has several suggestions, which we now survey.

PARTIES AS FIRMS. Many scholars envision parties as being similar to the firms depicted in the literature on industrial organization (cf. Alchian and Demsetz 1972; Tirole 1988), in that they involve delegation to central agents (party leaders) in order to reduce transaction costs and ameliorate collective action problems. Scholars in this tradition implicitly accept the industrial organization literature's focus on hierarchical firms with single chief executive officers.

PARTIES AS PARTNERSHIPS. In the case of the political party, we believe a more fruitful analogy is to partnerships, such as law or accountancy firms, in which various gradations of senior partners provide overall strategic and tactical direction to the firm. The "senior partners" in our story—at least as regards the majority party—will be committee and subcommittee chairs, majority party floor leaders, campaign finance committee chairs, and the like. Agenda-setting and other powers are distributed across the offices held by these senior partners rather than fully concentrated in the hands of the speaker, just as the right to recruit new clients and take on new jobs is distributed among the senior partners in a law or accountancy firm, rather than fully concentrated in the hands of the firm's president. Similarly, just as the job of ensuring that no senior partner's actions impinge too unfavorably on a law firm's overall reputation falls not just on the firm's president but also on the other senior partners collectively, so too the job of policing committee chairs falls partly to the speaker and partly to informal politics centered on the party caucus.

What Do Parties Do?

Once organized, what do parties do to mitigate the collective action problems that are assumed to be the reason for their existence?

PARTIES AS FLOOR VOTING COALITIONS.   Some partisan theories view parties primarily as floor voting coalitions. In such theories, the central issue is the degree to which parties can discipline their members, ensuring a cohesive voting bloc on the floor, even when there are internal disagreements over policy.

The best-known model that seeks to explain variations in American parties' ability to discipline their members, and hence enact programs, is the conditional party government model of Aldrich (1995), Rohde (1991), and Aldrich and Rohde (2001). In this model, majority party backbenchers delegate more power to their party leaders, when preferences vary less within each party and more between the parties. Party government is thus conditional on a sufficient disagreement in preferences between the parties (relative to their internal disagreements) arising. When this condition is met, American parties act more in accord with the traditional model of responsible party government.

PARTIES AS PROCEDURAL COALITIONS.   Other partisan theories, including our own, view parties primarily as procedural coalitions. For such theories, the central issue is the majority party's ability to control the legislative agenda, defined as the set of bills considered and voted on the floor.

How Do Majority Parties Control the Agenda?

Strict party discipline, at least on important votes, is one method for the majority party or coalition to control legislative outcomes. When party leaders have the means to impose discipline on their backbenchers, agenda control is attained by the extension of the will of the party leadership. But, where discipline is costly, other methods may be substituted. In considering these other methods, there is an important distinction to be made between positive and negative agenda power. Positive agenda power is the ability to push bills through the legislative process to a final-passage vote on the floor. Negative agenda power is the ability to block bills from reaching a final passage vote on the floor. Formal and informal models of legislative parties differ in whether they depict parties as controlling the agenda via the allocation of proposal rights (positive agenda power) or veto rights (negative agenda power).

PARTIES AS ALLOCATING PROPOSAL RIGHTS.   Two examples of theories in which proposal rights are the key resource allocated by parties to their members are Laver and Shepsle's (1996) model of ministerial government and Diermeier and Feddersen's (1998) model of the vote of confidence. In a common interpretation of Laver and Shepsle's model, multiparty coalition governments allocate ministerial portfolios to their various member parties, with each minister then possessing both positive and negative agenda power in his respective jurisdiction. Thus, each minister can make proposals directly to the assembly, without needing cabinet clearance. In Diermeier and Feddersen's model, coalitions of legislators allocate increased "recognition probabilities" to their members, thereby increasing their ability to make proposals. Once recognized, a given member of a coalition again needs no preclearance by other members of the coalition for his proposals: They go straight to a final-passage vote in the plenary.

PARTIES AS ALLOCATING VETO RIGHTS. An alternative view of parties is that they allocate negative agenda power, or veto rights, among their members. Tsebelis (2002) takes this view of parliamentary coalitions. Rather than view individual parties as possessing both negative and positive agenda power across a range of issues (those under the jurisdiction of the party's ministers), Tsebelis views parties as possessing a general veto over the entire range of issues the coalition must face—therefore no coalition partner possesses unilateral proposal power. Similarly, Cox and McCubbins (2002) view majority parties primarily as allocating veto (or delaying) power to various offices held by their senior partners, such as committee chairs and speakers, thus necessarily lessening the proposal power of any given party member or subset of members.

Procedural Cartel Theory

In this section, we list the assumptions and motivating principles of procedural cartel theory. Assumptions 1–5 are from our previous book, *Legislative Leviathan*, and are defended at length in the second edition of that volume. Assumption 6 is new to this reading, and, accordingly, we expand on it here. . . . After elaborating the assumptions of our theory, we sketch some of the intuitions that have steered our research (. . .) and conclude. . . .

Assumption 1: Members of Congress seek reelection to the House, internal advancement within the House, good public policy, and majority status.

In our previous work (Cox and McCubbins 1993), our formal statement of members' goals included three of the motivations just discussed: reelection, internal advancement, and majority status.[2] Key to our approach was the assumption that majority status confers substantial benefits. In particular, advancement to committee chairs and other key posts in the House is possible only if one's party gains a majority, and advancement of one's legislative projects is greatly facilitated by majority status.[3] Thus, majority status is arguably an essential gateway to internal advancement and policy goals. The more substantial the benefits of majority status are, the more incentive they provide to the senior partners in a given party to pursue majority status—hence to undertake the sorts of agenda-setting actions that we describe in the remainder of the reading.

Assumption 2: The reputation (or brand name) of a member's party affects both the member's personal probability of reelection and, more substantially, the party's probability of securing a majority.

We have discussed this premise at length in our previous work (see Cox and McCubbins 1993, Chapter 5). To the extent that this assumption holds, a political party's reputation is a *public good* to all candidates sharing the party's label. More specifically, if a party's reputation improves or worsens, all members benefit or suffer together, regardless of whether they contributed to the improvement or worsening.

Assumption 3: A party's reputation depends significantly on its record of legislative accomplishment.

The policies with which a particular party and its leaders are associated—both those it promotes and those it opposes—can significantly affect the party's reputation. A recent example of this is the budget battle waged between Speaker of the House Newt Gingrich and President Bill Clinton in 1995. This battle led to the opening of the new fiscal year without a federal budget, causing the closure of nonessential government services. For present purposes, the important point about this budgetary stand-off is simply that it led to a sharp reduction in the popularity of congressional Republicans and their leaders, as measured by thermometer ratings in mass surveys (Jacobson 1996). In other words, in this instance a leader's legislative policy—that of refusing to compromise on the budget—led directly to a decline in the party's overall popularity.

We assume that this anecdote points to a more general phenomenon, in which legislative actions taken by various members of the party can affect the overall party's reputation on the margin. There is some disagreement about how much and how quickly party identification incorporates new events and evaluations. For our purposes, we need simply to assert a position similar to that adopted by V. O. Key (1966), in which parties' legislative actions *do* consequentially affect voters' behavior. Whether the path by which legislative actions influence votes is through party reputations (party identification) or through some shorter-term partisan pathways is less important.

Assumption 4: Legislating—hence compiling favorable records of legislative accomplishment—is akin to team production and entails overcoming an array of cooperation and coordination problems.

Achieving their goals—reelection, internal advancement, and majority status—requires passage of legislation, yet legislators' ability to accomplish things on their own is quite limited. Legislation must be accepted by majorities in both houses of Congress and be signed by the president to become law.[4] To get through even one house, moreover, a bill needs to get scarce floor time and the support of a majority coalition, both of which are costly and difficult to achieve. Legislating thus requires that members somehow join forces, cooperate, and engage in "team production" (Alchian and Demsetz 1972).

Team production, however, means confronting and overcoming a variety of collective action and coordination problems. For example, all members would like to spend more money on their own districts than might be optimal from their party's perspective (Cox and McCubbins 1993); all members would like to have free access to floor time, but the result could be that nothing can get done reliably; divergent national, regional, and partisan interests might lead members to pursue different policies in the absence of some coordinating mechanism. Most important for our theory, as noted above, the party label itself is a public good (for party members) that is subject to free-rider problems. Managing the party label is the primary collective action problem that members of a party must solve, and their collective goal of solving this and other collective action problems is the sense in which they are members of a partnership.

> **Assumption 5:** The primary means by which a (majority) party regulates its members' actions, in order to overcome problems of team production in the legislative process, is by delegating to a central authority.

Though other solutions for collective action problems exist, the most common solution seems to be delegation to a central authority—an idea that appears in a wide variety of literatures.[5] Three common elements in all these works are that the central authority to whom power is delegated monitors individual behavior, controls carrots and sticks with which to reward and punish individuals, and is motivated to solve the collective action problem(s) faced by the group. Along these lines, the core point of our previous book (Cox and McCubbins 1993) is that majority party members delegate to party leaders the authority to manage legislative resources and the legislative process in order to solve the cooperation and coordination problems they face, including maintaining the value of the party label.[6]

How are party leaders motivated to use their delegated powers for collective, rather than purely personal, gain? We argue that members wishing to hold important offices in the House (such as the speakership and committee chairs) know that the only realistic route to getting these offices is for their party to attain a majority of seats and for them to be in sufficiently good standing with their caucus to be (re)nominated for such offices.[7] Thus, the more valuable are the top posts going to the majority party's senior members, the more motivated are those members to ensure the party's continued majority status (and their own good standing).

[W]e believe that political parties are more fruitfully analogized to legal or accountancy partnerships than to strictly hierarchical single-leader firms (or armies). Thus, when we speak of delegation to a central authority, we do not mean literally to a single person but instead to a group of "senior partners."

> **Assumption 6:** The key resource that majority parties delegate to their senior partners is the power to set the legislative agenda; the majority party forms a procedural cartel that collectively monopolizes agenda-setting power.

This is our key assumption, and our point of departure from most of the previous literature. A *procedural cartel* is a coalition of legislators who constitute a majority in the assembly, share a common label (at least in the United States), and cartelize the agenda via the following basic strategy. First, the cartel creates (or, more typically, inherits) a set of offices endowed with special agenda-setting powers. In the case of the U.S. House, the main agenda-setting offices are the committee chairs, slots on the Rules Committee, and the speakership.[8] Second, the cartel ensures that its members get all, or nearly all, of the agenda-setting offices.[9] Third, cartel members expect those appointed to agenda-setting offices to *always* obey "the first commandment of party leadership"—*Thou shalt not aid bills that will split thy party*—and to sometimes obey the second commandment—*Thou shalt aid bills that most in thy party like.* Fourth, cartel members expect rank-and-file members to support the agenda-setting decisions rendered by officeholders when those decisions are made in conformity to the expectations just noted. Fifth, the cartel's leadership takes action to maintain cooperation and coordination within the cartel.

We use the term "cartel" because procedural cartels, like economic cartels, seek to establish a collective monopoly on a particular resource (in this case, agenda-setting power), seek to restrict supply of products made with this resource (in this case, bills that are placed on the floor agenda), and face problems of free-riding (in this case, members reluctant to vote for a party measure when such a vote will not sell well back home, or members eager to use their delegated agenda powers for personal gain). We have also used the term "legislative leviathan" to describe party organizations within legislatures, in order to emphasize their sometimes considerable degree of centralized authority.[10] Indeed, even during their relatively decentralized periods, parties in the U.S. House have been more hierarchical and stable than the typical economic cartel. Even though neither term's connotations are fully satisfactory, in this reading we will refer to party organizations as forming procedural cartels (and we will stress the analogy of a group of senior partners directing a law or accountancy firm rather than of a CEO running a corporation or a general commanding an army).

How Does the Majority Cartelize the Agenda?

In this section, we reconsider the defining features of "procedural cartels," as mentioned in Assumption 6. At this point, we wish only to argue that these features *plausibly* characterize the modern (i.e., post-Reed) House of Representatives; we will return to them in greater detail later in the reading.

The Structure of Agenda-Setting Offices

An initial question is whether there exist offices endowed with special agenda-setting powers in the House and whether these offices' powers were in some sense chosen by the majority party. By "special agenda-setting powers," or agenda power for short, we refer to any *special* ability to determine which bills are considered on the floor and under what procedures. Because any member can participate in an attempt to discharge a bill, we would not count "the ability to participate in a discharge attempt" as an "agenda power" in our sense. Such an ability is not special; it is general. In contrast, only members of the Rules Committee can participate in fashioning special rules,[11] and only chairs can delay bills merely by not scheduling them—to mention two examples of agenda power as we define it.

Given this definition, there obviously do exist offices in the House endowed with agenda power. As noted previously, the most important of these include the committee and subcommittee chairs, the seats on the Rules Committee, and the speakership.

Did the majority party in some sense choose the level of agenda power delegated to the various agenda-setting offices? Yes, in two senses.

First, the House adopts rules anew in each Congress. These rules are proposed by the majority party and are usually adopted on a straight party-line vote. Thus, among other things, the majority chooses (or reaffirms) the delegation of agenda power in those rules.

Second, the modern structure of agenda power in the House was erected in the period 1880–94 to enable the majority party to legislate, even against the wishes of the minority. . . . We will show that the House's rules have not, since 1894, changed so as to erase the majority party advantages accrued in this period. In particular, the minority party's ability to delay has not been restored, nor has the central position of the Rules Committee been significantly altered.[12] The powers of the speaker have waxed and waned, but when they have changed, they have simply been redistributed within the majority party, not allocated to any minority party members. In this sense, the majority party chose the structure of agenda power and the majority's overall advantage has remained largely constant since the 1890s (a claim we defend at length). . . .

Who Gets the Agenda-Setting Offices?

A second question is whether the majority party sets up a procedure for selecting the occupants of the agenda-setting offices that is likely to lead in principle, and does lead in practice, to its members winning most of the agenda-setting offices. The answer in practice is clear: the majority party secures all chairs, the speakership, and a super-proportional share of seats on the Rules Committee. It also secures super-proportional shares on the major committees that enjoy privileged access to the floor and on conference committees (which also exercise special agenda-setting powers) (Cox and McCubbins 1993).

As for the procedures regulating access to the House's agenda-setting posts, they all include an initial stage in which each party decides on nominees for the various posts, followed by a choice between, or ratification of, the parties' nominees in the House. The choice of a speaker is largely unregulated, as this is the first vote in each Congress and occurs before the adoption of rules. The choice of all other agenda-setting posts—committee positions of various sorts—is regulated. In particular, since 1917 the procedure has been as follows. First, the majority party informs the minority of how many seats each party will receive on each committee. Second, each party submits a slate specifying its nominees for its designated committee positions. Third, the two party slates are combined into a single resolution that is then voted up or down (since 1917 it has not been permissible to amend the slates on the floor). Given these procedures, it is not surprising that the majority party has never failed to secure a monopoly on chairs, the speakership, and a disproportionally large share of seats on the control and conference committees.[13]

Fiduciary Behavior of Officeholders

A third question is whether party members expect that party officeholders will exercise their official powers partly for the benefit of the party, rather than purely to pursue personal goals, and whether officeholders who do not act as expected are sanctioned in some way. Since agenda cartelization entails delegation of authority from party backbenchers to party leaders, cartelization creates the possibility of mischief by party leaders (i.e., not serving the collective interests of the party). Much of the literature implicitly adopts a strict standard by which to judge when officeholders act in the interest of their party, according to which they must aid legislation favored by significant majorities of their party. For example, the well-known accounts of Judge Smith's tenure on the Rules Committee point out—quite accurately—that he frequently obstructed legislation desired by large portions of his own party, and they conclude from this that Smith was acting in pursuit of his own or his faction's interests, not his party's.

Delay or outright obstruction of bills that significant portions of one's party want to turn into "party issues" represents an agency loss, but it does not mean that the persons in question have utterly abandoned representing or serving their party. After all, the wets in Thatcher's government delayed and obstructed when they could, and many other examples of hard bargaining over tough issues in coalition governments involve such tactics. Are we to conclude from every instance of persistent obstruction by elements of the governing coalition that the coalition is entirely toothless?

We think that would be premature. There are less stringent standards that might serve as "lines in the sand," demarcating behavior that is minimally fiduciary from behavior that is treasonous. Here, we wish to characterize such a standard, one that we believe has been expected of officeholders in the House at least since the late nineteenth century. This standard focuses on crimes of commission—pushing legislation one's party mostly dislikes—not on crimes of omission—failing to aid (or actively blocking) legislation one's party mostly likes. Crimes of commission increase in seriousness (1) with the proportion of the party that dislikes it and (2) if the bill actually passes. As a specific benchmark, *we claim that officeholders are expected never to push bills that would pass despite the opposition of a majority of their party*. We call such an event—passage of a bill against the votes of a majority of a given party— a *roll* of that party. If the majority's officeholders are not held to even the minimal standard of not using their powers to roll their own party, then they do indeed look like nonpartisan figures willing (and able with impunity) to build shifting coalitions in support of their projects.

An example of a violator of our proposed standard is Representative Phil Gramm (D-TX) who, during the negotiations leading to the first Reagan budget, clearly used his position in a way intended to roll his own party. In this specific instance, Democratic party leaders branded Gramm's behavior as unconscionable after they discovered it and took quick actions to sanction him, including stripping him of the posts he had abused (Roberts 1983a).[14]

Other similar examples can be cited. In 1924, eight Republicans on the Rules Committee cooperated on the passage of a strengthened discharge procedure, which most majority party members opposed; six of them were removed from the committee in the next Congress (in which the offending rule was also eviscerated cf. Hasbrouck 1927: 163–64). In 1975, Chairman Richard Ichord of the Internal Security Committee, a longtime thorn in the side of liberal Democrats, found that the committee had essentially been disestablished, due largely to actions taken in the Democratic Caucus (Jacobs 1995). In all these cases, the majority party caucus essentially *denied renomination* to wayward officeholders. There was no House vote needed to ratify the majority's decision; moreover, it would have been difficult to reject those decisions in the House, given that each party's slate of committee nominations is unamendable under House rules. To the extent that threats to deny renomination are credible, they induce officeholders to abandon, or at least sweeten, bills that substantial portions of their party dislike.

Our position is that these anecdotes generalize. In any period of congressional history, an officeholder behaving as Gramm did would have met with comparable reactions. In any period, it would be common knowledge that the standard of "not conspiring, explicitly or implicitly, with the enemy to roll one's own party" would apply to officeholders and that violators of this standard could expect to lose their offices and/or face other sanctions.

Many in the congressional literature seem to believe that sanctions against officeholders, especially against committee chairs, were simply not feasible in the period from 1937 to 1960. If this were so, then one should expect that Southern Democrats in this period used their agenda powers with impunity to push bills that they and the Republicans agreed on. Such "conservative coalition" bills, moving policy rightward, would have provoked splits in committees chaired by Southerners—with Northern Democrats outvoted by a combination of Southern Democrats and Republicans. Moreover, such bills would easily have made it to the floor, with the help of a Rules Committee often seen as controlled by the conservative coalition in this period. Once on the floor, conservative coalition bills would have *both* split the majority party *and* passed. Passage would follow as long as the number of conservative Southern Democrats plus regular Republicans exceeded the number of Northern Democrats plus liberal Republicans. Put another way, as long as the policy being changed lay to the left of the House median, the conservative coalition would have outvoted a majority of the Democratic Party. We assess the impact of the conservative coalition in detail, and evaluate these predictions. . . . For now, suffice it to say that we do not find significant evidence of Southern Democrats defecting from their party and joining with Republicans to successfully push an agenda unpalatable to Northern Democrats.

Loyalty from the Rank and File

A final question is: how does a procedural cartel ensure that its rank-and-file members support the agenda-setting decisions of its officeholders, even though at least some members' short-term interests would be better served by voting against those decisions? A key to the answer is that votes taken on procedural decisions (e.g., a vote to ratify a special rule proposed by the Rules Committee or to sustain a decision rendered by the speaker) are more obscure to constituents than are ordinary substantive votes (cf. Froman and Ripley 1965). If a member votes for a bill her constituents oppose on final passage, she runs a clear risk. If she supports a special rule filled with arcane boilerplate that helps ensure the bill's success, she runs a smaller risk.[15] Thus, party pressures can affect members' decisions on procedure more than their decisions on substance, even though all legislators know that procedural motions directly affect substantive outcomes.[16]

Another key point is that the cartel does not need the loyalty of every member on every vote. Often, it needs only enough votes to snatch victory from the jaws of defeat on close and important votes (cf. King and Zeckhauser 2003). This is a much more limited and manageable task than enforcing some minimum standard of cohesion across the board, which some mistakenly take to be what any "partisan" model must predict.

Is there evidence that cartels in the U.S. House do demand loyalty? Alexander (1970 [1916]: 210) notes that, soon after Reed's elevation of the Rules Committee to its modern status, members chafed under the expectation that "one must support whatever the Rules Committee brought forward or become irregular." More recently, Republican Whip Tom DeLay (R-TX) has made the party's expectations regarding behavior on procedural motions clear to his freshmen (Burger 1995).

To buttress such anecdotal evidence that majority parties do expect loyalty on key procedural votes, one can also point to more systematic evidence that the majority party's rank and file support their officeholders' agenda-setting decisions, while minority party members oppose them. First, after the packing of the Rules Committee in 1961 (and especially after the procedural reforms of 1973), members have voted with their parties significantly more than would be expected on the basis of their left–right position on a wide range of procedural and organizational votes (Cox and Poole 2002).[17] Second, in the postreform Congress, majority party members have been prone to support special rules, even when they then vote against the bill in question, while minority party members have exhibited the opposite tendency (Sinclair 2002). Sinclair's interpretation of this evidence is that majority party members are supporting their leaders' agenda-setting decisions, even when they oppose the substance of the proposals aided by the special rule in question, while minority party members oppose the Rules Committee's resolutions, even when they support the measure being aided. Third, more evidence of parties' influence over their members' voting behavior is reviewed. . . .

In addition, party leaders reward party members' loyalty on key votes, and especially on "agenda votes" in which the leaders of the two parties take opposing positions.[18] More loyal members are more likely to be appointed to the most desirable committees and to have committee transfers granted than are less loyal party members (Cox and McCubbins 1993, Chapter 7).

In summary, majority party leaders make clear their expectations of loyalty on certain key procedural votes; there is evidence that party pressures are greater on such votes; and there is evidence that more loyal members get better committee assignments. These findings are all consistent with a picture in which majority party leaders both *expect* and *get* "loyalty on the margin," enough to make the difference between winning and losing on close votes (King and Zeckhauser 2003).

Nevertheless, it is the very costliness of enforcing discipline in the U.S. House that helps to explain why U.S. parties principally rely on controlling the legislative agenda to achieve their legislative goals. In the model of responsible party government (American Political Science Association 1950), parties ensure cohesive voting blocs through a combination of control over nominations and disciplining their members. U.S. parties, however, have relatively weak nominating powers. Similarly, discipline is weaker in the United States than in some other countries. This puts more emphasis on agenda control, or influencing the bills and motions on which members must vote, as the single most powerful mechanism by which legislative outcomes can be affected in the U.S. House. By using agenda control, the party can prevent votes on which its disciplinary abilities would be strained or broken.

What about Quitting the Party?

In the discussion of fiduciary behavior and loyalty . . . , we did not address the issue of why members of a cartel do not quit their party, join the other side, and form a new cartel (with a better share of the spoils for themselves). In particular, one might wonder why centrist members cannot extract a better deal. Why are not all the committee chairs centrists, for example? Alternatively, why are not centrist chairs free to exercise agenda power in any way they see fit, subject only to majoritarian and not specifically partisan constraints?

There are three points we would urge in answer to this line of inquiry. First, it is rare for a single member to be pivotal (Senator James Jeffords in May 2001 being the most notable exception). Typically, several members must simultaneously switch parties in order to bring down the current cartel. Potential defectors must thus *coordinate*, not just in the sense of jumping at the same time but also in the sense of negotiating, *before* actually defecting, with their prospective new partners over the division of the spoils.[19]

Second, and more important, it is ex ante costly to switch parties. The Grenvillite faction in late eighteenth-century English politics could pivot freely, little constrained by electoral considerations, because they literally owned their seats. In the modern U.S. House, however, elections are partisan, and party labels count for a lot. When a member switches party labels, can he communicate that fact—and at what cost—to his constituents? How many voters in his former party will continue out of habit or loyalty to support that party? How many voters in the new party will remember that he used to be in the other party and refuse to support him on that ground? Among those voters who do learn of the member's switch, how many will view it as purely opportunistic, making the representative seem unreliable? Can he combat such ideas at low cost? How many names on the member's donor list will stop contributing? Who has been planning to run for the other party and how will they react to the incumbent's switch? All these questions about electoral ramifications—and more besides—would have to be considered by prospective defectors, at least if they are prudent.

Third, it is ex post costly to switch parties. Grose and Yoshinaka (2003) report "that incumbent legislators who switch parties have poorer showings after their switch in both general and primary election contests." Moreover, if one regresses the number of terms remaining in a legislator's career in

Congress t on her seniority (i.e., the number of terms already served through Congress t) and a dummy variable equal to 1 if the member switched parties in Congress t, one finds the switched party dummy variable to have a statistically significant coefficient of roughly –3. In other words, by one crude estimate, the cost of switching parties is three fewer terms in the House than would otherwise be expected, given a member's current seniority.[20]

These various costs help explain why actual party switching has been rare in the House and Senate. To the extent that the exogenous electoral costs of switching are large, moreover, it would follow that the threat of switching parties would not be as effective as it would be in a pure spatial representation of politics.

CONCLUSION

. . . [W]e have laid out the main assumptions underpinning our theory of legislative parties. In our view, U.S. legislators seek not just reelection but also advancement in the internal hierarchy of posts within the House, good public policy, and majority status for their parties. Their parties compete in mass elections, as business firms compete in mass markets, by developing brand names. The value of a party's brand name depends on its legislative record of accomplishment. Thus, a key problem for majority parties is to manage the legislative process, in order to secure the best possible record, hence contributing to the best possible reputation.

This much was already evident in our original exploration of congressional organization, *Legislative Leviathan*. In this reading, we develop several additional themes.

First, we portray agenda control as the key to the majority party's influence over the legislative process. In the responsible party government model, the primary mechanisms by which a party overcomes collective action problems, so that it can enact a program, are screening candidates and disciplining legislators. In the U.S. context, however, both screening and discipline are—although utilized to some extent—relatively costly. This raises the importance of a third technique to manage conflicts between collective and individual goals; controlling the agenda so that the sharpest conflicts are never even considered on the floor.

How does a legislative majority party work to control the agenda? The mechanism is similar to that portrayed in *Legislative Leviathan*. Certain members of the party—whom we have here dubbed the "senior partners"— are given valuable offices wielding substantial agenda-setting powers. In order to secure their party's (re)nomination for these offices, senior partners are expected to obey a minimal commandment of party loyalty—namely, not using their official powers in order to promote bills that will, if considered on the floor, lead to serious splits in the party. . . . The rank and file, meanwhile, are also expected to obey a minimal commandment of party loyalty—namely, supporting their officeholders' agenda-setting decisions, especially on the more procedurally arcane (yet substantively critical) votes. Their incentive to support such procedural maneuvers is the prospect of better internal advancement and a greater chance of majority status for the party as a whole.

Analogizing parties to partnerships is our second main point of departure from *Legislative Leviathan,* where we more often focused on the speaker and the top few leaders rather than the entire set of party members holding agenda-setting offices. Law and accountancy partnerships are designed to allow their senior partners considerable autonomy. By stressing the analogy to a partnership and the importance of agenda power, our approach naturally raises the question of how specific agenda powers are distributed among senior partners.

There are many theoretical possibilities, such as allocating *all* agenda power to the top party leader, allocating proposal power(s) to various senior partners, or allocating veto power(s) to various senior partners. We have argued that, whatever the details of agenda-power allocation, all majority parties in the U.S. House since adoption of Reed's Rules have structured agenda power in such a way that it is very difficult to roll them.

Closely related to the issue of what powers are distributed to which senior partners is the question of what standards of behavior those partners are expected to uphold. At one theoretical extreme, senior partners may have no fiduciary responsibilities to their parties. Agenda power is clearly allocated in these models but officeholders are then free to act in pursuit of their own interests, with neither formal checks (e.g., the necessity of securing their party's renomination) nor informal norms to constrain them. At the other theoretical extreme, senior partners may be expected completely to subordinate their personal goals to the party's. This is implicitly the case, for example, in Ranney's (1951) or the American Political Science Association's (1950) portrayal of responsible party government. Agenda power is not mentioned in such models, but officeholders are clearly enjoined to marshal their parties behind a coherent party platform.

We have opted for a theoretical middle ground of sorts, in which the norm to which senior partners are held depends on the internal homogeneity of the party. If the party is extremely heterogeneous (perhaps similar to a multiparty coalition government in other countries), then only a minimal standard can be realistically enforced: that of not using one's official powers to push legislation that will roll the party. As the party becomes more homogeneous, its senior partners are held to a higher standard, in which they must also use their official posts to help push legislation that most in the party support. Thus, for example, Jamie Whitten (D-MI) continued as chair of the powerful Appropriations Committee in the 1970s because he considerably increased his willingness to cooperate with the party leadership in pushing through Democratic priorities, even those he personally found distasteful (Crook and Hibbing 1985).

Why does the fiduciary standard become higher for more homogeneous parties? This prediction is entailed by our theory because procedural cartels, as we describe them, primarily distribute veto power among the senior partners of the party. Distributing veto power necessarily interferes with pushing through an ambitious program of legislation, as each senior partner with a veto in a particular policy area has to be brought on board. Thus, the ability of a procedural cartel to legislate necessarily depends on how similar their senior partners' preferences are.

Even when a majority's senior partners disagree on a wide range of issues, however, it becomes no easier to roll the majority party (i.e., pass bills that most majority party members dislike) because some senior partner or partners with relevant veto power will derail the bill. Thus, even internally divided majority parties do not surrender their *negative* agenda-setting power. They simply avoid bills that cannot be passed and move on to bills that can be passed, which tend to be less ideological and more porcine. The minority benefits from the internal divisions of the majority, in the sense that the bills the senior partners can agree on are less likely to have a clear ideological bite to them, hence less likely to roll the minority. But the minority is no more successful in dismantling the majority's previous accomplishments than before. Nor does it benefit by receiving a larger share of chairs, of staff, or of pork.

Because negative agenda power is the bedrock and "first story" of party government, in our view, most of this reading considers the consequences of such power. We return to the "second story" of party government, and discuss when a majority party might wish to build up such a story by readjusting the mix of positive and negative agenda power.

NOTES

1. Quoted in Babington (2004).

2. We did not there formally incorporate the third of Fenno's (1973) famous trio of goals: the pursuit of good public policy. . . . [H]owever, we adapt the standard spatial model of policy making for much of our argument, and this model is sufficiently abstract so that one can easily read personal policy goals into it. Thus, one can add the pursuit of policy as one of the goals that is consistent with the model we present here—although we do not insist on that interpretation.

3. As an example of the importance of majority status for members' legislative projects, consider the statements that Representative Ralph Hall made as he switched from being a member of the Democratic minority to being a member of the Republican majority: "This is the first time, I've just been zeroed out [by the Appropriations Committee]. . . . I've always said that if being a Democrat hurt my district, I'd either resign, retire or switch parties. . . . And it hurt my district this time [because I was denied funds]" (Wolf 2004).

4. Alternatively, of course, a bill can be vetoed, and the veto can be overridden by two-thirds of both houses.

5. Among the other solutions suggested in the literature are preplay communication, repeated play, and property rights (Tirole 1988; Friedman 1971).

6. Describing the authority associated with party leadership, Dennis Hastert stated, "So I have two functions. One is governmental, the other political. The governmental function is to run the House, move legislation through, make sure the chairmen and the committees are all operating smoothly. . . . The other function is political. I have to recruit the best possible candidates for Congress and make sure they have the financial and other resources they need to run or, if they're already in Congress, to make sure they have enough to stave off potential challengers" (Hastert 2004: 181–82).

7. Speaker Dennis Hastert clearly recognized the importance of majority status and being in good standing with his party. He emphasized, "Stripped to its essentials, my job is to run the House and make sure we [Republicans] hold the House" (Hastert 2004: 181).

8. Although the speakership is a constitutional office, its agenda-setting powers, as well as those of the other offices mentioned, are stipulated in House rules and precedents. The cartel controls the allocation of agenda power to the various offices to the extent that it can control votes on the adoption of rules.

9. In the United States, the cartel ensures a near-monopoly on agenda-setting offices to the extent that it can control the relevant votes on the floor (on election of the speaker and appointment of committees). To aid in controlling these floor votes, the cartel establishes an intracartel procedure to decide on the nominee for speaker and on a slate of committee appointments.

10. The role of the majority party has also been analogized to former Soviet Congresses. Indeed, as Hastert (2004: 250) notes, "Representative David Obey . . . compares the way the House is run today to 'the old Soviet Congresses—stamp of approval and ratify' rather than using your own judgment. Well, Obey was here when Democrats ran the place. . . . Talk about rubber stamps and domination by a party that had lots of votes and squish room. They were ruthless. They did things like the old Soviet Congresses, such as removing offenders from their hideaway offices, grabbing their office furniture, and taking their parking spots away."

11. A "special rule" is a resolution reported by the Rules Committee that regulates the consideration of a bill or resolution.

12. We are talking here about the powers of the Rules Committee, not its membership.

13. Decrying this monopoly power of the majority party, Dennis Hastert stated, "The truth is that since the last time we had a majority in 1954 only one Republican, Missouri's Bill Emerson, had ever stood on the House Floor—and he stood there as a page. We [the Republicans] had been in the wilderness so long that nobody remembered anything about being in the leadership. We didn't even know where the special back rooms were; we didn't even know where the *keys* to those rooms were" (Hastert 2004: 118).

14. A number of his coconspirators, the so-called Boll Weevils, were also punished by then-Speaker Tip O'Neill. For example, John Breaux of Louisiana and Roy Dyson of Maryland failed to win spots on the Budget and Appropriations committees, respectively (Roberts 1983a). In Breaux's place, the Democratic Party awarded the Budget Committee position to Martin Frost, a Texas Democrat who had "proven himself to be a national Democrat" (Roberts 1983b). Although G. V. Montgomery of Mississippi was reelected chairman of Veterans' Affairs, he lost 53 votes in the party caucus and remarked that conservatives would henceforth likely be more cooperative with their party leaders in Congress (Roberts 1983a).

15. In Arnold's (1990) terms, procedural votes are less "traceable."

16. Nokken's (2004) analysis demonstrates that departing members of Congress in lame duck sessions increasingly vote with their party (as opposed to their constituency). The explanation for this phenomenon is that when constituency constraints are severed (as they are in this situation), members vote with their party in hopes that the party will reward them for their loyalty by aiding them in their future career moves.

17. Quantitatively, Cox and Poole estimate about five to 10 votes switching on key procedural votes, which is consistent with qualitative evidence regarding vest pocket votes.

18. Loyalty is always important in committee assignments, but during times of high homogeneity within the majority party, there may be an increased premium placed on legislative competence. High levels of intraparty homogeneity decrease the relative importance of high loyalty and increase the importance of competence (Wawro 2000, Crook and Hibbing 1985).

19. The Jeffords case is informative here, as it demonstrates the costs of negotiating a defection. The Democrats gave Senator Jeffords the chairmanship of the Environment and Public Works Committee as an inducement to switch parties, which required Harry Reid to give up his status as the ranking Democrat on the committee (Lancaster 2001).

20. The analysis covers only the 80th through 100th Congresses. It is a crude estimate for two main reasons. First, the (negative) correlation between whether a member switches parties and how long that member continues in the House may be only partly due to switching being bad, per se. Perhaps members who switched had very poor electoral prospects, had they remained in their parties, and switched for this reason. So far as we know, however, there is no systematic evidence that party switchers did face greater electoral risks than the typical nonswitching member. Indeed, Ansolabehere, Snyder, and Stewart (2001) find qualitative evidence that discomfort with being ideological misfits accounts for legislators' switching; however, Castle and Fett (2000: 236–37) find that switching is more likely the more ideologically out of step a member is with his copartisans, controlling for a measure of primary electoral risk. Second, our data do not include the full number of terms served by members whose careers continue past the 100th Congress. For these members, the number of terms remaining is coded as zero. As there were no members who switched parties in the 100th Congress, this defect of the data biases our estimate of the cost of switching downward. In other words, if we knew the correct total terms remaining for all members whose careers reached the 100th Congress, the difference between switchers and nonswitchers would be even larger than we report here.

BIBLIOGRAPHY

Alchian, Armen, and Harold Demsetz. 1972. "Production, Information Costs, and Economic Organization." *The American Economic Review* 62: 777–95.

Aldrich, John H. 1995. *Why Parties? The Origin and Transformation of Party Politics in America.* Chicago: University of Chicago Press.

Aldrich, John H., and David W. Rohde. 2001. "The Logic of Conditional Party Government." In *Congress Reconsidered*, 7th ed., eds. Lawrence C. Dodd and Bruce I. Oppenheimer, 269–92. Washington, DC: Congressional Quarterly.

Alexander, DeAlva Stanwood. 1970 [1916]. *History and Procedure of the House of Representatives.* New York: Houghton Mifflin Company.

American Political Science Association. 1950. *Toward a More Responsible Party System: A Report.* New York: Rinehart.

Ansolabehere, Stephen, James Snyder, and Charles Stewart. 2001. "The Effects of Party and Preferences on Congressional Roll-Call Voting." *Legislative Studies Quarterly* 26: 533–72.

Arnold, R. Douglas. 1990. *The Logic of Congressional Action.* New Haven, CT: Yale University Press.

Babington, Charles. 2004. "Hastert Launches a Partisan Policy." Downloaded 11/27/04 from: www.washingtonpost.com.

Burger, Timothy. 1995. "After a Defeat, House Leaders Must Regroup." *Roll Call,* July 17.

Castle, David, and Patrick Fett. 2000. "Member Goals and Party Switching in the U.S. Congress." In *Congress on Display, Congress at Work*, ed. William T. Bianco, 231–42. Ann Arbor: University of Michigan Press.

Cox, Gary W., and Mathew D. McCubbins. 1993. *Legislative Leviathan: Party Government in the House.* Berkeley: University of California Press.

———. 2002. "Agenda Power in the U.S. House of Representatives, 1877 to 1986." In *Party, Process, and Political Change in Congress: New Perspectives on the History of Congress*, eds. David Brady and Mathew D. McCubbins. Stanford, CA: Stanford University Press.

Cox, Gary W., and Keith T. Poole. 2002. "On Measuring Partisanship in Roll-Call Voting: The U.S. House of Representatives, 1877–1999." *American Journal of Political Science* 46: 477–89.

Crook, Sara Brandes, and John R. Hibbing. 1985. "Congressional Reform and Party Discipline: The Effects of Changes in the Seniority System on Party Loyalty in the U.S. House of Representatives." *British Journal of Political Science* 15: 207–26.

Diermeier, Daniel, and Timothy J. Feddersen. 1998. "Cohesion in Legislatures and the Vote of Confidence Procedure." *American Political Science Review* 92: 611–21.

Fenno, Richard F. 1973. *Congressmen in Committees.* Boston: Little, Brown.

Friedman, James. 1971. "A Non-cooperative Equilibrium for Supergames." *Review of Economic Studies* 38: 1–12.

Froman, Lewis A., Jr., and Randall B. Ripley. 1965. "Conditions for Party Leadership: The Case of the House Democrats." *American Political Science Review* 59: 52–63.

Grose, Christian, and Antoine Yoshinaka. 2003. "The Electoral Consequences of Party Switching by Incumbent Members of Congress, Incumbent Legislators Who Switched Parties, 1947–2000." *Legislative Studies Quarterly* 27(1): 55–75.

Hasbrouck, Paul DeWitt. 1927. *Party Government in the House of Representatives.* New York: Macmillan.

Hastert, Dennis. 2004. *Speaker: Lessons from Forty Years in Coaching and Politics.* Washington, DC: Regnery.

Jacobs, John. 1995. *A Rage for Justice.* Berkeley: University of California Press.

Jacobson, Gary C. 1996. "The 1994 House Elections in Perspective." *Political Science Quarterly* 111: 203–23.

Key, V. O. 1966. *The Responsible Electorate.* Cambridge, MA: Harvard University Press.

King, David C., and Richard Zeckhauser. 2003. "Congressional Vote Options." *Legislative Studies Quarterly* 28: 387–411.

Lancaster, John. 2001. "Senate Republicans Try to Regroup: GOP Caucus Unites Behind Lott as Leader in the Wake of Jeffords's Defection," *The Washington Post*, May 26, p. A.18

Laver, Michael, and Kenneth A. Shepsle. 1996. *Making and Breaking Governments: Cabinets and Legislatures in Parliamentary Democracies.* Cambridge and New York: Cambridge University Press.

Nokken, Timothy P. 2004. "Roll Call Behavior in the Absence of Electoral Constraints: Shirking in Lame Duck Sessions of the House of Representatives, 1879–1933." Unpublished paper.

Ranney, Austin. 1951. "Toward A More Responsible Two-Party System: A Commentary." *American Political Science Review* 45: 488–99.

Roberts, Steven V. 1983a. "The Democrats Get Even." *New York Times*, January 9, p. E1.

———. 1983b. "Democrats Reward Loyalty in Giving Assignments," *New York Times*, January 6, p. A25.

Rohde, David W. 1991. *Parties and Leaders in the Postreform House.* Chicago: University of Chicago Press.

Sinclair, Barbara. 2002. "Do Parties Matter?" In *Party, Process, and Political Change: New Perspectives on the History of Congress*, eds. David Brady and Mathew D. McCubbins, 36–63. Stanford, CA: Stanford University Press.

Tirole, Jean. 1988. *The Theory of Industrial Organization.* Cambridge, MA: MIT Press.

Tsebelis, George. 2002. *Veto Players: How Political Institutions Work.* Princeton, NJ: Princeton University Press.

Wawro, Gregory. 2000. *Legislative Entrepreneurship in the U.S. House of Representatives.* Ann Arbor: University of Michigan Press.

Wolf, Jim. 2004. "Veteran Texas Democrat Switches to Republicans." Washington, DC: Reuters.

5.4

WILLIAM BERNHARD AND TRACY SULKIN

From *Legislative Style*

*Members of Congress (MCs) fall into five distinct patterns of behavior that Bern-
hard and Sulkin describe as legislative "styles." Almost a third of MCs are policy
specialists, while about a quarter each are district advocates and party soldiers.
The remainder are party builders and ambitious entrepreneurs. These styles
occur about equally between Republicans and Democrats. While a common
pattern is for MCs to behave using one specific style their whole careers, a substantial proportion of MCs begin their careers in the House of Representatives as
party soldiers and later gravitate toward becoming policy specialists.*

THE STYLES

> The mix of actual member activities is, in one sense, determined by the
> Constitution's job description for House and Senate members, but in
> another sense it is empirical. You have to look and see.
>
> —David Mayhew, *America's Congress* (2000, 10)

The first step in understanding legislative style is to describe the five styles that
emerge from our analysis: What characterizes the Members of Congress (MCs)
who fall into each style, and what distinguishes a particular style from the
others? Such descriptions assist us in determining whether the styles we
uncover are valid—that is, if our analysis yields meaningful groupings of MCs.

■　■　■

The distribution of the five styles is presented in Figure [1]. As shown, there
are three relatively large clusters (comprising about one-quarter to one-third
of MC-congress observations each) and two smaller clusters.[1]

Policy Specialists

The largest cluster, at 31.4% of observations, is distinguished by representatives who have the highest scores of any group on the policy focus (i.e., they

From William Bernhard and Tracy Sulkin, *Legislative Style* (Chicago, IL: Chicago University Press,
2018).

FIGURE [1]   Distribution of Legislative Styles

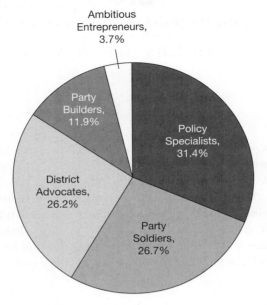

NOTE: Proportion of observations (an MC-congress) that fall into each of the five legislative styles. $N = 4276$

have focused agendas, generally targeting issues within the jurisdiction of their committee assignments), and who vote and co-sponsor regularly with their parties. They have the lowest score of any on the showboat index and hence do not engage in much speech-making or other publicly visible activities, and they do not raise or redistribute much money. We call this cluster the "policy specialists."

To illustrate how this policy specialist style manifests itself, consider a few of the 158 MCs with this style in the 110th Congress (2007–08), the congress from which all of our examples in this chapter will be drawn. Some of these legislators have reputations for concentrated investments in a particular issue. Carolyn McCarthy (D-NY), for example, who first took office in 1996, was motivated to run for the House on a gun control platform after her husband was killed and her son injured in a mass shooting on a Long Island Railroad commuter train in 1993. Once in office, she devoted the majority of her legislative efforts to gun violence, becoming known as "the fiercest gun-control advocate in Congress" (Toeplitz 2011).

Similarly, Henry Waxman (D-CA) is best known for his career-long interest in health and environmental issues, including pesticides, clean air, food and drug safety, and tobacco regulation. These issues fall largely within the jurisdiction of the Energy and Commerce committee, which, in the 110th Congress, was chaired by Waxman. Waxman held a seat on this committee since his first election to Congress in 1974, where he was one of the lucky few freshmen to receive a first-choice assignment to a relatively prestigious committee. His interests in these issues date back to his service as a member of the California State Assembly. As Waxman himself describes it:

> Early on, I decided that in order to become an effective legislator, I should develop an area of expertise, which would enable me to exert outsized influence whenever that subject arose. Because my district was home to a large elderly population, health policy struck me as a good specialization (Waxman and Green 2009, 20).

Accordingly, the decision to specialize was, for Waxman, largely a strategic one, enabling him to carve out a niche for himself as a policy expert.

Paul Ryan (R-WI), who explicitly identified as a specialist, claiming, "I've always been one of the House policy wonks" (Wallace 2012), also falls into this style in the 110th Congress. Like Waxman, Ryan's interests developed early—his first job on the Hill was as a staff economist to Senator Bob Kasten (R-WI). Upon entering Congress in 1999, he quickly earned a reputation for his interest and expertise in fiscal issues, rising, by 2007, to the ranking member of the House Budget Committee. He became the voice of the Republican Party on budget issues, serving as chief author of its budget proposals, and eventually achieving even greater national prominence as Mitt Romney's vice presidential running mate in 2012 and then, in 2015, becoming Speaker of the House.[2]

While McCarthy, Waxman, and Ryan devoted themselves to particular issues, other policy specialists in the sample are distinguished by a more general focus on policy making. For example, Rosa DeLauro (D-CT) and Thaddeus McCotter (R-MI), chairs of their parties' steering and policy committees in the 110th Congress, are both policy specialists in that congress. And, of course, many other MCs who go (relatively) quietly about their business, attending to their committee assignments and doing their jobs as MCs, fall into this style.

What, then, makes policy specialists distinct from MCs with other styles? The differences in patterns of behavior become most clear when we draw direct comparisons with the activity of those MCs who fall into one of the other four clusters.

Party Soldiers

The second-largest cluster, comprising 26.7% of observations, consists of MCs we refer to as "party soldiers." These legislators vote regularly with their parties and only rarely cross the aisle to cosponsor bills introduced by the other party. They engage in considerably more showboat activity than do policy specialists, and they raise a fair amount of money, but they do not redistribute it. In short, these MCs are loyal backbenchers and members of the party team who can be counted on to toe the party line and participate in the legislative process, but who do not appear to be particularly invested in policy specialization or in fund-raising activities that would help them rise through the hierarchy.

This cluster includes several of the longest-serving MCs, such as Edward Markey (D-MA) and Dale Kildee (D-MI), both elected in 1976, and Dan Burton (R-IN), elected in 1982. As expected, all are party stalwarts, with Burton, for example, described by the *Almanac of American Politics* as "an active and enthusiastic Republican" (Barone and Cohen 2007, 614). All three of these MCs accumulated records of legislative accomplishment, though perhaps with less focus than many of their policy specialist colleagues, and also without the positions of power of some of their colleagues with other styles. However, this did not keep them from seeking and attaining visibility. Indeed, several hold reputations as gadflies. The same holds true of many of the midcareer party soldiers, such as Dennis Kucinich (D-OH), described by the *Almanac* as "unrepentant" about pushing Cleveland into default when he was mayor in the 1970s (2008, 1302); Mike Pence (R-IN), who "quickly made his mark as one of the House's more outspoken conservative members" (2008, 617); and Jim Moran (D-VA), "known for his short temper and quick tongue" (2008, 1685).

The real heart of the party soldiers group, however, is relative newcomers to Congress. In fact, in the 110th Congress, half of the eighty-five MCs with the party soldier style were in their first or second terms, and 63% of the newly elected representatives in that congress adopted the party soldier style. This suggests that this style may be a way station of sorts for many new MCs, who begin as party soldiers and then move on to other styles.

District Advocates

The third cluster, with 26.2% of observations, includes those MCs we call "district advocates." These legislators have a high mean score on the home front . . . and the lowest on party voting. Indeed, they also often cosponsor with members of the opposite party. They also receive low scores on the showboat index and are the lowest of the five clusters on party giving and lawmaking. In sum, these MCs are not a part of the party fold and operate largely beneath the radar. Instead, they devote their energy and resources to cultivating their districts.[3]

Included in this cluster are a number of long-serving MCs whose partisan leanings run against those of their states, such as Southern Democrats Bud Cramer (D-AL) and Gene Taylor (D-MS) and New England Republicans Christopher Smith (R-NJ) and James Walsh (R-NY).[4] It also includes some MCs known for their focus on pork projects and earmarks for their districts, such as Stephanie Herseth Sandlin, included as a "top earmarker" in 2008 by the Center for Responsive Politics, and Alan Mollohan (D-WV), named "Porker of the Year" by Citizens Against Government Waste in 2006. In response, Mollohan proudly noted:

The founding fathers gave Congress the power of the purse recognizing that the people's representatives were in a far better position than the executive branch to be responsive to the needs of people and communities. . . . I am pleased to receive recognition for my efforts to support West Virginia, which is as deserving as any other state to receive federal assistance for community and economic development (Barone and Cohen 2007, 1749).

The district advocates cluster also includes a number of early career MCs ensconced in what Fenno (1978) referred to the "expansionist" stage of their careers (i.e., wherein they attempt to expand their base of support within the district), including, in the 110th, freshmen such as Gabrielle Giffords (D-AZ) and Heath Shuler (D-NC).

Party Builders

MCs in the fourth cluster share with their party soldier and policy specialist colleagues a focus on party loyalty. They vote at the highest rates with their parties and do not often cosponsor measures introduced by the other party. However, their loyalty is not limited to their legislative actions—they also redistribute campaign contributions to their party organizations and to copartisans, receiving the highest score of any group on the "party giving" index. In addition, they are quite active in the law-making process and are publicly visible, scoring highly on the showboat index. However, they have the lowest score of any of the groups for home front attention. We name this cluster the "party builders." They comprise 11.9% of observations in the sample, and they include many movers and shakers—those MCs who are strong party supporters, serve as its public face, and engage in heavy lifting legislatively.

In the 110th Congress, this cluster includes nearly all of the legislative leaders and whips (Nancy Pelosi [D-CA], Eric Cantor [R-VA], Steny Hoyer [D-MD], James Clyburn [D-SC]); the financiers (Chris Van Hollen [D-MD] and Tom Cole [R-OK], who chaired the Democratic and Republican campaign committees); and some long-serving members such as John Conyers (D-MI). However, this cluster is not limited to senior MCs, and it also includes some relative newcomers, such as up and coming sophomores Debbie Wasserman Schultz (D-FL) and Tom Price (R-GA). Schultz's efforts on behalf of the party in her first term in office in the 109th Congress earned her a seat on the Appropriations Committee and a position as Chief Deputy Whip in the 110th, and she went on to become chair of the DNC. Price quickly established himself in the conservative wing of the Republican Party, joining the Republican Study Committee and Republican Policy Committee (both of which he would later chair), and rising to prominence in the 111th Congress as the main sponsor of the Empowering Patients First Act, the Republican competitor to Obamacare (i.e., the Affordable Care Act).

Ambitious Entrepreneurs

The fifth and smallest cluster, with just 3.7% of observations, consists of MCs we label "ambitious entrepreneurs." These legislators score the highest of any of the five clusters on money raised, show-boating, and in the volume of law-making activity. They edge out district advocates on the home front index and come in second to them on voting against their parties, but are the most likely of the five groups to cross the aisle in their cosponsorship coalitions. However, this behavior does not necessarily indicate that they are moderate. Instead, some are part of idiosyncratic coalitions, either steering their own individual course or trying to build reputations in the chamber and beyond to enable them to rise to positions of power. In the 110th, this group includes progressively ambitious MCs such as the newly elected Kirsten Gillibrand (D-NY), who would serve just one full term in the House before being appointed to a Senate seat and then winning reelection for that seat, and Bobby Jindal (R-LA), who was in his second term in the House following a failed run for the governorship in 2003, but who would run again for governor, this time successfully, during the 110th Congress.

Importantly, this style is not just the province of the (imminently) progressively ambitious. In the 110th, it also includes more senior iconoclasts such as John Murtha (D-PA), Ralph Hall (R-TX), and James Obserstar (D-MN). In earlier congresses, Newt Gingrich (R-GA), Ron Paul (R-TX), Dan Rostenkowski (D-IL), Bernie Sanders (I-VT),[5] and James Traficant (D-OH) occupied this cluster.

■   ■   ■

Patterns in Style across Parties and Congresses

. . . The contemporary Democratic and Republican parties do differ on some important dimensions that could bear on their styles. The Republicans, for example, display less ideological dispersion than do the Democrats (see Bonica 2013), and, under Newt Gingrich, began increasing centralization of power in the leadership (Davidson et al. 2014, 137). However, the resurgence of partisanship in voting and as an organizing force in Congress has affected both Democrats and Republicans. Moreover, we view style as more fundamentally about individual differences in how to approach the job of MC. We expect these differences to precede party, occurring for both Democrats and Republicans. Accordingly, we hypothesize that differences in the distribution of style across parties will be small in magnitude.

The results in Figure [2] confirm this expectation. To assess overall party differences, we compared the mean proportion of each of the five styles for Democrats and Republicans. We find that styles are relatively evenly distributed across the parties. Slightly more Republicans than Democrats are ambitious entrepreneurs (4.5% vs. 3.0%, $t = 2.5$) and party soldiers (28.2% vs. 25.3%, $t = 2.1$); and a larger proportion of Democrats than Republicans are policy spe-

FIGURE [2]   Distribution of Styles by Party

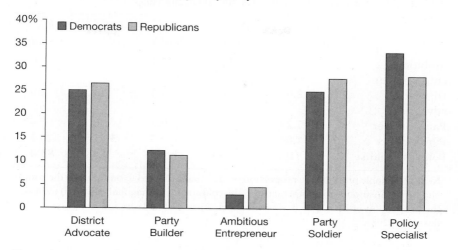

NOTE: Proportion of Democrats and Republicans (where the observation is the MC-congress) who adopted each of the styles. $N = 4276$

cialists (33.4% vs. 28.8%, $t = 3.6$), but these differences are not large in magnitude, and the rank ordering of the styles by relative size is the same for both parties. Thus, partisanship does not drive cluster assignments.

▪   ▪   ▪

[W]e expect that overall, individual MCs' styles should be relatively stable. Research on legislative behavior shows that dimensions of activity such as roll call voting patterns (Poole and Rosenthal 2007), bill introductions and cosponsorships (Ragsdale and Cook 1987), and presentational styles (Fenno 2000; Grimmer 2013) tend to display consistency across time. Thus, if most MCs were in different clusters in every congress, or if they were regularly moving between clusters that were largely incompatible with one another (e.g., from party builder to district advocate), then we might question the validity of our approach and of the styles we uncover. On the other hand, we do not expect style to be constant, especially over the long term. As we discuss below, much can happen to MCs across a period of years that could lead to a shift in goals, capacity, and priorities, and hence a transition in style.

Table [1] presents the proportion of MCs by cluster who maintained or shifted style in the next congress. To calculate these figures, we take MCs' styles in each congress (time t) and examine their distribution of styles in the next (time $t + 1$). Thus, the diagonal in the table reveals the amount of consistency for each style (for example, the proportion of party builders in congress t who remained party builders in congress $t + 1$).

TABLE [1] Transition Patterns from Cluster to Cluster (%)

	Ambitious entrepreneur	*District advocate*	*Party builder*	*Party soldier*	*Policy specialist*
Ambitious entrepreneur	**50.0**	18.3	22.1	9.6	0
District advocate	2.0	**91.5**	1.3	2.4	2.9
Party builder	7.2	4.2	**79.2**	2.0	7.4
Party soldier	1.0	5.1	6.5	**58.1**	29.3
Policy specialist	0	5.1	6.6	4.9	**83.4**

NOTE: This table presents the proportion of MCs that belonged to one cluster (the rows) and then transitioned to another cluster (the columns). The diagonals (in bold) indicate the proportion of MCs who maintained a consistent style from one congress to the next. $N = 3298$

There is an impressive amount of stability. It is highest for district advocates, 92% of whom remain so from one congress to the next. This makes sense, as the decision to be a district advocate is likely a function of (unchanging) constituency constraints. Policy specialists and party builders follow closely after (at 83% and 79%, respectively). Party soldiers and ambitious entrepreneurs lag behind, with consistency rates of 58% and 50%. Since ambitious entrepreneurs often have their sights set on career goals outside the chamber, they may be likely to shift their patterns of activity to accommodate changing circumstances.[6] Similarly, the party soldiers cluster, occupied by many freshman and sophomore legislators, likely serves as a starting point for many new MCs who then settle into different styles.[7]

NOTES

1. We conducted robustness checks to confirm that our clusters held with slight tinkering to the inputs (e.g., rolling the cosponsorship variable into the party voting index) and to different numbers of congresses. While there are, as expected, some small differences, the same general pattern of clusters emerges.

2. It is likely that in the congresses after our data collection ends, Ryan's ascent up the leadership ladder and increasingly public persona corresponded to a transition in style.

3. Ideally, we would have access to data on pork and other district benefits delivered by each representative. Unfortunately, such data are not available for our time frame. However, anecdotal evidence does suggest that district advocate MCs are active in efforts to bring money to their districts.

4. We have data on these four MCs for nine or ten of the congresses in the sample. With the exception of Smith, who falls into another cluster in one of the congresses, all maintain the district advocate style in every congress for which we have information.

5. Because Sanders caucused with the Democrats, we consider him a Democrat for purposes of our analyses.

6. They are also the smallest group, so a shift of a handful of MCs can result in large percentage shifts. Not surprisingly, they have the highest standard deviation on consistency of any group.

7. The table also reveals some other interesting patterns in transitions—e.g., ambitious entrepreneurs never transition (directly) to the policy specialist style and policy specialists never transition to become ambitious entrepreneurs. We also see that party soldiers who change style from one congress to the next tend to become policy specialists, while ambitious entrepreneurs become district advocates or party builders.

WORKS CITED

Barone, Michael, and Richard E. Cohen. 2001. *The Almanac of American Politics 2002*. Washington, D.C.: National Journal Group.

Bonica, Adam. 2013. "Ideology and Interests in the Political Marketplace." *American Journal of Political Science* 57(2): 294–311.

Davidson, Roger H., Walter J. Olezsek, Frances E. Lee, and Eric Schickler. 2014. *Congress and Its Members*. 14th ed. Thousand Oaks: CQ Press.

Fenno, Richard F. 2000. *Congress at the Grassroots: Representational Change in the South, 1970–1998*. Chapel Hill: University of North Carolina Press.

Grimmer, Justin. 2013. *Representational Style in Congress: What Legislators Say and Why It Matters*. New York: Cambridge University Press.

Poole, Keith T. and Howard Rosenthal. 2007. *Ideology and Congress*. New Brunswick: Transaction Publishers.

Ragsdale, Lyn, and Timothy E. Cook. 1987. "Representatives' Actions and Challengers' Reactions: Limits to Candidates Connections in the House." *American Journal of Political Science* 31(1): 45–81.

Toeplitz, Shira. 2011. "McCarthy Unveils Gun-Control Bill." *Politico*, January 13. Accessed April 1, 2016. http://www.politico.com/story/2011/01/mccarthy-unveils =gun-control=bill-047565.

Wallace, Gregory. 2012. "Ryan: 'Wonk' Is a Compliment." *CNN*, November 13. Accessed April 1, 2016. http://politicalticker.blogs.cnn.com/2012/11/13/ryan-wonk-is-a-com pliment/.

Waxman, Henry, and Joshua Green. 2009. *The Waxman Report: How Congress Really Works*. New York: Hachette.

5.5

FRANCES E. LEE

From *Insecure Majorities: Congress and the Perpetual Campaign*

Competition for majority status in the U.S. Congress is close and intense. Unlike previous eras (such as 1964–94), today members of both major political parties in Congress believe that majority party control can easily switch in the next election. Lee shows that this close competition unifies the party members in Congress around focused messaging that touts party accomplishments and disparages the other party. It also makes bipartisan lawmaking more difficult because of the focus on party messaging and defeating opponents. The parties in Congress spend their time competing to gain or keep majority status rather than seeking to build coalitions to adopt new laws.

THE LOGIC OF CONFRONTATION

Competition for majority status affects strategic decisions in Congress. When there is little competition for party control of Congress, members will, of course, weigh how the politics of various issues might affect their own individual electoral interests. But there will be less collective strategizing about how to influence the parties' overall image, reputation, and public standing. When control of Congress hangs in the balance, however, members will ponder how they might affect their party's common fate. As one former staffer put it, "When you think you have a chance [to win the majority], you're just going to go all out."[1] Members competing for majority-party status thus take a wider view of politics beyond their own reelection. They will be more likely to view issues and political decisions with an eye toward partisan (as well as personal) advantage.

[I]ncreased competition for control of Congress fuels a more confrontational style of partisanship, as parties in their quest for power seek to define the stakes for voters. I begin by laying out a logic of partisan confrontation: why members of Congress perceive political benefits from defining and dramatizing party differences and how they go about doing so. *Messaging* is the term that congressional insiders use to describe their efforts to highlight party differences. Next, I examine how party messaging disrupts bipartisanship. Finally, I analyze how a party's incentives to engage in strategies of partisan differentiation are

From Frances E. Lee, *Insecure Majorities: Congress and the Perpetual Campaign* (Chicago, IL: University of Chicago Press, 2016).

affected by its institutional position in the constitutional system (e.g., majority vs. minority status, unified vs. divided party control, House vs. Senate). . . .

The Quest for Majority Control

What is the job of [a] Republican leader in the minority? It's to hold the job for as short a time as possible.

—Rep. John A. Boehner (R-OH) in a 2006 letter to House
Republican colleagues.[2]

There is no question that members care about which party holds a majority. When I asked interview subjects whether majority status mattered to members, I would often get an incredulous look. "Without the majority, you have nothing," responded one senior Senate aide.[3] "Absolutely! It matters hugely," answered another. "Every senator in the majority party will get a gavel [of at least a subcommittee]."[4] When Republicans lost the majority in 2001, he continued, Republican senators' reactions "were as if someone had taken a beloved old dog out and shot him. These are all alpha males, Type A personalities. They want the ball." A staffer serving during the immediate aftermath of the 1994 elections recalled former House Energy and Commerce chairman John Dingell's (D-MI) reaction to his new minority status: "At first, he asked *'What do I do now?'* He couldn't set the agenda; he couldn't legislate. It was as if he had died, or as if they'd cut off both legs and both arms."[5] When I asked one senior Senate aide if his boss closely watched elections outside his own state, he said that "[his boss] would be chair if Republicans won a majority, which would mean a major change for him, a very big deal. There is a lot riding on the outcome."[6] Members are "acutely aware" of the stakes in the quest for majority control, said another Senate staffer.[7]

▪ ▪ ▪

Defining and Dramatizing Party Differences

[The 1992 election] is our shot. . . . We've just got to go all out. We've got every reason to define the differences between the parties.

—House Minority Leader Bob Michel (R-IL), 1991[8]

Control of Congress will be the issue in 1982. We've got to give Democratic voters a sense that they have something at stake in 1982: their jobs, their homes, their children's future, their retirement.

—Kirk O'Donnell, chief aide to House Speaker
Tip O'Neill (D-MA), 1982[9]

In waging these party message battles, members and leaders have one primary goal: to give voters reasons to choose their own party over its opposition. Underneath this strategy is an implicit view of voters as rational actors. Put in Downsian terms, party messaging aims to increase the "expected party differential": the difference voters perceive in utility between each party being in power.

The underlying belief is that voters need to be convinced that the parties are different and that they should care about which party holds the reins of power. Politicians seeking to help their party win and hold majorities operate under the assumption that they must be able to offer clear reasons as to why voters should choose their party over the alternative. They want sharp contrasts so as to motivate supporters to make the effort to turn out to vote or to engage in more demanding forms of political activity, such as donating to campaigns.

Making the case for one's own party thus involves an active quest for issues to differentiate the two parties. "We committed to fashioning an alternative to every bill or amendment the Democrats proposed," explained former House Republican Whip Tom DeLay (R-TX) about his party's efforts in the lead-up to the 1994 elections. "This proved to be an effective strategy. . . . It illustrated to the American people that they had a choice" (DeLay and Mansfield 2007, 93). One former senior Senate leadership aide stated, "The key to effective party messaging is finding a way to illustrate the differences between the parties, finding a concrete example."[10] "To the extent that you're not drawing distinctions, you're making it harder to make your case," said a former House leadership staffer.[11]

▪ ▪ ▪

A sense of shared threat or opportunity generates incentive for fellow partisans to work past disagreements and unite around a party message. Message discipline does not generally happen by accident. It occurs because members believe they have a common stake in the outcome of the effort. One longtime Senate staff director said, "Only years of getting our clock cleaned got us to our political consensus now that we work together on messaging. Unless there's an issue that is uniquely personal to your state, you work with the party. . . . There are some members who are complainers. But generally speaking, members don't take their criticisms of the leadership out on the talk circuit. They raise their issues in caucus, but then present a unified front to outsiders."[12] Asked how Minority Leader Nancy Pelosi (D-CA) was able to build agreement around a party message for the lead-up to the 2006 elections, another staffer echoed this point: "In the end, no one else, aside from Pelosi, had a road back [to the majority]. So Democrats were able to sublimate their own personal ideological and programmatic goals to the common agenda."[13] A Republican leadership staffer made the same observation: "If [Minority Leader] McConnell says, 'Let's avoid self-inflicted wounds,' [members] get the stakes. They get the importance. This is true for members generally, not just those in line to be chairmen."[14] In short, a competitive context in which the majority is perceived to be in contention strengthens members' incentives to accept some message discipline.

▪ ▪ ▪

Trade-Offs between Legislating and Messaging

Drawing clear lines between the parties stands at odds with the conciliatory efforts that are typically necessary to legislate, especially in a political system with so many veto points. Bicameralism, separation of powers, and other aspects of American national institutions almost always force congressional leaders to legislate by assembling large, bipartisan coalitions. Important legislation rarely passes on the strength of one party alone (Krehbiel 1998; Mayhew 2005).

Bipartisan participation in legislating, however, undercuts party messaging efforts. This is a theme that emerged repeatedly in interviews, and it often crops up in members' quoted comments in published media as well. How can members legislate across party lines on important issues and then proclaim to voters that it makes a big difference which party controls Congress? How will a party draw clear contrasts with the opposition while voting to pass major legislation on a bipartisan basis? How does a minority party vote in support of the bills the majority party leadership brings to the floor and then convincingly denounce the majority's performance in a campaign for change in party control? "You just apparently don't want to be caught being bipartisan," said Rep. Sander Levin (D-MI). "It's going to blur the political message" (Hulse 2010, A18).

■　　■　　■

The tension between legislating and messaging is a key reason so many present and former members of Congress express anxiety about the trade-offs between governing and messaging. "We're all frustrated. We all wish there was more legislating and less messaging," said Sen. Max Baucus (D-MT; Kane 2013). "Today, Congress is constantly campaigning. Governing has fallen by the wayside," wrote retiring Rep. Elton Gallegly (R-CA) in a 2013 op-ed. "They keep saying, 'the election,'" said Sen. Olympia Snowe (R-ME). "And I say that's a year and a half from now. In the meantime, could we just sort of legislate?" (Mitchell 1999, E1). "What is disturbing about our current situation is that we seem to have forgotten the concept of legislative compromise," said Sen. Robert C. Byrd (D-WV). "There is no give and take. Instead, members seem more concerned with sowing the landscape with political seeds that can be cultivated and harvested during next year's election campaigns."[15] Each of these statements explicitly acknowledges perceived conflicts between the requirements of message politics and legislative deal making.

■　　■　　■

In order to clearly define "us versus them," roll-call votes designed for messaging purposes will force members to select between simplistic "either/or" alternatives. As such, messaging does not entail an effort to wrestle with policy complexity or to identify inclusive "both/and" solutions. As a Senate leadership staffer put it. "With messaging, you're setting up simple choices: pay equity, motherhood, and apple pie. Are you for it, or are you against it? Of course, you and I know that these issues are not so simple. But they're designed for use in the thirty second ad."[16]

■　　■　　■

Power, Responsibility, and Weighing the Trade-Offs between Messaging and Legislating

> Ain't opposition fun? We don't have to be responsible. All we have to do is watch them self-destruct.
> —Anonymous Democratic Congressman, 1995[17]

When faced with trade-offs between legislating and messaging, members have to make strategic choices about their priorities. They have to decide whether to make legislative deals or to withdraw from negotiations and instead focus on setting up issues for electoral purposes. "The classic legislative dilemma is how far you go in participating in a compromise," observed Rep. Henry Waxman (D-CA) during a 1985 Democratic intraparty debate over how to respond to President Reagan's budget (Cohen 1985, 2588). As Rep. Vic Fazio (D-CA) explained, "We were divided on the question of whether we wanted to win [a partial victory] or go down in glorious defeat" (Cohen, 1985, 2588).

To prioritize messaging over legislating means abjuring opportunities to influence policy in the present moment while looking with hope toward a future electoral victory. Rep. Barney Frank (D-MA) explained the dilemma: "Am I better off making a deal and making the policy better? Or am I better off just opposing?"[18] After Republicans won control of the House in the 2010 elections, they debated among themselves whether to try to strike an agreement with President Obama to reduce the budget deficit. Even though it might have been possible for Republicans in 2011 to advance some of their fiscal goals in exchange for concessions, a contingent of House Republicans pressed Speaker John A. Boehner (R-OH) to cease negotiations with the president altogether. "It's no longer policy season," said one Republican member in January 2011, nearly two years before the 2012 elections. "It's message season" (Stanton 2011).

■   ■   ■

Through calculations such as these, the zero-sum logic of electoral competition encroaches into the legislative process. To the extent that a party in power benefits from legislative successes, in a two-party system the party with less power and responsibility for outcomes will perceive political gains from legislative failures.

■   ■   ■

The clear picture that emerges is that members of Congress generally believe it is necessary to define and dramatize party differences in order to energize their supporters and to persuade undecided voters to prefer their party to the opposition. Drawing partisan differences, however, stands in tension with successful legislating for a variety of reasons. Most importantly, the bipartisanship typically necessary to legislate in a separated system with many veto points fundamentally undercuts efforts to clarify how and where the parties differ. When faced with such trade-offs, members must make choices about their priorities. Where parties stand in the separation-of-powers system (e.g., as majorities or minorities, in control of the presidency or not) is likely to affect the relative weight they will place on legislating versus messaging. But, as the interviews and perspectives consulted for this chapter reveal, the quest for partisan majorities inhibits legislative cooperation across party lines, particularly for parties dissatisfied with their share of institutional power.

Intensified competition for party control of Congress after 1980 and 1994 makes the trade-offs between legislating and messaging more acute. Competition focuses members' attention on the pursuit of partisan political advantage. During a period when party control of Congress appeared a settled fact of political life, trade-offs between legislating and messaging were less salient. Indeed, members had little reason to consider how they might affect their party's chances of winning or holding control when majority status was seemingly not in doubt. As one staff veteran of the House in the 1960s and 1970s observed, "The era of maximum [bipartisan] cooperation was when Democrats had an overwhelming majority. Under those circumstances, they could afford to give amendments to Republicans, to make concessions. [But] this kind of co-operation only prevails when the minority is resigned to minority status."[19] On the other hand, as Rep. Vic Fazio (D-CA) observed in 2002, "I'm afraid that when your majority is so small, if you were to overlook the priority of the next election, you would be derelict in your duties" (Nather 2002, 1922).

In the contemporary Congress, neither party is resigned to being a permanent minority. As such, members of both parties are likely to carefully weigh their choices between focusing on politics and focusing on policy—between messaging and legislating. In this context, Sen. Joe Manchin (D-WV) has bemoaned what he perceives as an excessive focus on winning partisan advantage. "Politics rules the day," he said. "Don't worry about policy; don't worry about good government, just worry about politics: who has 51 [in the Senate] and who's got 218 [in the House]" (Everett 2014).

NOTES

1. Interview 32.
2. Quoted in Hulse 2006.
3. Interview 9.
4. Interview 1.
5. Interview 25.
6. Interview 12.
7. Interview 28.
8. Quoted in Hallow (1991).
9. Quoted in Farrell (2001).
10. Interview 1.
11. Interview 20.
12. Interview 7.
13. Interview 20.
14. Interview 28.
15. *Congressional Record*, December 15, 1995, S18698.
16. Interview 11.

17. Quoted in Klein (1995, 37).
18. Interview 2.
19. Interview 24.

REFERENCES

Cohen, Richard E. 1977. "Hour Republicans under Rhodes—Divided They Stand and Fret." *National Journal*, October 29, 1686.

DeLay, Tom D., and Stephen Mansfield. 2007. *No Retreat, No Surrender: One American's Fight*. New York: Sentinel.

Everett, Burgess. 2014. "Congress Punts on Issues That Pile Up." *Politico*. July 22, I.

Hulse, Carl. 2010. "Legislative Hurdles in an Era of Conflict, Not Compromise." *New York Times*, June 20, A20.

Kane, Paul. 2013. "Congress's Committee Chairmen Push to Reassert Their Power." *Washington Post*, February 16, A4.

Krehbiel, Keith. 1998. *Pivotal Politics: A Theory of U.S. Lawmaking*. Chicago: University of Chicago Press.

Mayhew, David R. 2005. *Divided We Govern: Party Control, Lawmaking, and Investigations, 1946–2002*. 2nd ed. New Haven, CT. Yale University Press.

Mitchell, Alison. 1999. "Compromise Takes a Holiday." *New York Times*, August 8, E1.

Nather, David. 2002. "Daschle's Soft Touch Lost in Tough Senate Arena." *CQ Weekly*, July 20, 1920–22.

Stanton, John. 2011. "Boehner's Pursuit of Big Deal Irks GOP." *Roll Call*, December 15, http://www.rollcall.com/issues57_75/Boehner-Pursuit-of-Big-Deal-Irks-GOP-211077-1.html?pos=hftxt.

DISCUSSION QUESTIONS

1. If Mayhew is right—that members of Congress can be assumed to seek reelection above all other goals—how does Congress occasionally pass meaningful, long-lasting legislation that affects many people across the country?

2. What are some effective ways that members of Congress increase their support within their districts to secure reelection?

3. Describe the difference between negative and positive agenda control and describe how the majority political party uses the former (negative) to maintain unity against the opposition.

4. Among the different legislative styles that Bernhard and Sulkin find in Congress, the policy specialist category tends to grow over the course of a member's career. Why would that be the case?

5. Why, in Lee's argument, do minority party members avoid bipartisan compromise? Give an explanation that contrasts the minority party's interests with the majority party's interests.

6. Are the political parties in the U.S. Congress effective in serving the needs of their own members within Congress? Are they effective in serving the needs of the general public? Why or why not?

6

THE PRESIDENCY

6.1

RICHARD E. NEUSTADT

From *Presidential Power and the Modern Presidents: The Politics of Leadership from Roosevelt to Reagan*

In leading a vast executive branch with millions of employees, the president cannot monitor all those who work for him, nor can he or she compel many people to act. This excerpt from the famous book by Neustadt makes the simple point that presidents lead by persuading others that their interests coincide with the president's interests. According to Neustadt, presidential power ebbs and flows with each president's credibility as a persuader.

THE POWER TO PERSUADE

. . . The Constitutional Convention of 1787 is supposed to have created a government of "separated powers." It did nothing of the sort. Rather, it created a government of separated institutions *sharing* powers. "I am part of the legislative process," Eisenhower often said in 1959 as a reminder of his veto. Congress, the dispenser of authority and funds, is no less part of the administrative process. Federalism adds another set of separated institutions. The Bill of Rights adds others. Many public purposes can only be achieved by voluntary acts of private institutions; the press, for one, in Douglass Cater's phrase, is a "fourth branch of government." And with the coming of alliances abroad, the separate institutions of a London, or a Bonn, share in the making of American public policy.

From Richard E. Neustadt, *Presidential Power and the Modern Presidents: The Politics of Leadership from Roosevelt to Reagan* (New York: The Free Press, 1990).

What the Constitution separates our political parties do not combine. The parties are themselves composed of separated organizations sharing public authority. The authority consists of nominating powers. Our national parties are confederations of state and local party institutions, with a headquarters that represents the White House, more or less, if the party has a President in office. These confederacies manage presidential nominations. All other public offices depend upon electorates confined within the states. All other nominations are controlled within the states. The President and congressmen who bear one party's label are divided by dependence upon different sets of voters. The differences are sharpest at the stage of nomination. The White House has too small a share in nominating congressmen, and Congress has too little weight in nominating presidents for party to erase their constitutional separation. Party links are stronger than is frequently supposed, but nominating processes assure the separation.

The separateness of institutions and the sharing of authority prescribe the terms on which a President persuades. When one man shares authority with another, but does not gain or lose his job upon the other's whim, his willingness to act upon the urging of the other turns on whether he conceives the action right for him. The essence of a President's persuasive task is to convince such men that what the White House wants of them is what they ought to do for their sake and on their authority. (Sex matters not at all; for *man* read *woman*.)

Persuasive power, thus defined, amounts to more than charm or reasoned argument. These have their uses for a President, but these are not the whole of his resources. For the individuals he would induce to do what he wants done on their own responsibility will need or fear some acts by him on his responsibility. If they share his authority, he has some share in theirs. Presidential "powers" may be inconclusive when a President commands, but always remain relevant as he persuades. The status and authority inherent in his office reinforce his logic and his charm.

Status adds something to persuasiveness; authority adds still more. . . . In Walter Bagehot's charming phrase, "no man can *argue* on his knees." Although there is no kneeling in this country, few men—and exceedingly few cabinet officers—are immune to the impulse to say "yes" to the President of the United States. It grows harder to say "no" when they are seated in his Oval Office at the White House, or in his study on the second floor, where almost tangibly he partakes of the aura of his physical surroundings. In Sawyer's case, moreover, the President possessed formal authority to intervene in many matters of concern to the secretary of commerce. These matters ranged from jurisdictional disputes among the defense agencies to legislation pending before Congress and, ultimately, to the tenure of the secretary, himself. . . .

A President's authority and status give him great advantages in dealing with the men he would persuade. Each "power" is a vantage point for him in the degree that other men have use for his authority. From the veto to appointments, from publicity to budgeting, and so down a long list, the White House now controls the most encompassing array of vantage points in the American political system. With hardly an exception, those who share in governing this country are aware that at some time, in some degree, the doing of *their* jobs, the furthering of *their* ambitions, may depend upon the President of the United States. Their need for presidential action, or their fear of it, is bound to be recurrent if not actually continuous. Their need or fear is his advantage.

A President's advantages are greater than mere listing of his "powers" might suggest. Those with whom he deals must deal with him until the last day of his term. Because they have continuing relationships with him, his future, while it lasts, supports his present influence. Even though there is no need or fear of him today, what he could do tomorrow may supply today's advantage. Continuing relationships may convert any "power," any aspect of his status, into vantage points in almost any case. When he induces other people to do what he wants done, a President can trade on their dependence now and later.

The President's advantages are checked by the advantages of others. Continuing relationships will pull in both directions. These are relationships of mutual dependence. A President depends upon the persons whom he would persuade; he has to reckon with his need or fear of them. They, too, will possess status, or authority, or both, else they would be of little use to him. Their vantage points confront his own; their power tempers his.

▪   ▪   ▪

The power to persuade is the power to bargain. Status and authority yield bargaining advantages. But in a government of "separated institutions sharing powers," they yield them to all sides. With the array of vantage points at his disposal, a President may be far more persuasive than his logic or his charm could make him. But outcomes are not guaranteed by his advantages. There remain the counter pressures those whom he would influence can bring to bear on him from vantage points at their disposal. Command has limited utility; persuasion becomes give-and-take. It is well that the White House holds the vantage points it does. In such a business, any President may need them all—and more.

II

This view of power as akin to bargaining is one we commonly accept in the sphere of congressional relations. Every textbook states and every legislative session demonstrates that save in times like the extraordinary Hundred Days of 1933—times virtually ruled out by definition at midcentury—a President will often be unable to obtain congressional action on his terms or even to halt action he opposes. The reverse is equally accepted: Congress often is frustrated by the President. Their formal powers are so intertwined that neither will accomplish very much, for very long, without the acquiescence of the other. By the same token, though, what one demands the other can resist. The stage is set for that great game, much like collective bargaining, in which each seeks to profit from the other's needs and fears. It is a game played catch-as-catch-can, case by case. And everybody knows the game, observers and participants alike.

■   ■   ■

In spheres of party politics the same thing follows, necessarily, from the confederal nature of our party organizations. Even in the case of national nominations, a President's advantages are checked by those of others. In 1944, it is by no means clear that Roosevelt got his first choice as his running mate. In 1948, Truman, then the President, faced serious revolts against his nomination. In 1952, his intervention from the White House helped assure the choice of Adlai Stevenson, but it is far from clear that Truman could have done as much for any other candidate acceptable to him. In 1956, when Eisenhower was President, the record leaves obscure just who backed Harold Stassen's efforts to block Richard Nixon from renomination as vice president. But evidently everything did not go quite as Eisenhower wanted, whatever his intentions may have been. The outcomes in these instances bear all the marks of limits on command and of power checked by power that characterize congressional relations. Both in and out of politics these checks and limits seem to be quite widely understood.

Influence becomes still more a matter of give-and-take when Presidents attempt to deal with allied governments. A classic illustration is the long unhappy wrangle over Suez policy in 1956. In dealing with the British and the French before their military intervention, Eisenhower had his share of bargaining advantages but no effective power of command. His allies had their share of counterpressures, and they finally tried the most extreme of all: action despite him. His pressure then was instrumental in reversing them. But had the British government been on safe ground at home, Eisenhower's wishes might have made as little difference after intervention as before. Behind the decorum of diplomacy—which was not very decorous in the Suez affair—relationships among allies are not unlike relationships among state delegations at a national convention. Power is persuasion, and persuasion becomes bargaining. The concept is familiar to everyone who watches foreign policy.

In only one sphere is the concept unfamiliar: the sphere of executive relations. Perhaps because of civics textbooks and teaching in our schools, Americans instinctively resist the view that power in this sphere resembles power in all others. Even Washington reporters, White House aides, and congressmen are not immune to the illusion that administrative agencies comprise a single structure, "the" executive branch, where presidential word is law, or ought to be. . . . When a President seeks something from executive officials his persuasiveness is subject to the same sorts of limitations as in the case of congressmen, or governors, or national committeemen, or private citizens, or foreign governments. There are no generic differences, no differences in kind and only sometimes in degree. The incidents preceding the dismissal of MacArthur and the incidents surrounding seizure of the steel mills make it plain that here, as elsewhere, influence derives from bargaining advantages; power is a give-and-take.

Like our governmental structure as a whole, the executive establishment consists of separated institutions sharing powers. The President heads one of these; cabinet officers, agency administrators, and military commanders head others. Below the departmental level, virtually independent bureau chiefs head many more. Under midcentury conditions, federal operations spill across dividing lines on organization charts; almost every policy entangles many agencies; almost every program calls for interagency collaboration. Everything somehow involves the President. But operating agencies owe their existence least of all to one another—and only in some part to him. Each has a separate statutory base; each has its statutes to administer; each deals with a different set of subcommittees at the Capitol. Each has its own peculiar set of clients, friends, and enemies outside the formal government. Each has a different set of specialized careerists inside its own bailiwick. Our Constitution gives the President the "take-care" clause and the appointive power. Our statutes give him central budgeting and a degree of personnel control. All agency administrators are responsible to him. But they also are responsible to Congress, to their clients, to their staffs, and to themselves. In short, they have five masters. Only after all of those do they owe any loyalty to each other.

"The members of the cabinet," Charles G. Dawes used to remark, "are a president's natural enemies." Dawes had been Harding's budget director, Coolidge's vice president, and Hoover's ambassador to London; he also had been General Pershing's chief assistant for supply in World War I. The words are highly colored, but Dawes knew whereof he spoke. The men who have to serve so many masters cannot help but be somewhat the "enemy" of any one of them. By the same token, any master wanting service is in some degree the "enemy" of such a servant. A President is likely to want loyal support but not to relish trouble on his doorstep. Yet the more his cabinet members cleave to him, the more they may need help from him in fending off the wrath of rival masters. Help, though, is synonymous with trouble. Many a cabinet officer, with loyalty ill rewarded by his lights and help withheld, has come to view the White House as innately hostile to department heads. Dawes's dictum can be turned around.

A senior presidential aide remarked to me in Eisenhower's time: "If some of these cabinet members would just take time out to stop and ask themselves, 'What would I want if I were President?' they wouldn't give him all the trouble he's been having." But even if they asked themselves the question, such officials often could not act upon the answer. Their personal attachment to the President is all too often overwhelmed by duty to their other masters.

Executive officials are not equally advantaged in their dealings with a President. Nor are the same officials equally advantaged all the time. . . . The vantage points conferred upon officials by their own authority and status vary enormously. The variance is heightened by particulars of time and circumstance. In mid-October 1950, Truman, at a press conference, remarked of the man he had considered firing in August and would fire the next April for intolerable insubordination:

> Let me tell you something that will be good for your souls. It's a pity that you . . . can't understand the ideas of two intellectually honest men when they meet. General MacArthur . . . is a member of the Government of the United States. He is loyal to that Government. He is loyal to the President. He is loyal to the President in his foreign policy. . . . There is no disagreement between General MacArthur and myself.

MacArthur's status in and out of government was never higher than when Truman spoke those words. The words, once spoken, added to the general's credibility thereafter when he sought to use the press in his campaign against the President. And what had happened between August and October? Near victory had happened, together with that premature conference on postwar plans, the meeting at Wake Island.

If the bargaining advantages of a MacArthur fluctuate with changing circumstances, this is bound to be so with subordinates who have at their disposal fewer powers, lesser status, to fall back on. And when officials have no powers in their own right, or depend upon the President for status, their counterpressure may be limited indeed. White House aides, who fit both categories, are among the most responsive men of all, and for good reason. As a director of the budget once remarked to me, "Thank God I'm here and not across the street. If the President doesn't call me, I've got plenty I can do right here and plenty coming up to me, by rights, to justify my calling him. But those poor fellows over there, if the boss doesn't call them, doesn't ask them to do something, what *can* they do but sit?" Authority and status so conditional are frail reliances in resisting a President's own wants. Within the White House precincts, lifted eyebrows may suffice to set an aide in motion; command, coercion, even charm aside. But even in the White House a President does not monopolize effective power. Even there persuasion is akin to bargaining. A former Roosevelt aide once wrote of cabinet officers:

> Half of a President's suggestions, which theoretically carry the weight of orders, can be safely forgotten by a Cabinet member. And if the President asks about a suggestion a second time, he can be told that it is being investigated. If he asks a third time, a wise Cabinet officer will give him at least part of what he suggests. But only occasionally, except about the most important matters, do Presidents ever get around to asking three times.

The rule applies to staff as well as to the cabinet, and certainly has been applied *by* staff in Truman's time and Eisenhower's.

Some aides will have more vantage points than a selective memory. Sherman Adams, for example, as the assistant to the President under Eisenhower, scarcely deserved the appelation "White House aide" in the meaning of the term before his time or as applied to other members of the Eisenhower entourage. Although Adams was by no means "chief of staff" in any sense so sweeping—or so simple—as press commentaries often took for granted, he apparently became no more dependent on the President than Eisenhower on him. "I need him," said the President when Adams turned out to have been remarkably imprudent in the Goldfine case, and delegated to him, at least nominally, the decision on his own departure. This instance is extreme, but the tendency it illustrates is common enough. Any aide who demonstrates to others that he has the President's consistent confidence and a consistent part in presidential business will acquire so much business on his own account that he becomes in some sense independent of his chief. Nothing in the Constitution keeps a well-placed aide from converting status into power of his own, usable in some degree even against the President—an outcome not unknown in Truman's regime or, by all accounts, in Eisenhower's.

The more an officeholder's status and his powers stem from sources independent of the President, the stronger will be his potential pressure on the President. Department heads in general have more bargaining power than do most members of the White House staff; but bureau chiefs may have still more, and specialists at upper levels of established career services may have almost unlimited reserves of the enormous power which consists of sitting still.

■　　■　　■

In the right circumstances, of course, a President can have his way with any of these people. [There were] three instances where circumstances were "right" and a presidential order was promptly carried out. But one need only note the favorable factors giving those three orders their self-executing quality to recognize that as between a President and his "subordinates," no less than others on whom he depends, real power is reciprocal and varies markedly with organization, subject matter, personality, and situation. The mere fact that persuasion is directed at executive officials signifies no necessary easing of his way. Any new congressman of the Administration's party, especially if narrowly elected, may turn out more amenable (though less useful) to the President than any seasoned bureau chief "downtown." *The probabilities of power do not derive from the literary theory of the Constitution.*

III

There is a widely held belief in the United States that were it not for folly or for knavery, a reasonable President would need no power other than the logic of his argument. No less a personage than Eisenhower has subscribed to that belief in many a campaign speech and press-conference remark. But faulty reasoning and bad intentions do not cause all quarrels with Presidents. The best of reasoning and of intent cannot compose them all. For in the first place, what the President wants will rarely seem a trifle to the people he wants it from. And in the second place, they will be bound to judge it by the standard of their own responsibilities, not his. However logical his argument according to his lights, their judgment may not bring them to his view.

Those who share in governing this country frequently appear to act as though they were in business for themselves. So, in a real though not entire sense, they are and have to be. When Truman and MacArthur fell to quarreling, for example, the stakes were no less than the substance of American foreign policy, the risks of greater war or military stalemate, the prerogatives of Presidents and field commanders, the pride of a proconsul and his place in history. Intertwined, inevitably, were other stakes as well: political stakes for men and factions of both parties; power stakes for interest groups with which they were or wished to be affiliated. And every stake was raised by the apparent discontent in the American public mood. There is no reason to suppose that in such circumstances men of large but differing responsibilities will see all things through the same glasses. On the contrary, it is to be expected that their views of what ought to be done and what they then should do will vary with the differing perspectives their particular responsibilities evoke. Since their duties are not vested in a "team" or a "collegium" but in themselves, as individuals, one must expect that they will see things for themselves. Moreover, when they are responsible to many masters and when an event or policy turns loyalty against loyalty—a day-by-day occurrence in the nature of the case—one must assume that those who have the duties to perform will choose the terms of reconciliation. This is the essence of their personal responsibility. When their own duties pull in opposite directions, who else but they can choose what they will do?

When Truman dismissed MacArthur, the latter lost three posts: the American command in the Far East, the Allied command for the occupation of Japan, and the United Nations command in Korea. He also lost his status as the senior officer on active duty in the United States armed forces. So long as he held those positions and that status, though, he had a duty to his troops, to his profession, to himself (the last is hard for any man to disentangle from the rest). As a public figure and a focus for men's hopes he had a duty to constituents at home, and in Korea and Japan. He owed a duty also to those other constituents, the UN governments contributing to his field forces. As a patriot he had a duty to his country. As an accountable official and an expert guide he stood at the call of Congress. As a military officer he had, besides, a duty to the President, his constitutional commander. Some of these duties may have manifested themselves in terms more tangible or more direct than others. But it would be nonsense to argue that the last negated all the rest, however much it might be claimed to override them. And it makes no more sense to think that anybody but MacArthur was effectively empowered to decide how he himself would reconcile the competing demands his duties made upon him.

■   ■   ■

The essence of a President's persuasive task, with congressmen and everybody else, is to induce them to believe that what he wants of them is what their own appraisal of their own responsibilities requires them to do in their interest, not his. Because men may differ in their views on public policy, because differences in outlook stem from differences in duty—duty to one's office, one's constituents, oneself—that task is bound to be more like collective bargaining than like a reasoned argument among philosopher kings. Overtly or implicitly, hard bargaining has characterized all illustrations offered up to now. This is the reason why: persuasion deals in the coin of self-interest with men who have some freedom to reject what they find counterfeit.

6.2

CHARLES M. CAMERON

From *Veto Bargaining: Presidents and the Politics of Negative Power*

The president is the executive of the national government, but he has a key leg-islative power that allows him to influence Congress: the veto. Cameron shows how presidents can use the veto effectively to shape legislation. The threat of a presidential veto can be enough; Congress will often write legislation specifically to avoid a veto.

"Presidential power" is a deceptive phrase. It suggests that the capacity to shape policy is an attribute of the *president*, and a single attribute at that. But power is not an attribute of an individual, like her height or weight. Instead, "power" describes something about the outcome of a strategic interaction (a "game"). In particular, a president has power in a game when its outcome resembles what the president wants and he causes the outcome to be that way.[1]

This way of thinking about power shifts attention from the attributes of presidents to the characteristics of the games they play. Among these many games are the Supreme Court nominations game, the veto game, the executive order game, the treaty ratification game, the legislative leadership game, the agency supervision and management game, the commander-in-chief game, the staffing game, the executive reorganization game, the opinion leadership game, and the impeachment game. *Understanding the presidency means under-standing these games.* I am tempted to add, "and that is all it means," but that would be too strong. Skill, personality, and charisma seem to matter, or so many people believe. But they always operate within the confines of specific games and strategic circumstances. Understanding the games presidents play is fundamental for understanding presidential power.

Presidents participate in so many games that it is hard to characterize them in a simple way. Broadly speaking, though, when presidents interact with Con-gress, they often play *coordination games* or *bargaining games*. Loosely speak-ing, coordination games require many players to act in one of several possible ways if they are to benefit themselves. If they do not all act in the same way, they work at cross-purposes. The politics of such games involve selecting the "focal points" coordinating the players' actions. A majority party setting its

From Charles M. Cameron, *Veto Bargaining: Presidents and the Politics of Negative Power* (New York: Cambridge University Press, 2000).

legislative agenda in Congress is a prime example of this situation, because many players—across committees in both houses and in the leadership—must focus on a few priorities if they are to accomplish much. Oft times, the selection of focal points involves loose norms and improvisation rather than formal procedures specified in law or the Constitution; this lies outside what Neustadt called the "literary theory of the Constitution," though hardly outside the reach of social science.

In contrast, bargaining games require players to divide among themselves a "pie," or set of benefits. The politics of bargaining involves gambits increasing one's share of the pie. Examples include haggling over the content of laws, pulling and hauling to determine the direction and vigor of agency decisions, and bickering over the appointment of executive officials and judges. These activities all involve give-and-take across the branches of government. Many bargaining games in which the president participates are quite formal, with a structure specified by the Constitution, by law, or by norms of long-standing precedent.[2]

▪ ▪ ▪

PRESIDENTIAL BARGAINING GAMES: WHAT DO WE KNOW?

Given the importance of bargaining games for the contemporary presidency, an obvious question is: What does the empirical record tell us about presidential bargaining games? This seems like it should be an easy question to answer, but unfortunately it is not. The problem is that data on the *process* of bargaining—the number of vetoes, of nominees rejected by Congress, the number of oversight hearings, the number of policy proposals in State of the Union messages, the number of bills introduced in Congress, the number of executive orders reversed by Congress, and so on—are relatively easy to collect but hard to interpret (I'll explain why shortly). Conversely, data on the *outputs* from bargaining games—for example, the number and content of important laws, executive orders, and treaties, the intensity and import of bureaucratic action, the ideological tenor and meaning of court decisions—are very hard to collect but much easier to interpret.

Why are process measures so much harder to interpret compared to output measures? The problem is that power in bargaining games often operates through *anticipation*. Congress anticipates a veto if it goes too far: in order to avoid the veto, it trims back a policy initiative. No veto occurs, but the president's preferences have altered what Congress would have done if [it] could have operated without constraint. In other words, the game's structure allows the president to exercise power over the outcome, even absent a veto. As a second example, suppose the president anticipates a torrent of opposition if he nominates a controversial activist to head a regulatory agency. Accordingly, he eschews the controversial nominee in favor of a more moderate one, though he would prefer to put the activist in charge if he could do so without cost. The nomination then flies through Congress. In this case, the structure of the game allows Congress to exercise some power over the nominee's ideology, even with no direct evidence of this in the public record.

Situations like this involve the "second face of power," power operating through anticipated response.[3] These situations are notoriously difficult to study using process measures since participants maneuver to avoid the most easily measured consequences of disagreement.

How can one find the traces of power when the second face of power is at work? There are two methods: the first direct, the second indirect. The direct method involves measuring policy outputs and relating them to the actors' preferences. If the president actually exercises power over the output, even without taking visible action, then a switch from a liberal president to a conservative one should result in a change in policy, *ceteris paribus*. If one collects data on policy outputs and proxies for preference changes (e.g., partisan affiliation of the president and key congressional actors), and the policy outputs change in a clear and simple way in response to changes in the preference proxies, then one has strong circumstantial evidence of power being exercised. Obviously, one needs to control for confounding influences, but the principle is clear enough.[4]

The indirect approach is more convoluted. It begins with process data, such as vetoes, rejected nominees, reversed executive orders, and blocked agency initiatives. The problem is interpreting such data. In order for events like vetoes to occur, there must be policy disagreement between the actors. But this is only a *necessary* condition. It is certainly not a *sufficient* condition, as arguments about the second face of power indicate. Instead, a process marker like a veto, a rejected nominee or treaty, or a reversed executive order, represents the impact of policy disagreement, *plus something else beyond mere disagreement*. Let us call this additional element "Factor X."[5] The essence of the indirect approach is to build an explicit model of bargaining *incorporating Factor X*. Using this model, one can interpret the process measures and even draw conclusions about presidential power. Absent such a model, all that can be concluded from process measures like counts of vetoes is that policy disagreement occurred—a very weak conclusion since policy disagreement may not trigger a veto without Factor X.[6]

■   ■   ■

The Indirect Approach: Studying Veto Bargaining

Absent a model of vetoes (actual vetoes, not just veto power), any number of vetoes is equally compatible with little, some, or a great deal of presidential power over legislative outputs. No vetoes may mean that Congress has capitulated to the president, or the president has capitulated to Congress; or that Congress has made some compromises before submitting the bill to the president, who compromises somewhat by accepting it. Many vetoes are equally ambiguous. The lesson is a general one—data on process measures simply do not speak for themselves. The idea of the indirect approach is to combine process measures with explicit models of bargaining, in the hope the data will speak more distinctly.

Veto Threats

Matthews provides an elegant model of veto threats, beginning with a standard model of one-shot, take-it-or-leave-it bargaining over political issues.[7] Then he adds an explicit "Factor X"—congressional uncertainty about the president's policy preferences. In other words, Matthews assumes the president has a policy reputation, but the reputation is not so precise that Congress can predict with pinpoint accuracy the response of the president to every conceivable bill. Disagreement between the president and Congress, *plus* congressional uncertainty about how far it can push the president before triggering a veto, allows vetoes to occur within the model—they occur when the president turns out to be somewhat tougher (that is, more extreme) than Congress anticipated. Finally, Matthews allows the president to issue a veto threat before Congress writes a bill. Using quite sophisticated game theory, Matthews works out predictions about the behavior of Congress and president.

Within the confines of the model, one can evaluate the impact of the "institution" of the veto threat on presidential power. Broadly speaking, veto threats often enhance presidential power (relative to a world without veto threats), because they help the president and Congress strike bargains that they might not otherwise forge, for want of congressional concessions. Moreover, the concessions induced by threats often work to the advantage of the president.[8]

In our own research, my collaborators and I present systematic data on veto threats, congressional concessions after threats, and vetoes after threats, and use Matthews's model to interpret the data (and, to some extent, use the data to test the model).[9] The universe for the study consists of the 2,284 "nonminor" bills presented to the president between 1945 and 1992. We collected data on a random sample of 281 nonvetoed bills from the universe, stratified across three levels of "legislative significance" derived from an approach similar to Mayhew's. We also collected data on all vetoed bills in the universe, some 162 bills, for a total of 443 bills in all. We compiled data on threats and concessions from legislative histories of the bills, the public papers of the presidents, and newspaper accounts.

Statistical analysis of the data revealed the following patterns:

1. During unified government, veto threats rarely occur regardless of the significance of the legislation.
2. During divided government, veto threats occur frequently and increase in frequency with legislative significance. The frequency of veto threats for important legislation during divided government is surprisingly high: 34 percent of such bills received veto threats.

3. If a bill is not threatened, a veto is unlikely though not impossible.
4. If a bill is threatened, the probability of a veto increases dramatically, especially during divided government and at higher levels of legislative significance. But vetoes are not certain even after a threat.
5. Veto threats usually bring concessions.
6. Concessions deter vetoes. The bigger the concession the less likely a threatened bill is to be vetoed.

Although some of these findings lie outside the scope of Matthews's model (e.g., the importance of legislative significance), for the most part these findings strongly resemble what the model predicts. Thus, the model "explains" the data, in the sense that it provides a detailed causal mechanism for the process. If one combines the import of the model—veto threats often enhance presidential power—with the data on the actual frequency of threats, one obtains a picture in which veto threats assume considerable importance in the armamentarium of presidents serving in periods of divided party government.

NOTES

1. This conclusion follows from the canonical definition of power: "power is a causal relationship between preferences and outcomes." For a thorough discussion, see Jack Nagal, *The Descriptive Analysis of Power* (New Haven, CT: Yale University Press, 1975).

2. The distinction I am drawing between coordination and bargaining is rooted more in presidential politics than abstract game theory. For example, there are bargaining games in which coordination is critical (e.g., Nash bargaining games, with a multitude of equilibria). So I am not drawing a logical or mathematical distinction but instead pointing to the character of different activities.

3. Peter Bachrach and Morton Baratz, "The Two Faces of Power," *American Political Science Review* (1962) 56: 947–52.

4. This method of studying power is laid out in the classics of the power literature, see Robert A. Dahl, *Modern Political Analysis*, 2nd ed. (Englewood Cliffs, NJ: Prentice-Hall, 1970), and Jack Nagal, *The Descriptive Analysis of Power* (New Haven, CT: Yale University Press, 1975). It was first applied to studying presidential power in Terry Moe, "An Assessment of the Positive Theory of 'Congressional Dominance' of Bureaucracy," *Legislative Studies Quarterly* (1987) 12: 475, and Barry R. Weingast, and Mark J. Moran, "Bureaucracy Discretion or Congressional Control? Regulatory Policymaking by the Federal Trade Commission," *Journal of Political Economy* (1983) 91: 765–800.

5. For those who don't like suspense: "Factor X" often turns out to be some type of uncertainty, including uncertainty about what others will do (e.g., in the form of mixed strategies) or what they want (e.g., incomplete information about actors' preferences) and thus what they will do.

6. One cannot even conclude that vetoes are evidence of the most important or most intense disagreements. Drawing that conclusion requires a model of vetoes in which the statement is true; absent the model, it is not a valid inference.

7. Steven Matthews, "Veto Threats: Rhetoric in a Bargaining Game," *Quarterly Journal of Economics* (1989) 103: 347–69.

8. They don't always do so, for sometimes the concessions are inadequate to head off a veto. In this case, concessions don't actually advantage the president (neglecting veto overrides).

9. Charles M. Cameron, *Veto Bargaining: Presidents and the Politics of Negative Power* (New York: Cambridge University Press, 2000), and Charles Cameron, John S. Lapinski, and Charles Riemann, "Testing Formal Theories of Political Rhetoric," *Journal of Politics* (Winter 2000).

6.3

BRANDICE CANES-WRONE

From *Who Leads Whom? Presidents, Policy, and the Public*

Do presidents follow public opinion even when they believe it is wrong? Or do presidents do what they think is right even when doing so is unpopular? Canes-Wrone describes three important cases when presidents pandered; that is, they followed public opinion rather than do what they thought was the right thing to do. She argues that this happens often.

EXAMPLES OF POLICY PANDERING AND LEADERSHIP

Why did Jimmy Carter, a long-time proponent of expanding humanitarian assistance, suddenly propose to scale back the program? Why did Ronald Reagan, who was philosophically opposed to tax increases, recommend an unpopular one? And why did George H. W. Bush veto a bill extending unemployment benefits only to sign similar bills over the course of the following eight months?

. . . [T]he cases illustrate the behaviors of *policy pandering* and *policy leadership*. Pandering reflects circumstances in which a president supports a popular policy option despite the fact that he expects it to harm citizens' interests. Policy leadership, in comparison, occurs when a president endorses an unpopular option that he believes will advance societal welfare.

■   ■   ■

Case Selection

The primary motivation for developing the Conditional Pandering Theory was to assess the incentives of the president to pander to public opinion when forced to choose between endorsing a popular course of action or one he believes will produce a good outcome for society. Given this substantive aim, I focus the narrative analysis on executive decisions for which the president's beliefs regarding the optimal policy choice differed from those of the mass public. As previously discussed, the concept of policy pandering does not require that a president's beliefs regarding the optimal course of action are

From Brandice Canes-Wrone, *Who Leads Whom? Presidents, Policy, and the Public* (Chicago: University of Chicago Press, 2005).

necessarily correct. Accordingly, in the cases, the fact that a president deemed the mass citizenry to be misguided does not mean that the reader will necessarily agree with the president's assessment.

The need to ascertain the president's beliefs in relation to public opinion made the selection of cases contingent on the availability of historical evidence on these factors. Even so, I imposed a number of additional restrictions regarding the selection. First, to illustrate how the theoretical predictions vary according to the president's popularity relative to that of his likely competition, I ensured that one case concerned a president far ahead of his likely competition, one a president far behind, and one a president who could expect a tight race. . . . [A]t least one case involved a highly popular president, one an unpopular chief executive, and one a marginally popular president. Thus, in the narratives, presidential approval ratings are often employed as a proxy for a chief executive's popularity relative to that of his potential competition. Prior research establishes that this factor is correlated with a president's likelihood of retaining office (e.g., Brody and Sigelman 1983; Sigelman 1979). By comparison, trial heats are not particularly accurate assessments of a president's electoral prospects until the final months of a race; indeed, trial heats are not even routinely available throughout a president's term.

The second restriction is that the universe of potential cases was limited to the decisions of presidents since Nixon. The literature suggests that these presidents have been more likely than their predecessors to involve the mass public in policymaking (e.g., Kernell 1997; Skowronek 1993); the restriction enables showing that the Conditional Pandering Theory is germane to these presidencies. Third, to demonstrate that the theory is not limited in applicability to a given administration or personality, I selected a different chief executive for each case. Fourth, I chose only policy decisions that were significant enough to receive coverage in the *Congressional Quarterly Almanac*. This restriction was inspired by a desire to establish that the theory is relevant to relatively important policy decisions. Finally, the selection was influenced by the fact that presidents can more easily change public opinion in foreign as compared with domestic affairs. Because of this asymmetry, one might suppose that presidential pandering would be uncommon in foreign affairs and common in domestic matters. To demonstrate the relevance of the Conditional Pandering Theory across both domains, I illustrate the behavior of policy pandering with decisions involving foreign affairs and the behavior of policy leadership with decisions on domestic matters.

A substantial portion of each narrative is devoted to describing why seemingly plausible alternative explanations do not explain the sequence of events. This attention to alternative explanations is partially a function of the fact that one would not necessarily anticipate truth revelation by presidents and their advisors. Chief executives are not likely to admit, even in retrospect, that they followed public opinion despite having evidence suggesting the action would produce harmful effects. (Nor are presidents particularly likely to state that electoral motivations were what led them to take an unpopular position, as occurs in the Conditional Pandering Theory when first-term presidents exercise policy leadership.) The narratives accordingly do not revolve around "smoking guns" of admissions by presidents but, instead, careful attention to their long-standing beliefs, public opinion, and possible alternative accounts.

President Carter and Foreign Aid: The Trustee Panders

Carter is reputed to have placed the public interest above other political objectives. For example, Erwin Hargrove (1988, 11) assesses in his biography of Carter: "The key of Carter's understanding of himself as a political leader was his belief that the essential responsibility of leadership was to articulate the good of the entire community rather than any part of it. . . . Rather than being antipolitical or nonpolitical leadership, this was, for him, a different kind of leadership that eschewed the normal politician's preoccupation with representing private interests, bargaining, and short-term electoral goals." Similarly, Charles Jones (1988) characterizes Carter's regime as the "trusteeship presidency," in which the chief executive viewed himself as a trustee of the people and sought to enact policies he believed were in the public interest even when they were not politically expedient. Precisely because of this reputation, I illustrate the behavior of pandering with a case study that concerns President Carter. By establishing that the Conditional Pandering Theory has relevance for his policy decisions, I show it is applicable even to presidents who are not thought to cater to public opinion.

The case study focuses on Carter's budgetary proposal for the policy issue of humanitarian assistance in 1980, the year he ran for reelection. Upon taking office, Carter had pledged to switch U.S. policy toward communist containment in the Third World. Instead of responding militarily whenever conflicts over communism arose, Carter espoused a "preventive" approach. He sought to lessen the appeal of communism to the citizens of Third World nations by solving their underlying problems (e.g., Deibel 1987; Skidmore 1996). Development assistance comprised a key component of this preventive approach.

For the first three years of Carter's term, his proposals for humanitarian assistance, or economic aid, were consistent with this philosophy. In each year, Carter requested an increase and he invariably achieved one, even if not for the full amount he had requested. He pursued this expansion despite a lack of public support for the program; according to responses to the General Social Survey, throughout his administration over 65 percent of the populace believed the United States spent too much on foreign aid.[1]

Carter knew that his policy position was unpopular. He acknowledged as much during a call-in radio show he hosted during the first few months in office. Stating his policy stance to a caller, Carter began, "Well, John [the caller], I'm going to take a position that's not very popular, politically speaking."[2] Likewise, in a session with media representatives during the second year of the administration, Carter remarked, "I don't know of any issue that has less political support than that program itself, foreign aid in all its forms."[3]

Carter's lack of pandering over foreign aid during his first three years in office is consistent with his reputation for placing the public interest above other, more political objectives. His behavior also, however, comports with the Conditional Pandering Theory. The theory suggests that a president will not pander to public opinion if he does not soon face a contest for reelection or if he is highly popular or unpopular. In the early months of 1977 and 1978, when Carter submitted his foreign aid proposals as a part of his annual budgetary requests, the presidential election was relatively distant. By the outset of 1979, when Carter offered his humanitarian aid proposal for the following fiscal year, the electoral race was approaching but Carter's popularity was weak. His public approval ratings for the past year had averaged 43 percent, a very low level by historical standards. His decision to exercise policy leadership is thus consistent with the Conditional Pandering Theory.

Of course, that Carter's policymaking on foreign aid between 1977 and 1979 comports with the Conditional Pandering Theory does not eliminate the possibility that his actions were entirely the consequence of his character. For this reason, we focus on the humanitarian aid proposal Carter offered in 1980, when he reversed his previous position and recommended that the United States cut economic assistance. Specifically, in his budget of January 1980 (which was for fiscal year 1981), Carter proposed cutting economic assistance by 2 percent in nominal terms. The cut constituted a nominal decline of 26 percent relative to his recommendation in the previous budget. Moreover, given the inflation rate predicted by the administration, his request signified a real reduction of 11 percent from the appropriations of last year and 39 percent from his earlier proposal.

The descriptive summaries accompanying the numbers in Carter's budgets reflect the change in his policy position. The budget submitted in 1979 stated that it contained "increases in foreign aid with emphasis on long-term development of poor countries, and reducing widespread poverty." In contrast, the budget submitted in 1980 characterized the proposals for foreign affairs as "designed to help meet the near-term challenges to stability." This budget was also printed in the colors of Carter's reelection campaign, emphasizing the linkage between the document and election year politics (Hargrove 1988).

When Carter submitted his election-year budget, he had reason to believe the impending presidential race would be competitive. His approval ratings were respectable at 58 percent but not remarkably high by historical standards. Moreover, economists were forecasting an imminent recession that would cause double-digit inflation and an increase in unemployment. Carter knew that the recession, assuming it materialized, could cause him serious problems in his campaign for reelection. As a result, he very much wanted his budget to appeal to voters (Kaufman 1993, 168–69).

Carter's policy reversal on foreign aid helped to achieve this goal. By proposing a reduction in economic assistance, he ensured that his position on this program would be consonant with public opinion. According to a Roper survey taken the month before he submitted his budget, 72 percent of the population thought foreign assistance should be decreased.[4] Had Carter continued trying to expand economic aid, he would have handed challengers an easy issue on which to criticize him.

Thus consistent with the Conditional Pandering Theory, Carter switched his position in the direction of public opinion once he was marginally popular and soon faced a contest for reelection. He could reasonably expect that the effects of cutting economic assistance would not be known by voters before the election, particularly since appropriations bills are not typically enacted until summer at the earliest. Moreover, the anticipated competitiveness of the race meant that his policy choice might affect his likelihood of winning. As a result, Carter had an electoral incentive to take the popular position of cutting humanitarian assistance, even if he believed that increasing it was in America's long-term interest.

Among seemingly plausible alternative explanations, none receives support on careful examination. Perhaps the most natural justification, and one that would comport with Carter's reputation for pursuing the public interest, is that his beliefs about the value of humanitarian assistance had changed. In fact, as Michael Genovese (1994) observes, there is a good deal of evidence that Carter shifted from a "Wilsonian idealist" to a "Cold War confrontationist" as his term progressed. David Skidmore (1996) also describes this transformation in an analysis that is fittingly entitled *Reversing Course*. However, as these scholars acknowledge, the transformation began as early as 1978. Thus, if the change in philosophy were the primary cause of Carter's policy reversal on foreign aid, the policy reversal should have occurred earlier.

Moreover, the budget that Carter proposed in his final month in office, after his electoral defeat, reiterated his commitment to a substantial growth in humanitarian assistance. He recommended increasing it by 26 percent in nominal terms, which, given the projected inflation rate, comprised a real increase of 12 percent. The justification Carter gave for this request in his Budget Message highlighted his continued belief in the importance of humanitarian assistance. He stated, "I believe in the need for higher levels of aid to achieve foreign policy objectives, promote economic growth, and help needy people abroad. Foreign aid is not politically popular and represents an easy target for budget reduction. But it is not a wise one." Carter's election-year proposal to decrease development assistance therefore cannot be attributed to a fundamental change in his convictions regarding the benefits of foreign aid.

Given that the policy shift cannot be ascribed to a change in Carter's convictions, I consider whether it can be attributed to factors specific to the time period in which it occurred. These alternative explanations include the macroeconomy, anticipated congressional behavior, and international events. I consider each in turn.

In January 1980, inflation was a major concern for President Carter and the public. During the past year, the consumer price index had increased by 12.4 percent and according to Gallup's Most Important Problem survey, 36 percent of citizens (a plurality of respondents) considered inflation to be the most important problem in the nation.[5] Carter accordingly designed his election-year budget with the goal of curbing inflation (Hargrove 1988, 102–3; Kaufman 1993, 168–69). One could therefore argue that he proposed to cut humanitarian aid in order to help reduce inflation.

The key problem with this argument is that Carter's overall budget was not all that fiscally conservative. As Hargrove (1988, 103) assesses, the budget reflected that Carter was "not, in the final analysis, a conservative prepared to launch a period of austerity." In fact, Carter's budget entailed real increases in other, more popular programs. For example, Carter proposed conspicuous growth in funding for federal health programs and ground transportation, issues on which a majority of the public supported higher spending.[6] It is therefore difficult to conclude that Carter's desire to curb inflation was the primary determinant of his decision to recommend reducing humanitarian assistance.

A separate potential explanation for the policy shift involves Carter's congressional relations. In 1979, Congress failed to enact a Foreign Aid Appropriations Bill. The funding for international assistance programs came from continuing resolutions, which appropriated almost 20 percent less than the president had requested for the programs. Given these events, one might conjecture that Carter's policy reversal resulted from a change in his bargaining strategy.

The evidence suggests, however, that Carter's proposal to reduce international assistance did not reflect a general adjustment in his approach to budgetary negotiations. In fact, in the same budget he proposed expanding programs for which Congress had in the previous year appropriated far less than he had requested. For example, in 1979 Carter obtained 23 percent less funding than he had proposed for the District of Columbia, but in 1980 he still requested 9 percent more than he had in the previous budgetary cycle. Likewise, Congress appropriated 9 percent less than Carter recommended for agricultural spending in 1979, yet in 1980 the president recommended an increase of 20 percent relative to his proposal of the previous year. Carter thus did not systematically lower his budgetary requests in response to previous failures to expand the programs.

In keeping with this evidence that Carter's legislative negotiations differed by policy area, I consider as a final rationale for his policy shift an explanation particular to foreign aid. Specifically, I examine the possibility that an international event induced the president to desire a lower level of humanitarian assistance. In 1979, there were two major international incidents that affected

U.S. interests: the abduction of American hostages in Iran in November 1979 and the Soviet invasion of Afghanistan in the following month. Ostensibly, these incidents could have affected Carter's beliefs concerning the value of bilateral assistance to the Soviet Union and Iran.

Regardless of the president's beliefs about such bilateral assistance, however, his proposal to reduce humanitarian aid could not be the consequence of them. As documented in the 1981 *Country Report on Human Rights Practices* prepared by the State Department, the United States offered no bilateral assistance to the Soviet Union or Iran in 1979.[7] Thus, Carter could not recommend cutting assistance to these countries.[8] A related possibility is that the Soviet invasion of Afghanistan and the Iranian hostage crisis induced the president to disfavor the use of humanitarian aid as a means of solving the problems of the Third World. Yet, as previously discussed, soon after the 1980 elections, Carter proposed a massive increase in humanitarian assistance. Thus the international events seem to have, if anything, strengthened the president's belief that humanitarian assistance would promote U.S. interests.[9]

In sum, Carter's policy reversal on foreign aid in 1980 cannot be attributed to a change in his belief system, the state of the economy, congressional relations, or to the major foreign events of the day. Nor is the shift consistent with his subsequent policy proposals on foreign aid. The decision does, however, comport with the Conditional Pandering Theory. When the election was distant or Carter's approval ratings were low, he pursued the course of action he believed to be in the public interest. Yet when the election was near and his public standing was such that he seemed likely to face a tight race, the president pandered to public opinion.

President Bush and Unemployment Benefits: Policy Leadership from Ahead and Pandering

Throughout the summer of 1991, President Bush looked likely to sail to reelection. His approval ratings had hit historically high levels in the wake of the Gulf War victory earlier that year and still hovered in the high 60s and low 70s.[10] Front-runners for the Democratic nomination decided one after another not to challenge the president. By September, Al Gore, Richard Gephardt, and Jay Rockefeller IV had all dropped out of the race. As Robert E. Denton and Mary E. Stuckey (1994, 19) surmise, "Bush simply seemed unbeatable."

This popularity was noteworthy given the lackluster economy over which the president was presiding. The gross national product (GNP) had increased only 0.4 percent during the second quarter of 1991, and this relatively meager growth followed nine months of GNP retraction.[11] As of June, the unemployment rate was approaching 7 percent.[12] Much of the unemployment involved middle-management workers who had been downsized by corporations. These managers were having a particularly difficult time finding alternative employment; many remained jobless at the time their unemployment benefits expired. The unemployment rate thus reflected a substantial number of workers who were not only out of work but also not receiving government assistance. For instance, in July 1991 unemployment compensation expired for 350,000 jobless Americans (Cohen 1997, 218).

It was in this environment that Congress enacted a series of bills extending unemployment benefits. The first of these bills to reach Bush's desk was HR 3201, which arrived August 17. The legislation provided up to 20 weeks of extra benefits through July 1992 at an estimated cost of $5.3 billion. The legislation specified that for the compensation to be distributed, the president had to declare a state of emergency. Bush signed the bill but did not declare an emergency, thereby preventing the expenditure of the benefits.

The second unemployment bill to reach Bush's desk was S 1722, entitled the Emergency Unemployment Compensation Act of 1991. The bill, which was passed by Congress on October 1, again offered up to 20 weeks of extended benefits and had an estimated cost of $6.4 billion. Unlike the earlier legislation, S 1722 did not allow the president the option of signing the legislation without obligating the additional benefits. Bush could thus either veto the bill or enact the temporary extension.[13]

Surveys conducted around the time that Congress passed S 1722 suggest the bill was quite popular. A *Los Angeles Times* poll taken September 21 through 25 found that 63 percent of respondents favored the legislation strongly or at least somewhat, and only 33 percent opposed it.[14] Likewise, a Harris poll conducted September 27 through October 2 found that only 37 percent of respondents would rate the president's opposition to the bill as "excellent" or "pretty good."[15] These survey data suggest that to the extent Bush wished to placate the mass public, he had an incentive to endorse the legislation.

Bush's incentives were not straightforward, however, because he did not believe that the extension of unemployment benefits would promote a strong economy. As David Mervin (1996, 87) describes, the president was "particularly averse to government interference in the economy." This belief repeatedly put him in conflict with the Democratic-controlled Congress. Nicholas Calio, who was in charge of Bush's legislative relations, describes how the White House perceived congressional efforts to control the economy: "There were many things that, in our view, Congress got involved in [which] it really shouldn't [have]—in micro managing markets. . . . There were a lot of things we felt needed to be stopped."[16]

The legislation S 1722, the Emergency Unemployment Compensation Act, was apparently one of those things. While the legislation was being considered, Bush openly referred to it as part of "a bunch of garbage" that the Democrats were sending his way.[17] In a news conference, he argued that the measure would ultimately harm taxpayers. Furthermore, he exhorted citizens to implore their representatives to "do something that the President can sign that will help us with unemployment benefits but will also protect the other taxpayer."[18] On October 11, Bush vetoed S 1722, declaring in an accompanying memorandum that it would "threaten economic recovery and its associated job creation." He continued, "the Congress has . . . ignored my call for passage of measures that will increase the nation's competitiveness, productivity and growth.[19]

For all of this strong language, Bush agreed to a measure quite similar to S 1722, HR 3575, less than two months later. HR 3575 extended unemployment benefits for up to 20 weeks through mid-June at an estimated cost of $5.3 billion. When the president signed the bill on November 15, his electoral vulnerability was much greater than it had been when he had vetoed S 1722. Headlines from the preceding weeks had declared "Democrats Find Bush Is Vulnerable" and "Democrat Hopefuls See Bush Weakness."[20] Correspondingly, his popularity ratings had dropped to 56 percent.[21]

The possibility that Bush switched his policy position for electoral reasons did not go unnoticed at the time. For example, Senator George Mitchell of Maine, referring to Bush's apparent reversal, asserted the president was in "panic city."[22] The administration rebuked such criticism and claimed the legislative negotiations had, in fact, culminated in a victory for the president over the details of how the unemployment benefits would be funded. According to the administration, the bill that Bush had originally vetoed would have increased the deficit and thus violated the 1990 Budget Act, which required that any new program not add to the deficit. The bill he signed, in comparison, supposedly paid for itself through tax increases on the wealthy, the renewal of an employer tax, and a new policy of income confiscation from individuals who defaulted on school loans.[23]

Such a justification for Bush's action would have been more credible had the president not soon thereafter approved another temporary extension of unemployment benefits, HR 4095, which many believed would increase the deficit. Bush signed this subsequent legislation on February 7, 1992, after his popularity ratings had been hovering in the mid-40s for the past month.[24] HR 4095 provided an additional thirteen weeks of benefits, paying for them primarily through a "surplus" that the Office of Management and Budget (OMB) predicted would arise from 1991 tax bills.[25] The Congressional Budget Office (CBO) disputed the prediction of a surplus, and critics ridiculed the forecast.[26] For example, Representative Thomas J. Downey, a Democrat from Long Island, chided that "Only in the land of Oz could you take a $350 billion deficit and find $2 billion in savings."[27]

The claim that Bush did not switch his position seemed even more disingenuous in July 1992. On July 3, when the president was running neck-and-neck with Bill Clinton and Ross Perot in the pre-election polls, the president signed HR 5260, which permanently changed the unemployment system by allowing nonemergency benefits to take effect more easily during times of high unemployment. As recently as April, Bush had opposed making such permanent changes to the system.[28] Even the day before signing HR 5260, the president had threatened to veto the permanent expansion.[29] The champion of the bill in Congress, Representative Thomas J. Downey, offered an explanation for Bush's actions during the brief House debate over the legislation. He predicted, "The President is going to sign this bill for two reasons. Unemployment is up, and his popularity is down."[30]

Does the variation in Bush's policy decisions over unemployment benefits correspond to the predictions of the Conditional Pandering Theory? The theory suggests that a president will endorse policies that he believes are in the public interest when he is quite popular relative to his likely electoral competition, when he is relatively unpopular, or when he does not soon face a contest for reelection. In this case, Bush supported an unpopular policy that he believed would advance a strong economy so long as his electoral prospects were strong. Once he seemed vulnerable, however, he changed course and issued popular decisions that did not reflect his belief that preventing government interference in the economy would harm it and, by consequence, societal welfare. This variation in executive behavior is exactly what the Conditional Pandering Theory would predict.

Some readers may take issue with the notion that Bush was trying to advance societal welfare by vetoing unemployment benefits. It is accordingly worth reemphasizing that the Conditional Pandering Theory does not require that a president is actually advancing citizens' interests, only that he believes he is doing so; the president can be wrong in this assessment. The preceding description of events documented that Bush believed economic recovery, as well as long-term growth, would be best advanced by limiting government interference in the macroeconomy. The question of whether these beliefs were accurate, or whether they are in part a function of ideological biases, is not paramount to analyzing the predicative power of the theory. In the concluding section of this reading, I return to the issue of whether presidents are likely to have better information than citizens do about the expected consequences of policies. For now, I have a more precise goal, which is to show that the Conditional Pandering does a better job at predicting the variation in Bush's policy decisions than seemingly likely alternative explanations.

To realize this goal, four alternative rationales are evaluated, the last two of which are evaluated jointly. First, I examine whether Bush altered his policy beliefs in response to economic events. Second, the possibility that his claims of policy consistency were correct is considered. Third, I analyze executive-legislative negotiations that occurred after Clinton had taken a clear lead in order to assess whether Bush's likelihood of pandering was simply greater the sooner the election; and fourth, whether this likelihood was greater the lower his chances of retaining office.

During the course of the executive-legislative negotiations over the extension of unemployment benefits, the unemployment rate itself varied noticeably. When the president vetoed an extension of benefits in October 1991, the Labor Department had just announced that the rate had dropped a tenth of a percentage point to 6.7 percent. A month later, when Bush approved a temporary extension, the rate had risen back up to 6.8 percent. Furthermore, at the subsequent bill signings in February and July, the rate was estimated to be 7.1

percent and 7.8 percent, respectively. It therefore seems plausible that changes in the economic situation caused Bush to believe greater government intervention in the economy was warranted.

Yet the evidence suggests otherwise. In June 1991, the unemployment rate was 6.9 percent, and legislation temporarily extending compensation to the jobless was already making its way through Congress. Bush, who was enjoying approval ratings in the mid-70s, did not lend support to the bill. Then in July 1992, Bush threatened to veto a permanent expansion of unemployment benefits even after the Labor Department had announced that the unemployment rate was 7.8 percent, the highest level in eight years.[31]

Finally, Bush never intimated that he reversed course because of changes in the economy. Instead, he consistently stated that his willingness to approve extensions of compensation depended on whether they would increase the deficit. For example, during a news conference in August 1991, he promoted Senator Dole's proposed extension of unemployment benefits, which was less expensive than the Democratic proposals, claiming that the Dole plan had "fiscal integrity."[32] At a fundraising luncheon in November, the president expounded his position further, declaring:

> The Democratic leaders know that I've been ready since August to sign an extension, but to sign one as proposed by most of the Republicans in the Senate and House that lives within the budget agreement. We don't have to add to the ever-increasing deficit and still do what is compassionate and correct. They passed a bill. They wanted to embarrass me politically. I vetoed that bill . . . Unemployed workers deserve this kind of support, but we need a change in the Congress if we're going to do it in a way that lives within the budget agreement.[33]

These assertions comport with the ones Bush gave eight months later with regards to permanently extending unemployment compensation. When the president was asked by Congressman Robert H. Michel, the Minority Leader of the House, whether he might veto such legislation, Bush responded that he had a "certain custodianship for trying to support reasonable expenditures." He continued, "If [Democratic congressional members] send me something that we view and the leadership here views as too expensive, we'll have to send it back and urge them to get one down there that we can support."[34]

In sum, Bush's actions as well as rhetoric indicate that changes in the unemployment rate did not alter his fundamental beliefs about the appropriateness of extending benefits to the jobless. The president's rhetoric highlights a separate alternative explanation, however, which is that substantive differences among the assorted bills explain the variation in his willingness to sign them. The president's decisions could accordingly be construed as an example of what Cameron (2000) terms "veto bargaining." This rationale for the seemingly disparate decisions has some merit. In fact, had the legislative matter ended after Bush's approval of the extension of benefits in November 1991, it would be relatively straightforward to argue that his policy actions reflected an aversion to increasing the deficit.

The president's behavior in February 1992 suggests that this alternative explanation cannot completely account for his behavior, however. As discussed previously, the extension Bush approved in February paid for itself only under highly disputed assumptions about unexpected revenues. In fact, during a congressional hearing on the legislation, Republican House members recommended that the unemployment trust fund be taken off-budget so that it could not affect the official deficit.[35] Bush's ostensible fiscal restraint thus not only entailed questionable assumptions about unexpected surpluses but also coincided with Republicans recommending score-keeping changes in the accounting of unemployment benefits. Given these circumstances, Bush's supposed fiscal responsibility appears more superficial than substantial. His desire for restraint may well have been sincere, but this desire appears to have been superseded by an impetus to enact a popular policy once he was facing a competitive electoral contest.

The final alternative hypotheses I consider are that Bush was simply more likely to pander to public opinion as the election neared, independent of his popularity; and that he was simply more likely to pander as his popularity declined, and thus would have pandered even if the preelection polls had indicated he was quite likely to lose reelection. The events described thus far do not allow one to distinguish between these explanations and the Conditional Pandering Theory. However, subsequent events shed light on the matter.

Clinton took a substantial lead in the polls following the Democratic Party Convention in mid-July. Throughout the remainder of the race, Bush was consistently the underdog, trailing the competition by as much as twenty-five points and sustaining approval ratings no higher than 40 percent.[36] While Congress did not enact other unemployment legislation during this period, the chambers did pass several bills that involved substantial government regulation of the private sector.

That legislation included the Family and Medical Leave Act of 1992 (S 5), which Congress enacted on September 10, and the Cable Television Consumer Protection and Competition Act of 1992 (S 12), which was sent to the president on September 22. The first bill granted workers up to twelve weeks of unpaid leave in order to care for a new baby or sick relative.[37] The second aided competitors to the cable industry, as well as bestowed the federal government with the power to set rates for the lowest-priced cable package.[38] Each of these bills appealed to popular sentiment. For instance, in a survey of registered voters, 63 percent of respondents stated that they would support a law requiring businesses to grant up to three months of unpaid leave for a new child or medical emergency, while only 31 percent opposed such a law.[39] Likewise, a Harris survey found that 87 percent of the national adult population believed most cable companies could overcharge customers owing to a lack of competition, and 70 percent favored allowing local telephone companies to provide cable services so that the cable industry would be more competitive.[40]

Despite the popularity of the policy issues, Bush vetoed the bills. In each case, his expressed rationale for doing so was consistent with his belief that government interference in the economy would harm it. The president professed that the Family and Medical Leave Act, if enacted, would become a "government-dictated mandate that increases costs and loses jobs."[41] He predicted the cable bill would "cost the economy jobs, reduce consumer programming choices, and retard the deployment of growth-oriented investment critical to the future of our Nation's communications infrastructure."[42]

Bush issued each veto within seven weeks of the election, by which time Clinton held a convincing lead in the preelection polls. When Bush delivered the Family Leave veto on September 22, Clinton maintained a ten percentage point advantage according to the Gallup trial heat.[43] At the time of the Cable Bill veto, on October 3, Bush trailed by eleven to twelve percentage points.[44] That the president vetoed the bills under these conditions suggests that he did not continually pander to public opinion as the election approached or as his popularity declined relative to his electoral competition.

Instead, as predicted by the Conditional Pandering Theory, Bush endorsed the policies he believed to be the right ones when he was unpopular compared with his electoral opposition. In combination with his decisions on unemployment legislation, Bush's behavior illustrates the theoretically predicted relationship between the likelihood of pandering and presidential popularity. When he was highly popular or unpopular relative to his competition, he supported the policies he believed would produce the best outcomes for the nation, despite the proximity of the presidential election. Only when he was in the midst of a seemingly tight race did he enact popular laws that he did not believe would ultimately advance citizens' interests.

Reagan and the Contingency Tax Proposal: Policy Leadership from Behind

In the beginning of 1983, Reagan's personal popularity was quite low. Throughout the month of January, his approval ratings hovered in the mid-30s.[45] This lack of popularity reflected the economic situation. In the previous year, the GNP had fallen 1.8 percent, the largest annual reduction since 1946.[46] Unemployment stood at 10.8 percent, the highest level since 1950.[47]

Many economists, including ones working in the executive branch, believed the projection of large deficits for years to come was holding back an economic recovery. As of January 1983, the projected deficits for the next five years were in the range of $185 to $300 billion, approximately 7 percent of GNP. In comparison, the deficit of the last full year before Reagan entered office was $60 billion, around 2 percent of GNP.[48] Paul Volcker, the Chairman of the Federal Reserve, publicly expressed his concerns about the projected deficits in January. He observed, "We are exposed to fears of 'out-of-control' structural deficits, and the result is upward pressure on interest rates."[49] Martin Feldstein, chairman of the Council of Economic Advisors, agreed with Volcker that the projection of large deficits was boosting interest rates and therefore impeding an economic recovery, particularly in sectors dependent on borrowing, such as housing and automobiles.[50] Indeed, interest rates were quite high; the prime rate was 11 percent and the rate for a conventional home loan was 13.25 percent.[51]

Reagan was deeply concerned about the economy and, moreover, realized that he would not win reelection in 1984 unless conditions improved. He acknowledged that if his administration could not move the country into a recovery it "obviously . . . would be a sign" that he should retire after one term.[52] Reagan also recognized the projected deficits as a problem. For example, in an administration briefing in May 1982, he claimed that "the only thing that's keeping the interest rates up and preventing a speedier recovery is the lack of confidence on the part of the private sector that government will stay the course" by progressing toward a balanced budget.[53]

Curbing the deficit was not a simple matter for the president, however. He desired significant increases in defense spending and the preservation of his recently enacted income tax cuts (e.g., Dallek 1984, 105; Feldstein 1994, 26 and 36–37). Furthermore, Reagan did not want to obtain the needed reductions through changes to Medicare, Social Security, or federal employee retirement programs, which together constituted a majority of the budget (Dallek 1984, 72–73). The president was willing, indeed wanted, to decrease spending on social welfare programs (e.g., Hogan 1990, 225), but congressional leaders had indicated that they would be unwilling to curtail these programs substantially.[54]

It was in this setting that Reagan proposed standby taxes that would be triggered in a couple of years if the deficit did not decline by then; specifically, the taxes were scheduled to take effect on October 1, 1985, if the estimated deficit for fiscal year 1986 turned out to be greater than 2½ percent of the GNP and Congress had approved the president's spending cuts. The taxes included an excise fee on oil of approximately five dollars a barrel as well as an increase in corporate and personal income tax payments of approximately 1 percent of taxable income.[55] Reagan promoted this proposal in his State of the Union address, a radio address, and several targeted addresses during the first two months of 1983.[56]

The evidence suggests that Reagan believed the policy was in citizens' interests because it would help to control the deficit and thereby improve the economy by reducing interest rates. Martin Feldstein, who helped to design the plan along with Reagan's domestic policy adviser Ed Harper, describes how the president came to espouse the idea. Feldstein recounts that the president supported the policy over the objections of others within the White House because, ultimately, he "recognized the need to project declining deficits and an eventual budget balance" (Feldstein 1994, 28). The president's statements support this assertion. For example, in remarks to the St. Louis Regional Commerce and Growth Association on February 1, the president promoted the standby tax proposal by claiming that "it will reassure many of those out in the money markets today that we do mean to control inflation and interest rates."[57]

Despite Reagan's public espousal of the policy, it was quite unpopular. In fact, survey data suggest it was even less popular than the option of eliminating Reagan's income tax reductions. When citizens were asked whether they would support "a standby program of increased personal and business taxes—as well as a special tax on oil" for the years 1986–88 in order to reduce the budget deficit, 60 percent opposed the proposal.[58] In comparison, only 39 percent of the population believed that "July's tax cut should be put into effect despite the size of the government deficit."[59]

Reagan's promotion of the contingency tax proposal is thus not a case of a president following public opinion. Instead, consistent with the Conditional Pandering Theory, Reagan advocated a policy he believed would serve the public interest even though it was unpopular. As documented earlier, the president knew that without an economic recovery, he would be unlikely to win reelection. He believed that the standby taxes, if enacted, would help the economy and thereby increase his likelihood of winning the upcoming race. His electoral incentive was therefore to promote the proposal despite its lack of popular support.

Of course, it remains plausible that Reagan's behavior was consistent with the Conditional Pandering Theory but that he promoted the proposal for other reasons. I discuss three plausible alternative explanations: that Reagan had a propensity to follow his policy beliefs regardless of the political circumstances; that the president was somehow catering to his conservative base; and that he was playing blame-game politics with the Democrats over who was responsible for the budget deficit. None of these explanations is corroborated under scrutiny.

A seemingly credible rationale for Reagan's behavior is that he generally advocated policies he thought were in the public interest, regardless of their popularity. Indeed, this claim receives some support from officials who worked for him. For example, Edwin Meese III, Reagan's attorney general from February 1985 through August 1988, observes that "Reagan was remarkably steadfast when pursuing his key objectives" (Meese 1992, 330). Martin Anderson, the chief domestic and policy adviser to the president in 1981 and 1982, similarly assesses that Reagan would "never alter his course" when he felt strongly about a decision (Pemberton 1997, 110).

Notwithstanding Reagan's dedication to his beliefs, there is evidence that he was not above catering to public opinion. For example, he was more than willing to fire agency heads who became unpopular while following his agenda. William Pemberton (1997, 121) notes that after the White House pressured Ann Gorsuch Burford to resign her post as head of the Environmental

Protection Agency, she "felt betrayed" by the president because he had "abandoned her when she came under fire for carrying out his policy." Likewise, when James Watt, Reagan's first Secretary of Interior, told the president that he would probably have to fire Watt at some point because of the unpopular agenda Watt would be implementing, "Reagan, eyes sparkling with laughter, replied, 'I will'" (Pemberton 1997, 119).

Robert Dallek (1984, 33) reconciles the apparent tension between Reagan's faithfulness to his beliefs and capacity to make tactical modifications. "If Goldwater was ready to stand or fall on principle," Dallek observes, "Reagan, in his determination to be liked and to gain his personal goals, will compromise." As this assessment and Reagan's dealings with his officials imply, the president's support for the contingency taxes cannot be attributed to a universal unwillingness to take positions for purely political reasons.

Conclusion

The narratives on Carter's humanitarian assistance proposals, Bush's policy decisions on unemployment compensation, and Reagan's proposal for standby taxes establish that the Conditional Pandering Theory has explanatory power. In all of these analyses, the predictions of the theory were consistent with the president's policy decisions. Furthermore, the theory made sense of seemingly puzzling events; in each case a president switched positions and/or supported policies counter to his ideological leanings. In contrast, conventional explanations of presidential decision making—character, inside the beltway bargaining, and the appeasement of core constituencies, for example—did not account for the executive behavior.

NOTES

1. The survey asked, "We are faced with many problems in this country, none of which can be solved easily or inexpensively. I'm going to name some of these problems, and for each one I'd like you to tell me whether you think we're spending too much money on it, too little money, or about the right amount. Are we spending too much money, too little money, or about the right amount on foreign aid?"

2. Jimmy Carter, "'Ask President Carter' Remarks During a Telephone Call-in Program on the CBS Radio Network," March 5, 1977, *Public Papers of the Presidents of the United States, 1977 Book 1* (Washington, DC: Government Printing Office, 1977).

3. Jimmy Carter, "Remarks and a Question-and-Answer Session with a Group of Editors and News Directors," May 19, 1978, *Public Papers of the Presidents of the United States, 1978 Book 1* (Washington, DC: Government Printing Office, 1978).

4. Survey conducted December 1–8, 1979. The question wording is identical to that in note 1.

5. Survey conducted by the Gallup organization January 25–28, 1980. The survey asked the standard most important problem question, "What do you think is the most important problem in the nation today?" Responses were open-ended.

6. Carter proposed real increases of 9 percent in health programs and 4 percent in ground transportation. The public opinion data are from a Roper survey conducted

December 1–8, 1979. Respondents were asked the (by-now familiar) question, "We are faced with many problems in this country, none of which can be solved easily or inexpensively. I'm going to name some of these problems, and for each one I'd like you to tell me whether you think we're spending too much money on it, too little money or about the right amount." For health, the question ended with "improving and protecting the nation's health" and for ground transportation, it ended with "improving the public transportation." The responses suggest that 59 percent of adults believed the government was spending too little on health and that 50 percent believed too little was being spent on public transportation.

7. *Country Reports on Human Rights Practices*, report submitted to the Committee on Foreign Relations, U.S. Senate, and Committee on Foreign Affairs, U.S. House of Representatives, by the Department of State, February 2, 1981.

8. Carter did impose an embargo on the sale of grain to the Soviet Union, but this embargo did not affect appropriations for foreign assistance.

9. Nor did Carter shift his requests for humanitarian aid into security assistance; in nominal terms, Carter proposed a measly 0.002 percent increase in security aid.

10. Ragsdale (1998, 213).

11. Peter G. Gosselin, "Economy Rolling Again . . . But Slowly: Slight Gain in Gross National Product Worries Analysts," *Boston Globe*, July 27, 1991, 12.

12. U.S. Department of Labor, Bureau of Labor Statistics.

13. *Congressional Quarterly Almanac*, vol. 47 (1991), 304–8.

14. The question was: "Congress recently passed a bill to extend unemployment benefits beyond the regular 25-week period. To provide the $6.4 billion dollars needed to extend benefits, a budget emergency would have to be declared that President Bush says is not justified. Would you like to see Bush sign this bill into law, or do you think he should veto it?"

15. The question was: "Now let me ask you some specifics about President Bush. How would you rate him on . . . his opposition to a bill that would extend for 20 weeks unemployment insurance to unemployed workers whose benefits have run out . . . excellent, pretty good, only fair or poor?" The responses of "only fair" and "poor" are reported jointly by Harris, with 59 percent of the population assigning Bush one of these ratings.

16. Quoted in Mervin (1996, 114).

17. George Bush, "Remarks at a Republican Party Fundraising Dinner in East Brunswick, New Jersey," September 24, 1991, *Public Papers of the Presidents, 1991 Book 2* (Washington, DC: Government Printing Office, 1992).

18. George Bush, "The President's News Conference," October 4, 1991, *Public Papers of the Presidents, 1991 Book 2.*

19. George Bush, "Memorandum of Disapproval for the Emergency Unemployment Compensation Act of 1991," October 11, 1991, *Public Papers of the Presidents, 1991 Book 2.*

20. Andrew J. Glass, "Democrats Find Bush Is Vulnerable," *Atlanta Journal and Constitution*, November 3, 1991, O5; Adam Pertman, "Democrat Hopefuls See Bush Weakness," *Boston Globe*, November 3, 1991, 213.

21. Ragsdale (1998, 213).

22. Michael Kranish, "Bush Bristles at Claims He Has Shifted," *Boston Globe*, November 17, 1991, 1.

23. *Congressional Quarterly Almanac*, vol. 48 (1992), 347–48.

24. Ragsdale (1998, 213).

25. *Congressional Quarterly Almanac*, vol. 48 (1992), 347.

26. Ibid.

27. To deal with the possibility that the additional unemployment compensation would add to the deficit, Congress voted to waive the 1990 Budget Act, which required that every new program pay for itself (*Congressional Quarterly Almanac*, vol. 48 [1992], 352).

28. Adam Clymer, "Bush Fights Long-Term Change in Jobless Benefits," *New York Times*, April 9, 1992, D20.

29. Adam Clymer, "Congress Passes Jobless Aid and Bush Says He Will Sign," *New York Times*, July 3, 1992, A13.

30. Ibid.

31. Jill Zuckman, "Bush Relents, Agrees to Sign Jobless Benefits Extension," *Congressional Quarterly Weekly*, July 4, 1992, 1961–62.

32. George Bush, "The President's News Conference," August 2, 1991, *Public Papers of the Presidents, 1991 Book 2*.

33. George Bush, "Remarks at a Bush-Quayle Fundraising Luncheon in New York City," November 12, 1991, *Public Papers of the Presidents, 1991 Book 2*.

34. George Bush, "Remarks and an Exchange with Reporters in a Meeting with the House Republican Conference on Health Care," July 2, 1992, *Public Papers of the Presidents, 1992–93 Book 1* (Washington, DC: Government Printing Office, 1993).

35. Ways and Means Committee Subcommittee on Human Resources Hearing. "Extending Unemployment Benefits." Panel of Congressional Witnesses, B-318 Rayburn House Office Building, January 23, 1992.

36. The 1992 Gallup Poll Presidential Candidate Trial Heats are available in the Roper Center for Public Opinion Research database on polls and surveys (commonly referred to as RPOLL). For Bush's approval ratings, see Ragsdale (1998, 213–14).

37. Jill Zuckman, "Family Leave Act Falls Again: Veto Override Fails in House," *Congressional Quarterly Weekly*, October 3, 1992, 3059.

38. Mike Mills, "Bush Asks for a Sign of Loyalty: Congress Changes the Channel," *Congressional Quarterly Weekly*, October 10, 1992, 3149–51.

39. NBC News and Wall Street Journal Poll conducted September 12–15, 1992. The survey asked: "Congress has passed a law that would require companies to give employees up to three months of unpaid leave for the birth or adoption of a child, or to care for a seriously ill family member, while protecting their job. Would you favor or oppose this law, even if it means additional costs for business?"

40. Harris survey conducted March 19–24, 1992. The first question was, "Here are some statements people have made about the cable television industry in America today. For each one, please tell me whether you agree or disagree. . . . Because most cable T.V. companies have local monopolies, they can charge too much for the service they provide." The second question was, "Would you favor or oppose changing the regulations so that your telephone company could provide cable television service in competition with the company that provides now?"

41. George Bush, "Remarks and an Exchange with Reporters on Family Leave Legislation," September 16, 1992, *Public Papers of the Presidents, 1992–93 Book 2*.

42. George Bush, "Letter to Congressional Leaders on Cable Television Legislation," September 17, 1992, *Public Papers of the Presidents, 1992–93 Book 2*.

43. Each of the following trial heats, conducted September 17–20 of registered voters and those who could vote without having yet registered, gave Clinton a ten-point lead. The questions were, "If the (1992) presidential election were being held today, would you vote for the Republican ticket of George Bush and Dan Quayle or for the

Democratic ticket of Bill Clinton and Al Gore? (If Perot (vol.)/Other (vol.)/Don't know/ Refused, ask:) As of today, do you lean more to Bush and Quayle, the Republicans, or to Clinton and Gore, the Democrats?" and "If the (1992) presidential election were being held today, would you vote for the Republican ticket of George Bush and Dan Quayle or for the Democratic ticket of Bill Clinton and Al Gore?" In the first case, Clinton received support from 50 percent of respondents, and in the second, he received support from 44 percent.

44. These trial heats were conducted by the Gallup Organization on October 1–3 using the questions in the format of note 43. The only difference in the questions is that Ross Perot was explicitly mentioned as a candidate, a result of the fact that he had reentered the race. In the survey that did not urge the leaners to make a choice, Clinton was favored by 47 percent of respondents and Bush by 35 percent. In the survey that pushed the leaners to choose a candidate, Clinton received support from 44 percent of the respondents and Bush from 33 percent.

45. Ragsdale (1998, 210).

46. Anantole Kaletsky, "GNP in U.S. Fell 1.8% Last Year," *Financial Times* (London ed.), January 20, 1983, I1.

47. "Unemployment Claims Rose at End of the Year," *New York Times*, January 14, 1983, D15.

48. Jonathan Fuerbringer, "Do Deficits Impede Recovery?" *New York Times*, January 20, 1983, D1.

49. Volcker's statement was made at a meeting of the American Council for Capital Formation. Kenneth B. Noble, "Deficits Criticized by Volcker," *New York Times*, January 21, 1983, D3.

50. Fuerbringer, "Do Deficits Impede Recovery?"

51. "Current Interest Rates," *New York Times*, January 10, 1983, D7; Kenneth R. Harney, "Interest Rates May Rise Along with Economy," *Washington Post*, January 15, 1983, F1.

52. Rich Jaroslovsky, "Economic Upturn Aids President's Popularity, but It Is Not Panacea," *Wall Street Journal*, April 28, 1983, 1. Cited in Kernell (1997, 224).

53. Ronald Reagan, "Meeting with Editors from the Midwestern Region," May 10, 1982, *Public Papers of the Presidents, 1982 Book 1* (Washington, DC: Government Printing Office, 1983).

54. Hedrick Smith, "Deficit in the $185 Billion Range Expected in 1984 Reagan Budget," *New York Times*, January 18, 1983, A1.

55. Robert D. Hershey Jr., "President to Seek Contingent Taxes," *New York Times*, January 26, 1983, A15.

56. These addresses include the State of the Union on January 25, a national radio address entitled "Fiscal Year 1984 Budget" on January 29, "Remarks and a Question-and-Answer Session at the St. Louis Regional Commerce and Growth Association" on February 1, "Remarks and a Question-and-Answer Session via Satellite to the Young Presidents Organization" on February 14. All of these addresses are in the *Public Papers of the Presidents, 1983 Book 1* (Washington, DC: Government Printing Office, 1984).

57. Ibid.

58. Cambridge Reports, Research International survey conducted in January of 1983. The full question was "Last month, in his State of the Union and Budget Messages to Congress, President (Ronald) Reagan proposed the following actions as ways of reducing these budget deficits for the next few years. Please tell me whether you

would favor or oppose each of them. . . . Putting in effect a standby program of increased personal and business taxes—as well as a special tax on oil—for the years 1986–88."

59. Roper survey conducted January 8–22, 1983. The full question was, "A 5% cut in income taxes took effect in October 1981, and another 10% cut in income taxes took effect this past July. An additional 10% cut in income taxes is due to take effect this coming July. Do you think next July's tax cut should be put into effect despite the size of the government deficit, or do you think next July's tax cut should be cancelled to help reduce the deficit?"

REFERENCES

Brody, Richard A., and Lee Sigelman. 1983. "Presidential Popularity and Presidential Elections: An Update and Extension." *Public Opinion Quarterly* 47: 325–28.

Cameron, Charles M. 2000. *Veto Bargaining: President and the Politics of Negative Power.* Cambridge, UK: Cambridge University Press.

Cohen, Jeffrey E. 1997. *Presidential Responsiveness and Public Policy-Making: The Public and the Policies that Presidents Choose.* Ann Arbor: University of Michigan Press.

Dallek, Robert. 1984. *Ronald Reagan: The Politics of Symbolism.* Cambridge, MA: Harvard University Press.

Deibel, Terry L. 1987. *Presidents, Public Opinion, and Power: The Nixon, Carter and Reagan Years.* New York: Foreign Policy Association.

Denton, Robert E., Jr., and Mary E. Stuckey. 1994. "A Communication Model of Presidential Campaigns: A 1992 Overview." In *The 1992 Presidential Campaign: A Communication Perspective,* ed. Robert E. Denton, Jr., 1–42. Westport, CT: Praeger.

Feldstein, Martin. 1994. Introductory chapter of *American Economic Policy in the 1980s,* ed. Martin Feldstein, 1–79. Chicago: University of Chicago Press.

Genovese, Michael A. 1994. "Jimmy Carter and the Age of Limits: Presidential Power in a Time of Decline and Diffusion." In *The Presidency and Domestic Politics of Jimmy Carter,* ed. Herbert D. Rosenbaum and Alexej Ugrinsky, 187–221. Westport, CT: Greenwood Press.

Hargrove, Erwin C. 1988. *Jimmy Carter as President: Leadership and the Politics of the Public Good.* Baton Rouge: Louisiana State University Press.

Hogan, Joseph. 1990. *The Reagan Years: The Record in Presidential Leadership,* ed. Joseph Hogan. New York: Manchester University Press.

Jones, Charles O. 1988. *The Trusteeship Presidency: Jimmy Carter the United States Congress.* Baton Rouge: Louisiana State University Press.

Kaufman, Burton Ira. 1993. *The Presidency of James Earl Carter, Jr.* Lawrence: University Press of Kansas.

Kernell, Samuel. 1997. *Going Public: New Strategies of Presidential Leadership,* 3rd ed. Washington, DC: Congressional Quarterly Press.

Meese, Edwin III. 1992. *With Reagan: The Inside Story.* Washington, DC: Regnery Gateway.

Mervin, David. 1996. *George Bush and the Guardianship Presidency.* New York: St. Martin's Press.

Pemberton, William E. 1997. *Exit with Honor: The Life and Presidency of Ronald Reagan.* Armonk, NY: M. E. Sharpe.

Ragsdale, Lyn. 1998. *Vital Statistics on the Presidency: Washington to Clinton.* Washington, DC: Congressional Quarterly, Inc.

Sigelman, Lee. 1979. "Presidential Popularity and Presidential Elections." *Public Opinion Quarterly* 43: 532–34.

Skidmore, David. 1996. *Reversing Course: Carter's Foreign Policy, Domestic Politics, and the Failure of Reform.* Nashville, TN: Vanderbilt University Press.

Skowronek, Stephen. 1993. *The Politics Presidents Make: Leadership from John Adams to George Bush.* Cambridge, MA: Harvard University Press.

6.4

WILLIAM G. HOWELL

From *Power without Persuasion:*
The Politics of Direct Presidential Action

Presidents have increasingly used unilateral actions, such as executive orders, to make policy independent of Congress. Howell describes the trends in these unilateral actions and offers a historical explanation. Over the course of the twentieth century, both Congress and the Supreme Court permitted presidents more latitude because the problems they faced became more complicated.

PRESIDENTIAL POWER IN THE MODERN ERA

. . . Throughout the twentieth century, presidents have used their powers of unilateral action to intervene in a whole host of policy arenas. Examples abound:

- During World War II, Roosevelt issued dozens of executive orders that nationalized aviation plants, shipbuilding companies, thousands of coal companies, and a shell plant—all clear violations of the Fifth Amendment's "taking" clause. The courts overturned none of these actions.
- With executive order 9066, Roosevelt ordered the evacuation, relocation, and internment of over 110,000 Japanese Americans living on the West Coast.
- In 1948, Truman desegregated the military via executive order 9981.
- After congressional efforts to construct a program that would send American youth abroad to do charitable work faltered three years in a row, Kennedy unilaterally created the Peace Corps and then financed it using discretionary funds.
- Johnson instituted the first affirmative action policy with executive order 11246.
- Preempting Congress, Nixon used an executive order to design the Environmental Protection Agency not as an independent commission, as Congress would have liked, but as an agency beholden directly to the president.
- By subjecting government regulations to cost-benefit analyses with executive order 12291, Reagan centralized powers of regulatory review.

From William G. Howell, *Power without Persuasion: The Politics of Direct Presidential Action* (Princeton, NJ: Princeton University Press, 2003).

▪ In 1992, George Bush federalized the National Guard and used its members to quell the Los Angeles riots.

While the majority of unilateral directives may not resonate quite so loudly in the telling of American history, a growing proportion involve substantive policy matters. Rather than being simply "daily grist-of-the-mill diplomatic matter," presidential directives have become instruments by which presidents actually set all sorts of consequential domestic and foreign policy (Paige 1977). . . .

Between 1920 and 1998, presidents issued 10,203 executive orders, or roughly 130 annually. As might be expected, presidents issued more civil service orders than orders in any other policy arena. On average, presidents issued thirty-three such orders, most of which dealt with the management of government personnel. This proportion, however, declined precipitously after World War II, when executive orders were no longer used to perform such trivial administrative practices as exempting individuals from mandatory retirement requirements.

Outside of those orders relating directly to the civil service, each year presidents issued on average thirty-two orders in foreign affairs, another eight on social welfare policy, sixteen on regulations of the domestic economy, and fully thirty-three that concerned the management of public lands and energy policy, though the number in this last category has declined markedly over the past few decades. The majority of orders, it seems, have substantive policy content, both foreign and domestic.

These figures only concern executive orders, which represent but one tool among many that presidents have at their disposal. When negotiating with foreign countries, presidents can bypass the treaty ratification process by issuing executive agreements; not surprisingly, the ratio of executive agreements to treaties, which hovered between zero and one in the nineteenth century, now consistently exceeds thirty (King and Ragsdale 1988). If presidents choose to avoid the reporting requirements Congress has placed on executive orders, they can repackage their policies as executive memoranda, determinations, administrative directives, or proclamations. And if they prefer to keep their decisions entirely secret, they can issue national security directives, which neither Congress nor the public has an opportunity to review (Cooper 2002).

The U.S. Constitution does not explicitly recognize any of these policy vehicles. Over the years, presidents have invented them, citing national security or expediency as justification. Taken as a whole, though, they represent one of the most striking, and underappreciated, aspects of presidential power in the modern era. Born from a truly expansive reading of Article II powers, these policy mechanisms have radically impacted how public policy is made in America today. The president's powers of unilateral action exert just as much influence over public policy, and in some cases more, than the formal powers that presidency scholars have examined so carefully over the past several decades.

▪   ▪   ▪

If we want to account for the influence that presidents wield over the construction of public policy, we must begin to pay serious attention to the president's capacity to create law on his own.

"Presidential Power Is the Power to Persuade"

The image of presidents striking out on their own to conduct a war on terrorism or revamp civil rights policies or reconstruct the federal bureaucracy stands in stark relief to scholarly literatures that equate executive power with persuasion and, consequently, place presidents at the peripheries of the lawmaking process.

Richard Neustadt sets the terms by which every student of American politics has come to understand presidential power in the modern era. When thinking about presidents since FDR, Neustadt argues, "weak remains the word with which to start" (1991 [1960], xix). Presidents are much like Shakespearean kings, marked more by tragedy than grandeur. Each is held captive by world events, by competing domestic interests and foreign policy pressures, by his party, his cabinet, the media, a fickle public, and partisan Congress. To make matters worse, the president exercises little control over any of these matters—current events and the political actors who inhabit them regularly disregard his expressed wishes. As a result, the pursuit of the president's policy agenda is marked more by compromise than conviction; and his eventual success or failure (as determined by either the public at the next election or historians over time) ultimately rests with others, and their willingness to extend a helping hand.

The public now expects presidents to accomplish far more than their formal powers alone permit. This has been especially true since the New Deal, when the federal government took charge of the nation's economy, commerce, and the social welfare of its citizens. Now presidents must address almost every conceivable social and economic problem, from the impact of summer droughts on midwestern farmers to the spread of nuclear weapons in the former Soviet Union. Armed with little more than the powers to propose and veto legislation and recommend the appointment of bureaucrats and judges, however, modern presidents appear doomed to failure from the very beginning. As one recent treatise on presidential "greatness" puts it, "modern presidents bask in the honors of the more formidable office that emerged from the New Deal, but they find themselves navigating a treacherous and lonely path, subject to a volatile political process that makes popular and enduring achievement unlikely" (Landy and Milkis 2000, 197).

If a president is to enjoy any measure of success, Neustadt counsels, he must master the art of persuasion. Indeed, according to Neustadt, power and persuasion are synonymous. The ability to persuade, to convince other political actors that his interests are their own, defines political power and is the key to presidential achievement. Power is about bargaining and negotiating; about brokering deals and trading promises; and about cajoling legislators, bureaucrats, and justices to do things that the president cannot accomplish on his own. . . . The president wields influence when he manages to enhance his bargaining stature and build governing coalitions; and the principal way to accomplish as much, Neustadt claims, is to draw upon the bag of experiences, skills, and qualities that he brings to the office.

Intentionally or not, Neustadt set off a behavioral revolution. . . . Self-confidence, an instinct for power, an exalted reputation within the Washington community, and prestige among the general public were considered the foundations of presidential success. Without certain personal qualities, presidents could not hope to build the coalitions necessary for action. Power was contingent upon persuasion, and persuasion was a function of all the personal qualities individual presidents bore; and so, the argument ran, what the presidency was at any moment critically depended upon who filled the office.

By these scholars' accounts, a reliance on formal powers actually signals weakness. What distinguishes great presidents is not a willingness to act upon the formal powers of the presidency but an ability to rally support precisely when and where such formal powers are lacking. As Neustadt argues, formal powers constitute a "painful last resort, a forced response to the exhaustion of other remedies, suggestive less of mastery than of failure—the failure of attempts to gain an end by softer means" (1991 [1960], 24). Presidents who veto bill after bill (think Ford) do so because their powers to persuade have faltered. The presidents who effectively communicate (Reagan) or who garner strong professional reputations (Roosevelt) stand out in the eyes of history.

Although the notion of the personal presidency dominated the field for decades, its influence is on the decline. The principal reason is that it no longer matches up with the facts. The personal presidency became a popular theoretical notion just as the American presidency was experiencing tremendous growth and development as an institution: in its staffing, its budget, and the powers delegated to it by Congress. As time went on, it became increasingly clear that the field needed to take more seriously the formal structures and powers that define the modern presidency.

If the personal presidency literature is correct, executive power should rise and fall according to the personal qualities of each passing president. Presidential power should expand and contract according to the individual skills and reputations that each president brings to the office. The constituent elements of the personal presidency may be important. Prestige and reputation may matter. But if we are to build a theory of presidential power, it seems reasonable to start with its most striking developments during the modern era. And these developments have little to do with the personalities of the men who, since Roosevelt, have inhabited the White House.

By virtually any objective measure, the size and importance of the "presidential branch" has steadily increased over the past century (Hart 1995). According to Thomas Cronin, "for almost 150 years the executive power of the presidency has steadily expanded" (1989, 204). Edward Corwin echoes this sentiment, arguing that "taken by and large, the history of the Presidency is a history of aggrandizement" (1957, 238). How can such trends persist if presidential powers are fundamentally personal in nature? It cannot be that the caliber of presidents today is markedly higher than a century ago, and for that reason alone presidents have managed to exert more and more influence. Does it really make sense to say that successful twentieth-century presidents (e.g., the Roosevelts or Reagan) distinguish themselves from great nineteenth-century presidents (e.g., Jackson, Polk, or Lincoln) by exhibiting stronger personalities? And if not, how can we argue that the roots of modern presidential power are fundamentally personal in nature? While Neustadt may illuminate short-term fluctuations at the boundaries of presidential influence—skill in the art of persuasion surely plays some part in political power—he cannot possibly explain the general growth of presidential power.

During the past twenty years, scholars have revisited the more formal components of presidential power. Work on the institutional presidency has regained the stature it held in political science during the first half of the twentieth century. This work is far more rigorous than the personal presidency literature and, for that matter, the institutional literature's earlier incarnations. A science of politics is finally taking hold of presidential studies: empirical tests now are commonplace; theoretical assumptions are clearly specified; and hypotheses are subject to independent corroboration. Perhaps more important than its methodological contributions, though, the institutional literature has successfully refocused scholarly attention on the office of the presidency and the features that make it distinctly modern: its staff and budget, the powers and responsibilities delegated to it by Congress, and the growth of agencies and commissions that collect and process information within it.

Nothing in the institutional literature, however, fundamentally challenges Neustadt's original claim that "presidential power is the power to persuade" (1991 [1960], 11). Scholars continue to equate presidential power with an ability to bargain, negotiate, change minds, turn votes, and drive legislative agendas through Congress. Not surprisingly, the president remains secondary throughout this work. He continues to play second fiddle to the people who make real policy decisions: committee members writing bills, congressional representatives offering amendments, bureaucrats enforcing laws, judges deciding cases.

To legislate, to build a record of accomplishments about which to boast at the next election, and to find their place in history, presidents above all rely upon Congress—so the institutional literature argues. Without Congress's active support, and the endorsement of its members, presidents cannot hope to achieve much at all. . . . The struggle for votes is perennial; and success is always fleeting. Should Congress lock up, or turn away, the president has little or no recourse. Ultimately, presidents depend upon Congress to delegate authority, ratify executive decisions, and legislate when, and where, presidents cannot act at all.

■   ■   ■

Because of his unique position within a system of separated powers, the president has numerous opportunities to take independent action, with or without the expressed consent of either Congress or the courts. Sometimes he does so by issuing executive orders, proclamations, or executive agreements; other times by handing down general memoranda to agency heads; and still other times by dispensing national security directives. The number of these unilateral directives, and of opportunities to use them, has literally skyrocketed during the modern era (Moe and Howell 1999a, 1999b). While presidents freely exercise these powers during periods of national crises, as the events following September 11th have made clear, they also rely upon executive orders and executive agreements during periods of relative calm, effecting policy changes that never would survive the legislative process. And to the extent that presidents use these "power tools of the presidency" more now than they did a century ago, the ability to act unilaterally speaks to what is distinctively "modern" about the modern presidency (Cooper 1997, 2002).

Rather than hoping to influence at the margins what other political actors do, the president can make all kinds of public policies without the formal consent of Congress. While the growth of the presidency as an institution (its staffs, budgets, departments, and agencies) augments presidential power, it is the ability to set policy unilaterally that deserves our immediate and sustained attention.

■   ■   ■

Thinking about Unilateral Powers

From the beginning, it is worth highlighting what makes unilateral powers distinctive. For the ability to act unilaterally is unlike any other power formally granted the president. Two features stand out.

The most important is that the president moves policy first and thereby places upon Congress and the courts the burden of revising a new political landscape. Rather than waiting at the end of an extended legislative process to sign or veto a bill, the president simply sets new policy and leaves it up to Congress and the courts to respond. If they choose not to retaliate, either by passing a law or ruling against the president, then the president's order stands. Only by taking (or credibly threatening to take) positive action can either adjoining institution limit the president's unilateral powers.

. . . By moving first, and anticipating the moves of future actors, legislators of all stripes and in very different political systems influence the kinds of policies governments produce. . . . But gains to the president are twice over. While agenda setters in Congress only propose bills, the president moves first and creates legally binding public policies. And he does so without ever having to wait on coalitions subsequently forming, committee chairs cooperating, or party leaders endorsing.

The second important feature of unilateral powers is that the president acts alone. There is no need to rally majorities, compromise with adversaries, or wait for some interest group to bring a case to court. Rather than depending upon Congress to enact his legislative agendas, the president frequently can strike out on his own, occasionally catching even his closest advisors off guard (recall Clinton's unilateral decision to bomb Iraq in the fall of 1998, the day before his scheduled impeachment hearing in the House Judiciary Committee). As the chief of state, the modern president is in a unique position to lead, to define a national agenda, and to impose his will in more and more areas of governance.

■　　■　　■

The ability to move first and act alone, then, distinguishes unilateral powers from all other sources of influence. In this sense, Neustadt is turned upside-down, for unilateral action is the virtual antithesis of bargaining and persuading. Here, presidents just act; their power does not hinge upon their capacity to "convince [political actors] that what the White House wants of them is what they ought to do for their sake and for their authority" (Neustadt 1991 [1960], 30). To make policy, presidents need not secure the formal consent of Congress, the active support of bureaucrats, or the official approval of justices. Instead, presidents simply set public policy and dare others to counter. For as long as Congress lacks the votes (usually two-thirds of both chambers) to overturn him, the president can be confident that his policy will stand.

The presidency literature's traditional distinction between formal and informal powers does not contribute much insight here. Because the Constitution does not mandate them, powers of unilateral action cannot be considered formal. It is by reference to what presidents have done (or gotten away with) that these powers take form. But nor are these discretionary powers informal. They are not rooted in personal qualities that vary with each passing president. Rather, these powers emerge from specific institutional advantages within the office of the presidency itself: its structure, resources, and location in a system of separated powers. The promise of a sustained analysis of unilateral powers, then, is great. To the extent that presidents act unilaterally with increasing frequency and effect in the postwar era, an institutional theory of unilateral action enables scholars to see beyond Neustadt's original conception of presidential influence in the modern era.

The Tool Chest

. . . Presidents in more modern times have manufactured a number of policy instruments that give shape and meaning to . . . prerogative powers. The most common include executive orders, proclamations, national security directives, and executive agreements. There are few hard and fast rules about how policies are classified, affording presidents a fair measure of liberty to select the instrument that best serves their objectives. Still, some basic distinctions generally apply.

Among all unilateral directives, "executive orders combine the highest levels of substance, discretion, and direct presidential involvement" (Mayer 2001, 35). Executive orders, for the most part, instruct government officials and administrative agencies to take specific actions with regard to both domestic and foreign affairs. "Executive orders are directives issued by the president to officers of the executive branch, requiring them to take an action, stop a certain type of activity, alter policy, change management practices, or accept a delegation of authority under which they will henceforth be responsible for the implementation of law" (Cooper 2002, 16). But while presidents direct executive orders to subordinates within the executive branch, the impact of these orders is felt well beyond the boundaries of the federal government. . . . Through executive orders, presidents have dictated the terms by which government contractors hire and fire their employees, set restrictions on where American citizens can travel abroad, frozen the financial holdings of private parties, reset trade, [set] tariffs, and determined the kinds of recreational activities that are allowed on public lands.

If executive orders are typically directed to officials within the federal government, presidential proclamations almost always target individuals and groups outside of the government. Because Article II of the Constitution does not endow the president with clear and immediate authority over private parties (as it does over the federal bureaucracy), it is not surprising that proclamations tend to be less consequential than executive orders, most involving ceremonial and commemorative affairs. There are, however, numerous exceptions, such as Nixon's 1971 proclamations and orders temporarily freezing all wages, rents, and prices as part of the national economic stabilization program; Ford's 1973 proclamation granting pardons to draft dodgers; and Carter's 1980 proclamations imposing new surcharges on imported oil.

■ ■ ■

Even the advent of the Cold War can be traced back to a national security directive. Issued in April 1950, N.S.C. 68 emphasized the historical importance of the mounting conflict between the United States and Soviet Union. The document, drafted by the director of the State Department's policy-planning staff, Paul Nitze, was a call to arms and defined the nation's military and political objectives as it waged an ongoing struggle against the world's only other superpower. . . . While it met some initial resistance within the Truman and Eisenhower administrations, N.S.C. 68, more than any other document, established the guiding doctrine for successive presidents' Cold War foreign policy.

Executive agreements stand apart from these other directives. While executive orders, proclamations, and (to a lesser degree) national security directives all are unilateral counterparts to legislation, executive agreements provide presidents with an alternative to the treaty ratification process. Rather than having to secure the consent of two-thirds of the Senate before entering into a bi- or multilateral agreement with foreign nations, presidents can use executive agreements to unilaterally commit the United States to deals involving such issues as international trade, ocean fishing rights, open air space, environmental standards, and immigration patterns. While most of these agreements concern very specific (and often technical) matters, the sheer number issued during the modern era has increased at such an astronomical rate that collectively they now constitute a vital means by which presidents unilaterally affect public policy.

When setting public policy, presidents frequently issue combinations of these various policy directives. To force the integration of schools in Little Rock, Arkansas, Eisenhower simultaneously issued a proclamation and an executive order. Carter relied upon a series of executive orders and executive agreements to negotiate the Iran Hostage Crisis. Presiding over World War II, the Korean War, and the Vietnam War, Roosevelt, Truman, Johnson, and Nixon all issued a wide array of secretive orders, national security directives and otherwise. Presidents frequently use executive orders, secretarial orders, and reorganization plans to create administrative agencies and then turn to other kinds of unilateral directives—for example, administrative directives, findings and determinations, and regulations—to monitor their behavior. The ease with which presidents can mix and match these unilateral directives to advance their policy goals is considerable.

The Legality of Unilateral Powers

The first Court challenge to a presidential order, *Little v. Barreme* (1804) concerned the legality of a seizure of a Danish ship, the *Flying Fish*. George Little, the captain of the *U.S.S. Boston,* had intercepted the ship at sea. At the time, Captain Little was complying with a John Adams presidential order that the Navy seize any and all ships sailing to or from French ports. Previously, however, Congress had only authorized the seizure of frigates sailing to French ports. Because the Danish brig was sailing *from* a French port and not *to* one (it was headed from Jérémie to St. Thomas), the Court for the first time had to resolve a discrepancy between a presidential order and congressional statute.

In a unanimous ruling written by Chief Justice John Marshall, the Court declared that had Adams' order stood alone, the Navy's actions would be constitutional. Because Congress had enacted a more restrictive statute, however, the Court was forced to rule in favor of the Danish captain. "Congressional policy announced in a statute necessarily prevails over inconsistent presidential orders. . . . Presidential orders, even those issued as Commander in Chief, are subject to restrictions by Congress." Marshall subsequently ordered Captain Little to pay damages. More importantly, though, Marshall established the clear principle that when an executive order blatantly conflicts with a law, the law prevails.

During the rest of the nineteenth century, the federal courts considered a host of challenges to unilateral directives issued by presidents, most of which involved military orders. It was not until the 1930s that the Supreme Court formally recognized the president's power to act unilaterally. Three cases—*United States v. Curtiss-Wright* (1936); *United States v. Belmont* (1937); and *United States v. Pink* (1942)—made the difference (Schubert 1973, 107).

Curtiss-Wright centrally involved the constitutionality of an executive agreement that forbade the sale of arms to countries involved in armed conflict. When it sold fifteen machine guns to the government of Bolivia, Curtiss-Wright Export Corporation was charged with violating the agreement. As part of its defense, the company argued that Congress had "abdicated its essential functions and delegated them to the Executive," and for that reason, the Court should overturn the executive agreement. Instead, the Supreme Court, in an oft-cited phrase, deemed the president the "sole organ of the federal government in the field of international relations" and upheld the constitutionality of this particular delegation of authority. Doing so, it formally recognized his legal right to issue executive agreements.

In *United States v. Belmont*, the Supreme Court extended this right to executive orders. When Russia reneged on debts owed to the United States in the 1930s, President Roosevelt seized Russian financial assets held in American banks. Arguing that Roosevelt's actions violated New York State law, a Russian investor asked the Court to overturn the executive order and to award compensation for his losses. The Court, however, refused. Doing so, it equated an executive order with federal law and reaffirmed its preeminence over state law.

The Supreme Court extended this reasoning to executive agreements in *United States v. Pink*, which again involved the seizure of Russian assets in American banks. This time, however, the focus concerned an exchange between the president and the Russian government known as the Litvinov Assignment. In a letter to Roosevelt, People's Commissar for Foreign Affairs Maxim Litvinov relinquished certain Russian claims to assets of Russian companies in New York banks. Roosevelt subsequently acknowledged the reassignment of property claims. In *Pink*, the question before the Court centered on the legal authority of this exchange. Ultimately, the Court ruled that because executive agreements have the same status as treaties, and because both override state laws, the plaintiffs could not use New York State law to try to recover their lost assets.

Collectively, *Curtiss-Wright, Belmont,* and *Pink* firmly established the president's authority to issue directives involving "external affairs." Their distinction between foreign and domestic policy, however, subsequently blurred. And for good reason. The list of exceptions to any definition of "foreign" or "domestic" policy is sufficiently long as to make the definitions themselves unworkable as elements of jurisprudence. "The original constitutional understanding that in domestic affairs Congress would make the law and presidents would see to its enforcement had never worked in practice and by the early 1990s it had largely been abandoned" (McDonald 1994, 314). The courts now fully recognize the president's power to issue executive orders and agreements that concern both foreign and domestic policy. Indeed, powers of unilateral action have become a veritable fixture of the American presidency in the modern era.

Writing Public Policy

Much can happen between the issuance of a presidential order and its implementation. Opportunities for shirking abound. Administrative agencies may read their mandates selectively; they may ignore especially objectionable provisions; they may report false or misleading information about initiatives' successes and failures. As we have already noted, the executive branch assuredly does not reduce to the president himself. Bureaucrats enjoy a fair measure of autonomy to do as they please.

Demanding a policy change does not make it so. As Neustadt himself forcefully argued, orders handed down from on high are not always self-executing (1991 [1960], 10–28). In 1948, for instance, Truman issued an executive order demanding the desegregation of the military, but decades passed before the outcome was finally realized. Presidents are engaged in a constant struggle to ensure compliance among members of the executive branch, and to advance the realization of their policy interests. Presidents appoint high-ranking officials who share their worldview, and whenever possible, presidents try to rally the support of their subordinates. This has important consequences for our understanding of presidential power; for when it comes to the implementation of public policy (whether enacted as a federal statute or issued as a unilateral directive), the power modern presidents wield very much depends upon their ability to persuade.

■   ■   ■

[W]hile presidents must build and sustain coalitions to pass laws, they can unilaterally issue policy directives over the vocal objections of congressional majorities. As one political observer instructs, "Forget Capitol Hill deliberations and back-room negotiations with industry titans. No need for endless debate and deal-making. For a president, an executive order can be as powerful as a law—and considerably easier to achieve." In the political fight over the content of public policy, presidents regularly exert power without persuasion.

■   ■   ■

CONCLUSION

■ ■ ■

Macrotrends in Unilateral Policy Making

Since George Washington issued the Neutrality Proclamation in 1793, presidents have relied upon their unilateral powers to effect important policy changes. In the nineteenth century, Jefferson followed up with the Louisiana Purchase and Lincoln with the Emancipation Proclamation. In the early twentieth century, Theodore Roosevelt established the national parks system and Wilson issued more than 1,700 executive orders to guide the nation through World War I.

For the past fifty years, however, the trajectory of unilateral policy making has noticeably increased. While it was relatively rare, and for the most part inconsequential, during the eighteenth and nineteenth centuries, unilateral policy making has become an integral feature of the modern presidency. Presidents issue more unilateral directives today than ever before, steadily expanding their influence over all kinds of public policies, foreign and domestic. While there remain important fluctuations from year to year, and from administration to administration, the time-series of significant executive orders and executive agreements unmistakably rises.

In part, this is due to the overwhelming demands placed upon modern presidents. The public holds presidents responsible for all kinds of activities that previously either did not concern the federal government or rested solely within the domain of Congress. Presidents now develop policies on medical practices, racial discrimination, social welfare, labor and management relations, international trade, and education—areas that few presidents, prior to FDR, ever addressed. Indeed, it is difficult to think of a single area of governance that modern presidents can safely ignore. Modern presidents, in this sense, do more simply because the public expects them to.

In addition, presidential powers have expanded over the past half-century because the checks placed on them by Congress have subsided. As political parties have weakened, subcommittees have proliferated, and ideological divisions within Congress have heightened, Congress's ability to legislate has waned. So much so, in fact, that gridlock, while not constant, has become "a basic fact of U.S. lawmaking" (Krehbiel 1998, 4). This development has important implications for presidential power. As Congress weakens, the check it places on presidential power relaxes, and new opportunities arise for the president to strike out on his own. An expansion of presidential power then signals a shift in the overall division of powers—tipping the balance in favor of the president, and against Congress.

Two additional factors probably contributed to the overall increase in unilateral policy making during the latter half of the twentieth century. First, the time-series takes off in the late 1930s, just after the Supreme Court issued a series of rulings—*United States v. Curtiss-Wright* (1936); *United States v. Belmont* (1937); and *United States v. Pink* (1942)—that collectively fortified the president's legal authority to issue executive orders and executive agreements. With the official sanctioning of the Court, modern presidents proceeded with a greater measure of confidence when issuing executive orders and other unilateral directives. Second, many of these orders either created new administrative agencies or directed existing agencies to perform new functions. In this sense, the general trajectory of the significant executive order time-series maps the steady growth of the administrative state. Modern presidents did more simply because more needed to be done. Compared to their predecessors, modern presidents oversee more agencies that employ more employees that perform more tasks. As a consequence, it is little wonder that modern presidents rely upon the unilateral powers with greater frequency.

These trends, however, need not continue forever. There is nothing in the logic of the unilateral politics model that requires presidential power to increase monotonically over time. Quite the contrary, should a new consensus about policy matters emerge in Congress and legislative productivity displace gridlock, opportunities for presidents to act unilaterally may decline. Similarly, should executive actions attract heightened public scrutiny, judges may feel emboldened to overturn presidents with greater frequency.

BIBLIOGRAPHY

Cooper, Phillip. 2002. *By Order of the President: The Use and Abuse of Executive Direct Action.* Lawrence: University Press of Kansas.

———. 1997. "Power Tools for an Effective and Responsible Presidency." *Administration and Society* 29 (5): 529–56.

Corwin, Edward. 1957. *The President, Office and Powers, 1787–1948: History and Analysis of Practice and Opinion.* New York: New York University Press.

Cronin, Thomas. 1989. *Inventing the American Presidency.* Lawrence: University of Kansas Press.

Hart, John. 1995. *The Presidential Branch From Washington to Clinton.* Chatham, NJ: Chatham House Publishers, Inc.

King, Gary, and Lyn Ragsdale. 1988. *The Elusive Executive: Discovering Statistical Patterns in the Presidency.* Washington, DC: Congressional Quarterly Press.

Krehbiel, Keith. 1998. *Pivotal Politics: A Theory of U.S. Lawmaking.* Chicago: University of Chicago Press.

Landy, Marc, and Sidney Milkis. 2000. *Presidential Greatness.* Lawrence: University of Kansas Press.

Mayer, Kenneth. 2001. *With the Stroke of a Pen: Executive Orders and Presidential Power.* Princeton, NJ: Princeton University Press.

McDonald, Forrest. 1994. *The American Presidency: An Intellectual History.* Lawrence: University of Kansas Press.

Moe, Terry, and William Howell. 1999a. "The Presidential Power of Unilateral Action." *Journal of Law, Economics and Organization* 15 (1): 132–79.

———. 1999b. "Unilateral Action and Presidential Power: A Theory." *Presidential Studies Quarterly* 29 (4): 850–72.

Neustadt, Richard E. 1991 [1960]. *Presidential Power and the Modern Presidents*. New York: Free Press.

Paige, Joseph. 1977. *The Law Nobody Knows: Enlargement of the Constitution—Treaties and Executive Agreements*. New York: Vantage Press.

Schubert, Glendon. 1973. *The Presidency in the Courts*. New York: Da Capo Press.

6.5

COREY ROBIN

From *The Reactionary Mind: Conservatism from Edmund Burke to Donald Trump*

This leftist critique of Donald Trump by Robin is more than merely a reaction to Trump's policies. Robin cites the many contradictions within Trump's own rhetoric but also between Trump's rhetoric and traditional conservatism. Trump, it is argued, is an odd conservative, relying on some of the core ideas of contemporary American conservativism but ultimately distorting them to harken an older version centered around Trump's unique style and career history. Trump, Robin argues, ultimately leans on the old-fashioned, muscular version of conservatism as opposed to the more modern, pro-capitalist version.

> But in the desert you shall be invincible and shall achieve the goal.
> —Arnold Schoenberg, *Moses und Aron*

Inconsistency has long been [Donald] Trump's style.[1] But where Trump's critics seize on that inconsistency as evidence of his unique liabilities, yet another instance of the difference between him and his respectable predecessors on the right, a happy avowal of contradiction has been a feature of the conservative tradition since the beginning. Originally, that avowal assumed a tonier form: as a counter to the simpleminded rationalism that was supposed to animate the left.[2] Against the belief that politics and society could be reduced to and made consistent with the austere rules of logic and reason, the conservative sought what Walter Bagehot called, in a different vein, "truth as a succession of perpetual oscillations, like the negative and positive signs of an alternate series, in which you were constantly more or less denying or affirming the same proposition."[3] The capacity to inhabit the twin poles of a proposition and its negation, without attempting to reconcile or overcome them, helped one appreciate and preserve the subtle textures of society. A complex social order, layered by centuries of submission and rule, would be ruined—made smaller, more tractable, less grand—by the leveling reason of the left.

■ ■ ■

From Corey Robin, *The Reactionary Mind: Conservatism from Edmund Burke to Donald Trump* (New York, NY: Oxford University Press, 2018).

Trump neither knows nor nods to this tradition. Yet as he ambles from one contradiction to the next, it's hard to avoid the suspicion that his indifference to consistency, his refusal to bow before the god of the flip-flop, is part of his appeal on the right. It advertises the image of the non-stuffed shirt that he, like so many conservatives before him, has long cultivated.[4] "Most people are surprised by the way I work," he says in *The Art of the Deal*. "I play it very loose. . . . You can't be imaginative or entrepreneurial if you've got too much structure. I prefer to come to work each day and just see what develops."[5] Trump doesn't need to make things tidy and neat. He's not afraid of a little chaos or disorder. He's also not afraid to give offense. He's as willing to defy the norms of political correctness as he is the rule of reason; those norms are a limitation on freedom as constraining as any socialist design.[6] Like George W. Bush, whose cowboy affect inspired the gushing title "Rebel in Chief," Trump plays the part of the happy buccaneer, forever impolitic, thumbing his nose at the prissy professor of principle—a part that invokes the right's age-old hostility to political arithmetic and moral geometry.[7] "Sometimes," as Trump says, "it pays to be a little wild."[8]

▪ ▪ ▪

Trump . . . is no mere carbon copy of his predecessors. In at least two respects he has revised the right's script. First, Trump reflects a tension between two visions on the right: what we might call the political and the economic. One vision prizes heroism, glory, and elite action, and is associated with the battlefield, high politics, and the hard affairs of state. The other celebrates the market and trade, the accumulation of wealth and exchange of commodities, and is associated with unfettered capitalism. The conflict between the warrior and the businessman is an old one, predating the rise of the right and capitalism.[9] But since the eighteenth century, that conflict has produced on the right an intense ambivalence about capitalism. One side of the right has propped up the spheres of war and high politics as antidotes to or escapes from the deadening effects of capitalism. Here, capitalism is not so much eliminated as it is downgraded, its place in society diminished in order to make room for what Nietzsche called *grosse Politik*. The other side, of which there are glimmerings in Burke and a more developed picture in Schumpeter and Hayek, has not denigrated capitalism but recast it. No longer the province of the comfortable bourgeois trader, capitalism comes to look, in this view, like the agonistic political world its early defenders and critics thought capitalism might displace. The businessman ceases to be an antidote to the warrior or the aristocrat; he becomes their sublimation.

The Cold War allowed—or forced—the right to hold these tensions between the warrior and the businessman in check. Against the backdrop of the struggle against communism abroad and welfare-state liberalism at home, the businessman became a warrior and the warrior a businessm[a]n.[10] With the end of the Cold War, that conflation or confusion of roles became difficult to sustain. In one precinct of the right, the market returned to its status as a deadening activity that stifled greatness, whether of the nation or the elite. In another precinct of the right, market activities were revalorized as acts of heroism by an economic class that saw itself and its work as the natural province of rule. Donald Trump hails from the second precinct, but with a twist: he suggests that its self-understanding can no longer be sustained.

Trump's second innovation upends the always-delicate relationship on the right between elite and mass, privilege and populism. Conservatism is an elitist movement of the masses, an effort to create a new-old regime that, in one way or another, makes privilege popular. Sometimes, conservatism has multiplied the ranks of privilege, creating ever-finer gradations between the worse off and the worst off. Here the model is the American firm, with its many tiers of middle and lower management.[11] Sometimes, conservatism has simplified those ranks into two: the white race and the black race of the white supremacist imagination. Sometimes, it has offshored society's inequalities, seeing in the people of an imperial state a unified rank of superiors, "a kind of nobility among nations" subjugating less civilized peoples abroad.[12] And sometimes it has turned elites into victims, encouraging the masses to see their abjection reflected in the higher misery of those above them. Regardless of the means, conservatism has always found a way to conscript the lower orders into its regime of lordly rule.

▪   ▪   ▪

Trump's critics often dismiss the anti-elitism of his economic rhetoric as incidental if not irrelevant. Yet Trump's critique of plutocracy, defense of entitlements, and articulated sense of the market's wounds were among the more noteworthy rhetorical innovations of his campaign—at least with respect to recent victorious strands of the electoral right (one can find precedents for Trump's mix of racial and economic populism in the less electorally successful campaigns of Father Coughlin, George Wallace, and Pat Buchanan).[13] If nothing else, those rhetorical innovations signal that the sun of Reaganomics—which saw in the unfettered market the answer to the political, economic, and cultural stagflation of the 1970s—no longer warms the lower orders of the right.[14] It's not "morning in America," Trump declared in a recent campaign book, invoking Reagan's famous tag line from 1984; we are now "*mourning for America.*"[15]

What these two innovations tell us is that the tensions that long buttressed the right—the countervailing pressures of the political versus the economic, elite versus mass—are no longer as taut as they once were. Those pressures don't support the movement; they don't give it the buoyancy it once had. The reason is the disappearance of the right's traditional antagonists—the freedom movements of the left, those subaltern assertions of agency and will, from the French Revolution through civil rights and women's lib, that sought individual emancipation through collective liberation and vice versa. "Conservatism does its best," the right-wing British philosopher Roger Scruton has written, "in times of crisis." For the right, the crisis is a dynamic and vibrant left, the challenge of movements of revolution or reform that force the right to think harder and better, to act smarter and with greater discipline and intentionality: not out of any Millian desire to get the better of an argument but out of dread necessity, the need to defend power and privilege in the face of a movement seeking their elimination. When the left is ascendant and genuinely threatening, the right gets tough, intellectually and politically; when the left is in abeyance, the right grows sclerotic and complacent, rigid and lazy. According to Hayek, the defense of the free market "became stationary when it was most influential." It "progressed" only when it was "on the defensive." While there are stirrings on the left—Occupy, Black Lives Matter, LGBTQ movements, and the Sanders campaign—none of these movements has yet achieved sufficient velocity or institutional traction to awaken and discipline a new right that would be able to do what its predecessors did. The right's greatest "burst of creative energy," according to Frank Meyer, one of its leading midcentury action intellectuals, occurred "simultaneously with a continuing spread of the influence of Liberalism in the practical political sphere."[16] Without a formidable enemy on the left, without an opponent to discipline and tutor the right, the long-standing fissures of the conservative movement are allowed to deepen and expand.

■　　■　　■

Trump's rhetoric is suffused with this conception of economic life as a struggle of the best men for power and position. Nothing provokes his ire more than the time-server, whether in the family or the firm. One of the men Trump has great admiration for is Conrad Hilton, who built a hotel empire on his own. Hilton believed "that inherited wealth destroys moral character and motivation." Trump agrees (in theory; from his earliest years, he had a trust fund, and he campaigned against the estate tax). That is why he takes such a jaundiced view of Hilton's son, who despite Conrad's warnings about inheritance, came to a position of great power in his father's industry. "It had nothing to do with merit," says Trump; "it's called birthright." . . .

In business, Trump prefers to deal with "the sharpest, toughest, and most vicious people in the world. I happen to love to go up against these guys, and I love to beat them." . . . Like the bloody battles of ancient Greece or medieval Europe, moments of economic combat belong to the more excellent, superior man. Not better in the sense of meritocratic achievement—institutional measures of worth can reward only the institution man—or in terms of an economic contribution—a new product, more jobs, higher shareholder value—but in the sense of besting another in the field of battle. Those moments reveal the "instincts" of the self. Those instincts may entail "a certain intelligence," but more important, they reflect a driving will to overcome, to overpower, to win. There are some who have great talent but who "will never find out how great they could have been. Instead, they'll be content to sit and watch stars perform on television." Such individuals "are afraid of success, afraid of making decisions, afraid of winning." The great man has no such compunctions; he has a driving will to win, to put that greatness into effect, to show it off to the world. And that, says Trump, is not something one can learn or develop; it is "an ability you're born with." It is what truly belongs to the original and originating self.[17]

▪   ▪   ▪

Trump is by no means the first man of the right (though he may be the first president, at least since Teddy Roosevelt) to reach that conclusion about capitalism. A great many neoconservatives found themselves stranded on the same beach after the end of the Cold War. As had many conservatives before that. Those conservatives, however, always found a redeeming vision in the state. Not the welfare state or the nanny state but The State of high politics, national greatness, imperial leadership, and war. Given the thrumming menace of Trump's rhetoric, his impatience with routine, his fetish for pomp and love of grandeur, this state, too, would seem the natural terminus of his predilections. As Bannon said, "A country's more than an economy. We're a civic society." Yet on closer inspection, the state of Trump's imagination looks less like The State than the deals he's not sure have added up to much.

Trump's 2011 proto-campaign statement *Time to Get Tough*—repackaged for the 2016 campaign with a new subtitle, *Make America Great Again!*®—plots this trajectory to a tee. It opens on that note of wounded nationalism for which Trump has come to be famous—

> Every day in business I see America getting ripped off and abused. We have become a laughingstock, the world's whipping boy, blamed for everything, credited for nothing, given no respect.[18]

—and it never lets up. Across nearly 200 pages, it recounts an epoch of national humiliation, presided over by decadent leaders like Barack Obama and—shades of McCarthyites talking about Dean Acheson—his band of "cream puff 'diplomats.'" We're sinking like a stone, growls Trump, we come to the rest of the world "on bended knee," Obama "practices 'pretty please' diplomacy," his statements are "drenched in weakness," China is our enemy, Obama is a traitor, we have to get tough, Let's Make America Great Again![19] So committed is Trump to America First that, after acknowledging that no American wants to drill for oil in his backyard, he cites as yet another example of our national humiliation the fact that we allow other nations to drill in their backyards. Like George C. Scott's General "Buck" Turgidson in *Dr. Strangelove*—"Mr. President, we must not allow . . . a mineshaft gap!"—Trump complains "the holes are going to get drilled into the planet anyway" so "we should drill them on our soil."[20]

▪   ▪   ▪

. . . [W]hat's remarkable about Trump's political vision is how economistic it can be, especially at moments when he hews most closely to a hard image of the state. Where anti-market conservatives historically flew into the arms (in both senses) of the state as an end run around the market, Trump often sees in matters of state nothing but the transactions of the market. Money is the instrument of state power. Money is the end of state power. Anyone aspiring to wield state power should be an adept of money: success or failure in the business world is the best test of one's political mettle. Even when Trump tries to talk the language of hard power—violence, coercion, rule—he cannot avoid sliding back into the idioms of the market he knows so well.

"China is our enemy," Trump says, and "the military threat from China is gigantic." As a result, "we've got to have a president who knows how to get tough with China."[21] Does that entail an arms race, more aggressive deployments in East Asia, nuclear brinksmanship? No, just the opposite.

■ ■ ■

At almost every step—from his opening salvo of a travel ban to his attempt to repeal Obamacare to his effort to build a wall to his budget proposal for the remainder of fiscal year 2017 and plans to overhaul the tax code—Trump's plans and purposes have been checked by opposition in the streets, the courts, the Democratic Party, and uncertainty and division within his own party.[22] Less than five months into his term, his voting base—whites, men, and white men and women without college degrees—has begun to erode.[23] With the important exceptions of rolling back his predecessor's regulatory regime and pushing a punitive immigration policy—the latter being an area where all presidents have independent power, a power the last two Democrats in the White House exercised with decreasing restraint[24]—Trump's program, thus far, has been mostly stymied. And despite Trump's campaign promise, repeated in his Inaugural Address, to govern as a new type of conservative, defending the interests of the working man, his practice has been overwhelmingly consistent with mainstream pro-business Republicanism.[25]

NOTES

1. Michael Kruse and Noah Weiland, "Donald Trump's Greatest Self-Contradictions," *Politico* (May 5, 2016), http://www.politico.com/magazine/story/2016/05/donald-trump -2016-contradictions-213869; Inae Oh, "Watch Donald Trump Contradict Himself on Every Major Campaign Issue," *Mother Jones* (August 9, 2016), http://www.motherjones .com/politics/2016/08/donald-trump-contradicting-himself-hypocrisy-video; David Bier, "Four Ways Trump Contradicts Himself with His New Travel Ban," *Newsweek* (March 9, 2017), http://www.newsweek.com/four-ways-trump-contradicts-himself-his -new-travel-ban-564902.

2. The most important statement of this position on the right remains Michael Oakeshott, *Rationalism and Politics and Other Essays* (Indianapolis: Liberty Fund, 1991). On Oakeshott's reflections on inconsistency, see Dale Hall and Tariq Modood, "Oake-

shott and the Impossibility of Philosophical Politics," *Political Studies* 30 (June 1982), 157–76.

3. Walter Bagehot, "Intellectual Conservatism," in *The Works and Life of Walter Bagehot*, Vol. 9 (London: Longmans, Green, and Co., 1915), 254.

4. Kevin Mattson, *Rebels All! A Short History of the Conservative Mind in Postwar America* (New Brunswick: Rutgers University Press, 2008).

5. Trump, *Art of the Deal*, I.

6. Andrew Prokop, "Trump backers hate 'political correctness.' That's why gaffes don't hurt him," *Vox* (February 29, 2016), http://www.vox.com/2016/2/29/11133796/donald -trump-political-correctness; Lauren Berlant, "Trump, or Political Emotions," *The New Inquiry* (August 5, 2016), https://thenewinquiry.com/features/trump-or-political -emotions/.

7. Fred Barnes, *Rebel in Chief: Inside the Bold and Controversial Presidency of George W. Bush* (New York: Crown, 2006). About this book, and the general reputation Bush sought to cultivate among his conservative base, historian Kevin Mattson writes, "Barnes does not see Bush as a statesman (or as stately); rather, his idealized president looks like Marlon Brando mounting his motorcycle and raising hell in the iconic 1953 film *The Wild One*. For Barnes. Bush is 'defiant of the press, scornful of the conventional wisdom, and keen to reverse or at least substantially reform long-standing policies.' The president is 'edgy' and 'blunt'; he leads an army of insurgents.'" Mattson, 2.

8. Trump, *Art of the Deal*, 5.

9. Albert O. Hirschman, *The Passions and the Interests: Political Arguments for Capitalism before Its Triumph* (Princeton: Princeton University, 1977).

10. Kim Phillips-Fein, *Invisible Hands: The Businessman's Crusade Against the New Deal* (New York: Norton, 2009).

11. David Gordon, *Fat and Mean: The Corporate Squeeze of Working Americans and the Myth of Managerial Downsizing* (New York: Free Press, 1996).

12. Hannah Arendt, *The Origins of Totalitarianism* (New York: Schocken, 1951), 232.

13. Alan Brinkley, *Voices of Protest: Huey Long, Father Coughlin, and the Great Depression* (New York: Knopf, 1982), 143–68, 287–88; Michael Kazin, *The Populist Persuasion: An American History* (New York: Basic, 1995), 109–33, 221–42; Dan T. Carter, *The Politics of Rage: George Wallace, the Origins of the New Conservatism, and the Transformation of American Politics* (New York: Simon and Schuster, 1995), 352, 281–83; Joseph E. Lowndes, *From the New Deal to the New Right* (New Haven: Yale University Press, 2008), 85, 101–4; Peter Kolozi, *Conservatives Against Capitalism: From the Industrial Revolution to Globalization* (New York: Columbia University Press, 2017), 167–89.

14. See Jonathan Chait, "What's Less Popular Than Donald Trump? Pretty Much Everything Paul Ryan and Mitch McConnell Are Doing," *New York* (May 29, 2017), http://nymag.com/daily/intelligencer/2017/05/whats-less-popular-than-donald-trump -paul-ryan-and-mitch-mcconnell.html; Jeff Stein, "Paul Ryan's Agenda has been a much bigger liability for the GOP than Trump's Scandals," *Vox* (May 23, 2017), https:// www.vox.com/policy-and-politics/2017/5/23/15674450/paul-ryan-special-election; Eric Levitz, "'Small Government' Conservatism Is Killing Republican Voters," *New York* (March 26, 2017), http://nymag.com/daily/intelligencer/2017/03/small-government-conser vatism-is-killing-republican-voters.html

15. Donald Trump, *Time to Get Tough: Make America Great Again!* (Washington, DC: Regnery, 2011, 2015), 4.

16. Roger Scruton, *The Meaning of Conservatism* (London: Macmillan, 1980, 1984), 11; Friedrich A. Hayek, *The Constitution of Liberty* (Chicago: University of Chicago

Press, 1960), 7; Frank Meyer, "Freedom, Tradition, Conservatism," in *In Defense of Freedom and Related Essays* (Indianapolis: Liberty Fund, 1996), 15.

17. Trump, *Art of the Deal*, 45–48, 63.

18. Trump, *Time to Get Tough*, 2.

19. Trump, *Time to Get Tough*, 8, 24, 27, 29, 33, 36, 41, 48; David K. Johnson, *The Cold War Persecution of Gays and Lesbians in the Federal Government* (Chicago: University of Chicago Press, 2006), 70.

20. Trump, *Time to Get Tough*, 26.

21. Trump, *Time to Get Tough*, 2, 45, 48.

22. See Ashley Parker, Phillip Rucker, and Sean Sullivan, "Trump Scrambles to Show Progress as the 100-day Mark Approaches," *Washington Post* (April 25, 2017), https://www.washingtonpost.com/politics/trump-scrambles-to-show-progress-as-the -100-day-mark-approaches/2017/04/25/9fc6803c-29d4 11c7-b605-33413c691853_story .html; David Lewis, "So Far Trump Is Struggling as a Chief Executive," *Washington Post* (April 27, 2017), https://www.washingtonpost.com/news/monkey-cage/wp/2017/04 /27/so-far-trump-gets-a-failing-grade-at-managing-the-executive-branch/; Billy House, Erik Wasson, and Laura Litvan, "Trump Says He'll Sign Congress Spending Deal That Jettisons His Goals," *Bloomberg Politics* (April 30, 2017), https://www.bloomberg.com /politics/articles/2017-05-01/congress-strikes-tentative-deal-on-1-1-trillion-spending -bill; Aaron Blake, "President Trump Just Had His Bluff Called—Again," *Washington Post* (April 25, 2017), https://www.washingtonpost.com/news/the-fix/wp/2017/04/25 /president-trump-just-had-his-bluff-called-again/; James Hohmann, "Trump Is Caving on Border Wall Funding after Showing His Base that He Tried," *Washington Post* (April 25, 2017), https://www.washingtonpost.com/news/powerpost/paloma/daily-202 /2017/04/25/daily-202-trump-is-caving-on-border-wall-funding-after-showing-his -base-that-he-tried/58fea413e9b69b3a72331ec4/; Amber Phillips, "Trump Is About to Be 0-4 on His Legislative Promises for His First 100 Days," *Washington Post* (April 27, 2017), https://www.washingtonpost.com/news/the-fix/wp/2017/04/27/trump-is-about-to -be-0-4-on-his-legislative-promises-for-his-first-100-days/; Patrick Jenkins and Barney Jopson, "Wall Street's hopes for deregulation switch from laws to watchdogs," *Financial Times* (May 7, 2017), https://www.ft.com/content/8d46739c-31ac-11e7-9555-23ef563 ecf9a; Ben White and Annie Karni, "America's CEOs fall out of love with Trump," *Politico* (June 3, 2017), http://www.politico.com/story/2017/06/03/donald-trump-ceos-corporate -relationship-239080.

23. Matthew Yglesias, "The 3 different things we talk about when we talk about 'Trump voter,'" *Vox* (December 7, 2016), https://www.vox.com/policy-and-politics/2016 /12/7/13854512/who-are-trump-supporters; Benjy Sarlin, "United States of Trump," *NBC News* (June 20, 2016), https://www.nbcnews.com/specials/donald-trump-republican -party; Justin Gest, "The Two Kinds of Trump Voters," *Politico* (February 8, 2017), https://www.politico.com/magazine/story/2017/02/trump-voters-white-working-class -214754; Nate Cohn, "A 2016 Review: Turnout Wasn't the Driver of Clinton's Defeat," *New York Times* (March 28, 2017), https://www.nytimes.com/2017/03/28/upshot/a-2016 -review-turnout-wasnt-the-driver-of-clintons-defeat.html; Nicholas Carnes and Noam Lupu, "It's Time to Bust the Myth: Most Trump Voters Were Not Working Class," *Washington Post* (June 5, 2017), https://www.washingtonpost.com/news/monkey-cage/wp /2017/06/05/its-time-to-bust-the-myth-most-trump-voters-were-not-working-class/.

24. Leighton Akio Woodhouse, "Obama's Deportation Policy Was Even Worse Than We Thought," *The Intercept* (May 15, 2017), https://theintercept.com/2017/05/15/obamas -deportation-policy-was-even-worse-than-we-thought/; Aviva Chomsky, "Making Sense of the Deportation Debate," *TomDispatch.com* (April 25, 2017), http://www.tomdispatch

.com/blog/176271/; Alan Aja and Alejandra Marchevsky, "How Immigrants Became Criminals," *Boston Review* (March 17, 2017), http://bostonreview.net/politics/alan-j-aja-alejandra-marchevsky-how-immigrants-became-criminals.

25. Robin, "Trump's Inaugural Address versus Reagan's Inaugural Address."

DISCUSSION QUESTIONS

1. What kinds of evidence would support Neustadt's argument about presidential power? For instance, would Donald Trump's behavior and influence be evidence in favor of Neustadt's argument?

2. Describe the steps in veto bargaining. Explain why the actual use of the veto is not evidence that having the veto is influential.

3. According to Canes-Wrone, under what conditions do presidents pander to the public? Under what conditions do presidents try to lead the public or act against the public's wishes?

4. "By moving first," Howell says, presidents can have great influence over policy by issuing executive orders. Why are Congress and the federal courts disadvantaged when presidents act unilaterally?

5. Contrast Donald Trump's version of conservatism with the Republican Party's more mainstream conservatism.

6. Describe some of the real constraints on the president's capacity to act unilaterally. Then describe conditions under which the president can successfully act unilaterally.

7

THE BUREAUCRACY

7.1

JAMES Q. WILSON

From *Bureaucracy: What Government Agencies Do and Why They Do It*

Wilson writes convincingly that bureaucracies can vary greatly in their effectiveness. He pokes holes in standard complaints about bureaucracies by indicating how some of the inefficiencies that people complain about are either unavoidable or by design.

BUREAUCRACY AND THE PUBLIC INTEREST

The German army beat the French army in 1940; the Texas prisons for many years did a better job than did the Michigan prisons; Carver High School in Atlanta became a better school under Norris Hogans. These successes were the result of skilled executives who correctly identified the critical tasks of their organizations, distributed authority in a way appropriate to those tasks, infused their subordinates with a sense of mission, and acquired sufficient autonomy to permit them to get on with the job. The critical tasks were different in each case, and so the organizations differed in culture and patterns of authority, but all three were alike in one sense: incentives, culture, and authority were combined in a way that suited the task at hand.

By now, . . . the reader may find all this painfully obvious. If [these points] are obvious to the reader, then surely they are obvious to government officials.

From James Q. Wilson, *Bureaucracy: What Government Agencies Do and Why They Do It* (New York: Basic Books, 2006).

Intellectually perhaps they are. But whatever lip service may be given to the lessons . . . the daily incentives operating in the political world encourage a very different course of action.

Armies

Though the leadership and initiative of field officers and noncoms is of critical importance, the Pentagon is filled with generals who want to control combat from headquarters or from helicopters, using radios to gather information and computers to process it. Though the skill of the infantryman almost always has been a key to military success, the U.S. Army traditionally has put its best people in specialized units (intelligence, engineering, communications), leaving the leftovers for the infantry.[1] Though it has fought wars since 1945 everywhere except in Europe, the army continues to devote most of its planning to big-tank battles on the West German plains.

Prisons

The success of George Beto in the Texas DOC was there for everyone to see, but many observers gave the most favorable attention to prison executives who seemed to voice the best intentions (rehabilitation, prisoner self-governance) rather than the best accomplishments (safe, decent facilities).

Schools

Especially in big cities, many administrators keep principals weak and teachers busy filling out reports, all with an eye toward minimizing complaints from parents, auditors, interest groups, and the press. Teachers individually grumble that they are treated as robots instead of professionals, but collectively they usually oppose any steps—vouchers, merit pay, open enrollment, strengthened principals—that in fact have given teachers a larger role in designing curricula and managing their classrooms. Norris Hogans received little help from the Atlanta school system; politically, extra resources had to go to all schools "equally" rather than disproportionately to those schools that were improving the most.

These generals, wardens, administrators, and teachers have not been behaving irrationally; rather, they have been responding to the incentives and constraints that they encounter on a daily basis. Those incentives include the need to manage situations over which they have little control on the basis of a poorly defined or nonexistent sense of mission and in the face of a complex array of constraints that seems always to grow, never to shrink. Outside groups—elected officials, interest groups, professional associations, the media—demand a voice in the running of these agencies and make that demand effective by imposing rules on the agencies and demanding that all these rules be enforced all of the time. Moreover, habitual patterns of action—the lessons of the past, the memories of earlier struggles, the expectations of one's co-workers—narrow the area within which new courses of action are sought.

Bureaucrats often complain of "legislative micromanagement," and indeed it exists . . . with respect to the armed forces. There has been a dramatic increase in the number of hearings, reports, investigations, statutory amendments, and budgetary adjustments with which the Pentagon must deal.[2] But there also has been a sharp increase in presidential micromanagement. Herbert Kaufman notes that for a half century or more, the White House has feared agency independence more than agency paralysis, and so it has multiplied the number of presidential staffers, central management offices, and requirements for higher-level reviews. Once you start along the path of congressional or White House control, the process acquires a momentum of its own. "As more constraints are imposed, rigidities fixing agencies in their established ways intensify. As a result, complaints that they do not respond to controls also intensify. Further controls, checkpoints, and clearances are therefore introduced."[3] Much the same story can be told with respect to the growing involvement of the courts in agency affairs.

With some conspicuous exceptions, the result of this process has been to deflect the attention of agency executives away from how the tasks of their agencies get defined and toward the constraints that must be observed no matter what the tasks may be. Who then decides what tasks shall be performed? In a production agency with observable outputs and routinized work processes, the answer is relatively simple: The laws and regulations that created the agency also define its job. But in procedural, coping, and craft agencies, the answer seems to be nobody in particular and everybody in general. The operating-level workers define the tasks, occasionally by design, as in those cases where operator ideology makes a difference, but more commonly by accident, as in those instances where prior experiences, professional norms, situational and technological imperatives, and peer-group expectations shape the nature of the work.

From time to time a gifted executive appears at a politically propitious time and makes things happen differently. He or she creates a new institution that acquires a distinctive competence, a strong sense of mission, and an ability to achieve socially valued goals. The Army Corps of Engineers, the Social Security Administration, the Marine Corps, the Forest Service, the FBI: For many years after they were created, and in many instances still today, these agencies, along with a few others that could be mentioned, were a kind of elite service that stood as a living refutation of the proposition that "all bureaucrats are dim-witted paper-shufflers." And these are only the federal examples; at the local level one can find many school systems and police departments that have acquired a praiseworthy organizational character.

But one must ask whether today one could create from scratch the Marine Corps, or the FBI, or the Forest Service; possibly, but probably not. Who would dare suggest that a new agency come into being with its own personnel system (and thus with fewer opportunities for civil servants to get tenure), with a single dominant mission (and thus with little organizational deference to the myriad other goals outsiders would want it to serve), and with an arduous training regime designed to instill *esprit de corps* (and thus with less regard for those niceties and conveniences that sedentary people believe to be important)? Or how optimistic should we be that today we could organize a Social Security Administration in a way that would bring to Washington men and women of exceptional talent? Might not many of those people decide today that they do not want to risk running afoul of the conflict-of-interest laws, that they have no stomach for close media and congressional scrutiny, and that they would not accept the federal pay levels pegged to the salaries of members of Congress fearful of raising their own compensation?

It would be a folly of historical romanticism to imagine that great agencies were created in a golden age that is destined never to return, but it would be shortsighted to deny that we have paid a price for having emphasized rules and constraints to the neglect of tasks and mission. At the end of her careful review of the problems the SSA has had in managing disability insurance and supplemental security income, Martha Derthick makes the same point this way: "If the agencies repeatedly fall short, one ought at least to consider the possibility that there is a systematic mismatch between what they are instructed to do and their capacity to do it."[4] In recent years, when Congress has been creating new programs and modifying old ones at a dizzying rate, often on the basis of perfunctory hearings (or, as with the Senate's consideration of the 1988 drug bill, no hearings at all), a government agency capable of responding adequately to these endless changes would have to be versatile and adaptable, "capable of devising new routines or altering old ones very quickly." These qualities, she concludes, "are rarely found in large formal organizations."[5] I would only add that government agencies are far less flexible than formal organizations generally.

Things are not made much better by our national tendency to engage in bureaucrat-bashing. One has to have some perspective on this. It is true that bureaucracies prefer the present to the future, the known to the unknown, and the dominant mission to rival missions; many agencies in fact are skeptical of things that were "NIH"—Not Invented Here. Every social grouping, whether a neighborhood, a nation, or an organization, acquires a culture; changing that culture is like moving a cemetery: it is always difficult and some believe it is sacrilegious. It is also true, as many conservatives argue, that the government tries to do things that it is incapable of doing well, just as it is true, as many liberals allege, that the government in fact does many things well enough. As Charles Wolf has argued, both markets and governments have their imperfections; many things we might want to do collectively require us to choose between unsatisfactory alternatives.[6]

A Few Modest Suggestions that May Make a Small Difference

To do better we have to deregulate the government.[7] If deregulation of a market makes sense because it liberates the entrepreneurial energies of its members, then it is possible that deregulating the public sector also may help energize it.

The difference, of course, is that both the price system and the profit motive provide a discipline in markets that is absent in non-markets. Whether any useful substitutes for this discipline can be found for public-sector workers is not clear, though I will offer some suggestions. But even if we cannot expect the same results from deregulation in the two sectors we can agree at a minimum that detailed regulation, even of public employees, rarely is compatible with energy, pride in workmanship, and the exercise of initiative. The best evidence for this proposition, if any is needed, is that most people do not like working in an environment in which every action is second-guessed, every initiative viewed with suspicion, and every controversial decision denounced as malfeasance.

James Colvard, for many years a senior civilian manager in the navy, suggests that the government needs to emulate methods that work in the better parts of the private sector: "a bias toward action, small staffs, and a high level of delegation which is based on trust."[8] A panel of the National Academy of Public Administration (NAPA), consisting of sixteen senior government executives holding the rank of assistant secretary, issued a report making the same point:

> Over many years, government has become entwined in elaborate management control systems and the accretion of progressively more detailed administrative procedures. This development has not produced superior management. Instead, it has produced managerial overburden. . . . Procedures overwhelm substance. Organizations become discredited, along with their employees. . . . The critical elements of leadership in management appear to wither in the face of a preoccupation with process. The tools are endlessly "perfected"; the manager who is expected to use these tools believes himself to be ignored. . . . Management systems are not management. . . . The attitude of those who design and administer the rules . . . must be reoriented from a "control mentality" to one of "how can I help get the mission of this agency accomplished."[9]

But how can government "delegate" and "trust" and still maintain accountability? If it is a mistake to foster an ethos that encourages every bureaucrat to "go by the book," is it not an equally serious problem to allow zealots to engage in "mission madness," charging off to implement their private versions of some ambiguous public goal? (Steven Emerson has written a useful account of mission madness in some highly secret military intelligence and covert-action agencies.)[10] Given everything we know about the bureaucratic desire for autonomy and the political rewards of rule making, is there any reason to suppose that anybody will find it in his or her interest to abandon the "control mentality" and adopt the "mission accomplishment" mentality?

Possibly not. But it may be worth thinking about what a modestly deregulated government might look like. It might look as it once did, when some of the better federal agencies were created. At the time the Corps of Engineers, the Forest Service, and the FBI were founded much of the federal government was awash in political patronage, petty cabals, and episodic corruption. Organizing an elite service in those days may have been easier than doing so today, when the problems are less patronage and corruption than they are officiousness and complexity. But the keys to organizational success have not changed. The agencies were started by strong leaders who were able to command personal loyalty, define and instill a clear and powerful sense of mission, attract talented workers who believed they were joining something special, and make exacting demands on subordinates.

Today there is not much chance to create a new agency; almost every agency one can imagine already has been created. Even so, the lessons one learns from changing agencies confirm what can be inferred from studying their founding.

FIRST. Executives should understand the culture of their organizations—that is, what their subordinates believe constitute the core tasks of the agency—and the strengths and limitations of that culture. If members widely share and warmly endorse that culture the agency has a sense of mission. This permits the executive to economize on scarce incentives (people want to do certain tasks even when there are no special rewards for doing it); to state general objectives confident that subordinates will understand the appropriate ways of achieving them; and to delegate responsibility knowing that lower-level decisions probably will conform to higher-level expectations.

A good executive realizes that workers can make subtle, precise, and realistic judgments, but only if those judgments refer to a related, coherent set of behaviors. People cannot easily keep in mind many quite different things or strike reasonable balances among competing tasks. People want to know what is expected of them; they do not want to be told, in answer to this question, that "on the one hand this, but on the other hand that."

In defining a core mission and sorting out tasks that either fit or do not fit with this mission, executives must be aware of their many rivals for the right to define it. Operators with professional backgrounds will bring to the agency their skills but also their biases: lawyers, economists, and engineers see the world in very different ways. You cannot hire them as if they were tools that in your skilled hands will perform exactly the task you set for them. Black and Decker may make tools like that, but Harvard and MIT do not. Worker peer groups also set expectations to which operators conform, especially when the operators work in a threatening, unpredictable, or confrontational environment. You may design the ideal patrol officer or schoolteacher, but unless you understand the demands made by the street and the classroom, your design will remain an artistic expression destined for the walls of some organizational museum.

These advantages of infusing an agency with a sense of mission are purchased at a price. An agency with a strong mission will give perfunctory attention, if any at all, to tasks that are not central to that mission. Diplomats in the State Department will have little interest in embassy security; intelligence officers in the CIA will not worry as much as they should about counterintelligence; narcotics agents in the DEA will minimize the importance of improper prescriptions written by physicians; power engineers in the TVA will not think as hard about environmental protection or conservation as about maximizing the efficiency of generating units; fighter pilots in the USAF will look at air transport as a homely stepchild; and navy admirals who earned their flag serving on aircraft carriers will not press zealously to expand the role of minesweepers.

If the organization must perform a diverse set of tasks, those tasks that are not part of the core mission will need special protection. This requires giving autonomy to the subordinate tasks subunit (e.g., by providing for them a special organizational niche) and creating a career track so that talented people performing non-mission tasks can rise to high rank in the agency. No single organization, however, can perform well a wide variety of tasks; inevitably some will be neglected. In this case, the wise executive will arrange to devolve the slighted tasks onto another agency, or to a wholly new organization created for the purpose. Running multitask conglomerates is as risky in the public as in the private sector. There are limits to the number of different jobs managers can manage. Moreover, conglomerate agencies rarely can develop a sense of mission; the cost of trying to do everything is that few things are done well. The turf-conscious executive who stoutly refuses to surrender any tasks, no matter how neglected, to another agency is courting disaster; in time the failure of his or her agency to perform some orphan task will lead to a political or organizational crisis. Long ago the State Department should have got out of the business of building embassies. Diplomats are good at many things, but supervising carpenters and plumbers is not one of them. Let agencies whose mission is construction—the Army Corps of Engineers or the navy's Seabees—build buildings.

SECOND. Negotiate with one's political superiors to get some agreement as to which are the *essential* constraints that must be observed by your agency and which the marginal constraints. This, frankly, may be impossible. The decentralization of authority in Congress (and in some state legislatures) and the unreliability of most expressions of presidential or gubernatorial backing are such that in most cases you will discover, by experience if not by precept, that all constraints are essential all of the time. But perhaps with effort some maneuvering room may be won. A few agencies obtained the right to use more flexible, less cumbersome personnel systems modeled on the China Lake experiment, and Congress has the power to broaden those opportunities. Perhaps some enlightened member of Congress will be able to get statutory authority for the equivalent of China Lake with respect to procurement regulations. An executive is well advised to spend time showing that member how to do it.

THIRD. Match the distribution of authority and the control over resources to the tasks your organization is performing. In general, authority should be placed at the lowest level at which all essential elements of information are available. Bureaucracies will differ greatly in what level that may be. At one extreme are agencies such as the Internal Revenue Service or maximum-security prisons, in which uniformity of treatment and precision of control are so important as to make it necessary for there to be exacting, centrally determined rules for most tasks. At the other extreme are public schools, police departments, and armies, organizations in which operational uncertainties are so great that discretion must be given to (or if not given will be taken by) lower-level workers.

A good place in which to think through these matters is the area of weapons procurement. The overcentralization of design control is one of the many criticisms of such procurement on which all commentators seem [to have] agreed. Buying a new aircraft may be likened to remodeling one's home: you never know how much it will cost until you are done; you quickly find out that changing your mind midway through the work costs a lot of money; and you soon realize that decisions have to be made by people on the spot who can look at the pipes, wires, and joists. The Pentagon procures aircraft as if none of its members had ever built or remodeled a house. It does so because both it and its legislative superiors refuse to allow authority to flow down to the point where decisions rationally can be made.

The same analysis can be applied to public schools. As John Chubb and Terry Moe have shown, public and private schools differ in the locus of effective control.[11] At least in big cities, decisions in private schools that are made by headmasters or in Catholic schools that are made by small archdiocesan staffs are made in public schools by massive, cumbersome headquarters bureaucracies. Of course, there are perfectly understandable political reasons for this difference, but not very many good reasons for it. Many sympathetic critics of the public schools believe that the single most useful organizational change that could be made would be to have educational management decisions—on personnel, scheduling, and instructional matters—made at the school level.[12]

FOURTH. Judge organizations by results. This reading has made it clear that what constitutes a valued result in government usually is a matter of dispute. But even when fairly clear performance standards exist, legislatures and executives often ignore them with unhappy results. William E. Turcotte compared how two state governments oversaw their state liquor monopolies. The state that applied clear standards to its liquor bureaucrats produced significantly more profit and lower administrative costs than did the state with unclear or conflicting standards.[13]

Even when results are hard to assess, more can be done than is often the case. If someone set out to evaluate the output of a private school, hospital, or security service, he or she would have at least as much trouble as would someone trying to measure the output of a public school, hospital, or police department. Governments are not the only institutions with ambiguous products.

There are two ways to cope with the problem in government. One . . . is to supply the service or product in a marketlike environment. Shift the burden of evaluation off the shoulders of professional evaluators and onto the shoulders of clients and customers, and let the latter vote with their feet. The "client" in these cases can be individual citizens or government agencies; what is important is that the client be able to choose from among rival suppliers.

But some public services cannot be supplied, or are never going to be supplied, by a market. We can imagine allowing parents to choose among schools but we cannot imagine letting them choose (at least for most purposes) among police departments or armies. In that case one should adopt the second way of evaluating a public service: carry out a demonstration project or conduct a field experiment. (I will use the two ideas interchangeably, though some scholars distinguish between them.)[14] An experiment is a planned alteration in a state of affairs designed to measure the effect of the intervention. It involves asking the question, "If I change X, what will happen to Y, having first made certain that everything else stays the same?" It sounds easy, but it is not.

A good experiment (bad ones are worse than no experiment at all) requires that one do the following: first, identify a course of action to be tested; call it the treatment. A "treatment" can be a police tactic, a school curriculum, or a welfare program. Second, decide what impact the treatment is intended to have; call this the outcome. The outcome can be a crime rate, an achievement score, a work effort, a housing condition, or an income level. Third, give the treatment to one group (the experimental group) and withhold it from another (the control group). A group might be a police precinct, a class of students, the tenants in a housing project, or people who meet some eligibility requirement (say, having low incomes). It is quite important how the membership in these groups is determined. It should be done randomly; that is, all eligible precincts, schools, tenants, or people should be randomly sorted into experimental and control groups. Random assignment means that all the characteristics of the members of the experimental and control groups are likely to be identical. Fourth, assess the condition of each group before and after the treatment. The first assessment describes the baseline condition, the second the outcome condition. This outcome assessment should continue for some time after the end of the treatment, because experience has shown that many treatments seem to have a short-term effect that quickly disappears. Fifth, make certain that the evaluation is done by people other than those providing the treatment. People like to believe that their efforts are worthwhile, so much so that perhaps unwittingly they will gather data in ways that make it look like the treatment worked even when it did not.[15]

The object of all this is to find out what works. Using this method we have discovered that tripling the number of patrol cars on a beat does not lower the crime rate; that foot patrol reduces the fear of crime but not (ordinarily) its incidence; and that arresting spouse-beaters reduces (for a while) future assaults more than does counseling the assaulters.[16] We have learned that giving people an income supplement (akin to the negative income tax) reduces work effort and in some cases encourages families to break up.[17] We have learned that giving special job training and support to welfare mothers, ex-offenders, and school drop-outs produces sizable gains in the employment records of the welfare recipients but no gain for the ex-offenders and school drop-outs.[18] We have learned that a housing allowance program increases the welfare of poor families even though it does not improve the stock of housing. We have learned that more flexible pay and classification systems greatly benefit the managers of navy research centers and improve the work atmosphere at the centers.

There also have been many failed or flawed management experiments. In the 1930s, Herbert Simon carried out what may have been the first serious such experiment when he tried to find out how to improve the performance of welfare workers in the California State Relief Administration. Though elegantly designed, the experimental changes proved so controversial and the political environment of the agency so unstable that it is not clear that any useful inferences can be drawn from the project.[19] The attempt to evaluate educational vouchers at Alum Rock was undercut by the political need to restrict participation by private schools. . . . There are countless other "studies" that are evaluations in name only; in reality they are self-congratulatory conclusions written by program administrators. The administrative world is a political world, not a scientific laboratory, and evaluators of administration must come to terms with that fact. Often there are no mutually acceptable terms. But where reasonable terms can be struck it is possible to learn more than untutored experience can tell us about what works.

Such dry and dusty research projects probably seem thin fare to people who want Big Answers to Big Questions such as "How can we curb rampant bureaucracy?" or "How can we unleash the creative talents of our dedicated public servants?" But public management is not an arena in which to find Big Answers; it is a world of settled institutions designed to allow imperfect people to use flawed procedures to cope with insoluble problems.

FIFTH.   The fifth and final bit of advice flows directly from the limits on judging agencies by their results. All organizations seek the stability and comfort that comes from relying on standard operating procedures—"SOPs." When results are unknown or equivocal, bureaus will have no incentive to alter those SOPs so as better to achieve their goals, only an incentive to modify them to conform to externally imposed constraints. The SOPs will represent an internally defined equilibrium that reconciles the situational imperatives, professional norms, bureaucratic ideologies, peer-group expectations, and (if present) leadership demands unique to that agency. The only way to minimize the adverse effect of allowing human affairs to be managed by organizations driven by their autonomous SOPs is to keep the number, size, and authority of such organizations as small as possible. If none of the four preceding bits of advice works, the reader must confront the realization that there are no solutions for the bureaucracy problem that are not also "solutions" to the government problem. More precisely: all complex organizations display bureaucratic problems of confusion, red tape, and the avoidance of responsibility. Those problems are much greater in government bureaucracies because government itself is the institutionalization of confusion (arising out of the need to moderate competing demands); of red tape (arising out of the need to satisfy demands that cannot be moderated); and of avoided responsibility (arising out of the desire to retain power by minimizing criticism).

In short, you can have less bureaucracy only if you have less government. Many, if not most, of the difficulties we experience in dealing with government agencies arise from the agencies being part of a fragmented and open political system. If an agency is to have a sense of mission, if constraints are to be minimized, if authority is to be decentralized, if officials are to be judged on the basis of the outputs they produce rather than the inputs they consume, then legislators, judges, and lobbyists will have to act against their own interests. They will have to say "no" to influential constituents, forgo the opportunity to expand their own influence, and take seriously the task of judging the organizational feasibility as well as the political popularity of a proposed new program. It is hard to imagine this happening, partly because politicians and judges have no incentive to make it happen and partly because there are certain tasks a democratic government must undertake even if they cannot be performed efficiently. The greatest mistake citizens can make when they complain of "the bureaucracy" is to suppose that their frustrations arise simply out of management problems; they do not—they arise out of governance problems.

Bureaucracy and the American Regime

The central feature of the American constitutional system—the separation of powers—exacerbates many of these problems. The governments of the United States were not designed to be efficient or powerful, but to be tolerable and malleable. Those who devised these arrangements always assumed that the federal government would exercise few and limited powers. As long as that assumption was correct (which it was for a century and a half) the quality of public administration was not a serious problem, except in the minds of those reformers (Woodrow Wilson was probably the first) who desired to rationalize government in order to rationalize society. The founders knew that the separation of powers would make it so difficult to start a new program or to create a new agency that it was hardly necessary to think about how those agencies would be administered. As a result, the Constitution is virtually silent on what kind of administration we should have. At least until the Civil War thrust the problem on us, scarcely anyone in the country would have known what you were talking about if you spoke of the "problem of administration."

Matters were very different in much of Europe. Kings and princes long had ruled; when their authority was captured by parliaments, the tradition of ruling was already well established. From the first, the ministers of the parliamentary regimes thought about the problems of administration because in those countries there was something to administer. The centralization of executive authority in the hands of a prime minister and the exclusion (by and large) of parliament from much say in executive affairs facilitated the process of controlling the administrative agencies and bending them to some central will. The constitutions of many European states easily could have been written by a school of management.

Today, the United States at every level has big and active governments. Some people worry that a constitutional system well-designed to preserve liberty when governments were small is poorly designed to implement policy now that governments are large. The contrast between how the United States and the nations of Western Europe manage environmental and industrial regulation . . . is illuminating: here the separation of powers insures, if not causes, clumsy and adversarial regulation; there the unification of powers permits, if not causes, smooth and consensual regulation.

I am not convinced that the choice is that simple, however. It would take another book to judge the advantages and disadvantages of the separation of powers. The balance sheet on both sides of the ledger would contain many more entries than those that derive from a discussion of public administration. But even confining our attention to administration, there is more to be said for the American system than many of its critics admit.

America has a paradoxical bureaucracy unlike that found in almost any other advanced nation. The paradox is the existence in one set of institutions of two qualities ordinarily quite separate: the multiplication of rules and the opportunity for access. We have a system laden with rules; elsewhere, that is a sure sign that the bureaucracy is aloof from the people, distant from their concerns, and preoccupied with the power and privileges of the bureaucrats—an elaborate, grinding machine that can crush the spirit of any who dare oppose it. We also have a system suffused with participation: advisory boards, citizen groups, neighborhood councils, congressional investigators, crusading journalists, and lawyers serving writs; elsewhere this popular involvement would be taken as evidence that the administrative system is no system at all, but a bungling, jerry-built contraption wallowing in inefficiency and shot through with corruption and favoritism.

That these two traits, rules and openness, could coexist would have astonished Max Weber and continues to astonish (or elude) many contemporary students of the subject. Public bureaucracy in this country is neither as rational and predictable as Weber hoped nor as crushing and mechanistic as he feared. It is rule-bound without being overpowering, participatory without being corrupt. This paradox exists partly because of the character and mores of the American people: they are too informal, spontaneous, and other-directed to be either neutral arbiters or passionless Gradgrinds. And partly it exists because of the nature of the regime: our constitutional system, and above all the exceptional power enjoyed by the legislative branch, makes it impossible for us to have anything like a government by appointed experts but easy for individual citizens to obtain redress from the abuses of power. Anyone who wishes it otherwise would have to produce a wholly different regime, and curing the mischiefs of bureaucracy seems an inadequate reason for that. Parliamentary regimes that supply more consistent direction to their bureaucracies also supply more bureaucracy to their citizens. The fragmented American regime may produce chaotic government, but the coherent European regimes produce bigger governments.

In the meantime, we live in a country that despite its baffling array of rules and regulations and the insatiable desire of some people to use government to rationalize society still makes it possible to get drinkable water instantly, put through a telephone call in seconds, deliver a letter in a day, and obtain a passport in a week. Our Social Security checks arrive on time. Some state prisons, and most of the federal ones, are reasonably decent and humane institutions. The great majority of Americans, cursing all the while, pay their taxes. One can stand on the deck of an aircraft carrier during night flight operations and watch two thousand nineteen-year-old boys faultlessly operate one of the most complex organizational systems ever created. There are not many places where all this happens. It is astonishing it can be made to happen at all.

NOTES

1. Arthur T. Hadley, *The Straw Giant* (New York: Random House, 1986), 53–57, 249–52.

2. CSIS, *U.S. Defense Acquisition: A Process in Trouble* (Washington, D.C.: Center for Strategic and International Studies, March 1987), 13–16.

3. Herbert Kaufman, *The Administrative Behavior of Federal Bureau Chiefs* (Washington, D.C.: The Brookings Institution, 1981), 192.

4. Martha Derthick, *Agency Under Stress: The Social Security Administration and American Government* (Washington, D.C.: Brookings Institution, 1990).

5. Martha Derthick, *Agency Under Stress*, chap. 3.

6. Charles Wolf, Jr., *Markets or Governments: Choosing Between Imperfect Alternatives* (Cambridge, MA: MIT Press, 1988).

7. I first saw this phrase in an essay by Constance Horner, then director of the federal Office of Personnel Management: "Beyond Mr. Gradgrind: The Case for Deregulating the Public Sector," *Policy Review* 44 (Spring 1988): 34–38. It also appears in Gary C. Bryner, *Bureaucratic Discretion* (New York: Pergamon Press, 1987), 215.

8. James Colvard, "Procurement: What Price Mistrust?" *Government Executive* (March 1985): 21.

9. NAPA, *Revitalizing Federal Management: Managers and Their Overburdened Systems* (Washington, DC: National Academy of Public Administration, November 1983), vii, viii, 8.

10. Steven Emerson, *Secret Warriors* (New York: G. P. Putnam's Sons, 1988).

11. John E. Chubb and Terry M. Moe, "Politics, Markets, and the Organization of Schools," *American Political Science Review* 82 (1988): 1065–87.

12. Chester E. Finn, Jr., "Decentralize, Deregulate, Empower," *Policy Review* (Summer 1986): 60; Edward A. Wynne, *A Year in the Life of an Excellent Elementary School* (Lancaster, PA: Technomic, 1993).

13. William E. Turcotte, "Control Systems, Performance, and Satisfaction in Two State Agencies," *Administrative Science Quarterly* 19 (1974): 60–73.

14. Richard P. Nathan, *Social Science in Government: Uses and Misuses* (New York: Basic Books, 1988), chap. 3.

15. Matters are, of course, a bit more complicated than this summary might suggest. There is a small library of books on evaluative research that go into these matters in more detail; a good place to begin is Richard P. Nathan, *Social Science in Government* (New York: Basic Books, 1988). On the political aspects of evaluation, see Henry J. Aaron, *Politics and the Professors* (Washington, DC: The Brookings Institution, 1978). On the technical side see Thomas D. Cook and Donald T. Campbell, *Quasi-Experimentation* (Chicago: Rand McNally, 1979). There is even a journal, *Evaluation Review*, specializing in these issues.

16. These projects were all done by the Police Foundation and are described in James Q. Wilson, *Thinking About Crime*, rev. ed. (New York: Basic Books, 1983).

17. See Joseph A. Pechman and P. Michael Timpane, eds., *Work Incentives and Income Guarantees* (Washington, D.C.: Brookings Institution, 1975); and R. Thayne Robson, ed., *Employment and Training R&D* (Kalamazoo, MI: Upjohn Institute for Employment Research, 1984).

18. Nathan, *Social Science*, chap. 5; and Manpower Demonstration Research Corporation, *Summary and Findings of the National Supported Work Demonstration* (Cambridge, MA: Ballinger, 1980).

19. Clarence E. Ridley and Herbert A. Simon, *Measuring Municipal Activities* (Chicago: International City Managers' Association, 1938).

7.2

MATHEW D. McCUBBINS AND THOMAS SCHWARTZ

"Congressional Oversight Overlooked: Police Patrols versus Fire Alarms"

In this classic article, McCubbins and Schwartz compare two kinds of oversight of executive agencies by Congress. Under the police patrol model, Congress provides resources for constant monitoring of bureaucratic behavior. Under the fire alarm model, Congress waits for complaints from constituents and groups in society about the bureaucracies and then holds them accountable. The fire alarm model is often the more efficient method of oversight.

Scholars often complain that Congress has neglected its oversight responsibility: despite a large and growing executive branch, Congress has done little or nothing to oversee administrative compliance with legislative goals. As a consequence, we are told, Congress has largely lost control of the executive branch: it has allowed the executive branch not only to grow but to grow irresponsible. In popular debate as well as congressional scholarship, this neglect of oversight has become a stylized fact: widely and dutifully reported, it is often bemoaned, sometimes explained, but almost never seriously questioned.[1]

We question it. What has appeared to scholars to be a neglect of oversight, we argue, really is a preference for one form of oversight over another, less-effective form. In so arguing, we develop a simple model of congressional choice of oversight policy, offer evidence to support the model, and draw from it further implications regarding bureaucratic discretion and regulatory legislation. More generally, we model the choice by policy makers of an optimal enforcement strategy, given opportunity costs, available technology, and human cognitive limits.

THE MODEL

Congressional oversight policy concerns whether, to what extent, and in what way Congress attempts to detect and remedy executive-branch violations of legislative goals. Our model of congressional choice of oversight policy rests on a distinction between two forms or techniques of oversight:

From Mathew D. McCubbins and Thomas Schwartz, "Congressional Oversight Overlooked: Police Patrols versus Fire Alarms," *American Journal of Political Science* 28, no. 1 (February 1984): 165–79.

Police-Patrol Oversight

Analogous to the use of real police patrols, police-patrol oversight is comparatively centralized, active, and direct: at its own initiative, Congress examines a sample of executive-agency activities, with the aim of detecting and remedying any violations of legislative goals and, by its surveillance, discouraging such violations. An agency's activities might be surveyed by any of a number of means, such as reading documents, commissioning scientific studies, conducting field observations, and holding hearings to question officials and affected citizens.

Fire-Alarm Oversight

Analogous to the use of real fire alarms, fire-alarm oversight is less centralized and involves less active and direct intervention than police-patrol oversight: instead of examining a sample of administrative decisions, looking for violations of legislative goals, Congress establishes a system of rules, procedures, and informal practices that enable individual citizens and organized interest groups to examine administrative decisions (sometimes in prospect), to charge executive agencies with violating congressional goals, and to seek remedies from agencies, courts, and Congress itself. Some of these rules, procedures, and practices afford citizens and interest groups access to information and to administrative decision-making processes. Others give them standing to challenge administrative decisions before agencies and courts, or help them bring alleged violations to congressmen's attention. Still others facilitate collective action by comparatively disorganized interest groups. Congress's role consists in creating and perfecting this decentralized system and, occasionally, intervening in response to complaints. Instead of sniffing for fires, Congress places fire-alarm boxes on street corners, builds neighborhood fire houses, and sometimes dispatches its own hook-and-ladder in response to an alarm.

The distinction between police-patrol and fire-alarm oversight should not be confused with the distinction that sometimes is drawn between *formal* and *informal* oversight, which differ in that formal oversight activities have oversight as their principal and official purpose, whereas informal oversight activities are incidental to other official functions, such as appropriations hearings. Both can involve direct and active surveillance rather than responses to alarms. (See Dodd and Schott, 1979; Ogul, 1977.)

Our model consists of three assumptions:

Technological Assumption

Two forms of oversight are available to Congress: police-patrol oversight and fire-alarm oversight. Congress can choose either form or a combination of the two, making tradeoffs between them in two circumstances: (1) When writing legislation, Congress can include police-patrol features, such as sunset review, or fire-alarm features, such as requirements for public hearings. (2) When it evaluates an agency's performance, Congress can either call oversight hearings to patrol for violations of legislative goals or else wait for alarms to signal potential violations.

Motivational Assumption

A congressman seeks to take as much credit as possible for the net benefits enjoyed by his potential supporters—by citizens and interest groups, within his constituency and elsewhere, whose support can help him win reelection. This means, in part, that a congressman seeks to avoid as much blame as possible for the net costs borne by his potential supporters.

Institutional Assumption

Executive agencies act as agents of Congress and especially of those subcommittees on which they depend for authorizations and appropriations.

The Motivational Assumption is closely tied to Mayhew's celebrated reelection model (1974) and to the blame-shirking model of Fiorina (1982a). The Institutional Assumption is found in Baldwin (1975), Ferejohn (1981), Joskow (1974), McCubbins (1982a,b), and Mitnick (1980). Although not previously stated, the Technological Assumption seems to us to be uncontroversial.

That cannot be said of the Motivational Assumption, which depicts congressmen as pure politicians, single-mindedly pursuing reelection. To this picture, one might object that real congressmen are not just politicians but statesmen, pursuing justice and the public interest, acting according to various moral and ideological principles, even at some cost to their reelection prospects.

We will argue, however, that if the Motivational Assumption were replaced by the assumption that congressmen act strictly as statesmen, our conclusions regarding oversight would still be derivable, although in a somewhat different way. Our analysis has less to do with specific legislative goals than with optimal strategies for enforcing compliance with legislative goals of any sort.

CONSEQUENCES

Three important consequences follow from our model:

Consequence 1

To the extent that they favor oversight activity of any sort, congressmen tend to prefer fire-alarm oversight to police-patrol oversight.

Our argument for Consequence 1 is that a congressman's objective, according to the Motivational Assumption, is to take as much credit as possible for net benefits enjoyed by his potential supporters and that he can do so more efficiently under a policy of fire-alarm oversight than under a police-patrol policy, for three reasons:

First, congressmen engaged in police-patrol oversight inevitably spend time examining a great many executive-branch actions that do not violate legislative goals or harm any potential supporters, at least not enough to occasion complaints. They might also spend time detecting and remedying arguable violations that nonetheless harm no potential supporters. For this they receive scant credit from their potential supporters. According to the Motivational Assumption, then, their time is largely wasted, so they incur opportunity costs. But under a fire-alarm policy, a congressman does not address concrete violations unless potential supporters have complained about them, in which case he can receive credit for intervening. So a unit of time spent on oversight is likely to yield more benefit for a congressman under a fire-alarm policy than under a policy-patrol policy. As a result, a fire-alarm policy enables congressmen to spend less time on oversight, leaving more time for other profitable activities, or to spend the same time on more personally profitable oversight activities—on addressing complaints by potential supporters. Justly or unjustly, time spent putting out visible fires gains one more credit than the same time spent sniffing for smoke.

Second, under a realistic police-patrol policy, congressmen examine only a small sample of executive-branch actions. As a result, they are likely to miss violations that harm their potential supporters, and so miss opportunities to take credit for redressing grievances, however fair the sample. Under a fire-alarm policy, by contrast, potential supporters can, in most cases, bring to congressmen's attention any violations that harm them and for which they have received no adequate remedy through the executive or judicial branch.

Third, although fire-alarm oversight can be as costly as police-patrol oversight, much of the cost is borne by the citizens and interest groups who sound alarms and by administrative agencies and courts rather than by congressmen themselves. A congressman's responsibility for such costs is sufficiently remote that he is not likely to be blamed for them by his potential supporters.

Consequence 2

Congress will not neglect its oversight responsibility. It will adopt an extensive and somewhat effective (even if imperfect) oversight policy.

This is because one of the two forms of oversight—the fire-alarm variety—serves congressmen's interests at little cost. When his potential supporters complain of a violation of legislative goals, a congressman gains credit if he eliminates the cause of the complaint. By virtue of the Institutional Assumption, he often can be reasonably effective in eliminating such causes. Beyond establishing and perfecting the system and addressing some complaints, fire-alarm oversight is almost costless to congressmen: others bear most of the cost.

Consequence 3

Congress will adopt an extensive and somewhat effective policy of fire-alarm oversight while largely neglecting police-patrol oversight.

This just summarizes Consequences 1 and 2.

MISPERCEPTION

Faced with an apparent fact he finds puzzling, unfortunate, or otherwise worthy of attention, a scientist has two alternatives: (a) to accept the fact and try to explain it, or (b) to question the *apparent* fact and try to explain its appearance. In the case at hand, students of Congress have, for the most part, chosen (a): they have uncritically agreed that Congress neglects its oversight responsibility and have tried to explain this neglect.

Here are the three main explanations found in the literature, along with a brief critical comment on each:

Complexity

Because public-policy issues are so complex, Congress has had to delegate authority over them to a large, complex, technically expert bureaucracy, whose actions it is unable effectively to oversee (Lowi, 1969; Ogul, 1977; Ripley, 1969; Seidman, 1975; Woll, 1977).

Comment

Given sufficient incentives, as Fiorina (1982a) observes, Congress has found the capacity to tackle a number of complex issues itself. A striking example is the tax code (Jaffe, 1973, pp. 1189–90). What is more, there is no evident reason [for] why Congress should respond to the complexity of issues by creating a large, expert bureaucracy without also creating a large, expert congressional staff—one sufficiently large and expert, not only to help decide complex issues, but to help oversee a large, expert bureaucracy.

Good Government

To serve the public interest, Congress has established regulatory and other executive-branch agencies based on expertise and divorced from politics. Because these agencies are designed to serve the public interest, whereas Congress is influenced by special-interest lobbies, oversight not only is unnecessary but might be regarded as political meddling in processes that ought to remain nonpolitical (Lowi, 1969).

Comment

Whatever the original intent, it is no longer plausible in most cases to suppose that the public interest is best served by a bureaucracy unaccountable to Congress and, therefore, unaccountable to the electorate.

Decentralization

Because congressional decisions are made, for the most part, by a large number of small, relatively autonomous subcommittees with narrow jurisdictions, general oversight committees tend to be weak (Dodd and Schott, 1979).

Comment

At most, this explains why congressional oversight responsibilities are not centralized. It does not explain why they are neglected. If anything, subcommittee specialization should enhance congressional oversight over individual agencies. Subcommittees controlling authorizations and appropriations might be in a better position to do oversight than so-called oversight committees.

Regarding the apparent fact that Congress neglects oversight, we choose alternative (b) over (a): what appears to be a neglect of oversight can be explained as a preference by congressmen for fire-alarm over police-patrol oversight. We have already argued that congressmen have this preference. Scholars who decry the neglect of oversight have, we suggest, focused on a single form of oversight: they have looked only for police-patrol oversight, ignoring the fire-alarm alternative—and therewith the major part of actual oversight activity. Observing a neglect of *police-patrol* oversight, they have mistakenly concluded that *oversight* is neglected.

It has been suggested to us that scholars who have remarked congressional neglect of oversight were using the word more narrowly than we are—that they were *defining* "oversight" to mean police-patrol oversight, contrary to our Technological Assumption.

To this we have three replies: First, established usage equates oversight with the task of detecting and remedying violations of legislative goals by the executive branch.[2] No technique for accomplishing this task can be ruled out by definition. Second, the definitional equation of oversight with police-patrol oversight reflects the odd view that it is less important for Congress to make a serious attempt to detect and remedy violations of legislative goals than to employ a specific technique for doing so. Third, it would be odd to have a name for one way of detecting and remedying executive-branch violations of legislative goals but none for the general task of detecting and remedying such violations.

It has also been suggested to us that fire-alarm activities were never conceived or intended to be a form of oversight, whatever their effects.

We agree that congressmen rarely, if ever, refer to fire-alarm activities as "oversight," a term officially applied to subcommittees engaged in direct surveillance—in police-patrol oversight. Still, there is no evident reason for congressmen to engage in most fire-alarm activities unless they aim thereby to detect and remedy certain administrative violations of legislative goals.

Those who equate oversight with police-patrol oversight might argue that redressing grievances against the executive branch is not the same as enforcing compliance with congressional goals: the goals congressmen pursue in answering alarms related to particular laws need not be the goals they had in mind when they enacted those laws.

We see no reason to believe, however, that acts of legislation reflect well-defined or unalterable legislative goals—especially in view of the classical voting paradox and similar anomalies (Arrow, 1963; Plott, 1967; Schwartz, 1970, 1981, 1982a). Rather, legislative goals are refined, elaborated, and even changed over time in response to new problems—including complaints against executive agencies—and to changes in preferences and political alignments. In answering fire alarms, congressmen not only enforce compliance with legislative goals; they help decide what those goals are.

Possibly those who bemoan congressional neglect of oversight would agree that fire-alarm oversight is extensively practiced but argue that it is not *effective*.

We have argued already that fire-alarm oversight is likely to be somewhat effective. The evidence presented two sections hence supports this conclusion.

Even granting that fire-alarm oversight is extensively practiced and *somewhat* effective, hence that Congress does not *neglect* its oversight responsibility, one might still wonder which form of oversight is the *more* effective. To this question we now turn.

THE GREATER EFFECTIVENESS OF FIRE-ALARM OVERSIGHT

We will argue that fire-alarm oversight is likely to be more effective, on balance, than police-patrol oversight. But this requires two qualifications: first, we do not contend that the most effective oversight policy is likely to contain no police-patrol features, only that fire-alarm techniques are likely to predominate. Second, we do not contend that a predominantly fire-alarm policy is more likely than a predominantly police-patrol policy to serve the public interest, only that it is likely to secure greater compliance with legislative goals; whether such compliance serves the public interest depends on what those goals are.

A predominantly fire-alarm oversight policy is likely to be more effective—to secure greater compliance with legislative goals—than a predominantly police-patrol policy for two main reasons:

First, legislative goals often are stated in such a vague way that it is hard to decide whether any violation has occurred unless some citizen or group registers a complaint. Such a complaint gives Congress the opportunity to spell out its goals more clearly—just as concrete cases and controversies give courts the opportunity to elucidate legal principles that would be hard to make precise in the abstract.

Second, whereas a fire-alarm policy would almost certainly pick up any violation of legislative goals that seriously harmed an organized group, a police-patrol policy would doubtless miss many such violations, since only a sample of executive-branch actions would be examined.

One who agrees with this point might still argue, on behalf of the greater efficacy of police-patrol oversight, that the citizens harmed by violations of legislative goals are not always represented by organized groups and, hence, cannot always sound a loud enough alarm to secure a redress of grievances.

Our reply is fourfold: first, nowadays even "disadvantaged" groups often have public spokesmen. Second, as we show in the following section, sometimes Congress passes legislation, as part of its fire-alarm policy, that helps comparatively disorganized groups to act collectively. Third, congressmen's extensive constituent-service activities provide even individual citizens with an effective voice against administrative agencies: case work is part (but only part) of the fire-alarm system. Finally, if the point is merely that fire-alarm oversight can be biased in various ways, then the same is true of police-patrol oversight; and although a good enough police-patrol policy would avoid bias, so would a good enough fire-alarm policy.

To be sure, fire-alarm oversight tends to be *particularistic* in the sense of Mayhew (1974): it arguably emphasizes the interests of individuals and interest groups more than those of the public at large. This is an important difference—the essential difference, we think, between the respective products of police-patrol and fire-alarm oversight. But whether it is a shortcoming of fire-alarm oversight depends on one's ideological point of view: even if fire-alarm oversight deemphasizes some public-interest concerns, it gives special emphasis to a concern for the interests and rights of individual citizens and small groups—a concern well founded in American political values.

Although our model refers only to Congress, we hazard to hypothesize that as most organizations grow and mature, their top policy makers adopt methods of control that are comparatively decentralized and incentive based. Such methods, we believe, will work more efficiently (relative to accepted policy goals) than direct, centralized surveillance. This is sufficiently plausible that we wonder why students of Congress have generally assumed that congressional oversight must be of the direct, centralized police-patrol variety. Part of the reason, perhaps, is that Congress itself applies the label "oversight" to subcommittees charged with police-patrol responsibilities.

As we stated earlier, Consequences 1–3 do not depend on our Motivational Assumption, which depicts congressmen as pure politicians rather than statesmen. This is because statesmen, wishing to secure compliance with their legislative goals, would presumably adopt the most effective oversight policy, and that is likely to be one in which fire-alarm techniques predominate.

EVIDENCE

Evidence for Consequence 3—and therewith our model—is plentiful and well known. Scholars who bemoan congressional neglect of oversight have not ignored this evidence. Rather, they have missed its significance: lacking the concept of fire-alarm oversight, they have failed to see the details of our fire-alarm system as instances of oversight activity. Here is a brief summary of the available evidence:

1. Under a fire-alarm system, complaints against administrative agencies are often brought to the attention of congressional subcommittees by lobbyists for organized groups, and to the attention of administrative agencies by congressional subcommittees. The functioning of this "subgovernmental triangle" has been well documented (Dodd and Oppenheimer, 1977; Fenno, 1966, 1973a,b; Goodwin, 1970; Ornstein, 1975; Ripley, 1969; Huitt, 1973; Matthews, 1960; Ripley and Franklin, 1976).

2. Congress has passed legislation to help comparatively disorganized groups to press their grievances against the federal government. McConnell (1966) shows how the Agriculture, Labor, and Commerce Departments act as lobbyists for farm, labor, and small-business interests. Congress has also created new programs, such as the Legal-Services Corporation, to organize and press the claims of comparatively voiceless citizens.

3. Constituent-service activities are not limited to unsnarling procedural knots. As part of the fire-alarm system, district staff and casework help individuals and groups—some of them otherwise powerless—to raise and redress grievances against decisions by administrative agencies. This casework component of legislative policy making has been examined only recently, with a primary focus on the electoral connection (Cain, Ferejohn, and Fiorina, 1979a,b; Fenno, 1978; Fiorina, 1977a; Mayhew, 1974; Parker and Davidson, 1979) and with a secondary focus on policy consequences (Fiorina, 1977a, 1982b; Fiorina and Noll, 1978, 1979a,b).

4. Often the fire-alarm system allows for the redress of grievances by administrative agencies and courts; Congress itself need not always get involved. To facilitate such redress, Congress has passed several laws, notably the Administrative Procedures Act of 1946 and the Environmental Procedures Act of 1969, that have substantially increased the number of groups with legal standing before administrative agencies and district courts regarding bureaucratic controversies (Lowi, 1969).[3] Congress has also, as in sections 4–7 of the Toxic Substances Control Act of 1976, increased the courts' powers to issue injunctions in response to alarms and has required administrative agencies to hold hearings, publish information, and invite public comment on agency decision making (McCubbins, 1982a).

5. There are numerous cases in which violations of legislative goals were brought to the attention of Congress, which responded with vigorous remedial measures. For example, Congress dismantled the Area Redevelopment Administration (ARA) in 1963, even though it had just been authorized in 1961. The ARA was encouraging industries to relocate in redevelopment areas despite clear provisions in the law to the contrary. Congress also can redefine or reaffirm its goals by

redefining or explicating the jurisdictional authority of an administrative agency. This happened with the Federal Trade Commission when it first sought to regulate cigarette advertising, children's television, and funeral homes. Sometimes such congressional intervention is legislatively mandated. Before taking action on a pending case, for example, the National Labor Relations Board must consult with the appropriate congressional committees.

6. The general impression that Congress neglects oversight, we have argued, really is a perception that Congress neglects police-patrol oversight. That impression and the evidence adduced to support it constitute further evidence for Consequences 1 and 3: they show that congressmen tend to prefer an oversight policy in which fire-alarm techniques predominate.

FURTHER IMPLICATIONS: HAS BUREAUCRATIC DISCRETION INCREASED?

Hand in glove with our stylized fact (neglect of oversight) goes another: Congress has increasingly relinquished its legislative authority to the executive branch, allowing the bureaucracy to make law (Dodd and Schott, 1979; Hess, 1976; Lowi, 1969; Woll, 1977).[4]

Although Congress may, to some extent, have allowed the bureaucracy to make law, it may also have devised a reasonably effective and noncostly way to articulate and promulgate its own legislative goals—a way that depends on the fire-alarm oversight system. It is convenient for Congress to adopt broad legislative mandates and give substantial rule-making authority to the bureaucracy. The problem with doing so, of course, is that the bureacracy might not pursue Congress's goals. But citizens and interest groups can be counted on to sound an alarm in most cases in which the bureaucracy has arguably violated Congress's goals. Then Congress can intervene to rectify the violation. Congress has not necessarily relinquished legislative responsibility to anyone else. It has just found a more efficient way to legislate.

When legislators try to write laws with sufficient detail and precision to preclude administrative discretion, they quickly run up against their own cognitive limits: beyond a certain point, human beings just cannot anticipate all the contingencies that might arise. The attempt to legislate for all contingencies can entail unintended (and undesired) consequences. In his classic study of Anglo-American judicial reasoning, Levi (1948) makes this point about judges (lawmakers of a sort), who lay down imprecise rules, which they subsequently and gradually elaborate in response to concrete legal disputes. Oakeshott (1973) makes a similar point about political activity of all sorts: it cannot be based on precise, detailed blueprints, and so policy formulations can at best be rough summaries of experience, requiring elaboration and judicious application case by case.

The ostensible shifting of legislative responsibility to the executive branch may simply be the responsible adoption of efficient legislative techniques and the responsible acceptance of human cognitive limits—both facilitated by the fire-alarm system.

FURTHER IMPLICATIONS: THE CHOICE OF REGULATORY POLICY

When it decides regulatory issues, Congress tends to choose one of two types of regulatory instrument: command-and-control instruments and incentive-based instruments. Congress faces a similar choice when it decides, not how to regulate society, but how to regulate the regulators—when it decides, in other words, on oversight policy. For police-patrol oversight is similar to command-and-control regulatory instruments, while fire-alarm oversight is similar to incentive-based instruments.

Offhand, one might suppose that just as congressmen tend to prefer fire-alarm to police-patrol oversight policies, so they would tend to prefer incentive-based to command-and-control regulatory policies. Our observations, of course, do not support this supposition (Breyer, 1982; Fiorina, 1982a; Joskow and Noll, 1978; McCubbins, 1982a; McCubbins and Page, 1982; Schultze, 1977).

Paradoxically, Congress's very preference for fire-alarm oversight entails a preference for command-and-control regulatory policy. For command-and-control agencies are more susceptible of case-by-case congressional intervention in response to complaints, hence more susceptible of fire-alarm control, than are courts, taxing authorities, and private individuals and firms—the principal participants in incentive-based regulatory policy.

CONCLUSION

The widespread perception that Congress has neglected its oversight responsibility is a widespread mistake. Congressional scholars have focused their attention on police-patrol oversight. What has appeared to many of them to be a neglect of oversight is really a preference—an eminently rational one—for fire-alarm oversight. That a decentralized, incentive-based control mechanism has been found more effective, from its users' point [of] view, than direct, centralized surveillance should come as no surprise.

Besides criticizing the received wisdom regarding congressional oversight, we hope to have highlighted a neglected way of looking at congressional behavior. Sometimes Congress appears to do little, leaving important policy decisions to the executive or judicial branch. But appearances can deceive. A perfectly reasonable way for Congress to pursue its objectives is by ensuring that fire alarms will be sounded, enabling courts, administrative agencies, and ultimately Congress itself to step in, whenever executive compliance with congressional objectives is called in question. In examining congressional policies and their impact, do not just ask how clear, detailed, or far-sighted congressional legislation is. Ask how likely it is that fire alarms will signal putative violations of legislative goals and how Congress is likely to respond to such alarms.

NOTES

1. See Bibby, 1966, 1968; Dodd and Schott, 1979; Fiorina, 1977a,b, 1982b; Hess, 1976; Huntington, 1973; Lowi, 1969; Mitnick, 1980; Ogul, 1976, 1977; Ripley, 1978; Scher, 1963; Seidman, 1975; Woll, 1977. The following remarks by Pearson (1975) succinctly exemplify this view: "Paradoxically, despite its importance, congressional oversight remains basically weak and ineffective" (p. 281). "Oversight is a vital yet neglected congressional function" (p. 288).

2. A 1977 report by the U.S. Senate Committee on Government Operations stated that "Oversight involves a wide range of congressional efforts to review and control policy implementation . . ." (pp. 4–5). According to Dodd and Schott (1979), "Oversight . . . involves attempts by Congress to review and control policy implementation" (p. 156). Ogul (1976) defines oversight as the process by which Congress determines, among other things, whether agencies are complying with congressional intent. See also Bibby, 1966; Harris, 1964; Lees, 1977; Lowi, 1969; Ripley, 1978; Woll, 1977.

3. Ferejohn (1974) provides a good example of how the decision-making procedures of the Army Corps of Engineers were expanded to include wilderness, wildlife, and environmental group interests by the passage of the 1969 Environmental Procedures Act.

4. On related points see Fiorina (1977b), Weingast and Moran (1981), McCubbins (1982a,b), and McCubbins and Page (1982). Weingast has argued that Congress employs a number of its constitutionally defined powers in a decentralized and often unobserved way in order to exercise control over the actions of administrative agencies (Calvert, Moran, and Weingast, 1982; Weingast and Moran, 1981).

REFERENCES

Arrow, Kenneth. 1963. *Social Choice and Individual Values*. 2nd ed. New York: Wiley.

Baldwin, John. 1975. *The Regulatory Agency and the Public Corporation: The Canadian Air Transport Industry*. Cambridge, MA: Ballinger.

Bibby, John. 1966. "Committee characteristics and legislative oversight of administration." *Midwest Journal of Political Science*, 10 (February 1966): 78–98.

———. 1968. "Congress' Neglected Function." In *Republican Papers*, edited by Melvin Laird. New York: Praeger.

Breyer, Stephen. 1982. *Regulation and Its Reform*. Cambridge, MA: Harvard University Press.

Cain, Bruce, John Ferejohn, and Morris Fiorina. 1979a. "The Roots of Legislator Popularity in Great Britain and the United States." Social Science Working Paper No. 288, California Institute of Technology, Pasadena, CA.

———. 1979b. "Casework Service in Great Britain and the United States." California Institute of Technology, Pasadena, CA: Mimeo.

Calvert, Randall, Mark Moran, and Barry Weingast. 1982. "Congressional Influence over Policymaking: The Case of the FTC." Paper presented at the annual meeting of the American Political Science Association, Chicago, September 1982.

Dodd, Lawrence, and Bruce Oppenheimer, eds. 1977. *Congress Reconsidered*. New York: Praeger.

Dodd, Lawrence, and Richard Schott. 1979. *Congress and the Administrative State*. New York: Wiley.

Fenno, Richard, Jr. 1966. *The Power of the Purse*. Boston: Little, Brown.

———. 1973a. *Congressmen in Committees*. Boston: Little, Brown.

———. 1973b. "The Internal Distribution of Influence: The House." In *The Congress and America's Future*, 2nd ed., edited by David Truman, 52–76. Englewood Cliffs, NJ: Prentice-Hall.

———. 1978. *Home Style*. Boston: Little, Brown.

Ferejohn, John. 1974. *Pork Barrel Politics*. Stanford, Calif.: Stanford University Press.

———. 1981. "A Note on the Structure of Administrative Agencies." California Institute of Technology, Pasadena, CA: Mimeo.

Fiorina, Morris, 1977a. *Congress: Keystone of the Washington Establishment*. New Haven, CT: Yale University Press.

———. 1977b. "Control of the Bureaucracy: A Mismatch of Incentives and Capabilities." Social Science Working Paper No. 182, California Institute of Technology, Pasadena, CA.

———. 1982a. "Legislative Choice of Regulatory Forms: Legal Process or Administrative Process?" *Public Choice* 39 (September 1982): 33–66.

———. 1982b. "Group Concentration and the Delegation of Legislative Authority." California Institute of Technology, Pasadena, CA: Mimeo.

Fiorina, Morris, and Roger Noll. 1978. "Voters, Bureaucrats and Legislators: A Rational Choice Perspective on the Growth of Bureaucracy." *Journal of Public Economics* 9 (June 1978): 239–54.

———. 1979a. "Voters, Legislators and Bureaucracy: Institutional Design in the Public Sector." In *Problemi di Administrazione Publica, Centro di Formazione e Studi per il Messogiorno*, Naples, Italy, Formes 4 (2): 69–89.

———. 1979b. "Majority Rule Models and Legislative Election." *Journal of Politics* 41: 1081–1104.

Goodwin, George, Jr. 1970. *The Little Legislatures*. Amherst: University of Massachusetts Press.

Harris, Joseph. 1964. *Congressional Control of Administration*. Washington, D.C.: Brookings.

Hess, Stephen. 1976. *Organizing the Presidency*. Washington, D.C.: Brookings.

Huitt, Ralph. 1973. "The Internal Distribution of Influence: The Senate." In *The Congress in America's Future*, 2nd ed., edited by David Truman, 77–101. Englewood Cliffs, NJ: Prentice-Hall.

Huntington, Samuel. 1973. "Congressional Responses to the Twentieth Century." In *The Congress in America's Future*, 2nd ed., edited by David Truman, 5–31. Englewood Cliffs, NJ: Prentice-Hall.

Jaffe, Louis. 1973. "The Illusion of the Ideal Administration." *Harvard Law Review* 86: 1183–99.

Joskow, Paul. 1974. "Inflation and Environmental Concern: Structural Change Is the Process of Public Utility Price Regulation." *Journal of Law and Economics* 17 (October 1974): 291–327.

Joskow, Paul, and Roger Noll. 1978. "Regulation in Theory and Practice: An Overview." California Institute of Technology, Social Science Working Paper No. 213, Pasadena, CA.

Lees, John D. 1977. "Legislatures and Oversight: A Review Article on a Neglected Area of Research." *Legislative Studies Quarterly* (May 1977): 193–208.

Levi, Edward. 1948. *Legal Reasoning*. Chicago: University of Chicago Press.

Lowi, Theodore. 1969. *The End of Liberalism*. New York: Norton.

Matthews, Donald. 1960. *U.S. Senators and Their World*. Chapel Hill: University of North Carolina Press.

Mayhew, David. 1974. *Congress: The Electoral Connection*. New Haven, CT: Yale University Press.

McConnell, Grant. 1966. *Private Power and American Democracy*. New York: Vintage Books.

McCubbins, Mathew. 1982a. "Rational Individual Behavior and Collective Irrationality: The Legislative Choice of Regulatory Forms." Ph.D. dissertation, California Institute of Technology, Pasadena, CA.

———. 1982b. "On the Form of Regulatory Intervention." Paper presented at the 1983 Annual Meeting of the Public Choice Society, Savannah, GA, March 24–26, 1983.

McCubbins, Mathew, and Talbot Page. 1982. "On the Failure of Environmental, Health and Safety Regulation." Paper presented at the 1983 Annual Meeting of the Midwest Political Science Association, Chicago, IL, April 20–23, 1983.

Mitnick, Barry. 1980. *The Political Economy of Regulation*. New York: Columbia University Press.

Oakeshott, Michael. 1973. "Political Education." In *Rationalism in Politics*, edited by Michael Oakeshott, 110–36. New York: Basic Books, 1962. Reprinted in *Freedom and Authority*, edited by Thomas Schwartz, 362–80. Encino, CA: Dickenson.

Ogul, Morris. 1976. *Congress Oversees the Bureaucracy*. Pittsburgh: University of Pittsburgh Press.

———. 1977. "Congressional Oversight: Structure and Incentives." In *Congress Reconsidered*, edited by Lawrence Dodd and Bruce Oppenheimer, 207–21. New York: Praeger.

Ornstein, Norman, ed. 1975. *Congress in Change*. New York: Praeger.

Parker, Glenn, and Roger Davidson. 1979. "Why Do Americans Love Their Congressmen So Much More than Their Congress?" *Legislative Studies Quarterly* 4 (February 1979): 53–62.

Pearson, James. 1975. "Oversight: A Vital Yet Neglected Congressional Function." *Kansas Law Review* 23: 277–88.

Plott, Charles. 1967. "A Notion of Equilibrium and Its Possibility under Majority Rules." *American Economic Review* 57 (September 1967): 787–806.

Ripley, Randall 1969. *Power in the Senate*. New York: St. Martin's.

———. 1978. *Congress: Process and Policy*. 2nd ed. New York: Norton.

Ripley, Randall, and Grace Franklin. 1976. *Congress, the Bureaucracy and Public Policy*. Homewood, IL: Dorsey.

Scher, Seymour. 1963. "Conditions for Legislative Control." *Journal of Politics* 25 (August 1963): 526–51.

Schultze, Charles. 1977. *The Public Use of Private Interest*. Washington, DC: Brookings.

Schwartz, Thomas. 1970. "On the Possibility of Rational Policy Evaluation." *Theory and Decision* 1 (October 1970): 89–106.

———. 1981. "The Universal-Instability Theorem." *Public Choice* 37 (3): 487–501.

———. 1982a. "A Really General Impossibility Theorem." *Quality and Quantity* 16 (December 1982): 493–505.

———. 1982b. "The Pork Barrel Paradox." University of Texas, Austin, TX: Mimeo.

Seidman, Harold. 1975. *Politics, Position, and Power: The Dynamics of Federal Organization.* New York: Oxford.

U.S. Senate. Committee on Government Operations. 1977. *Study on Federal Regulation, Vol. II, Congressional Oversight of Regulatory Agencies.* Washington, D.C.: Government Printing Office.

Weingast, Barry, and Mark Moran. 1981. "Bureaucratic Discretion of Congressional Control: Regulatory Policymaking by the Federal Trade Commission." Washington University, St. Louis: Center of the Study of American Business. Mimeo.

Woll, Peter. 1977. *American Bureaucracy.* New York: Norton.

7.3

SUSAN L. MOFFITT

From *Making Public Policy: Participatory Bureaucracy in American Democracy*

In this selection, Moffitt summarizes how bureaucracies often create public committees that permit people and groups from outside the government to comment on proposed regulations. She argues that these public committees allow bureaucratic leaders to learn from members of the public, but also to learn in public. The latter purpose, learning in public, has not been well understood by scholars of bureaucracy, but it has crucial benefits. Public committees provide opportunities to show the processes by which bureaucratic leaders make decisions. They can enhance legitimacy for decisions and shield bureaucracies from charges of secrecy and unaccountability.

PORTALS OF DEMOCRACY IN AMERICAN BUREAUCRACY

"[K]nowledge is no longer an immobile solid; it has been liquefied; it is actively moving in all the currents of society itself."

—John Dewey[1]

"Advisory committees can be of great value. They contribute to the 'openness' of Governmental decision-making, and provide advice and information not otherwise available to the Government. Their functions range from providing policy advice on major national issues, to providing technical recommendations on particular problems."

—Federal Advisory Committees: Sixth Annual Report
of the President, 1978

"Imagine planning your day around your life, instead of your osteoarthritis pain," enticed Merck's advertising campaign for Vioxx, its blockbuster arthritis drug. The drug Merck promoted "for everyday victories" soon became a symbol of regulatory failure as evidence emerged linking Vioxx with serious cardiovascular side effects and deaths. At the beginning of Senate hearings

From Susan L. Moffitt, *Making Public Policy: Participatory Bureaucracy in American Democracy* (New York: Cambridge University Press, 2014).

convened in 2004 to investigate Vioxx's withdrawal from the market, Senator Charles Grassley (R-IA) alleged that the FDA had "allowed itself to be manipulated by Merck" and, more broadly, that "the FDA has a relationship with drug companies that is far too cozy."[2] The remedy for coziness with industry and for regulatory failure, Senator Grassley continued, would include "changes inside the FDA that [would] result in greater transparency and greater openness." In its 2007 review of American drug safety, the Institute of Medicine (IOM) similarly claimed, "the FDA's reputation has been hurt by a perceived lack of transparency and accountability to the public."[3] As part of its package of proposals to improve the agency's impaired reputation, the Institute of Medicine called on the FDA to make greater use of its public advisory committees—groups of nongovernmental medical practitioners, researchers, and stakeholder representatives that the FDA consults on matters such as drug approval and labeling—to supplement agency expertise and to enhance transparency in the drug approval process. These proposals suggested public engagement could render FDA decisions both more accountable and less prone to regulatory failure.

The FDA, however, *had* publicly reviewed and discussed Vioxx long before the drug's withdrawal, before Senator Grassley's rebuke, and before the Institute of Medicine's charge: the agency consulted with its Arthritis Drugs Advisory Committee about Vioxx's safety and efficacy both in 1999 and in 2001. Neither FDA staffers nor the firm sponsoring the drug served on the agency's drug advisory committees as voting members. Instead, the firm sponsoring the drug summarized evidence from drug trials and offered justifications for the drug's approval and labeling claims. Agency staffers presented their findings and concerns about drug applications in testimony before the committee as well. Both Vioxx meetings invited nonbinding advice from the committee in front of public audiences, and a portion of the 2001 deliberation included debate over whether Vioxx caused heart attacks and strokes.[4]

Public meetings like the ones convened by the FDA suggest potential portals for public participation in agency policymaking that can challenge key aspects of traditional bureaucratic administration. They can provide a public forum for agency critics, reveal details of agency decision making that an agency may prefer to keep private, produce information an agency may not want to consider, and compromise agency jurisdiction over the ultimate policy decision.[5] As part of public meetings convened in 2005 to discuss Vioxx's withdrawal from the market, a representative of the consumer advocacy group, Public Citizen, publicly charged that the FDA knew about cardiovascular risks associated with Cox-2 inhibitors such as Vioxx and failed to reveal that information promptly.[6] Long before Vioxx, AIDS activists and groups representing other disease sufferers started using FDA advisory committees to chastise the FDA publicly and viscerally. "The FDA is incapable of doing its job expeditiously," a member of the AIDS organization ACT-UP New York charged at the June 12, 1991, Antiviral Drugs Advisory Committee meeting reviewing the drug Foscavir. He continued in his address to the committee:

> Tell [FDA Commissioner] David Kessler, [Center for Drug Evaluation and Research Director] Carl Peck . . . that denying [Foscavir] to people who have nothing to lose because of their slow bureaucratic procedures is a moral outrage that this committee and the American public will not tolerate. Remind the FDA—and it is sick that they need to be reminded of this—but remind them that they work for us, the American taxpayers, and that we are dying because of their inefficiency.[7]

The conventional portrait of government bureaucrats depicts insatiable appetites for secrecy and exclusivity. This notorious closure fuels a fundamental and enduring tension facing American government: reconciling bureaucratic policy making with democratic accountability. Yet, bureaucrats in American agencies across the federal government frequently make their information public, open their policymaking processes to public advice, and, in doing so, expose themselves to public rebuke as in the case of Foscavir. If public participation poses a fundamental threat to bureaucratic power, why do bureaucrats open their doors to participation and *choose* to convene thousands of public meetings each year? Does public participation in agency policymaking, of the kind that emerged for the Vioxx review, improve policy outcomes and provide a portal for democratic governance, or does it merely yield an additional platform for industry influence and privilege in executive branch policymaking? More broadly, what effects does public participation have on bureaucratic administration, on policy outcomes, and on democratic accountability?

■　　■　　■

"This is an idiotic policy," a member of the National Assessment Governing Board bluntly charged at the Board's May 2002 public meeting, referring to the portion of the No Child Left Behind Act (NCLB) that made the test questions on the National Assessment of Educational Progress more readily available to public inspection.[8]

Since 1969, the National Assessment of Educational Progress (NAEP) has been routinely testing and reporting nationally on student achievement in reading, math, science, and other subjects.[9] It has earned the reputation as the "gold standard" for measuring student achievement across the United States, a reputation that depends on producing valid measures of student achievement. Such validity stems from the assessment's design, which has historically precluded teachers from teaching to the test.

From the view of agency leadership at the National Center for Education Statistics (the government agency responsible for helping administer the assessment) along with some members of the National Assessment Governing

Board (the public board that sets policy for the assessment), provisions of NCLB designed to make National Assessment test questions more broadly accessible and transparent to the public threatened to jeopardize the assessment's integrity. Addressing the National Assessment Governing Board at its March 2002 meeting, the Acting Commissioner of the National Center for Education Statistics warned:

> [L]et's say, for example . . . someone got all the [NAEP] booklets and put them on a web site. Well, that would basically as far as I'm concerned shut down our ability to conduct that assessment.[10]

Similarly, the public Board's executive director warned at the May 2002 meeting that these new requirements could "bring NAEP to its knees" and possibly damage the statistical integrity of the test.[11] The Board Chairman echoed these worries, stating that it might be the responsibility of board members to speak about these concerns. He remarked that if it appeared this part of the law would jeopardize NAEP's integrity, it could be the Board's job to say "Stop."[12]

For the past fifty years, public participation through public committees has figured prominently in the National Assessment's governance, design, and operation. Public committees helped design the original NAEP in the early 1960s. Public committees have helped design and review the questions that NAEP poses on assessments. Public committees have governed the assessment's policy decisions ever since the assessment began. Unlike the advisory committees the FDA consults, public boards for the National Assessment enjoy binding policymaking authority over some policy tasks.[13] And the relationship between the Governing Board and the education statistics agency has, at times, been fraught.[14] Yet, the Board found itself at odds with a portion of the president's signature education policy initiative and in agreement with bureaucratic leadership in the National Center for Education Statistics, the government agency: to protect the statistical integrity of the National Assessment by shielding it from unfettered public access to assessment questions. The conventional portrait of public committees suggests that public participation can interfere with agencies' abilities to deploy their technical knowledge in policy implementation, and that a trade-off exists between democratic control and agency expertise. In the case of the National Assessment of Educational Progress, public participation has instead appeared to help protect and promote the statistical integrity of the assessment, combining public participation and aspects of closure. When does public participation enhance expertise and when does it compromise the technical integrity of agency policymaking? When do bureaucratic administration and democratic governance appear fundamentally at odds, and when can they be reconciled through participation that offers both?

The Tension between Bureaucratic Administration and American Democracy

[These] narratives invite us to rethink and refine ideas about whether and when expert knowledge creates tension between bureaucratic administration and democratic accountability. Both secrecy and expertise represent traditional hallmarks of bureaucratic administration[15] and provide the crux of the Vioxx puzzle. Given the power that exclusive expert knowledge and closure can confer, why would the FDA open its policymaking process to outside advisers and to an audience of spectators? One conventional response looks for elected officials' fingerprints on agency structures and processes that yield greater openness. The idea that government agencies possess and capitalize on exclusive expert information is foundational to theories of oversight and delegation that strive to explain when elected officials cede policymaking to bureaucrats and what structures and procedures elected officials construct to prevent bureaucrats' policies from straying far from elected officials' wishes.[16] Given bureaucrats' presumed appetites for secrecy, the power such secrecy can confer and the potential threat it poses to democratic governance, American elected officials and government reformers have repeatedly sought ways to induce bureaucrats to reveal otherwise private information and provide organized groups opportunities to monitor bureaucratic policymaking. This includes requirements to share government records, to conduct open government meetings, and to require public participation in rulemaking.[17] The ensuing political influence over agency work, however, can threaten agency expertise and impair the quality of policy outcomes. Aspects of political control, for instance, appear to come at the expense of drug safety.[18] Some versions of democratic accountability can compromise bureaucratic administration, and vice versa, thus yielding an apparent trade-off between the two.[19]

These concerns about the tension between bureaucratic policymaking, in which unelected civil servants make significant policy decisions, and democratic oversight that vests governing authority in the public, have long been stitched into the fabric of American governance. This tension has taken on heightened significance, however, with the dramatic expansion and development of American bureaucracy since the nation's founding.[20] The American bureaucracy wields significant power, and some estimates suggest that agency administrators—not Congress or the president—create the majority of American laws through the rulemaking process.[21] With the growth of the American administrative state has come responsibility for policies, services, and decisions on which Americans' health, safety, and financial livelihood depend. Failures in bureaucratic expertise can produce devastating consequences.

Participatory Bureaucracy: Some Guiding Principles

When are federal-level bureaucrats more or less likely to seek public participation in agency policymaking? When is public participation more or less likely to support key features of bureaucratic administration: expertise and diverse support? [We should consider] bureaucrats as implementers broadly defined, who make policy in the course of implementation.[22] While putting policy into practice is a dynamic process,[23] knowledge and turf provide the backbones of bureaucratic task implementation. Considered in the context of U.S. federal-level policy, neither knowledge nor jurisdiction for task implementation is a general or fixed property of an agency. Instead, knowledge and turf vary by task. Conditions conducive to participatory bureaucracy thus depend on characteristics of a policy task, the fundamental unit of bureaucratic work.[24]

For instance, federal-level bureaucrats may have knowledge superior to family physicians on Vioxx's cardiovascular risks, but Merck might have better information than the bureaucrats, and researchers at the Cleveland Clinic might have better information yet. Instead of assuming monopoly information—on anyone's part—bureaucratic implementers confront a range of informational contexts, including when bureaucrats have more information, when outsiders have more information, when nobody has information, or when everyone is informed.[25] Government agencies also face a continuum of implementation contexts, ranging from fully in-house, such as a budget examination housed in the Office of Management and Budget, to well outside the agency's hierarchical reach. The federal government, for instance, enjoys relatively little formal authority over local public schools. The extent to which federal bureaucrats can implement policy in local school contexts typically depends on thousands of loosely connected implementers populating the vast governance space between the federal Department of Education and Valley View Elementary.

Consider the schema in Figure [1] that depicts variation on two crucial dimensions of implementation: information and turf. The horizontal axis represents the agency's information relative to task demands: the right side reflects full agency information, and the left side pegs at agency ignorance. The vertical axis represents a continuum from task independence to task interdependence. The top reflects full independence: the task is performed entirely within the agency's hierarchy. The bottom reflects fully interdependent implementations. Considerable scholarship on bureaucratic politics focuses on quadrants A and B, and with good reason. Quadrant A represents an ideal bureaucracy with perfect information and full authority over implementation, rather like Internal Revenue Service tax audits. This is where Weberian expertise and secrets may reside in harmony. In Quadrant B, bureaucrats enjoy authority over implementation, but their information is less complete relative to task demands. Here is where the tenets of Weberian power—technical knowledge and secrecy—may be at odds. The Atomic Energy Commission in the 1950s, for instance, enjoyed authority over the development of American nuclear power. When faced with insufficient information, the Commission engaged in private learning: talking behind closed doors with outsiders who had

FIGURE [1] Participation in American Bureaucracy by Task-Specific Information and Implementation Conditions

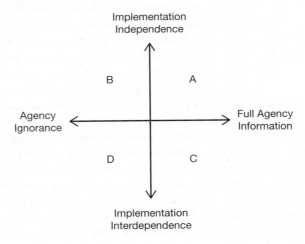

B: Private Agency Learning

D: Creating Knowledge
   Legitimating Knowledge

A: Agency Closure

C: Distributing Knowledge
   Allocating Responsibility

better information and more technical expertise than insiders.[26] Yet, Quadrant B is also where bureaucratic independence can allow bureaucrats to hide their ignorance: where secrecy enabled the Commission to avoid revealing their uncertainty over reactor safety, for instance. In his call for greater oversight of the Central Intelligence Agency in 1956, Senator Michael Mansfield (D-MT) lamented, "If we accept the idea of secrecy for secrecy's sake we will have no way of knowing whether we have a very fine intelligence service or a very poor one."[27] Secrecy can impair both expertise and democratic oversight.[28]

Task implementations that appear in Quadrants C and D foster greater incentives for bureaucrats not only to learn *from* the public but also to learn *in* public than in A and B. These are conditions of greater task interdependence, when bureaucrats depend fundamentally on implementers who reside outside the agency's hierarchical jurisdiction. To implement its task of ensuring drug safety and efficacy, for instance, the FDA depends on firms to gather and reveal appropriate information both to the FDA *and* to doctors and patients. The agency depends on physicians and patients to use therapies judiciously. It depends on firms and physicians to report adverse events to the agency. The FDA cannot command safe drug use: safety and efficacy are ultimately matters of practice that transcend the agency's organizational boundaries. While drug reviews present general conditions of interdependence, each drug review produces a different information and implementation context. . . .

Thus, one condition of participatory bureaucracy—public engagement in agency policymaking that supports both bureaucratic administration and democratic oversight—is *interdependent task implementation* that appears in Quadrants C and D. Interdependence renders the expertise or knowledge required for implementation contingent and emergent,[29] which creates incentives for public learning and learning *in* public, more so than for tasks with independent implementations. From a bureaucratic perspective, we would expect public participation to manifest in the same agency for some tasks but not for others. Participatory bureaucracy is less about whether or not the FDA reflects openness or closure overall, and more about whether and why openness appears for some tasks, such as drug reviews for novel indications, but not for others, such as drug reviews for supplemental indications. Participatory bureaucracy invites us to look beyond explanations that stop at the level of institutions and procedures and focus more closely on task-specific conditions.

Public participation can certainly occur for tasks that appear in Quadrants A and B, but participation in these contexts is more likely to yield participatory oversight than participatory bureaucracy. Public participation for tasks in Quadrants A and B [is] more likely to come at the expense of bureaucratic expertise and jurisdiction. The more that tasks are implemented in a traditional Weberian hierarchy—the more the tasks reside in Quadrants A and B—the less we would expect participatory bureaucracy to reconcile the democracy-bureaucracy tension, and the more we would expect the conventional trade-off, with more of one and less of another.[30] By some accounts, however, American government agency interdependence is both prevalent and expanding.[31] One estimate suggests that only 5 percent of "federal government activity" entails goods and services that government bureaucrats provide directly.[32] American government's reliance on third-party actors and public co-production renders public participation through public committees an increasingly feasible means of managing the bureaucracy-democracy tension.

However, complex tasks like those we would see in Quadrants C and D—such as regulator dependence on its regulatory target—can make agencies vulnerable to industry influence or capture,[33] which supports neither bureaucratic administration nor democratic oversight. Thus, a second condition for participatory bureaucracy is a public engagement process that yields *diverse expertise focused on implementation.* In the context of participatory bureaucracy, expert means possessing specialized knowledge that provides a baseline of knowledge or ability, but it does not inhere in fixed descriptive characteristics, such as being a woman or having a Ph.D. Instead, it can manifest from multiple sources, including the grassroots; and it depends on timing, location, and the nature of the policy task. Common critiques of participatory processes typically dichotomize "experts" and "public," defining expertise in terms of credentials or exclusive knowledge, and the public in terms of the mass that lacks formal credentials but has a potential interest in the issue. Participatory bureaucracy blurs the distinction between these categories. In participatory bureaucracy, disease sufferers may be expert in their ability to express how they are affected by disease, how they experienced pharmaceutical therapies, and their willingness to accept risk.[34] Expertise for participatory bureaucracy is not restricted to a particular profession or perspective, but evolves along with the implementation context: who is "expert" depends on the task.[35] Rather than dichotomies between the public and experts, participatory bureaucracy can embody significant overlap between the two.

Within the context of broadly defined expertise, diversity brings different *perspectives* and heuristics. This cognitive approach differs from traditional models of participation in bureaucratic policymaking that frame participation strictly as opportunities for communicating and advocating for particular *interests*.[36] Building on a broadly defined baseline of expertise, diverse perspectives and diverse cognitive heuristics render suboptimal policy decisions less likely. Suboptimal from the perspective of bureaucratic administration means policy outcomes that are costly to reverse and/or damaging to agency reputation.[37] Participatory bureaucracy is better equipped to manage the bureaucracy-democracy tension when it marshals diverse expertise keyed to the policy task. These conditions—diverse expertise focused on interdependent task implementation—render public participation amenable to supporting core elements of bureaucratic reputation: expertise and diverse support.[38]

Given the conditions it imposes on public participation, participatory bureaucracy clearly differs from participatory democracy's inclusiveness and empowerment.[39] Yet, participatory bureaucracy is amenable to democratic accountability when it "liquefies knowledge," to use Dewey's metaphor. Participatory bureaucracy that manages the bureaucracy-democracy tension is *indeterminate*: both the participatory process and its outcomes are fluid and evolving rather than fixed or foreordained. Participatory bureaucracy creates openness and access to policymaking that can expand beyond the scope of the particular task. Scholarship typically assesses the impact of participation on the individuals who participated in the policymaking process. Examples include Chicago's Alternative Policing Strategy that brought community members and police together to develop and implement priorities for the police, or environmental regulatory negotiations conducted through stakeholder participation.[40] The potential democratic contributions of participatory bureaucracy, however, exceed the scope of a singular decision or information exchange. Consistent with open-systems theories of organizations, participatory bureaucracy can transcend fixed jurisdictions and offer access to policymaking through visibility and through opportunities for engagement from governmental and nongovernmental sources.[41] The potential for accountability is ongoing: it does not end when the votes are cast and the meeting comes to an end. Open meetings can put knowledge into the public space that can, in turn, take on a life of its own. The promise of participatory bureaucracy resides in part in the ongoing portal it may create.

Skepticism toward participatory processes abounds. Imbalanced power can limit the extent and scope of participation and stifle discourse.[42] Insufficient connections between knowledge and subsequent action can limit the usefulness of public information for individual behavior or policy outcomes. Knowledge may drip rather than flow, and do so in ways that exacerbate political, social, and economic inequality. Yet, consider the counterfactuals of Quadrants A and B, where accountability may be even more remote *and* come at the expense of expert or competent implementation.

Participatory bureaucracy is not the sole solution for the bureaucracy-democracy tension, and can complement other governing approaches including representative bureaucracy and performance management. But it is distinct in notable ways. For one, bureaucrats may initiate, design, and administer participatory bureaucracy. Participatory bureaucracy is not necessarily imposed on the bureaucracy by elected officials. Rather than curtail agency autonomy, public participation creates room for government agencies to frame policy issues, shape alternatives for the public agenda, and cultivate favorable agency images. In this sense, participatory bureaucracy departs from congressional dominance views, which leave little room for bureaucratic autonomy and credit elected officials with institution building. While participatory bureaucracy offers room for representing interests, akin to pluralism or representative bureaucracy,[43] it also allows direct public access to information and policymaking, not just access mediated through representatives or groups.[44] Unlike pluralism and representative bureaucracy where the direction of influence and information flow is from the representatives to the policy decision, moreover, participatory bureaucracy can enable information to flow in multiple directions: from the agency to the various publics as well as from the public to the agency.[45] In contrast to some aspects of New Public Management,[46] participatory bureaucracy does not assume that the local level or the consumer has "better" information essential to policy implementation, just as it does not assume federal-level bureaucrats enjoy superior information. Information for implementation depends on the policy task.

Public participation's ability to manage the bureaucracy-democracy tension depends on the design of the policy task, on the design of participation, and on the broader context in which the policy is implemented and participation occurs. Managing the tension offers a potentially non-zero-sum approach to government administration. Instead of dichotomies between democratic governance and bureaucratic administration, between legislative and executive branch control, between public and private, or between public and expert, participatory bureaucracy offers potential complements. Rather than zero-sum, both elected officials and bureaucrats can reap rewards from permeable bureaucratic policymaking.[47] Both elected officials and bureaucrats can benefit from competent task implementation.[48] One way bureaucracy can abet competence is through public participation that assembles diverse expertise for interdependent task implementations.

Participatory bureaucracy shares several key features with the development of administrative expertise modeled in Gailmard and Patty's *Learning While Governing*. Both challenge the conventional assumption that bureaucrats enjoy superior or sufficient information relative to other policy actors. Both recognize the importance of information and authority for structuring bureaucratic incentives. Both recognize that bureaucratic expertise and democratic accountability are not necessarily at odds. Gailmard and Patty offer an important model for understanding organizational designs that induce bureaucrats to "acquire, share and elicit information," to use their terms.[49] Participatory bureaucracy focuses instead on task-specific variation in bureaucratic knowledge and jurisdiction that yield different incentives for learning *from* the public and learning *in* public across organizational and institutional arrangements. The analysis that follows suggests that systematic variation in task conditions goes far to explain some policy outcomes, whereas some prominent organizational and institutional differences do not.

The potential democratic mechanism in participatory bureaucracy also differs from principal-agent models. When learning in public liquefies knowledge, to use Dewey's metaphor, the potential for democratic accountability exceeds the scope of any singular policy decision. The transparency that can manifest from learning in public may assist democratic accountability not merely by holding the agency accountable but also by creating opportunities to hold other implementers outside the agency accountable upon whom task implementation depends. Accountability in participatory bureaucracy may manifest not only by holding the FDA solely responsible, for instance, but also by shining the spotlight on firms and inducing firms to behave in ways consistent with policy implementation.[50]

The policy conditions that make participatory bureaucracy promising, however, also render it fragile. Policies' interdependence can give way to imbalanced dependence, privilege, or even corruption. Emerging technologies and evolving expertise can expose nascent policies to unfounded attacks and equally unfounded sponsorship. The expansive, non-zero-sum potential of public knowledge generated through public participation can collide with zero-sum American politics. Appetites for secrecy persist. Public participation did not, for instance, prevent the arthritis drug Vioxx's post-marketing safety problems. Participatory bureaucracy is hard to pull off.

Given this mixed portrait of public participation in agency policymaking, this [reading] explores the following questions:

- When do different forms of public participation emerge: participatory oversight, private learning, and participatory bureaucracy?

- What are the implications of participatory bureaucracy for policy outcomes and bureaucratic reputations?
- What are the implications of participatory bureaucracy for democratic accountability?

Managing the challenge of expert bureaucratic administration amid democratic accountability confronts policymakers and implementers across policy domains, from pharmaceutical regulation, to education testing, to defense contracting, to financial services reform. The vast U.S. federal advisory committee system offers an enduring venue for examining public participation in agency policymaking, for assessing its potential to yield participatory bureaucracy, and for addressing this [reading's] guiding questions.

Participatory Bureaucracy through Public Advice

Federal public committees are uniquely positioned among forms of federal level public engagement, such as notice-and-comment procedures and freedom-of-information requests, to address the three guiding questions introduced in the previous section. Committees like the ones that contribute to policymaking for pharmaceutical regulation are part of a vast American system of public committees and represent a defining feature of the American administrative state.[51] Federal public boards and committees offer durable and prevalent venues for policy development and deliberation, with roughly 1,000 committees currently in operation across federal agencies, such as the FDA's Arthritis Drugs Advisory Committee. . . . Committees typically consist of individuals who are employed outside of government but who advise government agencies on topics ranging from aviation security to electronic medical records. Through the Federal Advisory Committee Act of 1972 and its amendments, common procedures govern advisory committee operations, including requirements for announcing meetings, setting committee agendas, transcribing meeting deliberations, and ensuring "balanced" committee membership. Although public meetings vary considerably, one common meeting format entails the agency presenting information on a policy, some nongovernmental individuals presenting information on that policy, some period of open public comment, and committee deliberation from members who are formally appointed to the public board and others in the room. Within the contours of Federal Advisory Committee Act provisions, committees vary considerably in terms of their meeting format, committee membership, meeting frequency, and their policy contributions.[52]

Federal public committees have the potential to make policy public in several ways. Committees are public in the sense that public officials—legislators, presidents, presidential appointees, bureaucrats—create them as portals for discussion and participation. Despite bureaucrats' legendary appetites for secrecy, government agencies have created nearly half of the approximately 1,000 federal advisory committees operating in 2010 and have played prominent roles in structuring many others, as Figure [2] illustrates.[53]

FIGURE [2] Count of Active Public Committees by Institutional Authority, 1974–2010

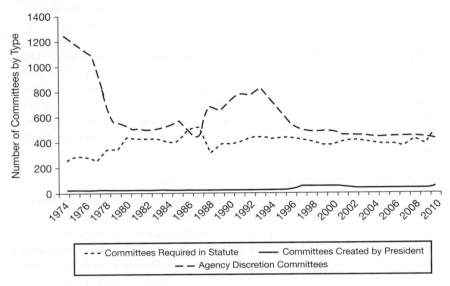

Committees are also public in the sense that they include members of the general public—individuals who work outside of government—in government policymaking.[54] This can provide individuals and interests a seat at government agencies' policymaking tables they would not otherwise enjoy.[55] Tens of thousands of people have served on public committees every year dating back to the 1950s. Some members serve as designated representatives of various interests. Other members serve as "special government employees" and are subject to government ethics provisions prohibiting conflicts of interest.

Committees are also public in the sense of promoting visibility: they can monitor and shine light on government agency policy processes. The Federal Advisory Committee Act contains provisions designed to promote committee transparency, such as requirements that advisory committees convene in public and make their meeting minutes publicly accessible, affording room for visibility and for knowledge to spread. Through their visibility, public committees can expand participation beyond the boundaries of the officially convened discussion: information and arguments from open public participation can disseminate to other sites of governance outside the agency.

Despite public committees' longevity and ubiquity in the landscape of American governance, they have faced steady criticism for failing to be sufficiently public or sufficiently participatory. Proponents argue public participation, in general, may legitimate policy, promote a capable citizenry, advance policy implementation, and generate new knowledge. Public committees, as one form of participation, may promote bureaucratic accountability to elected officials by allowing outsiders access to agency policymaking,[56] and can legitimize and encourage stable policy processes and outcomes.[57] Public participation in practice, however, habitually falls short of either a democratic or a bureaucratic ideal and has been described as "the most vilified approach to public involvement" in agency policymaking.[58] Participation can be constrained, opinions may become reinforced rather than evolve, and technical uncertainty can persist. Public advisory committees face enduring allegations of privileging particular interests, compromising agency expertise, promoting *secrecy* rather than transparency, or bringing validation, not participation, to agency work.[59] Public councils ranging from the Department of Justice Antitrust Division's advisory committees in the 1950s to the National Energy Policy Development Group convened by Vice President Cheney in 2001 chose to close their meetings to public inspection and to public audiences. Critics of the NASA Advisory Council have argued that the council operates as "spokesmen on the agency's behalf" rather than as a venue for meaningful participation.[60] The EPA's Science Advisory Board faced allegations of insufficiently rigorous measures for preventing conflicts of interest among board members.[61] Some estimates suggest that thousands of committee meetings are closed to general public audiences each year.[62]

■   ■   ■

Though transparency and public participation are typically cast as ways to curtail bureaucratic power, bureaucrats may benefit from and seek greater openness and engagement—and they may do so through public committees. Scholarship on public committees has helped us understand general committee operations and influence, committees' abilities to balance political and technical demands, elected officials' abilities to use committees as a way to monitor the bureaucracy, and representation on committees. Missing, however, is an account of public participation from a *bureaucratic perspective*: when public participation transforms into participatory bureaucracy and provides a potential means of managing the tension between democratic accountability and bureaucratic administration.

NOTES

1. John Dewey, *The School and Society and The Child and the Curriculum* (Chicago: University of Chicago Press, 1956), 25.

2. Statement of Senator Charles E. Grassley (R-IA), U.S. Congress, Senate, Committee on Finance, *FDA, Merck, and Vioxx: Putting Patient Safety First?* 108th Congress, 2nd Session, November 18, 2004 (Washington, DC: Government Printing Office, 2004), 3.

3. Institute of Medicine, *The Future of Drug Safety: Promoting and Protecting the Health of the Public* (Washington, DC: National Academy Press, 2007), 17.

4. Food and Drug Administration, "Arthritis Advisory Committee Meeting Transcript: Vioxx, April 20, 1999"; Food and Drug Administration, "Arthritis Advisory Committee Meeting Transcript: Vioxx, February 8, 2001."

5. Kenneth I. Kaitin, Ann Melville and Betsy Morris, "FDA Advisory Committees and the New Drug Approval Process," *Journal of Clinical Pharmacology* 29 (1989): 886–90; Steven J. Balla and John R. Wright, "Can Advisory Committees Facilitate Congressional Oversight of the Bureaucracy?" *Congress at Work, Congress on Display* (Ann Arbor: University of Michigan Press, 2000), 167–87; Steven J. Balla and John R. Wright, "Interest Groups, Advisory Committees, and Congressional Control of the Bureaucracy," *American Journal of Political Science* 45 (2001): 799–812.

6. See comments from Sidney Wolfe, "Food and Drug Administration, Joint Meeting of the Arthritis Advisory Committee and the Drug Safety and Risk Management Advisory Committee Transcript, Volume II, February 17, 2005," 240–41.

7. David Kessler was the FDA commissioner at the time. Carl Peck was the director of the Center for Drug Evaluation and Research, in charge of the drug review process. Statement of Derek Link, in Food and Drug Administration, "Antiviral Drugs Advisory Committee Transcript: Foscavir for treatment of cytomegalovirus retinitis in patients with AIDS, June 12, 1991," 6.

8. Author's field notes, May 17, 2002; see also National Assessment Governing Board, "Official Summary of Board Actions, Meeting of May 17–18, 2002," in August 2002 Briefing Book, 9–10; Lynn Olson, "Board Acts to Bring NAEP in Line with ESEA," *Education Week* 21 (2002): 22–24.

9. Assessments in Science, Writing, and Citizenship marked the first round of NAEP assessments, conducted in 1969–1970. Assessments in Reading and Literature began in 1970–71, followed by assessments in Music and Social Studies in 1971–72. The first assessment in Math was conducted in 1972–73. See National Center for Education Statistics, *Directory of NAEP Publications* (Washington, DC: U.S. Department of Education, 1999).

10. See National Assessment Governing Board, "Board Meeting Transcript, March 1, 2002." Page numbers are not reported on pages of the transcript.

11. Author's field notes, May 18, 2002. Participants at the meeting discussed the "good faith effort" the Board and agency had undertaken to implement the law.

12. Author's field notes, May 18, 2002. For further discussion, see National Assessment Governing Board, "Official Summary of Board Actions, Meeting of May 17–18, 2002," in August 2002 Briefing Book, 10.

13. P.L. 103–382 stipulates that "Only sections 10, 11, and 12 of the Federal Advisory Committee Act shall apply with respect to the Board." Those sections bear on procedures for calling meetings, holding open meetings, transcript availability, and financial reporting.

14. A historical review concludes NAGB and NCES "usually have worked closely and harmoniously together" despite "certain tensions and disputes." See Maris Vinovskis, *Overseeing the Nation's Report Card: The Creation and Evolution of the National Assessment Governing Board* (Washington, DC: National Assessment Governing Board, 1998), 31.

15. Max Weber, *From Max Weber: Essays in Sociology* (New York: Oxford University Press, 1946), 233; Max Weber, *The Theory of Social and Economic Organizations* (London: Free Press of Glencoe, Collier-MacMillian Ltd., 1947), 339. This book defines secrecy as concealing information and defines transparency as revealing information, consistent with Sissela Bok, *Secrets: On the Ethics of Concealment and Revelation* (New York: Random House, 1983).

16. See Mathew McCubbins and Thomas Schwartz, "Congressional Oversight Overlooked: Police Patrols vs. Fire Alarms," *American Journal of Political Science* 28 (1984): 165–79; Mathew McCubbins, Roger Noll, and Barry Weingast, "Structure and

Process, Policy and Politics: Administrative Arrangements and the Political Control of Agencies," *Virginia Law Review* 75 (1989): 431–82; David Epstein and Sharyn O'Halloran, *Delegating Powers: A Transaction Cost Politics Approach to Policy Making under Separate Powers* (New York: Cambridge University Press, 1999); John Huber and Charles R. Shipan, *Deliberate Discretion; The Institutional Foundations of Bureaucratic Autonomy* (New York: Cambridge University Press, 2002).

17. On regulatory notice and comment procedures and its limitations, see Cornelius Kerwin, *Rulemaking* (Washington, DC: CQ Press, 2003), 62–66; Jason Webb Yackee and Susan Webb Yackee, "Bias Toward Business?" *Journal of Politics* 68 (2006): 128–39; Steven J. Balla, "Administrative Procedures and Political Control of the Bureaucracy," *American Political Science Review* 92 (1998): 663–73. On the Freedom of Information Act provisions, see Alasdair Roberts, *Blacked Out* (New York: Cambridge University Press, 2006), 13–18.

18. Politics can never be fully separate from administration. However, imposing deadlines on the FDA to review drugs quickly—one manifestation of political influence over agency policymaking—can compromise the quality of the agency's regulatory process by putting drugs on the market that are more likely to pose safety problems associated with adverse events and deaths. Daniel Carpenter, Jacqueline Chattopadhyay, Susan Moffitt, and Clayton Nall, "The Complications of Controlling Agency Time Discretion: FDA Review Deadlines and Postmarket Safety," *American Journal of Political Science* 56 (2012): 98–114.

19. Kathleen Bawn, "Political Control Versus Expertise: Congressional Choices About Administrative Procedures," *American Political Science Review* 89 (1995): 62–73.

20. Stephen Skowronek, *Building a New American State: The Expansion of National Administrative Capacities, 1877–1920* (Cambridge: Cambridge University Press, 1982); William T. Gormley, Jr. and Steven J. Balla, *Bureaucracy and Democracy: Accountability and Performance* (Washington, DC: CQ Press, 2007).

21. Kenneth F. Warren, *Administrative Law in the Political System*, 4th ed. (Boulder, CO: Westview Press, 2004), 282, cited in Susan Webb Yackee, "Lifecycle of Medical Product Rules Issued by the Food and Drug Administration," *Journal of Health Politics, Policy and Law* (Forthcoming). For comprehensive scholarship on bureaucratic power, see Daniel P. Carpenter, *Reputation and Power: Organizational Image and Pharmaceutical Regulation at the FDA* (Princeton, NJ: Princeton University Press, 2010).

22. Though this view of implementation as creating policy is typically attributed to grassroots implementation, it applies to federal-level implementers as well. On grassroots implementation, see Michael Lipsky, *Street-Level Bureaucracy: Dilemmas of the Individual in Public Services* (New York: Russell Sage Foundation, 1980).

23. On the factors affecting implementation, see David K. Cohen and Susan L. Moffitt, *The Ordeal of Equality: Did Federal Regulation Fix the Schools?* (Cambridge, MA: Harvard University Press, 2009), 17–44.

24. On the importance of tasks within an organizational context, see James Q. Wilson, *Bureaucracy: What Government Agencies Do and Why They Do It* (New York: Basic Books, 1989), 25–26. The discussion that follows does not aim to provide an optimal strategy for bureaucrats or for elected officials. Instead, it focuses on the conditions when participation is more or less likely to be consistent with key features of bureaucratic reputation.

25. For important work on the development of bureaucratic information and expertise, see Sean Gailmard and John W. Patty, *Learning While Governing: Expertise and Accountability in the Executive Branch* (Chicago: University of Chicago Press, 2012).

26. On the Atomic Energy Commission, see Brian Balogh, *Chain Reaction: Expert Debate and Public Participation in American Commercial Nuclear Power, 1945–1975* (New York: Cambridge University Press, 1991).

27. Comments of Senator Michael Mansfield, (D-MT), *Congressional Record* Senate, April 9, 1956, 5930.

28. Francis E. Rourke, *Secrecy and Publicity: Dilemmas of Democracy* (Baltimore, MD: Johns Hopkins Press, 1961) 5, 10–11, 138; Michel Crozier, *The Bureaucratic Phenomenon* (Chicago: University of Chicago Press, 1964), 153; Daniel Patrick Moynihan, *Secrecy: The American Experience* (New Haven, CT: Yale University Press, 1998); Kenneth J. Meier and John Bohte, *Politics and the Bureaucracy: Policymaking in the Fourth Branch of Government* (Belmont, CA: Thomson Wadsworth, 2007), 66; Harold Wilensky, *Organizational Intelligence* (New York: Basic Books, 1969), 144; Jeffrey Pfeffer and Gerald R. Salancik, *The External Control of Organizations* (New York: Harper and Row, 2003), 104.

29. For careful distinction between the concepts of complexity, difficulty, and uncertainty, see Scott E. Page, "Uncertainty, Difficulty and Complexity," *Journal of Theoretical Politics* 20 (2008): 115–49. Task interdependence is consistent with public administration's concept of co-production and viewing the public as a partner. John Clayton Thomas, *Citizen, Customer, Partner: Engaging the Public in Public Management* (New York: M.E. Sharpe, 2012), 10–12, 85–101; Jeffrey Brudney and Robert England, "Toward a Definition of the Co-Production Concept," *Public Administration Review* 43 (1983): 59–65; Sean P. Osborne, "Delivering Public Services: Time for a New Theory?" *Public Management Review* 12 (2010): 1–10.

30. For related discussion on this point, see Thomas, *Citizen, Customer, Partner*, 129–30.

31. Kenneth J. Meier and Laurence J. O'Toole, *Bureaucracy in a Democratic State: A Governance Perspective* (Baltimore, MD: Johns Hopkins University Press, 2006).

32. Lester M. Salamon, *The Tools of Government: A Guide to the New Governance* (New York: Oxford University Press, 2002), 4.

33. Nolan McCarty, "Complexity, Capacity and Capture," in *Preventing Regulatory Capture: Special Interest Influence and How to Limit It*, edited by Daniel Carpenter and David Moss (Cambridge: Cambridge University Press, 2013), 99–123.

34. Usable knowledge arises from many sources. Charles Lindblom and David K. Cohen, *Usable Knowledge: Social Science and Social Problem Solving* (New Haven, CT: Yale University Press, 1979). For related discussion, see p. 18 of Archon Fung and Erik Olin Wright, "Deepening Democracy: Innovations in Empowered Participatory Governance," *Politics and Society* 29 (2001): 5–41.

35. For more discussion on the relativity of capability for policy implementation, see Cohen and Moffitt, *Ordeal of Equality*, 17–44.

36. For a summary, see Meier and Bohte, *Politics and the Bureaucracy*, 198–205. On the distinction between representing interests and including diverse professional and social perspectives on public committees, see Mark B. Brown, "Fairly Balanced: The Politics of Representation on Government Advisory Committees," *Political Research Quarterly* 61 (2008): 547–60.

37. For a review on group decision making, see Daan van Knippenberg and Michaéla C. Schippers, "Work Group Diversity," *Annual Review of Psychology* 58 (2007): 515–41. On the ability of diverse perspectives to render suboptimal policy less likely, see Scott E. Page, *The Difference: How the Power of Diversity Creates Better Groups, Firms, Schools and Societies* (Princeton, NJ: Princeton University Press, 2007). On the impact of diverse perspectives on the quality of deliberation, see James Bohman, *Public Deliberation:*

Pluralism, Complexity and Democracy (Cambridge, MA: MIT Press, 1996). On costly reversals and agency reputation, see Daniel P. Carpenter, "Groups, the Media, Agency Waiting Costs and FDA Drug Approval," *American Journal of Political Science* 46 (2002): 490–505.

38. Bureaucrats benefit from diverse support for their programs and policies, instead of support limited to a single dominant group. Carpenter, *The Forging of Bureaucratic Autonomy*, 14, 32; Francis E. Rourke, *Bureaucracy, Politics and Public Policy*, 2nd ed. (Boston: Little, Brown & Co, 1976), 55.

39. Carol Pateman, *Participation and Democratic Theory* (Cambridge: Cambridge University Press, 1970).

40. Archon Fung, *Empowered Participation: Reinventing Urban Democracy* (Princeton, NJ: Princeton University Press, 2004), 3. On debate over the durability of policy made through negotiated rulemaking, see Cary Coglianese, "Assessing Consensus: The Promise and Performance of Negotiated Rulemaking," *Duke Law Journal* 46 (1997): 1255–1349; Laura Langbein, "Responsive Bureaus, Equity and Regulatory Negotiation," *Journal of Public Policy Analysis and Management* 21 (2002): 446–65. For a review of reg-neg, see Peter H. Schuck and Steven Kochevar, "Reg Neg Redux: The Career of a Procedural Reform," *Theoretical Inquiries in Law* 15 (2014).

41. Richard M. Cyert and James G. March, *A Behavioral Theory of the Firm* (Englewood Cliffs, NJ: Prentice-Hall, 1963); Pfeffer and Salancik, *The External Control of Organizations*; Karl Weick, "Educational Organizations as Loosely Coupled Systems," *Administrative Science Quarterly* 21 (1976): 1–19.

42. For a classic illustration of power represented through "blue ribbon" advisory committees at the local level, see Robert Dahl, *Who Governs? Democracy and Power in an American City* (New Haven, CT: Yale University Press, 1961), 124.

43. Representative bureaucracy focuses on having individuals who serve in government reflect the broader population in terms of gender, race, ethnicity, sexual orientation, and other descriptive characteristics. When bureaucracy embodies the interests and preferences of the populace, it can offer a defensible substitute for more direct democratic accountability and can impact subsequent policy decisions. Meier and O'Toole, *Bureaucracy in a Democratic State*, 67–92; Kenneth J. Meier, Eric Gonzalez Juenke, Robert D. Wrinkle, and J. L. Polinard, "Structural Choices and Representational Biases: The Post-Election Color of Representation," *American Journal of Political Science* 49 (2005): 758–68; Lael R. Keiser, Vicky M. Wilkins, Kenneth J. Meier, and Catherine A. Holland, "Lipstick and Logarithms: Gender, Institutional Context and Representative Bureaucracy," *American Political Science Review* 96 (2002): 553–64.

44. As Thomas argues, representative bureaucracy offers a top-down, hierarchical approach to bringing broader community voice into agency policymaking, in contrast to co-production forms of engagement. Thomas, *Citizen, Customer, Partner*, 20–29.

45. On this point, see Thomas, *Citizen, Customer, Partner*, 177.

46. For a consumer-oriented view, see David Osborne and Ted Gaebler, *Reinventing Government: How the Entrepreneurial Spirit Is Transforming the Public Sector* (Reading, MA: Addison-Wesley, 1992).

47. For related argument on the non-zero-sum potential of group engagement, see Jane J. Mansbridge, "A Deliberative Theory of Interest Representation," in *The Politics of Interests: Interest Groups Transformed*, edited by Mark P. Petracca (Boulder, CO: Westview Press, 1992), 32–57. In her discussion of public boards from the perspective of democratic accountability, Mansbridge distinguishes between unitary and adversary issues (conflicting or common interests) as key to understanding different participa-

tory arrangements. Jane J. Mansbridge, *Beyond Adversary Democracy* (Chicago: University of Chicago Press, 1983), ix–x of the revised preface.

48. Competently performing policy tasks can offer one expression of accountability. For an important theoretical approach that combines administrative balance and rationality to yield accountability, see Anthony Bertelli and Laurence E. Lynn Jr., *Madison's Managers: Public Administration and the Constitution* (Baltimore, MD: Johns Hopkins University Press, 2006).

49. Gailmard and Patty, *Learning While Governing*, 11.

50. Recall that the extent to which participatory bureaucracy yields competent task implementation can also support democratic accountability.

51. Rourke, *Bureaucracy, Politics and Public Policy*, 123. On committees that advise French pharmaceutical regulation, see Philippe Urfalino, *Le Grand Méchant Loup Pharmaceutique* (Paris: Les éditions Textuel, 2005).

52. In *Organizational Intelligence*, Harold Wilensky offers a useful summary of the range of ways the government may use advisory committees, including representing constituencies, testing ideas, channeling public attention, mobilizing policy support, and broadening participation in the policymaking process. Harold Wilensky, *Organizational Intelligence* (New York: Basic Books, 1969), 169–72. On the development and use of public committees in various policy domains, see Sheila Jasanoff, *The Fifth Branch: Science Advisors as Policy Makers* (Cambridge, MA: Harvard University Press, 1990); Stephen Hilgartner, *Science on Stage: Expert Advice as Public Drama* (Stanford, CA: Stanford University Press, 2000); Rourke, *Bureaucracy, Politics and Public Policy*, 121–24; David Truman, *The Governmental Process* (New York: Knopf, 1951), 458; Martha Derthick, *Policymaking for Social Security* (Washington, DC: Brookings Institution Press, 1979), 100–101; Herbert Kaufman, *The Administrative Behavior of Federal Bureau Chiefs* (Washington, DC: The Brookings Institution, 1981), 39–40; William T. Gormley Jr., *The Politics of Public Utility Regulation* (Pittsburgh, PA: University of Pittsburgh Press, 1983); Thomas A. Wolanin, *Presidential Advisory Committees: Truman to Nixon* (Madison: University of Wisconsin Press, 1975); Don K. Price, *Government and Science: Their Dynamic Relation in American Democracy* (New York: Oxford University Press, 1962) 130; Anthony Downs, *Inside Bureaucracy* (Boston: Little, Brown Downs, 1967), 207–8; Bruce L. R. Smith, *The Advisers: Scientists in the Policy Process* (Washington, DC: Brookings Institution Press, 1992), 8; Steven P. Croley and William F. Funk, "The Federal Advisory Committee Act and Good Government," *Yale Journal on Regulation* 14 (1997): 451–557.

53. Jasanoff, *The Fifth Branch*, 84–88; Derthick, *Policymaking for Social Security*, 100–9. For a discussion of the ways in which committees are "public," see Wolanin, *Presidential Advisory Commissions*, 8–9.

54. For discussion on the state-society divide, see Jeffrey M. Sellers, "State-Society Relations," *The Sage Handbook of Governance*, edited by Mark Bevir (London: Sage, 2011), 124–41.

55. On the representation of interests on advisory committees, see Stéphane Lavertu, Daniel E. Walters, David L. Weimer, "Scientific Expertise and the Balance of Political Interests: MEDCAC and Medicare Coverage Decisions," *Journal of Public Administration Research and Theory* 22 (2012): 55–81.

56. Balla and Wright, "Can Advisory Committees Facilitate Congressional Oversight of the Bureaucracy?" 167–87.

57. Jasanoff, *The Fifth Branch*, 17; Hilgartner, *Science on Stage*; Heimann, *Acceptable Risks*, 154. Jasanoff discusses public committees' failures to achieve either democratic or technocratic ideals.

58. Thomas, *Citizen, Customer, Partner*, 173. Thomas notes that this critique "unfairly judges" some forms of participation.

59. For allegations of advisory committees creating barriers between government administration and the public, see U.S. Congress, Senate, *Advisory Committees*, Hearings before the Subcommittee on Intergovernmental Relations of the Committee on Government Operations, 92nd Congress, 1st Session, part 2 (Washington, DC: GPO, 1971), 497. The FDA's panel on cyclamates offers a well-known example of alleged validation.

60. Smith, *The Advisers*, 122.

61. U.S. General Accounting Office, *EPA's Science Advisory Board Panels: Improved Policies and Procedures Needed to Ensure Independence and Balance* (Washington, DC: GAO, 2001), 2.

62. Kevin D. Karty, "Closure and Capture in Federal Advisory Committees," *Business and Politics* 4 (2002): 213–38. However, other work suggests that most agencies "rarely close their meetings." See Croley and Funk, "The Federal Advisory Committee Act and Good Government," 505. Historically, peer review committees within the National Science Foundation and National Endowment for the Humanities constitute some of the most frequently closed committees.

DISCUSSION QUESTIONS

1. According to Wilson, what are some of the specific ways government bureaucracies are different than private bureaucracies that serve commercial business purposes?

2. Describe the differences between police patrol and fire alarm models of the federal bureaucracy's congressional oversight.

3. What does "learning in public" mean for Moffitt? Why is that beneficial to bureaucracies?

4. Using these readings, discuss several ways in which a bureaucratic leader in government needs to act like a politician—that is, seek public approval, stake out a claim about policy, build a constituency and protect it, publicize actions, and recognize and address oppositional forces within government.

8

THE JUDICIARY

8.1

GERALD N. ROSENBERG

From *The Hollow Hope: Can Courts Bring about Social Change?*

Rosenberg argues that courts in the United States are highly constrained in bring-ing about social change. Though many people think of the courts as "dynamic"—as drivers of social change—in Rosenberg's view, courts instead follow the other branches of government. They do not drive change but rather respond late to social changes and end up trying to catch up with trends in society.

INTRODUCTION

The Problem

■   ■   ■

To what degree, and under what conditions, can judicial processes be used to produce political and social change? What are the constraints that operate on them? What factors are important and why?

. . . Traditionally, most lawyers and legal scholars have focused on a related normative issue: whether courts *ought* to act. From the perspective of demo-cratic theory, that is an important and useful question. Yet since much of poli-tics is about who gets what, when, and how, and how that distribution is maintained, or changed, understanding to what extent, and under what condi-tions, courts can produce political and social change is of key importance.

From Gerald N. Rosenberg, *The Hollow Hope: Can Courts Bring about Social Change?* (Chicago: University of Chicago Press, 1991).

. . . In the last several decades, movements and groups advocating what I will shortly define as significant social reform have turned increasingly to the courts. Starting with the famous cases brought by the civil rights movement and spreading to issues raised by women's groups, environmental groups, political reformers, and others, American courts seemingly have become important producers of political and social change. Cases such as *Brown* (school desegregation) and *Roe* (abortion) are heralded as having produced major change. Further, such litigation has often occurred, and appears to have been most successful, when the other branches of government have failed to act. While officious government officials and rigid, unchanging institutions represent a real social force which may frustrate popular opinion, this litigation activity suggests that courts can produce significant social reform even when the other branches of government are inactive or opposed. Indeed, for many, part of what makes American democracy exceptional is that it includes the world's most powerful court system, protecting minorities and defending liberty, in the face of opposition from the democratically elected branches. Americans look to activist courts, then, as fulfilling an important role in the American scheme.[1] This view of the courts, although informed by recent historical experience, is essentially functional. It sees courts as powerful, vigorous, and potent proponents of change. I refer to this view of the role of the courts as the "Dynamic Court" view.

As attractive as the Dynamic Court view may be, one must guard against uncritical acceptance. Indeed, in a political system that gives sovereignty to the popular will and makes economic decisions through the market, it is not obvious why courts should have the effects it asserts. Maybe its attractiveness is based on something more than effects? Could it be that the self-understanding of the judiciary and legal profession leads to an overstatement of the role of the courts, a "mystification" of the judiciary? If judges see themselves as powerful; if the Bar views itself as influential, and insulated; if professional training in law schools inculcates students with such beliefs, might these factors inflate the self-importance of the judiciary? The Dynamic Court view may be supported, then, because it offers psychological payoffs to key actors by confirming self-images, not because it is correct.[2] And when this "mystification" is added to a normative belief in the courts as the guardian of fundamental rights and liberties—what Scheingold (1974) calls the "myth of rights"—the allure of the Dynamic Court view may grow.

Further, for all its "obviousness," the Dynamic Court view has a well-established functional and historical competitor. In fact, there is a long tradition of legal scholarship that views the federal judiciary, in Alexander Hamilton's famous language, as the "least dangerous" branch of government. Here, too, there is something of a truism about this claim. Courts, we know, lack both budgetary and physical powers. Because, in Hamilton's words, they lack power over either the "sword or the purse," their ability to produce political and social change is limited. In contrast to the first view, the "least dangerous" branch can do little more than point out how actions have fallen short of constitutional or legislative requirements and hope that appropriate action is taken. The strength of this view, of course, is that it leaves Americans free to govern themselves without interference from non-elected officials. I refer to this view of the courts as weak, ineffective, and powerless as the "Constrained Court" view.

The Constrained Court view fully acknowledges the role of popular preferences and social and economic resources in shaping outcomes. Yet it seems to rely excessively on a formal-process understanding of how change occurs in American politics. But the formal process doesn't always work, for social and political forces may be overly responsive to unevenly distributed resources. Bureaucratic inertia, too, can derail orderly, processional change. There is room, then, for courts to effectively correct the pathologies of the political process. Perhaps accurate at the founding of the political system, the Constrained Court view may miss growth and change in the American political system.

Clearly, these two views, and the aspirations they represent, are in conflict on a number of different dimensions. They differ not only on both the desirability and the effectiveness of court action, but also on the nature of American democracy. The Dynamic Court view gives courts an important place in the American political system while the older view sees courts as much less powerful than other more "political" branches and activities. The conflict is more than one of mere definition, for each view captures a very different part of American democracy. We Americans want courts to protect minorities and defend liberties, *and* to defer to elected officials. We want a robust political life *and* one that is just. Most of the time, these two visions do not clash. American legislatures do not habitually threaten liberties, and courts do not regularly invalidate the acts of elected officials or require certain actions to be taken. But the most interesting and relevant cases, such as *Brown* and *Roe*, occur when activist courts overrule and invalidate the actions of elected officials, or order actions beyond what elected officials are willing to do. What happens then? Are courts effective producers of change, as the Dynamic Court view suggests, or do their decisions do little more than point the way to a brighter, but perhaps unobtainable future? Once again, this conflict between two deeply held views about the role of the courts in the American political system has an obvious normative dimension that is worth debating.

■　　■　　■

THE DYNAMIC AND THE CONSTRAINED COURT

■　　■　　■

Structural Constraints: The Logic of the Constrained Court View

The view of courts as unable to produce significant social reform has a distinguished pedigree reaching back to the founders. Premised on the institutional structure of the American political system and the procedures and belief systems created by American law, it suggests that the conditions required for courts to produce significant social reform will seldom exist.

■   ■   ■

[T]he Constrained Court view holds that litigants asking courts for significant social reform are faced with powerful constraints. First, they must convince courts that the rights they are asserting are required by constitutional or statutory language. Given the limited nature of constitutional rights, the constraints of legal culture, and the general caution of the judiciary, this is no easy task. Second, courts are wary of stepping too far out of the political mainstream. Deferential to the federal government and potentially limited by congressional action, courts may be unwilling to take the heat generated by politically unpopular rulings. Third, if these two constraints are overcome and cases are decided favorably, litigants are faced with the task of implementing the decisions. Lacking powerful tools to force implementation, court decisions are often rendered useless given much opposition. Even if litigators seeking significant social reform win major victories in court, in implementation they often turn out to be worth very little. Borrowing the words of Justice Jackson from another context, the Constrained Court view holds that court litigation to produce significant social reform may amount to little more than "a teasing illusion like a munificent bequest in a pauper's will" (*Edwards* v. *California* 1941, 186).

Court Effectiveness: The Logic of the Dynamic Court View

The three constraints just presented are generated from the view of courts as unable to produce significant social reform. That view appears historically grounded and empirically plausible. Yet, on reflection, it has two main difficulties. First, it seems to overstate the limits on courts. After all, since the mid-twentieth century or so courts have been embroiled in controversies over significant social reform. Many lawyers, activists, and scholars have acted or written with the belief that the constraints are weak or non-existent and can easily be overcome. Indeed, the whole modern debate over judicial activism makes no sense if the Constrained Court view is correct. If courts are as impotent as the constraints suggest, then why has there been such political, academic, and judicial concern with the role of courts in modern America? Theory and practice are unaligned if the Constrained Court view is entirely correct. Second, examined carefully, its claim is that courts are *unlikely* to produce significant social reform; it does not deny the possibility. However, that doesn't help us understand when, and under what conditions, courts can produce significant social reform. The Constrained Court view is not the complete answer.

The Dynamic Court view may help. It maintains that courts can be effective producers of significant social reform. Its basic thrust is that not only are courts not as limited as the Constrained Court view suggests, but also, in some cases, they can be more effective than other governmental institutions in producing significant social reform.

Political, Institutional, and Economic Independence

▪ ▪ ▪

The Dynamic Court view provides a powerful alternative to the view of courts as the "least dangerous branch." Pointing to pathologies in the other branches, it places courts in a unique position to act. Acknowledging, perhaps, that the Constrained Court view was accurate at the Founding and for part of American history, it maintains that great change has occurred over the last few decades and that courts now have the tools to effectively produce significant social reform. Unlike the Constrained Court view, it is congruent with judicial activism and the modern use of the courts to produce significant social reform. While courts cannot solve all problems, the Dynamic Court view does see them as powerful and effective, unconstrained by the concentrations of power and bureaucratic inertia that stymie self-initiated change in the other branches.

▪ ▪ ▪

Yet for all their plausibility and surface appeal, and their seemingly accurate description of recent litigation, attempts to ground the Dynamic Court view empirically are not entirely satisfying. Unfortunately, studies of the sort referred to above neither completely validate it nor are particularly helpful in constructing hypotheses about courts' effectiveness in producing significant social reform. Often, they either focus on unrepresentative time periods, or on unimportant and noncontroversial cases, or they overstate their findings. In addition, many of the studies that support the Dynamic Court view are theoretical rather than empirical. They mistake what conceivably could happen with what actually has happened. Further, the empirical studies tend to examine only one case. The problem here, from the Constrained Court perspective, is that given the constraints on judges imposed by court rules and the legal culture, it is the rare judge who will become so actively engaged. Although the Dynamic Court view may be correct, the empirical evidence offered in its support does not seal the case.

▪ ▪ ▪

With special masters, again, actual case studies do not bear out claims on behalf of the Dynamic Court view. For example, introducing an edited compilation of seven studies of school desegregation, Kalodner concludes that "masters have seldom if ever been effective in the effort to find a solution that is both acceptable and constitutional" (Kalodner 1978, 9). Reviewing the use of masters in six school desegregation cases, Kirp and Babcock explicitly reject Aronow's optimistic conclusions (Kirp and Babcock 1981, 395). Finally, a lengthy and detailed study of institutional reform litigation points out that under court rules the use of special masters must "be the exception and not the rule. Consequently, there cannot be reference to masters as a matter of course" (Special Project 1978, 808). While special masters may be helpful in some cases, overall their record of use appears of limited effectiveness. And the crucial question of under what conditions special masters will be effective is left unanswered.

The Dynamic Court view, then, though in large part an effective retort to the unbending constraints of the Constrained Court view, does not get us very far in understanding the conditions under which courts can produce significant social reform. While its logic of independence and equal access makes good sense, its lack of generalizable empirical support is unhelpful. In sum, while courts may be more effective in producing significant social reform than the constraints of the Constrained Court view allow, the Dynamic Court view does not definitively demonstrate when, and under what conditions, court efficacy can be found.

Conditions for Court Efficacy

The thrust of the Dynamic Court view is that its competitor oversimplifies reality by *under*stating court effectiveness. However, it appears that the Dynamic Court view likewise oversimplifies, by *over*stating court effectiveness. Further, the views appear to be in conflict. For example, the Dynamic Court view proposes court action in the face of hostile or inert political institutions while the constraints of the Constrained Court view tell us that in such situations success is least likely. Along with conflict, however, each view appears to convey something of the truth. On an intuitive level, opposition from political elites is not conducive to court effectiveness. On the other hand, judicial isolation from many pressures allows courts to act when other institutions wish to but cannot. Surely it is naive to expect courts to be able to solve political and economic problems that the other branches cannot. But it appears equally short-sighted to deny that since mid-century courts have played an important role in producing significant social reform. It may well be that while each view captures part of the truth, neither is fine-grained enough to capture the conditions under which courts can effectively produce significant social reform.

. . . I suggest that this is the case; the constraints of the Constrained Court view generally limit courts, but when political, social, and economic conditions have become supportive of change, courts can effectively produce significant social reform. . . . [T]he conditions enabling courts to produce significant social reform will seldom be present because courts are limited by three separate constraints built into the structure of the American political system:

1. The limited nature of constitutional rights . . .
2. The lack of judicial independence . . .
3. The judiciary's lack of powers of implementation . . .

However, when certain conditions are met, courts can be effective producers of significant social reform. These conditions occur when:

1. . . . There is ample legal precedent for change; *and*,
2. . . . There is support for change from substantial numbers in Congress and from the executive; *and*,
3. . . . There is either support from some citizens, or at least low levels of opposition from all citizens.

NOTES

1. Not everyone, however, thinks such liberal judicial activism is a good thing. It has spawned a wave of attacks on the judiciary ranging from Nathan Glazer's warning of the rise of an "imperial judiciary" to a spate of legislative proposals to remove court jurisdiction over a number of issues. See Glazer (1975); *An Imperial Judiciary* (1979). And, of course, Presidents Nixon and Reagan pledged to end judicial activism by appointing "strict constructionists" to the federal courts.

2. As McCann (1986, 114) suggests, in the public-interest movement, lawyers are "quite naturally the most ardent spokespersons" for the use of courts to produce change.

CASE REFERENCES

Edwards v. *California*, 314 U.S. 160 (1941).
Brown vs. Board of Education of Topeka, 347 U.S. 483 (1954).
Roe v. *Wade*, 410 U.S. 113 (1973).

REFERENCES

Aronow, Geoffrey F. 1980. "The Special Master in School Desegregation Cases: The Evolution of Roles in the Reformation of Public Institutions through Litigation." 7 *Hastings Const. L. Q.* 739.

Glazer, Nathan. 1975. "Towards an Imperial Judiciary?" *The Public Interest* (Fall): 104–23.

An Imperial Judiciary: Fact or Myth? 1979. Washington, DC: American Enterprise Institute.

Kalodner, Howard I. 1978. Introduction. In *Limits to Justice*. Eds. Howard I. Kalodner, and James J. Fishman. Cambridge, MA: Ballinger. 1–24.

Kirp, David L., and Gary Babcock. 1981. "Judge and Company: Court Appointed Masters, School Desegregation, and Institutional Reform." In "Symposium, Judicially Managed Institutional Reform." 32 *Alabama L. Rev.* 317.

McCann, Michael. 1986. *Taking Reform Seriously: Perspectives on Public Interest Liberalism*. Ithaca: Cornell University Press.

Scheingold, Stuart A. 1974. *The Politics of Rights: Lawyers, Public Policy, and Political Change*. New Haven, CT: Yale University Press.

Special Project. 1978. "The Remedial Process in Institutional Reform Litigation." 78 *Colum. L. Rev.* 784.

8.2

Marbury v. Madison (1803)

This foundational Supreme Court decision was a bold move by the Court to establish its central role in the national government. In writing this opinion, Chief Justice John Marshall laid out the case in favor of the Supreme Court having the final say in determining whether a law or action of the government is constitutional. By declaring that "it is emphatically the province and duty of the judicial department to say what the law is," this opinion establishes judicial review as a fundamental aspect of American government.

MR. CHIEF JUSTICE MARSHALL delivered the opinion of the Court.

At the last term, on the affidavits then read and filed with the clerk, a rule was granted in this case requiring the Secretary of State to show cause why a mandamus should not issue directing him to deliver to William Marbury his commission as a justice of the peace for the county of Washington, in the District of Columbia.

No cause has been shown, and the present motion is for a mandamus. The peculiar delicacy of this case, the novelty of some of its circumstances, and the real difficulty attending the points which occur in it require a complete exposition of the principles on which the opinion to be given by the Court is founded.

These principles have been, on the side of the applicant, very ably argued at the bar. In rendering the opinion of the Court, there will be some departure in form, though not in substance, from the points stated in that argument.

If he has a right, and that right has been violated, do the laws of his country afford him a remedy?

The very essence of civil liberty certainly consists in the right of every individual to claim the protection of the laws whenever he receives an injury. One of the first duties of government is to afford that protection. In Great Britain, the King himself is sued in the respectful form of a petition, and he never fails to comply with the judgment of his court.

The Government of the United States has been emphatically termed a government of laws, and not of men. It will certainly cease to deserve this high

From *Marbury v. Madison*, 5 U.S. 137 (1803).

appellation if the laws furnish no remedy for the violation of a vested legal right.

By the act concerning invalids, passed in June, 1794, the Secretary at War is ordered to place on the pension list all persons whose names are contained in a report previously made by him to Congress. If he should refuse to do so, would the wounded veteran be without remedy? Is it to be contended that where the law, in precise terms, directs the performance of an act in which an individual is interested, the law is incapable of securing obedience to its mandate? Is it on account of the character of the person against whom the complaint is made? Is it to be contended that the heads of departments are not amenable to the laws of their country?

Whatever the practice on particular occasions may be, the theory of this principle will certainly never be maintained. No act of the Legislature confers so extraordinary a privilege, nor can it derive countenance from the doctrines of the common law.

It follows, then, that the question whether the legality of an act of the head of a department be examinable in a court of justice or not must always depend on the nature of that act.

If some acts be examinable and others not, there must be some rule of law to guide the Court in the exercise of its jurisdiction.

In some instances, there may be difficulty in applying the rule to particular cases; but there cannot, it is believed, be much difficulty in laying down the rule.

The power of nominating to the Senate, and the power of appointing the person nominated, are political powers, to be exercised by the President according to his own discretion. When he has made an appointment, he has exercised his whole power, and his discretion has been completely applied to the case. If, by law, the officer be removable at the will of the President, then a new appointment may be immediately made, and the rights of the officer are terminated. But as a fact which has existed cannot be made never to have existed, the appointment cannot be annihilated, and consequently, if the officer is by law not removable at the will of the President, the rights he has acquired are protected by the law, and are not resumable by the President. They cannot be extinguished by Executive authority, and he has the privilege of asserting them in like manner as if they had been derived from any other source.

The question whether a right has vested or not is, in its nature, judicial, and must be tried by the judicial authority. If, for example, Mr. Marbury had taken the oaths of a magistrate and proceeded to act as one, in consequence of which a suit had been instituted against him in which his defence had depended on his being a magistrate; the validity of his appointment must have been determined by judicial authority.

So, if he conceives that, by virtue of his appointment, he has a legal right either to the commission which has been made out for him or to a copy of that commission, it is equally a question examinable in a court, and the decision of the Court upon it must depend on the opinion entertained of his appointment.

It is then the opinion of the Court:

That, by signing the commission of Mr. Marbury, the President of the United States appointed him a justice of peace for the County of Washington in the District of Columbia, and that the seal of the United States, affixed thereto by the Secretary of State, is conclusive testimony of the verity of the signature, and of the completion of the appointment, and that the appointment conferred on him a legal right to the office for the space of five years.

That, having this legal title to the office, he has a consequent right to the commission, a refusal to deliver which is a plain violation of that right, for which the laws of his country afford him a remedy.

It remains to be inquired whether, he is entitled to the remedy for which he applies.

With respect to the officer to whom it would be directed. The intimate political relation, subsisting between the President of the United States and the heads of departments, necessarily renders any legal investigation of the acts of one of those high officers peculiarly irksome, as well as delicate, and excites some hesitation with respect to the propriety of entering into such investigation. Impressions are often received without much reflection or examination, and it is not wonderful that, in such a case as this, the assertion by an individual of his legal claims in a court of justice, to which claims it is the duty of that court to attend, should, at first view, be considered [p170] by some as an attempt to intrude into the cabinet and to intermeddle with the prerogatives of the Executive.

It is scarcely necessary for the Court to disclaim all pretensions to such a jurisdiction. An extravagance so absurd and excessive could not have been entertained for a moment. The province of the Court is solely to decide on the rights of individuals, not to inquire how the Executive or Executive officers perform duties in which they have a discretion. Questions, in their nature political or which are, by the Constitution and laws, submitted to the Executive, can never be made in this court.

But, if this be not such a question; if so far from being an intrusion into the secrets of the cabinet, it respects a paper which, according to law, is upon record, and to a copy of which the law gives a right, on the payment of ten cents; if it be no intermeddling with a subject over which the Executive can be considered as having exercised any control; what is there in the exalted station of the officer which shall bar a citizen from asserting in a court of justice his legal rights, or shall forbid a court to listen to the claim or to issue a mandamus directing the performance of a duty not depending on Executive discretion, but on particular acts of Congress and the general principles of law?

If one of the heads of departments commits any illegal act under colour of his office by which an individual sustains an injury, it cannot be pretended that his office alone exempts him from being sued in the ordinary mode of proceeding, and being compelled to obey the judgment of the law. How then can his office exempt him from this particular mode of deciding on the legality of his conduct if the case be such a case as would, were any other individual the party complained of, authorize the process?

It is not by the office of the person to whom the writ is directed, but the nature of the thing to be done, that the propriety or impropriety of issuing a mandamus is to be determined. Where the head of a department acts in a case in which Executive discretion is to be exercised, in which he is the mere organ of Executive will, it is again repeated, that any application to a court to control, in any respect, his conduct, would be rejected without hesitation.

But where he is directed by law to do a certain act affecting the absolute rights of individuals, in the performance of which he is not placed under the particular direction of the President, and the performance of which the President cannot lawfully forbid, and therefore is never presumed to have forbidden—as for example, to record a commission, or a patent for land, which has received all the legal solemnities; or to give a copy of such record—in such cases, it is not perceived on what ground the Courts of the country are further excused from the duty of giving judgment that right to be done to an injured individual than if the same services were to be performed by a person not the head of a department.

This opinion seems not now for the first time to be taken up in this country.

It is true that the mandamus now moved for is not for the performance of an act expressly enjoined by statute.

It is to deliver a commission, on which subjects the acts of Congress are silent. This difference is not considered as affecting the case. It has already been stated that the applicant has, to that commission, a vested legal right of which the Executive cannot deprive him. He has been appointed to an office from which he is not removable at the will of the Executive, and, being so appointed, he has a right to the commission which the Secretary has received from the President for his use. The act of Congress does not, indeed, order the Secretary of State to send it to him, but it is placed in his hands for the person entitled to it, and cannot be more lawfully withheld by him than by another person.

This is a plain case of a mandamus, either to deliver the commission or a copy of it from the record, and it only remains to be inquired:

Whether it can issue from this Court.

The act to establish the judicial courts of the United States authorizes the Supreme Court to issue writs of mandamus, in cases warranted by the principles and usages of law, to any courts appointed, or persons holding office, under the authority of the United States.

The Secretary of State, being a person, holding an office under the authority of the United States, is precisely within the letter of the description, and if this Court is not authorized to issue a writ of mandamus to such an officer, it must be because the law is unconstitutional, and therefore absolutely incapable of conferring the authority and assigning the duties which its words purport to confer and assign.

The Constitution vests the whole judicial power of the United States in one Supreme Court, and such inferior courts as Congress shall, from time to time, ordain and establish. This power is expressly extended to all cases arising under the laws of the United States; and consequently, in some form, may be exercised over the present case, because the right claimed is given by a law of the United States.

In the distribution of this power. it is declared that the Supreme Court shall have original jurisdiction in all cases affecting ambassadors, other public ministers and consuls, and those in which a state shall be a party. In all other cases, the Supreme Court shall have appellate jurisdiction.

It has been insisted at the bar, that, as the original grant of jurisdiction to the Supreme and inferior courts is general, and the clause assigning original jurisdiction to the Supreme Court contains no negative or restrictive words, the power remains to the Legislature to assign original jurisdiction to that Court in other cases than those specified in the article which has been recited, provided those cases belong to the judicial power of the United States.

If it had been intended to leave it in the discretion of the Legislature to apportion the judicial power between the Supreme and inferior courts according to the will of that body, it would certainly have been useless to have proceeded further than to have defined the judicial power and the tribunals in which it should be vested. The subsequent part of the section is mere surplusage—is entirely without meaning—if such is to be the construction. If Congress remains at liberty to give this court appellate jurisdiction where the Constitution has declared their jurisdiction shall be original, and original jurisdiction where the Constitution has declared it shall be appellate, the distribution of jurisdiction made in the Constitution, is form without substance.

Affirmative words are often, in their operation, negative of other objects than those affirmed, and, in this case, a negative or exclusive sense must be given to them or they have no operation at all.

It cannot be presumed that any clause in the Constitution is intended to be without effect, and therefore such construction is inadmissible unless the words require it.

If the solicitude of the Convention respecting our peace with foreign powers induced a provision that the Supreme Court should take original jurisdiction in cases which might be supposed to affect them, yet the clause would have proceeded no further than to provide for such cases if no further restriction on the powers of Congress had been intended. That they should have appellate jurisdiction in all other cases, with such exceptions as Congress might make, is no restriction unless the words be deemed exclusive of original jurisdiction.

When an instrument organizing fundamentally a judicial system divides it into one Supreme and so many inferior courts as the Legislature may ordain and establish, then enumerates its powers, and proceeds so far to distribute them as to define the jurisdiction of the Supreme Court by declaring the cases in which it shall take original jurisdiction, and that in others it shall take appellate jurisdiction, the plain import of the words seems to be that, in one class of cases, its jurisdiction is original, and not appellate; in the other, it is appellate, and not original. If any other construction would render the clause inoperative, that is an additional reason for rejecting such other construction, and for adhering to the obvious meaning.

To enable this court then to issue a mandamus, it must be shown to be an exercise of appellate jurisdiction, or to be necessary to enable them to exercise appellate jurisdiction.

The authority, therefore, given to the Supreme Court by the act establishing the judicial courts of the United States to issue writs of mandamus to public officers appears not to be warranted by the Constitution, and it becomes necessary to inquire whether a jurisdiction so conferred can be exercised.

This original and supreme will organizes the government and assigns to different departments their respective powers. It may either stop here or establish certain limits not to be transcended by those departments.

The Government of the United States is of the latter description. The powers of the Legislature are defined and limited; and that those limits may not be mistaken or forgotten, the Constitution is written. To what purpose are powers limited, and to what purpose is that limitation committed to writing, if these limits may at any time be passed by those intended to be restrained? The distinction between a government with limited and unlimited powers is abolished if those limits do not confine the persons on whom they are imposed, and if acts prohibited and acts allowed are of equal obligation. It is a proposition too plain to be contested that the Constitution controls any legislative act repugnant to it, or that the Legislature may alter the Constitution by an ordinary act.

Between these alternatives there is no middle ground. The Constitution is either a superior, paramount law, unchangeable by ordinary means, or it is on a level with ordinary legislative acts, and, like other acts, is alterable when the legislature shall please to alter it.

If the former part of the alternative be true, then a legislative act contrary to the Constitution is not law; if the latter part be true, then written Constitutions are absurd attempts on the part of the people to limit a power in its own nature illimitable.

Certainly all those who have framed written Constitutions contemplate them as forming the fundamental and paramount law of the nation, and consequently the theory of every such government must be that an act of the Legislature repugnant to the Constitution is void.

This theory is essentially attached to a written Constitution, and is consequently to be considered by this Court as one of the fundamental principles of our society. It is not, therefore, to be lost sight of in the further consideration of this subject.

If an act of the Legislature repugnant to the Constitution is void, does it, notwithstanding its invalidity, bind the Courts and oblige them to give it effect? Or, in other words, though it be not law, does it constitute a rule as operative as if it was a law? This would be to overthrow in fact what was established in theory, and would seem, at first view, an absurdity too gross to be insisted on. It shall, however, receive a more attentive consideration.

It is emphatically the province and duty of the Judicial Department to say what the law is. Those who apply the rule to particular cases must, of necessity, expound and interpret that rule. If two laws conflict with each other, the Courts must decide on the operation of each.

So, if a law be in opposition to the Constitution, if both the law and the Constitution apply to a particular case, so that the Court must either decide that case conformably to the law, disregarding the Constitution, or conformably to the Constitution, disregarding the law, the Court must determine which of these conflicting rules governs the case. This is of the very essence of judicial duty.

If, then, the Courts are to regard the Constitution, and the Constitution is superior to any ordinary act of the Legislature, the Constitution, and not such ordinary act, must govern the case to which they both apply.

Those, then, who controvert the principle that the Constitution is to be considered in court as a paramount law are reduced to the necessity of maintaining that courts must close their eyes on the Constitution, and see only the law.

This doctrine would subvert the very foundation of all written Constitutions. It would declare that an act which, according to the principles and theory of our government, is entirely void, is yet, in practice, completely obligatory. It would declare that, if the Legislature shall do what is expressly forbidden, such act, notwithstanding the express prohibition, is in reality effectual. It would be giving to the Legislature a practical and real omnipotence with the same breath which professes to restrict their powers within narrow limits. It is prescribing limits, and declaring that those limits may be passed at pleasure.

That it thus reduces to nothing what we have deemed the greatest improvement on political institutions—a written Constitution, would of itself be sufficient, in America where written Constitutions have been viewed with so much reverence, for rejecting the construction. But the peculiar expressions of the Constitution of the United States furnish additional arguments in favour of its rejection.

The judicial power of the United States is extended to all cases arising under the Constitution.

Could it be the intention of those who gave this power to say that, in using it, the Constitution should not be looked into? That a case arising under the Constitution should be decided without examining the instrument under which it arises?

This is too extravagant to be maintained.

In some cases then, the Constitution must be looked into by the judges. And if they can open it at all, what part of it are they forbidden to read or to obey?

There are many other parts of the Constitution which serve to illustrate this subject.

It is declared that "no tax or duty shall be laid on articles exported from any State." Suppose a duty on the export of cotton, of tobacco, or of flour, and a suit instituted to recover it. Ought judgment to be rendered in such a case? ought the judges to close their eyes on the Constitution, and only see the law?

The Constitution declares that "no bill of attainder or *ex post facto* law shall be passed."

If, however, such a bill should be passed and a person should be prosecuted under it, must the Court condemn to death those victims whom the Constitution endeavours to preserve?

"No person," says the Constitution, "shall be convicted of treason unless on the testimony of two witnesses to the same overt act, or on confession in open court."

Here, the language of the Constitution is addressed especially to the Courts. It prescribes, directly for them, a rule of evidence not to be departed from. If the Legislature should change that rule, and declare one witness, or a confession out of court, sufficient for conviction, must the constitutional principle yield to the legislative act?

From these and many other selections which might be made, it is apparent that the framers of the Constitution contemplated that instrument as a rule for the government of courts, as well as of the Legislature.

Why otherwise does it direct the judges to take an oath to support it? This oath certainly applies in an especial manner to their conduct in their official character. How immoral to impose it on them if they were to be used as the instruments, and the knowing instruments, for violating what they swear to support!

The oath of office, too, imposed by the Legislature, is completely demonstrative of the legislative opinion on this subject. It is in these words: I do solemnly swear that I will administer justice without respect to persons, and do equal right to the poor and to the rich; and that I will faithfully and impartially discharge all the duties incumbent on me as according to the best of my abilities and understanding, agreeably to the Constitution and laws of the United States.

Why does a judge swear to discharge his duties agreeably to the Constitution of the United States if that Constitution forms no rule for his government? if it is closed upon him and cannot be inspected by him?

If such be the real state of things, this is worse than solemn mockery. To prescribe or to take this oath becomes equally a crime.

It is also not entirely unworthy of observation that, in declaring what shall be the supreme law of the land, the Constitution itself is first mentioned, and not the laws of the United States generally, but those only which shall be made in pursuance of the Constitution, have that rank.

Thus, the particular phraseology of the Constitution of the United States confirms and strengthens the principle, supposed to be essential to all written Constitutions, that a law repugnant to the Constitution is void, and that courts, as well as other departments, are bound by that instrument.

The rule must be discharged.

8.3

Lawrence v. Texas (2003)

In 2003, 17 years after the Bowers v. Hardwick *decision that let stand state laws against sodomy, the Supreme Court reversed itself and declared that a Texas law banning homosexual sodomy was unconstitutional. The majority decided that state laws banning private sexual activity between consenting adults violated the constitutional right to privacy.*

JUSTICE KENNEDY delivered the opinion of the Court.

Liberty protects the person from unwarranted government intrusions into a dwelling or other private places. In our tradition the State is not omnipresent in the home. And there are other spheres of our lives and existence, outside the home, where the State should not be a dominant presence. Freedom extends beyond spatial bounds. Liberty presumes an autonomy of self that includes freedom of thought, belief, expression, and certain intimate conduct. The instant case involves liberty of the person both in its spatial and more transcendent dimensions.

I

The question before the Court is the validity of a Texas statute making it a crime for two persons of the same sex to engage in certain intimate sexual conduct.

In Houston, Texas, officers of the Harris County Police Department were dispatched to a private residence in response to a reported weapons disturbance. They entered an apartment where one of the petitioners, John Geddes Lawrence, resided. The right of the police to enter does not seem to have been questioned. The officers observed Lawrence and another man, Tyron Garner, engaging in a sexual act. The two petitioners were arrested, held in custody over night, and charged and convicted before a Justice of the Peace.

The complaints described their crime as "deviate sexual intercourse, namely anal sex, with a member of the same sex (man)." The applicable state law is Tex. Penal Code Ann. §21.06(a) (2003). It provides: "A person commits an

From *Lawrence v. Texas*, 539 U.S. 558 (2003).

offense if he engages in deviate sexual intercourse with another individual of the same sex." The statute defines "[d]eviate sexual intercourse" as follows:

> "(A) any contact between any part of the genitals of one person and the mouth or anus of another person; or
> "(B) the penetration of the genitals or the anus of another person with an object."

The petitioners exercised their right to a trial *de novo* in Harris County Criminal Court. They challenged the statute as a violation of the Equal Protection Clause of the Fourteenth Amendment and of a like provision of the Texas Constitution. Tex. Const., Art. 1, §3a. Those contentions were rejected. The petitioners, having entered a plea of *nolo contendere*, were each fined $200 and assessed court costs of $141.25.

The Court of Appeals for the Texas Fourteenth District considered the petitioners' federal constitutional arguments under both the Equal Protection and Due Process Clauses of the Fourteenth Amendment. After hearing the case en banc the court, in a divided opinion, rejected the constitutional arguments and affirmed the convictions. The majority opinion indicates that the Court of Appeals considered our decision in *Bowers v. Hardwick* (1986), to be controlling on the federal due process aspect of the case. *Bowers* then being authoritative, this was proper.

We granted certiorari, to consider three questions:

1. Whether Petitioners' criminal convictions under the Texas "Homosexual Conduct" law—which criminalizes sexual intimacy by same-sex couples, but not identical behavior by different-sex couples—violate the Fourteenth Amendment guarantee of equal protection of laws?
2. Whether Petitioners' criminal convictions for adult consensual sexual intimacy in the home violate their vital interests in liberty and privacy protected by the Due Process Clause of the Fourteenth Amendment?
3. Whether *Bowers v. Hardwick*, should be overruled?

The petitioners were adults at the time of the alleged offense. Their conduct was in private and consensual.

II

We conclude the case should be resolved by determining whether the petitioners were free as adults to engage in the private conduct in the exercise of their liberty under the Due Process Clause of the Fourteenth Amendment to the Constitution. For this inquiry we deem it necessary to reconsider the Court's holding in *Bowers*.

There are broad statements of the substantive reach of liberty under the Due Process Clause in earlier cases, including *Pierce v. Society of Sisters* (1925), and *Meyer v. Nebraska* (1923); but the most pertinent beginning point is our decision in *Griswold v. Connecticut* (1965).

In *Griswold* the Court invalidated a state law prohibiting the use of drugs or devices of contraception and counseling or aiding and abetting the use of contraceptives. The Court described the protected interest as a right to privacy and placed emphasis on the marriage relation and the protected space of the marital bedroom.

After *Griswold* it was established that the right to make certain decisions regarding sexual conduct extends beyond the marital relationship. In *Eisenstadt v. Baird* (1972), the Court invalidated a law prohibiting the distribution of contraceptives to unmarried persons. The case was decided under the Equal Protection Clause; but with respect to unmarried persons, the Court went on to state the fundamental proposition that the law impaired the exercise of their personal rights. It quoted from the statement of the Court of Appeals finding the law to be in conflict with fundamental human rights, and it followed with this statement of its own:

> It is true that in *Griswold* the right of privacy in question inhered in the marital relationship. . . . If the right of privacy means anything, it is the right of the *individual*, married or single, to be free from unwarranted governmental intrusion into matters so fundamentally affecting a person as the decision whether to bear or beget a child.

The opinions in *Griswold* and *Eisenstadt* were part of the background for the decision in *Roe v. Wade* (1973). As is well known, the case involved a challenge to the Texas law prohibiting abortions, but the laws of other States were affected as well. Although the Court held the woman's rights were not absolute, her right to elect an abortion did have real and substantial protection as an exercise of her liberty under the Due Process Clause. The Court cited cases that protect spatial freedom and cases that go well beyond it. *Roe* recognized the right of a woman to make certain fundamental decisions affecting her destiny and confirmed once more that the protection of liberty under the Due Process Clause has a substantive dimension of fundamental significance in defining the rights of the person.

In *Carey v. Population Services Int'l* (1977), the Court confronted a New York law forbidding sale or distribution of contraceptive devices to persons under 16 years of age. Although there was no single opinion for the Court, the law was invalidated. Both *Eisenstadt* and *Carey*, as well as the holding and rationale in *Roe*, confirmed that the reasoning of *Griswold* could not be confined to the protection of rights of married adults. This was the state of the law with respect to some of the most relevant cases when the Court considered *Bowers v. Hardwick*.

The facts in *Bowers* had some similarities to the instant case. A police officer, whose right to enter seems not to have been in question, observed Hardwick, in his own bedroom, engaging in intimate sexual conduct with another adult male. The conduct was in violation of a Georgia statute making it a criminal offense to engage in sodomy. One difference between the two cases is that the Georgia statute prohibited the conduct whether or not the participants were of the same sex, while the Texas statute, as we have seen, applies only to participants of the same sex. Hardwick was not prosecuted, but he brought an action in federal court to declare the state statute invalid. He alleged he was a practicing homosexual and that the criminal prohibition violated rights guaranteed to him by the Constitution. The Court, in an opinion by Justice White, sustained the Georgia law. Chief Justice Burger and Justice Powell joined the opinion of the Court and filed separate, concurring opinions. Four Justices dissented. (opinion of Blackmun, J., joined by Brennan, Marshall, and Stevens, JJ.); (opinion of Stevens, J., joined by Brennan and Marshall, JJ.).

The Court began its substantive discussion in *Bowers* as follows: "The issue presented is whether the Federal Constitution confers a fundamental right upon homosexuals to engage in sodomy and hence invalidates the laws of the many States that still make such conduct illegal and have done so for a very long time." That statement, we now conclude, discloses the Court's own failure to appreciate the extent of the liberty at stake. To say that the issue in *Bowers* was simply the right to engage in certain sexual conduct demeans the claim the individual put forward, just as it would demean a married couple were it to be said marriage is simply about the right to have sexual intercourse. The laws involved in *Bowers* and here are, to be sure, statutes that purport to do no more than prohibit a particular sexual act. Their penalties and purposes, though, have more far-reaching consequences, touching upon the most private human conduct, sexual behavior, and in the most private of places, the home. The statutes do seek to control a personal relationship that, whether or not entitled to formal recognition in the law, is within the liberty of persons to choose without being punished as criminals.

This, as a general rule, should counsel against attempts by the State, or a court, to define the meaning of the relationship or to set its boundaries absent injury to a person or abuse of an institution the law protects. It suffices for us to acknowledge that adults may choose to enter upon this relationship in the confines of their homes and their own private lives and still retain their dignity as free persons. When sexuality finds overt expression in intimate conduct with another person, the conduct can be but one element in a personal bond that is more enduring. The liberty protected by the Constitution allows homosexual persons the right to make this choice.

Having misapprehended the claim of liberty there presented to it, and thus stating the claim to be whether there is a fundamental right to engage in consensual sodomy, the *Bowers* Court said: "Proscriptions against that conduct have ancient roots." In academic writings, and in many of the scholarly *amicus* briefs filed to assist the Court in this case, there are fundamental criticisms of the historical premises relied upon by the majority and concurring opinions in *Bowers*. We need not enter this debate in the attempt to reach a definitive historical judgment, but the following considerations counsel against adopting the definitive conclusions upon which *Bowers* placed such reliance.

At the outset it should be noted that there is no longstanding history in this country of laws directed at homosexual conduct as a distinct matter. Beginning in colonial times there were prohibitions of sodomy derived from the English criminal laws passed in the first instance by the Reformation Parliament of 1533. The English prohibition was understood to include relations between men and women as well as relations between men and men. Nineteenth-century commentators similarly read American sodomy, buggery, and crime-against-nature statutes as criminalizing certain relations between men and women and between men and men. The absence of legal prohibitions focusing on homosexual conduct may be explained in part by noting that according to some scholars the concept of the homosexual as a distinct category of person did not emerge until the late 19th century. Thus early American sodomy laws were not directed at homosexuals as such but instead sought to prohibit nonprocreative sexual activity more generally. This does not suggest approval of homosexual conduct. It does tend to show that this particular form of conduct was not thought of as a separate category from like conduct between heterosexual persons.

Laws prohibiting sodomy do not seem to have been enforced against consenting adults acting in private. A substantial number of sodomy prosecutions and convictions for which there are surviving records were for predatory acts against those who could not or did not consent, as in the case of a minor or the victim of an assault. As to these, one purpose for the prohibitions was to ensure there would be no lack of coverage if a predator committed a sexual assault that did not constitute rape as defined by the criminal law. Thus the model sodomy indictments presented in a 19th-century treatise, addressed the predatory acts of an adult man against a minor girl or minor boy. Instead of targeting relations between consenting adults in private, 19th-century sodomy prosecutions typically involved relations between men and minor girls or minor boys, relations between adults involving force, relations between adults implicating disparity in status, or relations between men and animals.

To the extent that there were any prosecutions for the acts in question, 19th-century evidence rules imposed a burden that would make a conviction more difficult to obtain even taking into account the problems always inherent in prosecuting consensual acts committed in private. Under then-prevailing standards, a man could not be convicted of sodomy based upon testimony of a consenting partner, because the partner was considered an accomplice. A partner's testimony, however, was admissible if he or she had not consented to the act or was a minor, and therefore incapable of consent. The rule may explain in part the infrequency of these prosecutions. In all events that infrequency makes it difficult to say that society approved of a rigorous and systematic punishment of the consensual acts committed in private and by adults.

The longstanding criminal prohibition of homosexual sodomy upon which the *Bowers* decision placed such reliance is as consistent with a general condemnation of nonprocreative sex as it is with an established tradition of prosecuting acts because of their homosexual character.

The policy of punishing consenting adults for private acts was not much discussed in the early legal literature. We can infer that one reason for this was the very private nature of the conduct. Despite the absence of prosecutions, there may have been periods in which there was public criticism of homosexuals as such and an insistence that the criminal laws be enforced to discourage their practices. But far from possessing "ancient roots," American laws targeting same-sex couples did not develop until the last third of the 20th century. The reported decisions concerning the prosecution of consensual, homosexual sodomy between adults for the years 1880–1995 are not always clear in the details, but a significant number involved conduct in a public place.

It was not until the 1970s that any State singled out same-sex relations for criminal prosecution, and only nine States have done so. Post-*Bowers* even some of these States did not adhere to the policy of suppressing homosexual conduct. Over the course of the last decades, States with same-sex prohibitions have moved toward abolishing them.

In summary, the historical grounds relied upon in *Bowers* are more complex than the majority opinion and the concurring opinion by Chief Justice Burger indicate. Their historical premises are not without doubt and, at the very least, are overstated.

It must be acknowledged, of course, that the Court in *Bowers* was making the broader point that for centuries there have been powerful voices to condemn homosexual conduct as immoral. The condemnation has been shaped by religious beliefs, conceptions of right and acceptable behavior, and respect for the traditional family. For many persons these are not trivial concerns but profound and deep convictions accepted as ethical and moral principles to which they aspire and which thus determine the course of their lives. These considerations do not answer the question before us, however. The issue is whether the majority may use the power of the State to enforce these views on the whole society through operation of the criminal law. "Our obligation is to define the liberty of all, not to mandate our own moral code." *Planned Parenthood of Southeastern Pa. v. Casey* (1992).

Chief Justice Burger joined the opinion for the Court in *Bowers* and further explained his views as follows: "Decisions of individuals relating to homosexual conduct have been subject to state intervention throughout the history of Western civilization. Condemnation of those practices is firmly rooted in Judeao-Christian moral and ethical standards." 478 U.S. 196. As with Justice White's assumptions about history, scholarship casts some doubt on the sweeping nature of the statement by Chief Justice Burger as it pertains to private homosexual conduct between consenting adults. In all events we think that our laws and traditions in the past half century are of most relevance here. These references show an emerging awareness that liberty gives substantial protection to adult persons in deciding how to conduct their private lives in matters pertaining to sex. "[H]istory and tradition are the starting point but not in all cases the ending point of the substantive due process inquiry." *County of Sacramento v. Lewis* (1998) (Kennedy, J., concurring).

This emerging recognition should have been apparent when *Bowers* was decided. In 1955 the American Law Institute promulgated the Model Penal Code and made clear that it did not recommend or provide for "criminal penalties for consensual sexual relations conducted in private." It justified its decision on three grounds: (1) The prohibitions undermined respect for the law by penalizing conduct many people engaged in; (2) the statutes regulated private conduct not harmful to others; and (3) the laws were arbitrarily enforced and thus invited the danger of blackmail. In 1961 Illinois changed its laws to conform to the Model Penal Code. Other States soon followed.

In *Bowers* the Court referred to the fact that before 1961 all 50 States had outlawed sodomy, and that at the time of the Court's decision 24 States and the District of Columbia had sodomy laws. Justice Powell pointed out that these prohibitions often were being ignored, however. Georgia, for instance, had not sought to enforce its law for decades.

The sweeping references by Chief Justice Burger to the history of Western civilization and to Judeo-Christian moral and ethical standards did not take account of other authorities pointing in an opposite direction. A committee advising the British Parliament recommended in 1957 repeal of laws punishing homosexual conduct. Parliament enacted the substance of those recommendations 10 years later.

Of even more importance, almost five years before *Bowers* was decided the European Court of Human Rights considered a case with parallels to *Bowers* and to today's case. An adult male resident in Northern Ireland alleged he was a practicing homosexual who desired to engage in consensual homosexual conduct. The laws of Northern Ireland forbade him that right. He alleged that he had been questioned, his home had been searched, and he feared criminal prosecution. The court held that the laws proscribing the conduct were invalid under the European Convention on Human Rights. Authoritative in all countries that are members of the Council of Europe (21 nations then, 45 nations now), the decision is at odds with the premise in *Bowers* that the claim put forward was insubstantial in our Western civilization.

In our own constitutional system the deficiencies in *Bowers* became even more apparent in the years following its announcement. The 25 States with laws prohibiting the relevant conduct referenced in the *Bowers* decision are reduced now to 13, of which 4 enforce their laws only against homosexual conduct. In those States where sodomy is still proscribed, whether for same-sex or heterosexual conduct, there is a pattern of nonenforcement with respect to consenting adults acting in private. The State of Texas admitted in 1994 that as of that date it had not prosecuted anyone under those circumstances.

Two principal cases decided after *Bowers* cast its holding into even more doubt. In *Planned Parenthood of Southeastern Pa. v. Casey,* the Court reaffirmed the substantive force of the liberty protected by the Due Process Clause. The *Casey* decision again confirmed that our laws and tradition afford constitutional protection to personal decisions relating to marriage, procreation, contraception, family relationships, child rearing, and education. In explaining the respect the Constitution demands for the autonomy of the person in making these choices, we stated as follows:

> These matters, involving the most intimate and personal choices a person may make in a lifetime, choices central to personal dignity and autonomy, are central to the liberty protected by the Fourteenth Amendment. At the heart of liberty is the right to define one's own concept of existence, of meaning, of the universe, and of the mystery of human life. Beliefs about these matters could not define the attributes of personhood were they formed under compulsion of the State. (Ibid.)

Persons in a homosexual relationship may seek autonomy for these purposes, just as heterosexual persons do. The decision in *Bowers* would deny them this right.

The second post-*Bowers* case of principal relevance is *Romer v. Evans* (1996). There the Court struck down class-based legislation directed at homosexuals as a violation of the Equal Protection Clause. *Romer* invalidated an amendment to Colorado's constitution which named as a solitary class persons who were homosexuals, lesbians, or bisexual either by "orientation, conduct, practices or relationships," and deprived them of protection under state antidiscrimination laws. We concluded that the provision was "born of animosity toward the class of persons affected" and further that it had no rational relation to a legitimate governmental purpose.

As an alternative argument in this case, counsel for the petitioners and some *amici* contend that *Romer* provides the basis for declaring the Texas statute invalid under the Equal Protection Clause. That is a tenable argument, but we conclude the instant case requires us to address whether *Bowers* itself has continuing validity. Were we to hold the statute invalid under the Equal Protection Clause some might question whether a prohibition would be valid if drawn differently, say, to prohibit the conduct both between same-sex and different-sex participants.

Equality of treatment and the due process right to demand respect for conduct protected by the substantive guarantee of liberty are linked in important respects, and a decision on the latter point advances both interests. If protected conduct is made criminal and the law which does so remains unexamined for its substantive validity, its stigma might remain even if it were not enforceable as drawn for equal protection reasons. When homosexual conduct is made criminal by the law of the State, that declaration in and of itself is an invitation to subject homosexual persons to discrimination both in the public and in the private spheres. The central holding of *Bowers* has been brought in question by this case, and it should be addressed. Its continuance as precedent demeans the lives of homosexual persons.

The stigma this criminal statute imposes, moreover, is not trivial. The offense, to be sure, is but a class C misdemeanor, a minor offense in the Texas legal system. Still, it remains a criminal offense with all that imports for the dignity of the persons charged. The petitioners will bear on their record the history of their criminal convictions. Just this Term we rejected various challenges to state laws requiring the registration of sex offenders. We are advised that if Texas convicted an adult for private, consensual homosexual conduct under the statute here in question the convicted person would come within the registration laws of at least four States were he or she to be subject to their jurisdiction. This underscores the consequential nature of the punishment and the state-sponsored condemnation attendant to the criminal prohibition. Furthermore, the Texas criminal conviction carries with it the other collateral consequences always following a conviction, such as notations on job application forms, to mention but one example.

The foundations of *Bowers* have sustained serious erosion from our recent decisions in *Casey* and *Romer*. When our precedent has been thus weakened, criticism from other sources is of greater significance. In the United States criticism of *Bowers* has been substantial and continuing, disapproving of its reasoning in all respects, not just as to its historical assumptions. The courts of five different States have declined to follow it in interpreting provisions in their own state constitutions parallel to the Due Process Clause of the Fourteenth Amendment.

To the extent *Bowers* relied on values we share with a wider civilization, it should be noted that the reasoning and holding in *Bowers* have been rejected elsewhere. The European Court of Human Rights has followed not *Bowers* but its own decision in *Dudgeon v. United Kingdom*. Other nations, too, have taken action consistent with an affirmation of the protected right of homosexual adults to engage in intimate, consensual conduct. The right the petitioners seek in this case has been accepted as an integral part of human freedom in many other countries. There has been no showing that in this country the governmental interest in circumscribing personal choice is somehow more legitimate or urgent.

The doctrine of *stare decisis* is essential to the respect accorded to the judgments of the Court and to the stability of the law. It is not, however, an inexorable command. In *Casey* we noted that when a Court is asked to overrule a precedent recognizing a constitutional liberty interest, individual or societal reliance on the existence of that liberty cautions with particular strength against reversing course. The holding in *Bowers*, however, has not induced detrimental reliance comparable to some instances where recognized individual rights are involved. Indeed, there has been no individual or societal reliance on *Bowers* of the sort that could counsel against overturning its hold-ing once there are compelling reasons to do so. *Bowers* itself causes uncer-tainty, for the precedents before and after its issuance contradict its central holding.

The rationale of *Bowers* does not withstand careful analysis. In his dissent-ing opinion in *Bowers* Justice Stevens came to these conclusions:

> Our prior cases make two propositions abundantly clear. First, the fact that the governing majority in a State has traditionally viewed a particu-lar practice as immoral is not a sufficient reason for upholding a law prohibiting the practice; neither history nor tradition could save a law prohibiting miscegenation from constitutional attack. Second, indi-vidual decisions by married persons, concerning the intimacies of their physical relationship, even when not intended to produce offspring, are a form of "liberty" protected by the Due Process Clause of the Fourteenth Amendment. Moreover, this protection extends to intimate choices by unmarried as well as married persons. (footnotes and citations omitted)

Justice Stevens's analysis, in our view, should have been controlling in *Bowers* and should control here.

Bowers was not correct when it was decided, and it is not correct today. It ought not to remain binding precedent. *Bowers v. Hardwick* should be and now is overruled.

The present case does not involve minors. It does not involve persons who might be injured or coerced or who are situated in relationships where consent might not easily be refused. It does not involve public conduct or pros-titution. It does not involve whether the government must give formal recogni-tion to any relationship that homosexual persons seek to enter. The case does involve two adults who, with full and mutual consent from each other, engaged in sexual practices common to a homosexual lifestyle. The petitioners are entitled to respect for their private lives. The State cannot demean their exis-tence or control their destiny by making their private sexual conduct a crime. Their right to liberty under the Due Process Clause gives them the full right to engage in their conduct without intervention of the government. "It is a promise of the Constitution that there is a realm of personal liberty which the government may not enter." The Texas statute furthers no legitimate state interest which can justify its intrusion into the personal and private life of the individual.

Had those who drew and ratified the Due Process Clauses of the Fifth Amendment or the Fourteenth Amendment known the components of liberty in its manifold possibilities, they might have been more specific. They did not presume to have this insight. They knew times can blind us to certain truths and later generations can see that laws once thought necessary and proper in fact serve only to oppress. As the Constitution endures, persons in every generation can invoke its principles in their own search for greater freedom.

The judgment of the Court of Appeals for the Texas Fourteenth District is reversed, and the case is remanded for further proceedings not inconsistent with this opinion.

It is so ordered.

8.4

National Federation of Independent Business v. Sebelius (2012)

In this controversial decision, the Supreme Court upheld nearly all of the Afford-
able Care Act, the signature health care law of the Obama administration. Chief
Justice John Roberts wrote the majority opinion and split legal hairs. Aspects of
the law, he wrote, violate the commerce clause of the Constitution, but can be
upheld because they are consistent with Congress's power to tax. One provision of
the law on funding for Medicaid was declared unconstitutional, while the remain-
der of the law was permitted to stand. This decision will undoubtedly have deep
political consequences for many years, not only because of the implications for
health care policy, but also because of the Chief Justice's indication of his discom-
fort with the current legal status of the commerce clause. That clause has been
widely seen as opening the door to greater national power relative to the states,
and Roberts, in this opinion, signals that he thinks that door is open too wide.

CHIEF JUSTICE ROBERTS delivered the opinion of the Court.

Today we resolve constitutional challenges to two provisions of the Patient
Protection and Affordable Care Act of 2010: the individual mandate, which
requires individuals to purchase a health insurance policy providing a minimum level of coverage; and the Medicaid expansion, which gives funds to the
States on the condition that they provide specified health care to all citizens
whose income falls below a certain threshold. We do not consider whether the
Act embodies sound policies. That judgment is entrusted to the Nation's elected
leaders. We ask only whether Congress has the power under the Constitution to
enact the challenged provisions.

In our federal system, the National Government possesses only limited powers; the States and the people retain the remainder. Nearly two centuries ago,
Chief Justice Marshall observed that "the question respecting the extent of the
powers actually granted" to the Federal Government "is perpetually arising,
and will probably continue to arise, as long as our system shall exist." *McCull-*
och v. Maryland (1819). In this case, we must again determine whether the Constitution grants Congress powers it now asserts, but which many States and
individuals believe it does not possess. Resolving this controversy requires us

From *National Federation of Independent Business v. Sebelius*, 567 U.S. _____ (2012).

to examine both the limits of the Government's power, and our own limited role in policing those boundaries.

The Federal Government "is acknowledged by all to be one of enumerated powers." *Ibid*. That is, rather than granting general authority to perform all the conceivable functions of government, the Constitution lists, or enumerates, the Federal Government's powers. Congress may, for example, "coin Money," "establish Post Offices," and "raise and support Armies." Art. I, §8, cls. 5, 7, 12. The enumeration of powers is also a limitation of powers, because "[t]he enumeration presupposes something not enumerated." *Gibbons v. Ogden* (1824). The Constitution's express conferral of some powers makes clear that it does not grant others. And the Federal Government "can exercise only the powers granted to it." *McCulloch, supra*.

Today, the restrictions on government power foremost in many Americans' minds are likely to be affirmative prohibitions, such as contained in the Bill of Rights. These affirmative prohibitions come into play, however, only where the Government possesses authority to act in the first place. If no enumerated power authorizes Congress to pass a certain law, that law may not be enacted, even if it does not violate any of the express prohibitions in the Bill of Rights or elsewhere in the Constitution.

Indeed, the Constitution did not initially include a Bill of Rights at least partly because the Framers felt the enumeration of powers sufficed to restrain the Government. As Alexander Hamilton put it, "the Constitution is itself in every rational sense, and to every useful purpose, A BILL OF RIGHTS." *The Federalist*, No. 84. And when the Bill of Rights was ratified, it made express what the enumeration of powers necessarily implied: "The powers not delegated to the United States by the Constitution . . . are reserved to the States respectively, or to the people." U. S. Const., Amdt. 10. The Federal Government has expanded dramatically over the past two centuries, but it still must show that a constitutional grant of power authorizes each of its actions.

The same does not apply to the States, because the Constitution is not the source of their power. The Constitution may restrict state governments—as it does, for example, by forbidding them to deny any person the equal protection of the laws. But where such prohibitions do not apply, state governments do not need constitutional authorization to act. The States thus can and do perform many of the vital functions of modern government—punishing street crime, running public schools, and zoning property for development, to name but a few—even though the Constitution's text does not authorize any government to do so. Our cases refer to this general power of governing, possessed by the States but not by the Federal Government, as the "police power."

"State sovereignty is not just an end in itself: Rather, federalism secures to citizens the liberties that derive from the diffusion of sovereign power." *New York v. United States* (1992). Because the police power is controlled by 50 different States instead of one national sovereign, the facets of governing that touch on citizens' daily lives are normally administered by smaller governments closer to the governed. The Framers thus ensured that powers which "in the ordinary course of affairs, concern the lives, liberties, and properties of the people" were held by governments more local and more accountable than a distant federal bureaucracy. *The Federalist*, No. 45 (J. Madison). The independent power of the States also serves as a check on the power of the Federal Government: "By denying any one government complete jurisdiction over all the concerns of public life, federalism protects the liberty of the individual from arbitrary power." *Bond v. United States* (2011).

This case concerns two powers that the Constitution does grant the Federal Government, but which must be read carefully to avoid creating a general federal authority akin to the police power. The Constitution authorizes Congress to "regulate Commerce with foreign Nations, and among the several States, and with the Indian Tribes." Art. I, §8, cl. 3. Our precedents read that to mean that Congress may regulate "the channels of interstate commerce," "persons or things in interstate commerce," and "those activities that substantially affect interstate commerce." *United States v. Morrison* (2000). The power over activities that substantially affect interstate commerce can be expansive. That power has been held to authorize federal regulation of such seemingly local matters as a farmer's decision to grow wheat for himself and his livestock, and a loan shark's extortionate collections from a neighborhood butcher shop.

Congress may also "lay and collect Taxes, Duties, Imposts and Excises, to pay the Debts and provide for the common Defence and general Welfare of the United States." U.S. Const., Art. I, §8, cl. 1. Put simply, Congress may tax and spend. This grant gives the Federal Government considerable influence even in areas where it cannot directly regulate. The Federal Government may enact a tax on an activity that it cannot authorize, forbid, or otherwise control. And in exercising its spending power, Congress may offer funds to the States, and may condition those offers on compliance with specified conditions. These offers may well induce the States to adopt policies that the Federal Government itself could not impose.

The reach of the Federal Government's enumerated powers is broader still because the Constitution authorizes Congress to "make all Laws which shall be necessary and proper for carrying into Execution the foregoing Powers." Art. I, §8, cl. 18. We have long read this provision to give Congress great latitude in exercising its powers: "Let the end be legitimate, let it be within the scope of the constitution, and all means which are appropriate, which are plainly adapted to that end, which are not prohibited, but consist with the letter and spirit of the constitution, are constitutional." *McCulloch.*

Our permissive reading of these powers is explained in part by a general reticence to invalidate the acts of the Nation's elected leaders. "Proper respect for a coordinate branch of the government" requires that we strike down an Act of Congress only if "the lack of constitutional authority to pass [the] act in question is clearly demonstrated." *United States v. Harris* (1883). Members of this Court are vested with the authority to interpret the law; we possess neither the expertise nor the prerogative to make policy judgments. Those decisions are entrusted to our Nation's elected leaders, who can be thrown out of office if the people disagree with them. It is not our job to protect the people from the consequences of their political choices.

Our deference in matters of policy cannot, however, become abdication in matters of law. "The powers of the legislature are defined and limited; and that those limits may not be mistaken, or forgotten, the constitution is written." *Marbury v. Madison* (1803). Our respect for Congress's policy judgments thus can never extend so far as to disavow restraints on federal power that the Constitution carefully constructed. "The peculiar circumstances of the moment may render a measure more or less wise, but cannot render it more or less constitutional." "Chief Justice John Marshall, A Friend of the Constitution No. V," *Alexandria Gazette*, July 5, 1819, in John Marshall's *Defense of McCulloch v. Maryland*. And there can be no question that it is the responsibility of this Court to enforce the limits on federal power by striking down acts of Congress that transgress those limits. *Marbury v. Madison, supra.*

The questions before us must be considered against the background of these basic principles.

I

In 2010, Congress enacted the Patient Protection and Affordable Care Act, 124 Stat. 119. The Act aims to increase the number of Americans covered by health insurance and decrease the cost of health care. The Act's 10 titles stretch over 900 pages and contain hundreds of provisions. This case concerns constitutional challenges to two key provisions, commonly referred to as the individual mandate and the Medicaid expansion.

The individual mandate requires most Americans to maintain "minimum essential" health insurance coverage. The mandate does not apply to some individuals, such as prisoners and undocumented aliens. Many individuals will receive the required coverage through their employer, or from a government program such as Medicaid or Medicare. But for individuals who are not exempt and do not receive health insurance through a third party, the means of satisfying the requirement is to purchase insurance from a private company.

Beginning in 2014, those who do not comply with the mandate must make a "[s]hared responsibility payment" to the Federal Government. That payment, which the Act describes as a "penalty," is calculated as a percentage of household income, subject to a floor based on a specified dollar amount and a ceiling based on the average annual premium the individual would have to pay for qualifying private health insurance. In 2016, for example, the penalty will be 2.5 percent of an individual's household income, but no less than $695 and no more than the average yearly premium for insurance that covers

60 percent of the cost of 10 specified services (e.g., prescription drugs and hospitalization). The Act provides that the penalty will be paid to the Internal Revenue Service [IRS] with an individual's taxes, and "shall be assessed and collected in the same manner" as tax penalties, such as the penalty for claiming too large an income tax refund. The Act, however, bars the IRS from using several of its normal enforcement tools, such as criminal prosecutions and levies. And some individuals who are subject to the mandate are nonetheless exempt from the penalty—for example, those with income below a certain threshold and members of Indian tribes.

On the day the President signed the Act into law, Florida and 12 other States filed a complaint in the Federal District Court for the Northern District of Florida. Those plaintiffs—who are both respondents and petitioners here, depending on the issue—were subsequently joined by 13 more States, several individuals, and the National Federation of Independent Business. The plaintiffs alleged, among other things, that the individual mandate provisions of the Act exceeded Congress's powers under Article I of the Constitution. The District Court agreed, holding that Congress lacked constitutional power to enact the individual mandate. The District Court determined that the individual mandate could not be severed from the remainder of the Act, and therefore struck down the Act in its entirety.

The Court of Appeals for the Eleventh Circuit affirmed in part and reversed in part. The court affirmed the District Court's holding that the individual mandate exceeds Congress's power. The panel unanimously agreed that the individual mandate did not impose a tax, and thus could not be authorized by Congress's power to "lay and collect Taxes." U.S. Const., Art. I, §8, cl. 1. A majority also held that the individual mandate was not supported by Congress's power to "regulate Commerce . . . among the several States." *Id.*, cl. 3. According to the majority, the Commerce Clause does not empower the Federal Government to order individuals to engage in commerce, and the Government's efforts to cast the individual mandate in a different light were unpersuasive. Judge Marcus dissented, reasoning that the individual mandate regulates economic activity that has a clear effect on interstate commerce.

Having held the individual mandate to be unconstitutional, the majority examined whether that provision could be severed from the remainder of the Act. The majority determined that, contrary to the District Court's view, it could. The court thus struck down only the individual mandate, leaving the Act's other provisions intact.

Other Courts of Appeals have also heard challenges to the individual mandate. The Sixth Circuit and the D.C. Circuit upheld the mandate as a valid exercise of Congress's commerce power. The Fourth Circuit determined that the Anti-Injunction Act prevents courts from considering the merits of that question. That statute bars suits "for the purpose of restraining the assessment or collection of any tax." A majority of the Fourth Circuit panel reasoned that the individual mandate's penalty is a tax within the meaning of the Anti-Injunction Act, because it is a financial assessment collected by the IRS through the normal means of taxation. The majority therefore determined that the plaintiffs could not challenge the individual mandate until after they paid the penalty.

The second provision of the Affordable Care Act directly challenged here is the Medicaid expansion. Enacted in 1965, Medicaid offers federal funding to States to assist pregnant women, children, needy families, the blind, the elderly, and the disabled in obtaining medical care. In order to receive that funding, States must comply with federal criteria governing matters such as who receives care and what services are provided at what cost. By 1982 every State had chosen to participate in Medicaid. Federal funds received through the Medicaid program have become a substantial part of state budgets, now constituting over 10 percent of most States' total revenue.

The Affordable Care Act expands the scope of the Medicaid program and increases the number of individuals the States must cover. For example, the Act requires state programs to provide Medicaid coverage to adults with incomes up to 133 percent of the federal poverty level, whereas many States now cover adults with children only if their income is considerably lower, and do not cover childless adults at all. The Act increases federal funding to cover the States' costs in expanding Medicaid coverage, although States will bear a portion of the costs on their own. If a State does not comply with the Act's new coverage requirements, it may lose not only the federal funding for those requirements, but all of its federal Medicaid funds.

Along with their challenge to the individual mandate, the state plaintiffs in the Eleventh Circuit argued that the Medicaid expansion exceeds Congress's constitutional powers. The Court of Appeals unanimously held that the Medicaid expansion is a valid exercise of Congress's power under the Spending Clause. And the court rejected the States' claim that the threatened loss of all federal Medicaid funding violates the Tenth Amendment by coercing them into complying with the Medicaid expansion. We granted *certiorari* to review the judgment of the Court of Appeals for the Eleventh Circuit with respect to both the individual mandate and the Medicaid expansion. Because no party supports the Eleventh Circuit's holding that the individual mandate can be completely severed from the remainder of the Affordable Care Act, we appointed an *amicus curiae* to defend that aspect of the judgment below. And because there is a reasonable argument that the Anti-Injunction Act deprives us of jurisdiction to hear challenges to the individual mandate, but no party supports that proposition, we appointed an *amicus curiae* to advance it.

II

Before turning to the merits, we need to be sure we have the authority to do so. The Anti-Injunction Act provides that "no suit for the purpose of restraining the assessment or collection of any tax shall be maintained in any court by any person, whether or not such person is the person against whom such tax was assessed." This statute protects the Government's ability to collect a consistent stream of revenue, by barring litigation to enjoin or otherwise obstruct the collection of taxes. Because of the Anti-Injunction Act, taxes can ordinarily be challenged only after they are paid, by suing for a refund.

The penalty for not complying with the Affordable Care Act's individual mandate first becomes enforceable in 2014. The present challenge to the mandate thus seeks to restrain the penalty's future collection. *Amicus* contends that the Internal Revenue Code treats the penalty as a tax, and that the Anti-Injunction Act therefore bars this suit.

The text of the pertinent statutes suggests otherwise. The Anti-Injunction Act applies to suits "for the purpose of restraining the assessment or collection of any *tax*." (emphasis added). Congress, however, chose to describe the "[s]hared responsibility payment" imposed on those who forgo health insurance not as a "tax," but as a "penalty." There is no immediate reason to think that a statute applying to "any tax" would apply to a "penalty."

Congress's decision to label this exaction a "penalty" rather than a "tax" is significant because the Affordable Care Act describes many other exactions it creates as "taxes." Where Congress uses certain language in one part of a statute and different language in another, it is generally presumed that Congress acts intentionally.

Amicus argues that even though Congress did not label the shared responsibility payment a tax, we should treat it as such under the Anti-Injunction Act because it functions like a tax. It is true that Congress cannot change whether an exaction is a tax or a penalty for constitutional purposes simply by describing it as one or the other. Congress may not, for example, expand its power under the Taxing Clause, or escape the Double Jeopardy Clause's constraint on criminal sanctions, by labeling a severe financial punishment a "tax."

The Anti-Injunction Act and the Affordable Care Act, however, are creatures of Congress's own creation. How they relate to each other is up to Congress, and the best evidence of Congress's intent is the statutory text. We have thus applied the Anti-Injunction Act to statutorily described "taxes" even where that label was inaccurate.

Congress can, of course, describe something as a penalty but direct that it nonetheless be treated as a tax for purposes of the Anti-Injunction Act. For example, 26 U.S.C. §6671(a) provides that "any reference in this title to 'tax' imposed by this title shall be deemed also to refer to the penalties and liabilities provided by" subchapter 68B of the Internal Revenue Code. Penalties in subchapter 68B are thus treated as taxes under Title 26, which includes the Anti-Injunction Act. The individual mandate, however, is not in subchapter 68B of the Code. Nor does any other provision state that references to taxes in Title 26 shall also be "deemed" to apply to the individual mandate.

Amicus attempts to show that Congress did render the Anti-Injunction Act applicable to the individual mandate, albeit by a more circuitous route. Section 5000A(g)(1) specifies that the penalty for not complying with the mandate "shall be assessed and collected in the same manner as an assessable penalty under subchapter B of chapter 68." Assessable penalties in subchapter 68B, in turn, "shall be assessed and collected in the same manner as taxes." According to *amicus*, by directing that the penalty be "assessed and collected in the same manner as taxes," §5000A(g)(1) made the Anti-Injunction Act applicable to this penalty.

The Government disagrees. It argues that §5000A(g)(1) does not direct courts to apply the Anti-Injunction Act, because §5000A(g) is a directive only to the Secretary of the Treasury to use the same "methodology and procedures" to collect the penalty that he uses to collect taxes. Brief for United States 32–33.

We think the Government has the better reading. As it observes, "Assessment" and "Collection" are chapters of the Internal Revenue Code providing the Secretary authority to assess and collect taxes, and generally specifying the means by which he shall do so. Section 5000A(g)(1)'s command that the penalty be "assessed and collected in the same manner" as taxes is best read as referring to those chapters and giving the Secretary the same authority and guidance with respect to the penalty. That interpretation is consistent with the remainder of §5000A(g), which instructs the Secretary on the tools he may use to collect the penalty. The Anti-Injunction Act, by contrast, says nothing about the procedures to be used in assessing and collecting taxes.

Amicus argues in the alternative that a different section of the Internal Revenue Code requires courts to treat the penalty as a tax under the Anti-Injunction Act. Section 6201(a) authorizes the Secretary to make "assessments of all taxes (including interest, additional amounts, additions to the tax, and *assessable penalties*)." (Emphasis added.) *Amicus* contends that the penalty must be a tax, because it is an assessable penalty and §6201(a) says that taxes include assessable penalties.

That argument has force only if §6201(a) is read in isolation. The Code contains many provisions treating taxes and assessable penalties as distinct terms. There would, for example, be no need for §6671(a) to deem "tax" to refer to certain assessable penalties if the Code already included all such penalties in the term "tax." Indeed, *amicus*'s earlier observation that the Code requires assessable penalties to be assessed and collected "in the same manner as taxes" makes little sense if assessable penalties are themselves taxes. In light of the Code's consistent distinction between the terms "tax" and "assessable penalty," we must accept the Government's interpretation: §6201(a) instructs the Secretary that his authority to assess taxes includes the authority to assess penalties, but it does not equate assessable penalties to taxes for other purposes.

The Affordable Care Act does not require that the penalty for failing to comply with the individual mandate be treated as a tax for purposes of the Anti-Injunction Act. The Anti-Injunction Act therefore does not apply to this suit, and we may proceed to the merits.

III

The Government advances two theories for the proposition that Congress had constitutional authority to enact the individual mandate. First, the Government argues that Congress had the power to enact the mandate under the Commerce Clause. Under that theory, Congress may order individuals to buy health insurance because the failure to do so affects interstate commerce, and could undercut the Affordable Care Act's other reforms. Second, the Government argues that if the commerce power does not support the mandate, we should nonetheless uphold it as an exercise of Congress's power to tax. According to the Government, even if Congress lacks the power to direct individuals to buy insurance, the only effect of the individual mandate is to raise taxes on those who do not do so, and thus the law may be upheld as a tax.

A

The Government's first argument is that the individual mandate is a valid exercise of Congress's power under the Commerce Clause and the Necessary and Proper Clause. According to the Government, the health care market is characterized by a significant cost-shifting problem. Everyone will eventually need health care at a time and to an extent they cannot predict, but if they do not have insurance, they often will not be able to pay for it. Because state and federal laws nonetheless require hospitals to provide a certain degree of care to individuals without regard to their ability to pay, hospitals end up receiving compensation for only a portion of the services they provide. To recoup the losses, hospitals pass on the cost to insurers through higher rates, and insurers, in turn, pass on the cost to policy holders in the form of higher premiums. Congress estimated that the cost of uncompensated care raises family health insurance premiums, on average, by over $1,000 per year.

In the Affordable Care Act, Congress addressed the problem of those who cannot obtain insurance coverage because of preexisting conditions or other health issues. It did so through the Act's "guaranteed-issue" and "community-rating" provisions. These provisions together prohibit insurance companies from denying coverage to those with such conditions or charging unhealthy individuals higher premiums than healthy individuals.

The guaranteed-issue and community-rating reforms do not, however, address the issue of healthy individuals who choose not to purchase insurance to cover potential health care needs. In fact, the reforms sharply exacerbate that problem, by providing an incentive for individuals to delay purchasing health insurance until they become sick, relying on the promise of guaranteed and affordable coverage. The reforms also threaten to impose massive new costs on insurers, who are required to accept unhealthy individuals but prohibited from charging them rates necessary to pay for their coverage. This will lead insurers to significantly increase premiums on everyone.

The individual mandate was Congress's solution to these problems. By requiring that individuals purchase health insurance, the mandate prevents cost-shifting by those who would otherwise go without it. In addition, the mandate forces into the insurance risk pool more healthy individuals, whose premiums on average will be higher than their health care expenses. This allows insurers to subsidize the costs of covering the unhealthy individuals the reforms require them to accept. The Government claims that Congress has power under the Commerce and Necessary and Proper Clauses to enact this solution.

1

The Government contends that the individual mandate is within Congress's power because the failure to purchase insurance "has a substantial and deleterious effect on interstate commerce" by creating the cost-shifting problem. Brief for United States 34. The path of our Commerce Clause decisions has not always run smooth, but it is now well established that Congress has broad authority under the Clause. We have recognized, for example, that "[t]he power of Congress over interstate commerce is not confined to the regulation of commerce among the states," but extends to activities that "have a substantial effect on interstate commerce." *United States v. Darby* (1941). Congress's power, moreover, is not limited to regulation of an activity that by itself substantially affects interstate commerce, but also extends to activities that do so only when aggregated with similar activities of others.

Given its expansive scope, it is no surprise that Congress has employed the commerce power in a wide variety of ways to address the pressing needs of the time. But Congress has never attempted to rely on that power to compel individuals not engaged in commerce to purchase an unwanted product. Legislative novelty is not necessarily fatal; there is a first time for everything. But sometimes "the most telling indication of [a] severe constitutional problem . . . is the lack of historical precedent" for Congress's action. *Free Enterprise Fund v. Public Company Accounting Oversight Bd.* (2010). At the very least, we should "pause to consider the implications of the Government's arguments" when confronted with such new conceptions of federal power. *United States v. Lopez* (1995).

The Constitution grants Congress the power to "*regulate* Commerce." Art. I, §8, cl. 3 (emphasis added). The power to regulate commerce presupposes the existence of commercial activity to be regulated. If the power to "regulate" something included the power to create it, many of the provisions in the Constitution would be superfluous. For example, the Constitution gives Congress the power to "coin Money," in addition to the power to "regulate the Value thereof." *Id.*, cl. 5. And it gives Congress the power to "raise and support Armies" and to "provide and maintain a Navy," in addition to the power to "make Rules for the Government and Regulation of the land and naval Forces." *Id.*, cls. 12–14. If the power to regulate the armed forces or the value of money included the power to bring the subject of the regulation into existence, the specific grant of such powers would have been unnecessary. The language of the Constitution reflects the natural understanding that the power to regulate assumes there is already something to be regulated.

Our precedent also reflects this understanding. As expansive as our cases construing the scope of the commerce power have been, they all have one thing in common: They uniformly describe the power as reaching "activity." It is nearly impossible to avoid the word when quoting them.

The individual mandate, however, does not regulate existing commercial activity. It instead compels individuals to become active in commerce by purchasing a product, on the ground that their failure to do so affects interstate commerce. Construing the Commerce Clause to permit Congress to regulate individuals precisely because they are doing nothing would open a new and potentially vast domain to congressional authority. Every day individuals do not do an infinite number of things. In some cases they decide not to do something; in others they simply fail to do it. Allowing Congress to justify federal regulation by pointing to the effect of inaction on commerce would bring countless decisions an individual could potentially make within the scope of federal regulation, and—under the Government's theory—empower Congress to make those decisions for him.

Applying the Government's logic to the familiar case of *Wickard v. Filburn* shows how far that logic would carry us from the notion of a government of limited powers. In *Wickard*, the Court famously upheld a federal penalty imposed on a farmer for growing wheat for consumption on his own farm. That amount of wheat caused the farmer to exceed his quota under a program designed to support the price of wheat by limiting supply. The Court rejected the farmer's argument that growing wheat for home consumption was beyond the reach of the commerce power. It did so on the ground that the farmer's decision to grow wheat for his own use allowed him to avoid purchasing wheat in the market. That decision, when considered in the aggregate along with similar decisions of others, would have had a substantial effect on the interstate market for wheat.

Wickard has long been regarded as "perhaps the most far reaching example of Commerce Clause authority over intrastate activity," *Lopez*, 514 U.S., but the Government's theory in this case would go much further. Under *Wickard* it is within Congress's power to regulate the market for wheat by supporting its price. But price can be supported by increasing demand as well as by decreasing supply. The aggregated decisions of some consumers not to purchase wheat have a substantial effect on the price of wheat, just as decisions not to purchase health insurance have on the price of insurance. Congress can therefore command that those not buying wheat do so, just as it argues here that it may command that those not buying health insurance do so. The farmer in *Wickard* was at least actively engaged in the production of wheat, and the Government could regulate that activity because of its effect on commerce. The Government's theory here would effectively override that limitation, by establishing that individuals may be regulated under the Commerce Clause whenever enough of them are not doing something the Government would have them do.

Indeed, the Government's logic would justify a mandatory purchase to solve almost any problem. To consider a different example in the health care market, many Americans do not eat a balanced diet. That group makes up a larger percentage of the total population than those without health insurance. The failure of that group to have a healthy diet increases health care costs, to a greater extent than the failure of the uninsured to purchase insurance. Those increased costs are borne in part by other Americans who must pay more, just as the uninsured shift costs to the insured. Congress addressed the insurance problem by ordering everyone to buy insurance. Under the Government's theory, Congress could address the diet problem by ordering everyone to buy vegetables.

People, for reasons of their own, often fail to do things that would be good for them or good for society. Those failures—joined with the similar failures of others—can readily have a substantial effect on interstate commerce. Under the Government's logic, that authorizes Congress to use its commerce power to compel citizens to act as the Government would have them act.

That is not the country the Framers of our Constitution envisioned. James Madison explained that the Commerce Clause was "an addition which few oppose and from which no apprehensions are entertained." *The Federalist*, No. 45. While Congress's authority under the Commerce Clause has of course expanded with the growth of the national economy, our cases have "always recognized that the power to regulate commerce, though broad indeed, has limits." *Maryland v. Wirtz* (1968). The Government's theory would erode those limits, permitting Congress to reach beyond the natural extent of its authority, "everywhere extending the sphere of its activity and drawing all power into its impetuous vortex." *The Federalist*, No. 48 (J. Madison). Congress already enjoys vast power to regulate much of what we do. Accepting the Government's theory would give Congress the same license to regulate what we do not do, fundamentally changing the relation between the citizen and the Federal Government.

To an economist, perhaps, there is no difference between activity and inactivity; both have measurable economic effects on commerce. But the distinction between doing something and doing nothing would not have been lost on the Framers, who were "practical statesmen," not metaphysical philosophers. *Industrial Union Dept., AFL–CIO v. American Petroleum Institute* (1980). As we have explained, "the framers of the Constitution were not mere visionaries, toying with speculations or theories, but practical men, dealing with the facts of political life as they understood them, putting into form the government they were creating, and prescribing in language clear and intelligible the powers that government was to take." *South Carolina v. United*

States (1905). The Framers gave Congress the power to regulate commerce, not to compel it, and for over 200 years both our decisions and Congress's actions have reflected this understanding. There is no reason to depart from that understanding now.

The Government sees things differently. It argues that because sickness and injury are not only unpredictable but unavoidable, "the uninsured as a class are active in the market for health care, which they regularly seek and obtain." Brief for United States 50. The individual mandate "merely regulates how individuals finance and pay for that active participation—requiring that they do so through insurance, rather than through attempted self-insurance with the back-stop of shifting costs to others." *Ibid.*

The Government repeats the phrase "active in the market for health care" throughout its brief, but that concept has no constitutional significance. An individual who bought a car two years ago and may buy another in the future is not "active in the car market" in any pertinent sense. The phrase "active in the market" cannot obscure the fact that most of those regulated by the individual mandate are not currently engaged in any commercial activity involving health care, and that fact is fatal to the Government's effort to "regulate the uninsured as a class." Our precedents recognize Congress's power to regulate "class[es] of *activities,*" *Gonzales v. Raich* (2005) (emphasis added), not classes of individuals, apart from any activity in which they are engaged.

The individual mandate's regulation of the uninsured as a class is, in fact, particularly divorced from any link to existing commercial activity. The mandate primarily affects healthy, often young adults who are less likely to need significant health care and have other priorities for spending their money. It is precisely because these individuals, as an actuarial class, incur relatively low health care costs that the mandate helps counter the effect of forcing insurance companies to cover others who impose greater costs than their premiums are allowed to reflect. If the individual mandate is targeted as a class, it is a class whose commercial inactivity rather than activity is its defining feature.

The Government, however, claims that this does not matter. The Government regards it as sufficient to trigger Congress's authority that almost all those who are uninsured will, at some unknown point in the future, engage in a health care transaction. Asserting that "[t]here is no temporal limitation in the Commerce Clause," the Government argues that because "[e]veryone subject to this regulation is in or will be in the health care market," they can be "regulated in advance." Tr. of Oral Arg. 109 (Mar. 27, 2012).

The proposition that Congress may dictate the conduct of an individual today because of prophesied future activity finds no support in our precedent. We have said that Congress can anticipate the effects on commerce of an economic activity. But we have never permitted Congress to anticipate that activity itself in order to regulate individuals not currently engaged in commerce. Each one of our cases, including those cited by Justice Ginsburg, *post,* involved preexisting economic activity.

Everyone will likely participate in the markets for food, clothing, transportation, shelter, or energy; that does not authorize Congress to direct them to purchase particular products in those or other markets today. The Commerce Clause is not a general license to regulate an individual from cradle to grave, simply because he will predictably engage in particular transactions. Any police power to regulate individuals as such, as opposed to their activities, remains vested in the States.

The Government argues that the individual mandate can be sustained as a sort of exception to this rule, because health insurance is a unique product. According to the Government, upholding the individual mandate would not justify mandatory purchases of items such as cars or broccoli because, as the Government puts it, "[h]ealth insurance is not purchased for its own sake like a car or broccoli; it is a means of financing health care consumption and covering universal risks." Reply Brief for United States 19. But cars and broccoli are no more purchased for their "own sake" than health insurance. They are purchased to cover the need for transportation and food.

The Government says that health insurance and health care financing are "inherently integrated." Brief for United States 41. But that does not mean the compelled purchase of the first is properly regarded as a regulation of the second. No matter how "inherently integrated" health insurance and health care consumption may be, they are not the same thing: They involve different transactions, entered into at different times, with different providers. And for most of those targeted by the mandate, significant health care needs will be years, or even decades, away. The proximity and degree of connection between the mandate and the subsequent commercial activity is too lacking to justify an exception of the sort urged by the Government. The individual mandate forces individuals into commerce precisely because they elected to refrain from commercial activity. Such a law cannot be sustained under a clause authorizing Congress to "regulate Commerce."

2

The Government next contends that Congress has the power under the Necessary and Proper Clause to enact the individual mandate because the mandate is an "integral part of a comprehensive scheme of economic regulation"—the guaranteed-issue and community-rating insurance reforms. Brief for United States 24. Under this argument, it is not necessary to consider the effect that an individual's inactivity may have on interstate commerce; it is enough that Congress regulate commercial activity in a way that requires regulation of inactivity to be effective.

The power to "make all Laws which shall be necessary and proper for carrying into Execution" the powers enumerated in the Constitution, Art. I, §8, cl. 18, vests Congress with authority to enact provisions "incidental to the [enumerated] power, and conducive to its beneficial exercise," *McCulloch*, 4 Wheat. Although the Clause gives Congress authority to "legislate on that vast mass of incidental powers which must be involved in the constitution," it does not license the exercise of any "great substantive and independent power[s]" beyond those specifically enumerated. *Id.* Instead, the Clause is "merely a declaration, for the removal of all uncertainty, that the means of carrying into execution those [powers] otherwise granted are included in the grant." *Kinsella v. United States* (1960).

As our jurisprudence under the Necessary and Proper Clause has developed, we have been very deferential to Congress's determination that a regulation is "necessary." We have thus upheld laws that are "'convenient, or useful' or 'conducive' to the authority's 'beneficial exercise.'" *United States v. Comstock* (2010). But we have also carried out our responsibility to declare unconstitutional those laws that undermine the structure of government established by the Constitution. Such laws, which are not "consist[ent] with the letter and spirit of the constitution," *McCulloch, supra,* are not "proper [means] for carrying into Execution" Congress's enumerated powers. Rather, they are, "in the words of *The Federalist,* 'merely acts of usurpation' which 'deserve to be treated as such.'" *Printz v. United States* (1997).

Applying these principles, the individual mandate cannot be sustained under the Necessary and Proper Clause as an essential component of the insurance reforms. Each of our prior cases upholding laws under that Clause involved exercises of authority derivative of, and in service to, a granted power. For example, we have upheld provisions permitting continued confinement of those already in federal custody when they could not be safely released, *Comstock, supra*; criminalizing bribes involving organizations receiving federal funds, *Sabri v. United States* (2004); and tolling state statutes of limitations while cases are pending in federal court, *Jinks v. Richland County* (2003). The individual mandate, by contrast, vests Congress with the extraordinary ability to create the necessary predicate to the exercise of an enumerated power.

This is in no way an authority that is "narrow in scope," *Comstock, supra,* or "incidental" to the exercise of the commerce power, *McCulloch, supra.* Rather, such a conception of the Necessary and Proper Clause would work a substantial expansion of federal authority. No longer would Congress be limited to regulating under the Commerce Clause those who by some preexisting activity bring themselves within the sphere of federal regulation. Instead, Congress could reach beyond the natural limit of its authority and draw within its regulatory scope those who otherwise would be outside of it. Even if the individual mandate is "necessary" to the Act's insurance reforms, such an expansion of federal power is not a "proper" means for making those reforms effective.

The Government relies primarily on our decision in *Gonzales v. Raich.* In *Raich,* we considered "comprehensive legislation to regulate the interstate market" in marijuana. Certain individuals sought an exemption from that regulation on the ground that they engaged in only intrastate possession and consumption. We denied any exemption, on the ground that marijuana is a fungible commodity, so that any marijuana could be readily diverted into the interstate market. Congress's attempt to regulate the interstate market for marijuana would therefore have been substantially undercut if it could not also regulate intrastate possession and consumption. *Id.* Accordingly, we recognized that "Congress was acting well within its authority" under the Necessary and Proper Clause even though its "regulation ensnare[d] some purely intrastate activity." *Id. Raich* thus did not involve the exercise of any "great substantive and independent power," *McCulloch, supra,* of the sort at issue here. Instead, it concerned only the constitutionality of "individual *applications* of a concededly valid statutory scheme." *Raich, supra* (emphasis added).

Just as the individual mandate cannot be sustained as a law regulating the substantial effects of the failure to purchase health insurance, neither can it be upheld as a "necessary and proper" component of the insurance reforms. The commerce power thus does not authorize the mandate.

B

That is not the end of the matter. Because the Commerce Clause does not support the individual mandate, it is necessary to turn to the Government's second argument: that the mandate may be upheld as within Congress's enumerated power to "lay and collect Taxes." Art. I, §8, cl. 1.

The Government's tax power argument asks us to view the statute differently than we did in considering its commerce power theory. In making its Commerce Clause argument, the Government defended the mandate as a regulation requiring individuals to purchase health insurance. The Government does not claim that the taxing power allows Congress to issue such a command. Instead, the Government asks us to read the mandate not as ordering individuals to buy insurance, but rather as imposing a tax on those who do not buy that product.

The text of a statute can sometimes have more than one possible meaning. To take a familiar example, a law that reads "no vehicles in the park" might, or might not, ban bicycles in the park. And it is well established that if a statute has two possible meanings, one of which violates the Constitution, courts should adopt the meaning that does not do so. Justice Story said 180 years ago: "No court ought, unless the terms of an act rendered it unavoidable, to give a construction to it which should involve a violation, however unintentional, of the constitution." *Parsons v. Bedford* (1830). Justice Holmes made the same point a century later: "[T]he rule is settled that as between two possible interpretations of a statute, by one of which it would be unconstitutional and by the other valid, our plain duty is to adopt that which will save the Act." *Blodgett v. Holden* (1927).

The most straightforward reading of the mandate is that it commands individuals to purchase insurance. After all, it states that individuals "shall" maintain health insurance. Congress thought it could enact such a command under the Commerce Clause, and the Government primarily defended the law on that basis. But, for the reasons explained above, the Commerce Clause does not give Congress that power. Under our precedent, it is therefore necessary to ask whether the Government's alternative reading of the statute—that it only imposes a tax on those without insurance—is a reasonable one.

Under the mandate, if an individual does not maintain health insurance, the only consequence is that he must make an additional payment to the IRS when he pays his taxes. That, according to the Government, means the mandate can be regarded as establishing a condition—not owning health insurance—that triggers a tax—the required payment to the IRS. Under that theory, the mandate is not a legal command to buy insurance. Rather, it makes going without insurance just another thing the Government taxes, like buying gasoline or earning income. And if the mandate is in effect just a tax hike on certain taxpayers who do not have health insurance, it may be within Congress's constitutional power to tax.

The question is not whether that is the most natural interpretation of the mandate, but only whether it is a "fairly possible" one. *Crowell v. Benson* (1932). As we have explained, "every reasonable construction must be resorted to, in order to save a statute from unconstitutionality." *Hooper v. California* (1895). The Government asks us to interpret the mandate as imposing a tax, if it would otherwise violate the Constitution. Granting the Act the full measure of deference owed to federal statutes, it can be so read, for the reasons set forth below.

C

The exaction the Affordable Care Act imposes on those without health insurance looks like a tax in many respects. The "[s]hared responsibility payment," as the statute entitles it, is paid into the Treasury by "taxpayer[s]" when they file their tax returns. It does not apply to individuals who do not pay federal income taxes because their household income is less than the filing threshold in the Internal Revenue Code. For taxpayers who do owe the payment, its amount is determined by such familiar factors as taxable income, number of dependents, and joint filing status. The requirement to pay is found in the Internal Revenue Code and enforced by the IRS, which—as we previously explained—must assess and collect it "in the same manner as taxes." This process yields the essential feature of any tax: it produces at least some revenue for the Government. Indeed, the payment is expected to raise about $4 billion per year by 2017.

It is of course true that the Act describes the payment as a "penalty," not a "tax." But while that label is fatal to the application of the Anti-Injunction Act, it does not determine whether the payment may be viewed as an exercise of Congress's taxing power. It is up to Congress whether to apply the Anti-Injunction Act to any particular statute, so it makes sense to be guided by Congress's choice of label on that question. That choice does not, however, control whether an exaction is within Congress's constitutional power to tax.

Our precedent reflects this: In 1922, we decided two challenges to the "Child Labor Tax" on the same day. In the first, we held that a suit to enjoin collection of the so-called tax was barred by the Anti-Injunction Act. Congress knew that suits to obstruct taxes had to await payment under the Anti-Injunction Act; Congress called the child labor tax a tax; Congress therefore intended the Anti-Injunction Act to apply. In the second case, however, we held that the same exaction, although labeled a tax, was not in fact authorized by Congress's taxing power. That constitutional question was not controlled by Congress's choice of label.

We have similarly held that exactions not labeled taxes nonetheless were authorized by Congress's power to tax. In the License Tax Cases, for example, we held that federal licenses to sell liquor and lottery tickets—for which the licensee had to pay a fee—could be sustained as exercises of the taxing power. And in *New York v. United States* we upheld as a tax a "surcharge" on out-of-state nuclear waste shipments, a portion of which was paid to the Federal Treasury. We thus ask whether the shared responsibility payment falls within Congress's taxing power, "[d]isregarding the designation of the exaction, and viewing its substance and application." *United States v. Constantine* (1935).

Our cases confirm this functional approach. For example, in *Bailey v. Drexel Furniture Co.* (1922), we focused on three practical characteristics of the so-called tax on employing child laborers that convinced us the "tax" was actually a penalty. First, the tax imposed an exceedingly heavy burden—10 percent of a company's net income—on those who employed children, no matter how small their infraction. Second, it imposed that exaction only on those who knowingly employed underage laborers. Such scienter requirements are typical of punitive statutes, because Congress often wishes to punish only those who intentionally break the law. Third, this "tax" was enforced in part by the Department of Labor, an agency responsible for punishing violations of labor laws, not collecting revenue.

The same analysis here suggests that the shared responsibility payment may for constitutional purposes be considered a tax, not a penalty: First, for most Americans the amount due will be far less than the price of insurance, and, by statute, it can never be more. It may often be a reasonable financial decision to make the payment rather than purchase insurance, unlike the "prohibitory" financial punishment in *Drexel Furniture*. Second, the individual mandate contains no scienter requirement. Third, the payment is collected solely by the IRS through the normal means of taxation—except that the Service is not allowed to use those means most suggestive of a punitive sanction, such as criminal prosecution. The reasons the Court in *Drexel Furniture* held that what was called a "tax" there was a penalty support the conclusion that what is called a "penalty" here may be viewed as a tax.

None of this is to say that the payment is not intended to affect individual conduct. Although the payment will raise considerable revenue, it is plainly designed to expand health insurance coverage. But taxes that seek to influence conduct are nothing new. Some of our earliest federal taxes sought to deter the purchase of imported manufactured goods in order to foster the growth of domestic industry. Today, federal and state taxes can compose more than half the retail price of cigarettes, not just to raise more money, but to encourage people to quit smoking. And we have upheld such obviously regulatory measures as taxes on selling marijuana and sawed-off shotguns. Indeed, "[e]very tax is in some measure regulatory. To some extent it interposes an economic impediment to the activity taxed as compared with others not taxed." *Sonzinsky v. United States* (1937). That §5000A seeks to shape decisions about whether to buy health insurance does not mean that it cannot be a valid exercise of the taxing power.

In distinguishing penalties from taxes, this Court has explained that "if the concept of penalty means anything, it means punishment for an unlawful act or omission." *United States v. Reorganized CF&I Fabricators of Utah, Inc.* (1996). While the individual mandate clearly aims to induce the purchase of health insurance, it need not be read to declare that failing to do so is unlawful. Neither the Act nor any other law attaches negative legal consequences to not buying health insurance, beyond requiring a payment to the IRS. The Government agrees with that reading, confirming that if someone chooses to pay rather than obtain health insurance, they have fully complied with the law.

Indeed, it is estimated that four million people each year will choose to pay the IRS rather than buy insurance. We would expect Congress to be troubled by that prospect if such conduct were unlawful. That Congress apparently regards such extensive failure to comply with the mandate as tolerable suggests that Congress did not think it was creating four million outlaws. It suggests instead that the shared responsibility payment merely imposes a tax citizens may lawfully choose to pay in lieu of buying health insurance.

The plaintiffs contend that Congress's choice of language—stating that individuals "shall" obtain insurance or pay a "penalty"—requires reading §5000A as punishing unlawful conduct, even if that interpretation would render the law unconstitutional. We have rejected a similar argument before. In *New York v. United States* we examined a statute providing that "[e]ach State shall be responsible for providing . . . for the disposal of . . . low-level radioactive waste." A State that shipped its waste to another State was exposed to surcharges by the receiving State, a portion of which would be paid over to the Federal Government. And a State that did not adhere to the statutory scheme faced "[p]enalties for failure to comply," including increases in the surcharge. *New York* urged us to read the statute as a federal command that the state legislature enact legislation to dispose of its waste, which would have violated the Constitution. To avoid that outcome, we interpreted the statute to impose only "a series of incentives" for the State to take responsibility for its waste. We then sustained the charge paid to the Federal Government as an exercise of the taxing power. We see no insurmountable obstacle to a similar approach here.

The joint dissenters argue that we cannot uphold §5000A as a tax because Congress did not "frame" it as such. In effect, they contend that even if the Constitution permits Congress to do exactly what we interpret this statute to do, the law must be struck down because Congress used the wrong labels. An example may help illustrate why labels should not control here. Suppose Congress enacted a statute providing that every taxpayer who owns a house without energy efficient windows must pay $50 to the IRS. The amount due is adjusted based on factors such as taxable income and joint filing status, and is paid along with the taxpayer's income tax return. Those whose income is below the filing threshold need not pay. The required payment is not called a "tax," a "penalty," or anything else. No one would doubt that this law imposed a tax, and was within Congress's power to tax. That conclusion should not change simply because Congress used the word "penalty" to describe the payment. Interpreting such a law to be a tax would hardly "[i]mpos[e] a tax through judicial legislation." Rather, it would give practical effect to the Legislature's enactment.

Our precedent demonstrates that Congress had the power to impose the exaction in §5000A under the taxing power, and that §5000A need not be read to do more than impose a tax. That is sufficient to sustain it. The "question of the constitutionality of action taken by Congress does not depend on recitals of the power which it undertakes to exercise." *Woods v. Cloyd W. Miller Co.* (1948).

Even if the taxing power enables Congress to impose a tax on not obtaining health insurance, any tax must still comply with other requirements in the Constitution. Plaintiffs argue that the shared responsibility payment does not do so, citing Article I, §9, clause 4. That clause provides: "No Capitation, or other direct, Tax shall be laid, unless in Proportion to the Census or Enumeration herein before directed to be taken." This requirement means that any "direct Tax" must be apportioned so that each State pays in proportion to its population. According to the plaintiffs, if the individual mandate imposes a tax, it is a direct tax, and it is unconstitutional because Congress made no effort to apportion it among the States.

Even when the Direct Tax Clause was written it was unclear what else, other than a capitation (also known as a "head tax" or a "poll tax"), might be a direct tax. Soon after the framing, Congress passed a tax on ownership of carriages, over James Madison's objection that it was an unapportioned direct tax. This Court upheld the tax, in part reasoning that apportioning such a tax would make little sense, because it would have required taxing carriage owners at dramatically different rates depending on how many carriages were in their home State. The Court was unanimous, and those Justices who wrote opinions either directly asserted or strongly suggested that only two forms of taxation were direct: capitations and land taxes.

That narrow view of what a direct tax might be persisted for a century. In 1880, for example, we explained that "direct taxes, within the meaning of the Constitution, are only capitation taxes, as expressed in that instrument, and taxes on real estate." *Springer v. United States* (1881). In 1895, we expanded our interpretation to include taxes on personal property and income from personal property, in the course of striking down aspects of the federal income tax. *Pollock v. Farmers' Loan & Trust Co.* (1895). That result was overturned by the Sixteenth Amendment, although we continued to consider taxes on personal property to be direct taxes.

A tax on going without health insurance does not fall within any recognized category of direct tax. It is not a capitation. Capitations are taxes paid by every person, "without regard to property, profession, or *any other circumstance.*" *Hylton v. United States* (1796) (emphasis altered). The whole point of the shared responsibility payment is that it is triggered by specific circumstances—earning a certain amount of income but not obtaining health insurance. The payment is also plainly not a tax on the ownership of land or personal property. The shared responsibility payment is thus not a direct tax that must be apportioned among the several States.

There may, however, be a more fundamental objection to a tax on those who lack health insurance. Even if only a tax, the payment under §5000A(b) remains a burden that the Federal Government imposes for an omission, not an act. If it is troubling to interpret the Commerce Clause as authorizing Congress to regulate those who abstain from commerce, perhaps it should be similarly troubling to permit Congress to impose a tax for not doing something.

Three considerations allay this concern. First, and most importantly, it is abundantly clear the Constitution does not guarantee that individuals may avoid taxation through inactivity. A capitation, after all, is a tax that everyone must pay simply for existing, and capitations are expressly contemplated by the Constitution. The Court today holds that our Constitution protects us from federal regulation under the Commerce Clause so long as we abstain from the regulated activity. But from its creation, the Constitution has made no such promise with respect to taxes.

Whether the mandate can be upheld under the Commerce Clause is a question about the scope of federal authority. Its answer depends on whether Congress can exercise what all acknowledge to be the novel course of directing individuals to purchase insurance. Congress's use of the Taxing Clause to encourage buying something is, by contrast, not new. Tax incentives already promote, for example, purchasing homes and professional educations. Sustaining the mandate as a tax depends only on whether Congress has properly exercised its taxing power to encourage purchasing health insurance, not whether it can. Upholding the individual mandate under the Taxing Clause thus does not recognize any new federal power. It determines that Congress has used an existing one.

Second, Congress's ability to use its taxing power to influence conduct is not without limits. A few of our cases policed these limits aggressively, invalidating punitive exactions obviously designed to regulate behavior otherwise regarded at the time as beyond federal authority. More often and more recently we have declined to closely examine the regulatory motive or effect of revenue-raising measures. We have nonetheless maintained that "there comes a time in the extension of the penalizing features of the so-called tax when it loses its character as such and becomes a mere penalty with the characteristics of regulation and punishment." *Department of Revenue of Mont. v. Kurth Ranch* (1994) (quoting *Drexel Furniture, supra*).

We have already explained that the shared responsibility payment's practical characteristics pass muster as a tax under our narrowest interpretations of the taxing power. *Supra.* Because the tax at hand is within even those strict limits, we need not here decide the precise point at which an exaction becomes so punitive that the taxing power does not authorize it. It remains true, however, that the "power to tax is not the power to destroy while this Court sits." *Oklahoma Tax Comm'n v. Texas Co.* (1949).

Third, although the breadth of Congress's power to tax is greater than its power to regulate commerce, the taxing power does not give Congress the same degree of control over individual behavior. Once we recognize that Congress may regulate a particular decision under the Commerce Clause, the Federal Government can bring its full weight to bear. Congress may simply command individuals to do as it directs. An individual who disobeys may be subjected to criminal sanctions. Those sanctions can include not only fines and imprisonment, but all the attendant consequences of being branded a criminal: deprivation of otherwise protected civil rights, such as the right to bear arms or vote in elections; loss of employment opportunities; social stigma; and severe disabilities in other controversies, such as custody or immigration disputes.

By contrast, Congress's authority under the taxing power is limited to requiring an individual to pay money into the Federal Treasury, no more. If a tax is properly paid, the Government has no power to compel or punish individuals subject to it. We do not make light of the severe burden that taxation—especially taxation motivated by a regulatory purpose—can impose. But imposition of a tax nonetheless leaves an individual with a lawful choice to do or not do a certain act, so long as he is willing to pay a tax levied on that choice.

The Affordable Care Act's requirement that certain individuals pay a financial penalty for not obtaining health insurance may reasonably be characterized as a tax. Because the Constitution permits such a tax, it is not our role to forbid it, or to pass upon its wisdom or fairness.

D

Justice Ginsburg questions the necessity of rejecting the Government's commerce power argument, given that §5000A can be upheld under the taxing power. But the statute reads more naturally as a command to buy insurance than as a tax, and I would uphold it as a command if the Constitution allowed it. It is only because the Commerce Clause does not authorize such a command that it is necessary to reach the taxing power question. And it is only because we have a duty to construe a statute to save it, if fairly possible, that §5000A can be interpreted as a tax. Without deciding the Commerce Clause question, I would find no basis to adopt such a saving construction.

The Federal Government does not have the power to order people to buy health insurance. Section 5000A would therefore be unconstitutional if read as a command. The Federal Government does have the power to impose a tax on those without health insurance. Section 5000A is therefore constitutional, because it can reasonably be read as a tax.

IV

A

The States also contend that the Medicaid expansion exceeds Congress's authority under the Spending Clause. They claim that Congress is coercing the States to adopt the changes it wants by threatening to withhold all of a State's Medicaid grants, unless the State accepts the new expanded funding and complies with the conditions that come with it. This, they argue, violates the basic principle that the "Federal Government may not compel the States to enact or administer a federal regulatory program." *New York*.

There is no doubt that the Act dramatically increases state obligations under Medicaid. The current Medicaid program requires States to cover only certain discrete categories of needy individuals—pregnant women, children, needy families, the blind, the elderly, and the disabled. There is no mandatory coverage for most childless adults, and the States typically do not offer any such coverage. The States also enjoy considerable flexibility with respect to the coverage levels for parents of needy families. On average, States cover only those unemployed parents who make less than 37 percent of the federal poverty level, and only those employed parents who make less than 63 percent of the poverty line.

The Medicaid provisions of the Affordable Care Act, in contrast, require States to expand their Medicaid programs by 2014 to cover all individuals under the age of 65 with incomes below 133 percent of the federal poverty line. The Act also establishes a new "[e]ssential health benefits" package, which States must provide to all new Medicaid recipients—a level sufficient to satisfy a recipient's obligations under the individual mandate. The Affordable Care Act provides that the Federal Government will pay 100 percent of the costs of covering these newly eligible individuals through 2016. In the following years, the federal payment level gradually decreases, to a minimum of 90 percent. In light of the expansion in coverage mandated by the Act, the Federal Government estimates that its Medicaid spending will increase by approximately $100 billion per year, nearly 40 percent above current levels.

The Spending Clause grants Congress the power "to pay the Debts and provide for the . . . general Welfare of the United States." U.S. Const., Art. I, §8, cl. 1.

We have long recognized that Congress may use this power to grant federal funds to the States, and may condition such a grant upon the States' "taking certain actions that Congress could not require them to take." *College Savings Bank*, 527 U.S. Such measures "encourage a State to regulate in a particular way, [and] influenc[e] a State's policy choices." *New York, supra.* The conditions imposed by Congress ensure that the funds are used by the States to "provide for the . . . general Welfare" in the manner Congress intended.

At the same time, our cases have recognized limits on Congress's power under the Spending Clause to secure state compliance with federal objectives. "We have repeatedly characterized . . . Spending Clause legislation as 'much in the nature of a contract.'" *Barnes v. Gorman* (2002) (quoting *Pennhurst State School and Hospital v. Halderman* (1981)). The legitimacy of Congress's exercise of the spending power "thus rests on whether the State voluntarily and knowingly accepts the terms of the 'contract.'" *Pennhurst, supra.* Respecting this limitation is critical to ensuring that Spending Clause legislation does not undermine the status of the States as independent sovereigns in our federal system. That system "rests on what might at first seem a counterintuitive insight, that 'freedom is enhanced by the creation of two governments, not one.'" *Bond*, 564 U.S. (quoting *Alden v. Maine* (1999)). For this reason, "the Constitution has never been understood to confer upon Congress the ability to require the States to govern according to Congress's instructions." *New York, supra.* Otherwise, the two-government system established by the Framers would give way to a system that vests power in one central government, and individual liberty would suffer.

That insight has led this Court to strike down federal legislation that commandeers a State's legislative or administrative apparatus for federal purposes. It has also led us to scrutinize Spending Clause legislation to ensure that Congress is not using financial inducements to exert a "power akin to undue influence." *Steward Machine Co. v. Davis* (1937). Congress may use its spending power to create incentives for States to act in accordance with federal policies. But when "pressure turns into compulsion," *ibid.*, the legislation runs contrary to our system of federalism. "[T]he Constitution simply does not give Congress the authority to require the States to regulate." *New York.* That is true whether Congress directly commands a State to regulate or indirectly coerces a State to adopt a federal regulatory system as its own.

Permitting the Federal Government to force the States to implement a federal program would threaten the political accountability key to our federal system. "[W]here the Federal Government directs the States to regulate, it may be state officials who will bear the brunt of public disapproval, while the federal officials who devised the regulatory program may remain insulated from the electoral ramifications of their decision." *Id.* Spending Clause programs do not pose this danger when a State has a legitimate choice whether to accept the federal conditions in exchange for federal funds. In such a situation, state officials can fairly be held politically accountable for choosing to accept or refuse the federal offer. But when the State has no choice, the Federal Government can achieve its objectives without accountability, just as in *New York* and *Printz*. Indeed, this danger is heightened when Congress acts under the Spending Clause, because Congress can use that power to implement federal policy it could not impose directly under its enumerated powers.

We addressed such concerns in *Steward Machine*. That case involved a federal tax on employers that was abated if the businesses paid into a state unemployment plan that met certain federally specified conditions. An employer sued, alleging that the tax was impermissibly "driv[ing] the state legislatures under the whip of economic pressure into the enactment of unemployment compensation laws at the bidding of the central government." 301 U.S. We acknowledged the danger that the Federal Government might employ its taxing power to exert a "power akin to undue influence" upon the States. *Id.* But we observed that Congress adopted the challenged tax and abatement program to channel money to the States that would otherwise have gone into the Federal Treasury for use in providing national unemployment services. Congress was willing to direct businesses to instead pay the money into state programs only on the condition that the money be used for the same purposes. Predicating tax abatement on a State's adoption of a particular type of unemployment legislation was therefore a means to "safeguard [the Federal Government's] own treasury." *Id.* We held that "[i]n such circumstances, if in no others, inducement or persuasion does not go beyond the bounds of power." *Ibid.*

In rejecting the argument that the federal law was a "[weapon] of coercion, destroying or impairing the autonomy of the states," the Court noted that there was no reason to suppose that the State in that case acted other than through "her unfettered will." *Id.* Indeed, the State itself did "not offer a suggestion that in passing the unemployment law she was affected by duress." *Id.*

As our decision in *Steward Machine* confirms, Congress may attach appropriate conditions to federal taxing and spending programs to preserve its control over the use of federal funds. In the typical case, we look to the States to defend their prerogatives by adopting "the simple expedient of not yielding" to federal blandishments when they do not want to embrace the federal policies as their own. *Massachusetts v. Mellon* (1923). The States are separate and independent sovereigns. Sometimes they have to act like it.

The States, however, argue that the Medicaid expansion is far from the typical case. They object that Congress has "crossed the line distinguishing encouragement from coercion," *New York, supra*, in the way it has structured the funding: Instead of simply refusing to grant the new funds to States that will not accept the new conditions, Congress has also threatened to withhold those States' existing Medicaid funds. The States claim that this threat serves no purpose other than to force unwilling States to sign up for the dramatic expansion in health care coverage effected by the Act.

Given the nature of the threat and the programs at issue here, we must agree. We have upheld Congress's authority to condition the receipt of funds on the States' complying with restrictions on the use of those funds, because that is the means by which Congress ensures that the funds are spent according to its view of the "general Welfare." Conditions that do not here govern the use of the funds, however, cannot be justified on that basis. When, for example, such conditions take the form of threats to terminate other significant independent grants, the conditions are properly viewed as a means of pressuring the States to accept policy changes.

In *South Dakota v. Dole*, we considered a challenge to a federal law that threatened to withhold 5 percent of a State's federal highway funds if the State did not raise its drinking age to 21. The Court found that the condition was "directly related to one of the main purposes for which highway funds are expended—safe interstate travel." 483 U.S. At the same time, the condition was not a restriction on how the highway funds—set aside for specific highway improvement and maintenance efforts—were to be used.

We accordingly asked whether "the financial inducement offered by Congress" was "so coercive as to pass the point at which 'pressure turns into compulsion.'" *Id.* By "financial inducement" the Court meant the threat of losing 5 percent of highway funds; no new money was offered to the States to raise their drinking ages. We found that the inducement was not impermissibly coercive, because Congress was offering only "relatively mild encouragement to the States." *Dole*, 483 U.S. We observed that "all South Dakota would lose if she adheres to her chosen course as to a suitable minimum drinking age is 5 [percent]" of her highway funds. *Ibid.* In fact, the federal funds at stake constituted less than half of 1 percent of South Dakota's budget at the time. In consequence, "we conclude[d] that [the] encouragement to state action [was] a valid use of the spending power." *Ibid.* Whether to accept the drinking age change "remain[ed] the prerogative of the States not merely in theory but in fact." *Id.*

In this case, the financial "inducement" Congress has chosen is much more than "relatively mild encouragement"—it is a gun to the head. Section 1396c of the Medicaid Act provides that if a State's Medicaid plan does not comply with the Act's requirements, the Secretary of Health and Human Services may declare that "further payments will not be made to the State." A State that opts out of the Affordable Care Act's expansion in health care coverage thus stands to lose not merely "a relatively small percentage" of its existing Medicaid funding, but all of it. *Dole, supra.* Medicaid spending accounts for over 20 percent of the average State's total budget, with federal funds covering 50 to 83 percent of those costs. The Federal Government estimates that it will pay out approximately $3.3 trillion between 2010 and 2019 in order to cover the costs of pre-expansion Medicaid. In addition, the States have developed intricate statutory and administrative regimes over the course of many decades to implement their objectives under existing Medicaid. It is easy to see how the *Dole* Court could conclude that the threatened loss of less than half of 1 percent of South Dakota's budget left that State with a "prerogative" to reject Congress's desired policy, "not merely in theory but in fact." The threatened loss of over 10 percent of a State's overall budget, in contrast, is economic dragooning that leaves the States with no real option but to acquiesce in the Medicaid expansion.

Justice Ginsburg claims that *Dole* is distinguishable because here "Congress has not threatened to withhold funds earmarked for any other program." *Post*. But that begs the question: The States contend that the expansion is in reality a new program, and that Congress is forcing them to accept it by threatening the funds for the existing Medicaid program. We cannot agree that existing Medicaid and the expansion dictated by the Affordable Care Act are all one program simply because "Congress styled" them as such. *Post*. If the expansion is not properly viewed as a modification of the existing Medicaid program, Congress's decision to so title it is irrelevant.

Here, the Government claims that the Medicaid expansion is properly viewed merely as a modification of the existing program because the States agreed that Congress could change the terms of Medicaid when they signed on in the first place. The Government observes that the Social Security Act, which includes the original Medicaid provisions, contains a clause expressly reserving "[t]he right to alter, amend, or repeal any provision" of that statute. So it does. But "if Congress intends to impose a condition on the grant of federal moneys, it must do so unambiguously." *Pennhurst*. A State confronted with statutory language reserving the right to "alter" or "amend" the pertinent provisions of the Social Security Act might reasonably assume that Congress was entitled to make adjustments to the Medicaid program as it developed. Congress has in fact done so, sometimes conditioning only the new funding, other times both old and new.

The Medicaid expansion, however, accomplishes a shift in kind, not merely degree. The original program was designed to cover medical services for four particular categories of the needy: the disabled, the blind, the elderly, and needy families with dependent children. Previous amendments to Medicaid eligibility merely altered and expanded the boundaries of these categories. Under the Affordable Care Act, Medicaid is transformed into a program to meet the health care needs of the entire nonelderly population with income below 133 percent of the poverty level. It is no longer a program to care for the neediest among us, but rather an element of a comprehensive national plan to provide universal health insurance coverage.

Indeed, the manner in which the expansion is structured indicates that while Congress may have styled the expansion a mere alteration of existing Medicaid, it recognized it was enlisting the States in a new health care program. Congress created a separate funding provision to cover the costs of providing services to any person made newly eligible by the expansion. While Congress pays 50 to 83 percent of the costs of covering individuals currently enrolled in Medicaid, once the expansion is fully implemented Congress will pay 90 percent of the costs for newly eligible persons. The conditions on use of the different funds are also distinct. Congress mandated that newly eligible persons receive a level of coverage that is less comprehensive than the traditional Medicaid benefit package.

As we have explained, "[t]hough Congress's power to legislate under the spending power is broad, it does not include surprising participating States with postacceptance or 'retroactive' conditions." *Pennhurst, supra.* A State could hardly anticipate that Congress's reservation of the right to "alter" or "amend" the Medicaid program included the power to transform it so dramatically.

Justice Ginsburg claims that in fact this expansion is no different from the previous changes to Medicaid, such that "a State would be hard put to complain that it lacked fair notice." *Post.* But the prior change she discusses— presumably the most dramatic alteration she could find—does not come close to working the transformation the expansion accomplishes. She highlights an amendment requiring States to cover pregnant women and increasing the number of eligible children. *Ibid.* But this modification can hardly be described as a major change in a program that—from its inception—provided health care for "families with dependent children." Previous Medicaid amendments simply do not fall into the same category as the one at stake here.

The Court in *Steward Machine* did not attempt to "fix the outermost line" where persuasion gives way to coercion. 301 U.S. The Court found it "[e]nough for present purposes that wherever the line may be, this statute is within it." *Ibid.* We have no need to fix the line either. It is enough for today that wherever that line may be, this statute is surely beyond it. Congress may not simply "conscript state [agencies] into the national bureaucratic army," *FERC v. Mississippi* (1982), and that is what it is attempting to do with the Medicaid expansion.

B

Nothing in our opinion precludes Congress from offering funds under the Affordable Care Act to expand the availability of health care, and requiring that States accepting such funds comply with the conditions on their use. What Congress is not free to do is to penalize States that choose not to participate in that new program by taking away their existing Medicaid funding. Section 1396c gives the Secretary of Health and Human Services the authority to do just that. It allows her to withhold all "further [Medicaid] payments . . . to the State" if she determines that the State is out of compliance with any Medicaid requirement, including those contained in the expansion. In light of the Court's holding, the Secretary cannot apply §1396c to withdraw existing Medicaid funds for failure to comply with the requirements set out in the expansion.

That fully remedies the constitutional violation we have identified. The chapter of the United States Code that contains §1396c includes a severability clause confirming that we need go no further. That clause specifies that "[i]f any provision of this chapter, or the application thereof to any person or circumstance, is held invalid, the remainder of the chapter, and the application of such provision to other persons or circumstances shall not be affected thereby." Today's holding does not affect the continued application of §1396c to the existing Medicaid program. Nor does it affect the Secretary's ability to withdraw funds provided under the Affordable Care Act if a State that has chosen to participate in the expansion fails to comply with the requirements of that Act.

This is not to say, as the joint dissent suggests, that we are "rewriting the Medicaid Expansion." *Post*. Instead, we determine, first, that §1396c is unconstitutional when applied to withdraw existing Medicaid funds from States that decline to comply with the expansion. We then follow Congress's explicit textual instruction to leave unaffected "the remainder of the chapter, and the application of [the challenged] provision to other persons or circumstances." When we invalidate an application of a statute because that application is unconstitutional, we are not "rewriting" the statute; we are merely enforcing the Constitution.

The question remains whether today's holding affects other provisions of the Affordable Care Act. In considering that question, "[w]e seek to determine what Congress would have intended in light of the Court's constitutional holding." *United States v. Booker* (2005). Our "touchstone for any decision about remedy is legislative intent, for a court cannot use its remedial powers to circumvent the intent of the legislature." *Ayotte v. Planned Parenthood of Northern New Eng.* (2006). The question here is whether Congress would have wanted the rest of the Act to stand, had it known that States would have a genuine choice whether to participate in the new Medicaid expansion. Unless it is "evident" that the answer is no, we must leave the rest of the Act intact. *Champlin Refining Co. v. Corporation Comm'n of Okla.* (1932).

We are confident that Congress would have wanted to preserve the rest of the Act. It is fair to say that Congress assumed that every State would participate in the Medicaid expansion, given that States had no real choice but to do so. The States contend that Congress enacted the rest of the Act with such full participation in mind; they point out that Congress made Medicaid a means for satisfying the mandate and enacted no other plan for providing coverage to many low-income individuals. According to the States, this means that the entire Act must fall.

We disagree. The Court today limits the financial pressure the Secretary may apply to induce States to accept the terms of the Medicaid expansion. As a practical matter, that means States may now choose to reject the expansion; that is the whole point. But that does not mean all or even any will. Some States may indeed decline to participate, either because they are unsure they will be able to afford their share of the new funding obligations, or because they are unwilling to commit the administrative resources necessary to support the expansion. Other States, however, may voluntarily sign up, finding the idea of expanding Medicaid coverage attractive, particularly given the level of federal funding the Act offers at the outset.

We have no way of knowing how many States will accept the terms of the expansion, but we do not believe Congress would have wanted the whole Act to fall, simply because some may choose not to participate. The other reforms Congress enacted, after all, will remain "fully operative as a law," *Champlin, supra*, and will still function in a way "consistent with Congress's basic objectives in enacting the statute," *Booker, supra*. Confident that Congress would not have intended anything different, we conclude that the rest of the Act need not fall in light of our constitutional holding.

▪   ▪   ▪

The Affordable Care Act is constitutional in part and unconstitutional in part. The individual mandate cannot be upheld as an exercise of Congress's power under the Commerce Clause. That Clause authorizes Congress to regulate interstate commerce, not to order individuals to engage in it. In this case, however, it is reasonable to construe what Congress has done as increasing taxes on those who have a certain amount of income, but choose to go without health insurance. Such legislation is within Congress's power to tax.

As for the Medicaid expansion, that portion of the Affordable Care Act violates the Constitution by threatening existing Medicaid funding. Congress has no authority to order the States to regulate according to its instructions. Congress may offer the States grants and require the States to comply with accompanying conditions, but the States must have a genuine choice whether to accept the offer. The States are given no such choice in this case: They must either accept a basic change in the nature of Medicaid, or risk losing all Medicaid funding. The remedy for that constitutional violation is to preclude the Federal Government from imposing such a sanction. That remedy does not require striking down other portions of the Affordable Care Act.

The Framers created a Federal Government of limited powers, and assigned to this Court the duty of enforcing those limits. The Court does so today. But the Court does not express any opinion on the wisdom of the Affordable Care Act. Under the Constitution, that judgment is reserved to the people.

The judgment of the Court of Appeals for the Eleventh Circuit is affirmed in part and reversed in part.

It is so ordered.

8.5

TRACEY E. GEORGE AND LEE EPSTEIN

"On the Nature of Supreme Court Decision Making"

George and Epstein contrast two models of Supreme Court decision making. One, the legal model, focuses attention on the role of past law including precedents in shaping Supreme Court decisions. The other, the extralegal model, focuses attention on the political pressures facing the Court as well as the policy preferences of the justices. George and Epstein incorporate both the legal and extralegal models into a unified model and study capital punishment (execution) cases before the Supreme Court over two decades, the 1970s and 1980s. They show that legal factors predict Court decisions better earlier in the period while extralegal factors predict Court decisions later in the period.

How does the U.S. Supreme Court reach decisions? [Scholars] answer that question quite differently. [One], grounded in positivist jurisprudence, [may] suggest that the rule of law *stare decisis* is the key determinant. [Another], reflecting political jurisprudence, [may] posit the converse—that an array of sociological, psychological, and political factors having little to do with legal doctrine produce judicial outcomes. These perspectives represent the mainstream—albeit highly divergent—responses to the question we pose. . . .

Can two highly divergent conceptualizations of judicial decision making coexist? Empirical evidence suggests that at minimum, each can account for variations in behavior. . . .

Yet for all the research conducted and all the years this debate has raged, it is almost startling to find that scholars have yet to compare these basic models systematically.[1] . . .

How legal and extralegal models of judicial decision making perform in head-to-head competition forms our central concern here. Using Court cases involving the imposition of the death penalty, we estimate and evaluate the ability of each to account for decisional outcomes.

■　■　■

From Tracey E. George and Lee Epstein, "On the Nature of Supreme Court Decision Making," *The American Political Science Review* 86 no. 2 (June 1992): 323–337.

THE LEGAL MODEL

At its core, legalism centers around a rather simple assumption about judicial decision making, namely, that legal doctrine, generated by past cases, is the primary determinant of extant case outcomes. It views judges as constrained decision makers who "will base their opinions on precedent and will adhere to the doctrine of *stare decisis*" (Wasby 1988, 210). Some scholars label this *mechanical jurisprudence*, because the process by which judges reach decisions is highly structured. . . . Legal education and scholarship adopted this as a paradigm—the process by which judges and lawyers should proceed.

■   ■   ■

THE EXTRALEGAL MODEL

[N]ew perspectives emerged from the ranks of the nation's judiciary and law schools. In general, these thinkers denounced legalism as mechanical. . . . Instead, they beckoned judges to consider more dynamic factors as bases for decisions. . . . It was Pound (1931), however, who catalyzed the first strain of extrajudicialism, sometimes called *sociological jurisprudence*. In his seminal *Harvard Law Review* article, Pound drew his now-famous distinction between "law in books" and "law in action," behooving judges to adopt the latter, without necessarily abandoning the former. Cardozo and many others followed suit.

■   ■   ■

So began a long line of thinkers who harshly critiqued legal reasoning for its inadequacy as a basis for judicial decision making, an inadequacy stemming from various considerations. . . . It would be extraordinary, they claimed, to think that judges, just because they don black robes, were any less susceptible to such influences. Indeed, justices may be even more vulnerable than other decision makers because the rules of law are "typically available to support either side" (Pritchett 1969, 31). In making choices between competing precedents, then, other factors are bound to come into play.

■   ■   ■

MODELS: CURRENT STATUS

Over the past decades, countless efforts have viewed court decisions as a function of personal attributes (e.g., Tate 1981), attitudes (Rohde and Spaeth 1976), and role conceptions (Gibson 1978). In general, however, most of these depict a Court driven by single-minded seekers of legal policy, justices who wish to etch into law their personal views.

Though the basic tenets of behavioralism continue to shape our vision of the judicial process, we have made some attempts at refining that conceptualization. In general, we now know that Court decisions are a product of factors not only internal but also external to the Court.

Political scientists recognize that pressures emanating from outside the legal system can affect case outcomes. In particular, we believe that the Court is responsive to the larger political environment. Some suggest that its rulings reflect the wishes of the citizenry (e.g., Barnum 1985).

▪ ▪ ▪

ESTIMATING THE MODELS

Since both legal and extralegal models are well established theoretically and analytically, we evaluate each on . . . the ability to classify Court decisions correctly. For this examination, we focus on almost two decades' worth of cases involving capital punishment (N = 64), measuring Court outcomes as a simple binary choice [of] whether it affirmed the imposition of the penalty (coded 1) or not (coded 0). Data are from the *U.S. Reports* for the 1971–88 terms.

▪ ▪ ▪

EVALUATING THE MODELS: CATEGORIZATIONS AND PREDICTIONS

As we depict in Table [1], . . . both models start off quite well, postdicting nearly 100% of the 20 cases decided during the first two natural courts. Equally satisfying is that both categorize correctly 10 of the 14 cases occurring in Natural Court 4. Perhaps most important, however, is that their ability to generate correct predictions for the latest round of death penalty cases was nearly as good as those for the first. Our models correctly categorized all three cases decided in 1972. During the 1988 term, the Court decided seven cases involv-

TABLE [1] Evaluating the Predictions of Legal and Extralegal Models Over Time

	Number of Cases Predicted Correctly		
Natural Court Era	*Legal Model*	*Extralegal Model*	*Total Number of Cases*
1 (1971–74)	3 (100)	3 (100)	3
2 (1975–80)	16 (94)	17 (100)	17
3 (1981–86)	19 (63)	22 (73)	30
4 (1987–88)	10 (71)	10 (71)	14
Total	48 (75)	52 (81)	64

NOTE: Prediction equations are probits using estimates displayed in Table 1. Percentages are in parentheses.

ing imposition of the death penalty. If we withhold those cases and reestimate the models, each accurately forecasts the outcomes in five of the seven.

Although no erosion occurred in the utility of either model, a more detailed examination reveals the presence of two nontrivial problems. First, as we can see in Table [2], which depicts the percentage of liberal and conservative outcomes produced during each natural court (in contrast to the actual outcomes), our models possess ideological biases. The political model becomes increasingly and *incorrectly* prone toward conservatism. For Natural Court 1, it correctly classified all outcomes as liberal; by Natural Court 4, it placed only 21% of cases into that category, when half actually belonged there. Thus, despite initial appearances, by Natural Court 4 the political model is overestimating conservatism, an important finding, to which we will return.

The legal model exhibits precisely the opposite propensity. Beginning in Natural Court 3, the legal model overestimates the *liberal* inclination of the Court. As Table [1] indicates, it yielded its worst predictions in Natural Court 3. As we can see in Table [2], it produced those errors because it overcategorized liberal outcomes. Natural Court 4 presents much the same picture. It classified all seven cases decided in favor of the defendant accurately, but only three of the seven outcomes supporting the state. In short, our doctrinal model predicts more prodefendant outcomes over time than actually occurred, while the extralegal one is moving in the opposite direction. This reaches a point of virtual juxtaposition in Natural Court 4, when the legal model suggested that 79% of the cases would fall into the liberal column, while its extralegal counterpart placed 79% into the conservative one.

TABLE [2] Evaluating the Predictions of Legal and Extralegal Models by Ideology

		% Predicted			
		Natural Court Era			
		1 (1971–74)	2 (1975–86)	3 (1981–86)	4 (1987–88)
Liberal (Against Death Penalty)	Legal	100	76	66	79
	Extralegal	100	82	43	21
	Actual % Liberal	100	82	36	50
Conservative (for Death Penalty)	Legal	0	24	33	21
	Extralegal	0	18	56	79
	Actual % Conservative	0	18	63	50
Total Number of Cases		3	17	30	14

NOTE: Prediction equations are probits using estimates displayed in Table 1.

■　■　■

Not only are the models exhibiting trended ideological behavior, but (a related problem) they also seem to be working at cross purposes. Consider that the legal model incorrectly classified 16 cases, the extralegal one 13. If the cases missed by the models were simply idiopathic, we would expect many of the total 29 to be shared errors; but in fact, they had only 4 missed cases in common. Put in somewhat different terms, of the 16 outcomes incorrectly classified by the legal model, the extralegal one picked up 12. Conversely, the legal model accurately categorized 9 of the 13 errors produced by the extralegal one.

Hence, what emerges (taken in conjunction with previous findings) is that while the overall fits are quite good, the models exhibit disturbing propensities and, interestingly, ones that move in precisely opposing directions. The political model becomes increasingly conservative, the legal model increasingly liberal. Thus, the errors they produce are largely idiosyncratic. . . . Taken together, then, the legal and extralegal models seem to be working at cross purposes, producing opposing categorizations over time.

■　■　■

AN INTEGRATED MODEL

[B]oth models possess weaknesses—weaknesses that run diametrically to one another. The legal perspective, which overpredicts liberal outcomes, needs to be tempered by a consideration of political forces. Conversely, the extralegal model should be checked by doctrinal constraints. Given these weaknesses, should we abandon both models as incomplete portrayals of Court decision making? We think not. Rather, they should be considered codependent explanations. The legal model assumes that the Court cannot ignore its role as an adjudicative body, that it is bound by precedent. The extralegal model assumes that the Court heeds political forces and must do so to retain its institutional legitimacy. Over time, those models may diverge, applying diametric pressure of the Court. For capital punishment cases, the legal model exerts a liberalizing influence on the justices as attorneys capitalize on existing doctrine. The extralegal exerts influence toward a more conservative posture as the external and political environments move in that direction. To this extent, legal and extralegal models present interdependent explanations of judicial decision making.

Seen in this light, then, our most prudent approach, analytically speaking, is to combine the two into an integrated model of decision making, one informed by both legal and extralegal factors.

■　■　■

[G]iven the relative weight of extralegal factors (nonexistent), the data do tell us something about the nature of judicial decision making. When the justices placed the relatively novel issue of capital punishment on their agenda in 1972, they were apparently more influenced by the extant legal claims than by political and societal forces, which had yet to gel sufficiently. Such a finding seems to support what others have written about those early death penalty cases.

■   ■   ■

CONCLUSION

■   ■   ■

Taken as a whole, what does our model reveal about the nature of Supreme Court decision making? Can we now address our original research question, How does the Supreme Court reach decisions? On some level, its answer is obvious: the most complete explanation of judicial outcomes should incorporate legal and extralegal factors. Seen in this light, the views of neither the classical legal thinkers nor the behavioralists are incorrect; but they are incomplete. Both law and politics, as we would intuitively expect, play significant roles in the Supreme Court's decision-making process.

On another level, however, these roles may not necessarily be equivalent. Our analysis of capital cases reveals that legal factors have the greatest impact at the early stages of an issue's life; as it evolves, however, extralegal variables dominate.

NOTES

1. On the other hand, we could argue that this is more the "norm" than it is an anomaly; that is, research on the judicial process rarely compares models of decision making. Two of the few exceptions are Gibson 1978 and Johnson 1987. The latter, especially, is relevant to our study. Johnson sought to determine whether a legal or political model accounted for "more variation in the use of Supreme Court decisions by lower federal courts" (1987, 325). In the end, his analysis lends support to "those who argue that legal factors in part account for judicial behavior, especially in lower courts" (339).

REFERENCES

Barnum, David G. 1985. "The Supreme Court and Public Opinion: Judicial Decision Making in the Post–New Deal Period." *Journal of Politics* 47:652–65.

Cardozo, Benjamin N. 1921. *The Nature of the Judicial Process.* New Haven: Yale University Press.

Gibson, James L. 1978. "Judges' Role Orientations, Attitudes, and Decisions: An Interactive Model." *American Political Science Review* 72:911–24.

Pound, Roscoe. 1931. "The Call for a Realist Jurisprudence." *Harvard Law Review* 44:697–711.

Pritchett, C. Herman. 1969. "The Development of Judicial Research." In *Frontiers of Judicial Research*, ed. Joel B. Grossman and Joseph Tanenhaus. New York: Wiley.

Rohde, David W., and Harold J. Spaeth. 1976. *Supreme Court Decision Making*. San Francisco: Freeman.

Tate, C. Neal. 1981. "Personal Attribute Models of Voting Behavior of U.S. Supreme Court Justices: Liberalism in Civil Liberties and Economic Decisions, 1946–1978." *American Political Science Review* 75:355–67.

Wasby, Stephen L. 1988. *The Supreme Court in the Federal Judicial System*. Nelson Hall.

DISCUSSION QUESTIONS

1. Contrast the constrained court and dynamic court views of the federal judiciary.

2. What task, according to this ruling, is "emphatically the province and duty of the Judicial Department"? Why does Marshall not consider this a "political power"?

3. What elements of the Constitution does Kennedy use to justify this ruling overturning *Bowers*?

4. What elements of the Constitution does Roberts use to justify this ruling upholding the main aspects of the Affordable Care Act?

5. Compare the legal and extra-legal models of Supreme Court decision-making.

6. How insulated is the Supreme Court from broader political pressures from the other branches and from the general public? Provide evidence from these readings.

9

PUBLIC OPINION

9.1

ARTHUR LUPIA AND MATHEW D. McCUBBINS

From *The Democratic Dilemma: Can Citizens Learn What They Need to Know?*

Some observers have concluded that Americans do not know enough about politics and government to make wise choices in voting and other political decisions. The "dilemma" in the title is that citizens are quite uninformed but are being asked to make weighty decisions, like who should be president. Lupia and McCubbins argue that most of the time, under normal conditions, citizens get enough information to make reasonable decisions.

> Knowledge will forever govern ignorance: And a people who mean to be their own Governors, must arm themselves with the power which knowledge gives. A popular Government, without popular information, or the means of acquiring it, is but a Prologue to a Farce or a Tragedy; or, perhaps both.
>
> —James Madison[1]

The founders of the American republic, and many of their contemporaries around the world, believed that democracy requires citizens to make reasoned choices. Reasoned choice, in turn, requires that people know the consequences of their actions.

From Arthur Lupia and Mathew D. McCubbins, *The Democratic Dilemma: Can Citizens Learn What They Need to Know?* (New York: Cambridge University Press, 1998).

Can voters, legislators, and jurors make reasoned choices? Many observers conclude that they cannot. The evidence for this conclusion is substantial—study after study documents the breadth and depth of citizen ignorance. Making matters worse is the fact that many people acquire what little information they have from thirty-minute news summaries, thirty-second political advertisements, or eight-second sound bites. From this evidence, it seems very likely that "Men of factious tempers, of local prejudices, or of sinister designs, may, by intrigue, by corruption, or by any other means, first obtain the suffrages, and then betray the interests, of the people" (Madison, *Federalist* 10).

It is widely believed that there is a mismatch between the requirements of democracy and most people's ability to meet these requirements. If this mismatch is too prevalent, then effective self-governance is impossible. The *democratic dilemma* is that the people who are called upon to make reasoned choices may not be capable of doing so.

[W]e concede that people lack political information. We also concede that this ignorance can allow people "of sinister designs" to deceive and betray the underinformed. We do not concede, however, that democracy *must* succumb to these threats. Rather, we conclude that:

- Reasoned choice does not require full information; rather, it requires the ability to predict the consequences of actions. We define this ability as knowledge.[2]
- People *choose* to disregard most of the information they could acquire and base virtually all of their decisions on remarkably little information.
- People often *substitute* the advice of others for the information they lack. This substitution can give people the capacity for reasoned choice.
- Relying on the advice of others involves tradeoffs. Although it decreases the costs of acquiring knowledge, it also introduces the possibility of deception.
- A person who wants to gain knowledge from the advice of others must choose to follow some advice while ignoring other advice. People make these choices in systematic and predictable ways.
- Political institutions can help people choose which advice to follow and which advice to ignore. Institutions do this when they *clarify* the incentives of advice givers.
- Understanding how people learn not only helps us better identify when presumed democratic dilemmas are real but also shows us how we might begin to resolve these dilemmas. . . .

DEMOCRACY, DELEGATION, AND REASONED CHOICE

Democracy is a method of government based upon the choices of the people. In all modern democracies, the people elect or appoint others to represent them. Legislative assemblies, executives, commissions, judges, and juries are empowered by the people to make collective decisions on their behalf. These delegations form the foundation of democracy.

But there are dangers. As Dahl (1967: 21) warns, the principal danger is that uninformed decision makers, by failing to delegate well, will transform democracy into a *tyranny of experts:* "there are decisions that require me to *delegate* authority to others . . . but if I delegate, may I not, in practice, end up with a kind of aristocracy of experts, or even false experts?"

Must democracy become a tyranny of experts? Many observers answer yes, because those who delegate seem uninformed when compared with those to whom they delegate.

The principal democratic delegation, that of the people electing their governors, seems most susceptible to tyranny. Cicero's observation that "in the common people there is no wisdom, no penetration, no power of judgment" is an apt summary of modern voting studies (see Berelson 1952, Campbell et al. 1960, Converse 1964, Kinder and Sears 1985, Lane and Sears 1964, Luskin 1987, McClosky 1964, Neuman 1986, Schattschneider 1960, Schumpeter 1942, Zaller 1992, Zaller and Feldman 1992; for a survey, see Delli Carpini and Keeter 1996). Many scholars argue that voters, because of their obstinance or their inability to educate themselves, become the unwitting puppets of campaign and media puppet-masters (Bennett 1992, Sabato 1991). Iyengar (1987: 816) summarizes the literature on voting and elections: "the low level of political knowledge and the absence of ideological reasoning has lent credence to the charges that popular control of government is illusory." These studies suggest that voters who lack information cannot use elections to control their governors.

Other observers make similar arguments about elected representatives. Weber, for example, argues that legislators cannot control bureaucrats:

> Under normal conditions, the power position of a fully developed bureaucracy is always overtowering. The "political master" finds himself in the position of the "dilettante" who stands opposite the "expert," facing the trained official who stands within the management of administration. This holds whether the "master" whom the bureaucracy serves is a "people," equipped with the weapons of "legislative initiative," the "referendum," and the right to remove officials, or a parliament, elected on a more aristocratic or more "democratic" basis and equipped with the right to vote a lack of confidence, or with the actual authority to vote it. (Weber quoted in Gerth and Mills 1946: 232)

Niskanen (1971) continues that public officials' inability to contend with the complexities of modern legislation places them at the mercy of self-serving special interests and bureaucrats. Lowi (1979: xii) concludes, "actual policymaking will not come from voter preferences or congressional enactments but from a process of tripartite bargaining between the specialized administrators, relevant members of Congress, and the representatives of self-selected organized interests."

Jurors also seem to lack the information they need. Posner (1995: 52), for example, argues, "As American law and society become ever more complex, the jury's cognitive limitations will become ever more palpable and socially costly." Other observers characterize the legal system, not as a forum where citizens make reasoned choices, but as a stage for emotional appeals where style and deception overwhelm knowledge. As Abramson (1994: 3) laments,

> The gap between the complexity of modern litigation and the qualifications of jurors has widened to frightening proportions. The average jury rarely understands the expert testimony in an anti-trust suit, a medical malpractice case, or an insanity defense. Nor do most jurors know the law or comprehend the judge's crash course of instructions on it. Trial by jury has thus become trial by ignorance.

Although the critiques of democracy's delegations are myriad and diverse, all have a common conclusion—*reasoned choice does not govern delegation.* As Schumpeter (1942: 262) argues, "the typical citizen drops down to a lower level of mental performance as soon as he enters the political field. He argues and analyzes in a way which he would readily recognize as infantile within the sphere of his real interests. He becomes a primitive again. His thinking is associative and affective. . . . [T]his may prove fatal to the nation."

If voters, legislators, and jurors lack the capability to delegate effectively, then democracy may be "but a prologue to a farce or a tragedy." Like the scholars just quoted, we find this possibility alarming. Unlike these scholars, however, we argue that the capabilities of the people and the requirements of democracy are not as mismatched as many critics would have us believe. In what follows, we will identify the conditions under which this mismatch does and does not exist.

A PREVIEW OF OUR THEORY

We argue that *limited information need not prevent people from making reasoned choices.* Of course, we are not the first analysts to make this type of argument. In the 1950s, for example, Berelson, Lazarfeld, and McPhee (1954) and Downs (1957) argued that voters rely on opinion leaders and political parties to overcome their information shortfalls. More recently, a generation of scholars has further countered the view that the "democratic citizen is expected to be well informed about political affairs" (Berelson, Lazarsfeld, and McPhee 1954: 308). Collectively, these scholars have demonstrated that voters can use a wide range of simple cues as substitutes for complex information. We concur with the basic insight of each of these studies—people can use substitutes for encyclopedic information.

However, we want to do more than argue that limited information need not prevent people from making reasoned choices. We want to argue that *there are specific conditions under which people who have limited information can make reasoned choices.* Therefore, in addition to showing that people *can* use cues, we want to answer questions about *when* and *how* people use cues, *when* cues are effective substitutes for detailed information, and *when* cues are detrimental. To understand who is (and who is not) capable of reasoned choice, we must be able to answer questions such as:

- When do people use simple cues?
- When do people ignore simple cues and seek more detailed information instead?
- When are simple cues sufficient for reasoned choice?
- When can people who offer simple cues manipulate or deceive those who use them?
- What factors determine why a person relies on some simple cues while ignoring many others?
- How do political institutions affect the use and effectiveness of simple cues?

To answer these questions, we construct theories of attention, persuasion, and delegation. . . . [O]ur theory has the rare advantage of being relevant to the usually separate debates on learning, communication, and choice held in cognitive science, economics, political science, and psychology. Next, we describe our theory and preview the answers it gives to the questions listed previously.

Knowledge and Information

We begin by developing a theory of attention. The purpose of our theory is to explain how humans cope with complexity and scarcity. As Simon (1979: 3) argues, "human thinking powers are very modest when compared with the complexities of the environments in which human beings live." Making matters worse is the fact that many of the resources people need to survive are scarce.

Ironically, for many political issues, information is not scarce; rather it is the cognitive resources that a person can use to process information that are scarce. For example, political information appears in the newspapers, in the mail, on community bulletin boards, and on television and radio and is relayed to us in person by friends and family. People often lack the time and energy needed to make sense of all this information. As a consequence, people often have only incomplete information. Fortunately, reasoned choice does not require complete information. Instead, it requires *knowledge: the ability to predict the consequences of actions.*[3]

Implicit in many critiques of democracy is the claim that people who lack *information* are incapable of reasoned choice. By contrast, we argue that people who lack information solve enormously complex problems every day. They do so by making effective use of the information available to them, sorting that which is useful from that which is not.

Information is useful only if it helps people avoid costly mistakes. By contrast, if more information does not lead people to change their decisions, then it provides no instrumental benefit and they should ignore it. Indeed, ignoring useless information is necessary for humans and other species to survive and prosper (Churchland and Sejnowski 1992).

Those who find such statements surprising should consider the almost boundless range of actions, both mundane and grand, for which people ignore available information. For example, people take medication without knowing all of the conditions under which it might be harmful. They also buy houses based on limited information about the neighborhoods around them and with little or no information about the neighbors. People make choices in this way not because the information is unavailable but because the costs of paying attention to it exceed the value of its use.[4]

Although reasoned choice does not require complete information, it does require the ability to predict the consequences of actions. In many cases, simple pieces of information can provide the knowledge people need. For example, to navigate a busy intersection successfully, you must *know* where all of the other cars are going to be sure that you can avoid crashing into them. Advocates of complete information might argue that successful automotive navigation requires as much information as you can gather about the intentions of other drivers and the speed, acceleration, direction, and mass of their cars. At many intersections, however, there is a simple substitute for *all* of this information—a traffic signal. At these intersections, traffic signals are substitutes for more complex information and reduce the amount of information required to make a reasoned choice. At intersections without working traffic signals or other simple cues, reasoned choices require more information. Using similar logic, it follows that limited information precludes reasoned choice only if people are stuck at complex political intersections and lack access to effective political traffic signals.

Persuasion, Enlightenment, and Deception

People who want to make reasoned choices need knowledge. There are two ways to acquire knowledge. The first way is to draw from personal experience. People who exercise this option use their own observations of the past to derive predictions about the future consequences of their actions. The second way is to learn from others. People who exercise this option substitute other people's observations of the past for the personal experience they lack.

In many political settings, only the second option is available. This is true because politics is often abstract and its consequences are remote. In these settings, personal experience does not provide sufficient knowledge for reasoned choice. For many political decisions, reasoned choice requires learning from others.

There are many explanations of how people learn from others. Indeed, a generation of scholars, starting with Knight, Simon, Berelson et al. and Downs, suggest numerous heuristics—simple means for generating information substitutes.[5] . . .

Individually, each of these explanations of how we learn from others is valuable and enlightening. Each reveals a source of the judgmental shortcuts that people undoubtedly use. However, as Sniderman, Brody, and Tetlock (1991: 70) argue, "The most serious risk is that . . . every correlation between independent and dependent variables [is] taken as evidence of a new judgmental shortcut." We agree. We need a theory that explains when or how people choose among the shortcuts listed in the preceding paragraph. To understand how people learn from others, we must be able to explain *how people choose whom to believe*.

■ ■ ■

[N]otice that any attempt to learn from others leads to one of three possible outcomes.

- The first outcome is *enlightenment*. When someone furnishes us with knowledge, we become enlightened. Enlightenment, then, is the process of becoming enlightened. If we initially lack knowledge sufficient for reasoned choice and can obtain such knowledge only from others, then we can make reasoned decisions only if others enlighten us.
- The second outcome is *deception*. Deception is the process by which the testimony we hear reduces our ability to predict accurately the consequences of our actions. For example, we are deceived when someone lies to us *and* we believe that individual.
- The third outcome is that we *learn nothing*. When we learn nothing, our beliefs go unchanged and we gain no knowledge.

Both enlightenment and deception, in turn, require *persuasion: a successful attempt to change the beliefs of another*. The key to understanding whether people become enlightened or deceived by the testimony of others is to understand the conditions under which they can persuade one another.

Most scholars of communication and politics, dating back to Aristotle, focus on a speaker's *internal character* (e.g., honesty, ideology, or reputation) as a necessary condition for persuasion. If a speaker lacks the right character, then these scholars conclude that the speaker will not be persuasive. [W]e present a different set of necessary and sufficient conditions for persuasion. We argue that persuasion need not be contingent upon personal character; rather, *persuasion requires that a listener perceive a speaker to be both knowledgeable and trustworthy.* Although a perception of trust can arise from a positive evaluation of a speaker's character, we show that *external forces can substitute for character* and can thus generate persuasion in contexts where it would not otherwise occur.

An example of an external force that generates trust and persuasion is a listener's observation of a speaker's costly effort. From this observation, the listener can learn about the intensity of a speaker's preferences. This particular condition is also very much like the adage that actions speak louder than words. When speaker costs have this effect, they can provide a basis for trust by providing listeners with a window to speaker incentives.

To see how costly effort affects persuasion, consider the following situation. First, suppose that a listener knows a speaker to have one of three possible motivations—he is a conservative with intense preferences, a conservative with non-intense preferences, or a liberal with non-intense preferences. Second, suppose that the listener does not know which of the three motivations the speaker actually has. Third, suppose that the listener can make a reasoned choice only if he or she knows whether the speaker is liberal or conservative. Fourth, suppose that if the listener observes that the speaker paid a quarter of his or her income to affect a policy outcome, then the listener can conclude that the speaker has intense preferences. If all four suppositions are true, then the speaker's costly effort persuades the listener. As a result, the listener can make a reasoned choice because she can infer that the speaker is a conservative.

Another example of a trust-inducing external force is a penalty for lying. Penalties for lying, whether explicit, such as fines for perjury, or implicit, such as the loss of a valued reputation, can also generate trust by revealing a speaker's incentives. That is, although a listener may believe that a speaker has an interest in deception, the presence of a penalty for lying may lead the listener to believe that certain types of lies are prohibitively costly, rendering certain types of statements very likely to be true.

Our conditions for persuasion show when forces such as costly effort and penalties for lying are, and are not, effective substitutes for a speaker's character.[6] These conditions reveal that you do not necessarily learn more from people who are like you, nor do you learn more from people you like. This is why most people turn to financial advisors, instead of their mothers, when dealing with mutual funds, and back to Mom when seeking advice about child rearing.

Unlike most well-known theories of persuasion and strategic communication, our conditions for persuasion also clarify how and when people suffer as a result of substituting simple cues for complex information. For example, our theory allows us to identify conditions under which a speaker can deceive a listener (i.e., conditions under which a speaker lies *and* a listener believes the lie). These conditions are important because many critics of democracy claim that uninformed citizens are ripe for manipulation at the hands of slick political salesmen.

■   ■   ■

More generally, our conditions for persuasion show why some statements are persuasive and others are not. The obvious reason for these differences is that statements vary in content. The less obvious reason is that the context under which a speaker makes a statement also affects persuasion considerably. Two people making precisely the same statement may not be equally persuasive if only one is subject to penalties for lying.

Our conditions for persuasion further imply that not everyone can persuade. People listen to some speakers and not others. They read some books and not others. They buy some products, even though the manufacturers spend very little money on advertising, while refusing to buy others supported by celebrity endorsements. Similarly, people respond to the advice of some experts or interest groups and not that of others. Our conditions for persuasion explain how people make these choices.

Our results also reveal the bounds on the effectiveness of the heuristics mentioned earlier. Consider, for example, the use of ideology as a heuristic. When there is a high correlation between a speaker's ideology and that speaker's knowledge and trustworthiness, then people are likely to find ideological cues useful. By contrast, when there is no clear correlation, ideology is useless. Similar arguments can be made about other heuristics, such as party, reputation, and likability. In sum, *concepts such as reputation, party, or ideology are useful heuristics only if they convey information about knowledge and trust. The converse of this statement is not true*—knowledge and trust are the fundamental factors that make cues persuasive; the other factors are not.

■   ■   ■

Successful Delegation and the Institutions of Knowledge

. . . Two reasons are commonly cited for the failure of delegation: principals and agents have *conflicting interests* over the outcome of delegation, and agents have *expertise* regarding the consequences of the delegation that principals do not. When delegation occurs under these conditions, agents are free to take any action that suits them, irrespective of the consequences for the principal, and the principal cannot cause them to do otherwise.

We find that delegation succeeds if two conditions are satisfied: the knowledge condition and the incentive condition. The knowledge condition is satisfied in one of two ways. First, it is satisfied when the principal's personal experience allows her to distinguish beneficial from detrimental agent actions. Second, it is satisfied when the principal can obtain this knowledge from others. Therefore, the knowledge condition does not require the principal to know everything the agent knows; it requires only that the principal know enough to distinguish welfare-enhancing from welfare-decreasing agent actions.

The incentive condition is satisfied when the agent and the principal have at least some goals in common. In many cases, satisfaction of the knowledge condition is sufficient for satisfaction of the incentive condition: A principal who becomes enlightened with respect to the consequences of delegation either can motivate the agent to take actions that enhance her welfare or can reject the agent's actions that do not enhance her welfare.

We find that the outcome of delegation is not determined by whether or not the principal can match the agent's technical expertise. Instead, it is determined by the principal's ability to use the testimony of others effectively. If the principal has this ability, then delegation can succeed despite the information she lacks. If the principal lacks information about the agent and lacks the ability to learn from others, then delegation is doomed.

Moreover, we argue that, if democratic principals can create the context in which knowledgeable and persuasive speakers can inform them of the consequences of their agent's actions, then they can facilitate successful delegation. We argue that institutions, such as administrative procedure, rules of evidence, and statutory law, provide the context in which principals can learn about their agent's actions. Institutions can, if properly structured, offer principals a way to better judge their agent's actions. When institutions are poorly designed, or the incentives they induce are opaque, then the political consequence of limited information is likely to be failed delegation. By contrast, when these institutions properly and clearly structure incentives, then they facilitate enlightenment, reasoned choice, and successful delegation even in complex circumstances.

Conclusion

The mismatch between what delegation demands and citizens' capabilities constitutes the democratic dilemma. If people are not capable of reasoned political choices, then effective self-governance is an illusion. After observing that voters, legislators, and jurors are ignorant of many of the details of the decisions they face, many scholars and political commentators conclude that the illusion is real and argue for some type of reform. If their conclusion is correct, then effective self-governance may indeed require political reform. If their conclusion is incorrect, their reforms may restrain the truly competent and do more harm than good.

Other scholars have argued that people are quite capable of making complex decisions with very little information. They point to instances in which people use heuristics and conclude that such heuristics are sufficient for reasoned choice. If these conclusions are correct, then successful delegation does not require reform and the critics mentioned previously are akin to democracy's Chicken Littles. If, however, these latter conclusions are incorrect, then the optimistic scholars are akin to democracy's

Pollyannas, advocating the perpetuation of ineffective and harmful systems of governance.

Both sides of this debate recognize that people are often ignorant about the details of the choices they make. They also both recognize the existence of information shortcuts, cues, and heuristics. What is missing from this debate is an understanding of when ignorance of details prevents reasoned choice, how people choose among potential heuristics, and when these heuristics provide effective substitutes for the detailed information people lack. Only when we have these understandings will we be able to make constructive use of the common observation that people lack information. At that point, we can separate the Chicken Littles from the Pollyannas and build effective solutions to the democratic dilemma.

NOTES

1. From Hunt (1910: 103). Madison expressed similar beliefs in *Federalist 57* and in a speech before the Virginia Ratifying Convention, where he argued that it is necessary that the people possess the "virtue and intelligence to select men of virtue and wisdom" (Riemer 1986: 40).

2. There exists a centuries-old debate about what democracy *should* do. This debate has involved many great minds, is wide ranging, and is totally unresolved. We do not believe ourselves capable of resolving this debate. However, we strongly believe that we can make the debate more constructive. We can do so by clarifying the relationship between what information people have and what types of decisions they can make. Our reading is firmly about determining the capabilities of people who lack political information. It is designed to resolve debates about how much information voters, jurors, and legislators need in order to perform certain tasks. So, although our reading may help to clarify debates about what democracy should do, it will not resolve these debates.

We mention this because our relationship to the debate about what democracy should do motivates our definition of reasoned choice. Our definition of reasoned choice allows the reader to define an amount of knowledge that is required for reasoned choice. Some readers may argue that a reasoned choice requires knowledge of very technical matters, whereas others may argue that a reasoned choice requires less knowledge. Note that the difference between these viewpoints reduces to different views on what democracy should do. Therefore, our definition of reasoned choice is purposefully precise with respect to the relationship between information, knowledge, and choice and is purposefully vague with respect to most normative debates about what democracies *should* do.

3. For example, knowing which of two products is "better" than the other is often sufficient for us to make the same choice we would have made had we been completely informed about each product.

4. Furthermore, beyond being useless, some types of information cause people to make the wrong (i.e., welfare-reducing) choices when they would have otherwise made the right (i.e., welfare-increasing) ones with less information. For example, a person who votes for Jones instead of Smith because a newspaper endorses Jones may regret having attended to this additional information when Jones later opposes a policy that both she and Smith support.

5. Also, see Key (1966) and Tversky and Kahneman (1974).

6. A third external force that can induce a listener to trust a speaker arises when the speaker's statements are subject to some chance of being externally verified.

REFERENCES

Abramson, Jeffrey. 1994. *We, the Jury: The Jury System and the Ideal of Democracy.* New York: Basic Books.

Bennett, W. Lance. 1992. *The Governing Crisis: Media, Money, and Marketing in American Elections.* New York: St. Martin's Press.

Berelson, Bernard. 1952. "Democratic Theory and Public Opinion." *Public Opinion Quarterly* XVI: 313–30.

Berelson, Bernard, Paul F. Lazarfeld, and William N. McPhee. 1954. *Voting: A Study of Opinion Formation in a Presidential Campaign.* Chicago: University of Chicago Press.

Campbell, Angus, Philip E. Converse, Warren E. Miller, and Donald E. Stokes. 1960. *The American Voter.* New York: Wiley.

Churchland, Patricia S., and Terrence J. Sejnowski. 1992. *The Computational Brain.* Cambridge, MA: MIT Press.

Converse, Philip E. 1964. "The Nature of Belief Systems in Mass Publics." In *Ideology and Discontent,* edited by David E. Apter. New York: Free Press.

Dahl, Robert A. 1967. *Pluralist Democracy in the United States: Conflict and Consent.* Chicago: Rand McNally.

Delli Carpini, Michael X., and Scott Keeter. 1991. "Stability and Change in the United States Public's Knowledge of Politics." *Public Opinion Quarterly* 55: 583–612.

Downs, Anthony. 1957. *An Economic Theory of Democracy.* New York: Harper.

Gerth, H. H., and C. Wright Mills, eds. 1946. *From Max Weber: Essays in Sociology.* New York: Oxford University Press.

Hunt, Gaillard, ed. 1910. *The Writings of James Madison.* New York: Putnam.

Iyengar, Shanto. 1987. "Television News and Citizens' Explanations of National Affairs." *American Political Science Review* 81: 815–32.

Key, V. O. 1966. *The Responsible Electorate: Rationality in Presidential Voting, 1936–1960.* Cambridge, MA: Belknap Press of Harvard University Press.

Kinder, Donald R., and David O. Sears. 1985. "Public Opinion and Political Participation." In *Handbook of Social Psychology,* edited by G. Lindzey and E. Aronson. Reading, MA: Addison-Wesley.

Lane, Robert E., and David O. Sears. 1964. *Public Opinion.* Englewood Cliffs, NJ: Prentice-Hall.

Lowi, Theodore J. 1979. *The End of Liberalism: The Second Republic of the United States.* 2nd ed., New York: Norton.

Luskin, Robert C. 1987. "Measuring Political Sophistication." *American Journal of Political Science* 31: 856–99.

Madison, James. *Federalist.* In Clinton Rossiter, ed., *The Federalist Papers.* New York: Penguin.

McClosky, Herbert. 1964. "Consensus and Ideology in American Politics." *American Political Science Review* 58: 361–82.

Neuman, W. Russell. 1986. *The Paradox of Mass Politics: Knowledge and Opinion in the American Electorate.* Cambridge, Mass.: Harvard University Press.

Niskanen, William A. 1971. *Bureaucracy and Representative Government.* Chicago: Aldine-Atherton.

Posner, Richard. 1995. "Juries on Trial." *Commentary* 99: 49–52.

Riemer, Neal. 1986. *James Madison: Creating the American Constitution*. Washington, DC: Congressional Quarterly.

Sabato, Larry J. 1991. *Feeding Frenzy*. New York: Free Press.

Schattschneider, Elmer Eric. 1960. *The Semisovereign People: A Realist's View of Democracy in America*. New York: Holt, Rinehart and Winston.

Schumpeter, Joseph Alois. 1942. *Capitalism, Socialism, and Democracy*. New York: Harper.

Simon, Herbert A. 1979. *Models of Thought*. New Haven, CT: Yale University Press.

Sniderman, Paul M., Richard A. Brody, and Philip E. Tetlock. 1991. *Reasoning and Choice: Explorations in Political Psychology*. Cambridge: Cambridge University Press.

Tversky, Amos, and Daniel Kahneman. 1974. "Judgment under Uncertainty: Heuristics and Biases." *Science* 185: 1124–31.

Zaller, John. 1992. *The Nature and Origins of Mass Opinion*. Cambridge: Cambridge University Press.

Zaller, John, and Stanley Feldman. 1992. "A Simple Theory of the Survey Response: Answering Questions Versus Revealing Preferences." *American Journal of Political Science* 36: 579–616.

9.2

JOHN R. ZALLER

From *The Nature and Origins of Mass Opinion*

A large literature in political science examines what voters know and whether they have enough information to make informed choices in elections. Zaller proposes a model for how voters acquire information. Using this model, he argues that voters vary in the degree to which they are receptive to new information, depending on their underlying political predispositions and levels of knowledge about politics. His model lends insight into why some voters are swayed by public discourse and others stay firm in their attitudes.

HOW CITIZENS ACQUIRE INFORMATION AND CONVERT IT INTO PUBLIC OPINION

The comprehensive analysis of public opinion requires attention to two phenomena: how citizens learn about matters that are for the most part beyond their immediate experience, and how they convert the information they acquire into opinions.

. . . [I] propose a model of both phenomena. The model does not provide a fully accurate account of how people process information and form attitude statements. No model that is both parsimonious and testable on typical mass opinion data—the two most important constraints on my enterprise—could possibly do so. But the proposed model, as I hope to persuade the reader, does a plausible job of approximating what must actually occur, and a quite excellent job of accounting for the available survey evidence across a wide range of phenomena.

■　■　■

Some Definitions

I begin the statement of the model with definitions of primitive terms. The first is *consideration*, which is defined as any reason that might induce an individual to decide a political issue one way or the other.[1] Considerations, thus,

From John R. Zaller, *The Nature and Origins of Mass Opinion* (New York: Cambridge University Press, 1992).

are a compound of cognition and affect—that is, a belief concerning an object and an evaluation of the belief. . . .

Second, I define two types of political messages: persuasive messages and cueing messages. Persuasive messages are arguments or images providing a reason for taking a position or point of view; if accepted by an individual, they become considerations, as the term was just defined. . . .

Note that there is nothing in this account that implies that either political messages or the considerations that result from them must be coldly rational. On the contrary, messages may involve subtle or even subliminal images, and considerations may involve feelings or emotions. . . .

Cueing messages, which are the second type of message carried in elite discourse, consist of "contextual information" about the ideological or partisan implications of a persuasive message. The importance of cueing messages is that, as suggested by Converse (1964), they enable citizens to perceive relationships between the persuasive messages they receive and their political predispositions, which in turn permits them to respond critically to the persuasive messages.

▪   ▪   ▪

The Model

The model itself consists of four assertions, or axioms, about how individuals respond to political information they may encounter. Each is stated first as a general theoretical position and then elaborated and justified in more precise terms.

▪   ▪   ▪

A1. *RECEPTION AXIOM. The greater a person's level of cognitive engagement with an issue, the more likely he or she is to be exposed to and comprehend—in a word, to receive—political messages concerning that issue.*[2]

The messages people may receive include all types: that is, persuasive messages and cueing messages. . . .

Although cognitive engagement is the right specification for my model, it is a cumbersome and somewhat precious phrase. Therefore, I will, through most of the analysis that follows, use a simpler phrase, namely *political attentiveness* or *political awareness*. But cognitive engagement, political attentiveness, and political awareness are meant to convey the same meaning.

▪   ▪   ▪

A2. *RESISTANCE AXIOM. People tend to resist arguments that are inconsistent with their political predispositions, but they do so only to the extent that they possess the contextual information necessary to perceive a relationship between the message and their predispositions.*

The key to resistance, in this formulation, is *information* concerning the relationship between arguments and predispositions, where the requisite information is carried in cueing messages. According to the Reception Axiom, the probability of individuals acquiring cueing information depends on their levels of awareness of each given issue. Thus, A1 and A2 together imply that the likelihood of resisting persuasive communications that are inconsistent with one's political predispositions rises with a person's level of political attentiveness. Or, to put it the other way, politically inattentive persons will often be unaware of the implications of the persuasive communications they encounter, and so often end up "mistakenly" accepting them.

■ ■ ■

A3. *ACCESSIBILITY AXIOM. The more recently a consideration has been called to mind or thought about, the less time it takes to retrieve that consideration or related considerations from memory and bring them to the top of the head for use.*

Conversely, the longer it has been since a consideration or related idea has been activated, the less likely it is to be accessible at the top of the head; in the limit, a long unused set of considerations may be completely inaccessible, which is to say, forgotten.

This axiom appropriates for use in the model one of the best-established empirical regularities in cognitive psychology. General support for the basic idea is overwhelming and, as far as I can tell, undisputed. When an idea or concept has been recently used, seen, heard, or indirectly referenced, it is significantly more likely to be available for reuse than if it has not been recently activated.

■ ■ ■

A4. *RESPONSE AXIOM. Individuals answer survey questions by averaging across the considerations that are immediately salient or accessible to them.*

This axiom, which completes the statement of my proposed model, implies that persons who have been asked a survey question do not normally canvass their minds for all considerations relevant to the given issue; rather, they answer the question on the basis of whatever considerations are accessible "at the top of the head." In some cases, only a single consideration may be readily accessible, in which case individuals answer on the basis of that consideration; in other cases, two or more considerations may come quickly to mind, in which case people answer by averaging across accessible considerations.

An important feature of the Response Axiom is that it permits different people to respond to issue questions on the basis of different considerations—one, for example, emphasizing ideological concerns, another gut-level likes and dislikes, and yet another self-interest.

▪ ▪ ▪

Perhaps the most apt description of a survey response within the proposed model is "opinion statement." This term implies that the expression of opinion is genuine without also implying that it either represents prior reflection or is destined for a long half-life. The phrase "attitude report" has similar virtues.

Opinion statements, as conceived in my four-axiom model, are the outcome of a process in which people *receive* new information, decide whether to *accept* it, and then *sample* at the moment of answering questions. For convenience, therefore, I will refer to this process as the Receive-Accept-Sample, or RAS, Model.

How the Model Is Used

The model I have outlined consists of four very general claims about how people acquire information from the political environment (in the form of persuasive arguments and cues) and transform that information into survey responses.

▪ ▪ ▪

The argument to be made from the RAS model may be previewed as follows. It follows from the Response Axiom that the probability that a person will support or oppose a given policy depends on the mix of positive and negative considerations available in the person's mind at the moment of answering a question about it. If, for the moment, we overlook the probability of nonresponse (which occurs when no considerations are immediately salient in memory), and assume also that every consideration a person has internalized is as likely to be sampled as any other, then the probability of a liberal response by a given person is

$$Prob(Liberal\ response) = \frac{L}{L + C}$$

where L and C refer to the number of liberal and conservative considerations available in the person's mind. (I reiterate that here, as elsewhere in this book, liberal and conservative are simply *labels* for the directional thrust of ideas; a person may use a liberal consideration as the basis for a liberal response even though she is not, in any deeper sense, "a liberal.")

The balance of liberal and conservative considerations in people's minds depends on both society-level and individual-level variables. The key societal variables are the intensities of liberal and conservative information flows in the political environment with respect to a given issue. The key individual variables are political awareness and political predispositions. More aware persons will be exposed to more political communications (via the Reception

Axiom) but will be more selective in deciding which communications to internalize as considerations (via the Resistance Axiom). Thus, politically aware citizens will tend to fill their minds with large numbers of considerations, and these considerations will tend to be relatively consistent with one another and with the citizens' predispositions. Less aware persons will internalize fewer considerations and will be less consistent in doing so. As a result, more aware people will be more likely to be able to state opinions, and more likely to state opinions that are ideologically consistent with their predispositions.

NOTES

1. This term is a borrowing from Kelley (1983), who showed that individuals appear to make vote decisions in presidential elections on the basis of a net score across numerous competing "likes" and "dislikes" about the candidates, which he called "considerations."

2. These terms derive from McGuire, 1969.

REFERENCES

Converse, Philip. 1964. "The Nature of Belief Systems in Mass Publics." In *Ideology and Discontent*, edited by David Apter, 206–61. New York: Free Press.

Kelley, Stanley, Jr. 1983. *Interpreting Elections*. Princeton, NJ: Princeton University Press.

McGuire, William J. 1969. "The Nature of Attitudes and Attitude Change." In *Handbook of Social Psychology*, 2d ed. edited by G. Lindzey and E. Aronson, 136–314. Reading, MA.: Addison-Wesley.

9.3

DONALD R. KINDER AND CINDY D. KAM

From *Us Against Them: Ethnocentric Foundations of American Opinion*

In this excerpt from their book, Us Against Them: Ethnocentric Foundations of American Opinion, *Kinder and Kam show strong evidence that many Americans hold deep-seated prejudices against people who are of a different race. Furthermore, those prejudices are manifestations of ethnocentrism—seeing the world as "us and them." Ethnocentrism has meaningful political consequences. It can shape the different political attitudes and partisanship of people from different racial groups, affecting their voting behavior and the nature of their political participation.*

AMERICAN ETHNOCENTRISM TODAY

. . . [E]thnocentrism is an attitude that divides the world into two opposing camps. From an ethnocentric point of view, groups are either "friend" or they are "foe." Ethnocentrism is a general outlook on social difference; it is prejudice, broadly conceived.

■   ■   ■

Measuring Ethnocentrism

Ethnocentrism is commonly expressed through *stereotypes*. Stereotypes refer to the beliefs we possess about social groups—what we know or what we think we know about "poets, professors, professional wrestlers, and film stars" (Brown 1965, p. 188), among others. Stereotypes capture the characteristics that define a social group, that set it apart from others. Most often, such characteristics have to do with underlying dispositions—temperament, intelligence, trustworthiness—the deep core of human nature. When we say that "Jews are pushy" or that "blacks are lazy," we are trafficking in stereotypes.[1]

Stereotyping is often held up for reprimand, but it is an inevitable aspect of human cognition. To negotiate and make sense of the world, we need stereotypes. "Life is so short," as Gordon Allport once put it, "and the demands upon us for practical adjustments so great, that we cannot let our ignorance detain us in our daily transactions. We have to decide whether objects are good or

From Donald R. Kinder and Cindy D. Kam, *Us Against Them: Ethnocentric Foundations of American Opinion* (Chicago: University of Chicago Press, 2010), Chapter 3.

bad by classes. We cannot weigh each object in the world by itself. Rough and ready rubrics, however coarse and broad, have to suffice" (1954, p. 9).

If stereotypes are grounded in ordinary cognitive processes and if they reduce the social world to manageable size, they are, of course, very much a mixed blessing. For one thing, stereotypes exaggerate differences and sharpen boundaries: in-groups and out-groups appear more different from each other than they actually are. . . . For another, stereotypes tend to portray members of out-groups as though they were all the same: individual variation is flattened, anomalous cases are set aside. . . . Third, stereotypes are permeated by affect. To say that "Jews are pushy" or that "blacks are lazy" is not only to make a judgment but also to express an emotion. And fourth, stereotypes are easily activated and, once activated, influence judgment and behavior in a variety of ways.[2]

▪　▪　▪

How common is in-group favoritism in a fully modern setting? Do Americans attribute favorable characteristics more to their own group than they do to out-groups? Or, put the other way around, do they attribute undesirable characteristics less to their own group than they do to out-groups?

To answer these questions, consider Table [1]. There we have summarized results for a single characteristic (lazy versus hard-working) taken from a single survey (the 1992 NES). The columns of the table are defined by the group that is being rated. In the 1992 NES, the columns refer to ratings of whites, blacks, Hispanics, and Asians. The rows of the table are defined by

TABLE [1]　In-Group Favoritism Expressed through Stereotypes (Lazy versus Hard-Working)

Assessments by:	Assessments of:			
	Whites	*Blacks*	*Hispanics*	*Asians*
Whites	0.32	−0.06	0.02	0.29
	(1627)	(1609)	(1538)	(1511)
Blacks	0.20	0.24	0.16	0.25
	(264)	(268)	(249)	(239)
Hispanics	0.33	−0.01	0.28	0.30
	(168)	(168)	(167)	(157)
Asians	0.38	−0.18	0.02	0.63
	(28)	(27)	(27)	(28)

NOTE: Table entry is the average assessment of each group, among respondents in each racial/ethnic group, on the lazy versus hard-working trait question. The trait assessments are coded from −1 (Nearly all are lazy) to +1 (Nearly all are hard-working). Number of observations appears in parentheses.
SOURCE: 1992 NES.

the group that is providing the rating: ratings by whites, blacks, Hispanics, and Asians. The main elements of the table are mean scores on the trait, coded from –1 (almost all are lazy) to +1 (almost all are hard-working), with 0 representing the midpoint. A positive score indicates a favorable judgment, just as a negative score indicates an unfavorable judgment. The table also provides the number of cases (in parentheses) for each calculation. In some instances, this number is small (for Asian Americans, the number is perilously small).

Do whites, as predicted, attribute the characteristic of hard-working more to their own group than they do to blacks, Hispanics, and Asians? The first row of Table [1] shows that they do. Asian Americans display in-group favoritism too, and even more conspicuously (fourth row of Table [1]). The results for blacks and Hispanics are different, however. Both blacks and Hispanics see their own group as generally hard-working—but they generally see other groups as hard-working, too. As a result, in-group favoritism among black and Hispanic Americans is partial or limited. It shows up in just one respect. Black Americans believe blacks to be more hard-working than Hispanics, and Hispanics, returning the favor, believe that Hispanics are more hard-working than blacks.

The pattern of results shown in Table [1] is entirely general. It is just what we see elsewhere, in other NES and GSS surveys, and on other characteristics: intelligence, patriotism, self-reliance, trustworthiness, propensity for violence, and more. Everywhere we look, we find general in-group favoritism among white and Asian Americans, and partial in-group favoritism among black and Hispanic Americans.[3]

▪   ▪   ▪

Correlates of Ethnocentrism

Next we examine ethnocentrism's place among a standard set of social and political predispositions. We have argued that ethnocentrism represents a distinctive way of looking at the world. From an ethnocentric point of view, groups are either "friend" or "foe." As such, ethnocentrism might be correlated with other political predispositions—with certain varieties of conservatism, say—but it cannot be interchangeable with them. If that turned out to be true, then we would have no reason to proceed, no warrant for arguing that the understanding of public opinion has been diminished by the failure, up until now, to take ethnocentrism seriously. To see how closely ethnocentrism is associated with standard political predispositions, we rely on our primary measure of ethnocentrism, the one based on stereotypes (E), though the results would be no different were we to use the alternative measure based on group sentiment (E*).

We start with partisanship, first among equals when it comes to political predispositions. Most Americans think of themselves as Democrats or as Republicans. Party identification is a standing decision, a "durable attachment, not readily disturbed by passing events and personalities" (Campbell et al. [1960] 1980, p. 151). And it is consequential: "To the average person, the affairs of government are remote and complex, and yet the average citizen is asked periodically to formulate opinions about these affairs. . . . In this dilemma, having the party symbol stamped on certain candidates, certain issue positions, certain interpretations of reality is of great psychological convenience" (Stokes 1966, pp. 126–27; also see Bartels 2000; Converse 1966; Green, Palmquist, and Schickler 2002). To the extent that issues . . . from the war on terrorism to affirmative action in college admissions generate strong and durable disagreements between Democratic and Republican elites, we would expect Democrats and Republicans in the general public to disagree as well. Put differently, partisanship is likely to play an important part in our analysis of public opinion. True enough, but whatever part partisanship plays in opinion must be independent of the part ethnocentrism plays. As Table [2] reveals, partisanship and ethnocentrism are virtually uncorrelated.[4]

What about the relationship between ethnocentrism and views on the size and scope of government authority? Compared to citizens of other developed democracies, Americans are, on average, "suspicious of government, skeptical about the benefits of government authority, and impressed with the virtue of limiting government" (Kingdon 1999, p. 29). Moreover, differences among Americans on broad questions of governmental authority generate corresponding differences on a wide range of specific policy questions. Limited government is an important idea—but as Table [2] shows, it has no association with ethnocentrism.[5]

TABLE [2] The Relationship between Ethnocentrism and Social and Political Predispositions

	Full sample	Whites	Blacks	Hispanics
Partisanship	−0.06	−0.00	0.02	0.03
	(4923)	(3931)	(598)	(394)
Limited government	−0.03	−0.09	−0.05	−0.02
	(4947)	(3951)	(604)	(392)
Egalitarianism	−0.19	−0.18	0.07	−0.02
	(4974)	(3964)	(609)	(401)
Ideological identification	−0.07	−0.07	0.02	0.03
	(4945)	(3951)	(599)	(395)
Social trust	−0.08	−0.17	−0.02	−0.07
	(4898)	(3901)	(602)	(395)

NOTE: Table entry is the Pearson correlation coefficient. Number of observations appears in parentheses.
SOURCES: 1992, 1996, 2000, and 2004 NES.

Alongside the American taste for limited government, and to some degree in opposition to it, is a preference for egalitarianism—what [Alexis de] Tocqueville called the American "passion" for equality. Americans seem to take egalitarian beliefs—that everyone is fundamentally the same under the skin, that everyone deserves the same chance in life—seriously, and such general beliefs appear to influence what they think government should do (if anything) about poverty, health care, discrimination, and more. As might be expected, and as Table [2] shows, egalitarianism and ethnocentrism are negatively correlated. Ethnocentric Americans are inclined, slightly but consistently, to reject egalitarian principles.[6]

Next we consider ideological identification. It turns out that when asked directly, many American[s] are willing to describe themselves in ideological terms—as liberals or (more often) as conservatives—and these descriptions appear to be, if not sophisticated or philosophical, politically meaningful. Self-identified liberals tend to favor redistributive policies and social change; self-identified conservatives tend to celebrate the market and express misgivings about racial integration (Conover and Feldman 1981; Levitin and Miller 1979). Liberals and conservatives also differ when it comes to ethnocentrism—Americans who think of themselves as conservative are a bit more ethnocentric, on average, than are those who think of themselves as liberal—though the difference is tiny, as shown in Table [2].[7]

▪   ▪   ▪

In sum, partisanship, limited government, equality, ideological identification, and social trust are often treated as important ingredients in American public opinion. Our analysis of opinion will certainly take them into account. But the findings presented in Table [2] make clear that we can put away the worry that ethnocentrism brings nothing new to political analysis—that ethnocentrism is just another word for conservatism or anti-egalitarianism or the like. Ethnocentrism represents a distinctive outlook on social life, one that . . . has a distinctive and independent impact on public opinion.

NOTES

1. On the definition of stereotype, see Allport (1954); McCauley, Stitt, and Segal (1980); and Stangor and Lange (1994).

2. For evidence on the power of stereotypes to shape judgment and behavior, see M. Brewer (1988); Devine (1989); Fazio and Dunton (1997); and Fiske (1998).

3. Other surveys include 1996 NES, 2000 NES, 2004 NES, 1990 GSS, and 2000 GSS.

4. Partisanship is measured with v923634, v960420, v000523, v043116. It ranges from 0 (strong Republican) to 1 (strong Democrat).

5. On this theme, see Tocqueville ([1848] 1994), Myrdal (1944), Lipset (1959), Hofstadter (1948), and especially Louis Hartz's *The Liberal Tradition in America* (1955). Limited government is measured by a three-item scale that has become a regular part of NES, thanks to research and development work by Gregory Markus (2001).

In 1992 NES, the limited government scale consists of an additive index of v925729–v925731. In 1996 NES, it consists of v961144–v961146. In 2000 NES, it comprises v0001420–v001422. In 2004 NES, it consists of v045150–v045152. The scale is fairly reliable (*alpha* averages 0.73 across the years). The index ranges from 0 (want more active government) to 1 (want less active government).

6. On the meaning and measurement of equality, see Feldman (1988); Kinder and Sanders (1996); Feldman and Zaller (1992); McClosky and Zaller (1984); Schlozman and Verba (1979); and Sears, Henry, and Kosterman (2000).

In 1992 NES, the egalitarianism scale consists of an additive index of v926024–v926029. In 1996 NES, it consists of v961229–v961234. In 2000 NES, it comprises v001521–v001526. In 2004 NES, it consists of v045212–v045217. The scale is reasonably reliable (*alpha* averages 0.70 across the years). The index ranges from 0 (not) to 1 (egalitarian).

7. Ideological identification is measured with v923509, v960365, v001368, and v045117. It ranges from 0 (extremely conservative) to 1 (extremely liberal).

REFERENCES

Allport, Gordon W. 1954. *The Nature of Prejudice*. Cambridge, MA: Addison-Wesley.

Bartels, Larry M. 2000. "Partisanship and Voting Behavior, 1952–1996." *American Journal of Political Science* 44 (1): 35–50.

Brewer, Marilynn B. 1988. "A Dual Process Model of Impression Formation." In *Advances in Social Cognition*, vol. 1, ed. T. K. Srull and R. S. Wyer, 1–36. Hillsdale, NJ: Erlbaum.

Brown, Roger. 1965. *Social Psychology*. New York: Free Press.

Campbell, Angus, Philip E. Converse, Warren E. Miller, and Donald E. Stokes. [1960] 1980. *The American Voter*, unabridged ed. Chicago: Midway Reprint.

Conover, Pamela, and Stanley Feldman. 1981. "The Origins and Meaning of Liberal/Conservative Self-Identification." *American Journal of Political Science* 25 (4): 617–45.

Converse, Philip E. 1966. "Information Flow and the Stability of Partisan Attitudes." In *Elections and the Political Order*, edited by Angus Campbell, Philip E. Converse, Donald Stokes, and Warren E. Miller, 136–57. New York: Wiley.

Devine, Patricia G. 1989. "Stereotypes and Prejudice: Their Automatic and Controlled Components." *Journal of Personality and Social Psychology* 56 (1): 5–18.

Fazio, Russell H., and B. C. Dunton. 1997. "Categorization by Race: The Impact of Automatic and Controlled Components of Racial Prejudice." *Journal of Experimental Social Psychology* 33: 451–70.

Feldman, Stanley. 1988. "Structure and Consistency in Public Opinion: The Role of Core Beliefs and Values." *American Journal of Political Science* 32 (2): 416–40.

Feldman, Stanley, and John R. Zaller. 1992. "The Political Culture of Ambivalence." *American Journal of Political Science* 36 (1): 268–307.

Fiske, Susan T. 1998. "Stereotyping, Prejudice, and Discrimination." In *Handbook of Social Psychology*, 4th ed., edited by Daniel Gilbert, Susan T. Fiske, and Gardner Lindzey, 357–411. Boston: McGraw-Hill.

Green, Donald P., Bradley Palmquist, and Eric Schickler. 2002. *Partisan Hearts and Minds*. New Haven, CT: Yale University Press.

Hartz, Louis, 1955. *The Liberal Tradition in America*. New York: Harcourt Brace.

Hofstadter, Richard. 1948. *The American Political Tradition and the Men Who Made It*. New York: Knopf.

Kinder, Donald R., and Lynn M. Sanders. 1996. *Divided by Color*. Chicago: University of Chicago Press.

Kingdon, John W. 1999. *America the Unusual*. Belmont, CA: Wadsworth.

Levitin, Teresa E., and Warren E. Miller. 1979. "Ideological Interpretations of Presidential Elections." *American Political Science Review* 73: 751–71.

Lipset, Seymour Martin. 1959. *Political Man: The Social Bases of Politics*. Baltimore: Johns Hopkins University Press.

Markus, Gregory B. 2001. "American Individualism Reconsidered." In *Citizens and Politics: Perspectives from Political Psychology*, edited by James H. Kuklinski, 401–32. New York: Cambridge University Press.

McCauley, C., C. L. Stitt, and M. Segal. 1980. "Stereotyping: From Prejudice to Prediction." *Psychological Bulletin* 87: 195–208.

McClosky, Herbert M., and John Zaller. 1984. *The American Ethos: Public Attitudes toward Capitalism and Democracy*. Cambridge, MA: Harvard University Press.

Myrdal, Gunnar. 1944. *An American Dilemma: The Negro Problem and Modern Democracy*. New York: Harper and Row.

Schlozman, Kay Lehman, and Sidney Verba. 1979. *Insult to Injury: Unemployment, Class, and Political Response*. Cambridge, MA: Harvard University Press.

Sears, David O., P. J. Henry, and Rick Kosterman. 2000. "Egalitarian Values and Contemporary Racial Politics." In *Racialized Politics*, edited by David O. Sears, Jim Sidanius, and Lawrence Bobo, 75–117. Chicago: University of Chicago Press.

Stangor, Charles, and James E. Lange. 1994. "Mental Representations on Social Groups: Advances in Understanding Stereotypes and Stereotyping." *Advances in Experimental Social Psychology* 26: 357–416.

Stokes, Donald E. 1966. "Party Loyalty and the Likelihood of Deviating Elections." In *Elections and the Political Order*, edited by Angus Campbell, Philip E. Converse, Warren E. Miller, and Donald E. Stokes, 125–35. New York: Wiley.

Tocqueville, Alexis de. [1848] 1994. *Democracy in America*. New York: Knopf.

9.4

KATHERINE J. CRAMER

From *The Politics of Resentment: Rural Consciousness in Wisconsin and the Rise of Scott Walker*

Cramer dove deep into the Wisconsin countryside to listen to people in rural areas talk about politics and government. In this striking reading, she reveals the complexities of political attitudes among rural people. Many of them feel alienated from government and shut out of national and state conversations about the future direction of the country. She argues that their attitudes, often simplified and ridiculed, and sometimes ignored, deserve to be taken seriously. These people may feel forgotten, but when they find candidates that appeal to them, they make big waves that can roil national and state politics.

REPUBLICAN AND RURAL: NOT JUST A CORRELATION

Scholars and political pundits have known for decades, over a century even, that there is a correlation between votes and rural-urban location in the United States. [Scholars know] very little about the way rural-versus-urban divides function *as a perspective* through which some people think about politics.

Since the mid-twentieth century, Wisconsin has looked pretty much like national electoral maps: blue cities and red rural places. In Wisconsin, the Democratic Party's success in the larger cities is due in part to stronger union organizing (Fowler 2008, 184) and the concentration of African Americans in those places. Also, some of the Republicanism in the rural areas may be a holdover from anti–Democratic Party attitudes that rose up during World War I and II. Many Wisconsinites have German relatives somewhere in their family—43 percent of residents claimed German heritage in 2000 (Fowler 2008, 205). German American voters were strongly isolationist during World War I and II and, therefore, likely to vote against the Democrats, especially in rural areas, where unions had little influence (Fowler 2008).

Rural-urban divides have been an important part of Wisconsin's politics for at least a century. One of our famous quirks is that we were home to both

From Katherine J. Cramer, *The Politics of Resentment: Rural Consciousness in Wisconsin and the Rise of Scott Walker* (Chicago: University of Chicago Press, 2016).

Joe McCarthy and Bob La Follette, two decidedly different characters. McCarthy was the U.S. senator who is responsible for "McCarthyism"—the post–World War II anticommunist scare that led to the interrogations of many Americans, particularly government employees, people in the entertainment industry, and those involved in labor unions. La Follette, in contrast, is the father of Progressivism. He served in the U.S. House, the U.S. Senate, and was governor of the state in the first few decades of the twentieth century.

Some say that rural-urban tensions help explain how both of these folks were successful in the same state. Granted, the fact that La Follette and McCarthy were both from Wisconsin is a little less mysterious when you consider that they both started out as Republicans. Wisconsin was overwhelmingly Republican for much of the first half of the twentieth century (Epstein 1958). But the rural-urban divide helps solve part of the La Follette–McCarthy mystery, too. Both of them tapped into rural consciousness to win votes. When La Follette's Progressivism took hold, Wisconsin was mainly a nonmetropolitan state—as it is now. In that context, skepticism of party organizations among rural residents was a stronger force than was support of political machines among urban residents (Epstein 1958). Some scholars argue that McCarthy won his Senate seat by exploiting the skepticism that small-town residents had of globalization and distant institutions. Even the breakthrough of the modern Democratic Party—the election of Democrat William Proxmire to the Senate in a special election after McCarthy's death—is commonly understood as the result of Proxmire's successful appeal to "rural discontent" (Fowler 2008, 173). Also, he is the senator who devised the monthly Golden Fleece Award, an award he bestowed on a public official who had made an excessive government expenditure. Although a member of the Democratic Party, the party typically associated with "big government," he was a champion of government frugality.

For some time, then, there has been a correlation in Wisconsin, as in most of the United States, between rural and Republican. But that correlation is not inevitable and is not simply the result of people voting the same way their parents did. People have perspectives and understandings that make support for Republican candidates seem appropriate and natural.

. . . The perspective I am calling rural consciousness . . . had three main elements. First, rural consciousness was about perceptions of power, or who makes decisions and who decides what to even discuss. Second, it showed up with respect to perceptions of values and lifestyles. Third and finally, it involved perceptions of resources or who gets what.

These are the outlines of the rural consciousness I encountered. Every expression of this perspective did not sound exactly the same. As with all identities, people in particular places put their own twist on who they are. . . .

WHERE IS "RURAL" IN WISCONSIN?

. . . The two main metropolitan areas of the state . . . are Madison, the state capital and home to the flagship public university, and . . . Milwaukee, the main industrial area of the state. They are both located in the southern part of Wisconsin. The places outside these metro areas are sometimes referred to as "Outstate" or "out-state Wisconsin" (though this name annoys some people who live in those areas of the state) and the northern tier of the state, largely a tourist area, is typically called "up north."

This division of the state into Madison and Milwaukee versus the rest of the state was common knowledge to the people I encountered outside of Madison and Milwaukee. When talking about the big issues of the day, many of the people I visited in small towns automatically referred to this geography.

■ ■ ■

The rural consciousness perspective I heard was most common in communities one would readily identify as rural—lots of green space, few stoplights, and far from an urban center. But it also emerged in areas best described as nonmetro: more populous areas but beyond the major metro centers of Madison and Milwaukee. Rural consciousness was a matter of degree. Sometimes, for convenience, I use the term "rural" to refer broadly to all areas outside the two major metro areas in the state.

POWER

. . . The place-based sense of injustice among rural residents [could be] heard . . . in many of the groups I spent time with outside the Madison and Milwaukee areas. . . .

The rural consciousness perspective . . . was more than just identity as a rural person. Besides place identity, it encompassed perceptions of power, values and lifestyles, and resources. . . . When I heard people talking about rural consciousness in these conversations, they were often talking about several of these central elements.

. . . A good place to start is . . . education. [The] complaint that Wisconsin's funding formula for education unfairly hurt rural communities was a common concern across groups meeting in rural places. For example, on my first visit to [a] dice game group in central west Wisconsin, I started out with my "what are your big concerns here" question:

KJC: Anything—it can be any kind of concerns—I'll ask you more directly about the UW later on. What kind of issues? Partly the reason I want to know is that we do a phone survey at the UW and usually when we decide which topics to—

MARK: One thing we were bitching about yesterday is that you—is the state's penchant for unfunded mandates—what three times, two times they got a referenda in the community that was not wanted. And so now—they keep jamming the cost down to the county so they can avoid spending it on the state's nickel, that has to stop.

ERNIE: Things that are mandated should be paid for.

MARK: Yeah, the tax structure in this state is weird. I think that is a fundamental problem with the state is that they have to reorganize their tax structure. Local schools, local municipalities, and of course the state—what they're doing is they're just redirecting tax burden on the local taxes which ends up being more evident to the locals, so they more complain and then what ends up happening is they say it isn't their fault.

RICHARD: We don't have the economic base here to pay the kind of taxes that comes out of Madison. You know I mean down there if things go up 1 percent it doesn't—but 1 percent means a hell of a lot more here than it does in Madison or what Henry calls south of the Mason Dixon Line, the line east and west going through Wausau.

DALE: Or Portage [a city about an hour's drive north of Madison].

RICHARD: Well—

MARK: But I mean you know, right down to the tax form or the support form for the schools—why is a kid worth fourteen thousand dollars in Mequon [a suburban Milwaukee city] and what is he up here, Henry? Seven?

HENRY: Oh yeah—the consistency in schools that we're spending money—ridiculous. . . . Why don't they give each school X number of dollars per kid? If they want to spend eleven thousand dollars on a kid, tax the school district for the difference.

ERNIE: Have it averaged.

HENRY: Yeah, have it averaged. Everybody gets eight thousand dollars and if you want to spend eleven, tax the local district for it. Comprehensive plan.

MARK: This goes with the schools, in terms of facilities—facilities are gorgeous because they have the money to spend on it.

HENRY: If you take the state of Wisconsin and take a ruler and start at Green Bay and diagonally and just go fifty miles north of Madison, right over to the corner of the state, all your money lies in the south end of the state, your votes weight there. You're never going to get nothing changed to the north.

DAVE: That is absolutely correct.

HENRY: That's it.

MARK: That's not just the schools.

HENRY: We listen to the—being on the school board, we went several times to testify to the legislature to tell you that the formula was wrong, but they don't change it, because we haven't—if anybody on the south end would say change the formula for the schools, they never would get elected another two years and that's why all they are is looking for their own job.

Somebody makes a comment about the University of Wisconsin–Madison, and then Henry offers up his thoughts.

HENRY: And another thing, every time the state has a program, where do they, where do they implement it? Madison, Lake Geneva, in Milwaukee. They give everything to Milwaukee. You know all the programs in education—they want to try a new program, where do they put it? Milwaukee. Dead at the start. Why don't they put it out here where we can do something with it? Dead at the start.

RICHARD: Far as I can—like with—kept their schools up, Milwaukee let theirs fall down, and then they take our tax money to deal with the schools after we kept ours up. And they let theirs fall down.

HENRY: First of all, they oughta take that formula they give Milwaukee—they give Milwaukee a whole wad of money right off the top first and whatever is left, we divide by the other 425 schools in the state, which is wrong. Let Milwaukee do their own—get their fair—same share as we get, don't give a whole wad of it to them and then turn around and divide the rest among the rest of us.

In this conversation, the men complain about taxes and unfunded mandates—complaints that could come from someone in any type of municipality—but then they talk about this unfairness in terms of geography, namely, that a 1 percent tax increase "means a hell of a lot more here" than it does in the metro areas. They perceive that the decision making or the exercise of power in the major cities victimizes people in small towns by giving them less than their fair share of resources. In their eyes, decisions about funding for schools mean that small communities are the victims of distributive injustice.

Across the state, in a north-central tourist town, I asked a group of people at a diner counter early in the morning if they "feel like you're paying your fair share up here? Or heck no?"

NELSON: Well we'd like to keep more of our money for our school districts up here instead of sending it down below.

HELLEN [*The only other woman at the counter at that moment who is somewhat a little apologetic that she is about to leave me alone with them*]: I'm going to leave you with them.

KJC: Nice to meet you.

HELLEN: Good luck with these guys.

KJC: Oh thank you. So I'm sorry [to interrupt]—the schools. . . .

NELSON: They're taking so much of our money away from us. Want to close our schools and that sort of stuff, and the schools in Milwaukee and Madison and everyplace south of us, they've got all the foreign languages and every-thing else, and they got their curriculum is so much better than what we can give—because the fact that the state is not allowing us to have our money to educate our kids the way we should.

TREVOR: Talking about state schools? I thought that money came from here.

NELSON: Yeah—all of our money goes to Madison gets distributed back down to us.

KJC: A chunk of it—I don't know what percent but a good chunk of it.

NELSON: Yeah—the bureaucracy gets bigger and bigger. Their secretaries have to have secretaries . . .

PETE: Gotta figure with all the out-of-staters here, pay a lot of taxes.

NELSON: Oh sure—exactly true. People come up here to retire, the taxes eat 'em up. They have to move off [the lakes], but that's been their dream to get up here.

KJC: Oh no kidding.

NELSON: You know, as far as I'm concerned, I pay it, I don't protest, but I would like it if the city, the state would get fairer with the money. Why can't we have a foreign languages and that sort of stuff? Prepare for life after high school. They [kids from our community] get down to the colleges [which are almost all located south of this town], they are behind. . . .

Conversations about school funding often echoed the view that the rural areas were not getting their fair share. In such comments, people conveyed their identity as rural folks as well as their sense of injustice over the distribution of power and resources. I heard the claim that people in rural communities are helpless to change these funding formulas because no one downstate is listening to their concerns. They perceived that politicians and government in general are tone deaf to people outside the major cities.

Resentment about a lack of power compared to city people came through on many topics besides education. A group of people meeting in a gas station in a gorgeous hamlet on the Wisconsin River in southwest Wisconsin [was] very critical of what they saw as the state government's concern for tourists from the major cities and the Chicago area rather than themselves . . . :

GLENN: Just like everything else in Wisconsin, the most important thing to politicians in Wisconsin and in the state government is getting the tourists in here and the people out of Illinois. . . . You go to a boat landing around here and hell you can't unload your boat because there will be a dozen Illinois people there and they are top priority to the state and anybody with a supposed tourist label on 'em.

LARRY: Be there with their canoes, bring their food with 'em, their water, all they leave on the sand bars is shit.

[*Laughter*]

Four years later, their animosity toward the state government's neglect of their community's concerns came out as a complaint against unfunded mandates.

GEORGE: And where I see a lot of wasted money is garbage that I receive in the mail that doesn't have . . . I've been on the town board for about thirty-five years already . . .

KJC: Oh bless your heart.

GEORGE: And all the garbage I get, mail that doesn't even have anything to do with this area here whatsoever.

KJC: Huh. What kind of stuff?

GEORGE: Oh, from the state. Mandating everything, you know, do this, do that and our township doesn't have any curbs and gutters, there's so much stuff that the rural area doesn't even have that, you know, people in Milwaukee and Madison think, you know, that it's a big deal, but out here it's nothing.

As far as this group was concerned, city folks sent little to their community but junk mail and poop.

Even in a left-leaning group of retired women in an artsy community in northern Wisconsin, many of the members thought government paid no attention to their concerns.

KJC: OK, "How much attention do you feel the government pays to what the people think when it decides what to do? A good deal, some, or not much?"

[*Long pause*]

SUE: I think they're starting to get, that they're starting to listen with all this mess [the Great Recession].

KJC: Some. Yeah?

SUE: Before this I don't think. . . . I think it's changing.

DOROTHY: I think it's in the Beltway and out the Beltway. I mean Madison might listen to Madison people. Washington, DC, is a country unto itself. I know it; I spent time there. They haven't got a clue what the rest of the nation is up to, they're so absorbed studying their own belly button.

It is not a stretch to say that people in many places—not just rural areas—feel ignored by the government. But the complaints I heard in rural areas were not simply distrust of government—people in rural areas often perceived that government was *particularly* dismissive of the concerns of people in rural communities. Half of the groups outside the major metro areas expressed that belief. These attitudes were antigovernment thoughts, but they were rooted in residents' place identities.

. . . In a logging town in northwestern Wisconsin, during the run-up to the 2008 presidential election, I had this conversation with the two men remaining that morning out of a group that gathers in the back of the grocery store/gas station/liquor store/gift shop/hardware store:

KJC: Do you . . . what are your hopes for this presidential election? How would you like it to turn out in November?

Both of them laughed in response to the question before answering as follows:

SCOTT: Doesn't make any difference to me . . . Never has. I'm not a big political . . . I can't stand it because I've been around it for thirty-four years. County boards and stuff. I have no use for any of it. I'm sorry, I just—I'm sorry. That may be kind of a horseshit attitude, but I just, I'm sorry, I just don't.

KJC: A lot of people feel that way. The presidential candidates, you know, sometimes Wisconsin—

SCOTT: I can't see the difference it's gonna make up here anyway. We've been in a recession up here for thirty years, forty years. We don't know any different. People talk about recession, you oughta come up here.

KJC: Yeah?

SCOTT: Doesn't get any different.

Scott thought candidates did not care about his community and that his community, his place, had been ignored for decades. This was part of a widespread perception that small towns like his were generally overlooked. A group of women meeting for lunch in a central-west village on the day of the gubernatorial recall election in 2012 felt small communities like theirs had been "hung out to dry." I fumbled around with the question, but they ran with it.

KJC: Who do you think represents your concerns? I mean . . . do you . . . are there . . . does . . . do you feel like your state senator or state assembly person? Do you feel like anybody—

GLADYS: I think we are just hung out there to dry.

DOLORES: Great. I would agree with you. [*chuckles*]

KJC: That was the answer I feared, I mean—

DOLORES: There isn't anyone, I don't think, that really addresses the concerns of the smaller communities.

BEVERLY: No. I don't think so.

GLADYS: And being an agricultural dairy state, I understand that some of these farmers haven't got a lot more or maybe right in the same ballpark that they get for their milk that we got when we were farming twenty-three years ago and look at what else has gone up. The money it costs for the crops to go up . . . Nobody . . . We got the news. OK. "This big building burned in some area." It's all over the news. [But if] some farmer loses his barn, which is probably the same amount of money and the same catastrophe, it barely gets three seconds. It's not good.

Ignored by government and by the news media, these folks felt neglected by the powers that be. One way I noticed this was in the way they reacted to me. Several groups could not quite believe that I had made the effort to come "all the way from Madison" to talk with them. For example, in the town with the dice game in the central-west city, I spent time with a group that met up in the *early*, early morning at a gas station . . . :

KJC: Nice to meet you. Here's a football schedule for you—would you like one? Football schedule? Good for three years. Convenient, yeah? You're welcome. I would love to come back like January or February to talk to you guys again, could I?
[*"Sure!"*]
MARK: I think we need more input out of Madison in your small areas. Even like your senators, and everything. I mean they've gotta get around to do things like this.

Even higher income people in places outside the Madison and Milwaukee metro areas expressed this kind of surprise. They saw themselves as less important than people in the metro areas in the eyes of politicians and other decision makers. For example, one group of professionals meeting for coffee every morning in a diner in a central Wisconsin city said they were surprised that I, a university employee from Madison, was taking the time to drive around the state to listen to people like them: "I think that we are impressed [that you come up here to visit with us]. Because most of us, particularly in a state like Wisconsin where politicians—none of the national ones come and see us—you know we only have ten electoral votes. I mean none of the politicians come to see us at all." The Downtown Athletic Club perceived that the focus of politicians on cities rather than rural areas was a fact of politics nationwide:

KJC: Well, what's your take on the presidential election?
JOHN: You don't even want to know.
[*Fred laughs*]
KJC: Yes, I do! Sure I do. I don't want to start any fights. I want to know what you think.
JOHN: I don't know. How's that?
KJC: Oh you, yes you do. Why don't you . . .
JOHN: You had the state of Ohio, what was it? No. Pennsylvania. Where four precincts voted nineteen thousand some odd to nothing. For Obama. That just doesn't make a lot of sense, does it?
FRED: I didn't hear that story.
KJC: A little fishy. I didn't either.
JOHN: There was like four or so precincts where Romney never got a vote. Not one. You would think that any precinct that there'd be one person contrary to the norm. And at least I would.

MATT: Yeah, makes you wonder there, don't it.

JOHN: But uh no, I don't know. The election? The president knew where to campaign. He campaigned in all the metropolitan areas. The cities and stuff. That's where all the vote was. If you looked at, I go back to Ohio cause that was the swing state they all talked about all the time, and if you look at it on the map, I'm going to say there's sixty-five counties and Romney—so characteristic throughout the whole nation won—the vast majority of territory, he did not win the cities. I mean that's . . . somebody was attacking—

FRED: By square miles he'd have won.

KJC: Here in Wisconsin, too, right?

JOHN: Easily. What the . . . what did they say? All you have to do is win eleven cities and you can win the election?

KJC: Really?

JOHN: Someone was just saying that. The populist . . . the vote is that manner [set up in a way] that if you win eleven cities, you can win the election. I don't know if that's true but. . . .

To me, much of what is getting talked about here is power, and that power comes in several layers. The most obvious example of this power is the ability of governments to force rural places to abide by laws they dislike. This is the classic definition of power—the ability of A to get B to do something B otherwise would not do (Dahl 1961). "Unfunded mandates" is one example. But there is another dimension of power getting talked about here, too: control over which concerns even get recognized and discussed (Bachrach and Baratz 1962). I heard people in rural areas say many times that all of the major decisions are made in the urban areas, by urban people, and dictated outward. They complained that authority flowed out from Madison and Milwaukee but never in reverse. They felt that they did not have the power to get people to listen to their concerns.

While the inability to get their concerns heard is a subtle instance of feeling powerless, it is nonetheless important. Power is partly about respect, recognition, and listening. People whose voices are never heard by decision makers have no power. When those in power listen to some group, they convey that they are worthy of attention and, implicitly, that they share their power.

Many of the people I spent time with in rural areas felt like their towns were drying up and blowing away because the spigot of resources had been turned off. In addition, though, there was also a sense that these more subtle forms of power had been denied them as well.

One member of a group of retired and working women meeting for breakfast in a rural, far northern resort community explained:

THERESA: As a former educator, I resented, highly, comments such as, "There is no education north of Highway 8 [a U.S. highway that runs East-West across the middle of the state]. These kids aren't—" and we send them

such absolutely excellent and well-prepared students there that they—
the attitude that the hick area of the state—was painful.

KJC: So who did you get that from? Recruiters?

THERESA: Professors.

KJC: Really? When they would visit?

THERESA: Yeah, or publish in newspaper articles or other, you know—and that
was a little distressful because I think northern Wisconsin feels a little far
away from Madison anyway. And we keep waving our hands and saying,
"Yoo-hoo, there's another half of a state up here! Up north is not Wausau
[the main city in the central part of the state]!"

This is not just alienation, or a lack of trust, or low efficacy with respect to
powerful institutions. These sentiments are tightly bound to a sense of place
identity. Simply put, many folks I met in small places identified as rural
people and equated membership in that category with being a person who is
systematically ignored and left out of the exercise of power.

VALUES AND LIFESTYLES

When people talked about public affairs from a rural consciousness perspective they were telling me that city people have a lack of listening skills, exhibit
a chronic lack of respect for the rural way of life, and regularly ignore rural
communities. Many people talked about this as part and parcel of a fundamental aspect of the rural-versus-urban divide: city people just don't seem to
get it. They don't understand rural life or pay attention to it.

Part of the reason people in rural areas felt misjudged by urbanites were
the widely known stereotypes of rural folks. Many rural residents believed
that city dwellers thought they were just "a bunch of rednecks," for example.
A third of groups ($N = 18$) in places with populations under ten thousand
assumed that public decision makers in the major metro areas held common
negative stereotypes of rural residents, such as "hicks," "country bumpkins,"
"rednecks," and uneducated folks (Creed and Ching 1997; Jarosz and Lawson
2002). One group that I interviewed even went so far as to call themselves the
"Mediocre Redneck Coffee Klatch."

They were defensive, but they were also proud. And they had their own stereotypes of city folk. Slightly more than a third of these groups ridiculed
urbanites' lack of common sense. Many of them made a point of emphasizing
that in contrast to city folk, they understood how to really hunt and fish and
knew what it was like to really interact with nature. Also, many people took
enormous pride in using their hands rather than what they saw as what most
city folks did for work: sitting behind a desk all day.

This combination of pride in one's group and sense that their group is
deprived relative to other groups is characteristic of group consciousness in
general. So notice that although many rural residents resented cities, they did

not necessarily want to live in one. Conversations in eleven of the twenty-one groups located in places with populations of less than ten thousand included comments to the effect that, despite the hardships of rural life, they preferred their lifestyles to rootless, fast-paced city living. "Down in the cities, they don't even know their neighbors most of 'em!" one man exclaimed to me. People took pride in the face-to-face nature of their interactions, as opposed to the bureaucracy and technology they perceived to be typical of urban life. For example, one woman in a small town explained to me that, in her community, people do not do inspections when selling a house. "It's seen as insulting," she said. "If I give you my word that the house is in good shape, why would you need to inspect it?"

This perception of differing lifestyles for rural and urban residents fed the belief that city dwellers could not make decent decisions on behalf of rural communities. Such concerns were more focused on differences in ways of life and values than on differences in partisanship—that, say, city folks were Democrats and rural folks were Republican. In particular, many rural residents perceived a different pace of life in cities and were downright mad about attempts to appeal to tourists by urbanizing their own towns. For example, in [a] group of loggers in [a] northwestern village, during my first visit, I asked a general anything-else-I-should-know question, and here's what the group offered up:

KJC: But is there something else I oughta know about—I don't know—your lives in [this town] or what is going on up here? I know you can learn a whole lot in half an hour, but this is really helpful, actually.

[*Long pause*]

SAM: Well it's a lot less rat race than Madison.

KJC: Yeah, really peaceful.

JOHNNY: Yeah it's nice. I wouldn't live anywhere else.

KJC: Yeah you want to stay here—I can see that.

SAM: Drives to work, his house within a mile you're in the country—I mean not that [far] even.

KJC: Aw, it's beautiful.

SAM: Yeah, it's a lot less hectic. When you grow up this way. I guess if you grow up in the city, people say they can't stand it here. But if you grow up here—

KJC: Well, I think even city people, when they come up here, it's just like, "Wow it's so relaxing!" or they'll say things like—

SAM: Then they want to change everything. Have you been to Minocqua [a popular northern tourist town]?

KJC: Yeah.

SAM: Or Hayward [another popular northern tourist town]?

KJC: Not in a long time.

SAM: Hayward was like [this town] twenty years ago, and now it's got Walmart.

KJC: Hayward has a Walmart?

SAM: McDonald's, Menards, Subway—you turn around, you make a little Madison. Just strip malls. Downtown turns into antique stores because everything is out at Walmart. Lost all your businesses. Like this was all stores [as he waves his arm at the boarded-up Main Street outside].

A few hours west of that group of loggers, I met up two times in the town hall with a handful of leaders from the local government and the public schools who would turn on the lights and the Mr. Coffee machine and huddle together there every morning. The men resented outsiders' desire to urbanize northern Wisconsin.

DEAN: What generally happens is that one or the other likes it here, either the husband likes it here or the wife, and the other just hates it because they want to go downtown every day and shop. But if they wanna go shopping they have to drive twenty miles. So eventually, we've got like two- or three-million-dollar homes built, and they were there like five years, and one or the other of 'em didn't like it, and they sold out and went back to Florida.

KJC: Wow, did somebody buy that home? I mean, who's gonna? . . .

JACK: Oh yeah.

KJC: Really.

JACK: They had, you know, snowmobiles, all kinds of equipment, fishing rods and boats and all that, but she hated it here. Well, just to be in that party system in the city, and you come up here in the wintertime, there's nothing. I think that more spread between the very, very wealthy who move up here, and, it seems like to me, what we might call the middle class is shrinking, and the ones on the bottom. I don't have any facts, but that's the way I look at it.

Although most of the commentary about the contrast in urban and rural lifestyles was not overtly political, sometimes people did bring in politics directly. The men who gathered around the Mr. Coffee shared this:

FRANK: Well, we're very conservative in the Northwoods and they're very, very, very, very, very, very, very left in those cities. Just think if Madison and Milwaukee and La Crosse did not vote in an election. What would've happened? I mean our votes mean nothing because of the population and the votes [the large number of votes coming from cities, as opposed to small towns]. That's how I look at it. Same reason [upper] Michigan years ago wanted to leave lower Michigan. Form their own state.

KJC: So you feel like the show is pretty much run by the people—

FRANK: Oh yes, oh yeah. Yeah. We don't have any say.

KJC: So how about with the DNR [state Department of Natural Resources]? When you were working with the DNR?

FRANK [sarcastically]: Fine group of men. [laughs]

KJC: No, because the reason I ask is because connected with the state government did you feel like in your job you still didn't have much of a say—it was pretty much the folks in Madison telling you what you—

DEAN: You work long enough you have something political—we had decent working conditions—

AL: And that was the end of it. Now the governor appoints all the big shots and they don't know, before a guy had to work from the bottom all the way up and then become the head of the DNR. Now they just pick some guy off the street.

JACK: Oh yeah.

AL: A buddy of the governor and . . . That's the way I think about it. The DNR's changed.

Most of the people in this group were themselves elected officials or vocal commentators on public affairs. Their resentment toward the decisions people made in the cities had a clear partisan tone.

But when people talked about the inability of city dwellers to adequately represent rural concerns, partisanship was not front and center. Even for the group around the Mr. Coffee, they referenced "conservatism" not "Republicanism." There was a sense that urban residents lived differently. They were carving up the world into "us" and "them," but partisanship was not the key divider.

In addition, when they talked as if city people lived by different values, they were not emphasizing abortion, or gay marriage, or the things that are typically pointed to as the cultural issues that divide lower-income whites from the Democratic Party. Instead, the values they talked about were intertwined with economic concerns. When they talked about city folks being unable to understand rural life, those conversations were typically about how they had no understanding of the economic realities of rural life and how hard people had to work to make ends meet in small towns.

Here is one example of rural residents talking about how they struggled harder to get by than did people in cities. This exchange took place among a group of women meeting for lunch in the central-west town where the dice game takes place. They brought up the topic of health care and complained about politicians making choices out of step with ordinary people like themselves.

DOLORES: I have this feeling that—I don't know who mentioned this it might have been Bill Cosby—that if all of these senators and congressmen and all of these people took a cut in their wages, you know, and their benefits . . . and took the benefits that we have to take—

GLADYS: Yeah!

DOLORES: Live on the kind of salary that we have to live on, you know. They have no idea what small, rural America is like . . . small towns, you know! They couldn't begin to fathom what's it like to live on the incomes that we live on.

KJC: Do you feel that way about the state politicians too?
DOLORES: Up to a point. Yeah. You know, their thing is to win . . .

In a tiny town in the northwestern part of the state I met with a group of people that gathers in the basement of the local church every Tuesday morning: stay-at-home moms and some kids, retirees, and people taking a break from work. For a good chunk of time, the first time I met them, they complained about how disrespectful one of their state legislative representatives was and about how clueless state inspectors are. One example they gave me was the time an inspector checked the temperature of food in a salad bar in a restaurant a few towns over by sticking her thermometer in the ice.

When I asked them what the University of Wisconsin–Madison does not do well, they stated bluntly that people in Madison and Milwaukee have qualitatively different lifestyles than do people in the rural parts of the state.

KJC: What do you think the University of Wisconsin–Madison does not do well? When you think about [it] . . .
MARTHA: Represents our area. I mean we are like, we're strange to Madison. They want us to do everything for Madison's laws and the way they do things, but we totally live differently than the city people live. So they need to think more rural instead of all this city area.
DONNA: We can't afford to educate our children like they can in the cities. Simple as that. Don't have the advantages.
ETHEL: All the things they do, based on Madison and Milwaukee, never us.
MARTHA: Yeah, we don't have the advantages that they give their local people there, I think a lot of times. And it is probably because they don't understand how rural people live and what we deal with and our problems.
KJC: I think that's right. I think there is a whole lot of distance between— especially this corner of the state.
MARTHA: Oh we're, like, we're lost up here!
ROSEMARY: They don't even understand how we live in [our community]!
[*Laughter*]
MARTHA: Yeah that's right! It's very true. They won't even come and help us with our roads until you demand it.

In that conversation, in response to my question about the main concerns in their community, they had talked about their representative in Madison as someone unlike themselves, and about the state workers that regulated their livelihoods as oblivious to the basics of their businesses. The sense of being "strange to Madison" and living "differently than the city people live" was about fundamental differences in lived experience. And much of that difference was tied to economics: "We don't have the advantages that they give their local people there," Martha had said.

■   ■   ■

RESOURCES

When people in small towns claimed that they lived differently and had different values than city folks, they were often simultaneously claiming that they were people facing unique economic challenges. I want to ho[m]e in on their perceptions of economic injustice to show you the depth of these understandings. When people perceived that rural life was economically tough, this carried with it many complaints: about the injustice in the distribution of public dollars, unfair taxation, and more. Those complaints were intertwined with other aspects of rural consciousness, in particular, with their sense of being ignored and disrespected and of having fundamentally different values and lifestyles than city dwellers.

Here is a common narrative for how people wove these perceptions together: Rural life was a source of pride for many because it was different from urban living—it involved different lifestyles and values, including a special emphasis on hard work. That rural hard work ethic was a point of pride, but for many, it was a problem because in order to work hard, you needed a job, and rural communities were on the short end of the stick in terms of jobs. Why? Because rural communities had no power. Politicians and others with the ability to make the decisions to bring good-paying jobs to their communities paid no attention to the[se] places.

In the rural communities I visited, I often heard people stating, as though a matter of fact, that jobs, wealth, and taxpayer dollars are in "the M&Ms," as people sometimes referred to Madison and Milwaukee. They complained that rural areas are being left on their own to fight a losing battle. Conversations in seventeen of the twenty-five groups outside the Madison and Milwaukee areas included statements conveying that their communities did not receive their fair share of resources and that metro residents did not understand this. Their comments conveyed that the rural-versus-urban distinction was *the* main way to characterize the distribution of taxation, wealth, and the cost of goods and services in the state. In short, many people in small towns perceived that their tax dollars are "sucked in" by Madison and spent on that city or Milwaukee, never to be seen again.

On this mapping, wealthy people live in the cities (cf. Bell 1992, 78). "Everybody in [the] northern [part of the state] makes money off of tourists . . . [the tourists] bring some of that fresh money up," one man in the diner group in the north-central tourist town told me. On a different visit to the same group, another man said simply, "When you get down in the city, people are making more money."

Many people equated the cities with wealth because they perceived that the cities are where the good jobs are. One man in the group meeting in the small town on the Wisconsin River explained to me during my first visit, "Our salaries are less than what they are in Madison, by far, our hourly wages. And I would think salaried jobs as well. People here don't make as much, but there again, it's—that's why we don't have . . . that's why a lot of our young people have gone someplace else." About four years later, I heard a similar conversation in that group:

RANDY: I'd like to see, you know, I'd like to see a lot of new young families move into town . . . That's one thing you do see is too many older, retired persons in your communities—to be real active it makes a difference . . .

GLENN: A lack of good-paying jobs for the younger people to live on. You know it takes money to live or play or anything else and you get into a town like this and the people who are on the boards and stuff are people who usually own their homes and have a job and their interests are more in the parks and the fire departments and different things like that where it takes jobs for these young people to keep 'em around. And, you got jobs, you get young people, you get homes being built, and you get things being done.

RANDY: That's the problem with rural America.

GLENN: Right.

RANDY: You start here, go down along the river or whatever, you pick any of these communities, we're fortunate in [this town] . . . we're fortunate here that we got two or three good industries in town which we're very fortunate to have.

[. . .]

GLENN: In any of these towns. You go around Madison, thirty-, forty-mile radius, the majority of 'em are driving to Madison you know and it's, you know, they want to live in a small town but they gotta have a job, a decent paying job. With four-dollar gas, that's gonna make it tough.

Along with complaints about gas prices, I often heard concerns about utility bills in rural areas. For example, in the breakfast group of women in a rural tourist town:

SALLY: The cost of the water and sewer here is outrageous compared to what they pay in Madison. So here is big rich Madison, with all the good high-paying jobs, getting the cheapest water, and we have people up here who have three months of employment [because of the short tourist season], what are they paying? And I feel like there should be more sharing—less taxes going to Madison to help offset—

DOROTHY: I just moved from [a city in the central part of the state]. A quarter of water in [that city] is seventy bucks . . . seventy dollars every *three* months for [that] water. Up here, which we constantly have been paying, every second month, the bill—and sometimes we're not here—is seventy dollars every *second* month.

A bit later in the conversation, they continued on this theme.

SALLY: You've also got to look at Madison and the growth of Madison. There's new sewers going in every single day, the result of the businesses. You go down there and you don't know where Madison starts and Mount Horeb—I mean it is just one big sewer. . . . Like Walmart, buy it in volume, get it cheaper. But I think we don't look at places here—I mean I was coming up here eighteen years ago with a business, and I was shocked at how little the people got for services here. You pay for your garbage collection here on top of paying high taxes. I mean Madison, I throw out sofas [and don't have to pay]. There should be more sharing with these communities that are really struggling with stuff like that.

SHIRLEY: But in Madison there are all these big businesses that are paying taxes that we don't have here.

SUE: Exactly, but it should be a shared thing. I mean, why can't we look at that? Or at least put a state office building up here, with all the communication.

[*Agreement all around: "That would help."/ "That's a thought."/ "Great idea."/ "Absolutely."*]

SALLY: We could. I've worked for the state of Wisconsin, in a lot of offices, and a lot of offices could be—

DOROTHY: Outsource it to northern Wisconsin!

LAURA [*to me*]: You could be here all the time!

[*Laughter*]

KJC: That would be delightful—I would love it.

In the rural consciousness perspective, not only were the cities wealthier but they were also advantaged in terms of gas prices, utility bills, and infrastructure like sewers. These perceptions of injustice burned so brightly because they carried perceptions of blame. It was not just that cities were advantaged, but also that decision makers in them were intentionally overlooking the smaller communities in the state.

A man in the northwest logging group lamented, "I mean, rightfully so, you know, population centers, that's where the majority of the stuff has eventually got to go. It just makes sense. But you can't ignore everything up here either, you know." Likewise, a group of men at a diner in a rural northern-central tourist town almost laughed at the notion that the Obama administration stimulus proposal would help their community. They assumed none of the funds would focus on rural areas. One man said, "But the trickle down won't get to here because we don't have any business. So the trickle down will stop at Green Bay, Wausau [cities south of where they live] . . ."

Taxation was a seriously raw issue for many people in small communities. In general, the perception was that taxation hurt rural areas. At least one person in ten of the twenty-five groups outside the Milwaukee and Madison metro areas assumed that people in those cities are taxed at much lower rates than rural residents are.

Property taxes in particular were treated like an invasive species killing off native life forms. And people were sure it had come from the cities. Many rural folks blamed urbanites for driving up property values in their communities by purchasing expensive vacation homes. Some claimed this had driven locals out of their own communities or, at least, away from their lifetime dreams of finally buying a house on a local lake. They described these rising property values, driven by urbanites, as a threat to their personal and community identities (cf. Bell 1992, 76). For example, on the first morning that I met with the group of women in the rural northwest tourist town, one member showed me a list she had written in a small notebook of sixty people who had been forced out of their homes by urbanites buying expensive vacation homes. "The old-time families have left or are leaving," she said. "The character of the town is changing, and it is just too bad."

In Door County, the "thumb" of Wisconsin, I heard a similar thing from a woman taking part in a conversation after a church service:

Having been raised and grown up here, it has gotten to the point that I think Door County is becoming very elitist. Thank God I have a home. I was lucky enough that my husband and I had worked for it and paid for it before he died. On my wages, I could not have bought a home by myself. The cost of all of the surrounding land has become so expensive because of all the people who don't live here more than six weeks out of the year, and build three-quarter-million-dollar homes, million-dollar homes, and basically visit, and so they've driven the property values so high that those people who have lived in a home their whole lives and were able to afford, can no longer afford because the tax rate has gone up so high. The wage scale is not that great in Door County. People say, "Well, you know, you make a good living." No. And they somehow get the impression that we go to the gas station and we pay less for our gas, and pay less for our food because we live here. Ah, wrong! We pay the same price [*laughter*], but we don't make the wages, and we're paying for what has been driven up, and it's—I see it as a real hardship. I'm fortunate, but I look at my children and my grandchildren and I wonder will they be able to live here and own a home? Maybe they'll be able to rent, but to live here and own a home and take pride in that? That's scary. Really is scary.

The sentiment that city people were oblivious to the economic hardships that rural residents face was simmering on the back burner in many of these conversations. People living in tourist communities acknowledged the income that tourism generated but resented the perception that people living "up north" led leisurely lives. A woman in a northwest rural town said to me, "Just remember that up here many people have two and three part-time jobs to survive." Across the state, one man explained to me that, yes, he lived in a beautiful wilderness area, but when the weather got nice enough to be outside, he hardly had time to enjoy it. It was during those summer months that he and most of the people he knew had to work multiple jobs to get by throughout the rest of the year: "I live on a lake—lived there twenty-three years. I've fished it three times. Just not enough time. When we want to fish, we go to Canada or Minnesota to get away from it all."

Four years earlier, some people in his breakfast group expressed exasperation at how clueless city people were about the economic realities of tourist towns.

NELSON: Yeah—people in town here, they sell their home in Milwaukee or Madison or Illinois and they come up here and buy one of these small businesses. Christ!
PETE: Yeah—wake up!
NELSON: You won't make any money for twenty years, if you can stay in business for that long, pay your taxes and everything else.
KJC: Wow.
NELSON: It's a different world up here than it is in the southern part of the state.
PETE: Looks great in the summer time!
NELSON: Yeah looks great.
PETE: Nine months are winter, and three months are tough sledding.

In Door County, the "tough sledding" sounded like this:

PAM: What you make in six months has to stretch all year.
BECKY: And many of 'em are working two and three jobs during this period of time.
PAM: Exactly.
BECKY: Yeah, they're not doing just one job.
PAM: You don't really have a summer—it consists of working. When my kids were home, I worked two jobs, so you know—it goes by quickly.
SHELLY: People always say, "You are so lucky to live [here] in the summertime!" Well, any of us who live here, live here and work here and never enjoy it. First of all we're irritated [*half-jokingly*] because we can't get to our job because of these tourists driving so slow.
KJC: I'm sorry! [*Apologizing for being a slow-driving tourist.*]
SHELLY: And then when we get there we work, leave that and go to another job and come home and then we are following another tourist to come home [*laughter*], and so we really don't get to enjoy what everybody else does, although I am so appreciative that I can live here, I really can't imagine—I just thank God every day that I am able to live here in [this town] where I was born.
DON [*sarcastically*]: You don't want to go to Milwaukee and live there?
SHELLY: No and I'm willing to give up a lot to do that, and I think a lot of us have done that.

The way they described it, making a living in a tourist community was a challenge, characterized by constant hardship and uncertainty. And they believed that urbanites just did not understand this.

People resented the economic hardships they faced, the fact that city people and those who held the reins of power did not seem to recognize these hardships, and, also, the unfulfilled promise of tourism. They did not necessarily like city people coming in to their communities but were willing to put up with it in order to make a living. In some places, however, people talked about city people infiltrating their communities, yet not helping the local economy in any way. Local residents would complain that tourists passed right through without spending any money. One example was the "all they leave on the sandbars is shit" comment noted earlier. Randall, from the group of loggers in the northwest corner of the state, also expressed this objection: "A lot of people tell me, well, if it wasn't for tourists, your taxes would be higher. Well, they don't spend much money here. They bring their own gas, they bring their own food, they might stay in a motel, you know. We're not really gaining anything from tourism."

In these conversations, the distinctiveness of rural economies was obvious to people living in them. In one case, a woman gave this a label—"the rural class." "If you look at the *rural class* [emphasis added] . . . we've never had jobs here, it's not like this is part of the economy that there are no jobs, but I think one of our big concerns is the coming tourist season and the decrease in funding from the state for tourist-related activities, cause so many people here rely entirely on tourists coming so it's just a real uneasy feeling about what's gonna happen this year."

Talk concerning rural economies ranged from this "uneasy feeling" to downright anger. Sometimes the resentment about the economic inequality between the major cities and small communities was so strong I wondered if I should end the conversation and get out. Other times it was downright comical. One group in west-central Wisconsin actually imagined a geographic line that represented this unfairness. . . .

This is the gang of men who played dice every morning before work. The first time I visited this group, when a local attorney led me through the curtain at the back of the diner to the group sitting at their L-shaped table, they stopped playing dice for a while and talked with me. At the end of our conversation, they asked me if I knew how to play Ship, Captain, and Crew. I said, proudly, "Why, yes I do." My Wisconsinness came in handy here, as I had played this dice game many times with my family growing up. They asked me to "turn off that machine [my recorder] and we'll shake for a buck" in their dollar round (before most of them left and went to work or their other tasks for the day), and I promptly lost. They asked me to "come back and shake dice" and "bring your quarters." It was clear that I was welcome to come back, but I had better plan on playing dice when I did.

On my third visit, there was a horse auction going on in town, and the group members joked with me about buying a horse. This led to some colorful comments about Madison. When several of them asked me if I was going to check out the auction, I answered:

KJC: I think I will go up once, yeah, I went up—I looked through the fence yesterday evening.
HENRY: Why don't you buy one of them horses? I got a trailer.
KJC: Not sure where I'd keep him. [They knew by this point that I lived right in Madison, a mile from the football stadium at the time, where there was room for them to park next time they come down for a game. But there is certainly no room to keep a horse.]
HENRY: Huh?
KJC: I'm not sure where I'd keep him!
HENRY: Keep him in Madison. That's where they keep all the bullshit.

After everyone got a good laugh out of that one, Henry continued on:

HENRY: Well, basically all you gotta do is buy the front end of the horse, they got the back end in Madison!

The group laughed, and I almost snorted my coffee, but then I started to get uncomfortable—not because of the anti-Madison comments, but because I had been winning round after round in the dice game. Most of the members of the group thought this was funny, but at least one was visibly irritated. To try to soften the situation, I joked,

KJC: I come and ask for your thoughts and I take your money!
RICHARD: I'll tell you what, that's good though. Because we have so little of it.
KJC: And it all goes to Madison anyway [*joking along with them*].
HOWARD: We expect nothing less from Madison!
RICHARD: It won't cost any postage to get it down there now!

This resentment was good-natured, but it was ubiquitous across the rural communities I visited. It didn't seem temporary, either, and wasn't just a product of the Great Recession. People talked about economic injustice as a fact of rural life.

ISN'T THIS REALLY JUST ABOUT RACE?

Many people in these small towns perceived that someone or something was responsible for the decline of their communities. Someone or something was siphoning off their money, they told me. They believed that wherever their tax dollars were going they sure were not going to their own towns.

Who or what was doing this? Who was getting their hard-earned money? "They" often had something to do with cities: decision makers, wealthy people, liberals, and the undeserving.

Cities represent a lot in American life. One thing they conjure up is race. In short, cities are often shorthand for people who are not white. When the dice game group in central Wisconsin referred to the line dividing rural Wisconsin from the metropolitan centers in the southern part of the state as the Mason-Dixon line, the racial implications of that term were probably not accidental.

The urban-versus-rural divide is undoubtedly in part about race. Cities have perhaps always "been the places where we have first and most fully confronted the task of living alongside people who do not necessarily belong to our own tribe" (Conn 2014, 4). There is a widening policy conflict between urban and rural areas, and it is no secret that it is driven in part by racial mobilization (Gimpel and Schuknecht 2003). Research on implicit racial priming tells us that the term "inner city" is racialized—that this term activates racial attitudes (Hurwitz and Peffley 2005). It is likely the term "urban" does so as well. This may be especially the case in Wisconsin, which is extremely racially segregated. Only 29 percent of the state's African American population lives outside the cities of Milwaukee and Madison, and most of the state has little experience to date with Latino immigration. Also, the Milwaukee metro area is extremely segregated with respect to African Americans and Latinos. According to a Brookings Institute analysis of 2005–09 data from the Census Bureau's American Community Survey, the Milwaukee metro area is one of the most racially segregated in the country (Frey 2010).

So yes, it is highly likely that when people refer to "those people in Milwaukee" they are often referring to racial minorities. But notice how complex this is. The urbanites that rural folks were referring to were not predominantly racial minorities. When white outstaters (i.e., those living outside the major metropolitan areas) complained of the laziness in the cities in these conversations, their comments were almost always directed at white people: government bureaucrats and faculty members at the flagship public university.

In that way, antiurban resentment is not simply resentment against people of color. At the same time, given the way arguments against government redistribution in the United States have historically been made by equating deservingness with whiteness, these conversations are about race even when race is not mentioned. Also, animosity toward public workers and wealthy folks in the city may be driven by conservative views on race. Since the cities, particularly Madison, are perceived as liberal and vote Democratic in elections, people who harbor racial resentment may indeed be equating city people with racial liberalism. Now, as in the past, racial animosity is directed toward groups of whites that help minorities, such as government employees and academics.

When rural folks did make openly racist comments, they did so about Native Americans, an overwhelmingly rural population in Wisconsin. There are eleven reservations in Wisconsin, located primarily in the northern third of the state. Hostility toward Native Americans did not arise often in these conversations, but it is no secret that relations between Native Americans and whites in Wisconsin have been tense historically and in recent history. Violent protests erupted in response to a series of federal court decisions in the 1980s, beginning in 1983. Those decisions affirmed spearfishing treaty rights to the Chippewa tribe and imposed no limits on how many fish tribal members could harvest (Bobo and Tuan 2006, chap. 2). White residents protested at boat landings, held demonstrations and rallies, and called for the end to treaty rights as well as the reservation system. Much of this opposition was rooted in racism, as social science research has documented (Bobo and Tuan 2006).

In recent years, these tensions have become salient to the broader population again, as the Walker administration has passed legislation that is facilitating the start of an iron ore mine in northwestern Wisconsin. To some, the mine signifies hundreds of jobs for people in the area who are sorely lacking them, but to others it means extensive disturbance to the way of life and natural environment and health of Native Americans on the adjacent Bad River Reservation (Seely 2011).

It is very possible that the lack of references to urban racial minorities in the conversations I observed is a manifestation of the threat hypothesis, or the idea that racial prejudice is heightened when people of different racial backgrounds are in proximity to one another (Key 1949; Blalock 1967). Given the extreme racial segregation in Wisconsin, there is little interaction here between whites and people of color. Thus the immediate racial tensions in most rural areas are not between whites and African Americans and Latinos but, instead, with Native Americans and, in a few communities, with Hmong refugees, who were relocated to Wisconsin in the decades since the Vietnam War.

The point I want to make is this: race is a part of rural consciousness. However, I ask the reader to notice the complexity of these perspectives and not think of them as simply about race. If we boil rural consciousness down to race, we ignore the ways in which these perspectives comprise many things: identities with place, a sense of oneself as a person of a particular place in the class hierarchy, identities as people with particular values, and sometimes ideology. Resentment is operating because people perceive they are not getting their fair share. They are making sense of this injustice by resenting those whom they think are getting more than they deserve, and perceptions of who works hard and who is deserving are infected with racism (Winter 2006, 2008). But those notions of distributive justice are *intertwined* with race—neither separate from nor synonymous with a simple distinction of white versus other.

Finally, if we conclude that rural consciousness is just racism dressed up in social science jargon, it allows us to overlook the role of antigovernment attitudes and preferences for small government here. Tea Party messaging appeals to racism (Burghart and Zeskind 2010; Parker and Barreto 2013), but it also resonates with many of the perceptions of inequality and alienation from government observed in the conversations presented [here]. As I have argued, attitudes about redistribution rest on a long history of racial discrimination in the United States. But that long history has enabled an accretion of meaning around attitudes of injustice.

This is how the politics of resentment operates—it works through seemingly simple divisions of us versus them, but it has power because in these divisions are a multitude of fundamental understandings: who has power, who has what values and which of those values are right, who gets what, and perceptions of the basic fairness of all of this. It is opposition to other people, and the overlap of urban and racially "other" is a powerful combination.

This is part of the reason racism is so persistent. Because it is intertwined with other fundamental attitudes, it can be invoked and expressed in seemingly socially acceptable ways (Mendelberg 2001). In the conversations I observed, when people expressed racist sentiments, they did so while weaving them with values and allegiances of which they were sufficiently certain and proud that they were willing to express them in front of me, a relative stranger. Take for example these comments to me, by a man in the group of loggers in northwest Wisconsin . . . :

RON: Yeah. You know. Well like him that just left, that was here before to get coffee?

KJC: Yeah.

RON: He's an American Indian. [One sentence deleted for confidentiality.]

KJC: Oh really?

RON: He's a good guy.

KJC: Yeah.

RON: Works hard. Yeah.

KJC: Well sure.

RON: But he won't live on the reservation where they get all the free housing and stuff, he's self-supporting, you know?

KJC: Yeah.

RON: And, there, there's too many programs down there for a bunch of people, you know to have it for them to want to go to work. You know? They got the casino down there shoving our money through 'em, they got the federal government shoving our money through 'em, and they wonder where they got drunken alcohol problems, they got nothing to do all day besides sitting around and do what they want to do. And they keep giving 'em money to do it, well how do you expect to get anything out of anybody? There's an old saying: A hungry dog hunts harder. Hey, you keep feeding a dog or a cat, they're not gonna hunt, they're not gonna look for food, they're gonna lay around and get fat.

If I said these comments in a classroom, I would expect to get accused of racism. But for Ron, this was about hard work and deservingness. To call this just plain racism misses the complexity of the sentiments involved here.

CONCLUSION

"Rural consciousness" is the term I am using to describe a strong sense of identity as a rural person combined with a strong sense that rural areas are the victims of injustice: the sense that rural areas do not get their fair share of power, respect, or resources and that rural folks prefer lifestyles that differ fundamentally from those of city people. . . .

When I argue that rural consciousness structures the way people understand politics, I am suggesting that something other than partisanship is driving their political preferences. Support for the Republican Party is not what causes people to have these complex, intertwined understandings of economic injustice, place identity, class identity, race, and values. And the complexities of this understanding do not inevitably lead to support for the Republican Party. You may have noticed that some of these rural groups contain a good number of Democrats. In fact, the northwestern and southwestern corners of Wisconsin, although predominantly rural, lean Democratic. Booth Fowler, one of the wisest scholars of politics in Wisconsin, reasons that this is due in part to high levels of poverty in those areas, the influence of the city of Superior and of Great Lake shipping unions in the northwest corner, and the effect of commuters or out-migrants from Madison in the southwest (Fowler 2008). Whatever the reason, it is clear that the correlation between where people live and how they vote are not set in stone. They are the product of people actively trying to make sense of their lives.

REFERENCES

Bachrach, Peter, and Morton Baratz. 1962. "Two Faces of Power." *American Political Science Review* 56: 947–52.

Bell, Michael. 1992. "The Fruit of Difference: The Rural-Urban Continuum as a System of Identity." *Rural Sociology* 57 (1): 65–82.

Blalock, Hubert M. 1967. *Toward a Theory of Minority-Group Relations*. New York: Wiley.

Bobo, Lawrence D., and Mia Tuan. 2006. *Prejudice in Politics: Group Position, Public Opinion, and the Wisconsin Treaty Rights Dispute*. Cambridge, MA: Harvard University Press.

Burghart, Devin, and Leonard Zeskind. 2010. *Tea Party Nationalism: A Critical Examination of the Tea Party Movement and the Size, Scope, and Focus of Its National Factions*. Kansas City, MO: Institute for Research and Education on Human Rights.

Conn, Steven. 2014. *Americans against the City: Anti-Urbanism in the Twentieth Century*. New York: Oxford University Press.

Creed, Gerald W., and Barbara Ching. 1997. "Recognizing Rusticity." In *Knowing Your Place: Rural Identity and Cultural Hierarchy*, edited by Barbara Ching and Gerald W. Creed, 1–28. New York: Routledge.

Dahl, Robert A. 1961. *Who Governs? Democracy and Power in an American City*. New Haven, CT: Yale University Press.

Epstein, Leon. 1958. *Politics in Wisconsin*. Madison: University of Wisconsin Press.

Fowler, Booth. 2008. *Wisconsin Votes: An Electoral History*. Madison: University of Wisconsin Press.

Frey, William H. 2010. "Census Data: Blacks and Hispanics Take Different Segregation Paths." http://www.brookings.edu/research/opinions/2010/12/16-census-frey.

Gimpel, James G., and Jason E. Schuknecht. 2003. *Patchwork Nation: Sectionalism and Political Change in American Politics*. Ann Arbor: University of Michigan Press.

Hurwitz, Jon, and Mark Peffley. 2005. "Playing the Race Card in the Post–Willie Horton Era." *Public Opinion Quarterly* 76 (2): 99–112.

Jarosz, Lucy, and Victoria Lawson. 2002. "'Sophisticated People vs. Rednecks': Economic Restructuring and Class Differences in America's West," *Antipode* 34 (1): 8–27.

Key, V. O., Jr. 1949. *Southern Politics in State and Nation*. New York: A. A. Knopf.

Mendelberg, Tali. 2001. *The Race Card: Campaign Strategy, Implicit Messages, and the Norm of Equality*. Princeton, NJ: Princeton University Press.

Parker, Christopher, and Matt A. Barreto. 2013. *Change They Can't Believe In: The Tea Party and Reactionary Politics in America*. Princeton, NJ: Princeton University Press.

Seely, Ron. 2011. "Mining in Wisconsin: Promise or Peril?" *Wisconsin State Journal*, October 9.

Winter, Nicholas. 2006. "Beyond Welfare: Framing and the Racialization of White Opinion on Social Security." *American Journal of Political Science* 50 (2): 400–20.

———. 2008. *Dangerous Frames: How Ideas about Race and Gender Shape Public Opinion*. Chicago: University of Chicago Press.

9.5

JAMES CAMPBELL

From *Polarized: Making Sense of a Divided America*

One way to measure the degree to which Americans have become more polarized is to use surveys to discover the proportion who consider themselves moderate in ideology. Campbell shows that many more Americans currently say that they are ideologically very liberal or very conservative than was the case in previous decades, with a shrinking proportion of moderates. He carefully shows that these measures from surveys reflect actual changes in American political attitudes with real consequences for politics.

Are Americans sharply divided in their politics or are they calmly gathered around a pragmatic political center? This is a tough question because the answer most probably lies somewhere in between. Americans are neither cantankerously polarized to the hilt nor blissfully of one mind. But the fact that Americans are not all at the outer edges of ideology or neatly clustered at the center does not mean that we can blithely split the difference and walk away thinking that the polarization questions are answered. We should be able to extract a more meaningful reading of polarization from the evidence.

IDEOLOGICAL DIFFERENCES

There is a long history of self-reported measures of political ideologies. Since at least the mid-1930s, surveys have asked respondents to declare their general ideological perspectives on politics as liberal or conservative. Data drawn from these questions played important roles in public opinion research in the late 1960s, but it was not until the early 1970s that surveys provided consistent question wordings offering response-options across the spectrum from liberal to moderate to conservative.

Where better to begin an investigation of the polarization of the public than with what citizens themselves say about their own ideological orientations? After all, self-declarations are the basis for measuring the other major

From James Campbell, *Polarized: Making Sense of a Divided America* (Princeton, NJ: Princeton University Press, 2016).

long-term political orientation of voters: individually in party identification and collectively in macropartisanship. The party identification of citizens is determined directly by asking respondents whether they think of themselves as Democrats, Republicans, independents, or something else rather than whether they routinely think or vote in a particular way, or [by] asking researchers how they would on some other basis classify a respondent's partisanship. The same measurement approach seems quite reasonable to follow with respect to ideology. Not all Republicans (or Democrats) think alike on all matters nor mean exactly the same thing in identifying with that party, and we would not expect that all conservatives (or liberals) are in lockstep either. Americans may not always label themselves correctly and no measure is without flaws, but the fact that individuals identify or associate themselves with a party or an ideology would seem highly credible, barring overwhelming evidence to the contrary.

Five Ideological Series

The direct evidence of ideological polarization is drawn from five highly respected national survey data series of ideological self-identifications. Each collected self-reported ideology data over a significant period. The five series include data from the American National Election Study (ANES), the General Social Survey (GSS), the CBS/*New York Times* polls (CBS/NYT), Gallup polls, and the National Exit Poll of voters conducted on election days. All have two important characteristics in common. Each series allows respondents to indicate whether they consider their views to be liberal or conservative, and each permits respondents to declare their views to be moderate or somewhere between liberals and conservatives.

Beyond these common characteristics, there are many differences. The surveys were conducted over different intervals and in different years. The longest series is ANES. It has been conducted, for the most part, in conjunction with biennial national elections and extends from 1972 to 2012 (19 observations). The joint CBS and *New York Times* surveys have been conducted more frequently but at irregular intervals. Their ideology question was asked in 304 surveys conducted between 1976 and 2015. For the sake of comparability with the other series, the medians of these polls within calendar years are used to collapse the 304 surveys into 40 annual observations. The GSS series is from 1974 to 2014 (missing a few years) and has 28 annual observations. Gallup got a late start in settling on its ideological question. Its data span [the period between] 1992 to 2014 (23 observations). The shortest of the five series is the exit polls. It covers the ten presidential election years from 1976 to 2012. Overall, the combined series covers the years from 1972 to 2015 and consists of 120 annual observations.

The five series differ in several other ways as well. Each has its own distinctive question wording and sampling frame. They also differ in their response options. CBS/NYT and the Exit Polls offer respondents three possible responses (liberal, moderate, or conservative). Others offer more gradations of liberal or conservative responses. Gallup's format allows respondents to place themselves on a five-point scale from "very liberal" to "very conservative." ANES and GSS present a seven-point scale (extremely liberal, liberal, or slightly liberal and the same on the conservative side). The five series also differ in how easily respondents can opt out of responding, with the ANES consistently generating the highest percentage of "don't knows" by explicitly offering respondents the "haven't thought much about it" option. . . .

Polarized Ideologies

What do these data reveal about ideological polarization in recent decades? What portions of these electorates were relatively polarized from one another? Polarization is measured here as the percentage of respondents claiming to be either liberal or conservative rather than moderate or not knowing their ideological orientation. A high percentage of liberals and conservatives would reflect a relatively polarized electorate. A high percentage of moderates or respondents unaware of their ideological perspectives would reflect a less polarized electorate. Figure [1] displays the combined percentage of liberals and conservatives (ideologicals) for each of the five series from 1972 to 2015.

As one would expect given the variety of question wordings, options offered, receptivity to "don't know" responses, and other differences as well as the normal sampling errors of surveys, there is variation across the series within each year. This is particularly the case in the 1970s and 1980s. In more recent years, the measures tend to converge. Some of the series start at higher levels of liberals and conservatives and others track greater changes in these levels over time. The GSS series is relatively flat in the high 50s. The ideological portion of the public was initially smaller in the ANES series and then grew at a higher rate. The CBS/*New York Times* and Exit Poll data fall in between.

Though they have their differences, the five different ideology series together support four important points about the extent and development of the public's polarization. First, at the outset in the 1970s and early 1980s, a large portion of the electorate already was fairly well polarized. At the low end of the range, ANES indicates that about 45% of Americans were neither moderates nor unaware of their ideological perspective. Generally about half the electorate in exit polls asserted liberal or conservative ideological orientations, and the CBS/NYT series normally found those declaring a liberal or conservative inclination to outnumber moderates. According to the GSS measure, nearly three of every five Americans declared an ideological viewpoint. Taken as a whole, those asserting liberal or conservative perspectives constituted anywhere from 45% to 60% of Americans in the 1970s. Whether this should be interpreted as high or low is open to question—at least at this point. What is not open to question is that roughly half of Americans or more claimed a non-centrist ideological viewpoint as early as the 1970s. Contrary to a good

FIGURE [1]   Ideologicals (Conservatives Plus Liberals) in the American
Electorate, 1972–2015

NOTE: The percentages are of all respondents. The data are from the American National Election Study, the General Social Survey, the CBS and *New York Times* Surveys, Gallup, and the national Exit Polls housed at the Roper Center.

deal of cavalier talk, *most* Americans were *not* moderates in the 1970s, probably no more than a bare majority were.

Second, the public has become more polarized and less centrist over time. In each series, the ideological portion of the electorate has grown. This is clearly visible in four of the five series, with the data plots moving to the upper right corner of the figure. . . .

There is no doubt more Americans adopted ideological orientations or became more cognizant of their orientations over the last few decades. There can be questions over whether the growth in polarization was as slight as the GSS series suggests or as strong as the Gallup and ANES series indicate, but there is no question that Americans became more polarized than they were, at least as reflected in their declared ideological viewpoints.

Third, though somewhat obscured by herky-jerky movements in the five data series, polarization has grown quite consistently since the 1970s. It has not been confined, as some might contend, to the contentious post-2000 period of the Bush II and Obama presidencies. Although the ideological clarity of more fully polarized parties may have pushed along polarization's increase in more recent times, the trend regression indicates that the public's polarization had increased significantly in the previous three decades and detects no substantial acceleration in this trend since 2000.

Fourth, while there is some variation in the pervasiveness of ideological orientations measured by the different series in the 1970s and 1980s (though all indicated that a large share of the electorate were ideological) and variation as well in the degree to which polarization grew in the intervening years (though all find some growth), there is a general consensus that nearly three of every five Americans now associate themselves with either a liberal or conservative perspective. The spread of the percentage of ideologicals in the five series in Figure [1] resembles a cone with a wide end on the left and a narrow end drawn to the upper right corner, approaching the 60% mark.

. . . Nearly half of Americans (49%) were either liberal or conservative in the early 1970s. This increased to about 56% by 2012. The ideological portion of the electorate expanded by approximately seven percentage points from the 1970s to the 2010s. This was accompanied, of course, by about a seven-percentage-point decline of non-ideologicals. These are the self-declared moderates and those who would not or could not associate themselves with an ideological view. A majority of the decline among the non-ideologicals occurred among those indicating that they did not know how to characterize their political perspectives. This was about five of the seven-point drop. Whether these respondents had been ideologicals all along and only became aware of it in more recent years, or whether they (or their successors) developed a less centrist perspective in later years is unclear. What is clear is that they had been unable or unwilling to identify themselves as liberals or conservatives in earlier years and now, rather than claiming moderation, they report their general political perspectives to be either liberal or conservative.

In effect, the nation changed from one in which ideologicals and non-ideologicals were about at parity in the 1970s (still a large number of ideologicals) to one in which those reporting an ideological perspective outnumbered centrists by 12 percentage points (56% to 44%) in the 2010s. If we were comparing election returns, the former would be a dead heat and the latter a near-landslide. This is substantial change.

Some to the Left, More to the Right

A good deal of the increase in polarization in recent decades has been the result of more Americans claiming to be conservative. The portions of the electorate who report themselves to be conservatives and liberals are presented respectively in Figures [2] and [3]. Self-declared conservatives made up nearly 31% of the electorate in the 1970s according to Figure [2]. By the 2010s, they were nearly 35% of the electorate. In four of the five series, the increase of conservatives is statistically significant and the increase just barely falls short of conventional significance levels in the fifth series (the exit polls). The change is greatest in the ANES series and weakest in the CBS/NYT data. The growing number of conservatives accounts for about four of the seven-percentage-point increase in ideologicals.

FIGURE [2] Conservatives in the American Electorate, 1972–2015

NOTE: The percentages are of all respondents. The data are from the American National Election Study, the General Social Survey, the CBS and *New York Times* Surveys, Gallup, and the national Exit Polls housed at the Roper Center.

FIGURE [3] Liberals in the American Electorate, 1972–2015

NOTE: The percentages are of all respondents. The data are from the American National Election Study, the General Social Survey, the CBS and *New York Times* Surveys, Gallup, and the national Exit Polls housed at the Roper Center.

The percentage of self-reported liberals in the electorate is plotted in Figure [3]. As a comparison to the previous figure shows, except for the GSS series in the early 1970s in which they are [at] near parity, conservatives otherwise substantially outnumber liberals. From 1972 to 1990, the mean conservative advantage over liberals was about ten percentage points. Since 2000, the mean gap grew to about 13 points. Though there was no discernible increase in the percentage of liberals in one series (GSS), the percentage of liberals increased slightly in two others (ANES and CBS/NYT) and more substantially in two series (Gallup and the Exit Polls). The pooled series indicates a significant increase of about two and a half percentage points in liberal ranks since the 1970s. The liberal trend is about two-thirds as large as the trend toward conservatives. In short, from the 1970s to the 2010s, Americans became less moderate and more polarized, with an increase in the ranks of liberals and a larger increase in the ranks of conservatives.

▪   ▪   ▪

Operational Ideology

Free and Cantril in the late 1960s were the first to notice the apparent discrepancy of professed ideology and issue preferences as a challenge to the self-report measure. They noticed that a few self-reported liberals held conservative issue positions, but many more self-described conservatives adopted liberal issue positions. A good number of self-reported conservatives wanted to maintain or increase funding for education, public housing, and urban renewal and thought that the government should do more to reduce unemployment. These self-identified conservatives holding apparently inconsistent policy positions were labeled by Free and Cantril as "operational liberals."

Ellis and Stimson have updated and substantially extended Free and Cantril's interpretation of political ideology in the public. Like Free and Cantril decades before, Ellis and Stimson found that many conservatives surprisingly supported *more* government spending for a wide range of purposes—from healthcare and education to mass transportation and the environment. They constructed an index of operational ideology from responses to ten GSS questions asking respondents whether government was spending too much, too little, or about the right amount on ten different public problems. These included foreign aid, urban problems, crime, drug addiction, education, the environment, welfare, health, and "the conditions of blacks." Anyone who favored increased spending rather than cuts on more problems (other than defense) was classified as an operational liberal. Operational liberals who reported that they thought of themselves as conservatives were classified as "conflicted conservatives."

An example of the kind of question that Ellis and Stimson use in their operational ideology index is an ANES question about preferences on changes in spending for dealing with crime. Table [1] presents 2012 ANES responses of self-reported liberals, moderates, and conservatives to possible spending changes for anti-crime programs. The data demonstrate that a plurality of liberals, moderates, *and* conservatives favor devoting more resources to dealing with crime (though they might well differ over what "dealing" with crime entails as well as the source of the additional spending—including whether the additional spending might come from spending reductions elsewhere). Very few respondents of any ideological bent favor reductions in spending on anti-crime programs. Ellis and Stimson interpret the substantial percentage of self-declared conservatives favoring more spending on government programs, in this case anti-crime programs, as evidence of operational liberalism at odds with their symbolic attachment to the conservative label.

To demonstrate what they interpret as the robustness of operational ideology, Ellis and Stimson also examine responses to issues other than those involved with preferences about changes in government spending. Whether the government should guarantee jobs for everyone is one such issue. Responses to the ANES version of that question in 2012 are presented in Table [2]. Liberals presumably would favor the government guarantee and conservatives would oppose it. As the table shows, a large majority of self-reported conservatives, as expected, opposed the proposed policy, while a plurality of liberals favored it. There were, however, some liberals adopting the expected conservative position and some conservatives taking the expected liberal position. In this particular instance, a larger percentage of liberals (24%) strayed from the liberal line than conservatives (15%) from the conservative position. As this case demonstrates, there are a good number of individuals who hold issue positions that would appear to be contrary to or inconsistent with their self-reported ideology.

TABLE [1] Self-Reported Ideology and Preferences for Change in Spending on Crime, 2012

Self-Reported Ideology	Preferred Change in Government Spending on Crime (%)			
	Increased	*About the Same*	*Decreased*	*Total*
Liberal (24%)	45	44	11	100
Moderate/DK (39%)	59	36	5	100
Conservative (37%)	47	42	11	100
Total	51	40	9	100

NOTE: The data are from the 2012 ANES study. The question wording is: "Next I am going to read you a list of federal programs. For each one, I would like you to tell me whether you would like to see spending increased or decreased. What about dealing with crime. Should federal spending on dealing with crime be increased, decreased, or kept about the same (kept the same)?"

Based on their evaluation of the associations between self-reported ideology and an array of both spending and non-spending issue positions, much like those examined in Table [1], Ellis and Stimson conclude that, though "perhaps sincerely and deeply" identifying with the conservative label, nearly two-thirds of self-reported conservatives are actually misguided or "conflicted conservatives" who "support liberal public policies" and that "there is little evidence that conflicted conservatives are actually 'conservative' in any sense beyond self-identification." Despite strong evidence to the contrary . . . Ellis and Stimson conclude that "Americans tend to want to call themselves 'conservative' while they advocate big government liberalism." Put differently, and though they do not use the term, they essentially claim that as many as two-thirds of conservatives are really what might be called CINOs or "conservatives-in-name-only."

These are bold claims. Some might say outlandish. There is no question that some people misidentify their political ideologies, but the idea that *two-thirds* of conservatives would be so confused seems implausible, especially in light of the considerable evidence of the self-reported ideology measure's validity. Many self-declared conservatives would no doubt be deeply insulted by the proposition that they were so ill-informed and misguided—or mesmerized by a shiny conservative label—that they could not accurately describe their own general political perspectives. Still, as seemingly radical as the claims are, they are made by highly regarded scholars examining a good deal of professionally gathered survey data. They deserve to be taken seriously. The question is whether they should be believed.

TABLE [2] Self-Reported Ideology and Preferences on the Issue of Government Guaranteed Jobs, 2012

Self-Reported Ideology	Government Guaranteed Jobs and Standard of Living (%)			
	Favor	Neutral	Opposed	Total
Liberal (25%)	46	29	24	100
Moderate/DK (38%)	36	29	35	100
Conservative (38%)	15	14	71	100
Total	31	23	46	100

NOTE: The data are from the 2012 ANES study. The question wording is: "Some people feel the government in Washington should see to it that every person has a job and a good standard of living. Suppose these people are at one end of a scale, at point 1. Others think the government should just let each person get ahead on their own. Suppose these people are at the other end, at point 7. And, of course, some other people have opinions somewhere in between, at points 2, 3, 4, 5, or 6. Where would you place yourself on this scale, or haven't you thought much about this?" Categories 1, 2, and 3 were grouped as favoring guaranteed jobs. Categories 5, 6, and 7 were grouped as opposing government guaranteed jobs. Category 4 was scored as neutral on the issue.

Mountain or Mole Hill?

How serious are these critiques of the self-reported ideology measure? Do they discredit their use for assessing polarization in the electorate? More specifically, are the claims that Americans are really more "operationally liberal" while being "symbolically conservative," that is, liberal with a conservative veneer, well supported? Are these claims against self-reported ideology a formidable mountain or a concocted mole hill?

Based on the analysis that follows, the answer is that *none* of these criticisms, including the "conflicted conservative" and "operational liberal" claims, raise[s] serious concerns about the basic declaration by respondents of their own political perspectives. There are variations in ideological outlooks, different degrees to which they are held, local variations, and various competing influences for how much they influence policy positions, but these variations and competing influences are just that and not evidence that the underlying political perspective is anything other than what respondents say [it is], especially in light of the substantial evidence of the measure's validity and reliability.

First, it is a certainty that ideological labels mean different things to different people at different times. All liberals and all conservatives may not even prioritize their values in the same way. This is to be expected. In itself, this does not amount to a challenge to the ideological concept or measure. Any two conservatives in the public are likely to disagree over what it means exactly to be a conservative, just as any two conservatives (or, for that matter, liberals) in Congress are likely to disagree about what that ideological label requires. I would venture to guess that all Democrats (or Republicans) do not share the same idea of what it means to be a Democrat (or Republican) or that all Communists, Libertarians, or self-declared moderates are on the same page regarding their essential attributes. Beyond the political realm, all Catholics or Protestants or Jews or Muslims do not have exactly the same idea about what it means to be members of those religions. Any group affiliation, particularly those based on beliefs rather than on a physical characteristic, is likely to allow some ambiguity or variation in its membership criteria. Moreover, there may be some significant variation in these definitions by time, region, and degree. What it means to be a liberal in 1950 in Mississippi may be a good deal different from what it means to be one in 2015 in New York. Any social group involves a somewhat moveable "big tent." This variation does not mean that the grouping is an empty symbol.

The Ellis and Stimson study illustrates the dangers inherent in imposing a definition of what it means to be an adherent of an ideology and then attempting to reconstitute ideological attachments from various attitudes and behaviors. Their operational ideology measure appears to assume that conservatism is reflected in the opposition to any increase at any time in government spending on a broad array of domestic programs and that liberalism is observed in the support for increased spending for these programs under any circumstance (the assumption is reversed for defense spending). Respondents favoring an increase in spending in one area may qualify as conservative, but only if they favor cuts in more programs. Many die-hard, true-blue conservatives who favor limited, efficient, frugal, affordable, and sensible government for truly public purposes, however, favor increased spending to improve the nation's health (e.g., cancer and heart disease research, infectious disease treatments), to improve the nation's educational system (e.g., school vouchers, more and better teachers), or to halt a rising crime rate (see Table [1]). From time to time, they might even also have some reservations about the need for ever higher defense budgets. Are they any less conservative because they want government to wisely spend more money to cure cancer or keep the streets safe? Of course not. That a large majority of self-described conservatives do not qualify as operational conservatives by Ellis and Stimson's litmus test might be better regarded as evidence that the operational ideology measure is itself problematic rather than that self-declared conservatives are not what they claim themselves to be. To be clear, this is not to question the assumption that conservatives favor less spending on domestic policies in general than liberals. They most certainly do. It is, however, to question where the lines in spending are drawn between conservatives, moderates, and liberals, both in individual policy areas and in a collection of policy areas. Conservatives do not always favor less spending than the status quo on everything (other than defense) as the operational ideology index supposes.

Beyond variations in the meaning of ideologies, differences in the degrees to which ideologies are held and the contexts in which the opinions are given, and various complications in the construction of the operational questions, respondents professing an ideological perspective may stray from their ideologically expected position for many other reasons. Even for highly committed ideologues, ideology is not the be-all and end-all. Other considerations often come into play in deciding where someone stands on an issue. Different perceptions, strategies, and priorities may lead people with strong ideological principles in common to take somewhat different policy positions on occasion. A conservative may have a personal commitment to reducing crime or fighting cancer or protecting the environment, for instance, and this may override, on occasion, a general and deeply held commitment to government frugality and restraint. Or, an ideological commitment may temper the extent of support for various spending priorities. In either case, neither the ideological nor public policy preference precludes the other. They can, and do, harmoniously coexist.

■   ■   ■

Self-reported ideology is a credible measure of the general political perspectives of Americans. There is solid evidence that a plurality, *not* a majority, of Americans are moderates (or don't knows) and their numbers have been on the *decline*. Many more Americans are conservative than liberal and though both ideological perspectives have been growing, growth has been a bit greater at the conservative end of the ideological spectrum than at the liberal end. The aggregate distribution of these perspectives indicates: (1) that Americans in the 1970s were already fairly well polarized, and (2) that the extent of polarization in the American public has grown significantly since that time.

9.6

LILLIANA MASON

From *Uncivil Agreement:*
How Politics Became Our Identity

There is considerable evidence that, more than in the past, Americans feel anger toward those of the opposite political party, rather than feeling calm in the presence of respectful disagreement. Mason shows evidence from surveys and experiments that partisans of both major parties—Republicans and Democrats—are isolated from each other and have deep-seated animosity toward the "other" partisans, even if they do not know many of them. She shows evidence that the recent surge of anger is a consequence of the alignment of people's ideologies and partisanship. It was not always the case that ideological conservatives were all Republicans and ideological liberals were all Democrats. But today, the high levels of partisan division in the general population are driven by very conservative Republicans and very liberal Democrats feeling tremendous anger toward their partisan opponents.

> Trump has gotten voters who are so angry that they are willing to put their ideological concerns aside. We have never seen voters do that to this extent. They're saying, "We're so ticked off that that's the only message that matters."
>
> —Patrick Murray, pollster, 2016 (quoted in Goldmacher 2016)

In April of 2014, the federal Bureau of Land Management (BLM) attempted to round up and repossess a herd of cows belonging to a man named Cliven Bundy. Bundy grazed his cattle on federal land in Nevada, for which he was legally required to pay grazing fees. He had refused to pay these fees since 1993, claiming ownership of the land. By 2014, the BLM estimated that Bundy owed the federal government $1 million. As members of the BLM began to round up Bundy's cattle, some members of Bundy's family began protesting and confronting federal officials. Within days, a protest camp formed at Bundy's farm with a sign at the entrance reading "[MILITIA SIGN IN]" (Fuller 2014). Hundreds of self-identified members of armed militias gathered on Bundy's land, preparing for a violent battle against the federal employees. They dressed in paramilitary gear, set up illegal checkpoints, aimed their weapons

From Lilliana Mason, *Uncivil Agreement: How Politics Became Our Identity* (Chicago, IL: Chicago University Press, 2018).

at law-enforcement officials and federal employees, and threatened to bomb and kill people at local businesses (MacNab 2014). The story exploded in the national media, with conservative news sources praising Bundy as a hero, and liberal news sources calling him a terrorist and a "big fat million dollar welfare dead beat" (Vyan 2014).

Conservatives were outraged at the federal government's treatment of Bundy. And, with guns drawn, hundreds of militiamen joined Bundy in expressing their anger, if not outright rebellion, against the government. An attorney named Larry Klayman wrote in support of Bundy:

> Before these government goons do come back, let this message go forth. Barack Hussein Obama, Harry Reid and the gutless Republican estab- lishment leaders in Congress who roll over to and further this continued government tyranny, We the People have now risen up and we intend to remove you legally from office. This country belongs to us, not you. This land is our land! And, we will fight you will [sic] all legal means, includ- ing exercising our legitimate Second Amendment rights of self-defense, to end your tyranny and restore freedom to our shores! (Klayman 2014)

The case of a local rancher who hadn't paid his taxes was quickly turned into a national fiasco, and a source of potent outrage among conservatives. How did Cliven Bundy so quickly become a national conservative icon? The answer—as Paul Waldman (2014) put it in the *Washington Post*—was that "when conservatives looked at Bundy . . . everything about him told them he was their kind of guy."

Bundy checked off many of the boxes that make up the Republican Party. A strong conservative, a white man, a rural southerner, he represented the con- vergence of the social identities that hold the Republican Party together. This convergence of identities made it much easier for Republicans to get angry on his behalf, and for Democrats to get angry at him. Conservatives, as they defended Bundy, did focus on a policy aspect of the conflict—the overreach of the federal government. But for many conservatives, particularly under Demo- cratic president Barack Obama, the federal government, as Larry Klayman decried, had become more of an enemy—a set of "goons"—than the foundation of a policy position.

This sort of intense anger is not rare in modern American politics. In 2009, when Congress was debating what would eventually become the Affordable Care Act, town hall meetings across America erupted with angry outbursts. *Politico* reported, "Screaming constituents, protesters dragged out by the cops, congressmen fearful for their safety—welcome to the new town-hall- style meeting, the once-staid forum that is rapidly turning into a house of hor- rors for members of Congress" (Isenstadt 2009). At the same time, members of the Tea Party held angry protests in Washington. In 2011, in New York City, a liberal group calling themselves Occupy Wall Street protested against a number of economic, political, and social injustices. The New York protests spread to dozens of other cities and were described by the *New York Times* as "Countless Grievances, One Thread: We're Angry" (Lacey 2011). Turn on almost any cable news station during the last ten years, and you can find a political pundit expressing anger at a new political development.

Perhaps the pinnacle of all of this anger has been the unexpected success of the 2016 presidential campaign of Donald Trump. According to a 2016 Pew poll, the Americans who expressed anger at the government tended strongly to be Trump supporters. Trump is a fascinating case because, as a candidate, his policy positions were well known to be quite flexible, if not nonexistent.

In a 2016 *Washington Post* article, Philip Rucker and Dan Balz wrote, "Donald Trump fits no simple ideological framework. The presidential candidate collects thoughts from across the spectrum. Added together, however, his ideas represent a sharp departure from many of the Republican Party's values and priorities dating back half a century or more. . . . Trump's presidential candidacy has been described as a hostile takeover of the Republican Party. In reality it appears more a movement that threatens to subsume the GOP behind a menu of ideas and instincts that might best be described as 'America Wins.'" In this sense, the Trump candidacy distilled perfectly what Tajfel found in his minimal group paradigm experiments. Winning grows increasingly important as identities grow stronger. To this point, Trump's support was also strongest among those voters who shared multiple Republican-linked identities (Mason and Davis 2016). These particularly include white and Christian identities. Trump's campaign did not tear the Republican Party apart; he spoke directly to the social groups that have aligned with the Republican Party in recent years, and he did so with little real policy content.

The alignment of multiple social identities can directly affect the degree of anger with which individuals respond to identity threats. As identities have moved into alignment in recent years, levels of anger at outgroup candidates have also increased. Though these are simply correlational trends, they serve to set up the story to come.

One crude way to examine average levels of anger over time is to look at one question asked by the American National Election Studies every year beginning in 1980. The item asks respondents whether each presidential candidate "has—because of the kind of person he is, or because of something he has done—made you feel angry." I coded this item so that it refers only to people's feelings of anger toward the outgroup candidate. The numbers in Figure [1] represent the percentage of people who have reported feeling angry at the outgroup candidate in each presidential election year.[1]

This is a rough measure and fluctuates widely depending on the context of the election. For example, Barack Obama's 2008 Yes We Can campaign was generally oriented toward hope and change and was the first election in which an African American was elected president. Republicans (those for whom Obama was the outgroup candidate) had little to openly express anger about.

FIGURE [1]   Anger Toward the Outgroup Presidential Candidate

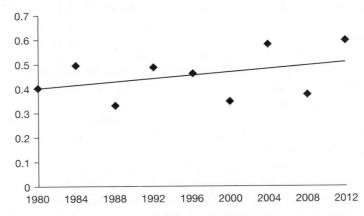

NOTE: Data drawn from the weighted ANES cumulative data file, 1948–2012. Numbers represent the percentage of people who reported feeling angry at the outgroup presidential candidate, coded as a presidential candidate of the party that the respondent does not belong to. Question was first asked in 1980. Pure independents are excluded.

Not only did social norms against racism briefly tamp down open partisan rancor, but it was, after all, a Republican president who had only months before presided over one of the greatest financial disasters in national history. Republicans may have been angry, but in that moment they were not angry at the relatively unknown Barack Obama. (That would come later.)

In the same election, John McCain, the Republican, had a reputation as a centrist, party-bucking politician who could be relied upon to make compromises. Democrats (those for whom McCain was the outgroup candidate) therefore had little to hold against him personally. Their ire was reserved for the sitting president, George W. Bush, who held some of the lowest approval ratings of all time.

An earlier drop in anger had registered in the election of 2000, when voters famously saw little difference between the two major party candidates. But these relatively low-anger elections did nothing to reduce anger in the following elections. If anything, the low-anger elections worked as sling-shots, pulling levels of anger down, only to shoot them back up in the following elections to unprecedented levels. Voters in recent years, when they do feel angry, feel angrier. In both 2004 and 2012, levels of anger reached 60 percent of the partisan population for the first time since the measure was introduced in 1980.

In Figure [1], the general trend over time is drawn as a straight line, which is moving upward, toward more anger. In 1980, 40 percent of partisans felt anger toward the opposing presidential candidate, and by 2012 that number had increased to 60 percent. Even accounting for fluctuations, the trend line indicates a 10 percentage point average increase in the proportion of people reporting angry feelings at their party's main opponent since 1980. The anecdotes of

FIGURE [2]   Enthusiasm for the Ingroup Presidential Candidate

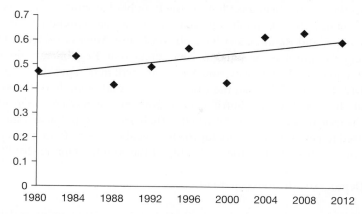

NOTE: Data drawn from the weighted ANES cumulative data file, 1948–2012. Numbers represent the percentage of people who reported feeling proud of the ingroup presidential candidate, coded as a presidential candidate of the party that the respondent does belong to. Pure independents are excluded.

partisan rancor and vitriol don't seem to be simply isolated events. There has been a modest but increasing trend toward angrier American politics.

This is not the entire story, however. Americans are not only angrier at their political opponents, they are also happier with their own team's candidates. Figure [2] shows trends in the percentages of Americans who claim they have felt "proud" of their ingroup presidential candidate.

Just as in the case of anger toward the outgroup candidate, pride for the ingroup candidate is steadily, if noisily, rising. The general trend from 1980 to 2012 is a mean increase in pride of 12 percentage points. In the three presidential elections since 2000, around 60 percent of partisans felt proud of their presidential candidate, compared to numbers hovering around 50 percent in the decades before. So, just as Americans are growing increasingly angry at their opponents' candidates, they are growing increasingly enthusiastic about their own.

Combine this anger and pride in every presidential election, and we see a picture of an electorate that is increasingly emotionally reactive. As time progresses, American partisans are more likely to feel angry at their opponents and proud of their own candidates. We are priming the pump for a very energetic battle.

▪   ▪   ▪

In the 2011 YouGov survey, I included an experiment in which respondents were randomly assigned to one of five conditions. Some respondents were asked to read a message that threatened their party. They were told it was taken from a political blog, but in fact I fabricated it based on a number of blog comments I had collected, in order to make the messages as comparable as possible. For Republicans, this message read:

2012 is going to be a great election for Democrats. Obama will easily win re-election against whatever lunatic the Republicans run, we are raising more money than Republicans, our Congressional candidates are in safer seats, and Republicans have obviously lost Americans' trust. Our current Congress is proving to Americans that Republicans do not deserve to be in the majority, and Americans will make sure they're gone in 2012. Finally, we'll take the Congress back and won't have to worry about the Republicans shutting down government anymore! I'm glad that Americans have finally returned to their senses. Republicans should get used to being the minority for the foreseeable future. Democrats will hold our central place in the leadership of the country. Obama 2012!!

For Democrats, the message read:

2012 is going to be a great election for Republicans. We're going to defeat the hardcore socialist Obama, we are raising more money than Democrats, our Congressional candidates are in safer seats, and Democrats have obviously lost Americans' trust. Our current Congress is proving to Americans that Democrats do not deserve to be in the majority, and Americans will make sure they're gone in 2012. Finally, we'll take the government back, and we won't have to worry about Democrats blocking us at every turn! I am so glad that Americans have finally returned to their senses. Democrats should not get used to running the government. Republicans will take back our central place in the leadership of the country. Defeat Obama in 2012!!

Other respondents were asked to read a "blog message" that threatened their party's cherished policy outcomes. For Republicans, this message read:

2012 is going to be a great election for responsible political ideas. After this election we can finally fix the economy using wise tax increases to pay for our indispensable social programs and infrastructure, so that we can create jobs instead of blindly throwing money to corporations and giving tax cuts to the millionaires who caused this mess. After this election we'll be able to improve the health care bill by adding a public option, make sure every woman has clear access to abortions, every child has a chance to learn evolutionary theory in school, and make it easier for all adults to get married if they want to, no matter who they are. Finally, our country will be on the right path again!

For Democrats, this message read:

2012 is going to be a great election for responsible political ideas. After this election we can finally fix the economy by enforcing personal responsibility, using a true free-market system to make sure people aren't handed more than they've earned. We'll be able to shrink the government and get it off our backs, and lower taxes so that hard-working people have a reason to work. After this election we'll be able to stop socialized medicine, prevent the abortions of innocent babies all over the country, bring God back into the public sphere, and make sure that we are a country that respects that marriage is between a man and a woman. Finally, our country will be on the right path again!

A fifth group did not read any message at all. The four messages were randomly assigned, so some Democrats would read the Republican threat message and some Republicans would read the Democratic threat message. When this occurred, I coded this as a message of support for the party.

After reading one of the messages, respondents were asked how the message had made them feel. They could answer A great deal, Somewhat, Very little, or Not at all to the following emotion items: Angry, Hostile, Nervous, Disgusted, Anxious, Afraid, Hopeful, Proud, and Enthusiastic. I combined their responses to the Angry, Hostile, and Disgusted items to form a scale of anger, and the Hopeful, Proud, and Enthusiastic responses to form a scale of enthusiasm. In comparison to the yes/no anger responses measured above, this measure created a scale of emotion that ranges relatively continuously from 0 to 1, creating much more variation in the amount of anger or enthusiasm a person could report.

Figure [3] illustrates the main effects of each experimental treatment on emotion. As expected, in the threat conditions, anger is substantially stronger than enthusiasm, and in the support conditions enthusiasm is the main result. The party-threat conditions included language that had the potential to generate stronger emotions than the issue conditions, but, as the data show, emotional reactions to the issue threats are relatively similar to the main emotional effects of party threats.

I measured sorting using the full social-sorting scale, including partisan, ideological, black, secular, evangelical, and Tea Party identities, measuring each, if present, using the four-item social-identification scale. This creates a much fuller measure of sorting by including multiple social identities that may come into play in determining how angry or enthusiastic each partisan can be.

I expected the most socially sorted partisans to be the most emotionally volatile. I thought they would react to the party-based threats with the most anger and to messages of support with the most enthusiasm. I also expected to find somewhat smaller results for partisan identity alone, and much smaller effects among those with the most extreme issue positions. In other words, I expected to see that a conglomeration of identities is most emotionally responsive to threat (particularly group-based threat), that one identity is slightly less so, and that a set of extreme issue positions generates the smallest emotional response to threat.

FIGURE [3] Main Effects of Experimental Treatment

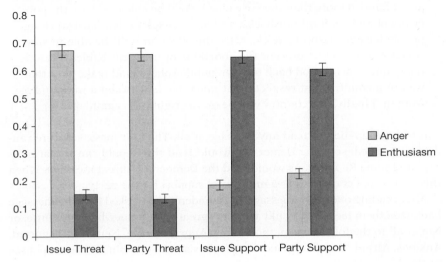

NOTE: Ninety-five percent confidence intervals shown. Bars represent mean levels of each emotion in each treatment, across the entire sample.

In order to give the issue positions a fair test, however, I included the threats that were devoid of partisan labels and only threatened policy outcomes. If anything were to anger those with strong issue positions, it should be these issue-based threats.[2] Furthermore, the issue measure used here accounts for not only issue extremity but also issue importance and issue constraint.[3] I refer to this measure as issue intensity, due to its inclusion of multiple elements of issue attitudes.[4]

Experimental Results

What I found was relatively consistent with expectations but also slightly surprising. The results are presented in Figures [4] and [5]. In short, the intensity of issue positions does, indeed, generate significant emotional reactions to issue-focused messages. When issue positions are threatened (Fig. [4a]) or reassured (Fig. [5a]), those with the most extreme, consistent, and salient issue positions respond by growing angrier and happier, respectively. However, when party defeat (Fig. [4b]) or victory (Fig. [5b]) is promised, issue extremity has no significant emotional effects. Issue-focused citizens are different from their issue-moderate counterparts in the degree to which they are angered and excited by practical goals but not by status threats regarding their own parties.

Partisanship has a different influence on emotion. Strong partisans are significantly angrier than weak partisans when the party is threatened (Fig. [4b]) but not when policy success is threatened (Fig. [4a]). They also grow significantly more enthusiastic than weak partisans when party victory is discussed

FIGURE [4] Predicted Angry Reactions to Messages

[4a] Issue Threat

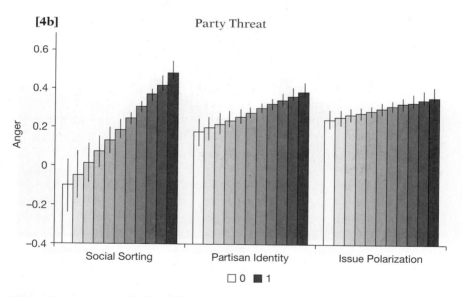

[4b] Party Threat

NOTE: Bars represent the predicted values of anger at each level of issue extremity, partisan identity, or sorting. Ninety-five percent confidence intervals shown.

FIGURE [5]   Predicted Enthusiastic Reactions to Messages

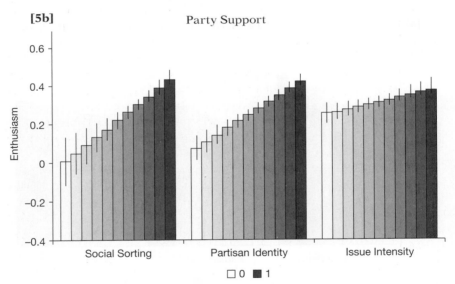

NOTE: Bars represent the predicted values of enthusiasm at each level of issue extremity, partisan identity, or sorting. Ninety-five percent confidence intervals shown.

(Fig. [5b]) but not when policy victory is promised (Fig. [5a]). It doesn't really matter to partisans whether their policy positions are threatened. Strong partisans are emotionally engaged by messages of support regarding their party's status—but not by the actual policy outcomes of that status.

Sorting is the unique variable in this sequence, in that it is capable of affecting emotion no matter what kind of message is presented. But this occurs in an interesting way. In Figure [4], social sorting does affect angry reactions to both issue-based and party-based messages of threat. Unlike either issue intensity or partisan identity alone, the difference between cross-cutting and well-sorted identities is apparent in response to both messages. However, one important point to note is that, in the issue-based threat condition, the highest levels of sorting do not generate anger that is significantly higher than the anger produced among the most issue intense. Similarly, in the party-based threat condition, the highest levels of sorting do not generate anger that is significantly higher than the anger produced among the strongest partisans. The main difference between the effects of sorting versus issue intensity and partisanship is found at the *low* end of the scale.

The people with the most cross-cutting identities respond to both types of threat with significantly *less* anger than either the least issue-intense or the least partisan individuals. In fact, for both types of threat, the cross-cut individuals respond with no anger in the case of party threat and with *negative* anger in the case of issue threat. In other words, when these cross-cut individuals read a threatening political message, they remain impassive. These data suggest that Americans are not growing increasingly angry because the best-sorted identities drive the highest levels of anger. They are growing angrier because the people who tend to respond without anger (those with cross-cutting identities) are disappearing. As the sorting continues, the people who have the best chance of remaining calm in the face of political conflict are shrinking as a proportion of the electorate.

A similar phenomenon is seen in the case of enthusiasm, shown in Figure [5]. In the presence of an issue-based message of victory [5a], the most socially sorted individuals are predicted to report no more enthusiasm than those who are the most issue intense. In this sense, sorting is not increasing enthusiasm beyond what it would already be among the most issue intense. However, at the low end of the spectrum, those with cross-cutting identities are significantly *less* enthusiastic than the least issue intense. The 95 percent confidence interval for the least-sorted group in Figure [5a] crosses zero, suggesting that, once again, those with cross-cutting identities have no emotional response whatsoever, even to a positive message.

In the case of party-based messages of victory, the same basic pattern arises. People who are highly socially sorted are no more enthusiastic after hearing a victory message than are the strongest partisans. In this one case, those with cross-cutting identities are statistically indistinguishable from very weak partisans. So the dampening effect of cross-cutting cleavages does not go beyond the dampening effect of simple weak partisanship. However, one difference does exist. The confidence interval around the predicted level of enthusiasm for those with the most cross-cutting identities includes zero, which means it is statistically probable that these people do not respond to encouraging messages with any enthusiasm at all. In comparison, the confidence interval for the weakest partisan's level of enthusiasm does *not* include zero (narrowly), and therefore, statistically speaking, a weak partisan is predicted to respond with some minimal level of enthusiasm.

Well-sorted citizens are broadly emotionally responsive. They get angry at any message of threat, and they get happy at any message of victory. Whether party-based or issue-based, highly sorted individuals react to political messages with emotional reactions that match those driven by the strongest partisans or the most issue-intense individuals. However, while the emotional reactions of highly sorted individuals match the maximum emotional reactions already found in the electorate, the reactions of cross-cut individuals are significantly less intense than the reactions of any other citizens measured here. Cross-cutting identities dampen emotional reactions to political messages, such that the most cross-cutting identities lead to a complete lack of emotional response. This lack of response exists only in the group of cross-cut citizens that are increasingly disappearing from the American electorate.

NOTES

1. In other analyses not shown, levels of anger toward the ingroup candidate have been decreasing over the same period. For more information on these trends, see Mason (2016).

2. I included each type of threat separately in a regression, controlling for demographic variables (race, gender, political knowledge, age, income, and church attendance), and included interactions between each variable of interest (sorting, partisan identity, issue extremity) and either party-based or issue-based threats. The interactions showed the effect of each of these variables only when the respondent had read a threatening message. In the sorting and partisan-identity models, issue extremity also interacted with threat in order to control for the effects of issue extremity more fairly. All other variables are held at their means or modes. Modes in this sample for the dichotomous variables are female and white.

3. The full set of issue positions is combined into a scale ranging from most liberal on all issues to most conservative on all issues. Each issue in the scale is weighted by its importance, as rated by the respondent. This full weighted scale is then folded in half, to range from the most conflicted/moderate/unimportant issues to the most consistent/extreme/important issue positions on either end of the ideological spectrum. This measure proved to generate the most powerful emotional results for issue positions and is therefore used here so as not to undersell the impact of issue positions. Broockman (2016) has argued that including constraint in the measure obscures important heterogeneity in extreme responses across ideological boundaries. This is true. However, the current measure is theoretically appropriate in the case of this particular experiment, as the models here are run under the assumption that issue positions are constrained. The

issue threats are full of party-consistent issue positions. Furthermore, parties constrain issues, and partisanship is a key element of the models. An unconstrained set of issues, for the purposes of this particular model, should be expected to reduce emotional reactivity due to their cross-cutting effects. Including constraint in the issue-polarization measure is therefore a decision that is intentional.

4. It should also be noted that in all the following models, those that examine the effects of sorting or partisan identity control for issue intensity. The issue-intensity models do not control for partisanship or sorting. These models therefore provide a particularly generous test of the effects of issue polarization. Also controlled for in all models are white race, sex, income, age, political knowledge, and church attendance. In the issue-intensity and partisanship models, black race is also controlled for, but, as it is included in the sociopartisan sorting measure, it is not separately controlled in the social-sorting models.

DISCUSSION QUESTIONS

1. According to Lupia's and McCubbins' theory, under what conditions can people with limited information make reasoned choices? Give a specific example of a situation in politics that satisfies these conditions.

2. What is the RAS model? What does the RAS model predict about the survey responses of people who do not pay much attention to politics? Why does it predict this?

3. Ethnocentrism is common, according to Kinder and Kam. Describe ethnocentrism and how it matters for contemporary American politics.

4. From the Cramer excerpt, use at least three quotes from people Cramer interviewed to depict rural consciousness that shows its distinctiveness from mainstream (i.e., urban or academic) views of American politics.

5. Campbell thinks certain arguments about polarization in the last few decades are wrong. Summarize how he uses data to refute these arguments and how he shows that Americans have actually become more polarized in recent decades.

6. What evidence does Mason use to show that Americans have become increasingly polarized by partisanship and ideology? What role does anger play in her arguments?

7. Among the phenomena discussed in Chapter 9—knowledge, ethnocentrism, rural consciousness, and polarization—which ones do you think stay constant over time, and which ones change over time given historical circumstances? Summarize specific evidence from the readings to support your claims.

10

PARTICIPATION

10.1

JANELLE WONG, S. KARTHICK RAMAKRISHNAN,
TAEKU LEE, AND JANE JUNN

From *Asian American Political Participation: Emerging Constituents and Their Political Identities*

Asian American is an increasingly influential demographic category in American politics. This study analyzes the relationship between self-identification as an Asian American and the propensity to participate in politics. The researchers find evidence that those who primarily identify themselves as Asian American, as opposed to a specific ethnic group like Filipino or Korean, have a higher probability of voting and participating in other forms of political activity.

NATIONAL ORIGIN, PAN-ETHNICITY, AND RACIAL IDENTITY

Identities are at once paradoxically personal and collective. My identity is what defines me personally and uniquely. Yet if my identity is Asian American, it is a fingerprint of individuality shared by roughly 15 million others. Consider for a moment any other trait or aspect you give as an answer to the defining identitarian question, "Who am I?" That answer will surely be shared.

The mystery that wraps this riddle is that the juxtaposition of Asian and American together does not lend itself to obvious interpretation, especially

From Janelle Wong et al., *Asian American Political Participation: Emerging Constituents and Their Political Identities* (New York: Russell Sage Foundation, 2011), Chapter 5.

under the rubric of a unitary, coherent collective identity. Lisa Lowe writes, "The American of Asian descent remains the symbolic 'alien,' the *metonym* for Asia who by definition cannot be imagined as sharing in America" (1996, 6). In some versions of Asian American, one identity dominates the other; in other versions, they coexist somewhere between détente and pluralist heaven, each retaining a willful integrity with respect to the other, and yet elsewhere they reconstitute in a hybrid identity—uniquely Asian American and neither Asian nor American.

Asian American is uncommonly diverse: Bengali, Chinese, Filipino, Indian, Indonesian, Japanese, Korean, Lao, Malay, Pakistani, Thai, Vietnamese, to mention just a few of the national origin groupings lumped together under this pan-ethnic rubric. An Asian American is Buddhist, Catholic, Confucian, Hindu, Muslim, Protestant, or one who eschews religious affiliation altogether. An Asian American may be a brand-new immigrant, just minutes through customs at Seattle-Tacoma International Airport, or the great-great-grandchild of immigrants from distant shores.

Sometimes an ethnic or racial label may emerge or crystallize as a result of identity-making work of doing politics together. . . .

■   ■   ■

Table [1] shows the distribution across the six major national origin groups in response to the following question: "People of Asian descent in the U.S. use different terms to describe themselves. In general do you think of yourself as . . . i) An Asian American, ii) A [Ethnic Group] (e.g., Korean), iii) A [Ethnic Group American] (e.g., Korean American), and iv) An Asian." The options were rotated so that respondents had an equal chance of getting one of these four group labels that relate to social identity. We gave respondents the option

TABLE [1]   Racial-Ethnic Self-Categorization (All Mentions)

	India	*China*	*Philippines*	*Japan*	*Korea*	*Vietnam*	*Total*
Ethnic American	36	40	46	44	64	69	47
Ethnic group	28	38	40	36	70	37	40
Asian American	21	20	15	13	43	20	21
Asian	12	17	15	12	48	16	19
American	6	4	3	5	2	1	4
Other	3	2	5	4	0	2	3

Survey question: "People of Asian descent in the U.S. use different terms to describe themselves. In general, do you think of yourself as . . . ?" [check all that apply; do not read "American" or "Other"]

SOURCES: Authors' compilation of data from the 2008 National Asian American Survey (Wong et al. 2011).

of saying yes or no to more than one of these categories, and we also recorded other answers that the respondent gave, including American and Other responses that were more open-ended. To avoid any confusion between the labels as offered in the survey and the terms we use throughout this book (such as Asian American, Vietnamese, and so on) we mark survey responses to the social identity question in italics. For example, in the case of a Filipino respondent, the four identity labels are *Filipino, Filipino American, Asian,* and *Asian American.*

As we can see in Table [1], nearly half of all survey respondents said they think of themselves as *Ethnic American,* with 47 percent saying yes to this descriptor. A slightly smaller proportion (40 percent) [said] they think of themselves as part of their *Ethnic Group,* while 21 percent identifie[d] as *Asian American,* and 19 percent as *Asian.* Because respondents could select more than one label, the proportions total more than 100 percent for the overall survey sample as well as for the various national-origin groups.

Looking across national-origin groups, we find some important differences. Those of Vietnamese and Korean descent [were] the ones most likely to identify as *Ethnic American* (that is, for example, Vietnamese American) (69 percent and 64 percent, respectively). A similarly large proportion of those with Korean ancestry (70 percent) [said] they identify as *Korean* alone. On identification with *Ethnic Group,* the other notable finding is that Indians stand out as the ones least likely to adopt this descriptor (28 percent). Indians [were] also more likely to identify as *Asian American* than Filipinos and Japanese Americans (21 percent versus 15 percent and 13 percent, respectively), and just as likely to identify with this pan-ethnic label as Chinese and Vietnamese Americans. This finding is important because it runs counter to the bias that many scholars have pointed out in the scholarship and politics surrounding Asian American activism and identity, with Indians and other immigrants from South Asia seen as wholly distinctive from other Asian American groups, and relatively marginal to Asian American identity and politics (Shankar and Srikanth 1998; Kibria 1998; Dave et al. 2000). What we find here is that Indian Americans are not at all distinctive with respect to adopting the *Asian American* label. Indeed, they are just as likely to adopt the pan-ethnic label as Chinese Americans, and are much more likely to do so than Japanese Americans, the group that arguably is most central to the historical development of an Asian American identity.

Finally, another important aspect of self-categorization that emerges from a comparison across national origins is that Koreans are much more likely to identify with multiple categories than members of other national origin groups. On average, Koreans in our survey identified with 2.2 categories. The next closest frequency is among Vietnamese, who on average identif[ied] with 1.4 categories. For the remaining groups, the average number of categories identified with ranges from 1.1 to 1.2. This discrepancy has important consequences because Koreans [had] the highest levels of identification in all four categories, with levels often twice as high as those found for other groups. Depending on the research question, it may make sense to standardize the four categories by the total number of mentions within each group before making comparisons across groups. Such a comparison would reveal, for instance, that the gap between *Ethnic Group* identification and *Asian American* identification is greatest for Filipinos and Japanese Americans, and least for Indian Americans. Regardless of the measure used, however, the data in Table [1] present a fairly clear storyline on self-categorization: a relatively small proportion of Asians in the United States self-identify as *Asian American*, a larger proportion as *Ethnic Group*, and the largest proportion as *Ethnic American*, which combines their national origin and American identities.

Self-identifying with a label, however, provides a limited view of identity and its link to politics. Take the example of the potential political significance of the pan-ethnic label *Asian American*. Perhaps during the height of the Asian American movement of the late 1960s and 1970s, the label carried clear political meaning (Wei 1993). Even [at] its height, this movement originated from elite educational institutions (Takagi 1998) and several decades of dramatic demographic change have occurred since then. Its current use more likely simply reflects popular usage of the label as a social convention. Rather than being a measure of a politicized pan-ethnicity, individuals who identify with the label *Asian American* may instead be acquiescing [to] and assimilating into dominant norms and conventions.

Several findings are worth noting, however, with respect to the relationship between the categories of self-identification and a sense of linked fate. The concept of linked fate has a distinguished pedigree in research on racial politics. The belief that one's personal lot in life is intimately intertwined with the lot of others in one's ethnic group has been shown to be an important feature of African American public opinion. Several studies have shown that it is this sense of linked fate that helps African Americans (and, to a large extent, Latinos) to overcome some of the political divisions that one might anticipate based on education and income within each of the groups. . . .

The National Asian American Survey includes two measures of linked fate. We asked respondents, "Do you think what happens generally to other groups of Asians in this country affects what happens in your life?" This measure is nearly identical to the measure that has been used in prior studies of African Americans. At the same time, given the high level of *Ethnic Group* and *Ethnic American* identification among Asian Americans, we also included a question on linked fate that has the respondent's ethnic group as the reference category.

Interestingly, those who say they think of themselves as Asian American are the most likely to say that their fate in politics is somewhat or very linked to other Asians in the United States. Among the four identity categories we measure, 54 percent of those who classify themselves as *Asian American* feel a sense of linked fate. This proportion is larger than among those who call themselves *Asian* (47 percent), *Ethnic American* (45 percent), or *Ethnic Group* (44 percent). Similarly, when asked the same question about a sense of linked fate but this time with respect to their ethnic group (rather than to the pan-ethnic *Asian American* group), the findings by [self-identified category] follow a similar but slightly less dramatic pattern. Fifty-seven percent of those who call themselves Asian Americans agree that they have some or a very strong linked fate with those in their ethnic group, followed by 54 percent of those who categorize themselves as Asian, 53 percent of those who say they are *Ethnic American*, and 52 percent who select the *Ethnic Group* term. However, in contrast to the findings above about the relatively strong sense of linked fate among those who choose the identity label of Asian American, we find that those who chose the *Ethnic Group* identity are the ones most likely to say they would vote for a co-ethnic candidate (66 percent) for political office. *Ethnic Americans* were next at 64 percent, *Asian Americans* at 62 percent, and *Asians* at 61 percent. These differences are modest, of course.

In addition to asking the higher-order question of how racial self-identification may relate to a sense of linked fate among Asian Americans, we also need to examine the more basic question of how linked fate varies across national origin groups. Table [2] displays the differences by national origin group on the two linked fate measures in the NAAS.

To the first question asking whether respondents think what happens generally to other groups of Asians in the United States affects what happens in

TABLE [2]   Pan-Ethnic and Ethnic Linked Fate

	India	China	Philippines	Japan	Korea	Vietnam	Total
Pan-ethnic linked fate							
Fate very linked	7	9	8	7	13	7	9
Fate somewhat linked	32	32	16	26	40	27	28
Fate not very linked	4	7	13	7	4	6	7
Fate not linked	49	43	60	50	35	47	48
Don't know	8	10	3	10	7	13	8
Ethnic linked fate							
Fate very linked	10	11	10	12	19	17	12
Fate somewhat linked	33	31	19	27	43	30	30
Fate not very linked	7	8	16	9	4	3	8
Fate not linked	42	40	50	43	28	42	42
Don't know	8	10	5	9	7	10	8

Survey questions: "Do you think what happens generally to other groups of Asians in this country affects what happens in your life?" "Do you think what happens generally to other [respondent's ethnic group] Americans affects what happens in your life?"

NOTE: Rates are in percentages.

SOURCE: Authors' compilation of data from the 2008 National Asian American Survey (Wong et al., 2011).

their lives, 44 percent agree to a sense of linked fate, but fewer than 10 percent feel that their fate is very linked to other Asians in this country. The variation among national origin groups is most substantial among Korean Americans: 57 percent agree with the concept of linked fate with other Asians in the United States; 13 percent of Koreans feel their fate is very closely linked. Filipinos and Vietnamese, by contrast, are the least likely to exhibit a linked fate orientation.

When the referent for the linked fate question is given as people who share the same ethnic or national-origin group, the overall sense of linked fate is somewhat stronger: half of the NAAS respondents agree that what happens to others in their national-origin group affects what happens in their life, and one in eight believe[s] that this link is strong. Again, Korean Americans are the strongest supporters of a sense of ethnic-group linked fate, nearly two-thirds agreeing and almost one in five agreeing strongly. On ethnic-group linked fate, Filipinos and Vietnamese no longer look so different from Asian Indians, Chinese, and Japanese Americans.

One final observation on Table [2] is the degree of similarity in the distribution of responses to our two linked fate measures. Despite differences in emphasis, the rank-order of responses is identical: the modal response is that fates (ethnic or pan-ethnic) are unlinked, followed in frequency by the view that fates are somewhat linked. Far less common are the views that fates are very linked or not very linked, or that the respondent simply does not know how to answer the question.

■　　■　　■

ETHNIC AND RACIAL IDENTITY AND POLITICAL ACTIVISM

. . . [We now] begin to consider the relationship between ethnic and racial identity and political participation. . . . this analysis lays out the basic relationship between measures of racial identification in terms of identity labels and forms of political participation. Although the NAAS measures numerous acts of participation, . . . we focus on several dimensions of political activity, including an overall voting index, a standard measure of protest activity, and three measures of political participation beyond voting.

The results of this initial analysis are suggestive (Table [3]). For the two measures of identity that connote some degree of integration or incorporation—*Asian American* and *Ethnic American* identity—the association between identity and four of our five key measures of participation appears to be positive. At the bivariate level, those who self-identify as *Asian American* or *Ethnic American* appear to vote, contribute money, contact government officials, and work with others in their community at higher levels than those who self-identify with their *Ethnic Group* or as *Asian*. Those who self-identify as *Asian*

TABLE [3] Ethnic and Self-Identified Categories by Political Participation

	Likely Voter	Political Contributor	Contact Government Officials	Protester	Community Activist
Asian American	49	15	10	4	24
Ethnic American	48	15	11	5	21
Ethnic group	42	9	6	4	17
Asian	44	9	7	4	16

NOTE: Rates are in percentages.
SOURCE: Authors' compilation of data from the 2008 National Asian American Survey (Wong et al., 2011).

TABLE [4] Rates of Political Participation by Ethnic Identification

	Likely Voter	Political Contributor	Contact Government Officials	Protester	Community Activist
Pan-ethnic linked fate					
Yes	46	15	11	6	24
No	45	11	8	4	20
Ethnic linked fate					
Yes	46	15	11	6	23
No	45	11	8	3	20
Commonality with Asians					
Yes	45	14	10	5	23
No	47	8	5	3	15
Political commonality with others					
Yes	46	14	10	5	23
No	39	6	3	2	12
Discriminated against					
Yes	44	17	13	6	27
No	46	10	7	4	18
Victim of hate crime					
Yes	42	16	17	8	29
No	46	12	9	4	21
All	43	13	9	4	21

NOTE: Rates are in percentages, representing the proportion of those with a specific score on the identity measure (linked fate, commonality with other Asians, and so forth) who also took part in the political activity.
SOURCE: Authors' compilation of data from the 2008 National Asian American Survey (Wong et al., 2011).

American or *Ethnic American* engage in these activities at more or less comparable rates vis-à-vis each other; similarly, those who identify as *Asian* or with their *Ethnic Group* appear to engage in these four activities at comparable rates. The relationship between racial or ethnic identification and protest activity appears to be minimal.

Although only a modest relationship (if any) is apparent between identity choices and the five forms of political engagement we analyze here, differences in participation by some other indicators of racial and ethnic identity are important. Table [4] summarizes the differences in level of participation in voting, contributing, contacting, protesting, and working with others in the community to solve problems by the two measures of linked fate, commonality with Asians and other racial groups, and experiences with discrimination and hate crimes.

In terms of voting, evidence of differences between respondents with varying levels of racial and political identity beyond the identity labels is scant. Only a sense of political commonality with other racial and ethnic groups has a positive relationship. In contrast, both of the commonality items—with Asians in this country and with other racial groups—are important with respect to contributions, with those holding a sense of commonality much more active in this form of engagement. Likewise, experiences with discrimination and hate crimes are also positively associated with making political contributions. Contacting officials shows a similar pattern to contributing, with strong relationships for the commonality and bias measures. This is also the case for activity with others in the community to solve problems. The same patterns are apparent, but to a lesser degree, for protest activity.

REFERENCES

Dave, Shilpa, Pawan Dhingra, Sunaina Maira, Partha Mazumdar, Lavina Dhingra Shankar, Jaideep Singh, and Rajini Srikanth. 2000. "De-Privileging Positions: Indian Americans, South Asian Americans, and the Politics of Asian American Studies." *Journal of Asian American Studies* 3 (1): 67–100.

Kibria, Nazli. 1998. "The Racial Gap: South Asian American Racial Identity and the Asian American Movement." In *A Part, Yet Apart: South Asians in Asian America, Asian American History and Culture*, edited by Lavina Dhingra Shankar and Rajini Srikanth. Philadelphia: Temple University Press.

Lowe, Lisa. 1996. *Immigrant Acts: On Asian American Cultural Politics*. Durham, NC: Duke University Press.

Shankar, Lavina Dhingra, and Rajini Srikanth, eds. 1998. *A Part, Yet Apart: South Asians in Asian America*. Philadelphia: Temple University Press.

Takagi, Dana Y. 1998. *The Retreat from Race: Asian-American Admissions and Racial Politics*. New Brunswick, NJ: Rutgers University Press.

Wei, William. 1993. *The Asian American Movement*. Philadelphia: Temple University Press.

10.2

JAN E. LEIGHLEY AND JONATHAN NAGLER

From *Who Votes Now? Demographics, Issues, Inequality, and Turnout in the United States*

A common conclusion from previous studies of non-voting was that voters and non-voters were not much different in terms of their attitudes about major political issues. Some concluded that it does not much matter who votes because popular pressure on the government would not change even if many more people voted. Leighley and Nagler offer an important corrective. They focus on issues of economic redistribution and find that voters and non-voters are actually quite different in their preferences over government-led redistribution. Voters are generally more conservative on economic redistribution issues than are non-voters, according to results from analysis of high-quality survey data.

Most discussions of the consequences of turnout focus on whether changes in the partisanship of the voters lead to changes in who wins the election. We believe it is also important to consider the governance consequences of turnout. Who wins an election is obviously important in a representative democracy. But once elected, officials have some flexibility to define their policy agendas and their policy priorities in ways that go beyond partisanship. . . . This argument shifts the focus from how representative voters are of nonvoters with respect to demographic characteristics to how representative voters are of nonvoters with respect to policy preferences.[1]

■ ■ ■

Given that nonvoters are disproportionately poor relative to voters, and have been since 1972, we expect to find sustained differences in the policy preferences of voters and nonvoters in presidential elections since 1972 on redistributive issues.

■ ■ ■

[E]lected officials are aware of the preferences of their supporters. [T]he poor and the wealthy might well support the same candidate and elect her; but when in office, she will pursue the policies preferred by voters (who are disproportionately wealthy) rather than those preferred by nonvoters (who

From Jan E. Leighley and Jonathan Nagler, *Who Votes Now? Demographics, Issues, Inequality, and Turnout in the United States* (Princeton, NJ: Princeton University Press, 2014).

are disproportionately poor). That means that for poor nonvoters to achieve substantive representation, it is not sufficient for rich voters to prefer the same *candidate* as poor nonvoters; they must also share the same *issue positions*. This possibility demands that we clearly understand whether voters hold the same policy positions as nonvoters if we are to understand the representational consequences of turnout.

We underscore the importance of this argument by noting that significant differences between voters and nonvoters have important electoral consequences even if voters and nonvoters have identical distributions of preferences across *candidates*. Imagine a world with two dimensions, and that voters who prefer the Republican candidate to the Democratic candidate do so based on economic issues, and voters who prefer the Democratic candidate to the Republican candidate do so based on social issues; but nonvoters who prefer the Republican candidate to the Democratic candidate do so based on social issues, and nonvoters who prefer the Democratic candidate to the Republican candidate do so based on economic issues. Assuming that equal proportions of voters and nonvoters prefer Republican candidates to Democratic candidates, it would make no difference to the *electoral outcome* whether the nonvoters stay home or whether they choose to become voters. But if we assume that elected officials know the preferences of those who vote for them and respond to those preferences, then it would make a tremendous difference to *governing outcomes* if the nonvoters choose to vote.

■   ■   ■

We consider citizens' preferences and attitudes as reflected in their political views, their preferences on redistributive issues, and their preferences on values-based issues. Figure [1] documents the policy differences between voters and nonvoters in presidential election years between 1972 and 2008, focusing on three redistributive policy questions: support for government spending on health; support for providing services; and support for government guaranteeing jobs.

We describe these questions as redistributive because they indicate the degree to which respondents support governmental services or policies that redistribute resources to the poor. For each question, respondents are asked to place themselves on a 7-point scale, with the high point indicating the most conservative policy position (opposing redistribution) and the low point indicating the most liberal policy position (supporting redistribution). In Figure [1] we plot the difference between the mean score of voters and the mean score of nonvoters on each issue. Positive values thus indicate that voters are more conservative than nonvoters, while negative values indicate that voters are more liberal than nonvoters.

As shown in Figure [1], we find consistent differences between voters and nonvoters on each of these issues. In each year since 1972, voters are more conservative than are nonvoters in their beliefs regarding how much the government should do to provide jobs, health insurance, and services. More

FIGURE [1] Differences between Voters' and Nonvoters' Attitudes on Redistributive Policies, 1972–2008

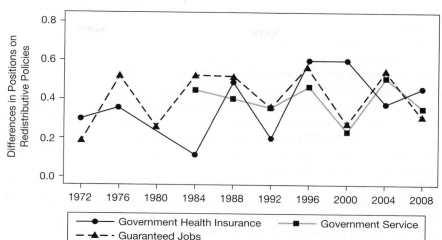

NOTE: Plotted values are the weighted mean difference between voters' and nonvoters' attitudes on each issue in the specified year. Values greater than 0 indicate that voters (as a group) are more conservative than nonvoters (as a group) on the specific policy question; values less than 0 indicate that voters are more liberal than nonvoters. All mean differences are significant at p < .05, except 1972 for guaranteed jobs, 1984 for government health insurance, and 2000 for government service. Computed by the authors using data from the American National Election Studies Time Series Cumulative File, 1972–2008.

specifically, except for the difference between voters and nonvoters on government health insurance and job guarantees in 1972 and on government health insurance in 1984, the difference between voters and nonvoters is statistically significant in each election. Substantively, the mean differences on all three issues are typically greater than .4 on a 7-point scale. This suggests that voters are about one-half a scale position more conservative than are nonvoters. As we expected, then, there are notable, consistent and substantial differences between voters and nonvoters on redistributive issues—and the conventional wisdom should be updated accordingly.

Next we consider the representativeness of voters on two different sets of issues that we refer to as values-based issues and political attitudes. We present these results in separate graphs. We expect the responses to the first set of questions, including party identification, party ideology, and candidate preference, to be most sensitive to the particular electoral context (i.e., the nature of the issues, campaign strategy, etc.). We therefore expect these attitudes—and candidate preference, in particular—to be most likely to change election by election.

In contrast, the second set of issues [is] largely motivated by some sense of "values": the role of women/women's equality, aid to blacks, and defense spending. While we are not arguing that this is a coherent set of opinions that share[s] common demographic or attitudinal sources, we do believe that each of these likely reflects more personal, fundamental symbolic beliefs than the other issues we consider. As such, we expect them to likely exhibit little sensitivity to election-specific contexts.

We turn to the representativeness of voters and nonvoters on political attitudes first. The party identification and political ideology measures are based on the standard NES 7-point party identification and political ideology questions. The vote preference measure is based on respondents' thermometer rankings of the two major presidential candidates in each election year. We first compute the difference between voters' evaluations of the Republican and Democratic candidates and then compute the same value for nonvoters. We then take the difference between these two scores and then, for graphing purposes, rescale it to be comparable to values on a 7-point scale.

Figure [2] presents the mean differences between voters and nonvoters on party identification, political ideology, and candidate vote preference for 1972 through 2008.[2] The values that are plotted for each attitude or preference (i.e., the vertical axis values) are the mean differences between voters and nonvoters for each attitude or preference. Based on our general knowledge of

FIGURE [2] Differences between Voters and Nonvoters on Ideology, Partisanship, and Vote Preference

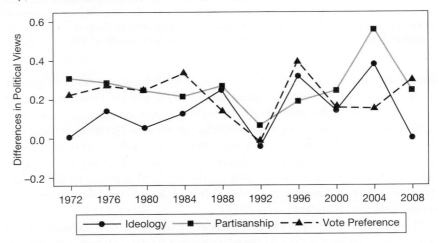

NOTE: Plotted values are the weighted mean difference between voters and nonvoters on each opinion item in the specified year. Values greater than 0 indicate that voters (as a group) are more conservative than nonvoters (as a group) on the specific attitude; values less than 0 indicate that voters are more liberal than nonvoters. Mean differences on partisanship (except 1992 and 1996) and vote preference (except 1988, 1992, 2000, and 2004) are significant at p < .05. Mean differences on ideology are significant at p < .05 only in 1988, 1996, and 2004. Computed by the authors using data from the American National Election Studies Time Series Cumulative File, 1972–2008.

the interrelationships among partisanship, ideology, and vote choice, we expected these three measures to move largely in sync with each other, and that is mostly what we see. And because vote preference is necessarily tied to candidate characteristics, we see this difference between voters and nonvoters varying the most from election to election, as we would expect.

We note that in many of these elections we observe statistically significant differences between voters and nonvoters on partisanship and vote preference. These differences are statistically significant in six of ten elections for vote preference and eight of ten elections for partisanship. Statistically significant differences between voters and nonvoters on ideology are less common, observed in only two elections, 1988 and 1996, though in seven of the ten elections voters in our sample are ideologically more conservative than nonvoters.[3] Thus we find that voters are more conservative than nonvoters on partisanship, candidate preference, and ideology, although the evidence is more robust for partisanship and candidate preference.

Figure [3] presents the mean differences between voters and nonvoters on values-based issues for 1972 through 2008. Our expectations of null findings

FIGURE [3]   Differences between Voters' and Nonvoters' Attitudes on Values-Based Issues

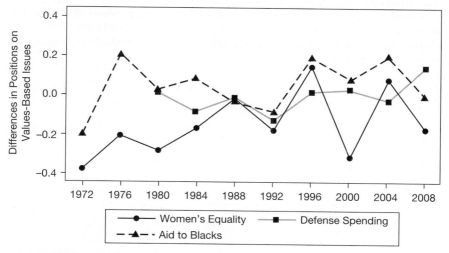

NOTE: Plotted values are the weighted mean difference between voters' and nonvoters' attitudes on each issue in the specified year. Values greater than 0 indicate that voters (as a group) are more conservative than nonvoters (as a group) on the specific policy question; values less than 0 indicate that voters are more liberal than nonvoters. Mean differences on women's equality are significant at $p < .05$ in 1972, 1980, 1992, and 2000. Mean differences on aid to blacks are significant at $p < .05$ in 1976. Computed by the authors using data from the American National Election Studies Time Series Cumulative File, 1972–2008.

here are generally supported. The magnitude of the difference between voters and nonvoters on aid to blacks and defense spending is generally less than 0.1. Larger differences between voters and nonvoters on women's equality are observed, and are statistically significant in four years (1972, 1980, 1992, and 2000), but even these differences disappear in the two most recent elections. Generally, then, we find little or no systematic differences between voters and nonvoters on these values-based issues.

■   ■   ■

We take issue with the claim that voters are indeed representative of non-voters. [I]n every election year from 1972 through 2008, voters and nonvoters differ substantively on most issues relating to the role of government in redistributive policies. In addition to these differences being evident in every election since 1972, we also note that the nature of the electoral bias is clear as well: voters are substantially more conservative than nonvoters on redistributive issues.

NOTES

1. See Erikson and Tedin (2011, fig. 7:1) for a simple demonstration of the differences between the preferences of voters and nonvoters on economic issues.

2. Mean differences are computed using the NES supplied weights.

3. Ideology could be interpreted differently by different respondents, and differently across elections. Some respondents might be emphasizing a social dimension in their evaluation of ideology; others might be emphasizing an economic dimension in their evaluation of ideology.

10.3

EITAN D. HERSH

From *Hacking the Electorate: How Campaigns Perceive Voters*

Technological advances have enabled campaign organizations and political parties to target specific individuals in "get out the vote" appeals. In eight states (all in the south), people indicate their race—white, black, Hispanic—when registering to vote. Hersh compares turnout rates between African Americans in these eight states to those in other similar states. He also compares turnout rates in the eight states among those who choose to identify their race and those who do not. Hersh finds compelling evidence that if campaigns can know a person's race, that person is more likely to be contacted by a campaign and more likely to turn out to vote. This shows how campaigns can increasingly focus on individual attributes in targeting their appeals specifically and directly, in contrast to previous attempts to campaign using broad themes in entire neighborhoods and sectors.

When public records of race are available to campaigns, campaigns focus more on mobilizing voters because of their racial identity and less on mobilizing voters because they live in racially segregated areas. . . . [C]ampaigns focus more attention on voters' races when public race data are available. [T]he patterns of voter turnout are consistent with the proposition that campaigns behave differently depending on the public data environment.

Public Records of Racial Identity

Voter registration databases in eight states, all in the south, contain records of racial identity. In these states, which include Alabama, Florida, Georgia, Louisiana, Mississippi, North Carolina, South Carolina, and Tennessee, the public record lists voters as Caucasian, Black, Hispanic, or by some other racial identifier. When citizens register to vote in these states, they are asked or required to indicate their race, and this designation becomes a public record. Because in the United States racial identity is highly correlated with partisan support, when a voter's race is listed in the public record, campaigns latch onto this data point as a key resource for engaging with voters. Because racial identity is difficult to predict in the absence of public race data, campaigns have a more

From Eitan D. Hersh, *Hacking the Electorate: How Campaigns Perceive Voters* (New York, NY: Cambridge University Press, 2015).

TABLE [1] Percentage of Registrants Identifying Their Race on Voter Registration Forms

State	Race Listed on Voter File	Total Obs. in Sample
Alabama	99.0%	56,176
Florida	96.7	192,856
Georgia	96.1	100,936
Louisiana	98.1	51,789
Mississippi	38.1	37,148
North Carolina	98.0	113,497
South Carolina	99.7	51,033
Tennessee	67.5	71,330

SOURCE: Two independently drawn Catalist 1% Analytics Samples, combined.

difficult time identifying and mobilizing voters by race in places that do not list voters by race in the public record.

In Table [1], the percentages of voters listed with a racial identifier in the public voter file in each state are shown. In six of these states (Alabama, Florida, Georgia, Louisiana, North Carolina, and South Carolina), more than 95 percent of registered voters are listed in the public record with a field indicating their racial identity. In Tennessee and Mississippi, indicating one's race on a registration application is optional, and as the table shows, fewer registrants in these states are listed with a racial identifier.

Why in these southern states, but not elsewhere in the country, are voters listed in the public record according to their race? The answer is in state-specific, historical idiosyncrasies.

▪ ▪ ▪

Clearly, politics in the south is more focused on race than politics outside the south, and the south has long tracked the race of residents for an array of administrative uses. However, state-specific explanations are at the root of the question of why the voters in these eight states are listed in the public record with their race while voters in other similar states are not.[1] No matter the origins of these laws, the fact is that some campaigns operate in environments where they have comprehensive lists of voters by racial identity while other campaigns operate in environments where such data are not available. This distinction, I argue, yields differences in strategies for engaging voters.

Perceiving Race without Public Identifiers

Quite clearly, campaigns would like to know the racial identities of voters. Race is highly predictive of partisan support, especially in the south. The American electorate is sensitive to overt race-focused appeals (Mendelberg, 2001; Valentino, Hutchings, and White, 2002), and so racial identifiers can enable campaigns to use direct contacting strategies to communicate with minority voters separately from white voters. This is particularly important for Democrats, who tend, in recent years anyway, to build coalitions across racial groups. Democratic campaigns want to mobilize African Americans with different kinds of messages than they use to appeal to whites. As a southern Democratic strategist explained to political scientist James Glaser, "you've got to approach the black vote surgically" (Glaser, 1996, p. 75). Some "surgical" approaches leverage segregated media environments, for example, by transmitting appeals to black voters through radio advertisements on stations that have pre-dominantly black audiences. But other surgical approaches involve using canvassers, phone bankers, and mailers to engage different racial groups in different ways.

In the states where 95 percent or more of registered voters are recorded in the public record with their racial identity, it is straightforward for campaigns to consider the race of voters in their direct contacting strategies and to use a surgical approach to target minorities differently than whites. But how do campaigns perceive the race of voters in the absence of individual-level racial data in voter files? One possibility is that campaigns might engage voters based on other characteristics that are correlated with partisan support, turnout likelihood, or persuadability. However, because identity as an African American or Latino is so highly predictive of partisan support, Democratic campaigns in particular do want to focus their direct contacting on minority groups.[2] Absent public records, they must use alternative tools for perceiving race. These tools, I argue, generate different strategies and result in different types of voters being mobilized than if public records of race were available.

Consider three alternatives that campaigns use to perceive voters' races when voters are not listed in public records by race. One alternative method is to use geography as a proxy. In the case of African Americans, a geographical strategy only reaches a portion of black voters, because half of all African Americans live in neighborhoods that are not majority black (Owens and Wright, 1998; Logan, 2001). As Kirk Clay, Director of Civic Engagement for the NAACP, explained to me in an interview, in a segregated black neighborhood a campaign can employ blanket mobilization strategies. In these neighborhoods, campaigns may send "sound trucks" around to broadcast reminders to vote via megaphones. But outside 90-percent-plus areas, campaigns do not use blanket mobilization strategies. Such strategies, geared toward black voters, are presumed not to be effective for white voters, and they may even be counterproductive from a campaign's perspective. Consequently, these strategies are not used except in areas that are overwhelmingly black.

A second alternative is to use networks, like churches, to mobilize minority voters. Churches have long been considered a centerpiece of black political mobilization (Harris, 1994; Leighley, 2001). However, as with a geographic strategy, a church-based strategy does not reach nearly as many African Americans as individual-level public records would permit. The political role of churches is somewhat overstated because many African Americans do not attend church, and among those who do, most do not attend the kind of politicized churches that tend to mobilize voters. One estimate suggests that, at most, only a quarter of blacks attend the kinds of politicized churches that increase turnout among attendees.[3]

A third alternative is to employ firms like Catalist to make statistical predictions about voters' races. Using the voter's name and the racial composition of the voter's neighborhood (which Catalist retrieves from the Census), Catalist estimates each voter's race.

■ ■ ■

The obvious takeaway from this discussion is that it is not as easy for campaigns to perceive voters by their racial identity without individual-level public records that are available in only eight states. But there is a more subtle and more important takeaway as well: *The kinds of minority voters who will be mobilized by Democratic campaigns will differ depending on the tools campaigns use to perceive their race.* In the absence of public identifiers, if a campaign focuses its efforts on geographic areas that are homogeneously black, then the kind of black person who is contacted by campaigns will be the kind of black person who lives in homogeneous black areas. Black voters who live in heterogeneous neighborhoods will be less likely to be contacted. Similarly, if a campaign uses a microtargeting model like Catalist's, it will tend to miss voters whose names and neighborhoods are not predictive of their racial group (e.g., middle-class blacks; Fryer Jr. and Levitt, 2007). If a campaign can use public records, it will be able to mobilize more blacks who live in heterogeneous neighborhoods and have names less distinctive from white names.

■ ■ ■

The data environment will affect a campaign's perceptions, the perceptions will affect their strategies, and the strategies will affect which voters are mobilized into the political process.

How do Racial Perceptions Affect Strategies?

In the eight states in which they can obtain racially identifying data from the election office, campaigns use these data to engage with voters based on the voters' races. Consider some anecdotal evidence from strategists. One Democratic operative who is involved in multiple southern campaigns explained that every time his campaigns pull lists of voters to contact in states that register voters by race, they screen the lists for race. Sometimes, they gear messages and events to African Americans; other times, they gear them to whites. But race is always part of the decision. Another southern Democratic strategist told me that in his state, "[GOTV] is really easy. You just go after black voters." In a third interview with a Florida-based field organizer from the Obama campaign, the operative told me that the campaign's goal was for voters who were listed on the registration rolls as African American to receive three in-person contacts from the Obama campaign. Three in-person visits to a voter is an aggressive use of resources, but because African Americans were leaning so strongly toward Obama *and because* nearly all registered voters in Florida are listed by race, the campaign deemed this strategy worthwhile.

On the Republican side, the efficient strategy in most southern elections is to ignore voters listed as African American, just as campaigns might ignore members of the opposite party in favor of focusing on independents and members of their own party. Efficiency simply means campaigns spend less time interacting with citizens whose votes they have little chance of winning. Given that black voters are upward of 90 percent likely to vote for Democrats, Republican campaigns can best employ their resources by focusing on white voters—deleting voters listed as black from their contact lists. While no Republican campaigner described this practice to me directly (no doubt owing to the sensitivity of the question), this use of race data is an entirely obvious and straightforward strategy for Republican campaigns. Data are not only useful to decide which voters to engage with; they are just as useful to decide which voters to ignore. Both parties use data in this way. A Democratic campaign manager told me that he uses public records about hunters and gun owners simply to exclude these voters from his contacting efforts, because gun owners lean Republican. Republican campaigns can be expected to use this same strategy with respect to racial identifiers.

Given that race data are a valuable resource for mobilization, what statistical evidence is there that the provision of public racial identifiers affects the way campaigns engage voters? In the Ground Campaign Project, I asked Obama campaign workers in 2012 to rank voter attributes in terms of their importance to the campaign's contacting strategies. Among the nine attributes offered was race. The other attributes included party, gender, age, income, and other such options. The survey question did not cue campaign workers to think about racial registration data in particular, but simply asked them to think about the voter characteristics that are used in contacting voters, whatever the source of those characteristics.

The results are shown in Figure [1]. The two 2012 swing states with racial registration data are North Carolina and Florida. In the swing states of North Carolina and Florida, campaign workers reported that race was a much more important voter characteristic than did campaign workers in other states. The average ranking for North Carolina and Florida is a point and a half higher than in the other states.

[T]he low level staffers and volunteers engaging with voters on behalf of the Obama campaign do not need to know the details of the campaign strategy to discern that their daily efforts are focused more on one or another kind of voter. Evidently, workers in Florida and North Carolina recognized that they were engaging with voters more based on their race than did workers in other states. This suggests that the strategy was indeed different in these two states than elsewhere. Figure [1] implies that the public data environment causes

FIGURE [1]   Importance of Voters' Race to Campaign Mobilizers in Different Data Environments

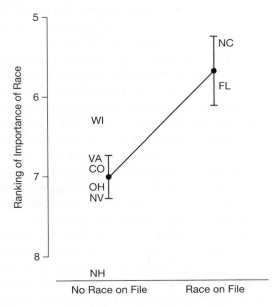

NOTE: Data from Ground Campaign Project. Data generated from 187 campaign workers in states with racial registration and 344 respondents in states without racial registration. The difference of means between campaigners in racial registration and non-racial registration states is statistically significant (p-value < 0.01). Virginia's position is emphasized to show its contrasting position to other southern states.

campaigns to pay more attention to race-based canvassing than [a] campaign would in the absence of public race records.

   To develop this argument, consider the state of Virginia in Figure [1]. Campaign workers in Virginia reported that race was as strategically important as did campaign workers in other nonracial registration states. But Virginia is a southern state . . . with a history of racialized politics, much like its neighbor North Carolina. Virginia was also a battleground state in 2012; the Obama campaign exerted a similar effort in Virginia and North Carolina, in terms of expenditures. Virginia and North Carolina are also similar in the percentage of their populations that are African American; both are approximately 20 percent black. But Virginia is very different from North Carolina in the importance of race to direct contacting strategies. Figure [1] shows that only campaigners in states with race data, and not similar states like Virginia, considered race to be a particularly important informational resource for direct contact. Likewise, Ohio, a northern swing state with large pockets of African-American voters, does not show an unusually strong focus on race in campaign efforts. The unusual position is reserved for the two states in the data in which voters are listed in the public record with their racial identities.

FIGURE [2]   Turnout in 2012 by Block Group Percentage Black in Virginia and North Carolina

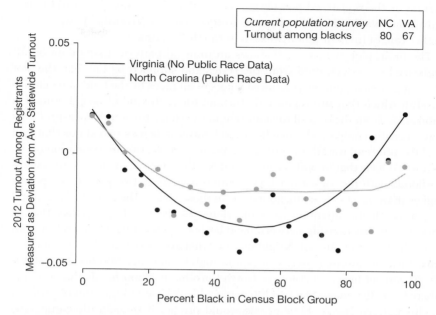

NOTE: Data are from the Catalist Q Tool. Each dot represents a 5-percentage-point range of block-group percentage black, from 0–5% black to 95–100% black. The full population of registered voters is observed including 5,233,943 registrants in Virginia and 6,433,168 registrants in North Carolina. The dot representing the fewest number of registrants represents 19,948 registrants.

CPS DATA SOURCE: United States Census Bureau, Current Population Survey, "Table 4b: Reported Voting and Registration, by Sex, Race and Hispanic Origin, for States: November 2012." Turnout for CPS is calculated based on citizens. If calculated based on reported registrants, turnout is 94.1% in North Carolina and 92.6% in Virginia.

Downstream Effects on Voters

Because of the similarities between North Carolina and Virginia in terms of region, battleground state status, and percentage black, I focus more on the comparison between these two states. If the Obama campaign in 2012 was active in both these states but had to engage voters differently in each state on account of the data environment, what evidence is there that different perceptions of blacks in these two states resulted in differential effects on the electorate?

Consider Figure [2]. In the upper-right of this figure, I note that according to the Census's Current Population Survey, turnout among blacks in North Carolina was higher than turnout among blacks in Virginia. Of course, citizens often lie about whether or not they voted, but I want only to draw attention to the *relative* turnout between these two states: turnout for blacks appears to have been higher in North Carolina than in Virginia. As indicated in the figure's note, this is true whether turnout is calculated based on the citizen population or the registered population. Given that the campaigns could target individual black voters in North Carolina but not Virginia, I expect this higher rate of turnout among blacks in North Carolina.

The main plot in Figure [2] shows an unusual pattern. Using data on all registered voters acquired from the states and supplied by Catalist, the plot estimates turnout among registered voters of all races by the kind of neighborhood in which they are registered. Turnout for each kind of neighborhood is subtracted from the overall turnout rate in the state. Turnout is measured this way to easily compare the neighborhood patterns across two states that had slightly different overall turnout rates. As an example, the interpretation of the leftmost dots is that in both Virginia and North Carolina, turnout in the neighborhoods with the lowest black population was about two percentage points higher than the statewide turnout rates in those states. The aspect of the graph to pay particular attention to is the slopes of the two lines. Notice that in Virginia, the relationship between neighborhood percentage black and turnout is much more pronounced. Neighborhoods that are more than 80 percent black have turnout approximately five points higher than neighborhoods that are 40–80 percent black. In contrast, North Carolina neighborhoods that are anywhere from 30 percent black to 100 percent black have similar rates of turnout.

This pattern is exactly what one would predict if Democratic campaigns target black individuals more in North Carolina (where racial data exists) but target black neighborhoods more in Virginia (where racial data does not exist). In the environment that lacks public records of race, turnout among blacks is not only lower; it is also *geographically contingent*. This suggests that the kind of black registrant who votes in Virginia is different from the kind who votes in North Carolina on account of campaigns' differential ability to perceive voters in each state. Black *perceived voters* in North Carolina are similar to the actual black electorate (since nearly all black voters are listed with their race in the public record), but black *perceived voters* in Virginia are a distorted version of the black electorate: they are blacks who live in black neighborhoods or who have racially distinct names and therefore can be identified as black in the absence of public records.

■ ■ ■

In eight states of the U.S. south, campaigns can perceive voters' races in public records. Absent these records, campaigns must find other resources to perceive race, such as a voter's neighborhood or a predictive model that estimates race using characteristics like a voter's name and Census block. I have argued that these different data tools generate different perceptions of racial cohorts and result in different strategies.

As evidence of differential strategies resultant from the data environment, I have shown that 2012 campaign workers in states that collect racial data considered race to be a more important characteristic in their voter engagement strategies than did campaign workers elsewhere in the country. Racial groups are targeted differently in the southern swing states of Florida and North Carolina than in states that are otherwise similar, like Virginia. When campaigns can perceive voters' races in public records, the evidence from the Ground Campaign Project suggests that they pay more attention to race in voter contact strategies as a result.

I have shown two downstream consequences of the racial data environment on voter turnout. Comparing North Carolina and Virginia, two states that have much in common except for that North Carolina collects racial data and Virginia does not, I have shown that 2012 turnout among blacks in North Carolina was higher and that turnout in Virginia was more geographically contingent. This evidence is consistent with the theory that campaigns direct more attention to black voters in the state where they have public data, and otherwise they use tools like geography to perceive blacks, which results in a different cohort of voters being engaged.

NOTES

1. It should be noted that I have asked dozens of legal experts, historians, and political scientists about the origins of these laws. While I can exclude the VRA and white primaries as the reasons, it is indeed a mystery to me why these states but not others collect race data.

2. See Fraga (2012) on race-based electoral coalitions.

3. This claim, it should be noted, comes from data from the 1990s, but to my knowledge, no newer, analogous data is available. About 60–75% of blacks claim in surveys that they attend church regularly (Verba, Schlozman, and Brady, 1995; Tate, 1996), and that number is surely inflated due to misreporting. More importantly, only 35% of black churchgoers report that they have heard any announcements or discussions in church about an upcoming presidential race (Calhoun-Brown, 1996). Calhoun-Brown finds that all effects of church mobilization on participation are concentrated among this 35% of churchgoers who attend a politicized church. As a back-of-the-envelope calculation, assuming (charitably) that 75% of blacks attend church regularly, but of these only 35% attend a politicized church, church-based mobilization strategies may be reaching at most 26% of blacks.

DISCUSSION QUESTIONS

1. Do more Asian Americans identify as Asian, or as a member of a specific ethnic group (e.g., Korean)? According to Wong, Ramakrishnan, Lee, and Junn, what are the political consequences of people having such identities?

2. A common conclusion from studies of nonvoters is that it would not matter to election or policy outcomes if more people voted because voters and

nonvoters have similar preferences. What evidence do Leighley and Nagler use to argue against this common conclusion?

3. Describe Hersh's reasoning for why campaign organizations and parties find it helpful to know the racial classification of individual voters. What are the implications for American democracy that campaigns and parties increasingly use mobilization efforts to target individuals based on race?

4. Discuss the following as determinants of political participation using the findings of these readings as evidence of the relative weight among them: identity, social capital, and mobilization.

11

INTEREST GROUPS

11.1

KEN KOLLMAN

From *Outside Lobbying: Public Opinion and Interest Group Strategies*

Kollman contrasts two types of lobbying: inside and outside. The inside game is more private and is played among people in Washington. The outside game is played by interest group leaders who bring people from outside Washington into the business of persuading members of Congress. Outside lobbying both signals existing public opinion to lawmakers and tries to shape that public opinion to an interest group's advantage.

INTRODUCTION

Outside lobbying is defined as attempts by interest group leaders to mobilize citizens outside the policymaking community to contact or pressure public officials inside the policymaking community. It represents a viable and effective strategy for many interest groups trying to influence representative government between elections. What better way is there to win favorable legislation in Congress, for example, than to mobilize a significant number of constituents to contact key legislators? Old-fashioned inside lobbying, the personal access and contact with legislators so necessary for maintaining good relations with government, may have only limited effectiveness today. Just as elected officials in Washington feel the need to monitor and assuage public opinion through polls and public relations, modern lobbying increasingly

From Ken Kollman, *Outside Lobbying: Public Opinion and Interest Group Strategies* (Princeton, NJ: Princeton University Press, 1998).

requires sophisticated methods of public mobilization. Lobbying in Washington is not just a game among well-paid lawyers, ideological activists, and legislators in the Capitol. The outside public is increasingly involved.

Mass expressions of public concern directed toward the federal government are rarely spontaneous. Behind most telephone calls, letters, faxes, and e-mails to members of Congress, behind marches down the Mall in Washington, D.C., and behind bus caravans to the Capitol, there are coordinating leaders, usually interest group leaders, mobilizing a select group of citizens to unite behind a common message. At the most basic level, an interest group leader seeks to persuade policymakers that what the members of the group want (as specified by the leader) is good public policy and/or good politics. And the leader uses outside lobbying to demonstrate first, that the members of the group are in fact united behind the leader, and second, that many other constituents agree with what the group leader wants. Faced with organized groups of constituents making noise about this or that policy issue, not many members of Congress could afford to ignore these efforts completely. Any leader who can organize thousands of citizens to write letters to their congressional representative, for example, can with some probability organize a good number of voters on election day to support or oppose the incumbent. For all the apparent benefits of outside lobbying to an interest group—sending a strong message to policymakers or reinforcing to voters that the group represents a credible source of political information—it is surprising nonetheless that outside lobbying is not undertaken more often by groups with an interest in controversial policy issues.

Outside lobbying, however, is in fact applied selectively, and lobbyists and interest group leaders spend precious hours and resources crafting careful public campaigns of persuasion. On some policy issues, groups on all sides use outside lobbying intensively. On other policy issues, only groups on one side of the issue use outside lobbying. There are many issues, even those considered extremely important to specific interest groups, where no groups use outside lobbying. And of course, groups try to time their public appeals for maximum effect. As every lobbyist (or salesperson, parent, or leader) knows, persuasion is a subtle business, and careless lobbying strategies can backfire. It is not always the case that outside lobbying, even when it generates a substantial public response, wins over the policymakers targeted.

The selective application and timing of outside lobbying strategies raises important questions. Obviously, outside lobbying is not always influential, even when interest group leaders on only one side of an issue use it. Who or what captures the attention of Washington policymakers? When are demonstrations of popular support effective in influencing policymakers? How do outside lobbying campaigns compare to financial donations or inside lobbying in influencing policymakers? V. O. Key raised similar questions nearly four decades ago, and he found answers difficult to come by. In the 1961 book *Public Opinion and American Democracy*, he expresses doubts about the influence of outside

lobbying activities. "Their function in the political process," he writes in reference to "propagandizing campaigns" by interest groups, "is difficult to divine"
(528). Outside lobbying activities are "rituals in obeisance to the doctrine that
public opinion governs" and are "on the order of the dance of the rainmakers. . . .
Sometimes these campaigns have their effects—just as rain sometimes follows
the rainmakers' dance. Yet the data make it fairly clear that most of these campaigns do not affect the opinion of many people and even clearer that they have
a small effect by way of punitive or approbative feedback in the vote" (528).

Why and when, Key is really asking, do policymakers pay attention to outside lobbying? Certainly many organizational leaders consider outside lobbying potentially influential; otherwise, they would not do it. The leaders of
the major labor unions, peak business organizations, and civil rights and
environmental groups use outside lobbying regularly enough to indicate that
they believe outside lobbying is more than the dancing of rainmakers. Even
corporate leaders use outside lobbying occasionally. And policymakers admit
that organized groups of constituents influence their decisions. One congressional staff member justified his boss's vote to repeal catastrophic health
insurance in 1990, little more than a year after voting for the insurance bill,
by explaining, "It was a no-brainer. He got over five thousand letters for the
repeal of the insurance, and literally eight letters in favor of the current insurance. He didn't have much choice really. He had to vote for repeal."

But beyond the relatively uninteresting claims that interest group leaders
consider outside lobbying effective and that policymakers sometimes consider
it influential, the topic deserves more attention than it receives. If, as most
observers claim, interest groups wield considerable power in Washington, and
if interest groups spend resources using outside lobbying fairly regularly, then
outside lobbying should be an important part of the process by which these
groups wield their power. Precisely when, why, or how outside lobbying operates to enhance group influence, however, is not well understood.

Our evaluations of the normative effects of outside lobbying are similarly imprecise. We know very little about whether outside lobbying serves to
improve the correspondence between what constituents want and what their
representatives do or whether it merely confuses representatives with meaningless information or reinforces inequalities in access to representatives
that accrue from campaign contributions and other less edifying activities of
interest groups. Surprisingly, many depictions of outside lobbying in the
national press are as unfavorable as those of lobbying in general. The image
of fat-cat lobbyists shoving money in the pockets of legislators has been sup-
plemented by negative images of farmers, teachers, truckers, or public
employees demonstrating at the Capitol or flooding Congress with telephone
calls for a bigger slice of the budgetary pie, or of business lobbyists spending
money to generate so-called astroturf (in contrast to real grass-roots support)
to save a valuable tax provision. The press depiction of interest group activities has had either a large influence on Americans or has tapped into deeply

negative sentiments among the general population. Recent polls show that a vast majority of Americans are cynical about the power of special interests. In the 1992 American National Election Study (ANES), when asked whether "the government is pretty much run by a few big interests looking out for themselves or [if] it is run for the benefit of all the people," 78 percent of those offering a response answered, "a few big interests." Common wisdom, it appears, holds that some interest groups have their way in Washington, and that outside lobbying either reinforces existing inequalities in access or is irrelevant to the real game of special interest lobbying.

The cynicism of the press and the general public toward interest groups is not shared by many political scientists. Studies have tended to describe a more sanguine climate of bargaining and information gathering between interest groups and policymakers in Washington. Descriptions of interest group activities and influence from the last four decades range from the near impotence of business lobbyists during legislative conflicts over free trade to subtle forms of persuasion and pressure that influence legislation marginally. Many studies of policymaking or interest groups have concluded that other pressures on policymakers besides interest group lobbying—colleagues in the House or Senate, public opinion in the district, the White House, party leaders—were more important in determining policy. Even those who ascribe considerable power to special interests suggest that that power is wielded subtly or silently, without the intense lobbying activity so common in Washington.

One reason the press and the general public may tend to exaggerate the influence of interest groups is that the news overemphasizes dramatic instances of graft, exploited campaign finance loopholes, or extraordinary pressure exerted on members of Congress by organizations like the National Rifle Association. Successful outside lobbying campaigns and increasingly large campaign contributions due to the reporting of the Federal Election Commission attract attention and are visible manifestations of group power. Inside lobbying in the form of interpersonal contacts, while an everyday occurrence for nearly all interest groups, is harder for the mass media to observe on a regular basis and has more of the flavor of relationship building and coordination among lobbyists and legislators than of outright pressure. Thus, the media fail to report adequately on the effects of inside strategies, and if they were to do so, it would probably bring the popular evaluation of interest group power more into balance.

In contrast, some of the conclusions of political scientists about the muted influence of interest groups may have something to do with the lack of research on outside lobbying. Researchers have tended to focus on inside lobbying, campaign contributions, and especially organizational formation. For each of these subjects, conclusions of researchers have highlighted the limitations of organized interests. Inside lobbying rarely changes legislators' positions on policy issues. Campaign contributions seem to correlate only weakly with legislative or electoral success. And groups are hard to form because of collective action problems. Given all the obstacles interest groups presumably face, one wonders why there are more than seven thousand registered organizations in Washington, and why so many of them spend precious resources trying to influence policymakers. Interest groups work hard to influence legislation, and it is difficult to believe that their money and efforts go to waste.

Part of the problem for political scientists may be that they fail to see the role that outside lobbying serves in enhancing the inside lobbying of interest groups. Interest groups choose lobbying strategies at the same time policymakers are trying to please constituents. Groups thus choose strategies intended to convince policymakers that group goals align with constituent goals. If successfully wielded, these strategies can enable interest group leaders to be quite influential in shaping public policies. While this seems apparent, outside lobbying does not get the attention it deserves in interest group research. Simply put, outside lobbying has rarely been studied systematically. The kinds of interest group activities the mass media tend to highlight are precisely those that political scientists tend to understudy, and the differences in coverage among the two affect conclusions about interest group power. This reading, in attempting to answer three questions—Why do groups use outside lobbying? When does outside lobbying work? Who benefits from outside lobbying?—is an effort to rectify the imbalance in interest group research.

Of course, interest group leaders are not the only ones who find it in their interests to mobilize citizens to pressure American policymakers. Political party leaders, politicians (especially the president), and even newspapers and mass media personalities actively encourage citizens to contact their elected representatives. The question of when it is advantageous in a democracy to mobilize citizens to pressure policymakers is considerably more general than the more specific question of when interest groups should do so. Many of the ideas in this reading about outside lobbying by interest groups should certainly apply to other actors in the political system.

Overview

Outside lobbying is important because it is a common means (perhaps the most common means except for elections) for elite policymakers to experience pressure in the form of popular participation. Were it not for outside lobbying from interest groups, many policy decisions would take place solely among a relatively insulated group of Washington insiders. Instead, interest group leaders call upon people outside of Washington to remind policymakers that a sizable portion of their constituents is paying attention. At least potentially, outside lobbying can pressure policymakers to adopt more popularly supported policies than they would in the absence of outside lobbying.

Outside lobbying accomplishes two tasks simultaneously. First, at the elite level it communicates aspects of public opinion to policymakers. The many forms of outside lobbying—publicizing issue positions, mobilizing constituents to contact Congress, protesting or demonstrating—have the common purpose of trying to show policymakers that the people the group claims to represent really do care about some relevant policy issue. These tactics say, in effect, "See, we told you constituents were angry about policy X, and now you can hear it from them."

I refer to this role for outside lobbying as *signaling* because it has many characteristics of basic signaling models in game theory. An interest group (the sender) tries to signal its popular support (its type) to a policymaker (the receiver). . . . When do the signals sent by interest group leaders actually influence policymakers' behavior?

The noteworthy characteristic of outside lobbying, however, is that it is not just an elite-level phenomenon. It is intended to influence members of the mass public as well. The second role for outside lobbying is to influence public opinion by changing how selected constituents consider and respond to policy issues. I shall call this its *conflict expansion* role in reference to the theoretical legacy of Schattschneider, who wrote in 1960 that the "most important strategy of politics is concerned with the scope of the conflict. . . . Conflicts are frequently won or lost by the success that the contestants have in getting the audience involved in the fight or in excluding it, as the case may be" (3–4). As Schattschneider emphasized, political elites, when faced with intransigent opposition, can bring attention to their cause, invite constituents to participate in the policy process, and hope to swing momentum to their side.

For both of these roles, the salience of policy issues to constituents, an often-overlooked characteristic of public opinion, lies at the center of interest group politics. It is not the popularity of policies that is mostly communicated or altered through outside lobbying. For one, the popularity of policies tends to stay relatively fixed over long periods of time, even given the outside lobbying activities of interest groups. But even more important, policymakers tend to have good information on the popularity of policies, primarily through opinion polls, but also because such popularity stays relatively constant and they can learn about it over time. Salience, however, defined as the relative importance people attach to policy issues, is an aspect of public opinion that policymakers perpetually running for reelection want to know but cannot learn about from ordinary opinion polls and experience. Policymakers want to know what proportion of constituents, when voting in the next election, will weigh the actions of their elected representatives on a particular policy issue. More salient policy issues will weigh more heavily on voting decisions than will less salient policy issues, and policymakers rely to a considerable extent on interest groups for current information on which issues rank high on salience. Because they can mobilize constituents to speak for themselves and can occasionally increase the salience of issues to those constituents, interest group leaders have a comparative advantage in sending credible signals on this precious information.

In sum, interest group leaders can turn their informational and leadership advantages into policy influence. They can try through inside lobbying to convince policymakers that voters care about an issue and are on the side of their group on the issue. But outside lobbying goes a step further in making a costly, public demonstration that, one, the issue is in fact salient to voters and, two, the interest group can make the issue even more salient.

The distinction between the two roles can be quite fuzzy, especially in practice. Consider two analogous situations. An opposition leader in an authoritarian regime wants to hold a large rally in the capital. The rally, if it successfully gathers hundreds of thousands of people as planned, accomplishes the two tasks just specified. It both communicates to the current regime the swelling sentiment among the population that the current regime is offensive *and* coordinates or mobilizes the opposing citizens on a particular course of action: support the opposition leader and work to topple the current government. To the government the rally signals the status of the opposition, and to the citizens in the rally it reinforces the notion that the effort to topple the regime is important and worthy of risky collective action.

Outside lobbying is also similar to the marketing behavior of business entrepreneurs promoting new product ideas to consumers and investors at the same time. Entrepreneurs do their own brand of inside lobbying among investors, hawking their product ideas and wooing support among a small group of people. At the same time, they gauge consumer demand for their products, communicate that level of demand to potential investors, and even try to stimulate more demand among consumers. Success among one audience (consumers) will likely lead to success among the other audience (investors). Just as investors try to assess potential consumer response to the entrepreneur's marketing efforts because future investments will succeed or fail based on consumer behavior, elected officials look to constituents' responses to outside lobbying because reelection efforts may hinge on the interest group success in mobilizing constituents. For interest groups, as with entrepreneurs, there are two audiences in mass marketing, but the overall goals converge because one audience relies very much on the other audience. . . .

The duality of purpose makes outside lobbying a powerful tool in the hands of interest groups. It can simultaneously fan the flames of constituent anger and bring the heat of those flames to the attention of representatives far away, whose job it is to put out or contain the fire. However, while the two roles can get mixed together in practice, there are important conceptual distinctions between them. In the signaling role, the salience of a policy issue must be considered *exogenous* in that there is something fixed and unknown to policymakers about salience that the group claims to be able to demonstrate through outside lobbying. Perhaps it is the potential salience of an issue that interest groups want to communicate. In this case, the "fixed" element of public opinion being communicated is the latent salience of an issue. The group is confident it can expand the conflict to a certain point, and it wants to communicate that confidence through outside lobbying. In the conflict expansion role, the salience of a policy issue is *endogenous*, in that the strategy is intended to influence the very characteristic of public opinion that is being communicated in the signaling role.

■   ■   ■

Communication costs in particular are relevant to the study of outside lobbying because the costs of successful outside lobbying are related systematically to the existing state of public salience on an issue. Precisely because outside lobbying is costly, and the strategies of interest groups conditional on those costs offer clues to the underlying public salience groups are trying to communicate, outside lobbying can influence policymakers. Policymakers learn about salience by making inferences from the revealed efforts of interest groups.

When group leaders are confident they can expand the conflict—raise public awareness of an issue or frame issues in different ways to their advantage—additional considerations besides the advantages of signaling to policymakers become important. What information should a group present to constituents to convince them the issue is worth costly collective action? When in the course of legislation should conflict expansion happen for maximum impact? How should a group frame the advantages of one policy over another policy? In general, when there are opportunities to expand the conflict, decision making over strategies turns on how potential increases in salience (or sometimes popularity) will benefit interest group goals, rather than on how the current level of popular support will play with policymakers.

As a first cut at understanding conflict expansion, we might think it benefits groups that do not have ready access to policymakers. Much of our understanding of this comes from Schattschneider. Schattschneider believed not only that outsider groups would want to outside lobby, but also that such groups tend to have advantages in the realm of public opinion. According to Schattschneider, "It is the weak who want to socialize conflict, i.e., to involve more and more people in the conflict until the balance of forces is changed" (1960, 40), the assumption being that groups with concentrated wealth or power would eschew politics involving broad popular participation and do not stand to gain from increased salience.

Schattschneider's ideas, however, do not completely square with contemporary interest group politics. In an age when all kinds of organizations, including large corporations, wealthy trade associations, and professional groups outside lobby on policy issues of great concern to millions of Americans, clearly there are times when the strong and those groups with considerable inside access want to expand the scope of the conflict as well. . . .

Two aspects of the policy context that influence outside lobbying are discussed in detail: the stage of legislation and the policy alternatives confronting policymakers. The stage of legislation—whether a policy problem is just being introduced to the government or whether well-defined alternatives are being considered by legislators—will have a large effect on both signaling and conflict expansion decisions (Kingdon 1984). In decisions over lobbying strategies or tactics, groups facing policies in earlier stages, when they merely try to raise consciousness on a new policy issue, will be less concerned about popular support for their policy positions than will groups facing policies in later stages, when they fight to swing a few key votes in a congressional committee. The stage of legislation shapes the way public opinion constrains interest group strategies mostly by varying the benefits groups attain in signaling the current salience of an issue versus in trying to increase the salience of that issue or the popularity of specific policies.

Policy alternatives, or more specifically the relative popularity of policy alternatives, matter a great deal because they also determine whether increasing salience is a good idea for a group. What may not be overwhelmingly popular—say, needle exchange programs—may be more popular than the most prominent policy alternative, increased spending on drug rehabilitation programs. Thus, as for influencing outside lobbying decisions, the popularity of policies must be regarded as relative, not absolute, a consideration that carries implications about whether a group benefits from conflict expansion.

■ ■ ■

Most [of] us would presumably like to see outside lobbying coming from groups supporting popular policies on salient issues. Instead, the empirical conclusions of this study are mixed. I find that outside lobbying, contrary to the view that most of it produces phony grass-roots support, is far from artificial. It is actually a good way for policymakers to learn what their constituents care about. My data show that outside lobbying on average works as a policymaker might hope: it communicates fairly accurately the salience of policy issues to large numbers of constituents, and it often influences the salience of policy issues to benefit the more popular side of an issue. At the same time, however, and more often than we would like, outside lobbying springs forth from intense groups pursuing relatively unpopular policies (especially early in the legislative process), and in this regard, it falls somewhat short in reinforcing the majority's preferences. Outside lobbying, in sum, does not distort the policymaking process nearly as much as many people like to claim, but it does a better job in communicating salience information than in bolstering popular pressure for majoritarian policies.

■ ■ ■

TACTICS AND STRATEGIES

The Story of the Hat Trick

One beautiful August morning in 1989, Leona Kozien took the bus from near her home in Chicago to the Copernicus Center for senior citizens on the city's northwest side. Kozien, who was sixty-nine years old, had no idea at the time that she was going to become a brief media star and a figure of political lore.

All she knew was that she was angry with the politicians in Washington. In particular, she felt betrayed by her congressman, Dan Rostenkowski, chairman of the Ways and Means Committee of the House of Representatives. Kozien was upset by a new policy from Washington that caused her husband to pay a surtax for catastrophic health care insurance. In her mind, it was an unfair attempt by the federal government to make senior citizens pay unreasonably for health care.

Rostenkowski knew many seniors were angry, but he did not know the extent of the anger. Since the unveiling of the policy a year earlier, a policy that he and the largest seniors lobby, the American Association of Retired Persons (AARP), had sponsored and supported all through the legislative process, he had been reluctant to meet with smaller senior citizens' groups, even those from his own district. National groups separate from the AARP, especially the National Committee to Preserve Social Security and Medicare, run by James Roosevelt, son of President Franklin D. Roosevelt, had been mobilizing grass-roots opposition to the policy for more than a year. The AARP then decided to oppose the new policy. Partly as a concession and partly as a compromise, Rostenkowski had agreed to meet with a few of the leaders of local senior citizens groups. The meeting was held at the Copernicus Center, right in the heart of Rostenkowski's district.

After prodding by her husband (who could not attend), Kozien joined approximately one hundred seniors who waited in the main hall of the center for Rostenkowski to emerge from the meeting with the group leaders. She and other seniors had been given signs to wave at Rostenkowski. The signs indicated displeasure with the current policy: Congressman Rostenkowski, Don't Tax the Seniors, and Read My Lips: Catastrophic Act Is a Seniors Tax.

While Rostenkowski met with group leaders, Kozien and her own group were holding a meeting of their own in the main hall. Participants were taking turns telling the rest of the group why the catastrophic health policy was bad for seniors. The group waiting for Rostenkowski agreed that the catastrophic "tax" had to go, but they also agreed on something else. They wanted Rostenkowski to speak to them in person.

"A lot of people felt they were owed something," one local interest group leader recalls. "They just wanted to see him. He was right there, and they felt this was their opportunity [to tell him what they thought of the policy]."

Rostenkowski emerged from his meeting and headed for the exit. The group waiting for him booed and hissed. Before the congressman could get to the door, a television crew stopped him to ask questions about events in Poland, a topic of keen interest to many of his constituents. This pause gave a small group of seniors enough time to run out of the building and surround Rostenkowski's car. Kozien led the charge.

Kozien shouted, "Where's his car parked? I'm going to make him talk to us!"

A small mob followed Kozien outside, and pretty soon there were fifteen to twenty seniors surrounding the congressman's car, while television crews stood nearby. Rostenkowski, meanwhile, fought through the crowd and got in the car.

"Coward!" "Shame!" "Impeach Rottenkowski!" The seniors stood in front of the car and waved placards. The congressman's driver honked the horn and moved the car a few inches. The front bumper brushed against Kozien's thigh, and she staggered a bit. Some man shouted, "You knocked her down! You hurt her!" This same man then turned to Kozien and said quietly, "Lay down under the car."

"Are you crazy? No way, he'd run me over!" retorted Kozien, who was barely over five feet tall. The car moved again, and this time Kozien fell on the hood of the car. Her face was inches from Rostenkowski's, with glass separating them. She was still carrying her placard, and from inside the car, Rostenkowski saw her placard, her face, and her body sprawled across the windshield.

"Killer! Killer!" the crowd shouted.

Rostenkowski then got out of the car and ran through a parking lot while angry seniors chased after him. The driver maneuvered through the crowd, drove around the block, and caught up with Rostenkowski down the street from the center. Rostenkowski jumped in, and the car sped off.

"It was a funny picture," recalled one local politician present, "because it was a true chase. The seniors would move faster, and Rosty would move faster. He gets in the car, and they stand in front of the car."

The scene made for dramatic television. The Chicago film crews, delighted with the footage, distributed it immediately to the national networks. All three major television news shows carried the story prominently that evening, earning the interest group leaders what they call "a hat trick," in reference to a hockey player scoring three goals in one game.

Kozien, meanwhile, the activist and agitator for that day, was an unlikely hero. She had never before been active in politics. She knew little about the seniors groups at the Copernicus Center. Her relatives called that evening, expressing amazement at their "crazy Aunt Leona." Over the next several years politicians, prior to speaking at senior citizen events, would ask her to accompany them onstage. She always refused.

She likewise downplayed her heroism. "We just wanted answers. Had he answered our questions, there would have been no incident." Yet the incident was a bonanza for the leaders of the interest groups. The image of Kozien on the hood of Rostenkowski's car was used for years afterward on network news to symbolize the potency of the senior citizen lobby.

The catastrophic insurance program, which had passed the House in June 1988 by a vote of 328 to 72, was soon after repealed. The vote was not even close. The House voted 360 to 66 in favor of repeal in October 1989. Incidentally, Rostenkowski stood firm, voting to oppose repeal.

Many members of Congress had heard from people like Kozien, though presumably not from atop the hoods of their cars. Two Florida legislators reported getting more than seventy-five thousand pieces of mail, each opposing the policy. One staffer reported to me that his boss received more than two thousand mail pieces in favor of repeal, and eight mail pieces against repeal. The turn of events on catastrophic health insurance had people shaking their heads.

To some, the outside lobbying gave a large voice to a small number of people. "It was a case of the House of Representatives being stampeded by a small, vocal group of seniors," said Pete Stark, a Democratic congressman from California. "Ambushed is how a lot of people here feel now," Tim Penny, a Democrat from Minnesota, said at the time. "Every member of Congress was getting accosted at town meetings," said [the late] Senator John McCain, Republican from Arizona.

Others were more positive about the outcome, preferring to think that the outside lobbying tapped into a widespread sentiment. "We made a mistake last year [in 1988]," said Brian Donnelly, a Democratic congressman from Massachusetts. "This time, we listened to the voters."

Significance of the Story

The story of the Rostenkowski incident in north Chicago, while hardly typical of stories of outside lobbying, is useful for several reasons. For one, it shows in dramatic fashion how interest groups can instigate or facilitate collective action through outside lobbying. Contrary to what interest group leaders were claiming afterward, the mobbing of Rostenkowski was not all that spontaneous. The meeting between Rostenkowski and the interest group leaders was set up by the interest group leaders, and seniors from around the neighborhood were encouraged to attend by the interest group leaders. The interest group leaders, not Rostenkowski's staff, had invited the networks to the meetings at the Copernicus Center. Rostenkowski's staff wanted to avoid media attention. And the interest group leaders made the placards and distributed them to Kozien and other seniors.

Interest group leaders also knew that the seniors attending were unusually angry about the new policy, and the leaders wanted to communicate that anger forcefully and make it seem less than fully staged. The seniors at the Copernicus Center were to represent the tip of the iceberg of constituent opinion. As for the seniors, their reactions could not have been better for the group leaders. The leaders provided a small, low-cost spark and let it turn into a conflagration. The behavior of Kozien and others was spontaneous and chaotic enough to indicate that the seniors were just plain mad. After all the preparations, events got out of control at the right time and at the right level. "Just barely out of control" might be the optimum level of behavioral response interest group leaders want from constituents in an outside lobbying campaign.

Therefore, what was communicated loudly and clearly to policymakers was the ease with which interest group leaders mobilized Kozien and her fellow seniors. The low costs involved for the interest groups to get hundreds of seniors to stampede the car of a powerful committee chairman counted for much more than the stampede itself. In trying to signal the "true" level of public salience over an issue, an interest group that succeeds with little effort can gain credibility.

Most of the conflict expansion on the issue had occurred well before that fateful day. National seniors organizations like the Gray Panthers and the National Committee to Preserve Social Security and Medicare had been running advertisements for months, and they had successfully framed the issue as one of unfair taxation for all seniors as opposed to one of health care benefits for a vast majority of seniors. By one reasonable interpretation, through the summer of 1989 interest groups had increased the level of salience among seniors on the issue. Then, as the salience of the issue peaked in late summer, interest group leaders had only to signal to policymakers the salience of the issue among those seniors who opposed the new policy. The Rostenkowski incident was timed perfectly. The conflict had been expanded, and the time had come to let policymakers know about it.

The story also neatly illustrates the roles assumed by the main players. Interest group leaders, the ones who had invited people like Kozien in the first place, set the stage for the famous confrontation (though they got lucky when it succeeded beyond their expectations). A policymaker, in this case a powerful House committee chairman, found himself the target of outside lobbying efforts by interest group leaders and constituents. And the ordinary constituents like Kozien, who behaved in both an organized and disorganized manner, made the lives of policymakers more difficult through simple expressions of anger.

The story is useful as well for highlighting the potential influence of outside lobbying. The renegade senior citizens groups, those distinguishing themselves early on from the AARP on the catastrophic health care policy, appear to have had an effect on Rostenkowski's colleagues in the House. As Table [1] indicates, 240 members of the House switched their votes from supporting

TABLE [1] Reconsidering Catastrophic Health Insurance: Number of Members of the House of Representatives Voting For or Against Original Bill and Repeal

	Original Bill	
Repeal	*Yea*	*Nay*
Yea	240	64
Nay	60	1

NOTE: This takes into account turnover from the 100th to 101st Congress, in that only members who voted on both bills are included. One member, Larry Hopkins, a Republican from Kentucky, voted against the original proposal and against repeal. The original bill was HR 2470, Catastrophic Health Insurance/Rule. The repeal was HR 3299, Amendment to Budget Reconciliation, Repealing Catastrophic Health Insurance Surtax.

catastrophic coverage in June 1988 to supporting repeal of catastrophic coverage sixteen months later. This is a remarkable instance of collective reconsideration. Only 124 members, or approximately half of the number that switched votes, voted the "same" way for both bills—that is, 124 either voted against the original bill and for repeal, or they voted for the original bill and against repeal. The latter vote, on the amendment to repeal the Catastrophic Coverage Act, was the first time Congress had ever voted to repeal a major social benefit it had created.

"An event of about 150 elderly people changed the tide of the thing," recalled Jan Schakowsky, at the time a leader of the Illinois State Council of Senior Citizens, one of the groups that mobilized seniors on that day. "It was a pivotal event." It was pivotal not because it changed Rostenkowski's mind (which it did not), but because it had such an influence on his colleagues. As the story and its aftermath remind us, a well-publicized event among a small number of people can send very strong signals about, and enhance the reputation of, a group numbering many thousands or even millions of people. More than five years later, members of Congress referred to the Rostenkowski incident as cementing the reputation of the senior citizens lobby. This, according to people in Washington who are inclined to slight hyperbole, is one group in the population they do not want to cross.

Another revealing aspect of the story is that the Rostenkowski event happened because of a grave miscalculation on the part of the chairman and his colleagues. They enacted the original policy because they were led to believe that seniors were behind it, but they gambled and lost when interest groups tapped into a[n] undiscovered level of antipathy among certain groups of seniors.[1] In general, legislators try to estimate the policy preferences and issue salience among their constituents, yet these estimates are shots in the dark on many controversial issues. They never know how some groups will respond, or which issues their next electoral opponent will use against them. They need to do the near impossible: anticipate how latent constituent opinion will manifest itself in the coming years. Rostenkowski was probably warned when he led his committee to recommend the original policy. Like anyone facing a difficult decision, however, he listened to the people who had previously established a credible reputation for electoral power, the AARP. Yet until Kozien and her fellow seniors let him know loudly and clearly their preferences, he could not have been certain about the consequences of his previous actions. The response among seniors led Rostenkowski and other policymakers to move toward repeal.

The Rostenkowski story is unusual, of course. Rarely are outside lobbying efforts as successful. Famous examples, such as this one, become lore around the Capitol. Another example from the early 1980s still generates discussion around Washington. During the successful outside lobbying efforts in 1982 by the American Bankers Association to repeal tax withholding from interest-bearing accounts, 22 million postcards from depositors flooded into Congress within days of the passage of the tax bill containing the provision. Every congressional district responded, according to the staff of Robert Dole, the chair of the Senate Finance Committee at the time. The marvel is that bankers, of all people, were able to make an issue more salient through conflict expansion, and at the same time were able to signal that salience to policymakers with a successful outside lobbying campaign. They did all of this without hiding their identities as bankers, indicating that latent salience among constituents is a great resource for all groups, not just for those with popular images or credibility as electoral powerhouses.

NOTE

1. In truth, even the AARP was caught off guard. Dissident elderly groups, those opposed to the policy all along, began stirring opposition until the AARP changed its policy on the issue. Then, once the AARP was opposed to the policy, it galvanized further action by the dissident elderly groups.

BIBLIOGRAPHY

Key, V. O. 1961. *Public Opinion and American Democracy*. New York: Alfred Knopf.
Kingdon, John. 1984. *Agendas, Alternatives, and Public Policies*. Boston: Little, Brown.
Schattschneider, E. E. 1960. *The Semi-Sovereign People*. Hinsdale, IL: Dryden Press.

11.2

LARRY M. BARTELS

From *Unequal Democracy: The Political Economy of the New Gilded Age*

Different income groups (rich, middle class, poor) pressure the government through organizations that represent their respective interests. Bartels argues that the policies of the national government resulting from this pressure have had a major impact on income inequality in the United States. Income inequality has increased over the last three and a half decades, with most of the increases occurring during Republican presidential administrations. Bartels argues that this reflects the success of organizations pressuring the government in favor of the rich, the different economic philosophies of the two major parties, and the different political interests of partisan voters.

THE PARTISAN POLITICAL ECONOMY

> . . . as our economy grows, market forces work to provide the greatest rewards to those with the needed skills in the growth areas. . . . This trend . . . is simply an economic reality, and it is neither fair nor useful to blame any political party.
>
> —Treasury Secretary Henry Paulson, 2006[1]

The tendency to think of economic outcomes as natural and inevitable is politically significant because it discourages systematic critical scrutiny of their causes and consequences. If escalating inequality is "simply an economic reality," it seems pointless to spend too much energy worrying about how and why it arises. Moreover, if "there has always been extreme income inequality" under Republicans and Democrats alike, it seems pointless to hope that public policies might mitigate that inequality. As prominent policy analyst Lawrence Mead rather breezily put it, in a response to the report of the American Political Science Association's Task Force on Inequality and American Democracy, . . . "The causes [of growing economic inequality] are not well understood and have little tie to government."[2]

My aim . . . is to refute the notion that the causes of economic inequality in contemporary America "have little tie to government." Indeed, I suggest that

From Larry M. Bartels, *Unequal Democracy: The Political Economy of the New Gilded Age* (Princeton, NJ: Princeton University Press, 2008).

the narrowly economic focus of most previous studies of inequality has caused them to miss what may be the most important single influence on the changing U.S. income distribution over the past half-century—the contrasting policy choices of Democratic and Republican presidents. Under Republican administrations, real income growth for the lower- and middle-income classes has consistently lagged well behind the income growth rate for the rich—and well behind the income growth rate for the lower and middle classes themselves under Democratic administrations.

. . . [T]he dramatic differences in patterns of income growth under Democratic and Republican presidents are quite unlikely to have occurred by chance; nor can they be attributed to oil price shocks or changes in the structure of the labor force or other purely economic factors, or to cyclical corrections by each party of the other party's policy excesses. Rather, they reflect consistent differences in policies and priorities between Democratic and Republican administrations. In the first half of the post-war era, these differences were expressed primarily in macroeconomic policies and performance, with Democrats presiding over significantly less unemployment and significantly more overall economic growth than Republicans. Since the 1970s some of these macroeconomic differences have been muted, but significant partisan differences in tax and transfer policies have continued to produce significant partisan disparities in patterns of post-tax income growth, with the middle class and, especially, the working poor experiencing significantly more income growth under Democratic presidents than under Republican presidents.

The cumulative effect of these partisan differences has been enormous. My projections based on the historical performance of Democratic and Republican presidents suggest that income inequality would actually have *declined* slightly over the past 50 years . . . had the patterns of income growth characteristic of Democratic administrations been in effect throughout that period. Conversely, continuous application of the patterns of income growth observed during periods of Republican control would have produced a much greater divergence in the economic fortunes of rich and poor people than we have actually experienced.

▪   ▪   ▪

The average rate of real income growth during 1948–2005 was higher for affluent families than for those lower in the income distribution. . . . What may be surprising is that this pattern of differential growth is entirely limited to periods in which Republicans controlled the White House.

. . . Figure [1] provides a graphical representation of . . . the starkly different patterns of income growth under Democratic and Republican administrations. . . . Under Democratic presidents, poor families did slightly better than richer families (at least in proportional terms), producing a modest net decrease in income inequality; under Republican presidents, rich families

FIGURE [1]   Income Growth by Income Level under Democratic and Republican Presidents, 1948–2005

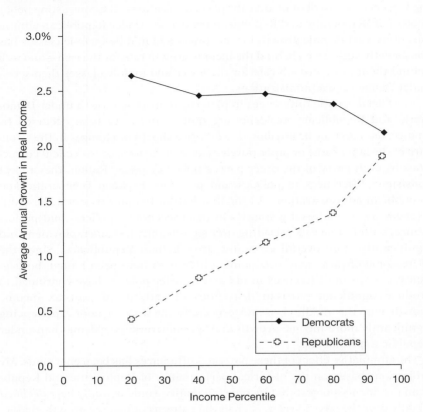

did vastly better than poorer families, producing a considerable net increase in income inequality. In both cases, the patterns are essentially linear over the entire range of family incomes represented in the figure (that is, for incomes ranging from about $25,000 to $200,000 in 2005).

▪   ▪   ▪

A Partisan Coincidence?

The partisan differences in characteristic rates of income growth documented in Figure [1] would seem to be of immense economic and political significance—if they are real. They suggest that middle-class and poor families in the postwar era have routinely fared much worse under Republican presidents than they have under Democratic presidents. By this accounting, economic inequality in contemporary America is profoundly shaped by partisan politics.

But to what extent are these patterns really attributable to partisan politics rather than to accidental historical factors? One way to address this question

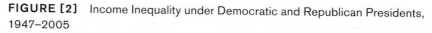

FIGURE [2]   Income Inequality under Democratic and Republican Presidents, 1947–2005

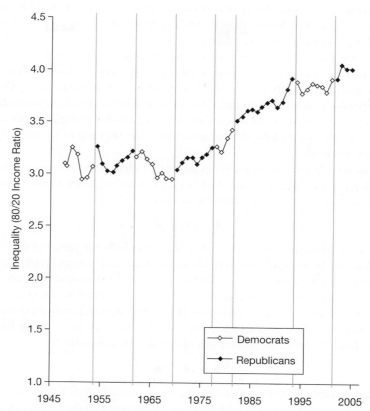

is to examine their consistency across a range of presidents and circumstances. To that end, Figure [2] shows the level of income inequality in each year of the post-war period as reflected in one standard measure of inequality, the ratio of incomes at the 80th percentile of the income distribution to those at the 20th percentile.

By this measure, income inequality was essentially constant from the late 1940s through the late 1960s, with families at the 80th percentile of the income distribution earning about three times as much as families at the 20th percentile. Inequality increased fairly steadily through the 1970s and 1980s before leveling off once again in the 1990s. These broad temporal trends reinforce the impression that growing inequality is significantly related to long-term technological and social changes.

Despite these long-term forces, distinguishing between Democratic and Republican administrations (the white [diamonds] and black diamonds in the figure, respectively) reveals the regularity with which Democratic presidents reduced and Republican presidents increased the prevailing level of economic inequality, regardless of the long-term trend. Indeed, the effect of presidential partisanship on income inequality turns out to have been remarkably consistent since the end of World War II. The 80/20 income ratio increased under each of the six Republican presidents in this period—Eisenhower, Nixon, Ford, Reagan, George H. W. Bush, and George W. Bush. In contrast, four of five Democratic presidents—all except Jimmy Carter—presided over declines in income inequality. If this is a coincidence, it is a very powerful one.[3] Even in the highly inegalitarian economic climate of the 1990s, Bill Clinton managed to produce slightly stronger income growth for families at the 20th percentile than at the 80th percentile, though families at the very top of the income distribution did even better.

The strikingly consistent partisan pattern of changes in income inequality in Figure [2] seems hard to attribute to a mere coincidence in the timing of Democratic and Republican administrations.

■　■　■

It may be tempting to suppose that the very different patterns of income growth under Democratic and Republican presidents in Figure [1] reflect a cycle of partisan equilibration in which Democrats pursue expansionary policies in reaction to Republican contractions and Republicans produce contractions as an antidote to Democratic expansions. However, a detailed analysis of the timing of partisan differences in income growth provides no support for that notion. Table [1] provides tabulations of average income growth.

■　■　■

[T]he partisan differences in average growth rates at every income level were about twice as large in terms with no partisan turnover as they were in the first terms of new partisan regimes. Democratic presidents generally presided over similar income growth rates for families in every part of the income distribution, regardless of whether they were in their first or second terms; but average income growth was consistently higher (by a little more than half a percentage point) when Democrats succeeded Democrats than when Democrats succeeded Republicans. Conversely, most families (except the most affluent) did better under first-term Republican presidents than in subsequent Republican administrations; these differences, too, were on the order of half a percentage point.

■　■　■

[T]he partisan pattern of post-tax income growth in Figure [3] is strikingly similar to the partisan pattern of pre-tax family income growth in Figure [1]. Households at every income level did about equally well under Carter and Clinton, with average growth rates ranging from 1.4% to 1.6%. On the other hand, Republican presidents presided over weaker income growth for

TABLE [1] The Impact of Partisan Turnover on Partisan Differences in Real Income Growth Rates, 1948–2005

Average annual real pre-tax income growth (%) for families at various points in the income distribution (with standard errors in parentheses). Partisan control measured from one year following inauguration to one year following subsequent inauguration. "Partisan turnover" refers to first-term Democrats who succeeded Republicans or first-term Republicans who succeeded Democrats.

	All Presidents	Democratic Presidents	Republican Presidents	Partisan Difference
Partisan turnover				
20th percentile	1.38 (.75)	2.28 (1.00)	.71 (1.08)	1.57 (1.52)
40th percentile	1.52 (.54)	2.07 (.75)	1.11 (.76)	.96 (1.09)
60th percentile	1.60 (.47)	2.00 (.63)	1.30 (.67)	.71 (.95)
80th percentile	1.80 (.45)	2.19 (.62)	1.51 (.63)	.68 (.91)
95th percentile	1.89 (.45)	1.93 (.69)	1.86 (.61)	.07 (.92)
N	28	12	16	28
No partisan turnover				
20th percentile	1.46 (.68)	2.95 (1.19)	.16 (.61)	2.80 (1.29)
40th percentile	1.56 (.56)	2.80 (.88)	.48 (.63)	2.31 (1.06)
60th percentile	1.86 (.51)	2.86 (.82)	.97 (.57)	1.89 (.98)
80th percentile	1.87 (.48)	2.55 (.78)	1.27 (.57)	1.28 (.95)
95th percentile	2.10 (.62)	2.28 (1.07)	1.95 (.70)	.34 (1.25)
N	30	14	16	30

SOURCE: Calculations based on data from Census Bureau Historical Income Tables.

households in the top half of the income distribution and little or no income growth for households in the bottom half of the income distribution. As with the partisan differences in pre-tax growth presented in Figure [1], these partisan differences in post-tax growth are concentrated in the second year of each administration, when the policy initiatives adopted in the "honeymoon" period immediately following Inauguration Day are most likely to take effect.[4]

▪   ▪   ▪

Democrats, Republicans, and the Rise of Inequality

Economists associate the escalation of inequality over the past 30 years with important structural changes in the American economy, including demographic shifts, globalization, and technological change. I see no reason to doubt that these factors have played an important role in increasing the income gap between rich and poor people in the contemporary United States; but if this is "simply an economic reality," as Treasury Secretary Paulson asserted,

FIGURE [3]   Post-Tax Income Growth under Democratic and Republican Presidents, 1980–2003

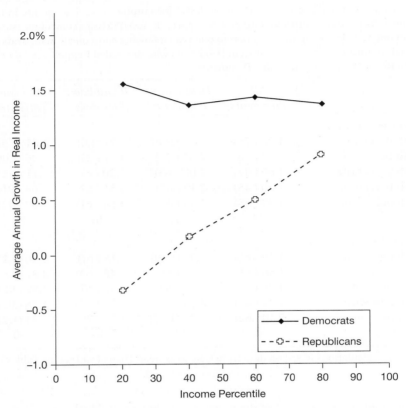

it does not follow that nothing can be done to mitigate the economic and social consequences of that reality. Nor does the fact that "there has always been extreme income inequality," as Ben Stein observed, imply that presidents and their policy choices can have no significant effect on the extent of inequality at any given time.

The cumulative impact of these partisan policy choices is illustrated in Figure [4]. The dotted line in the center of the figure represents the actual course of inequality over the past half-century, as measured by the ratio of family incomes at the 80th and 20th percentiles of the income distribution. (This portion of the figure is simply repeated from Figure [2].) The solid upper line represents the projected course of the 80/20 income ratio over the same period given the pattern of income growth that prevailed under Republican presidents during this period, while the lower line represents the projected course of the 80/20 income ratio under Democratic presidents. . . .

The projections in Figure [4] imply that continuous Democratic control would have produced an essentially constant level of economic inequality over the past

FIGURE [4] Projected Income Inequality under Republican and Democratic
Presidents, 1947–2005

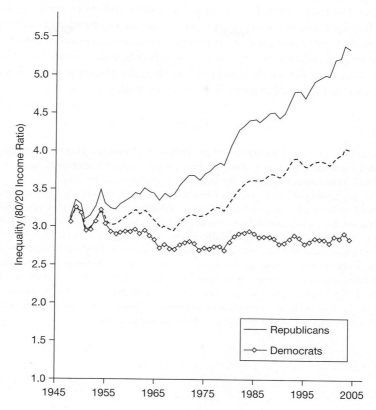

three decades, despite all the technological, demographic, and global competitive forces emphasized in economists' accounts of escalating inequality. In
contrast, continuous Republican control would have produced a much sharper
polarization between rich and poor than has actually occurred over the past
30 years, with the 80/20 income ratio reaching a level about one-third higher
than it actually did.[5]

The projections presented in Figure [4] are based on an arguably unrealistic assumption: that if either party had uninterrupted control of the White
House, it would do all the time what it in fact does only half the time. It is
impossible to know whether either party would actually have the political
will or the political power to produce economic redistribution of the cumulative magnitude suggested by these projections. Nevertheless, the cumulative differences portrayed in Figure [4] convey the fundamental significance
of partisan politics in ameliorating or exacerbating economic inequality
over the past half-century.

In the first 25 years of the post-war era, the partisan differences in income growth patterns documented [here] implied robust growth for middle-class and poor families under Democratic presidents and more modest growth under Republicans. In the less propitious economic circumstances prevailing in the early twenty-first century, not even a steady succession of Democratic presidents and policies would be likely to reproduce the robust broad-based income growth of the 1960s. However, that does not make the choice between Democrats and Republicans any less consequential.

NOTES

1. Remarks Prepared for Delivery by Treasury Secretary Henry H. Paulson at Columbia University, August 1, 2006, www.treas.gov/press/releases/hp41.htm.

2. Mead, "The Great Passivity," *Perspectives on Politics* 2 (2004): 671.

3. The probability of observing no more than one exception to the partisan pattern of increasing inequality under Republicans and decreasing inequality under Democrats in a random sequence of 11 increases and decreases would be $12 \div 2,048 = .006$.

4. In "honeymoon" years, the differences in average post-tax income growth between Democratic and Republican presidents range from 5.0% for households at the 20th percentile of the income distribution to 3.0% for households at the 80th percentile. The corresponding differences in nonhoneymoon years range from 0.9% to -0.3%.

5. The 80/20 income ratio increased by 27% between 1975 and 2005. The projections in Figure [4] suggest that it would have increased by 45% under continuous Republican control but by only 3% under continuous Democratic control.

11.3

BENJAMIN I. PAGE AND MARTIN GILENS

From *Democracy in America? What Has Gone Wrong and What We Can Do About It*

Page and Gilens offer a compelling narrative for how extraordinarily wealthy people have much more influence over government policy than everyone else. Not only do very wealthy people have different policy attitudes, especially about issues of government redistribution of wealth, taxation, and government-provided public goods, but they also go to great lengths to pressure policy makers to keep redistributive policies off the government's agenda. Wealthy people donate billions to campaigns, fund conservative think tanks, scholarship, and media outlets, and benefit from recent court decisions that will allow for even more money in politics. The influence of the wealthy, these authors argue, endangers our democracy.

[W]ealthy Americans wield a lot of influence. By investing money in politics, they can turn economic power into political power. Thus the United States suffers from what can be called "unequal democracy."[1]

The wealthy have won a number of important things from government: high-end tax cuts; minimal government spending; free-trade agreements; business subsidies and bank bailouts; "deregulation" of the economy. But ordinary citizens have not gotten much—especially citizens who feel pressured by economic globalization and low, stagnant incomes.

Our growing economic gap—with the fortunes of multimillionaires and billionaires soaring while most American families have been struggling to get by—has led to a widening *political* gap. The wealthy now have more to spend on politics. They have used their resources to lower their own taxes and to prevent any serious spending or regulatory efforts to ameliorate economic inequality. Thus economic inequality and political inequality mutually reinforce and increase each other. This mutual reinforcement threatens to cause a downward spiral that might continue indefinitely unless we make determined efforts to stop it.[2]

From Benjamin I. Page and Martin Gilens, *Democracy in America? What Has Gone Wrong and What We Can Do About It* (Chicago, IL: University of Chicago Press, 2017).

HOW MUCH POLITICAL INFLUENCE DO THE AFFLUENT HAVE?

Historians and journalists have always known that money plays a big part in influencing election outcomes and public policy in the United States. Examples are plentiful. Until very recently, however, no one has been able to use systematic data to figure out exactly *how much* influence the affluent have over a wide range of public policies.

Now, thanks to unique data covering 1,779 cases of federal government policy making over a twenty-year period, we have been able to estimate how much independent influence "affluent" Americans (the top 20 percent of income earners) have, while statistically taking into account the preferences of average Americans (those in the middle of the income distribution) and the alignments of major interest groups.[3]

As Figure [1] indicates, we have found that the affluent have substantial influence, far more than middle-income citizens do.[4] In sharp contrast to the flat line of (non)influence by average citizens, here the graph slopes rather steeply upward to the right. Taking into account the wishes of average citizens and interest groups, when a larger proportion of affluent Americans want[s] a policy change, that change is much more likely to happen.

But even the affluent often fail to get the policies they want from government. As the figure shows, when large majorities of the affluent want to *pre-*

FIGURE [1]   Affluent Americans Have Substantial Influence on Policy

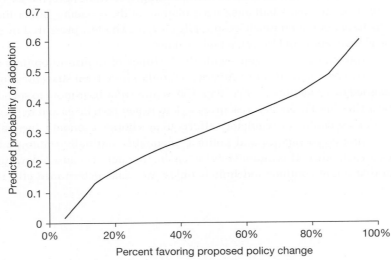

NOTE: Predicted probabilities of policy change, controlling for the preferences of average citizens and interest groups, based on 1,791 proposed policy changes between 1981 and 2002. See Gilens and Page 2014 for details.

vent a policy change, they can almost always do so. (Policies with very low affluent support, toward the left side of Figure [1], are rarely adopted.) But our political system has a strong, built-in bias against policy change, exacerbated in recent decades by partisan polarization and gridlock. So even policies with overwhelming support among the affluent (toward the right side of Figure [1]) have only about a fifty-fifty chance of being adopted.

Despite the difficulty that even affluent Americans face in getting the policies they want adopted, their preferences do significantly affect policy outcomes—in sharp contrast to the preferences of average citizens.

Our analysis shows that the affluent have influence over government policy making. But we cannot be sure exactly *who* among affluent citizens is exerting how much of that influence. Most of the "affluents" in our data are upper middle class, not really "rich." (Their median annual income of $160,000 [in 2016 dollars] may sound high to many readers, but it falls far short of the $500,000 or so needed to qualify for the top 1 percent of Americans.) We suspect that a lot of political inequality exists even among the affluent, just as it does in the general population. In fact, we suspect that much of the influence that we have detected is being wielded by a tiny group within the affluent: the "truly wealthy"—that is, multimillionaires and billionaires who can afford to donate thousands, even millions, of dollars to candidates and to superpowerful political action committees (PACs), or super PACs, that can accept unlimited donations.[5]

Although the *affluent* as a group frequently tend to agree with average Americans about public policy, we will see that the *truly wealthy* often disagree markedly. And the wealthy frequently get their way, especially in preventing policy changes that majorities of Americans favor. Money counts in politics. It makes sense that big money counts most.[6]

THE FLOOD OF MONEY IN U.S. ELECTIONS

One of the chief ways for wealthy individuals to influence political outcomes is to contribute money to election campaigns. Contributions can enable wealthy-friendly candidates to run. Withholding money can discourage candidates who are seen as threatening to the wealthy from running. Money can also grab candidates' attention and shape their priorities. It can help wealthy-friendly candidates win office and can shape their behavior once they get there.

U.S. elections are awash in money from affluent contributors.

■　　■　　■

At the national level, during the 2012 election cycle a total of $6.3 billion—that is more than *six thousand* million dollars—was spent by political parties, candidates, and supposedly "independent" groups to try to win elections. This amount easily set an all-time record for political spending in the United States—a record broken in 2016, in which early estimates placed total spending

FIGURE [2]   More Campaign Dollars Come from the Biggest Donors

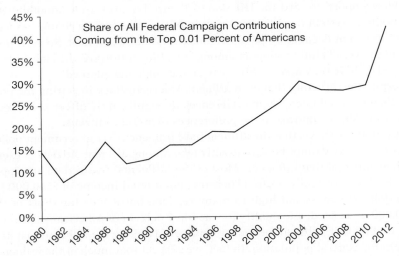

Share of All Federal Campaign Contributions Coming from the Top 0.01 Percent of Americans

Source: Bonica et al. 2013.

at just over $6.9 billion.[7] After adjusting for inflation, three times as much money was spent on congressional elections in 2012 as in 1980.[8] U.S. spending on elections is unmatched in the rest of the world. No other country comes close.

More important, perhaps, than the high cost of running for office is where the money comes from. In the United States, these vast sums of money come from *private* contributions rather than from the government, as is common in other countries.[9] This means that U.S. politicians are more dependent on private donors—especially the wealthy.

As Figure [2] shows, large donations from a tiny, extremely wealthy fraction of the American population have provided a larger and larger part of the money spent in national campaigns. In the 1980s, about 10 percent of all campaign spending came from one-tenth of one-tenth of 1 percent (0.01 percent) of the voting age population. By 2012, more than 40 percent of spending came from this tiny sliver of wealthy Americans.[10] Observers often fret that only six out of ten eligible voters turn out for presidential elections, and only four out of ten for off-year elections. But when it comes to money, an increasingly large proportion comes from a minuscule stratum of superrich contributors.

■   ■   ■

People in the top 1 percent of wealth holders (that is, people who have about $10 million or more in net worth), like the top billionaires, tilt their contributions toward the Republicans by about two to one. But these multimillionaire 1-percenters are an important source of cash for the Democrats, too. Individually, their political contributions come nowhere close to what billionaires can give, but there are many more 1-percenters than there are billionaires. The money adds up.[11]

Perhaps equally important to the Democratic Party have been hundreds of thousands of still smaller financial contributions from upper-middle-class professional people, including college teachers, lawyers, doctors, high-tech engineers, and computer experts. These professionals tend to be quite liberal on sociocultural issues such as civil rights for minorities, women's rights, gay rights, and civil liberties, but less so on equality-related economic issues such as progressive taxation.

In recent years, as substantial numbers of socially conservative working-class Americans have defected to the Republican Party, higher-income professional people have become a major part of the "base" of the Democratic Party. In 2012, for example, 55 percent of Americans with postgraduate degrees voted Democratic, while a majority of college graduates voted for the Republican presidential candidate.[12] In 2016, the Democratic share of highly educated (mostly high-income) people was even higher, while most whites without college degrees abandoned the Democratic Party.[13]

Some Democratic officials and party activists have seemed quite happy to raise money from a few multimillionaires and billionaires plus a large cadre of upper-middle-class professionals. They rejoiced that doing so made it possible to stay more or less financially competitive with the Republicans in several recent elections. Some, therefore, seemed to be complacent about our system of private financing of election campaigns. But such a view ignored serious problems for their party that came crashing down on them in 2016.

First, taken as a whole, the outpouring of private money in elections is a sure loser for the Democrats. Millionaires and billionaires tilt heavily Republican. Second, most of the wealthy or affluent Americans who *have* tended to support the Democrats have viewpoints that do not align with the labor unions and working-class Americans who once formed the core of Franklin Roosevelt's New Deal coalition. This difference in perspective has affected what the party stands for, in ways that have turned off many traditionally Democratic voters. As a result, many working-class people (especially less-educated white males) have been moving more and more Republican.[14]

We see these big problems of the Democrats—and much of the current turmoil and infighting within the Republican Party as well—as traceable to a tension between the need for big-money contributions and the need to appeal to ordinary voters. At the time we are writing, both parties are struggling to figure out what to do about this conflict. We have no crystal ball to predict what they will do. But it seems clear that private political money is a major problem for democracy in the United States.

THE CORRUPTION OF AMERICAN POLITICS

We believe that *both* major parties tend to be corrupted—and pushed away from satisfying the needs and wishes of ordinary Americans—by their reliance on wealthy contributors. We see this reliance as one of the major reasons for today's feeble state of democratic responsiveness. It is one of the main reasons that so many Americans are so angry at politicians. No wonder most Americans tell pollsters that public officials "don't care much what people like me think."[15]

When we say that both parties are "corrupted" by political money, we do not mean that public officials are regularly *bribed*, in quid pro quo ("this for that") exchanges of money for policy. Such bribery is a criminal offense. . . .

Much more pervasive is a broad pattern of undue influence that amounts to *systemic* corruption. . . . U.S. officials are clearly *dependent* on private money. Members of Congress spend an enormous amount of time raising campaign funds, in order to fend off opponents and get reelected. (In his wry preretirement "Confessions," Representative Steve Israel estimated that he had spent roughly 4,200 hours in "call time," whispering sweet nothings to potential donors; that he had attended about 1,600 fund-raisers for his own campaigns; and that he had raised nearly $20 million per election cycle.[16]) This means that officials are pulled away from doing the public's business by the need to spend time and energy soliciting money and pleasing major donors—especially since those donors tend to steer the conversation toward topics far from the concerns of most citizens, such as hedge fund managers' cherished "carried interest" tax break. As Lessig gently puts it, officials may develop "the wrong sensibilities."[17]

We would add that the flood of private money corrupts the U.S. policy-making process in another sense as well: it *affects what sorts of officials are elected* in the first place.[18] It gives us public officials whose values, experiences, economic interests, and policy preferences often diverge from those of the citizens they are supposed to represent. Research has shown that—despite the availability of numerous well-qualified Americans with blue-collar backgrounds—hardly any U.S. officials have had working-class experience. Nearly all are "white collar"— that is, fairly affluent, mostly professionals or businesspeople. They tend to think and vote quite differently from the few officials who do have working-class backgrounds.

NOTES

1. Bartels 2016.

2. See the discussions of downward spiral at the end of chapter 2 and in Kelly forth-coming.

3. See Gilens 2012, esp. chap. 2; Gilens and Page 2014, 568–70.

4. Here, and in Gilens and Page 2014, we measure the opinions of the "average citizen" in terms of the opinions of people in the middle (at the median) of the *income distribution*, as described in Gilens 2012. These people are conceptually distinct from, but empirically almost identical to, those at the medians of *opinion* distributions— that is, the Downsian "median voter" (Downs 1957).

5. To put this another way, in our analysis, the measured opinions of the affluent may be serving largely as an *indicator* of the opinions of the truly wealthy, which generally differ from ordinary citizens' opinions in the same direction—but by much greater amounts—than the affluents' opinions do.

6. Does this mean that the United States should be called a "plutocracy," or an "oligarchy"? We see the answer as depending both on how those terms are defined and on the results of future research. See Winters and Page 2009; Winters 2011.

7. Center for Responsive Politics 2017a.

8. Ornstein et al. 2017.

9. The U.S. tax "checkoff" system is moribund, providing too little money for presidential candidates to accept the cash and restrictions. As we will see, some states and localities do provide public money for their elections.

10. Bonica et al. 2013.

11. Page, Bartels, and Seawright 2013, 64. Multimillionaires polled in the Survey of Economically Successful Americans (SESA) were 58 percent Republican, 27 percent Democratic. This survey is discussed later in the text.

12. Sides et al. 2015, 371. Percentages of the 2012 presidential vote going to Obama over Romney were as follows: no high school, 64 percent; high school graduate, 51 percent; college graduate 47 percent; postgraduate, 55 percent.

13. *New York Times* 2016a, P9.

14. See T. Frank 2016.

15. In 2012, 61 percent of the citizenry agreed that officials "don't care much"; only 18 percent disagreed (Gilens 2015, 2).

16. Israel 2016. A leaked Democratic Congressional Campaign Committee "Model Daily Schedule" for incoming representatives included four hours of call time every day.

17. Lessig 2015, 19.

18. Jacobson 2013, 143–44.

DISCUSSION QUESTIONS

1. What is outside lobbying and how is it different than inside lobbying? Discuss the difference between the signaling role of outside lobbying and the conflict expansion role of outside lobbying.

2. Bartels argues that the political party that wins office influences income inequality. What evidence does he use to make that argument? Are you convinced that the different parties *cause* the different outcomes?

3. Describe the kinds of policy issues for which the truly wealthy (multimillionaires) have different preferences than the general public. How, according to Page and Gilens, do the truly wealthy get their way on policy?

12

POLITICAL PARTIES

12.1

JOHN H. ALDRICH

From *Why Parties? A Second Look*

Political parties are multifaceted organizations, and scholars have struggled to describe them and their functions in ways that make sense across eras and countries. In this important piece, Aldrich writes that, above all, parties are designed to serve the needs of ambitious politicians seeking public office. Parties have to be understood as solutions to a variety of collective dilemmas. They help government officials coordinate their actions so they can make public policy, candidates coordinate their behavior to win office, and voters overcome their collective action problems during elections.

POLITICS AND PARTIES IN AMERICA

■ ■ ■

The Political Party

■ ■ ■

My basic argument is that the major political party is the creature of the politicians, the partisan activist, and the ambitious office seeker and officeholder. They have created and maintained, used or abused, reformed or ignored the political party when doing so has furthered their goals and ambitions. The political party is thus . . . an institution shaped by these political actors.

From John H. Aldrich, *Why Parties? A Second Look* (Chicago: University of Chicago Press, 2011), Chapter 1.

Whatever its strength or weakness, whatever its form and role, it is the ambitious politicians' creation.

These politicians, we must understand from the outset, do not have partisan goals per se. Rather, they have more personal and fundamental goals, and the party is only the instrument for achieving them. Their goals are several and come in various combinations. Following Richard Fenno (1973), they include most basically the desire to have a long and successful career in political office, but they also encompass the desire to achieve policy ends and to attain power and prestige within the government. These goals are to be sought in government, not in parties, but they are goals that at times have best been realized *through* the parties. The parties are, as we will see, shaped by these goals in their various combinations, and particularly in the problems politicians most typically encounter when seeking to achieve their goals. Thus, there are three goals, three problems, and three reasons [for] why politicians often turn to the organized party in search for a sustainable way to solve these problems and thus be more likely to achieve these goals.

Ambitious politicians turn to the political party to achieve such goals only when parties are useful vehicles for solving problems that cannot be solved as effectively, if at all, through other means. Thus I believe that the political party must be understood not only in relation to the goals of the actors most consequential for parties, but also in relation to the electoral, legislative, and executive institutions of the government. Fiorina was correct: only given our institutions can we understand political parties.

The third major force shaping the political party is the historical setting. Technological changes, for instance, have made campaigning for office today vastly different than it was only a few decades ago, let alone in the nineteenth century. Such changes have had great consequences for political parties. In the nineteenth century, political parties were the only feasible means for organizing mass elections. Today's technologies allow an individual member of Congress to create a personal, continuing campaign organization, something that was simply unimaginable a century ago. But there is, of course, more to the historical context than technology.

Normative understandings have changed greatly. Even Ronald Reagan, who claimed that "government is not the solution to our problems, government *is* the problem," also held to the value of a "social safety net" provided by the government that is far larger than even the most progressive politician of the nineteenth century could have imagined. Ideas, in short, matter a great deal. Founders had to overcome antipathy verging on disgust over the very idea of political parties in order to create them in the first place, and Martin Van Buren's ideas about the nature and value of the "modern mass party" greatly shaped the nature of Jacksonian Democracy and political parties generally for more than a century. Neither Van Buren nor anyone else set out to create a system of competing mass parties (although he and others of that era recognized the importance of sustained partisan competition, they merely—but always—wanted to win that competition). But the creation of the modern mass party led quickly to the creation of the first modern mass two-party system.

History matters in yet another way, beyond the ideas, values, and technological possibilities available at any given historical moment. The path of development matters as well. Once a set of institutional arrangements is in place, the set of equilibrium possibilities is greatly reduced, and change from the existing equilibrium path to a new and possibly superior one may be difficult or impossible. In other words, once there are two major parties, their presence induces incentives for ambitious politicians to affiliate with one party or the other, and some of these incentives emerge only because of the prior existence of these two parties.

The combination of these three forces means that the fundamental syllogism for the theory of political parties to be offered here is just what Rohde and Shepsle (1978) originally offered as the basis for the rational-choice-based new institutionalism: political outcomes—here political parties—result from actors' seeking to realize their goals, choosing within and possibly shaping a given set of institutional arrangements, and so choosing within a given historical context.

▪   ▪   ▪

Previous Approaches to the Study of American Political Parties

Parties as Diverse Coalitions, Aggregating and Articulating the Interest in and of the Public

There are three basic views or understandings of major political parties in America. The first is most often associated with V. O. Key Jr. (e.g., 1964), Frank Sorauf (1964; now Hershey 2009), Samuel Eldersveld (1964, 1982), and others. The major American party, to them, is a broad and encompassing organization, a coalition of many and diverse partners, that is commonly called umbrella-like. In seeking to appeal to a majority of the public, the two parties are based on similar values, roughly defining the "American creed." McClosky (1969) said of political (which is to say partisan) elites, "The evidence suggests that it is the [political elites] rather than the public who serve as the major repositories of the public conscience and as the carriers of the Creed. Responsibility for keeping the system going, hence, falls most heavily upon them" (286). His basic finding was that such elites share most elements of this "creed."

On many policy issues, however, there are clear and sometimes sharply drawn lines between the two parties. What Benjamin I. Page (1978) referred to as "partisan cleavages" are possible, even likely. On civil rights, as on many other issues, the Democratic Party has been more liberal than the Republican Party for decades, and on New Deal economic issues even a generation longer.

▪   ▪   ▪

Each party is a coalition of many and diverse groups. This is most evident in the New Deal coalition Roosevelt forged in creating a working Democratic majority in the 1930s. It consisted of the then-solid South, cities, immigrants, blacks, ethnic and religious groups of many types, the working class and unions, and so on. Over half a century later this "coalition of minorities" has frayed considerably; some parts of it have exited from the coalition entirely, and the remnants are no longer capable of reaching majority size in presidential elections. Although some elements have left entirely or their loyalties have weakened, they have been replaced by others. For example, the Democratic coalition may no longer be home to as much of the South or as many blue-collar voters, but teachers' unions, women's groups, and organizations representing blacks, Hispanics, gays, environmentalists, and many others have been added since the 1960s to the panoply of voices seeking to be heard at their national convention. The Republican Party may once have been defined more easily by what wasn't included in the New Deal coalition, but it, too, has attracted a range of groups and interests. At Republican conventions one can find both Wall Street and Main Street fiscal conservatives, and westerners who seek to remove government interference in their lives (and lands), but also southerners who are social conservatives, the latter including pro-life groups, fundamentalist Christians, and so on, who seek active government intervention [o]n behalf of their central concerns.

Although there are good reasons [for] why these groups are allied with their particular parties, there is still great diversity within each party. There are even apparent contradictions latent—and at critical moments active—within each party. Blacks and white southerners may have found alliance comfortable when both were so deeply affected by the Great Depression, but when civil rights made it onto the national agenda in the 1950s and 1960s, the latent tensions in their respective views became active and divisive. Recent Republican conventions may have been noncontroversial, but fundamentalists and Wall Street business leaders, or other pairings, may well find that latent disagreements will become just as divisive when circumstances and the political agenda change. As of this writing, "tea party" and other conservative activists are engaging the Republican "regulars" on many such fronts.

In this view James Madison was correct. There is no small set of fixed interests; there are, rather, many and diverse interests in this extended Republic. He argued that a fundamental advantage of the new Constitution in creating a stronger federation was that the most evident and serious concern about majority rule—that a cohesive majority could tyrannize any minority—would be alleviated because there could be no cohesive majority in an extended republic. So, too, could no political party, no matter how large, rule tyrannically, because it must also be too diverse.

In a truly diverse republic, the problem is the opposite of majority tyranny. The problem is how to form *any* majority capable of taking action to solve pressing problems. A major political party aggregates these many and varied interests sufficiently to appeal to enough voters to form a majority in elections and to forge partisan-based, majority coalitions in government. In this view, parties are intermediaries that connect the public and the government. Parties also aggregate these diverse interests into a relatively cohesive, if typically compromise, platform, and they articulate these varied interests by representing them in government. The result, in this view, is that parties parlay those compromise positions into policy outcomes, and so they—a ruling, if nonhomogeneous and shifting, government majority—can be held accountable to the public in subsequent elections.

▪ ▪ ▪

The Responsible Party Thesis

. . . [T]he second view, that of responsible parties, is primarily normative and aspirational, with critique of the empirics of party politics thrown in. This thesis is most directly associated with E. E. Schattschneider (1942) and the Committee for a More Responsible Two-Party System, sponsored by the American Political Science Association, that he chaired (1950). But this view has deeper historical roots. Woodrow Wilson's *Congressional Government* (1881), for example, included a plea for parties more in the responsible party mold, and as Ranney (1975) and Epstein (1986) report, prominent political scientists at the beginning of the twentieth century were much enamored of this doctrine.

Ranney (1975, 43) lists four criteria that define responsible parties. Such parties (1) make policy commitments to the electorate, (2) are willing and able to carry them out when in office, (3) develop alternatives to government policies when out of office, and (4) differ sufficiently between themselves to "provide the electorate with a proper range of choice between alternative actions."[1] This doctrine derives from an idealized (and more closely realized) form of the British system, what Lijphart (1984, 1999) calls the "Westminster model." As a normative standard, it has several obvious defects. For example, it reduces choices for the public to exactly two. If the United States is a diverse and extended Madisonian republic, it is not obvious that the public would find its views adequately articulated by exactly two options, no matter how clear and distinct. A mélange of compromise proposals may be more suitable. Alternation of parties in office may also make policy trajectories shift dramatically back and forth. And if one party does capture a longtime working majority, majority tyranny could follow. This is a normative standard that thus places great weight on the accountability of elected officials, through their party's control of office, and less weight on interest articulation. In more practical terms, it is an idealization that fits more readily with a unified, essentially unicameral assembly that combines the legislative and executive branches and that is elected all at once. It fits more poorly with a government designed around the principles of separated but intermingled powers, with officials elected at different times from differently defined constituencies for the Madisonian purpose of making ambition check ambition.

. . . When the parties' candidates did address issues, it is often felt, they were too similar. Conservative Republicans in the 1940s and 1950s complained that the dominant, moderate wing of their party engaged in "me-too-ism"; whatever Democrats said, the moderate Republicans responded, "Me too!" Or as George Wallace, the once and future Democrat, claimed in his third-party presidential campaign in 1968, "there ain't a dime's worth of difference" between the two parties. It was not always so, responsible party advocates claimed. In other eras, parties were stronger, and they were stronger in the sense of responsible parties. At the very least they were sufficiently united in office to "be willing and able to carry out" whatever policy commitments the majority party chose. They may not have been then, and today may not truly be, responsible parties, consistent with that doctrine, but they once were stronger, more effective, and more easily held accountable. Perhaps they could become so again.

■ ■ ■

Parties and Electoral Competition

The third view of parties focuses on the importance of this competition for office. Of course both earlier views also saw electoral competition as a central characteristic of partisan politics. But this third view sees competition for office as the singular, defining characteristic of the major American political party. The most rigorous advocates of this position are Anthony Downs (1957) and Joseph A. Schlesinger (1991; see also Demsetz 1990). Both are rational choice theorists, positing that actors are goal seekers and that their actions, and eventually the institutional arrangements they help shape, are the product of their attempts to realize their goals. At the center of their theory are the partisan elites: the aspiring office seekers and the successful officeholders. Their theories rest, moreover, on a simple assumption about the goal of each such partisan elite, office seeking and holding per se. That is, party leaders are motivated to win elections. As a result a party is, in the words of Downs (1957, 25), "a team seeking to control the governing apparatus by gaining office in a duly constituted election." The political party therefore is the organization that team uses to realize its goals. Electoral victory is paramount; other motives are at most secondary. Most important, as Downs puts it, parties formulate policies to win elections rather than winning elections to promulgate policies. In a two-party system, the "health" of the system is measured by how competitive the two parties are for a wide range of elective offices over a long period. In Schlesinger's view (1991), the hallmark of a party is its ability to channel the competing career ambitions of its potential and actual officeholders, forming them into an effective electoral machine. More accurately, he argued that each office and its partisan seeker serves as one "nucleus" of a party, and a strong party is one that has many strong nuclei connected to each other for the purpose of supporting its ambitious partisan office seekers.

The genius of democracy, in this view, is rather like the genius Adam Smith found in the free market. In Smith's case, individuals acting in their own self-interest turn out to be guided, as if by some unseen hand, to act in the economic interests of the collective. In Schlesinger's case, ambitious politicians, seeking to have a long and successful career, are all led by the necessity of winning broad support in the face of stiff competition to reflect the desires of those citizens who support them. Without competition for office—without at least minimally strong political parties—career ambition is not necessarily harnessed to reflect the desires of the public. In elections, political parties serve the Madisonian principle of having ambition clash with, and thereby check, ambition. Seeking popular support in the face of competition yields officeholders who find it in their self-interest to respond to the wishes of the public so that that public will continually reelect them, thereby satisfying their career ambition. All else about parties flows from this Schumpeterian view. Office seekers will try to create a strong electoral machine for mobilizing the electorate, but only if competition forces them to do so. Thus will the party-as-organization flow from competition for office. So, too, will the party-in-government flow naturally from electoral competition—but only so long as it is in the long-term career interests of office seekers and holders to do so. Only so long, that is, as there is a shared, collective interest in working together in office, and doing so to remain in office. And that collective interest must come from a common electoral fate.

These, then, are the three major views or understandings of political parties. I will offer a fourth. . . . [I]t will be one that takes career ambitions of elective office seekers and holders as one of its central building blocks. It will differ, however, in seeing office seeking as only one of several goals held by those with political ambitions. To be sure, winning elections is an intermediary end on its way to achieving power and policy in addition to being an end in itself. Motivations for policy ends and for power and prestige in office, that is, require electoral victory. But for many, winning office per se is not the end of politics but the beginning. As we will see, this leads naturally and inevitably to drawing from the other views of parties, and it will be necessary to trace the historical . . . path of development. . . .

A Theory of Political Parties

These and other astute observers might come to very different conclusions, but they all agree that the political party is—or should be—central to the American political system. Parties are—or should be—integral parts of all political life, from structuring the reasoning and choice of the electorate, through all facets of campaigns and seemingly all facets of the government, to the very possibility of effective governance in a democracy.

▪ ▪ ▪

The "Fundamental Equation" of the New Institutionalism Applied to Parties
That parties are complex does not mean they are incomprehensible. Indeed, complexity is, if not an intentional outcome, at least an anticipated result of

those who shape the political parties. Moreover, they are so deeply woven into the fabric of American politics that they cannot be understood apart from either their own historical context and dynamics or those of the political system as a whole. Parties, that is, can be understood only in relation to the polity, to the government and its institutions, and to the historical context of the times.

The study of political parties is also necessarily a study of a major pair of political *institutions*. Indeed, the institutions that define the political party are unique, and as it happens they are unique in ways that make an institutional account especially useful. Their establishment and nature are fundamentally extralegal; they are nongovernmental political institutions. Instead of statute, their basis lies in the actions of ambitious politicians who created them and who maintain them. They are, in the parlance of the new institutionalism, *endogenous institutions*—in fact, the most highly endogenous political institutions of any substantial and sustained importance.

By endogenous I mean it was the actions of political actors that created political parties in the first place, and it is the actions of political actors that shape and alter them over time. And political actors have chosen to alter their parties dramatically at several times in our history, reformed them often, and tinkered with them constantly. Of all major political bodies in the United States, the political party is the most variable in its rules, regulations, and procedures—that is to say, in its formal organization—and in its informal methods and traditions. It is often the same actors who write the party's rules who then choose the party's outcomes, sometimes at nearly the same time and by the same method. Thus, for example, on one night, national party conventions debate, consider any proposed amendments, and then adopt their rules by a majority vote of credentialed delegates. The next night these same delegates debate, consider any proposed amendments, and then adopt their platform by majority vote, and they choose their presidential nominee by majority vote the following night.

Who, then, are these critical political actors? Many see the party-in-the-electorate as comprising major actors. To be sure, mobilizing the electorate to capture office is a central task of the political party. But America is a republican democracy. All power flows directly or indirectly from the great body of the people, to paraphrase Madison's definition. The public elects its political leaders, but it is that leadership that legislates, executes, and adjudicates policy. The parties are defined in relation to this republican democracy. Thus it is political leaders, those Schlesinger (1975) has called "office-seekers"—*those who seek and those who hold elective office*—who are the central actors in the party.

Ambitious office seekers and holders are thus the first and most important actors in the political party. A second set of important figures in party politics comprises those who hold, or have access to, critical resources that office seekers need to realize their ambitions. It is expensive to build and maintain the party and campaign organizations necessary to compete effectively in the electoral arena. Thomas Ferguson, for example, has made an extended argument for the "primary and constitutive role large investors play in American politics" (1983, 3; see also Ferguson 1986, 1989, 1991). Much of his research emphasizes this primary and constitutive role in party politics in particular, such as in partisan realignments. The study of the role of money in congressional elections has also focused in part on concentrations of such sources of funding, such as from political action committees (e.g., Sorauf 1988), which political parties have come to take advantage of (for early accounts see Herrnson 1988; Kayden and Mayhe 1985). Elections are also fought over the flow of information to the public. The electoral arm of political parties in the eighteenth century was made up of "committees of correspondence," which were primarily lines of communication among political elites and between them and potential voters, and one of the first signs of organizing of the Jeffersonian Republican Party was the hiring of a newspaper editor. . . . The press was first a partisan press, and editors and publishers from Thomas Ritchie . . . to Horace Greeley long were critical players in party politics. Today those with specialized knowledge relevant to communication, such as pollsters, media and advertising experts, and computerized fund-raising specialists, enjoy influence in party, campaign, and even government councils that greatly exceeds their mere technical expertise. . . .

In more theoretical terms, this second set of party actors include[s] those Schlesinger (1975) has called "benefit seekers," those for whom realization of their goals depends on the party's success in capturing office. Party activists shade from those powerful figures with concentrations of, or access to, large amounts of money and information, as described above, to the legions of volunteer campaign activists who ring doorbells and stuff envelopes and are, individually and collectively, critical to the first level of the party—its office seekers. All are critical because they command the resources, whether money, expertise, and information, or merely time and labor, that office seekers need to realize their ambitions. As a result, activists' motivations shape and constrain the behavior of office seekers, as their own roles are, in turn, shaped and constrained by the office seekers. . . . [T]he changed incentives of party activists have played a significant role in the fundamentally altered nature of the contemporary party, but the impact of benefit seekers will be seen scattered throughout this account.

Voters, however, are neither office seekers nor benefit seekers and thus are not a part of the political party at all, even if they identify strongly with a party and consistently support its candidates. Voters are indeed critical, but they are critical as the targets of party activities. Parties "produce" candidates, platforms, and policies. Voters "consume" by exchanging their votes for the party's product (see Popkin et al. 1976). Some voters, of course, become partisan benefit-seekers by becoming activists, whether as occasional volunteers, as sustained contributors, or even as candidates. But until they do so, they may be faithful consumers, "brand name" loyalists as it were, but they are still only the targets of partisans' efforts to sell their wares in the political marketplace.

Why, then, do politicians create and recreate the party, exploit its features, or ignore its dictates? The simple answer is that it has been in their interests to do so. That is, this is a *rational choice* account of the party, an account that presumes that rational, elective office seekers and holders use the party to achieve their ends.

I do not assume that politicians are invariably self-interested in a narrow sense. This is not a theory in which elective office seekers simply maximize their chances of election or reelection, at least not for its own sake. They may well have fundamental values and principles, and they may have preferences over policies as means to those ends. They also care about office, both for its own sake and for the opportunities to achieve other ends that election and reelection make possible. . . . Just as winning elections is a means to other ends for politicians (whether career or policy ends), so, too, is the political party a means to these other ends.

Why, then, do politicians turn to create or reform, to use or abuse, partisan institutions? The answer is that parties are designed as attempts to solve problems that current institutional arrangements do not solve and that politicians have come to believe they cannot solve. These problems fall into three general and recurring categories.

The Problem of Ambition and Elective Office Seeking

Elective office seekers, as that label says, want to win election to office. Parties regulate access to those offices. If elective office is indeed valuable, there will be more aspirants than offices, and the political party and the two-party system are means of regulating that competition and channeling those ambitions. Major party nomination is all but a necessary condition for election in America, and partisan institutions have been developed—and have been reformed and re-reformed—for regulating competition. Intrainstitutional leadership positions are also highly valued and therefore potentially competitive. There is, for example, a fairly well-institutionalized path to the office of Speaker of the House trod by Speakers from Sam Rayburn to Nancy Pelosi. It is, however, a Democratic Party institution. Elective politicians, of course, ordinarily desire election more than once. They are typically careerists who want a long and productive career in politics. Schlesinger's ambition theory (1966), developed and extended by others (see especially Rohde 1979), is precisely about this general problem. Underlying this theory, though typically not fully developed, is a problem. The problem is that if office is desirable, there will be more aspirants than there are offices to go around. When stated in rigorous form, it can be proved that in fact there is no permanent solution to this problem. And it is a problem that can adversely affect the fortunes of a party. In 1912, the Republican vote was split between William Howard Taft and Theodore Roosevelt. This split enabled Woodrow Wilson to win with 42 percent of the popular vote. Not only was Wilson the only break in Republican hegemony of the White House in this period, but in that year Democrats increased their House majority by sixty-five additional seats and captured majority control of the Senate. Thus, failure to regulate intraparty competition cost Republicans dearly.

For elective office seekers, regulating conflict over who holds those offices is clearly of major concern. It is ever present. And it is not just a problem of access to government offices but is also a problem internal to each party as soon as the party becomes an important gateway to office.

The Problem of Making Decisions for the Party and for the Polity

Once in office, partisans determine outcomes for the polity. They propose alternatives, shape the agenda, pass or reject legislation, determine how to implement what they enact, and oversee that implementation. The policy formation and execution process, that is, is highly partisan. The parties-in-government are more than mere coalitions of like-minded individuals, however; they are enduring institutions. Very few incumbents change their partisan affiliations. Most retain their partisanship throughout their careers, even though they often disagree (i.e., are not uniformly like-minded) with some of their partisan peers. When the rare incumbent does change parties, it is invariably to join the party more consonant with that switcher's policy interests. This implies that there are differences between the two parties at some fundamental and enduring level on policy positions, values, and beliefs. When incumbents do change parties, they almost invariably lament (often correctly) that they did not change their ideas or beliefs, but it was their party that changed and thus moved away from them. They were surprised by these important but occasional changes, reflecting the prevailing belief of partisan stability.

Thus, parties are institutions designed to promote the achievement of collective choices—choices on which the parties differ and choices reached by majority rule. As with access to office and ambition theory, there is a well-developed theory for this problem: social choice theory. Underlying this theory is the well-known problem that no method of choice can solve the elective officeholders' problem of combining the interests, concerns, or values of a polity that remains faithful to democratic values, as shown by the consequences flowing from Arrow's theorem (Arrow 1951). Thus, in a republican democracy politicians may turn to partisan institutions to solve the problem of collective choice. In the language of politics, parties may help achieve the goal of attaining policy majorities in the first place, as well as the often more difficult goal of maintaining such majorities. To the extent that this problem tends to reside most often in policy choices, it tends to be the problem that is confronted most often by legislative parties, although it certainly applies to electoral and organizational aspects of the parties, as well.

The Problem of Collective Action

The third problem is the most pervasive and thus the furthest-ranging in substantive content. The clearest example, however, is also the most important. To
win office, candidates need more than a party's nomination. Election requires
not only persuading members of the public to support that candidacy but also
mobilizing as many of those supporters as possible. Mobilizing is perhaps the
quintessential problem of collective action. How do candidates get supporters
to vote for them—at least in greater numbers than vote for the opposition—as
well as get them to provide the cadre of workers and contribute the resources
needed to win elections? The political party has long been the solution.

As important as wooing and mobilizing supporters are, collective action
problems arise in a wide range of circumstances facing elective office seekers. Party action invariably requires the concerted action of many partisans
to achieve collectively desirable outcomes. Jimmy Carter was the only president in the 1970s and 1980s to enjoy unified party control of government. Democrats in Congress, it might well be argued, shared an interest in achieving
policy outcomes. And yet Carter was all too often unable to get them to act in
their shared collective interests. In 1980, not only he but the Democratic congressional parties paid a heavy price for failed cooperation. The theory here,
of course, is the theory of public goods . . . and its consequence, the theory of
collective action. . . .

The Elective Office Seekers' and Holders' Interests Are to Win

Why should this crucial set of actors, the elective office seekers and officeholders, care about these three classes of problems? The short answer is that these
concerns become practical problems to politicians when they adversely affect
their chances of winning. Put differently, politicians turn to their political
party—that is, use its powers, resources, and institutional forms—when they
believe doing so increases their prospects for winning desired outcomes, and
they turn from it if it does not.

Ambition theory is about winning per se. The breakdown of orderly access
to office risks unfettered and unregulated competition. The inability of a party
to develop effective means of nomination and support for election therefore
directly influences the chances of victory for the candidates and thus for their
parties. The standard example of the problem of social choice theory, the "paradox of voting," is paradoxical precisely because all are voting to win desired
outcomes, and yet there is no majority-preferred outcome. Even if there happens to be a majority-preferred policy, the conditions under which it is truly a
stable equilibrium are extremely fragile and thus all too amenable to defeat.
In other words, majorities in Congress are hard to attain and at least as hard
to maintain. And the only reason to employ scarce campaign resources to
mobilize supporters is that such mobilization increases the odds of victory. Its
opposite, the failure to act when there are broadly shared interests—the prob-

lem of collective action—reduces the prospects of victory, whether at the ballot box or in government. Scholars may recognize these as manifestations of theoretical problems and call them "paradoxes," or "impossibility results," to emphasize their generic importance. Politicians recognize the consequences of these impossibility results by their adverse effects on their chances of winning—of securing what it is in their interests to secure.

So why have politicians so often turned to political parties for solutions to these problems? Their existence creates incentives for their use. It is, for example, incredibly difficult to win election to major office without the backing of a major party. It is only a little less certain that legislators who seek to lead a policy proposal through the congressional labyrinth will first turn to their party for assistance. But such incentives tell us only that an ongoing political institution is used when it is useful. Why form political parties in the first place? . . . A brief statement of three points will give a first look at the argument.

First, parties are institutions. This means, among other things, that they have some durability. They may be endogenous institutions, yet party reforms are meant not as short-term fixes but as alterations to last for years, even decades. Thus, for example, legislators might create a party rather than a temporary majority coalition to increase their chances of winning not just today but tomorrow and into the future. Similarly, a long and successful political career means winning office today, but it also requires winning elections throughout that career. A standing, enduring organization makes that goal more likely.

Second, American democracy chooses by plurality or majority rule. Election to office therefore requires broad-based support wherever and from whomever it can be found. So strong are the resulting incentives for a two-party system to emerge that the effect is called Duverger's Law (Duverger 1954). It is in part the need to win vast and diverse support that has led politicians to create political parties.

Third, parties may help officeholders win more, and more often, than alternatives. Consider the usual stylized model of pork barrel politics. All winners get a piece of the pork for their districts. All funded projects are paid for by tax revenues, so each district pays an equal share of the costs of each project adopted, whether or not that district receives a project. Several writers have argued that this kind of legislation leads to "universalism," that is, adoption of a "norm" that every such bill yields a project to every district and thus passes with a "universal" or unanimous coalition. Thus everyone "wins." Weingast proved the basic theorem (1979). His theorem yields the choice of the rule of universalism over the formation of a simple majority coalition, because in advance each legislator calculates the chances of any simple majority coalition's forming as equal to that of any other. As a result, expecting to win only a bit more than half the time and lose the rest of the time, all legislators prefer consistent use of the norm of universalism. But consider an alternative. Suppose some majority agree to form a more permanent coalition, to control outcomes now and into the future, and develop institutional means to encourage fealty to this agreement. If they successfully accomplish this, they will win regularly. Members of this institutionalized coalition would prefer it to universalism, since they always win a project in either case, but they get their projects at lower cost under the institutionalized majority coalition, which passes fewer projects. Thus, even in this case with no shared substantive interests at all, there are nonetheless incentives to form an enduring voting coalition—to form a political party. And those in the excluded minority have incentives to counterorganize. United, they may be more able to woo defectors to their side. If not, they can campaign to throw those rascals in the majority party out of office.

In sum, these theoretical problems affect elective office seekers and office-holders by reducing their chances of winning. Politicians therefore may turn to political parties as institutions designed to ameliorate them. In solving these theoretical problems, however, from the politicians' perspective parties are affecting who wins and loses and what is won or lost. And it is to parties that politicians often turn, because of their durability as institutionalized solutions, because of the need to orchestrate large and diverse groups of people to form winning majorities, and because often more can be won through parties. Note that this argument rests on the implicit assumption that winning and losing hang in the balance. Politicians may be expected to give up some of their personal autonomy only when they face an imminent threat of defeat without doing so or only when doing so can block opponents' ability to build the strength necessary to win.

This is, of course, the positive case for parties, for it specifies conditions under which politicians find them useful. Not all problems are best solved, perhaps even solved at all, by political parties. Other arrangements, perhaps interest groups, issue networks, or personal electoral coalitions, may be superior at different times and under different conditions (see Hansen 1991, for example). The party may even be part of the problem. In such cases, politicians turn elsewhere to seek the means to win. Thus this theory is at base a theory of ambitious politicians seeking to achieve their goals. Often they have done so through the agency of the party, but sometimes, this theory implies, they will seek to realize their goals in other ways.

The political party has regularly proved useful. The permanence of parties suggests that the appropriate question is not "When parties?" but "How much parties and how much other means?" That parties are endogenous implies that there is no single, consistent account of the political party—nor should we expect one. Instead, parties are but a (major) part of the institutional context in which current historical conditions—the problems—are set, and solutions are sought with permanence only by changing that web of institutional arrangements. Of these, the political party is by design the most malleable, and thus it is intended to change in important ways and with relatively great frequency. But it changes in ways that have, for most of American history, retained major political parties and, indeed, retained two major parties.

NOTE

1. Ranney is quoting Polsby and Wildavsky (1971, 225).

REFERENCES

APSA Committee on Political Parties. 1950. "A Report of the Committee on Political Parties." *American Political Science Review* 44 (September): i–xii, 1–99.

Arrow, Kenneth J. 1951. *Social Choice and Individual Values*. New York: Wiley.

Demsetz, Harold. 1990. "Amenity Potential, Indivisibilities, and Political Competition." In *Perspectives on Political Economy*, edited by James E. Alt and Kenneth A. Shepsle, 144–60. New York: Cambridge University Press.

Downs, Anthony. 1957. *An Economic Theory of Democracy*. New York: Harper and Row.

Duverger, Maurice. 1954. *Political Parties: Their Organization and Activities in the Modern State*. New York: Wiley.

Eldersveld, Samuel J. 1964. *Political Parties: A Behavioral Analysis*. Chicago: Rand McNally.

———. 1982. *Political Parties in American Society*. New York: Basic Books.

Epstein, Leon D. 1986. *Political Parties in the American Mold*. Madison: University of Wisconsin Press.

Fenno, Richard F. 1973. *Congressmen in Committees*. Boston: Little, Brown.

Ferguson, Thomas. 1983. "Party Realignment and American Industrial Structures: The Investment Theory of Political Parties in Historical Perspective." In *Research in Political Economy*, vol. 6, edited by Paul Zarembka, 1–82. Greenwich, CT: JAI Press.

———. 1986. "Elites and Elections, or: What Have They Done to You Lately?" In *Do Elections Matter?*, edited by Benjamin Ginsberg and Alan Stone, 164–88. Armonk, NY: Sharpe.

———. 1989. "Industrial Conflict and the Coming of the New Deal: The Triumph of Multinational Liberalism in America." In *The Rise and Fall of the New Deal Order, 1930–80*, edited by Steve Fraser and Gary Gerstle, 3–31. Princeton, NJ: Princeton University Press.

———. 1991. "An Unbearable Lightness of Being: Party and Industry in the 1988 Democratic Primary." In *Do Elections Matter?*, 2nd ed., edited by Benjamin Ginsberg and Alan Stone, 237–54. Armonk, NJ: Sharpe.

Hansen, John Mark. 1991. *Gaining Access: Congress and the Farm Lobby*. Chicago: University of Chicago Press.

Herrnson, Paul S. 1988. *Party Campaigning in the 1980s*. Cambridge, MA: Harvard University Press.

Hershey, Marjorie Randon. 2009. *Party Politics in America*. New York: Pearson Longman.

Kayden, Xandra, and Eddie Mayhe Jr. 1985. *The Party Goes On: The Persistence of the Two-Party System in the United States*. New York: Basic Books.

Key, V. O., Jr. 1964. *Politics, Parties, and Pressure Groups*. 5th ed. New York: Crowell.

Lijphart, Arend. 1984. *Democracies: Patterns of Majoritarian and Consensus Government in Twenty-One Countries*. New Haven, CT: Yale University Press.

———. 1999. *Patterns of Democracy: Government Forms and Performance in Thirty-Six Countries*. New Haven, CT: Yale University Press.

McClosky, Herbert. 1969. "Consensus and Ideology in American Politics." In *Empirical Democratic Theory*, edited by Charles F. Cnudde and Deane E. Neubauer, 268–302. Chicago: Markham. Originally published in *American Political Science Review* 58 (June 1964): 361–82.

Page, Benjamin I. 1978. *Choices and Echoes in Presidential Elections: Rational Man and Electoral Democracy.* Chicago: University of Chicago Press.

Polsby, Nelson W., and Aaron B. Wildavsky. 1971. *Presidential Elections: Strategies of American Electoral Politics.* 3rd ed. New York: Scribner.

Popkin, Samuel, John W. Gorman, Charles Phillips, and Jeffrey A. Smith. 1976. "Comment: What Have You Done for Me Lately? Toward an Investment Theory of Voting." *American Political Science Review* 70 (September): 779–805.

Ranney, Austin. 1975. *Curing the Mischiefs of Faction: Party Reform in America.* Berkeley and Los Angeles: University of California Press.

Rohde, David W. 1979. "Risk-Bearing and Progressive Ambition: The Case of the United States House of Representatives." *American Journal of Political Science* 23 (February): 1–26.

Rohde, David W., and Kenneth A. Shepsle. 1978. "Thinking about Legislative Reform." In *Legislative Reform: The Policy Impact,* edited by Leroy N. Rieselbach. Lexington, MA: Lexington Books.

Schattschneider, E. E. 1942. *Party Government.* New York: Rinehart.

Schlesinger, Joseph A. 1966. *Ambition and Politics: Political Careers in the United States.* Chicago: Rand McNally.

———. 1975. "The Primary Goals of Political Parties: A Clarification of Positive Theory." *American Political Science Review* 69 (September): 840–49.

———. 1991. *Political Parties and the Winning of Office.* Chicago: University of Chicago Press.

Sorauf, Frank J. 1964. *Party Politics in America.* Boston: Little, Brown.

———. 1988. *Money in American Elections.* Glenview, IL: Scott Foresman/Little, Brown.

Weingast, Barry R. 1979. "A Rational Choice Perspective on Congressional Norms." *American Journal of Political Science* 23 (May): 245–62.

Wilson, Woodrow. 1881. *Congressional Government: A Study in American Society.* Baltimore: Johns Hopkins University Press.

12.2

ANGUS CAMPBELL, PHILIP E. CONVERSE, WARREN E. MILLER,
AND DONALD E. STOKES

From *The American Voter: An Abridgement*

In this selection from the classic book The American Voter, *the authors depict partisanship as a deep psychological attachment to one of the two major parties, an attachment that largely determines individual voting decisions and shapes the way individuals evaluate policies and politicians. The authors demonstrate a way to measure partisanship in the population using surveys. Even though the original book was published in 1960, this conceptualization of partisanship and the method of measuring it are still widely used by scholars all over the world.*

THE IMPACT OF PARTY IDENTIFICATION

A general observation about the political behavior of Americans is that their partisan preferences show great stability between elections. . . . Often a change of candidates and a broad alteration in the nature of the issues disturb very little the relative partisanship of a set of electoral units, which suggests that great numbers of voters have party attachments that persist through time.

The fact that attachments of this sort are widely held is confirmed by survey data on individual people. In a survey interview most of our citizens freely classify themselves as Republicans or Democrats and indicate that these loyalties have persisted through a number of elections. Few factors are of greater importance for our national elections than the lasting attachment of tens of millions of Americans to one of the parties. These loyalties establish a basic division of electoral strength within which the competition of particular campaigns takes place. And they are an important factor in assuring the stability of the party system itself.

The Concept and Measurement of Party Identification

Only in the exceptional case does the sense of individual attachment to party reflect a formal membership or an active connection with a party apparatus. Nor does it simply denote a voting record, although the influence of party allegiance on electoral behavior is strong. Generally this tie is a psychological identification, which can persist without legal recognition or evidence of formal

From Angus Campbell et al., *The American Voter: An Abridgement* (New York: John Wiley & Sons, 1964).

membership and even without a consistent record of party support. Most Americans have this sense of attachment with one party or the other. And for the individual who does, the strength and direction of party identification are facts of central importance in accounting for attitude and behavior.

The importance of stable partisan loyalties has been universally recognized in electoral studies, but the manner in which they should be defined and measured has been a subject of some disagreement. In keeping with the conception of party identification as a psychological tie, these orientations have been measured in our research by asking individuals to describe their own partisan loyalties. Some studies, however, have chosen to measure stable partisan orientations in terms of an individual's past voting record or in terms of his attitude on a set of partisan issues. We have not measured party attachments in terms of the vote or the evaluation of partisan issues precisely because we are interested in exploring the *influence* of party identification on voting behavior and its immediate determinants. When an independent measure of party identification is used, it is clear that even strong party adherents at times may think and act in contradiction to their party allegiance. We could never establish the conditions under which this will occur if lasting partisan orientations were measured in terms of the behavior they are thought to affect.

Our measurement of party identification rests fundamentally on self-classification. Since 1952 we have asked repeated cross sections of the national population a sequence of questions inviting the individual to state the direction and strength of his partisan orientation.[1] The dimension presupposed by these questions appears to have psychological reality for virtually the entire electorate. The partisan self-image of all but the few individuals who disclaim any involvement in politics permits us to place each person in these samples on a continuum of partisanship extending from strongly Republican to strongly Democratic. The sequence of questions we have asked also allows us to distinguish the Independents who lean toward one of the parties from those who think of themselves as having no partisan coloration whatever.

The measure these methods yield has served our analysis of party identification in a versatile fashion. To assess both the direction and intensity of partisan attachments it can be used to array our samples across the seven categories shown in Table [1], which gives the distribution of party identification in the electorate during the years from 1952 to 1958.

In using these techniques of measurement we do not suppose that every person who describes himself as an Independent is indicating simply his lack of positive attraction to one of the parties. Some of these people undoubtedly are actually repelled by the parties or by partisanship itself and value their position as Independents. Certainly independence of party is an ideal of some currency in our society, and it seems likely that a portion of those who call themselves Independents are not merely reporting the absence of identification with one of the major parties.

Sometimes it is said that a good number of those who call themselves Independents have simply adopted a label that conceals a genuine psychological

TABLE [1]   The Distribution of Party Identification

	Oct. 1952	Sept. 1953	Oct. 1954	Apr. 1956	Oct. 1956	Nov. 1957	Oct. 1958
Strong Republicans	13%	15%	13%	14%	15%	10%	13%
Weak Republicans	14	15	14	18	14	16	16
Independent Republicans	7	6	6	6	8	6	4
Independents	5	4	7	3	9	8	8
Independent Democrats	10	8	9	6	7	7	7
Weak Democrats	25	23	25	24	23	26	24
Strong Democrats	22	22	22	19	21	21	23
Apolitical, don't know	4	7	4	10	3	6	5
Total	100%	100%	100%	100%	100%	100%	100%
Number of cases	1614	1023	1139	1731	1772	1488	1269

commitment to one party or the other. Accordingly, it is argued that a person's voting record gives a more accurate statement of his party attachment than does his own self-description. Our samples doubtless include some of these undercover partisans, and we have incorporated in our measure of party identification a means of distinguishing Independents who say they lean toward one of the parties from Independents who say they do not. We do not think that the problem of measurement presented by the concealed partisan is large. Rather it seems to us much less troublesome than the problems that follow if psychological ties to party are measured in terms of the vote.

This question can be illuminated a good deal by an examination of the consistency of party voting among those of different degrees of party identification, as is done in Table [2]. The proportion of persons consistently supporting one party varies by more than sixty percentage points between strong party identifiers and complete Independents. For the problem of the undercover partisan, the troublesome figure in Table [2] is the 16 percent of full Independents who have voted for the candidates of one party only. The importance of this figure diminishes when we remember that some of these persons have voted in very few presidential elections and could have supported one party consistently because of the way their votes fell, free of the influence of a genuine party tie.

■   ■   ■

The measurement of party identification in the period of our research shows how different a picture of partisan allegiance voting behavior and

TABLE [2] Relation of Strength of Party Identification to Partisan Regularity in Voting for President, 1956[*]

	Strong Party Identifiers	Weak Party Identifiers	Independents Leaning to Party	Independents
Voted always or mostly for same party	82%	60%	36%	16%
Voted for different parties	18	40	64	84
Total	100%	100%	100%	100%
Number of cases	546	527	189	115

[*] The question used to establish party consistency of voting was this: "Have you always voted for the same party or have you voted for different parties for President?"

self-description can give. Despite the substantial Republican majorities in the elections of 1952 and 1956, the percentages of Table [1] make clear that the Democratic Party enjoyed a three-to-two advantage in the division of party identification within the electorate in these same years. Moreover, Table [1] documents the stability of this division of party loyalty in a period whose electoral history might suggest widespread change. Except for the shifting size of the group of respondents refusing to be assigned any position on the party scale, there is not a single variation between successive distributions of party identification that could not be laid to sampling error.

The great stability of partisan loyalties is supported, too, by what we can learn from recall data about the personal history of party identification. We have asked successive samples of the electorate a series of questions permitting us to reconstruct whether an individual who accepts a party designation has experienced a prior change in his party identification. The responses give impressive evidence of the constancy of party allegiance.

The fact that nearly everyone in our samples could be placed on a unitary dimension of party identification and that the idea of prior movements on this dimension was immediately understood are themselves important findings about the nature of party support within the electorate. In view of the loose, federated structure of American parties it was not obvious in advance that people could respond to party in these undifferentiated terms. Apparently the positive and negative feelings that millions of individuals have toward the parties are the result of orientations of a diffuse and generalized character that have a common psychological meaning even though there may be a good deal of variation in the way party is perceived.

Party Identification and Political Attitude

The psychological function of party identification undoubtedly varies among individuals. Our interest here centers primarily on the role of party as a supplier of cues by which the individual may evaluate the elements of politics. The fact that most elements of national politics are far removed from the world of the common citizen forces the individual to depend on sources of information from which he may learn indirectly what he cannot know as a matter of direct experience. Moreover, the complexities of politics and government increase the importance of having relatively simple cues to evaluate what cannot be matters of personal knowledge.

In the competition of voices reaching the individual the political party is an opinion-forming agency of great importance. This is not to say that party leaders are able as a matter of deliberate technique to transmit an elaborate defense of their position to those in the electorate who identify with the party. To the contrary, some of the most striking instances of party influence occur with only the simplest kind of information reaching the party's mass support. For example, a party undoubtedly furnishes a powerful set of cues about a political leader just by nominating him for President. Merely associating the party symbol with his name encourages those identifying with the party to develop a more favorable image of his record and experience, his abilities, and his other personal attributes. Likewise, this association encourages supporters of the opposite party to take a less favorable view of these same personal qualities. Partisans in each camp may incorporate into their view of the candidates whatever detailed information they can, and the highly involved may develop an elaborate and carefully drawn portrait. But the impact of the party symbol seems to be nonetheless strong on those who absorb little of politics and whose image of the candidates is extremely diffuse.

Apparently party has a profound influence across the full range of political objects to which the individual voter responds. The strength of relationship between party identification and the dimensions of partisan attitude suggest that responses to each element of national politics are deeply affected by the individual's enduring party attachments.

▪   ▪   ▪

In the period of our studies, the influence of party identification on attitudes toward the perceived elements of politics has been far more important than the influence of these attitudes on party identification itself. We are convinced that the relationships in our data reflect primarily the role of enduring partisan commitments in shaping attitudes toward political objects. Our conviction on this point is rooted in what we know of the relative stability and priority in time of party identification and the attitudes it may affect. We know that persons who identify with one of the parties typically have held the same partisan tie for all or almost all of their adult lives. But within their experience since coming of voting age, many of the elements of politics have changed.

■   ■   ■

What is more, even the elements of politics that carry over from one election to another may be evaluated anew in later campaigns by part of the electorate. The involvement of many Americans in politics is slight enough that they may respond *de novo* to issues and personalities that have been present in earlier elections but that are salient to them only at the height of a presidential campaign. For many voters the details of the political landscape may be quite blurred until they are brought more into focus during the campaign period. The formative influence of party identification on these re-evaluations would not be essentially different from its influence on responses to newer elements of politics.

Because the influence of party identification extends through time, its workings cannot be fully disclosed by the relationships seen at a particular moment. For this reason, our statement of causal priorities is in the end an inference, but one for which the evidence is strong. If the inference is correct, the differences in attitude between those of differing partisan loyalties enlarge considerably our understanding of the configuration of forces leading to behavior.

■   ■   ■

Our hypothesis that party identification influences the voting act by influencing attitudes toward the objects to which this act relates needs to be modified for the person who has only the faintest image of these objects. If someone has little perception of the candidates, of the record of the parties, of public issues or questions of group interest, his attitudes toward these things may play a less important intervening role between party identification and the vote. Like the automobile buyer who knows nothing of cars except that he prefers a given make, the voter who knows simply that he is a Republican or Democrat responds directly to his stable allegiance without the mediating influence of perceptions he has formed of the objects he must choose between.

Party Identification and Electoral Choice

The role of general partisan orientations in molding attitudes toward the elements of politics is thus very clear. As a consequence of this role, party identification has a profound impact on behavior. . . . From the strength and direction of attitudes toward the various elements of politics we could order the individuals in our samples according to the probability of their voting Republican. That is, we could form an array extending from those most likely to vote Democratic to those most likely to vote Republican. Let us now make explicit the impact party identification has on behavior through its influence on attitude, by showing a separate array for each of five groups defined by our party identification scale. For each of the distributions shown in Figure [1] the

FIGURE [1]   Probable Direction of Vote by Party Identification Groups, 1956

◄——— Probably will vote Democratic   0.5   Probably will vote Republican ———►

Probability of Voting Republican Calculated from Evaluations of Elements of National Politics

horizontal dimension is the probability an individual will vote Republican; to the left this probability is low (that is, the likelihood the individual will vote Democratic is high), and to the right the probability that the individual will vote Republican is high. The effect of party is seen at once in the changing location of the distributions along this probability dimension as we consider successively Strong Democrats, Weak Democrats, Independents, Weak Republicans, and Strong Republicans. The moving positions of these arrays show clearly the impact of party identification on the forces governing behavior.

NOTE

1. The initial question was this: "Generally speaking, do you think of yourself as a Republican, a Democrat, an Independent, or what?" Those who classified themselves as Republicans or Democrats were also asked, "Would you call yourself a strong (Republican, Democrat) or a not very strong (Republican, Democrat)?" Those who classified themselves as Independents were asked this additional question: "Do you think of yourself as closer to the Republican or Democratic Party?" The concept itself was first discussed in George Belknap and Angus Campbell, "Political Party Identification and Attitudes toward Foreign Policy," *Public Opinion Quarterly*, XV (Winter 1952), 601–23.

12.3

MARTY COHEN, DAVID KAROL, HANS NOEL, AND JOHN ZALLER

From *The Party Decides: Presidential Nominations Before and After Reform*

In this piece, the authors challenge John Aldrich's portrayal of political parties as driven by the needs of ambitious politicians (see reading 12.1). They contend instead that American political parties are primarily driven by activists within the parties seeking certain policy goals. These activists determine which candidates will run under the party label and thus shape the policy direction of the party. Ambitious politicians seek the approval of these activists, and they need that approval before they can seek the approval of voters.

WHOSE PARTIES?

■ ■ ■

The Schwartz–Aldrich Model

In an important but unpublished essay, Schwartz (1989) imagined how a three-person legislature with no parties might structure its business. There would be a great temptation, Schwartz observed, for two legislators to gang up on the third by passing bills that help their constituents while shifting costs to constituents of the third. Schwartz called the winning coalition a "long coalition" to signify that it would form over a great many issues, always to the benefit of the same majority and the detriment of the same loser. The long coalition would be stable, because the two winning legislators would have every reason to continue cooperating over all business of mutual advantage. Voters, for their part, would be happy to reelect the two majority legislators because their interests would be well served by the long coalition. Schwartz generalized his argument to a large legislature, showing that the appeal of a "long coalition" of permanent winners would remain strong.

■ ■ ■

Schwartz's account is obviously quite spare, omitting important features of party organization in elections, local communities, and, the subject of most interest to us, presidential elections. In *Why Parties?* Aldrich builds on the Schwartz framework to fill in many of these features.

From Marty Cohen et al., *The Party Decides: Presidential Nominations Before and After Reform* (Chicago: University of Chicago Press, 2008), Chapter 2.

The most important idea in Aldrich's *Why Parties?*—the idea that comes up over and over and drives almost everything else—is that parties can be explained in terms of the benefits they provide to the ambitious politicians who form them. This is a change from Schwartz, who assumed that politicians formed parties in order to increase the flow of benefits to their districts. Aldrich thus writes that "the major political party is the creature of the politicians, the ambitious office seeker and the officeholder. They have created and maintained, used or abused, reformed or ignored the political party when doing so has furthered their goals and ambitions. The political party is thus an 'endogenous' institution—an institution shaped by these political actors" (1995, 4).

. . . Aldrich's ambitious office seekers are more than single-minded seekers of office: They also care about good public policy and about power and prestige within government. Yet, as Aldrich goes on to argue, politicians must win election before they can accomplish any of their other goals. Thus, Aldrich's parties, like those of Schumpeter, Downs, and Schlesinger, aim first of all to please voters.

What, then, are the benefits that politicians get from the parties they create? One of the most important is the reputation that parties develop with voters. Many voters pay too little attention to politics to learn what individual politicians stand for. By associating with a party that is well known, a politician wins the support of voters who know only the party. Parties also build electoral machinery that aids individual politicians. A party coalition thus attracts voter support in one election after another, providing politicians with a basis for long professional careers.

But before a party can develop a reputation with voters, its officeholders must somehow come together as a coalition. This does not happen easily. In a legislature that contains many points of view, there are likely to be many potential majorities rather than just one. Thus, one majority may favor B over A, and another majority may favor C over B, but then a third majority may favor A over C. In this way, one majority can beat another in a potentially endless cycle. Stopping cycling, even on different versions of the same bill, may take huge effort. But, as Aldrich points out, the formation of a long coalition—a group of legislators who vote together on many issues—saves legislators the "transaction costs" of creating stable majorities for each new bill and at the same time creates a partisan group that lasts long enough to acquire a reputation with voters.

A signature argument in *Why Parties?* is that parties serve the electoral needs of ambitious politicians in different ways now than in the past. Until about 1960, party organization consisted largely of patronage workers who mobilized voters for politicians in elections. (Patronage jobs are government jobs that are filled by followers of the winning party.) In the current period, patronage has largely disappeared, so parties help candidates through polling, training, fund-raising, and other electoral services. To use Aldrich's terminology, the "mass mobilization party" of the last century has given way to a contemporary party that is "in service" to politicians' needs. With the services thus provided, candidates create their own campaign organizations and follow their own political strategies, making for a candidate-centered style of party politics. But this difference does not seem fundamental: Neither the mass mobilization party nor the in-service party tries to constrain politicians or hold them to any particular policy position; both kinds of parties aim to help politicians do what prevailing theories say politicians want to do—get elected to office and stay in office.

The motives of party workers have also changed over time. Patronage workers of bygone years cared little about issues, but nowadays, party activists care greatly. In an incisive analysis, Aldrich explains why activists are more ideologically extreme than most voters and pressure politicians through the nomination process to take their extreme views. This seems a significant change: Rather than helping politicians to win election, activists constrain politicians in ways that can make election more difficult. The activists also provide helpful electoral resources, but the resources come at the cost of pressure that limits the flexibility of candidates to take the policy positions that will most please voters. Despite the pressure, however, Aldrich's argument remains that the modern party is "in service" to its officeholders, who are "the actual leaders of the party" (1995, 183).

We take the Schwartz-Aldrich model of politician-centered parties to be the most important contemporary treatment of American parties in the political science literature. It not only subsumes a vast amount of prior theorizing . . . it makes novel contributions of its own. Yet we also believe that a key feature of nearly all contemporary party theory—the central focus on the ambitious politician—is questionable. Departing from the bulk of recent theorizing, we think that a focus on group and activist demands for policy would provide a more useful starting point for theorizing about parties.

Volunteer Policy Demanders

We now commence to make that argument, beginning with an observation by Paul Allen Beck. After outlining the formal legal machinery of parties, Beck describes the role of regular party workers, as follows:

> The party organization is a grouping of people, most of them contributing their time and energy on a purely voluntary basis. Even paid professional party workers who increasingly staff the national and state offices share many of the attributes of volunteers. The statutes ignore these men and women of the party, their goals and ambitions, their interactions and relationships, the contributions they make to the organization, and the price they exact for their contributions. Yet, the activity and motivations of those men and women are closer to the real world of party politics than all the statutory paragraphs put together. (1997, 106)

A few pages later, Beck adds that "the desire to use the party as a means to achieve policy goals appears to be the major incentive attracting individuals to party work these days" (113).

We could not agree more with these observations. America has been, at least since the time of Tocqueville, a country in which citizens have flocked to voluntary civic and political institutions. Every activity that any number of people really cared about—whether social, political, religious, recreational, or self-improving—has become an object of cooperation among like-minded citizens. Some of these associations have grown into major social movements; others have remained merely local clubs. As Beck's remarks make clear, political parties are another important outlet for Americans' traditional impulse to get out and work for what they care about.

The notion that parties are, and may long have been, powered by large numbers of policy-oriented individuals does not explain why parties exist, or whether parties are organized as Traditional Party Organizations or in some other way, or what contribution activists make to parties. It is not, in short, a theory of parties. But it can be the foundation for one.

A Group-Centered Theory of Parties

The central idea in the Schwartz-Aldrich model is that officeholders form parties to organize legislative business, mobilize voters, and assure stable careers. Parties exist, in other words, because they serve the needs of the politicians who create them.

But why only politicians? What about interest groups, social movements, sectional interests, and citizen activists who are also prominent in political parties? Might these actors have needs that parties could serve? Might they wish to form parties? No one denies such groups play a big role in party politics. Yet they are absent or secondary in contemporary theorizing about party organization. The attitude seems to be that party organization can be studied separately from the political forces that underlie it. This seems mistaken. Parties are a central political institution—arguably *the* central institution—for organizing society's diverse demands and interests. The myriad political actors that care intensely about these matters do not stand idly by while politicians organize parties and choose nominees for office. To the contrary, they insert themselves into the middle of the process, trying mightily to shape every important aspect of parties and often succeeding.

Much of the energy in American politics comes from these "intense policy demanders." Examples are business and labor, slaveholders and abolitionists, feminists and religious traditionalists, greenbackers and gold bugs, farm groups, environmentalists, gun owners, civil rights workers, southern white segregationists, immigrant and ethnic organizations, and people commonly known as liberal and conservative activists. Many of the party workers described above by Beck would probably fall into this last category. Intense policy demanders agitate, organize, and work late into the night to get policies they want. Because these groups are often motivated by deep feelings of justice and moral necessity, they are not deterred by long odds.

We define intense policy demanders by three criteria. They are (1) animated by a demand or set of demands, (2) politically active on behalf of their demands, and (3) numerous enough to be influential. Formal organization is often present but not essential.

Many intense policy demanders are identifiable by social, economic, or demographic characteristics, but what is relevant for our theory is that they have the same policy demands. In some cases, intense policy demanders from the same social or demographic category make opposing demands. When this happens, we say that two (or more) groups of intense policy demanders exist. For example, most members of feminist organizations are intense policy demanders for a liberal view of women's rights. But some women do not care much about feminism, and some women actively oppose liberal feminism. In our theory, the relevant group is not "women," but "feminist women" and "traditional women." So it is with all intense policy demanders: They are defined by their demands, not their social or demographic characteristics.

Having said carefully what we mean by intense policy demanders, we now wish to provide a shorthand expression for it. The shorthand is *group*. When we use the word *group*, we will generally mean a *group of intense policy demanders, as defined by common demands*. The group may be a formally organized interest group, but also unorganized numbers of farmers, religious leaders, or ideological activists who make common demands.

Few, if any, groups of intense policy demanders are big enough to get what they want working alone. So they seek allies. But in joining party coalitions, groups do not put the good of the party ahead of their own goals. Parties are a means to an end, and the end is the group's own policy agenda. Groups cooperate in party business only insofar as cooperation serves their interests.

The most important party business is the nomination and election of office seekers *who will serve the interests of the party's intense policy demanders*. The italicized phrase marks the key difference between our theory and most other contemporary theorizing about parties. In our theory, parties—that is, the groups that constitute parties—do not care about winning for the sake of winning office. They care about the policy gains. And they make those gains not simply by the election of someone nominally affiliated with their party. They make them by the election of someone committed to the maximum feasible achievement of group goals.

In making nominations, the groups that constitute parties go beyond merely pressuring candidates to adopt positions closer to their own than most voters might prefer. They define basic party positions, decide how much electoral risk to take in pursuit of these positions, and choose which candidates to put forward under the party banner. Their purpose is to place reliable agents in government offices. Thus, intense policy demanders expect that their nominees will, if elected, provide loyal service on matters large and small. A variety of evidence indicates that they are not often disappointed in this expectation. For example, Karol (1999, 2001, 2009) shows that when groups within a party change their positions on issues, or when a new group joins a party coalition, top politicians routinely change their views to agree with the new group position. For example, when business and labor groups changed their positions on free trade around 1970, top Democratic and Republican officeholders changed with them. When social conservatives joined the Republican party in the 1980s, numerous top Republicans turned from pro-choice positions to pro-life ones. Groups did not punish this behavior as flip-flopping; they encouraged it with praise and support. In a different but related vein, Hall and Deardorff describe how special-interest lobbyists, most of whom have close relationships with a party, approach their work: "The proximate political objective of [lobbying] is not to change legislators' minds but to assist natural allies in achieving their own, coincident objectives" (2006, 69). In other words, lobbyists mainly just fill in details for goals that they and the officeholders share.

Our argument about the centrality of group demands in party politics has roots in an older tradition of theorizing by Arthur Bentley, E. E. Schattschneider, V. O. Key, and others. But it has been several decades since mainstream political science has taken seriously a group theory of parties. We therefore see value in working more fully through its logic. That done, we shall proceed to testing, as best we can, whether the modern politician-centered or the more venerable group-centered model gives a better account of how parties behave in presidential nominations.

Our development of the logic for group-centered parties takes the form of the "why parties?" analysis of Schwartz and Aldrich, except that it has a different starting point—instead of an imaginary legislature made up of politicians, we begin with an imaginary society having groups of intense policy demanders as well as politicians.

Why Groups Organize Parties

In our imaginary society, government consists of a policy dictator who is elected and serves a four-year term. Society has an abundance of ambitious politicians willing to promise whatever it takes to win this office.

Groups in our stylized society form when any large number of people wants either to change the status quo through government action or defend a status quo that is under attack. The number of intense policy demanders therefore varies across time and political circumstance. Intense policy demanders are the main source of campaign donations and campaign labor.

Voters in this society often hold strong political views but do not always attend to politics. As a result, some government actions fall into an "electoral blind spot" in which policies and their effects are invisible to voters. A degree of voter blindness is central to our analysis because it creates the possibility for politicians, or groups that may influence them, to convert public policies and resources to group purposes. If, for example, voters do not follow the details of regulatory politics, officeholders can sell regulatory policy to intense policy demanders in exchange for campaign resources. Selling policy to groups is tricky, because no one can estimate what voters will notice and punish. But exploitation of voter inattentiveness by groups of intense policy demanders is the principal reason groups become active in politics, whether in party politics or in other ways.

Having now outlined the main features of an imaginary society, let us figure out how its politics might work. We begin our analysis as the country is about to have its first election. With intense policy demanders controlling most campaign resources, the outcome will depend on whether they back a candidate. Would it make political sense to do so? Or would the intense policy demanders do better to wait to deploy their resources until the dictator has been chosen?

Let us suppose the groups decide to sit out the election. If, after the election, a group wants something, it will have to induce the dictator to go along. For policies that would make most voters better off, simple persuasion would be effective. But for policies the public doesn't favor and may even oppose, something more will be needed—the promise to donate money to the dictator's reelection. But the dictator may demand a high price, and if one group won't meet her price, she can do business with another group and adopt its policies instead. If the groups try to form an alliance against her, the dictator might refuse them all. Suppose, for example, a group wants extra trash pickups from the government trash service. The dictator might go along with the demand in exchange for campaign donations. Alternatively, the dictator might reassign trash workers to political duties that would help toward reelection. Either way, voters get less trash pickup for the taxes they pay, but probably not enough less to notice, and the dictator gets extra campaign support. The bottom line, then, is that an incumbent politician can drive hard bargains with groups that try to buy policy from her and may not sell on any terms.

Suppose, then, that one of the groups foresees this problem and decides to back someone in the initial election who will be friendly to its needs once she gets into office. With many politicians in the race and only one group offering campaign funds, the group has the upper hand and is almost sure to find a politician who will promise what it wants in exchange for campaign resources. Or better yet, the group may be able to find a politician with a proven record of working for the group or, in the group's ideal world, the politician may be an actual member of the group and hence share its values. Political scientists typically treat politicians as separate from the groups that back them for office, but the separation becomes somewhat artificial if, as groups might like to do, they choose politicians from their own group. A politician committed to group values will still value reelection, but she will be more likely to take initiatives and risks for the group than would one with a different background.

From this analysis, we infer that at least one group will decide to become active in the initial election by sponsoring—that is, nominating—a candidate for office. The advantages of being able to select the politician at the nomination stage, as [opposed to] buying her support at the postelection stage, are simply too great to pass up. But if one group becomes active, other groups will not want to stay on the sidelines while the first group picks the policy dictator. Many groups will therefore enter the electoral fray, which will create a new problem: If each group backs its own candidate, only one group will win and the rest will lose. These are bad odds.

The groups will therefore consider forming a coalition. They will consider, that is, combining forces behind a single politician who is committed to a program that gives each of the groups what it wants. If all the groups support the same candidate, they can be almost sure of winning, and they can probably do so for relatively little cost. However, the question arises: Can all the groups work together in a coalition?

This is another tricky issue. If each group wants a policy others don't care about—for example, one wants more trash pickup, another wants looser enforcement of liquor laws—cooperation is easy. The coalition just gives each group most, though perhaps not all, of what it wants. Qualification is necessary because no group can get so much that it unduly burdens other groups, and all group benefits must remain within the voters' blind spot. For example, the group getting extra trash pickup cannot get so much service that other groups don't get their trash picked up or that voters suffer a noticeable drop in service.

But conflict between groups need not be a barrier to a party coalition unless the conflict is severe. Indeed, if public resources are available to underwrite party pacts, a coalition can be the means for resolving group conflict.

From this analysis, we conclude that groups can often get more from government by funneling their resources through a party coalition to nominate and elect officeholders friendly to their interests than by buying policies one at a time from independent officeholders after they have taken office.

Having decided to unite behind a nominee, the groups must choose one. Who[m] they choose reflects who is in the coalition and who is not. Coalitions need to include enough groups to attract a majority of voters in the election, but not so many that it dilutes too much the benefits that any one group can get from being in the coalition.

A long coalition in a legislature can define itself bill by bill as it takes votes. A nominating coalition doesn't vote on individual bills, nor can it bind its nominee to any particular positions, since the nominee will be legally free to do whatever she wants once she gets into office. Hence, the parties must pick a nominee whose record or background demonstrates that the nominee can be trusted on all issues that groups in the coalition care about. In other words, the nominee must be acceptable to all members of the coalition. . . .

In our analysis, we have focused on election of a policy dictator, but our analysis would apply as well to the election of multiple officeholders. If, for example, we analyzed a case in which groups needed the support of scores of legislators as well as a president to enact policy, the efficiency gains from getting control of all these politicians at the nomination stage, when they were weak and disorganized, would be even more important than in the election of a policy dictator.

The advantage of party formation might be especially valuable to groups that sometimes come under popular attack. No group could expect an independent politician to stand up boldly for its interests when a majority is aroused against it. But if a politician has been selected to share group values, it will be individually rational for the politician to accept at least some electoral risk on behalf of the group. The problem with independent politicians is that they will jump ship in moments of danger; groups can expect greater steadfastness from politicians selected to share their values.

A final advantage of forming a party coalition, especially if no other party yet exists, is the opportunity to bias electoral procedures in favor of the group's party. We are not suggesting fraud, which is failure to follow rules, but rules that have a tilt to them. For example, if the party were strongest in cities, it might require voters to cast their ballots at urban locations. By such means, the first party to get control of government can create a permanent bias for its candidates. Even better than tilting the playing field is preventing an opposition party from forming in the first place. If only one party exists, it can quietly settle group differences internally, thereby increasing the range of policies in which voters will be blind to what groups are getting. As we argue in a later chapter, America's first party saw the opportunity for one-party politics and tried to seize it. The conditions under which party competition develops or fails to develop is an important but understudied problem in party politics (see, however, Masket, in press; Mickey 2008; Trounstine 2008).

In his original "Why Parties?" argument, Schwartz assumed that losing politicians would appeal to voters to win seats to become the majority. We make a similar assumption, except for groups. We assume, that is, that some initially inactive citizens will be directly hurt or angered by policies of the first party, become active as intense policy demanders, and form an opposition party. The result will be regular competition and rotation in office among group-dominated parties. Each party resembles one of Schwartz's long coalitions—a group of actors who vote together on a long list of issues.

It is natural to think of parties in a two-party system as majoritarian. Ours, however, are not. They want to win elections, but they do not necessarily wish to represent a majority of voters. As a by-product of their wish to govern, parties must offer a degree—perhaps a large degree—of responsiveness to popular majorities, but responsiveness to voters is not why parties exist. They exist to achieve the intense policy demands of their constituent groups. One might criticize parties for lack of deference to majority will, but their groups would not much care. Intense policy demanders nearly always believe their demands are just and that it is their duty to work for these demands whether or not most voters agree with them.

The theoretical analysis reported in this section grew out of our study of presidential nominations. We observed that party insiders seemed to control presidential nominations, but we could find no contemporary theory of party that would count their influence as party influence. Our theory of party has been created to explain why we believe it really is *party* influence.

REFERENCES

Aldrich, John H. 1995. *Why Parties? The Origin and Transformation of Political Parties in America.* Chicago: University of Chicago Press.

Beck, Paul Allen. 1997. *Party Politics in America.* 8th ed. New York: Longman.

Hall, Richard L., and Alan V. Deardorff. 2006. "Lobbying as Legislative Subsidy." *American Political Science Review* 100: 69–85.

Karol, David. 1999. "Realignment without Replacement: Issue Evolution and Ideological Change among Members of Congress." Paper given at the Midwest Political Science Association, Chicago, April 1999.

———. 2001. "How and Why Parties Change Positions on Issues: Party Policy Change as Coalition Management in American Politics." Paper given at the American Political Science Association, San Francisco, September 2001.

———. 2009. *Party Position Change in American Politics: Coalition Management.* New York: Cambridge University Press.

Mickey, Robert. 2008. *Paths Out of Dixie: The Democratization of Authoritarian Enclaves in America's Deep South, 1944–1972.* Princeton, NJ: Princeton University Press.

Schwartz, Thomas. 1989. *Why Parties?* Research memorandum, Department of Political Science, UCLA.

Trounstine, Jessica. 2008. *Political Monopolies in American Cities: The Rise and Fall of Bosses and Reformers.* Chicago: University of Chicago Press.

12.4

KEN KOLLMAN

"Who Drives the Party Bus?"

In this original essay, Kollman critiques the fundamental argument of the book
The Party Decides *in light of Donald Trump's candidacy for president as the*
Republican nominee in 2016, and his subsequent victory and behavior in office.
It is not enough, Kollman argues, to say that Trump was unusual or that some-
times unexpected things happen. The problem, he says, is that the authors of
The Party Decides *have the wrong theory of how political parties operate.*

There has been much discussion among journalists, pundits, and academics
about the book *The Party Decides*. The book, published in 2008 by Marty
Cohen, David Karol, Hans Noel, and John Zaller, four political science scholars whom I respect, made the following set of arguments: the two major political parties have at their core major funders, politicians, and party leaders who
share values and ideologies, and who steer the parties; this core group for, say,
the Republicans, has determined who wins the party's nomination as the presidential candidate. The candidate with the most endorsements among the key
party insiders has won the nomination in recent times. The party elites have
historically stacked the deck heavily in favor of establishment candidates and
have kept insurgents from gaining the nomination. The book has been widely
read as not only predicting that candidates like Donald Trump cannot win
the nomination, but also as highlighting the power of party insiders to get
their way on nominations, platforms, and the distribution of money among
party candidates.

Donald Trump's rise to become the Republican presidential candidate and
then president in 2016 directly contradicted the predictions of *The Party Decides*.
At least one of its authors gives a reasonable response. The party elites failed to
coordinate on an alternative to Trump. In response to criticism, Hans Noel
wrote in the *New York Times*, "Party leaders might have pushed aside Mr. Trump
if they'd had an easy choice among the acceptable candidates. Since they didn't,
the Trump distraction kept them from choosing anyone."[1]

When confronted with contradictory evidence for a theory, one could simply
claim that serendipity happens. Trump's rise was unexpected. Shrug the shoulders, concluding that unusual events happen. Trump's rise does not mean that
the overall theory is wrong. Perhaps if we were able to rerun the primary sea-

son many times, 95 out of 100 of those times Trump would not win the nomination, and thus never have become president. The likely event is that the favorite among party insiders would win. History throws unexpected events at us. The theory will predict better than other theories, but it will not always be correct.

The authors of *The Party Decides* probably have the right prediction most of the time—the most endorsed candidate usually wins the party's nomination for Republicans and Democrats. But the Trump nomination has exposed the real problem in their theory. The problem with *The Party Decides* is that it has the wrong theory of political parties.

Roughly two theories animate the academic study of political parties. To compare the theories, think of one as a story about a train and the other as a story about a bus. According to one view, exemplified by *The Party Decides*, the party elites structure the institutions of primary elections and caucuses and use their vast resources to determine the direction of the party. These party elites build the railroad tracks, place the train cars on the tracks, and then find the candidates to drive the trains in the direction predetermined.

The alternative view, as promulgated by political scientists Anthony Downs and John Aldrich, has political parties as more malleable and ultimately leaderless until candidates emerge. The candidates themselves, upon their choosing and their campaigning for office and ultimately governing, define what the party stands for and where it should go. The party is a bus that awaits a driver, and the candidate-driver can go in many different directions.

Another key difference between the theories is this: *The Party Decides* authors believe that the party elites, which include members of Congress, billionaire contributors, interest group leaders, and other stakeholders, can solve their internal conflicts *before* the nominating process and envision who or what kind of leader they need. Many experts on political parties believe that candidate nominating contests and campaigns are the *means* by which the various conflicting groups within parties temporarily solve their internal squabbles.

It takes an appealing candidate to bring together disparate factions within political parties. Funders and party intellectuals cannot unite parties because they create the factions that need to be brought together. Winning elections is what unites party factions.

Nixon, Reagan, Bill Clinton, George W. Bush, and Barack Obama were all successful at running for election in a manner that united their parties' factions. They found the rhetoric and policy ideas that brought success. No current theory of parties is able to predict events like the Trump surge well in advance. But a theory that places candidates at the center of decision-making better captures what actually happens in parties and gives more insight into the Trump phenomenon.

Trump, through his candidacy, proposed a way to solve the challenging contradictions within the Republican Party, and it proved surprisingly popular among primary voters and the general electorate. The party elites then played catch-up. The party ended up capturing the presidency. Sometimes parties are driven in an unpredicted direction and sometimes they win elections unexpectedly. Who drives the political parties? Candidates, not party elites.

NOTE

1. Hans Noel, "Why Can't the GOP Stop Trump?" *New York Times*, March 1, 2016. Available at http://www.nytimes.com/2016/03/01/opinion/campaign-stops/why-cant-the -gop-stop-trump.html (accessed November 3, 2016).

12.5

ERIC SCHICKLER

From *Racial Realignment: The Transformation of American Liberalism, 1932–1965*

A common argument about American partisan alignments from the 1930s until the late twentieth century is that the New Deal coalition for the Democrats—of working class whites, Southerners, liberals, and pro-regulation reformers—fell apart in the 1960s over civil rights and race. Republicans shifted to a more conservative stance on civil rights only in the 1970s as it incorporated Southern whites. Schickler challenges the historical timing of this common argument. Relying on new information about strategies of local politicians and party leaders, Schickler argues that civil rights for blacks and other minorities became a central part of grassroots politics within the Democrats in the 1930s, and that the New Deal coalition was always in flux throughout the mid- to late-twentieth century. The meaning and impact of liberalism was shifting in the direction of greater civil rights and liberties for minorities throughout the entire period, but mostly at the local level. This reshapes our understanding of how national party elites in both parties were slow to respond to political realities until the Civil Rights Movement forced them to pay attention to what was already happening locally.

Today political observers take for granted the idea that Democratic partisanship, economic liberalism, and racial liberalism cohere under a common programmatic banner, just as Republican partisanship is associated with economic conservatism and greater resistance to government programs to redress problems of racial inequality. But the emergence of these linkages is a relatively recent phenomenon. Prior to the 1930s, Republican elites provided greater (if often only tepid) support for civil rights than did their Democratic counterparts. By the mid-1960s, however, Democratic partisanship and economic liberalism were clearly identified with civil rights support and Republican conservatism had become identified with greater opposition to governmental action to redress racial inequalities.

The partisan transformation on race is often depicted as an elite-led, center-driven shift that occurred in the 1960s, breaking apart the New Deal coalition that had dominated American politics for more than a generation. By contrast, the realignment began with mass and midlevel party actors, that

From Eric Schickler, *Racial Realignment: The Transformation of American Liberalism, 1932–1965* (Princeton, NJ: Princeton University Press, 2016).

it was rooted in state and local politics rather than in Washington, DC, and that much of the important work was complete by the mid-1940s. . . .

THE CONVENTIONAL VIEW OF THE CIVIL RIGHTS REALIGNMENT

. . . [T]he conventional account treats the civil rights realignment as the disruption of one stable partisan alignment—rooted in the avoidance of racial issues—and its replacement by another alignment in which race played a defining role. The critical decisions driving this process occurred in the 1960s as national party elites grappled with the question of how to respond to pressure from civil rights activists and their opponents. The choices made at the center then reverberated throughout the political system, gradually remaking both parties at the mass and middle levels.

THE CIVIL RIGHTS REALIGNMENT: CONSTITUENCIES, LOCALLY ROOTED POLITICIANS, AND TIMING

In contrast to the conventional account, the partisan realignment on civil rights was rooted in changes in the New Deal coalition that emerged in the mid- to late 1930s, not the 1960s. Rather than realignment starting in Washington and diffusing out and down, state parties and locally oriented rank-and-file members of Congress provided a key mechanism for pro-civil rights forces—which first entered the New Deal coalition in the 1930s—to capture the Democratic Party from below. Far from spearheading the realignment, national party elites—that is, the leaders of political institutions of national scope, such as the president, top congressional leaders, and national party chairmen—feared the disruptive potential of civil rights issues for their respective partisan coalitions. As a result, these national leaders generally sought to straddle the civil rights divide and were actually among the last to move.

Constituency-Level Changes

Changes in the constituency base of the Democratic Party that took place in the 1930s set in motion the partisan realignment on race. While the New Deal's economic programs originally drew African Americans and Congress of Industrial Organizations (CIO) unions to the Democratic Party, their entry into the party coalition—and the reaction that entry provoked from southern Democrats—established important linkages between civil rights liberalism and New Deal liberalism that reverberated through the midlevels of the party and eventually forced the hand of top national leaders.

African Americans had voted Republican for decades but received little in return for their loyalty. By contrast, even as core features of the New Deal accommodated racial discrimination, Roosevelt's program offered real benefits to many northern African Americans, particularly when compared with the

Hoover administration's dismal record. Recognizing these gains, African Americans voted decisively for Roosevelt in 1936 and stuck with the president for the remainder of his term. The emergence of African Americans as a potentially important source of votes for northern Democrats gave at least some rank-and-file Democratic politicians an incentive to show concern for civil rights.[1]

While the number of northern states and congressional districts with a substantial African American population in the 1930s and early 1940s was modest, the meteoric rise of the CIO gave African Americans an important ally within the Democratic coalition. Before the formation of the CIO in 1935, the American Federation of Labor (AFL)–dominated labor movement had a poor record on civil rights. But from early on, the CIO stood out among white-led organizations in its support for civil rights. Even as rank-and-file union workers often shared in the racial prejudice that was prevalent in their communities, the union's leaders and organizers made racial equality a key facet of their program. This support was rooted both in the union's internal organizing imperatives and in its broader programmatic vision. The CIO's leaders and organizers believed that African American support was crucial for the union's prospects in industrial workplaces in which replacement workers were a constant threat. At the same time, many of these same union officials had roots in left-wing political movements committed to the idea that racial divisions undermined the class consciousness required to fight economic exploitation. These interests and beliefs led the CIO to fuse concerns about class and race, arguing that the cause of economic justice required an encompassing labor movement willing to use governmental power to tackle the mutually reinforcing problems of economic and racial inequality.

This fusion was especially important as observers on all sides quickly recognized that the CIO had developed into the central mobilization instrument outside the Democratic Party itself on behalf of liberalism. The CIO became the leading symbol—both for supporters and for opponents—of the most ambitious strands of New Deal liberalism in the United States, urging congressional Democrats and the executive branch to move to the left across a range of policies.[2] The CIO's outspoken civil rights advocacy meant that the group most associated with an expansive reading of the New Deal's goals was also associated with the civil rights cause.

These two constituency shifts provoked a furious reaction among southern Democrats, which had equally important implications for the future of New Deal liberalism. Southern Democrats had provided critical backing for the first and second New Deal.[3] But many southern politicians viewed African Americans' incorporation into both the Democratic Party and the labor movement as an existential threat to the racially oppressive "southern way of life."[4] Southern Democrats were soon the most consequential opponents of labor-sponsored expansions of the New Deal, cooperating with Republicans to push investigations and legislation that sought to undermine organized labor, and along with it, the liberal agenda more generally. Southern Democrats' fierce opposition both to the CIO and to civil rights meant that African Americans were no longer isolated claimants: their political enemies were increasingly identified as a crucial enemy of liberal advances, not just on civil rights but across a range of policy domains, including especially labor policy.

These changes gradually reshaped the meaning of New Deal liberalism. A new political alignment took shape in which the supporters of an ambitious reading of the New Deal's promise—CIO unions and African Americans, along with Jews and urban liberals more generally—found themselves opposed by southern Democrats who viewed both the CIO and African Americans as mortal threats. This alignment reached all the way down to the mass level of the parties, as economically liberal white northern Democrats were substantially more likely to back key civil rights initiatives by about 1940 than were economically conservative Republicans. The mass- and group-level developments had important implications for politicians: for Republicans to make civil rights their issue, they would have had to overcome the skepticism of their own economically conservative core partisans. For northern Democrats to skirt the issue, they would have had to ignore the views of their own core partisans— economic liberals and the growing number of African American Democrats.

Federalism and Geographical Decentralization

Northern state parties and rank-and-file members of Congress responded to these new constituency dynamics long before national party elites did.[5] Traditionally, liberals have interpreted the history of civil rights as the classic example of why one should be suspicious of states' rights and local politics. This analysis suggests that may be too hasty. While federalism and geographic representation certainly facilitated the development of the Jim Crow South, they also helped to precipitate its downfall. Locally rooted politicians played a crucial role as intermediaries between constituency-based pressures and elite decision-making arenas in the civil rights realignment.[6]

The nationally oriented party leaders who had the greatest stake in maintaining the Democrats' North-South coalition were generally slow to respond when advocates attempted to graft civil rights onto New Deal liberalism. But the independent power base of state and local parties and the election of House members through separate geographic districts channeled constituency pressure for civil rights, without requiring an immediate showdown with national party leaders. Even as many national political elites sought to avoid the civil rights issue, movement activists could appeal to rank-and-file members of Congress, mayors and other local officials, and state and local parties, each of which had its own, partly independent power base and constituency. These locally rooted politicians then contributed to civil rights activists' efforts to raise the salience of the issue.[7]

Specifically, Democratic partisanship and economic liberalism became associated with civil rights support among northern members of the House of Representatives starting in the late 1930s. By the end of World War II a substantial gap in civil rights support separated northern Democrats and economic liberals from northern Republicans and economic conservatives. Northern state Democratic parties displayed a similar pattern, adopting platforms and pursuing policies that were to the left of their GOP counterparts on civil rights by the mid-1940s, with the gap increasing gradually in the ensuing years. These mid-level party actors proved far more responsive to pressure to support civil rights than did most top national elites, who were preoccupied with holding together the increasingly precarious North-South coalition forged by Roosevelt.[8]

Federalism and the decentralized system of electing members of Congress thus provided key institutional mechanisms to facilitate the gradual incorporation of civil rights into the mainstream of the Democratic Party, undermining the implicit deal among national political leaders that had been a key foundation of the party for decades. Much like abolitionism in the 1830s–1840s and the currency issue in the 1870s–1880s, efforts by national party leaders to block a new issue ultimately failed and party lines were reshuffled.[9] Congress and state parties emerge from this case as potential vehicles for new interests to gain access; localism and geographic-based districts are often seen as bastions of conservatism, but in this case they provided institutional footholds for civil rights liberals.

Midlevel party actors also played an important role in the GOP's transformation on race. Growing southern Democratic disaffection with New Deal liberalism stirred Republican hopes of a realignment more than two decades before Barry Goldwater entered the political scene. The appeals to states' rights and limited government that became a staple of conservative Republican attacks on the New Deal in the 1930s were well suited to wooing southern Democrats worried about the threat posed by the CIO's brand of liberalism. But the moderate leaders atop the national GOP were wary of the implications of a wholesale alliance with southern conservatives. As a result, Republican presidential candidates generally sought to sidestep civil rights in the 1940s and 1950s.

Developments below the top leadership, however, gradually tilted the balance within the GOP in favor of racial conservatives during the 1940s and 1950s. Rank-and-file northern Republicans in Congress—facing little or no constituency pressure to back civil rights—drifted away from their earlier advocacy of civil rights legislation and even made common cause with southerners in fighting strong fair-employment practices legislation in the 1940s. At the state level, President Dwight Eisenhower's party-building efforts in the South—which aimed to create a suburban, moderate organization in his image—ironically created a new power base for his conservative rivals within the party. The Goldwater movement had deep roots in these earlier shifts within the party, which opened a pathway for racial conservatives to gain the upper hand and bring to fruition the long-standing conservative goal of drawing disaffected southern Democrats into the GOP.

For both Democrats and Republicans, the ability of state party organizations and rank-and-file members of Congress to adopt their own positions provided a mechanism for the parties' existing and new coalition partners and ideological allies to gain a power base at the local level in advance of capturing the national party as a whole. The leaders of social movements and their interest group allies need not first win over national party leaders in order to transform party politics. Rather, at least in the case of civil rights, a series of victories at the state level paved the way for a national realignment. The federal nature of American parties and, relatedly, the existence of important offices controlled by lower-level units thus emerge as key elements in the civil rights realignment.[10]

Timing

Rather than viewing the 1960s as the critical moment in the partisan realignment on race, much of the political work involved in bringing racial liberalism into the Democratic program was undertaken decades earlier. Efforts by the CIO, African American activists, and other urban liberals starting in the mid- to late 1930s had remade the Democratic Party, so that economic liberalism, Democratic partisanship, and support for civil rights were connected at both the mass and midlevels of the party throughout the North by the mid-1940s.

But winning over northern state parties and members of Congress was not itself sufficient to transform national alignments. A complete takeover of the national Democratic Party required overcoming the resistance not just of southern party leaders but also of the nationally oriented officials atop the party structure. With a few exceptions, top party leaders struggled mightily to tamp down the pressure to take a clear stand on civil rights. From 1944 to 1956, rank-and-file Democratic activists and convention delegates had been to the left of national leaders on civil rights, yet party elites generally succeeded in avoiding adoption of a platform or nomination of a presidential candidate that would alienate southern conservatives.

But civil rights movement activists—often acting in tandem with midlevel party actors—worked to force the issue to the top of the political agenda, eventually requiring leaders to take sides. Crucially, by the time the issue came to occupy center stage nationally, the liberals enjoyed a clear majority within the national party, while southern conservatives had become an isolated minority.

Long before Lyndon Johnson and Barry Goldwater took their opposing positions on civil rights, their parties had been remade beneath them. Below the surface a series of developments dating back to the 1930s and 1940s had transformed both parties so that the intraparty pressures in favor of an embrace of racial liberalism were much stronger on the Democratic side, while Republicans increasingly were pushed toward racial conservatism and a concomitant alliance with southern civil rights foes. African Americans and their allies in the CIO had done much of the work in bringing together New Deal liberalism and racial liberalism in the late 1930s and the 1940s. The civil rights movement of the late 1950s and the 1960s provided the catalyst to fulfill the promise of these earlier developments within the parties.

IMPLICATIONS

This reexamination of the civil rights realignment leads to a revised understanding of the New Deal coalition and of New Deal liberalism, which in turn suggests the need to revisit how we think about political parties as institutions. . . .

Splitting at the Seams: Race, Section, and the New Deal Coalition

▪   ▪   ▪

Rather than viewing the New Deal coalition as a stable equilibrium that was brought down by the disruptions of the 1960s, however, important actors within the Democratic Party were working to undermine the supposed "bargain" between northern liberals and southern racists starting in the late 1930s. Soon after the entry of the CIO and African Americans into the Democratic coalition in 1936, southern Democrats began to cooperate with Republicans to force antilabor investigations and bills onto the agenda that challenged one key pillar of the national Democratic coalition.[11] Meanwhile, northern Democrats were working to force civil rights bills onto the legislative agenda, thus threatening a second key pillar of that coalition.

In this sense, the New Deal coalition was being torn apart from within by about 1940: while most nationally oriented party leaders preferred to keep both issues off the agenda, southern members of Congress worked aggressively to exacerbate the party's split on labor policy, and northern members pushed civil rights policies that were anathema to their southern colleagues. The version of New Deal liberalism that CIO unions and other urban liberals articulated in the late 1930s—and that was incorporated into the commitments of rank-and-file northern members of Congress and state parties—was unacceptable to the southern wing of the party, and the southerners responded to this threat by seeking to weaken the same labor unions that were essential to electing northern Democrats.

Against the claim that racial liberalism was a belated 1960s addition to economic liberalism, this account suggests that New Deal liberalism—as articulated and developed by its firmest supporters starting in the late 1930s—had racially inclusive elements that ran counter to the well-documented exclusionary aspects of Roosevelt's program. The CIO and its allies fused "class" and "race" in an alignment that was forged amid the vast social and ideological turmoil of the 1930s and early 1940s. Most top party leaders resisted this fusion, but its impact nonetheless was evident in the behavior of rank-and-file members of Congress and state parties. It also was reflected in the southern shift away from the New Deal, and in conservative Republican efforts to demonstrate that their party's antistatism made it the natural home for disaffected southern Democrats. Modern liberalism and conservatism had their roots in these early battles over the future of the New Deal.[12]

The Civil Rights Realignment and Party Theory

The civil rights realignment also speaks directly to recent theories of political parties.

■   ■   ■

There is no single, overriding logic of party politics; instead, parties, like other political institutions, are historical composites shaped by multiple logics.[13] The need to nominate a single candidate for president—along with nationally oriented media coverage and fundraising—introduces an incentive for the groups associated with a party to coordinate on a common strategy and program. But at times groups with sharply opposed interests may end up in the same party coalition. Southern Democrats had been core members of the Democratic Party since its formation in the nineteenth century. The passage of the Wagner Act, which provided expansive collective bargaining rights for workers, brought labor unions into the Democratic coalition.[14] While a few prescient southerners anticipated the threat presented by early New Deal labor policies, most did not foresee the danger posed by incorporating unions into the New Deal coalition until after the rise of the CIO.[15] Southern Democrats and CIO unions entered the party for different reasons and at very different historical moments; once they became important players inside the party, each could draw on an independent institutional base to prosecute their battle for control over its future.

Once one sees that parties may at times encompass deep conflicts, privileging any single type of actor as *the* party becomes problematic.

■   ■   ■

The convergence of two initially distinct political trajectories over time thus shaped the civil rights realignment. It was a gradual process that started in the mid-1930s, gathered momentum in the 1940s as the war mobilization created a window of opportunity for civil rights activists to force fair employment laws onto the agenda, and received a final, decisive push from the reinvigorated civil rights movement of the late 1950s and the 1960s.

One needs to follow each of these trajectories—the remaking of the Democratic Party in the 1930s–1940s and the repeated efforts of grassroots movement activists to push civil rights onto the agenda—to understand the realignment's timing and meaning.

NOTES

1. David Karol, *Party Position Change in American Politics: Coalition Management* (New York: Cambridge University Press, 2009), 109–22.

2. William H. Riker, "The CIO in Politics, 1936–1946" (PhD diss., Harvard University, 1948).

3. The first New Deal featured the emergency recovery and relief legislation of 1933–34, while the second New Deal was highlighted by several landmark laws adopted in 1935: the Social Security Act, the National Labor Relations Act, the Wealth Tax Act, and the Emergency Relief Appropriation Act (which led to the Works Progress Administration). The labor, tax, and relief laws of the second New Deal became touchstones of partisan and ideological conflict and were seen as reflecting a turn away from Roosevelt's initial effort to forge an all-class alliance. See William E. Leuchtenburg, *Franklin D. Roosevelt and the New Deal, 1932–1940* (New York: Harper & Row, 1963), chaps. 4 and 7.

4. Sean Farhang and Ira Katznelson, "The Southern Imposition: Congress and Labor in the New Deal and Fair Deal," *Studies in American Political Development* 19 (2005): 1–30.

5. I define the "South" to include the eleven states of the Confederacy, along with Kentucky and Oklahoma. The remaining states are referred to as the "North."

6. See Richard P. Young and Jerome S. Burnstein, "Federalism and the Demise of Prescriptive Representation in the United States," *Studies in American Political Development* 9 (Spring 1995): 1–54, for the argument that federalism enhanced the influence of African Americans once the Great Migration created a critical mass in key northern states. See Theda Skocpol, *Protecting Soldiers and Mothers* (Cambridge, MA: Harvard University Press, 1992), for analysis of how federalism afforded groups the opportunity to mobilize at the grassroots level and through federated organizations to promote policy development in the realm of social welfare policy.

7. Urban politics often provided an entryway for African American politicians and voters into Democratic politics. See, e.g., James Q. Wilson, "Two Negro Politicians," *Midwestern Journal of Political Science* 4, 4 (1960): 346–69; Harold Gosnell, *Negro Politicians: The Rise of Negro Politics in Chicago* (Chicago: University of Chicago Press, 1967). As discussed in chapter 9, machine Democrats—newly sensitive to the increased number of African American voters in the wake of wartime migration—played a key role in the liberal triumph at the 1948 Democratic convention, when they sided with the pro–civil rights forces over the objections of national party leaders. See also Thomas Sugrue, *Sweet Land of Liberty: The Forgotten Struggle for Civil Rights in the North* (New York: Random House, 2008), 111–15.

8. The presidential ambitions characteristic of many senators give them a national orientation that cuts against the local roots emphasized here. As a result, senators constitute a mixed case: some northern Democrats downplayed civil rights in service of their national strategy (e.g., John Kennedy), while others, such as Hubert Humphrey, used civil rights advocacy as a launching pad to national prominence. Although the quantitative analysis focuses on the House, chapters 8–10 incorporate the maneuvering in both chambers.

9. The antislavery and currency cases are briefly discussed in chapter 11.

10. In countries with multiparty systems, third parties likely play a key role in bringing demands for new policies to the forefront when those policies threaten the leading parties' existing strategies. Given the institutional obstacles to third parties in the United States, it may be that federalism allows state parties to play a somewhat analogous role in providing a vehicle for new issue demands. In Canada, which had what has been called a two-and-a-half-party system for many years, the New Democratic Party (NDP) used its control of provincial governments as a showcase for health insurance reform, which contributed to eventual national-level policy innovation. (It is worth noting that Canada combines third parties *and* federalism; this combination may be especially potent as third parties are able to engage in provincial policy experimentation.) I thank Paul Pierson and Richard Valelly for suggesting this line of thinking.

11. Eric Schickler and Kathryn Pearson, "Agenda Control, Majority Party Power, and the House Committee on Rules, 1939–1952," *Legislative Studies Quarterly* 34, 4 (2009): 455–91.

12. As Farhang and Katznelson, "Southern Imposition," show, the New Deal changed in other ways as well in the late 1930s and the 1940s. The emphasis on government planning that many early New Deal advocates pushed gave way to a focus on fiscal policy in the 1940s. This turn away from planning was partly rooted in shifts in the South, though it also had roots in broader shifts in public opinion. See Eric Schickler and Devin Caughey, "Public Opinion, Organized Labor, and the Limits of New Deal Liberalism, 1936–1945," *Studies in American Political Development* 25, 2 (2011): 162–89. The move to fiscal policy did not, however, eliminate the threat posed by the CIO and African Americans' broad agenda to southern Democrats or temper southerners' eagerness to rein in the industrial labor movement.

13. Karen Orren and Stephen Skowronek, *The Search for American Political Development* (Cambridge: Cambridge University Press, 2004); Eric Schickler, *Disjointed Pluralism: Institutional Innovation and the Development of the U.S. House* (Princeton, NJ: Princeton University Press, 2001).

14. The Wagner Act is a good example of the idea that policy can "make" politics. In this case, a legislative change contributed to the growth of a new interest—industrial labor unions—that then transformed the balance of power within the Democratic Party and in American politics more generally. At the same time, the CIO's triumphs provoked a backlash in which the opponents of union power—southern Democrats and northern Republicans—coalesced to rein in organized labor. This opposition distinguishes the Wagner Act from some other landmark cases (such as Social Security) in which a policy created a self-sustaining politics. On policy feedback, see Andrea Campbell, "Policy Makes Mass Politics," *Annual Review of Political Science* 15 (2002): 333–51; see also David Plotke, "The Wagner Act, Again: Politics and Labor, 1935–1937," *Studies in American Political Development* 3 (1989): 104–56.

15. Devin Caughey, "Congress, Public Opinion, and Representation in the One-Party South, 1930s–1960s" (PhD diss., University of California, Berkeley, 2013).

DISCUSSION QUESTIONS

1. Describe the key roles that political parties play in American democracy. What "problems" do they solve, according to Aldrich?

2. Campbell, Converse, Miller, and Stokes describe how they measure party identification. What is party identification and why is it so important to understanding voting decisions?

3. Compare the Aldrich-Schwartz theory of political parties to the theory proposed by Cohen, Karol, Noel, and Zaller.

4. According to Kollman, what are the flaws in the theory of political parties proposed by Cohen, Karol, Noel, and Zaller?

5. Compare the traditional theory of the collapse of the New Deal coalition with Schickler's theory of changes in the Democratic Party. How does the *timing* of events matter in Schickler's theory?

6. Are political parties central to representative democracy? Why or why not? Would we be better off without political parties?

13

ELECTIONS

13.1

Citizens United v. Federal Election Commission (2010)

Justice Anthony Kennedy's majority opinion in this controversial Supreme Court decision establishes the key precedent that in matters of political speech, all organizations, including corporations and unions, are accorded First Amendment rights similar to those granted to individuals. Campaign finance regulations that treat corporations and unions as different from people and other kinds of organizations are at odds with the intent of the First Amendment. Thus, this decision strikes down portions of a campaign finance law that makes distinctions among the types of political organizations that can air political advertisements.

JUSTICE KENNEDY delivered the opinion of the Court.

Federal law prohibits corporations and unions from using their general treasury funds to make independent expenditures for speech defined as an "electioneering communication" or for speech expressly advocating the election or defeat of a candidate. Limits on electioneering communications were upheld in *McConnell v. Federal Election Comm'n*. The holding of *McConnell* rested to a large extent on an earlier case, *Austin v. Michigan Chamber of Commerce* (1990). *Austin* had held that political speech may be banned based on the speaker's corporate identity.

In this case we are asked to reconsider *Austin* and, in effect, *McConnell*. It has been noted that "*Austin* was a significant departure from ancient First Amendment principles," *Federal Election Comm'n v. Wisconsin Right to Life, Inc.* (2007) *(WRTL)*. We agree with that conclusion and hold that *stare decisis* does not

From *Citizens United v. Federal Election Commission*, 558 U.S. 310 (2010).

compel the continued acceptance of *Austin*. The Government may regulate corporate political speech through disclaimer and disclosure requirements, but it may not suppress that speech altogether. We turn to the case now before us.

Citizens United is a nonprofit corporation. It brought this action in the United States District Court for the District of Columbia. A three-judge court later convened to hear the cause. The resulting judgment gives rise to this appeal.

Citizens United has an annual budget of about $12 million. Most of its funds are from donations by individuals; but, in addition, it accepts a small portion of its funds from for-profit corporations.

In January 2008, Citizens United released a film entitled *Hillary: The Movie*. We refer to the film as *Hillary*. It is a 90-minute documentary about then-Senator Hillary Clinton, who was a candidate in the Democratic Party's 2008 Presidential primary elections. *Hillary* mentions Senator Clinton by name and depicts interviews with political commentators and other persons, most of them quite critical of Senator Clinton. *Hillary* was released in theaters and on DVD, but Citizens United wanted to increase distribution by making it available through video-on-demand.

Video-on-demand allows digital cable subscribers to select programming from various menus, including movies, television shows, sports, news, and music. The viewer can watch the program at any time and can elect to rewind or pause the program. In December 2007, a cable company offered, for a payment of $1.2 million, to make *Hillary* available on a video-on-demand channel called "Elections '08." Some video-on-demand services require viewers to pay a small fee to view a selected program, but here the proposal was to make *Hillary* available to viewers free of charge.

To implement the proposal, Citizens United was prepared to pay for the video-on-demand; and to promote the film, it produced two 10-second ads and one 30-second ad for *Hillary*. Each ad includes a short (and, in our view, pejorative) statement about Senator Clinton, followed by the name of the movie and the movie's Website address.

Citizens United desired to promote the video-on-demand offering by running advertisements on broadcast and cable television.

Before the Bipartisan Campaign Reform Act of 2002 (BCRA), federal law prohibited—and still does prohibit—corporations and unions from using general treasury funds to make direct contributions to candidates or independent expenditures that expressly advocate the election or defeat of a candidate, through any form of media, in connection with certain qualified federal elections.

BCRA §203 amended §441b to prohibit any "electioneering communication" as well. An electioneering communication is defined as "any broadcast, cable, or satellite communication" that "refers to a clearly identified candidate for Federal office" and is made within 30 days of a primary or 60 days of a general election. The Federal Election Commission's (FEC) regulations further define an electioneering communication as a communication that is "publicly distributed."

Corporations and unions are barred from using their general treasury funds for express advocacy or electioneering communications. They may establish, however, a "separate segregated fund" (known as a political action committee, or PAC) for these purposes. The moneys received by the segregated fund are limited to donations from stockholders and employees of the corporation or, in the case of unions, members of the union.

Citizens United wanted to make *Hillary* available through video-on-demand within 30 days of the 2008 primary elections. It feared, however, that both the film and the ads would be covered by §441b's ban on corporate-funded independent expenditures, thus subjecting the corporation to civil and criminal penalties under §437g. In December 2007, Citizens United sought declaratory and injunctive relief against the FEC. It argued that (1) §441b is unconstitutional as applied to *Hillary;* and (2) BCRA's disclaimer and disclosure requirements, BCRA §§201 and 311, are unconstitutional as applied to *Hillary* and to the three ads for the movie.

The District Court denied Citizens United's motion for a preliminary injunction. The court held that §441b was facially constitutional under *McConnell*, and that §441b was constitutional as applied to *Hillary* because it was "susceptible of no other interpretation than to inform the electorate that Senator Clinton is unfit for office, that the United States would be a dangerous place in a President Hillary Clinton world, and that viewers should vote against her." The court also rejected Citizens United's challenge to BCRA's disclaimer and disclosure requirements. It noted that "the Supreme Court has written approvingly of disclosure provisions triggered by political speech even though the speech itself was constitutionally protected under the First Amendment."

As the foregoing analysis confirms, the Court cannot resolve this case on a narrower ground without chilling political speech, speech that is central to the meaning and purpose of the First Amendment. It is not judicial restraint to accept an unsound, narrow argument just so the Court can avoid another argument with broader implications. Indeed, a court would be remiss in performing its duties were it to accept an unsound principle merely to avoid the necessity of making a broader ruling. Here, the lack of a valid basis for an alternative ruling requires full consideration of the continuing effect of the speech suppression upheld in *Austin*.

Citizens United stipulated to dismissing count 5 of its complaint, which raised a facial challenge to §441b, even though count 3 raised an as-applied challenge. The Government argues that Citizens United waived its challenge to *Austin* by dismissing count 5. We disagree.

First, even if a party could somehow waive a facial challenge while preserving an as-applied challenge, that would not prevent the Court from reconsidering *Austin* or addressing the facial validity of §441b in this case. And here, the District Court addressed Citizens United's facial challenge. In rejecting the claim, it noted that it "would have to overrule *McConnell*" for Citizens United to prevail on its facial challenge and that "[o]nly the Supreme Court may overrule its decisions." The District Court did not provide much analysis regarding the facial challenge because it could not ignore the controlling Supreme Court decisions in *Austin* or *McConnell*. Even so, the District Court did "pas[s] upon" the issue. Furthermore, the District Court's later opinion, which granted the FEC summary judgment, was "[b]ased on the reasoning of [its] prior opinion," which included the discussion of the facial challenge. After the District Court addressed the facial validity of the statute, Citizens United raised its challenge to *Austin* in this Court. In these circumstances, it is necessary to consider Citizens United's challenge to *Austin* and the facial validity of §441b's expenditure ban.

Second, throughout the litigation, Citizens United has asserted a claim that the FEC has violated its First Amendment right to free speech. All concede that this claim is properly before us. Citizens United's argument that *Austin* should be overruled is "not a new claim." Rather, it is—at most—"a new argument to support what has been [a] consistent claim: that [the FEC] did not accord [Citizens United] the rights it was obliged to provide by the First Amendment."

Third, the distinction between facial and as-applied challenges is not so well defined that it has some automatic effect or that it must always control the pleadings and disposition in every case involving a constitutional challenge. The distinction is both instructive and necessary, for it goes to the breadth of the remedy employed by the Court, not what must be pleaded in a complaint. The parties cannot enter into a stipulation that prevents the Court from considering certain remedies if those remedies are necessary to resolve a claim that has been preserved.

Citizens United has preserved its First Amendment challenge to §441b as applied to the facts of its case; and given all the circumstances, we cannot easily address that issue without assuming a premise—the permissibility of restricting corporate political speech—that is itself in doubt. As our request for supplemental briefing implied, Citizens United's claim implicates the validity of *Austin*, which in turn implicates the facial validity of §441b.

When the statute now at issue came before the Court in *McConnell*, both the majority and the dissenting opinions considered the question of its facial validity. The holding and validity of *Austin* were essential to the reasoning of the *McConnell* majority opinion, which upheld BCRA's extension of §441b. *McConnell* permitted federal felony punishment for speech by all corporations, including nonprofit ones, that speak on prohibited subjects shortly before federal elections.

The *McConnell* majority considered whether the statute was facially invalid. An as-applied challenge was brought in *Wisconsin Right to Life, Inc. v. Federal Election Comm'n*, and the Court confirmed that the challenge could be maintained. Then, in *WRTL*, the controlling opinion of the Court not only entertained an as-applied challenge but also sustained it. Three Justices noted that they would continue to maintain the position that the record in *McConnell* demonstrated the invalidity of the Act on its face. The controlling opinion in *WRTL*, which refrained from holding the statute invalid except as applied to the facts then before the Court, was a careful attempt to accept the essential elements of the Court's opinion in *McConnell*, while vindicating the First Amendment arguments made by the *WRTL* parties.

As noted above, Citizens United's narrower arguments are not sustainable under a fair reading of the statute. In the exercise of its judicial responsibility, it is necessary then for the Court to consider the facial validity of §441b. Any other course of decision would prolong the substantial, nation-wide chilling effect caused by §441b's prohibitions on corporate expenditures. Consideration of the facial validity of §441b is further supported by the following reasons.

First is the uncertainty caused by the litigating position of the Government. As discussed above, see Part II–D, *supra*, the Government suggests, as an alternative argument, that an as-applied challenge might have merit. This argument proceeds on the premise that the nonprofit corporation involved here may have received only *de minimis* donations from for-profit corporations and that some nonprofit corporations may be exempted from the operation of the statute. The Government also suggests that an as-applied challenge to §441b's ban on books may be successful, although it would defend §441b's ban as applied to almost every other form of media including pamphlets. The Government thus, by its own position, contributes to the uncertainty that §441b causes. When the Government holds out the possibility of ruling for Citizens United on a narrow ground yet refrains from adopting that position, the added uncertainty demonstrates the necessity to address the question of statutory validity.

Second, substantial time would be required to bring clarity to the application of the statutory provision on these points in order to avoid any chilling effect caused by some improper interpretation. It is well known that the public begins to concentrate on elections only in the weeks immediately before they are held. There are short timeframes in which speech can have influence. The need or relevance of the speech will often first be apparent at this stage in the campaign. The decision to speak is made in the heat of political campaigns, when speakers react to messages conveyed by others. A speaker's ability to engage in political speech that could have a chance of persuading voters is stifled if the speaker must first commence a protracted lawsuit. By the time the lawsuit concludes, the election will be over and the litigants in most cases will have neither the incentive nor, perhaps, the resources to carry on, even if they could establish that the case is not moot because the issue is "capable of repetition, yet evading review." Here, Citizens United decided to litigate its case to the end. Today, Citizens United finally learns, two years after the fact, whether it could have spoken during the 2008 Presidential primary—long after the opportunity to persuade primary voters has passed.

Third is the primary importance of speech itself to the integrity of the election process. As additional rules are created for regulating political speech, any speech arguably within their reach is chilled.

This regulatory scheme may not be a prior restraint on speech in the strict sense of that term, for prospective speakers are not compelled by law to seek an advisory opinion from the FEC before the speech takes place. As a practical matter, however, given the complexity of the regulations and the deference courts show to administrative determinations, a speaker who wants to avoid threats of criminal liability and the heavy costs of defending against FEC enforcement must ask a governmental agency for prior permission to speak. These onerous restrictions thus function as the equivalent of prior restraint by giving the FEC power analogous to licensing laws implemented in 16th- and 17th-century England, laws and governmental practices of the sort that the First Amendment was drawn to prohibit.

This is precisely what *WRTL* sought to avoid. *WRTL* said that First Amendment standards "must eschew 'the open-ended rough-and-tumble of factors,' which 'invit[es] complex argument in a trial court and a virtually inevitable appeal.'" Yet, the FEC has created a regime that allows it to select what political speech is safe for public consumption by applying ambiguous tests. If parties want to avoid litigation and the possibility of civil and criminal penalties, they must either refrain from speaking or ask the FEC to issue an advisory opinion approving of the political speech in question. This is an unprecedented governmental intervention into the realm of speech.

The ongoing chill upon speech that is beyond all doubt protected makes it necessary in this case to invoke the earlier precedents that a statute which chills speech can and must be invalidated where its facial invalidity has been demonstrated.

The First Amendment provides that "Congress shall make no law . . . abridging the freedom of speech." Laws enacted to control or suppress speech may operate at different points in the speech process.

The law before us is an outright ban, backed by criminal sanctions. Section 441b makes it a felony for all corporations—including nonprofit advocacy corporations—either to expressly advocate the election or defeat of candidates or to broadcast electioneering communications within 30 days of a primary election and 60 days of a general election. Thus, the following acts would all be felonies under §441b: The Sierra Club runs an ad, within the crucial phase of 60 days before the general election, that exhorts the public to disapprove of a Congressman who favors logging in national forests; the National Rifle Association publishes a book urging the public to vote for the challenger because the incumbent U.S. Senator supports a handgun ban; and the American Civil Liberties Union creates a Web site telling the public to vote for a Presidential candidate in light of that candidate's defense of free speech. These prohibitions are classic examples of censorship.

Section 441b is a ban on corporate speech notwithstanding the fact that a PAC created by a corporation can still speak. A PAC is a separate association from the corporation. Even if a PAC could somehow allow a corporation to speak—and it does not—the option to form PACs does not alleviate the First Amendment problems with §441b. PACs are burdensome alternatives; they are expensive to administer and subject to extensive regulations. For example, every PAC must appoint a treasurer, forward donations to the treasurer promptly, keep detailed records of the identities of the persons making donations, preserve receipts for three years, and file an organization statement and report changes to this information within 10 days.

PACs have to comply with these regulations just to speak. This might explain why fewer than 2,000 of the millions of corporations in this country have PACs.

Section 441b's prohibition on corporate independent expenditures is thus a ban on speech. As a "restriction on the amount of money a person or group can spend on political communication during a campaign," that statute "necessarily reduces the quantity of expression by restricting the number of issues discussed, the depth of their exploration, and the size of the audience reached." Were the Court to uphold these restrictions, the Government could repress speech by silencing certain voices at any of the various points in the speech process. If §441b applied to individuals, no one would believe that it is merely a time, place, or manner restriction on speech. Its purpose and effect are to silence entities whose voices the Government deems to be suspect.

Speech is an essential mechanism of democracy, for it is the means to hold officials accountable to the people. The right of citizens to inquire, to hear, to speak, and to use information to reach consensus is a precondition to enlightened self-government and a necessary means to protect it. The First Amendment "'has its fullest and most urgent application' to speech uttered during a campaign for political office."

For these reasons, political speech must prevail against laws that would suppress it, whether by design or inadvertence. Laws that burden political speech are "subject to strict scrutiny," which requires the Government to prove that the restriction "furthers a compelling interest and is narrowly tailored to achieve that interest."

Premised on mistrust of governmental power, the First Amendment stands against attempts to disfavor certain subjects or viewpoints. Prohibited, too, are restrictions distinguishing among different speakers, allowing speech by some but not others. As instruments to censor, these categories are interrelated: Speech restrictions based on the identity of the speaker are all too often simply a means to control content.

By taking the right to speak from some and giving it to others, the Government deprives the disadvantaged person or class of the right to use speech to strive to establish worth, standing, and respect for the speaker's voice. The

Government may not by these means deprive the public of the right and privilege to determine for itself what speech and speakers are worthy of consideration. The First Amendment protects speech and speaker, and the ideas that flow from each.

The Court has upheld a narrow class of speech restrictions that operate to the disadvantage of certain persons, but these rulings were based on an interest in allowing governmental entities to perform their functions. The corporate independent expenditures at issue in this case, however, would not interfere with governmental functions, so these cases are inapposite. These precedents stand only for the proposition that there are certain governmental functions that cannot operate without some restrictions on particular kinds of speech. By contrast, it is inherent in the nature of the political process that voters must be free to obtain information from diverse sources in order to determine how to cast their votes. At least before *Austin*, the Court had not allowed the exclusion of a class of speakers from the general public dialogue.

We find no basis for the proposition that, in the context of political speech, the Government may impose restrictions on certain disfavored speakers. Both history and logic lead us to this conclusion.

The Court has recognized that First Amendment protection extends to corporations. Under the rationale of these precedents, political speech does not lose First Amendment protection "simply because its source is a corporation." The Court has thus rejected the argument that political speech of corporations or other associations should be treated differently under the First Amendment simply because such associations are not "natural persons."

At least since the latter part of the 19th century, the laws of some States and of the United States imposed a ban on corporate direct contributions to candidates. Yet not until 1947 did Congress first prohibit independent expenditures by corporations and labor unions in §304 of the Labor Management Relations Act 1947. In passing this Act Congress overrode the veto of President Truman, who warned that the expenditure ban was a "dangerous intrusion on free speech."

In its defense of the corporate-speech restrictions in §441b, the Government notes the antidistortion rationale on which *Austin* and its progeny rest in part, yet it all but abandons reliance upon it. It argues instead that two other compelling interests support *Austin*'s holding that corporate expenditure restrictions are constitutional: an anticorruption interest, and a shareholder-protection interest.

The Government contends that *Austin* permits it to ban corporate expenditures for almost all forms of communication stemming from a corporation. If *Austin* were correct, the Government could prohibit a corporation from expressing political views in media beyond those presented here, such as by printing books.

Political speech is "indispensable to decision making in a democracy, and this is no less true because the speech comes from a corporation rather than an individual." This protection for speech is inconsistent with *Austin*'s antidistortion rationale. *Austin* sought to defend the antidistortion rationale as a means to prevent corporations from obtaining "an unfair advantage in the political marketplace" by using "resources amassed in the economic marketplace." But *Buckley* rejected the premise that the Government has an interest "in equalizing the relative ability of individuals and groups to influence the outcome of elections." *Buckley* was specific in stating that "the skyrocketing cost of political campaigns" could not sustain the governmental prohibition. The First Amendment's protections do not depend on the speaker's "financial ability to engage in public discussion."

The rule that political speech cannot be limited based on a speaker's wealth is a necessary consequence of the premise that the First Amendment generally prohibits the suppression of political speech based on the speaker's identity.

Either as support for its antidistortion rationale or as a further argument, the *Austin* majority undertook to distinguish wealthy individuals from corporations on the ground that "[s]tate law grants corporations special advantages—such as limited liability, perpetual life, and favorable treatment of the accumulation and distribution of assets."

Austin's antidistortion rationale would produce the dangerous, and unacceptable, consequence that Congress could ban political speech of media corporations. Media corporations are now exempt from §441b's ban on corporate expenditures. Yet media corporations accumulate wealth with the help of the corporate form, the largest media corporations have "immense aggregations of wealth," and the views expressed by media corporations often "have little or no correlation to the public's support" for those views. Thus, under the Government's reasoning, wealthy media corporations could have their voices diminished to put them on par with other media entities. There is no precedent for permitting this under the First Amendment.

Austin interferes with the "open marketplace" of ideas protected by the First Amendment. It permits the Government to ban the political speech of millions of associations of citizens. Most of these are small corporations without large amounts of wealth. This fact belies the Government's argument that the statute is justified on the ground that it prevents the "distorting effects of immense aggregations of wealth." It is not even aimed at amassed wealth.

The censorship we now confront is vast in its reach. The Government has "muffle[d]" the voices that best represent the most significant segments of the economy." By suppressing the speech of manifold corporations, both for-profit and nonprofit, the Government prevents their voices and viewpoints from reaching the public and advising voters on which persons or entities are hostile to their interests. Factions will necessarily form in our Republic, but the remedy of "destroying the liberty" of some factions is "worse than the disease."

The purpose and effect of this law is to prevent corporations, including small and nonprofit corporations, from presenting both facts and opinions to the public. When that phenomenon is coupled with §441b, the result is that smaller or nonprofit corporations cannot raise a voice to object when other corporations, including those with vast wealth, are cooperating with the Government. That cooperation may sometimes be voluntary, or it may be at the demand of a Government official who uses his or her authority, influence, and power to threaten corporations to support the Government's policies. Those kinds of interactions are often unknown and unseen. The speech that §441b forbids, though, is public, and all can judge its content and purpose. References to massive corporate treasuries should not mask the real operation of this law. Rhetoric ought not obscure reality.

Even if §441b's expenditure ban were constitutional, wealthy corporations could still lobby elected officials, although smaller corporations may not have the resources to do so. And wealthy individuals and unincorporated associations can spend unlimited amounts on independent expenditures. Yet certain disfavored associations of citizens—those that have taken on the corporate form—are penalized for engaging in the same political speech.

When Government seeks to use its full power, including the criminal law, to command where a person may get his or her information or what distrusted source he or she may not hear, it uses censorship to control thought. This is unlawful. The First Amendment confirms the freedom to think for ourselves.

What we have said also shows the invalidity of other arguments made by the Government. For the most part relinquishing the antidistortion rationale, the Government falls back on the argument that corporate political speech can be banned in order to prevent corruption or its appearance. In *Buckley*, the Court found this interest "sufficiently important" to allow limits on contributions but did not extend that reasoning to expenditure limits. When *Buckley* examined an expenditure ban, it found "that the governmental interest in preventing corruption and the appearance of corruption [was] inadequate to justify [the ban] on independent expenditures."

The *Buckley* Court, nevertheless, sustained limits on direct contributions in order to ensure against the reality or appearance of corruption. That case did not extend this rationale to independent expenditures, and the Court does not do so here.

The anticorruption interest is not sufficient to displace the speech here in question. Indeed, 26 States do not restrict independent expenditures by for-profit corporations. The Government does not claim that these expenditures have corrupted the political process in those States.

For the reasons explained above, we now conclude that independent expenditures, including those made by corporations, do not give rise to corruption or the appearance of corruption.

The Government contends further that corporate independent expenditures can be limited because of its interest in protecting dissenting shareholders from being compelled to fund corporate political speech. This asserted interest, like *Austin*'s antidistortion rationale, would allow the Government to ban the political speech even of media corporations. Assume, for example, that a shareholder of a corporation that owns a newspaper disagrees with the political views the newspaper expresses. Under the Government's view, that potential disagreement could give the Government the authority to restrict the media corporation's political speech. The First Amendment does not allow that power. There is, furthermore, little evidence of abuse that cannot be corrected by shareholders "through the procedures of corporate democracy."

Those reasons are sufficient to reject this shareholder-protection interest; and, moreover, the statute is both underinclusive and overinclusive. As to the first, if Congress had been seeking to protect dissenting shareholders, it would not have banned corporate speech in only certain media within 30 or 60 days before an election. A dissenting shareholder's interests would be implicated by speech in any media at any time. As to the second, the statute is overinclusive because it covers all corporations, including nonprofit corporations and for-profit corporations with only single shareholders. As to other corporations, the remedy is not to restrict speech but to consider and explore other regulatory mechanisms. The regulatory mechanism here, based on speech, contravenes the First Amendment.

Our precedent is to be respected unless the most convincing of reasons demonstrates that adherence to it puts us on a course that is sure error.

For the reasons above, it must be concluded that *Austin* was not well reasoned. The Government defends *Austin*, relying almost entirely on "the quid pro quo interest, the corruption interest or the shareholder interest," and not *Austin*'s expressed antidistortion rationale.

Austin is undermined by experience since its announcement. Political speech is so ingrained in our culture that speakers find ways to circumvent campaign finance laws. Our Nation's speech dynamic is changing, and informative voices should not have to circumvent onerous restrictions to exercise their First Amendment rights. Speakers have become adept at presenting citizens with sound bites, talking points, and scripted messages that dominate the 24-hour news cycle. Corporations, like individuals, do not have monolithic views. On certain topics corporations may possess valuable expertise, leaving them the best equipped to point out errors or fallacies in speech of all sorts, including the speech of candidates and elected officials.

Rapid changes in technology—and the creative dynamic inherent in the concept of free expression—counsel against upholding a law that restricts political speech in certain media or by certain speakers. Today, 30-second television ads may be the most effective way to convey a political message. Soon, however, it may be that Internet sources, such as blogs and social networking Web sites, will provide citizens with significant information about political candidates and issues. Yet, §441b would seem to ban a blog post expressly advocating the election or defeat of a candidate if that blog were created with corporate funds. The First Amendment does not permit Congress to make these categorical distinctions based on the corporate identity of the speaker and the content of the political speech.

Due consideration leads to this conclusion: *Austin* should be and now is over-ruled. We return to the principle established in *Buckley* and *Bellotti* that the Government may not suppress political speech on the basis of the speaker's corporate identity. No sufficient governmental interest justifies limits on the political speech of nonprofit or for-profit corporations.

Given our conclusion we are further required to overrule the part of *McConnell* that upheld BCRA §203's extension of §441b's restrictions on corporate independent expenditures. The *McConnell* Court relied on the antidistortion interest recognized in *Austin* to uphold a greater restriction on speech than the restriction upheld in *Austin*, and we have found this interest unconvincing and insufficient. This part of *McConnell* is now overruled.

Modern day movies, television comedies, or skits on Youtube.com might portray public officials or public policies in unflattering ways. Yet if a covered transmission during the blackout period creates the background for candidate endorsement or opposition, a felony occurs solely because a corporation, other than an exempt media corporation, has made the "purchase, payment, distribution, loan, advance, deposit, or gift of money or anything of value" in order to engage in political speech. Speech would be suppressed in the realm where its necessity is most evident: in the public dialogue preceding a real election. Governments are often hostile to speech, but under our law and our tradition it seems stranger than fiction for our Government to make this political speech a crime. Yet this is the statute's purpose and design.

Some members of the public might consider *Hillary* to be insightful and instructive; some might find it to be neither high art nor a fair discussion on how to set the Nation's course; still others simply might suspend judgment on these points but decide to think more about issues and candidates. Those choices and assessments, however, are not for the Government to make. "The First Amendment underwrites the freedom to experiment and to create in the realm of thought and speech. Citizens must be free to use new forms, and new forums, for the expression of ideas."

The judgment of the District Court is reversed with respect to the constitutionality of 2 U.S.C. §441b's restrictions on corporate independent expenditures.

It is so ordered.

13.2

Shelby County, Alabama v. Holder (2013)

A key part of the Voting Rights Act of 1965 was struck down in this 5–4 Supreme Court decision. The majority reasoned that the act singled out specific states and counties in the United States for special treatment in election administration based on 1960s data on racial discrimination. For Congress to continue to single out these same areas in the 2010s was in violation of the basic federal principles in the Constitution regarding states' equal authority to operate their own elections. This decision will likely grant states greater leeway in regulating the conduct of their elections, including requirements for voter eligibility. Critics of this decision claim that it negates the gains made in voting rights and once again gives states and counties license to discriminate against groups of voters as they had before the Voting Rights Act.

CHIEF JUSTICE ROBERTS delivered the opinion of the Court.

The Voting Rights Act of 1965 was enacted to address entrenched racial discrimination in voting, "an insidious and pervasive evil which had been perpetuated in certain parts of our country through unremitting and ingenious defiance of the Constitution." Section 2 of the Act, which bans any "standard, practice, or procedure" that "results in a denial or abridgement of the right of any citizen . . . to vote on account of race or color," applies nationwide, is permanent, and is not at issue in this case. Other sections apply only to some parts of the country. Section 4 of the Act provides the "coverage formula," defining the "covered jurisdictions" as States or political subdivisions that maintained tests or devices as prerequisites to voting, and had low voter registration or turnout, in the 1960s and early 1970s. In those covered jurisdictions, §5 of the Act provides that no change in voting procedures can take effect until approved by specified federal authorities in Washington, D.C. Such approval is known as "preclearance."

The coverage formula and preclearance requirement were initially set to expire after five years, but the Act has been reauthorized several times. In 2006, the Act was reauthorized for an additional 25 years, but the coverage formula was not changed. Coverage still turned on whether a jurisdiction had

From *Shelby County, Alabama v. Holder*, 570 U.S. ___ (2013).

a voting test in the 1960s or 1970s, and had low voter registration or turnout at that time. Shortly after the 2006 reauthorization, a Texas utility district sought to bail out from the Act's coverage and, in the alternative, challenged the Act's constitutionality. This Court resolved the challenge on statutory grounds, but expressed serious doubts about the Act's continued constitutionality. Petitioner Shelby County, in the covered jurisdiction of Alabama, sued the Attorney General in Federal District Court in Washington, D.C., seeking a declaratory judgment that §§ 4(b) and 5 are facially unconstitutional, as well as a permanent injunction against their enforcement. The District Court upheld the Act, finding that the evidence before Congress in 2006 was sufficient to justify reauthorizing §5 and continuing §4(b)'s coverage formula. The D.C. Circuit affirmed. After surveying the evidence in the record, that court accepted Congress's conclusion that §2 litigation remained inadequate in the covered jurisdictions to protect the rights of minority voters, that §5 was therefore still necessary, and that the coverage formula continued to pass constitutional muster.

The Voting Rights Act of 1965 employed extraordinary measures to address an extraordinary problem. Section 5 of the Act required States to obtain federal permission before enacting any law related to voting—a drastic departure from basic principles of federalism. And §4 of the Act applied that requirement only to some States—an equally dramatic departure from the principle that all States enjoy equal sovereignty. This was strong medicine, but Congress determined it was needed to address entrenched racial discrimination in voting, "an insidious and pervasive evil which had been perpetuated in certain parts of our country through unremitting and ingenious defiance of the Constitution." As we explained in upholding the law, "exceptional conditions can justify legislative measures not otherwise appropriate." Reflecting the unprecedented nature of these measures, they were scheduled to expire after five years. See Voting Rights Act of 1965, §4(a), 79 Stat. 438.

Nearly 50 years later, they are still in effect; indeed, they have been made more stringent, and are now scheduled to last until 2031. There is no denying, however, that the conditions that originally justified these measures no longer characterize voting in the covered jurisdictions. By 2009, "the racial gap in voter registration and turnout [was] lower in the States originally covered by §5 than it [was] nationwide." Since that time, Census Bureau data indicate that African-American voter turnout has come to exceed white voter turnout in five of the six States originally covered by §5, with a gap in the sixth State of less than one half of one percent.

At the same time, voting discrimination still exists; no one doubts that. The question is whether the Act's extraordinary measures, including its disparate treatment of the States, continue to satisfy constitutional requirements. As we put it a short time ago, "the Act imposes current burdens and must be justified by current needs."

In Northwest Austin, we stated that "the Act imposes current burdens and must be justified by current needs." 557 U.S., at 203. And we concluded that "a departure from the fundamental principle of equal sovereignty requires a showing that a statute's disparate geographic coverage is sufficiently related to the problem that it targets." Ibid. These basic principles guide our review of the question before us.

The Constitution and laws of the United States are "the supreme Law of the Land." U.S. Const., Art. VI, cl. 2. State legislation may not contravene federal law. The Federal Government does not, however, have a general right to review and veto state enactments before they go into effect. A proposal to grant such authority to "negative" state laws was considered at the Constitutional Convention, but rejected in favor of allowing state laws to take effect, subject to later challenge under the Supremacy Clause. Outside the strictures of the Supremacy Clause, States retain broad autonomy in structuring their governments and pursuing legislative objectives. Indeed, the Constitution provides that all powers not specifically granted to the Federal Government are reserved to the States or citizens. Amdt. 10. This "allocation of powers in our federal system preserves the integrity, dignity, and residual sovereignty of the States."

But the federal balance "is not just an end in itself: Rather, federalism secures to citizens the liberties that derive from the diffusion of sovereign power." Ibid. (internal quotation marks omitted). More specifically, "the Framers of the Constitution intended the States to keep for themselves, as provided in the Tenth Amendment, the power to regulate elections." Of course, the Federal Government retains significant control over federal elections. For instance, the Constitution authorizes Congress to establish the time and manner for electing Senators and Representatives. But States have "broad powers to determine the conditions under which the right of suffrage may be exercised."

Not only do States retain sovereignty under the Constitution, there is also a "fundamental principle of equal sovereignty" among the States. . . . Over a hundred years ago, this Court explained that our Nation "was and is a union of States, equal in power, dignity and authority." *Coyle v. Smith*, 221 U.S. 559, 567 (1911). Indeed, "the constitutional equality of the States is essential to the harmonious operation of the scheme upon which the Republic was organized."

The Voting Rights Act sharply departs from these basic principles. It suspends "all changes to state election law—however innocuous—until they have been precleared by federal authorities in Washington, D.C." States must beseech the Federal Government for permission to implement laws that they would otherwise have the right to enact and execute on their own, subject of course to any injunction in a §2 action. The Attorney General has 60 days to object to a preclearance request, longer if he requests more information. If a State seeks preclearance from a three-judge court, the process can take years.

And despite the tradition of equal sovereignty, the Act applies to only nine States (and several additional counties). While one State waits months or years and expends funds to implement a validly enacted law, its neighbor can typically put the same law into effect immediately, through the normal legislative process. Even if a noncovered jurisdiction is sued, there are important differences between those proceedings and preclearance proceedings; the preclearance proceeding "not only switches the burden of proof to the supplicant jurisdiction, but also applies substantive standards quite different from those governing the rest of the nation." All this explains why, when we first upheld the Act in 1966, we described it as "stringent" and "potent."

We recognized that it "may have been an uncommon exercise of congressional power," but concluded that "legislative measures not otherwise appropriate" could be justified by "exceptional conditions." We have since noted that the Act "authorizes federal intrusion into sensitive areas of state and local policymaking," and represents an "extraordinary departure from the traditional course of relations between the States and the Federal Government." As we reiterated in Northwest Austin, the Act constitutes "extraordinary legislation otherwise unfamiliar to our federal system."

In 1966, we found these departures from the basic features of our system of government justified. The "blight of racial discrimination in voting" had "infected the electoral process in parts of our country for nearly a century." Several States had enacted a variety of requirements and tests "specifically designed to prevent" African-Americans from voting. Case-by-case litigation had proved inadequate to prevent such racial discrimination in voting, in part because States "merely switched to discriminatory devices not covered by the federal decrees," "enacted difficult new tests," or simply "defied and evaded court orders." Shortly before enactment of the Voting Rights Act, only 19.4 percent of African-Americans of voting age were registered to vote in Alabama, only 31.8 percent in Louisiana, and only 6.4 percent in Mississippi. Id., at 313. Those figures were roughly 50 percentage points or more below the figures for whites. Ibid. In short, we concluded that "[u]nder the compulsion of these unique circumstances, Congress responded in a permissibly decisive manner." We also noted then and have emphasized since that this extraordinary legislation was intended to be temporary, set to expire after five years. At the time, the coverage formula—the means of linking the exercise of the unprecedented authority with the problem that warranted it—made sense. We therefore concluded that "the coverage formula [was] rational in both practice and theory." It accurately reflected those jurisdictions uniquely characterized by voting discrimination "on a pervasive scale," linking coverage to the devices used to effectuate discrimination and to the resulting disenfranchisement. The formula ensured that the "stringent remedies [were] aimed at areas where voting discrimination ha[d] been most flagrant."

Nearly 50 years later, things have changed dramatically. Shelby County contends that the preclearance requirement, even without regard to its disparate coverage, is now unconstitutional. Its arguments have a good deal of force. In the covered jurisdictions, "[v]oter turnout and registration rates now approach parity. Blatantly discriminatory evasions of federal decrees are rare. And minority candidates hold office at unprecedented levels." The tests and devices that blocked access to the ballot have been forbidden nationwide for over 40 years. Those conclusions are not ours alone. Congress said the same when it reauthorized the Act in 2006, writing that "[s]ignificant progress has been made in eliminating first generation barriers experienced by minority voters, including increased numbers of registered minority voters, minority voter turnout, and minority representation in Congress, State legislatures, and local elected offices." The House Report elaborated that "the number of African-Americans who are registered and who turn out to cast ballots has increased significantly over the last 40 years, particularly since 1982," and noted that "[i]n some circumstances, minorities register to vote and cast ballots at levels that surpass those of white voters." H.R. Rep. No. 109–478, p. 12 (2006). That Report also explained that there have been "significant increases in the number of African-Americans serving in elected offices"; more specifically, there has been approximately a 1,000 percent increase since 1965 in the number of African-American elected officials in the six States originally covered by the Voting Rights Act.

The 2004 figures come from the Census Bureau. Census Bureau data from the most recent election indicate that African-American voter turnout exceeded white voter turnout in five of the six States originally covered by §5, with a gap in the sixth State of less than one half of one percent. The preclearance statistics are also illuminating. In the first decade after enactment of §5, the Attorney General objected to 14.2 percent of proposed voting changes. In the last decade before reenactment, the Attorney General objected to a mere 0.16 percent.

There is no doubt that these improvements are in large part because of the Voting Rights Act. The Act has proved immensely successful at redressing racial discrimination and integrating the voting process.

When upholding the constitutionality of the coverage formula in 1966, we concluded that it was "rational in both practice and theory." The formula looked to cause (discriminatory tests) and effect (low voter registration and turnout), and tailored the remedy (preclearance) to those jurisdictions exhibiting both. By 2009, however, we concluded that the "coverage formula raise[d] serious constitutional questions."

As we explained, a statute's "current burdens" must be justified by "current needs," and any "disparate geographic coverage" must be "sufficiently related to the problem that it targets." Id., at 203. The coverage formula met that test in 1965, but no longer does so. Coverage today is based on decades-old data and eradicated practices. The formula captures States by reference to literacy tests and low voter registration and turnout in the 1960s and early 1970s. But such tests have been banned nationwide for over 40 years. And voter registration and turnout numbers in the covered States have risen dramatically in the years since. Racial disparity in those numbers was compelling evidence justifying the preclearance remedy and the coverage formula. There is no longer such a disparity. [H]istory did not end in 1965. By the time the Act was reauthorized in 2006, there had been 40 more years of it. In assessing the "current need" for a preclearance system that treats States differently from one another today, that history cannot be ignored. During that time, largely because of the Voting Rights Act, voting tests were abolished, disparities in voter registration and turnout due to race were erased, and African-Americans attained political office in record numbers. And yet the coverage formula that Congress reauthorized in 2006 ignores these developments, keeping the focus on decades-old data relevant to decades-old problems, rather than current data reflecting current needs.

The Fifteenth Amendment commands that the right to vote shall not be denied or abridged on account of race or color, and it gives Congress the power to enforce that command. The Amendment is not designed to punish for the past; its purpose is to ensure a better future. See *Rice v. Cayetano*, 528 U.S. 495, 512 (2000). ("Consistent with the design of the Constitution, the [Fifteenth] Amendment is cast in fundamental terms, terms transcending the particular controversy, which was the immediate impetus for its enactment.") To serve that purpose, Congress—if it is to divide the States—must identify those jurisdictions to be singled out on a basis that makes sense in light of current conditions. It cannot rely simply on the past. We made that clear in Northwest Austin, and we make it clear again today.

There is no valid reason to insulate the coverage formula from review merely because it was previously enacted 40 years ago. If Congress had started from scratch in 2006, it plainly could not have enacted the present coverage formula. It would have been irrational for Congress to distinguish between States in such a fundamental way based on 40-year-old data, when today's statistics tell an entirely different story. And it would have been irrational to base coverage on the use of voting tests 40 years ago, when such tests have been illegal since that time. But that is exactly what Congress has done.

Striking down an Act of Congress "is the gravest and most delicate duty that this Court is called on to perform." We do not do so lightly. That is why, in 2009, we took care to avoid ruling on the constitutionality of the Voting Rights Act when asked to do so, and instead resolved the case then before us on statutory grounds. But in issuing that decision, we expressed our broader concerns about the constitutionality of the Act. Congress could have updated the coverage formula at that time, but did not do so. Its failure to act leaves us today with no choice but to declare §4(b) unconstitutional. The formula in that section can no longer be used as a basis for subjecting jurisdictions to preclearance.

Our decision in no way affects the permanent, nationwide ban on racial discrimination in voting found in §2. We issue no holding on §5 itself, only on the coverage formula. Congress may draft another formula based on current conditions. Such a formula is an initial prerequisite to a determination that exceptional conditions still exist justifying such an "extraordinary departure from the traditional course of relations between the States and the Federal Government." Our country has changed, and while any racial discrimination in voting is too much, Congress must ensure that the legislation it passes to remedy that problem speaks to current conditions.

The judgment of the Court of Appeals is reversed.

It is so ordered.

13.3

RICHARD L. FOX AND JENNIFER L. LAWLESS

From "Gendered Perceptions and Political Candidacies: A Central Barrier to Women's Equality in Electoral Politics"

Using data from a survey of more than 2,000 people who were considered potential political candidates, Fox and Lawless provide evidence that shows that men's and women's self-perceptions differ in ways that matter a great deal in terms of political ambition. Men and women largely agree on the traits required to be successful in electoral politics, but women systematically believe that they themselves have fewer of those traits than men believe themselves to have. These differences go a long way toward explaining the persistence of a large gender disparity among elected politicians in the United States.

As of the 1970s, women occupied almost no major elective positions in U.S. political institutions. Ella Grasso, a Democrat from Connecticut, and Dixie Lee Ray, a Democrat from Washington, served as the only two women elected governor throughout the decade. Not until 1978 did Kansas Republican Nancy Kassebaum become the first woman elected to the Senate in her own right. By 1979, women comprised fewer than 5% of the seats in the U.S. House of Representatives, and only about 10% of state legislative positions across the country.

Although women's numeric representation is not quite as grave today, a striking gender imbalance persists. When the 111th Congress convened in January 2009, 83% of its members were men. Men occupy the governor's mansion in 44 of the 50 states, and they run City Hall in 93 of the 100 largest cities across the country. At least as important as women's continued underrepresentation in U.S. politics is evidence that points to stagnation in the numbers of women holding state and federal office. Since 2000, the number of women elected to state legislatures, which act as key launching pads to higher office, has reached a plateau. More Republican women won election to state assemblies in 1989 than in 2009. And even though the U.S. House of Representatives continues to experience incremental gains in female members, more women filed to run for Congress in 1992 than have ever since.

From Richard L. Fox and Jennifer L. Lawless, "Gendered Perceptions and Political Candidacies: A Central Barrier to Women's Equality in Electoral Politics," *American Journal of Political Science* 55, no. 1 (2011): 59–73.

Beginning in the 1970s, an academic subfield emerged to address women's political participation and representation. In particular, scholars began to offer a series of explanations for women's slow ascension into electoral politics. Much of the earliest research identified overt discrimination by voters and electoral gatekeepers as a critical impediment for women candidates (Diamond 1977; Githens and Prestage 1977; Rule 1981; Welch 1978). Other investigators pointed to "situational" factors as a prime explanation for the dearth of women in politics. Because women tended not to work in the fields of law and business—fields from which most congressional and state legislative candidates emerge—they often lacked the objective qualifications and economic autonomy to pursue elective office (Welch 1977). Political scientists also focused on structural barriers, most notably the incumbency advantage, which inhibited electoral opportunities for previously excluded groups such as women (Studlar and Welch 1990; Welch and Karnig 1979). Finally, scholars posited a broad socialization explanation for women's underrepresentation. Often reinforcing situational and structural obstacles, a culture of traditional gender role expectations hindered women's candidate emergence. Because women and men were expected to conform to traditional sex roles—women as the primary caretaker of the family and men as the public-oriented breadwinner—the notion of even well-situated women serving in positions of political power was anathema (Fowlkes, Perkins, and Tolleson Rinehart 1979; see also Jennings and Farah 1981).

Scholars in the women and politics subfield today continue to tackle the issue of women's underrepresentation. Indeed, since the 1970s, we have developed a much fuller understanding of the factors that impede women's election to public office. In the contemporary electoral environment, for instance, the explanatory power of overt discrimination has been largely discarded (e.g., Fox 2006; Lawless and Pearson 2008; Seltzer, Newman, and Leighton 1997).[1] Situational factors have also lost some of their strength in accounting for the low number of women in politics: women have substantially increased their presence in the pipeline professions that lead to political careers (American Bar Association 2006; Catalyst 2008). Even the power of institutional inertia has been called into question. Certainly, incumbency continues to pose a serious obstacle, particularly at the federal level (Palmer and Simon 2006). But 21 states enacted state legislative term limits throughout the 1990s, and scholars uncovered no evidence that combating incumbency with term limits improved women's representation (Kousser 2005). Thus, although structural barriers, situational factors, and, to a lesser degree, discrimination undoubtedly contribute to gender disparities in U.S. political institutions, the story is far more complicated.

As women's numeric representation continues to lag, despite their gains in educational and professional spheres, it is imperative to return to the one explanation that continues—at least in part—to elude us. We argue that one of the most fundamental barriers to women's representation derives from the patterns of traditional gender socialization to which scholars have long referred but have been limited in studying empirically. Scholars suggest that women's historical exclusion from the political sphere, coupled with tenacious traditional gender role expectations, foster a masculinized ethos in electoral politics (e.g., Carroll 1994; Enloe 2004). Flammang (1997) argues, for instance, that men's dominance in political institutions that traditionally resisted women's inclusion makes it difficult for women to embrace themselves as politicians. Further, whereas men are taught to be confident, assertive, and self-promoting, cultural attitudes toward women as political leaders continue to leave an imprint suggesting to women—if even only subtly—that it is often inappropriate or undesirable to possess these characteristics. A political consequence of these patterns of gender socialization is that, over time, men develop a greater sense of efficacy as candidates. As Thomas posits, traditional socialization results in women's "lower levels of confidence about becoming candidates for political office" (2005, 12). Even women who are well positioned to offer themselves for public office often cannot envision themselves as candidates.

The theoretical connection between women and men's perceived efficacy as candidates and prospects for gender equality and parity in politics, therefore, is well established. And the implications of women's lower self-evaluations are far-reaching. As long as women are more likely than men to express doubts about their ability to run for office, then gender parity in politics will never materialize. Moreover, the degree of comfort and freedom women articulate regarding their entry into electoral politics serves as an important barometer of their full integration into all aspects of political life in the United States. Yet virtually no research systematically examines the ways that traditional gender socialization affects women and men's perceptions of themselves as candidates. In our previous work, which focuses explicitly on gender differences in the decision to run for office, we find that "the most potent explanation" for the gender gap in political ambition is that women are less likely than men to view themselves as "qualified" to enter the electoral arena (Lawless and Fox 2010). But we acknowledge that we can do little more than establish this important "qualifications gap." We can pinpoint neither the specific factors on which women and men rely, nor the calculus they employ, to arrive at their sense of efficacy as candidates. Moreover, we cannot examine the extent to which gendered perceptions, as opposed to concrete differences in women and men's politically relevant credentials, experiences, and proximity to the political sphere, drive gender differences in self-efficacy. Hence, the next critical step in evaluating the evolution of women's candidacies and gauging prospects for women's full inclusion in the political system is to make a systematic assessment of the degree to which socialized beliefs about candidate efficacy persist.

[We] use data from the second wave of the Citizen Political Ambition Panel Study—a national survey of more than 2,000 "potential candidates" in 2008—

to provide the first thorough analysis of the manner in which gender affects efficacy to run for office. Our findings reveal that, despite comparable credentials, professional backgrounds, and political experience, highly accomplished women from both major political parties are substantially less likely than similarly situated men to perceive themselves as qualified to seek elective office. Importantly, we show that women and men rely on the same factors when evaluating themselves as candidates; but women are less likely than men to believe they meet these criteria. Not only are women more likely than men to doubt that they have the skills and traits necessary to succeed in electoral politics, but they are also more likely to doubt their abilities to engage in the mechanics involved in a political campaign. These empirical findings are critical because the perceptual differences we uncover account for much of the gender gap in potential candidates' self-efficacy, and ultimately hinder women's prospects for political equality.

THE GENDER GAP IN EFFICACY AS A CANDIDATE: BACKGROUND AND HYPOTHESES

Many of the perceptions women and men hold about the political process are deeply engrained by a culture that tends to reinforce traditional sex-role expectations and women's marginalization in politics (Enloe 2004; Freedman 2002). These perceptions are essential when investigating women and men's self-efficacy as candidates because they suggest that, regardless of the concrete qualifications and credentials women and men possess, they may not view themselves the same way. Among individuals who have already entered politics as candidates and elected officials, for instance, researchers uncover a gendered perceptual lens through which women and men perform their leadership roles and pursue their policy goals (Thomas 2005). Limited research also points to gender differences in how elected officials conceive of climbing the political career ladder (Bledsoe and Herring 1990; Fulton et al. 2006). And our earlier work provides anecdotal evidence that perceptions underpin gender differences in potential candidates' attitudes about their qualifications to run for office (Lawless and Fox 2010). For the most part, though, studies of political ambition tend to overlook gendered perceptions and examine, instead, the manner in which the political opportunity structure influences the decision to run for office. Consequently, Githens (2003) identifies potential candidates' perceptions of the electoral process and their prospects for participating in it as a critical, yet unexplored question in the study of women's candidate emergence.

In gauging how socialized gendered perceptions may affect efficacy to serve as a candidate, we rely on an array of empirical studies from political science, social psychology, business, economics, and education. This body of literature establishes at least two types of gendered perceptions that, even among successful professionals, may inhibit women's views of themselves and their prospects for electoral success.

Perceptions of Politically Relevant Skills and Traits. The first type of gendered perceptions that may affect efficacy to serve as a candidate pertains to individuals' assessments of their skills and traits. Evaluating oneself as a potential candidate, after all, involves personal reflection of talents and shortcomings. Though not directly related to politics, investigators from a variety of disciplines provide evidence to suggest that these self-assessments will ultimately depress women's levels of efficacy.

Turning first to gender differences in skills-based measures, researchers find that women are more likely than men to diminish and undervalue their professional skills and achievements. Studies of gender differences in academic abilities provide a clear example. By the time of adolescence, male students rate their mathematical abilities higher than female students do, despite no sex differences in objective indicators of competence (Wigfield, Eccles, and Pintrich 1996). In the areas of language arts, male and female students offer comparable self-assessments, although objective indicators reveal that female students are actually higher achieving in these fields (Pajares 2002). Many of these misconceptions persist into adulthood, percolating up even to high-level professionals who have succeeded in traditionally male domains (Beyer and Bowden 1997; Brownlow, Whitener, and Rupert 1998). Controlling for a series of job-related functions and work experience, for instance, female MBAs accepted salary offers that were lower than the offers accepted by their male counterparts (Bowles, Babcock, and McGinn 2005). In the absence of clear compensation standards, women are also more likely than men to express lower career-entry and career-peak pay expectations (Bylsma and Major 1992).

Gender differences exist not only in how women and men perceive their objective skills, but also in the confidence they exhibit regarding their credentials, backgrounds, propensity to take risks, and willingness to compete. Studies reveal that, in general, men are more likely than women to express confidence in skills they do not possess and overconfidence in skills they do possess (Kling et al. 1999). Men tend to be more "self-congratulatory," whereas women tend to be more modest about their achievements (Wigfield, Eccles, and Pintrich 1996). Men tend to overestimate their intelligence, while women tend to underestimate theirs (Beloff 1992; Furnham and Rawles 1995). Men often fail to incorporate criticism into their self-evaluations, whereas women tend to be strongly influenced by negative appraisals of their capabilities (Roberts 1991). Further, a review of 150 studies in psychology concludes that in almost all personal and professional decisions, women exhibit significantly higher levels of risk aversion than do men (Byrnes, Miller, and Schafer 1999). Perhaps because of this tendency, investigators find, when comparing professional performance in competitive and noncompetitive environments, that men are more likely than women to seek out competitive environments and to exude confidence when competing (Gneezy, Niederle, and Rustichini 2003; Niederle and Vesterlund 2007, 2010).

It follows, therefore, that any gender gap in potential candidates' self-efficacy may be driven by differences in how women and men perceive their politically relevant skills and traits.

Perceptions of Campaigns and the Electoral Environment. The second type of gendered perceptions that likely affect efficacy to serve as a candidate concerns the political environment in which women and men would compete. Not only must prospective candidates consider how they will be treated in the political sphere, but they also must assess how they would feel about engaging in the nuts and bolts of a campaign. Even though women perform as well as men on Election Day, women's historic exclusion from the political sphere may underscore their perceptions and work to women's detriment.

A small body of literature pertaining to perceptions of the political environment suggests that when women perceive gender bias in public life, they often withdraw. Political scientists have identified this pattern both within the bureaucracy (Dolan 2000; Naff 1995) and elective offices (Blair and Stanley 1991). This withdrawal, which may be a rational response to dealing with a political environment that has traditionally not embraced women, can also reinforce women's exclusion and perpetuate the notion that the electoral arena is biased against them. Indeed, as recently as 2008, pollsters uncovered that 51% of Americans believed that the country was not "ready to elect a woman to high office" (Pew 2008). Further, 40% of women did not think Hillary Rodham Clinton was treated fairly in her presidential campaign (Lifetime Network 2008). These aggregate levels of perceived bias likely contribute to the gender gap in candidate efficacy.

Gender differences in attitudes toward competition, coupled with the experiences of actual candidates, may further lead women to doubt their abilities to succeed. After all, female congressional candidates face more primary competition than do their male counterparts (Lawless and Pearson 2008). Geographic differences facilitate women's election in some congressional districts, but lessen their chances of success in others (Palmer and Simon 2006). Female candidates often recount bias in the press coverage they receive (Rausch, Rozell, and Wilson 1999). And women perceive fundraising as more difficult than men do (Fox 1997), ultimately devoting more time to it (Jenkins 2007). Certainly, women and men who have achieved high levels of professional success have, to some extent, already exhibited a willingness to compete. But if women are cognizant of a more difficult electoral process, then they may be more inclined than men to doubt that they would excel at typical campaign activities.

When assessing their efficacy as potential candidates, perceptions of gender bias, heightened electoral competition, and more challenging campaign dynamics may lead many women to conclude—perhaps rightfully so—that they have to be better than the average man to succeed. Accordingly, women may be less likely than men to express self-efficacy and consider themselves qualified to run for office.

Based on our review of research from a variety of disciplines, we test two central hypotheses. First, we expect to uncover a baseline gender gap in potential candidates' efficacy to run for office, regardless of their objective qualifications and credentials:

> *Gender Gap in Self-Efficacy Hypothesis*: There is a gender gap in self-efficacy among potential candidates, even after controlling for detailed measures of professional experiences, credentials, and political proximity.

Second, we expect that the deeply internalized perceptions of gender roles and politics that lead men to envision the notion of emerging as a candidate will lead women to doubt their abilities to enter the political sphere. We break this hypothesis into two parts:

> *Gendered Perceptions Hypothesis*: The gender gap in self-efficacy will be explained by:

> a. gender differences in potential candidates' perceptions of their political skills and traits.
> b. gender differences in potential candidates' perceptions of the campaign and electoral environments in which they would compete.

In short, and to borrow from Githens, we expect the "gendered nature of evaluative standards" (2003, 43) to remain problematic even for women who have already achieved high levels of success. Operationalizing these hypotheses allows for the first in-depth assessment of the manner in which patterns of traditional gender socialization influence potential candidates' views of their suitability to run for elective office.

RESEARCH DESIGN AND DATASET: THE CITIZEN POLITICAL AMBITION PANEL STUDY

We rely on data from the second wave of the Citizen Political Ambition Panel Study to examine potential candidates' self-efficacy. This national panel—the first wave of which we conducted in 2001, and the second wave of which we completed in 2008—serves as the only broad random sample of equally credentialed women and men who are well positioned to serve as future candidates for all elective offices. We drew our 2001 "candidate eligibility pool" from the professions that yield the highest proportion of political candidates for congressional and state legislative positions: law, business, education, and political activism (Dolan and Ford 1997; Moncrief, Squire, and Jewell 2001). We disproportionately stratified by sex, so the sample includes roughly equal numbers of women and men. The women and men are comparable in education, profession, income, and region, and they also hold similar employment roles, high degrees of professional success, and heightened levels of political interest and participation.[2]

The 2,036 respondents who completed the 2008 survey are a representative subsample of the original eligibility pool. Controlling for sex, race, and profession, individuals who expressed political ambition in 2001 were no more likely than respondents who had never considered a candidacy to complete the 2008 survey. Similarly, potential candidates who reported high levels of political interest and activism at the time of the 2001 survey were no more likely than those who did not to respond to the 2008 questionnaire (regression results not shown). No significant demographic or professional factors distinguish the 2001 and 2008 samples. Further, the women and men who completed the second survey are well matched in race, education, income, and geography. Women are, however, more likely to be Democrats, while men are more likely to be Republicans. The women are also, on average, three years younger than the men, a probable result of women's relatively recent entry into the fields of law and business. Our empirical analyses are sensitive to these differences and always control for them.

Our method and sample allow for a comprehensive assessment of gender differences in self-efficacy. The results from the 2001 survey uncovered the gender gap in respondents' perceptions of their qualifications to run for office. But the survey was limited in the extent to which it could shed light on the reasons for the gender gap. The original survey did not ask questions about respondents' objective credentials, political experiences, or proximity to the political arena. Similarly, it failed to gauge respondents' assessments of their own politically relevant skills and traits, or their perceptions of electoral competition. Thus, we included in the 2008 survey detailed batteries of questions about proximity to politics, political skills and traits, attitudes toward campaigning, and perceptions of electoral competition and the political process. Accordingly, our analysis relies on the data collected from only those respondents who completed the 2008 survey.

FINDINGS AND ANALYSIS

Establishing the Gender Gap in Self-Efficacy in the Candidate Eligibility Pool

To examine gender differences in how potential candidates assess their self-efficacy to run for office, we asked respondents a series of questions about their political qualifications. The broad measure of efficacy on which we rely gauges where potential candidates place themselves on a continuum from "not at all qualified" to "very qualified" to launch a candidacy. The data presented in the top half of Table [1] reveal that men are roughly 50% more likely than women to consider themselves "very qualified" to seek an elective position. Women are twice as likely as men to assert that they are "not at all qualified" to run for

TABLE [1]   Gender and Self-Efficacy in the Candidate Eligibility Pool

	Women	Men
How qualified are you to run for public office?		
Very Qualified	21%	33%
Qualified	35	40
Somewhat Qualified	32	21
Not at All Qualified	12	6
How qualified are you to hold public office?*		
Very Qualified	27%	40%
Qualified	36	40
Somewhat Qualified	27	17
Not at All Qualified	9	4
N	862	1,003

NOTE: Chi-square tests comparing women and men are significant at least at $p < .05$ for all comparisons.
*Numbers may not add up to 100 percent due to rounding.

office. Similar gender gaps appear when we consider women and men's assessments of whether they are qualified to perform the job of an elected official. Whereas 80% of men contend that they are "qualified" or "very qualified" to do the job of an officeholder, fewer than two-thirds of women assess themselves this way. Women are more than twice as likely as men to rate themselves as "not at all qualified" to perform the job. This gender gap in self-efficacy, which exists across professions, is roughly equal for Democrats and Republicans.[3] Further, the gap does not result from women envisioning running for higher offices than men. In fact, women are more likely than men to refer to local offices when expressing levels of political ambition (difference significant at $p < .01$).

The . . . gender gap in respondents' self-efficacy demonstrates that women are less likely than men to perceive themselves as qualified to enter the electoral environment. We would expect, however, that respondents who are politically involved may be more likely than those who are not to have a sense of efficacy to serve as candidates. In order to confirm the *Gender Gap in Self-Efficacy Hypothesis*, therefore, the gap must withstand a series of controls for measures of political proximity, campaign experience, and politically relevant credentials.

■　■　■

[Our] results indicate that differences in women and men's assessments of their political qualifications do not derive from differences in their actual credentials. The sex of the potential candidate remains a . . . predictor of self-efficacy and withstands the series of rigorous controls. Whereas the "average" male respondent has a 0.077 likelihood of considering himself "not at all qualified" to run for office, the "average" female respondent's likelihood of assessing this way is 0.122.[4] At the other end of [the] qualifications spectrum, a typical male potential candidate has a 0.174 predicted probability of considering himself "very qualified" to run for office, compared to a typical female potential candidate's predicted probability of 0.106. Put somewhat differently, women are nearly 60% more likely than similarly situated men to consider themselves "not at all qualified" to run for office; men are nearly two-thirds more likely than their female counterparts to evaluate themselves as "very qualified" to enter the electoral arena. Comparing the effect of sex relative to other factors highlights its importance; the independent, substantive effect of sex exceeds all of the political proximity and professional credentials variables. Indeed, the only predictor of qualifications with a larger relative effect than sex—albeit only slightly larger—is political recruitment.

■   ■   ■

When comparing women and men in the candidate eligibility pool, we confirm the *Gender Gap in Self-Efficacy Hypothesis.* The landscape for women candidates may be a shifting terrain with more women seeking and winning office than was the case 20 years ago. And women may have made progress in acquiring the backgrounds, experiences, and connections on which politicians traditionally have relied. Yet women remain less likely than men to report a sense of self-efficacy as a candidate. Because the gender gap persists despite professional and political similarities, we must move beyond objective credentials and assess respondents' perceptions of themselves navigating the political sphere.

EXPLAINING THE GENDER GAP IN SELF-EFFICACY IN THE CANDIDATE ELIGIBILITY POOL

Our *Gendered Perceptions Hypothesis* asserts that the gender gap in self-efficacy results from differences in women and men's perceptions of themselves and the electoral arena. Thus, we asked respondents 17 questions about a variety of activities and characteristics associated with being a candidate for elective office. The first series of questions we posed focuses on respondents' assessments of their political skills and traits. These measures allow us to test the first part of our hypothesis—that personal self-assessments drive the gender gap in self-efficacy. The second set of questions pertains to assessments of the political arena in which candidates compete. Here, we can examine the second part of the hypothesis—that perceptions of the political environment significantly affect efficacy to serve as a candidate. . . .

Turning first to perceptions of political skills and traits, women in our pool of potential candidates rate themselves less favorably than do men across the board. We uncover one of the largest gender differences when we focus on perceptions of political traits; women are 19 percentage points more likely than men to doubt that they have thick enough skin to run for office. Women are also less likely than men to perceive themselves as possessing all six of the skills about which we inquired. These perceptual differences are striking in light of women and men's actual skills and experiences. Women and men in the sample are . . . indistinguishable from one another in terms of the key skills necessary to run for office. Thirty-three percent of women and 35% of men have conducted extensive policy research; 65% of women and 69% of men regularly engage in public speaking; and 69% of women and 64% of men report experience soliciting funds. . . .

The gender differences are just as robust when we focus on respondents' perceptions of the electoral arena. . . . Women are significantly more likely than men to view most of the mechanics of running for office, particularly negative campaigning, as deterrents to a candidacy. Further, despite the fact that women and men in the sample are similarly dispersed geographically, women are more likely than men to perceive a biased and competitive electoral environment. . . .

It is important to recognize that the gender gap in self-efficacy may be a result not only of women's under-assessments of their skills and traits, but also men's tendency to overestimate their political skills. This phenomenon would be consistent with findings from the aforementioned studies in the fields of business and education. In a similar vein, men's longer-term presence and success in top positions in business and law may result in heightened levels of confidence about entering the political arena, also a male-dominated environment. In either case, though, women and men perceive political reality and their ability to succeed in the political system through a gendered lens.

■　■　■

CONCLUSION AND DISCUSSION

Based on the results of the second wave of the Citizen Political Ambition Panel Study, we establish and explicate the gender gap in self-efficacy among potential candidates. The women and men we surveyed share professional and educational backgrounds. They are well matched in objective indicators and experiences typical of actual candidates and officeholders. And they rely on the same calculus when evaluating their qualifications to run for office. Yet women are significantly more likely than men to dismiss their qualifications, and significantly less likely than their male counterparts to express self-efficacy to enter the electoral arena. Once we account for gender differences in perceptions of the skill sets and characteristics necessary to run for office, however, the gender gap in self-efficacy decreases considerably. In fact, a potential candidate's sex does not exert an independent effect on the likelihood of assessing [him or herself] as "not at all qualified" to run for office. The empirical findings delineate several factors that work to women's detriment; gender differences in perceptions of political skills and traits, as well as what it would be like to engage in the mechanics of a campaign, depress women's self-efficacy.

Our findings strongly suggest that traditional gender role socialization continues to perpetuate a culture in which women remain unaccustomed to entering the electoral arena. Women's lower self-assessments of their political skills are consistent with a political culture that has not embraced women in the public sphere. In addition, women's perceptions of their politically relevant traits reflect a heightened level of discomfort with entering politics, also a likely result of traditional gender role orientations that discourage women's candidacies.

■　■　■

[Our] results provide strong support for the *Gendered Perceptions Hypothesis*. Women and men who are equally and objectively qualified to run for office perceive neither themselves nor the political arena the same way. Similar professional credentials, economic autonomy, and political experience, alone, cannot close the gender gap in self-efficacy. These findings are vital because the socialized perceptual differences we uncover translate into a formidable hurdle women must overcome when behaving as strategic politicians and navigating the candidate emergence process. Self-efficacy, after all, is a statistically and substantively significant predictor of whether a respondent ever considered running for office, actually ran for office, took any concrete steps that tend to precede a campaign, or expressed interest in running for office at some point in the future (regression results not shown).

NOTES

1. In dismissing the impact of discrimination, we do not mean to overlook the pockets of bias that researchers continue to uncover or the complex role that gender continues to play in electoral politics. Surveys of local party officials reveal that some electoral gatekeepers appear to prefer male candidates (Niven 1998; Sanbonmatsu 2006). Examinations of campaigns show that gender stereotypes affect media coverage (Fowler and Lawless 2009; Fox 1997). And voters continue to rely on stereotypical conceptions of women and men's traits, issue expertise, and policy positions (Koch 2000; Lawless 2004).

2. See online supplemental information for a description of the research design and sample.

3. Republican women are twice as likely as Republican men to self-assess as "not at all qualified" (10% of women, compared to 5% of men), and 32% of Republican men, compared to 20% of Republican women, consider themselves "very qualified" to run for office. Among Democrats, 12% of women, compared to 7% of men, self-assess as "not at all qualified," and 35% of men, but only 20% of women, consider themselves "very qualified" to run for office.

4. Our analysis is based on setting all continuous independent variables to their sample means and dummy variables to their sample modes.

REFERENCES

American Bar Association. 2006. *Charting Our Progress: The Status of Women in the Profession Today.* Chicago: American Bar Association Commission of Women in the Profession.

Beloff, Halla. 1992. "Mother, Father and Me: Our IQ." *Psychologist* 5: 309–11.

Beyer, Sylvia, and Edward M. Bowden. 1997. "Gender Differences in Self-Perceptions: Convergent Evidence from Three Measures of Accuracy and Bias." *Personality and Social Psychology Bulletin* 23 (2): 157–72.

Blair, Diane D., and Jeanie R. Stanley. 1991. "Personal Relationships and Legislative Power: Male and Female Perceptions." *Legislative Studies Quarterly* 16 (4): 495–507.

Bledsoe, Timothy, and Mary Herring. 1990. "Victims of Circumstances: Women in Pursuit of Political Office." *American Political Science Review* 84 (1): 213–23.

Bowles, Hannah Riley, Linda C. Babcock, and Kathleen McGinn. 2005. "Constraints and Triggers: Situational Mechanics of Gender in Negotiation." *Journal of Personality and Social Psychology* 89 (6): 951–65.

Brownlow, Sheila, Rebecca Whitener, and Janet M. Rupert. 1998. "I'll Take Gender Differences for $1000! Domain-Specific Intellectual Success on 'Jeopardy.'" *Sex Roles: A Journal of Research* 38 (3): 269–86.

Bylsma, Wayne H., and Brenda Major. 1992. "Two Routes to Eliminating Gender Differences in Personal Entitlement: Social Comparisons and Performance Evaluations." *Psychology of Women Quarterly* 16 (2): 193–200.

Byrnes, James, David C. Miller, and William D. Schafer. 1999. "Gender Differences in Risk-Taking: A Meta-Analysis." *Psychological Bulletin* 125 (3): 367–83.

Carroll, Susan J. 1994. *Women as Candidates in American Politics.* 2nd ed. Bloomington: Indiana University Press.

Catalyst. 2008. "Catalyst 2008 Census of the Fortune 500." New York: Catalyst. December 10.

Diamond, Irene. 1977. *Sex Roles in the Statehouse.* New Haven, CT: Yale University Press.

Dolan, Julie. 2000. "The Senior Executive Service: Gender, Attitudes and Representative Bureaucracy." *Journal of Public Administration Research and Theory* 10 (3): 513–29.

Dolan, Kathleen, and Lynne E. Ford. 1997. "Change and Continuity among Women State Legislators: Evidence from Three Decades." *Political Research Quarterly* 50 (1): 137–51.

Enloe, Cynthia. 2004. *The Curious Feminist.* Berkeley: University of California Press.

Flammang, Janet. 1997. *Women's Political Voice: How Women Are Transforming the Practice and Study of Politics.* Philadelphia: Temple University Press.

Fowler, Linda L., and Jennifer L. Lawless. 2009. "Looking for Sex in All the Wrong Places: Press Coverage and the Electoral Fortunes of Gubernatorial Candidates." *Perspectives on Politics* 7 (3): 519–37.

Fowlkes, Diane L., Jerry Perkins, and Sue Tolleson Rinehart. 1979. "Gender Roles and Party Roles." *American Political Science Review* 73 (3): 772–80.

Fox, Richard L. 1997. *Gender Dynamics in Congressional Elections.* Thousand Oaks, CA: Sage.

Fox, Richard L. 2006. "Congressional Elections: Where Are We on the Road to Gender Parity?" In *Gender and Elections: Shaping the Future of American Politics*, edited by S. Carroll and R. Fox. New York: Cambridge University Press, 97–166.

Freedman, Estelle. 2002. *No Turning Back.* New York: Ballantine Books.

Fulton, Sarah A., Cherie D. Maestas, L. Sandy Maisel, and Walter J. Stone. 2006. "The Sense of a Woman: Gender, Ambition, and the Decision to Run for Congress." *Political Research Quarterly* 59 (2): 235–48.

Furnham, Adrian, and Richard Rawles. 1995. "Sex Differences in the Estimation of Intelligence." *Journal of Social Behavior and Personality* 10: 741–48.

Githens, Marianne. 2003. "Accounting for Women's Political Involvement: The Perennial Problem of Recruitment." In *Women and American Politics,* edited by S. Carroll. New York: Oxford University Press, 33–52.

Githens, Marianne, and Jewel L. Prestage. 1977. *A Portrait of Marginality: The Political Behavior of the American Woman.* New York: Longman.

Gneezy, Uri, Muriel Niederle, and Aldo Rustichini. 2003. "Performance in Competitive Environments: Gender Differences." *Quarterly Journal of Economics* 118 (3): 1049–74.

Jenkins, Shannon. 2007. "A Woman's Work Is Never Done? Fundraising Perceptions and Effort Among Female State Legislative Candidates." *Political Research Quarterly* 60 (2): 230–39.

Jennings, M. Kent, and Barbara G. Farah. 1981. "Social Roles and Political Resources: An Over-Time Study of Men and Women in Party Elites." *American Journal of Political Science* 25 (3): 462–82.

Kling, Kristen C., Janet Hyde, Carolin Showers, and Brenda N. Buswell. 1999. "Gender Differences in Self-Esteem: A Meta-Analysis." *Psychological Bulletin* 125 (4): 470–500.

Koch, Jeffrey W. 2000. "Do Citizens Apply Gender Stereotypes to Infer Candidates' Ideological Orientations?" *Journal of Politics* 62 (2): 414–29.

Kousser, Thad. 2005. *Term Limits and the Dismantling of State Legislative Professionalism.* New York: Cambridge University Press.

Lawless, Jennifer L. 2004. "Women, War, and Winning Elections: Gender Stereotyping in the Post September 11th Era." *Political Research Quarterly* 53 (3): 479–90.

Lawless, Jennifer L., and Richard F. Fox. 2010. *It Still Takes a Candidate: Why Women Don't Run for Office.* New York: Cambridge University Press.

Lawless, Jennifer L., and Kathryn Pearson. 2008. "The Primary Reason for Women's Under-Representation: Re-Evaluating the Conventional Wisdom." *Journal of Politics* 70 (1): 67–82.

Lifetime Networks. 2008. "New Lifetime Every Woman Counts Poll Sheds Light on Women's Reactions to Historic Presidential Election, Their Agenda for New Leaders and the Future of Female Candidates." *PR Newswire,* November 24.

Moncrief, Gary F., Peverill Squire, and Malcolm E. Jewell. 2001. *Who Runs for the Legislature?* Upper Saddle River, NJ: Prentice Hall.

Naff, Katherine C. 1995. "Subjective vs. Objective Discrimination in Government: Adding to the Picture of Barriers to the Advancement of Women." *Political Research Quarterly* 48 (3): 535–58.

Niederle, Muriel, and Lise Vesterlund. 2007. "Do Women Shy Away from Competition? Do Men Compete Too Much?" *Quarterly Journal of Economics* 122 (3): 1067–1101.

Niederle, Muriel, and Lise Vesterlund. 2010. "Explaining the Gender Gap in Math Test Scores: The Role of Competition." *Journal of Economic Perspectives* 24 (2).

Niven, David. 1998. "Party Elites and Women Candidates: The Shape of Bias." *Women & Politics* 19 (2): 57–80.

Pajares, Frank. 2002. "Gender and Perceived Self-Efficacy in Self-Regulated Learning." *Theory Into Practice* 41 (2): 116–25.

Palmer, Barbara, and Dennis Simon. 2006. *Breaking the Political Glass Ceiling: Women and Congressional Elections.* New York: Routledge.

Pew Research Center. 2008. "Men or Women? Who's the Better Leader?" *Social and Demographic Trends,* August 25.

Rausch, John D., Mark Rozell, and Harry L. Wilson. 1999. "When Women Lose: A Case Study of Media Coverage of Two Gubernatorial Campaigns." *Women & Politics* 20 (4): 1–22.

Roberts, T. 1991. "Gender and the Influences of Evaluation on Self-Assessment in Achievement Settings." *Psychological Bulletin* 109 (2): 297–308.

Rule, Wilma. 1981. "Why Women Don't Run: The Critical Contextual Factors in Women's Legislative Recruitment." *Western Political Quarterly* 34 (March): 60–77.

Sanbonmatsu, Kira. 2006. *Where Women Run: Gender and Party in the American States.* Ann Arbor: University of Michigan.

Seltzer, R. A., J. Newman, and M. Leighton. 1997. *Sex as a Political Variable.* Boulder, CO: Lynne Rienner.

Studlar, Donley T., and Susan Welch. 1990. "Multi-Member Districts and the Representation of Women: Evidence from Britain and the United States." *Journal of Politics* 52 (2): 391–412.

Thomas, Sue. 2005. "Introduction: Women and Elective Office: Past, Present, and Future." In *Women and Elective Office,* 2nd ed., edited by S. Thomas and C. Wilcox. New York: Oxford University Press, 3–25.

Welch, Susan. 1977. "Women as Political Animals? A Test of Some Explanations for Male-Female Political Participation Differences." *American Journal of Political Science* 21 (4): 711–30.

Welch, Susan. 1978. "Recruitment of Women to Public Office." *Western Political Quarterly* 31 (2): 372–80.

Welch, Susan, and Albert K. Karnig. 1979. "Correlates of Female Office Holding in City Politics." *Journal of Politics* 41 (2): 478–91.

Wigfield, Allan, Jacquelynne S. Eccles, and Paul R. Pintrich. 1996. "Development between the Ages of 11 and 25." In *Handbook of Educational Psychology,* edited by D. C. Berliner and R. C. Calfee. New York: Macmillan, 148–85.

13.4

CHRISTOPHER ACHEN AND LARRY M. BARTELS

From *Democracy for Realists: Why Elections Do Not Produce Responsive Government*

Achen and Bartels take a pessimistic view of whether voters in a democracy understand enough to choose their leaders wisely. The authors summarize decades of research showing that voters misunderstand the basic elements of democracy, that they are swayed at election time by irrelevant information, and that they often choose leaders against their own interests. This selection challenges us to depart from "romantic" views about democracy and instead to confront the reality that elections often do not work to produce effective, responsive government.

In the conventional view, democracy begins with the voters. Ordinary people have preferences about what their government should do. They choose leaders who will do those things, or they enact their preferences directly in referendums. In either case, what the majority wants becomes government policy—a highly attractive prospect in light of most human experience with governments. Democracy makes the people the rulers, and legitimacy derives from their consent. In Abraham Lincoln's stirring words from the Gettysburg Address, democratic government is "of the people, by the people, and for the people." That way of thinking about democracy has passed into everyday wisdom, not just in the United States but in a great many other countries around the globe. It constitutes a kind of "folk theory" of democracy, a set of accessible, appealing ideas assuring people that they live under an ethically defensible form of government that has their interests at heart.[1]

Unfortunately, while the folk theory of democracy has flourished as an ideal, its credibility has been severely undercut by a growing body of scientific evidence presenting a different and considerably darker view of democratic politics. That evidence demonstrates that the great majority of citizens pay little attention to politics. At election time, they are swayed by how they feel about "the nature of the times," especially the current state of the economy, and by political loyalties typically acquired in childhood. Those loyalties, not the facts of political life and government policy, are the primary drivers of

From Christopher Achen and Larry M. Bartels, *Democracy for Realists: Why Elections Do Not Produce Responsive Government* (Princeton, NJ: Princeton University Press, 2016).

political behavior. Election outcomes turn out to be largely random events from the viewpoint of contemporary democratic theory. That is, elections are well determined by powerful forces, but those forces are not the ones that current theories of democracy believe should determine how elections come out. Hence the old frameworks will no longer do.

We want to persuade the reader to think about democracy in a fundamentally different way. . . .

TWO CONTEMPORARY APPROACHES TO DEMOCRACY

What are the conventional notions of democracy that we argue have outlived their time? We consider two main types of theory, one popular with broad swatches of democratic society and a second whose appeal is largely confined to scholars specializing in the study of elections.[2]

The first model, which we refer to as the *populist* ideal of democracy, emphasizes the role of ordinary citizens in "determining the policies" of democratic communities (Dahl 1998, 37–38). As we will see, this populist notion of popular sovereignty has inspired a good deal of sophisticated academic thinking derived from Enlightenment concepts of human nature and the political views of 19th-century British liberalism. In its less rarified forms it has also undergirded the folk theory of democracy celebrated in much Fourth of July rhetoric. As the homespun poet of democracy Carl Sandburg (1936) proclaimed, "The People, Yes."

But *how* precisely shall the people govern according to the populist theory? [There are] two different accounts of how populist democracy might work. In one, the public "decide[s] issues through the election of individuals who are to assemble in order to carry out its will," as an unsympathetic critic of this account put it (Schumpeter 1942, 250). In the other, the people rule through "direct democracy," choosing policies themselves via initiative and referendum procedures. Both representative democracy and direct democracy loom large in popular understanding of democratic self-government. But as we shall see, the assumptions undergirding both versions of populist democracy are highly unrealistic.

The second contemporary model in defense of democracy is less widely popular, though more persuasive to most political scientists. This model focuses on elections as mechanisms for *leadership selection*. In contrast to the populist model, which he characterized as "the classical doctrine of democracy," Joseph Schumpeter (1942, 269) famously defined the democratic method as "that institutional arrangement for arriving at political decisions in which individuals acquire the power to decide by means of a competitive struggle for the people's vote."[3] Dispensing with the notion that "the people itself decide issues" by electing those who will "carry out its will," Schumpeter (1942, 284–285) insisted that "democracy does not mean and cannot mean that the people actually rule in any obvious sense of the terms 'people' and 'rule.' Democracy means only that the people have the opportunity of accepting or refusing the men who are to rule them."

Schumpeter gave little attention to the criteria by which voters would—or *should*—choose among potential rulers. However, subsequent scholars have fleshed out his account. The most influential model of democratic selection in contemporary political science is the *retrospective theory of voting*, which portrays "the electorate in its great, and perhaps principal, role as an appraiser of past events, past performance, and past actions" (Key 1966, 61). In this view, election outcomes hinge not on ideas, but on public approval or disapproval of the actual performance of incumbent political leaders. This model of democratic accountability appeals to skeptical scholars because it puts much less pressure on the voters to have elaborate, well-informed policy views. Ordinary citizens are allowed to drive the automobile of state simply by looking in the rearview mirror. Alas, we find that this works about as well in government as it would on the highway. Thus, we . . . argue that this second model of democracy, like the first, crumbles upon empirical inspection.

Hence we must think again. . . . A dramatically different framework is needed to make sense of how democracy actually works. We . . . argue that voters, even the most informed voters, typically make choices not on the basis of policy preferences or ideology, but on the basis of who they are—their social identities. In turn, those social identities shape how they think, what they think, and where they belong in the party system. But if voting behavior primarily reflects and reinforces voters' social loyalties, it is a mistake to suppose that elections result in popular control of public policy. . . . The [argument] may not be very comfortable or comforting. Nonetheless, we believe that a democratic theory worthy of serious social influence must engage with the findings of modern social science.

▪   ▪   ▪

THE CRITICAL TRADITION

The folk theory of democracy celebrates the wisdom of popular judgments by informed and engaged citizens. The reality is quite different. Human beings are busy with their lives. Most have school or a job consuming many hours of the day. They also have meals to prepare, homes to clean, and bills to pay. They may have children to raise or elderly parents to care for. They may also be coping with unemployment, business reverses, illness, addictions, divorce, or other personal and family troubles. For most, leisure time is at a premium. Sorting out which presidential candidate has the right foreign policy toward Asia is not a high priority for them. Without shirking more immediate and more important obligations, people cannot engage in much well-informed, thoughtful political deliberation, nor should they.

Recognizing that actual people are far from the unrealistic ideal citizens of the folk theory, disappointed observers have often adopted a judgmental tone, implicitly assuming that the folk theory provides the appropriate moral standard for citizens, which few meet. At the end of the 19th century, for example, James Bryce (1894, 250) observed "how little solidity and substance there is in the political or social beliefs of nineteen persons out of every twenty. These beliefs, when examined, mostly resolve themselves into two or three prejudices and aversions, two or three prepossessions for a particular leader or party or section of a party, two or three phrases or catchwords suggesting or embodying arguments which the man who repeats them has not analyzed." He might have added that the remaining one in twenty exhibit the limits of rationality, too. Nevertheless, however unaware of his own human limitations Bryce may have been, in our view he was not wrong about the fact of widespread citizen inattention. Indeed, the past century of political science has done remarkably little to alter the basic outlines of his portrait of public opinion. Even in the midst of the Progressive Era, the fundamental veracity of that portrait and its troubling implications for folk democratic theory were clear enough to those willing to see them. The great political scientist and Harvard University president A. Lawrence Lowell (1913, 233), for example, noted with respect to democracy that "there has probably never existed a political system of which men have not tried to demonstrate the perfection," but he dismissed as "fallacious" all theories "based on the assumption that the multitude is omniscient" and "all reforms that presuppose a radical change in human nature."

Three other distinguished scholars of the era also saw the tension between conventional democratic ideals and dreary reality. Schumpeter (1942, 262) acidly observed that citizens are especially prone "to yield to extra-rational or irrational prejudice and impulse" in the political sphere. By comparison with other realms of life, he argued (Schumpeter 1942, 261), "the typical citizen drops down to a lower level of mental performance as soon as he enters the political field. He argues and analyzes in a way which he would readily recognize as infantile within the sphere of his real interests."

Walter Lippmann (1914; 1922; 1925) faced more squarely than other commentators of his time the inevitable limits of human cognitive ability in politics. "Once you touch the biographies of human beings," he wrote (1914, 215), "the notion that political beliefs are logically determined collapses like a pricked balloon." He saw that the cherished ideas and judgments we bring to politics are stereotypes and simplifications with little room for adjustment as the facts change (1922, 16): "For the real environment is altogether too big, too complex, and too fleeting for direct acquaintance. We are not equipped to deal with so much subtlety, so much variety, so many permutations and combinations. And although we have to act in that environment, we have to reconstruct it on a simpler model before we can manage it." Lippmann remains the deepest and most thoughtful of the modern critics of the psychological foundations of the folk theory of democracy.

Reinhold Niebuhr (1932; 1944) noted that human judgment is not just over-whelmed by the complexity of the political world, as Lippmann emphasized, but in addition is profoundly warped by self-interest and the will to power. And he perceived clearly that the idealistic justification of democracy as human rationality in pursuit of the common good serves only too well to pro-vide cover for those who profit from the distortions and biases in the policy-making processes of actual democracies: "The will to power uses reason as kings used courtiers and chaplains to add grace to their enterprise" (Niebuhr 1932, 44).

These and other critical thinkers struggled to put democracy on an intel-lectually respectable foundation, taking account of human nature as they knew it. But in the era in which they wrote, few could hear. It was all too easy and convenient to dismiss the entire intellectual lineage as elitist and cynical, a mere literary tradition based on nothing but jaundiced interpretations of personal experience. Subsequent scholarly generations have also disliked the various racial and religious prejudices of the time, which these men some-times shared. By the 1950s and 1960s, skeptical writers like Wallas, Lowell, John Dickinson (1930), and even Lippmann and Niebuhr were no longer much read by students of politics.

Meanwhile, however, new tools emerged for investigating political behav-ior, most notably scientific survey research, whose findings were much harder to glibly dismiss. The pioneering survey research of Paul Lazarsfeld and his colleagues at Columbia University (Lazarsfeld, Berelson, and Gaudet 1948; Berelson, Lazarsfeld, and McPhee 1954), of Angus Campbell and his colleagues at the University of Michigan (Campbell et al. 1960), and of other early analysts of electoral choice produced a rather bleak portrait of habitual, socially deter-mined political behavior, once again calling into question whether citizens could perform the role that the folk theory of democracy seemed to require of them.

Philip Converse (1964) extended this seminal work, building a new, more formidable case for skepticism regarding the idealized image of democratic citizens, this time substituting random national samples for the insightful but less systematic observations of Bryce, Lippmann, Niebuhr, and Schumpeter. Converse's essay set off a vibrant decades-long critical discussion of his meth-odology and the inferences he drew from his findings, but few public opinion scholars disputed the central point he made—that judged by the standards of the folk theory, the political "belief systems" of ordinary citizens are gener-ally thin, disorganized, and ideologically incoherent.

. . . Converse's argument is, if anything, even better supported a half cen-tury later than it was when he wrote. A vast amount of supporting evidence has been added to his dispiriting comparison of actual human political cog-nition with the expectations derived from the folk theory of democracy. Well-informed citizens, too, have come in for their share of criticism, since their well-organized "ideological" thinking often turns out to be just a rather mechanical reflection of what their favorite group and party leaders have instructed them to think. Faced with this evidence, many scholars in the final chapters of their books continue to express idealistic hope that institutional reform, civic education, improved mass media, more effective mobilization of the poor, or stronger moral exhortation might bring public opinion into closer correspondence with the standards of the folk theory. But in sober moments most acknowledge the repeated failures of all those prescriptions.

Thus, scholars, too, persist uneasily in their schizophrenia, recognizing the power of the critical arguments but hoping against hope that those arguments can somehow be discredited or evaded, allowing the lackluster reality of democratic practice to be squared with conventional idealistic democratic thinking. Often, their attempts to bolster the tattered theoretical status quo bring them back to Winston Churchill's claim that "democracy is the worst form of government except all those others that have been tried from time to time."[4] But that is a distinctly un-idealistic defense of democracy—and no defense at all of the folk theory of democracy.

■   ■   ■

Our view is that conventional thinking about democracy has collapsed in the face of modern social-scientific research.

■   ■   ■

Unfortunately . . . Converse (1964) found that "the vast majority of Americans" are "thoroughly innocent of ideology" (Kinder 1983, 391)—and that finding has been "largely sustained" by subsequent scholarship (Kinder 1983, 401). The available evidence suggests that citizens of other advanced democracies are similar to Americans in this respect. Thus, Converse's work raises a significant challenge not only to the spatial model, but to a great deal of scholarly and popular thinking about how policy decisions might be justified on democratic grounds.

. . . A substantial body of scholarly work demonstrat[es] that most democratic citizens are uninterested in politics, poorly informed, and unwilling or unable to convey coherent policy preferences through "issue voting." How, then, are elections supposed to ensure ideological responsiveness to the popular will? In our view, they do not. The populist ideal of electoral democracy, for all its elegance and attractiveness, is largely irrelevant in practice, leaving elected officials mostly free to pursue their own notions of the public good or to respond to party and interest group pressures.

■   ■   ■

We conclude that group and partisan loyalties, not policy preferences or ideologies, are fundamental in democratic politics. Thus, a realistic theory of democracy must be built, not on the French Enlightenment, on British liberalism, or on American Progressivism, with their devotion to human rationality and monadic individualism, but instead on the insights of the critics of these traditions, who recognized that human life is group life.

■　　■　　■

THE CHALLENGE: TAKING ON THE DIVINE RIGHT OF THE PEOPLE

. . . Democracy is the justifying political ideology of our era. It is inevitably very difficult for any of us to recognize the intellectual constraints and contradictions entailed by our own preconceptions and normative commitments to it. As one of the preeminent contemporary scholars of American politics, James Stimson (2004, 170), wrote, "The word 'democracy' is bound up with symbolism, belief, patriotism, and a quasi-religious commitment. It is imbued with our self-identity as Americans. Democracy is the civil religion of America." Dahl (1961, 317) put it even more bluntly: "To reject the democratic creed is in effect to refuse to be an American."

Some useful perspective on this aspect of contemporary thinking about democracy may be provided by recalling political thought in early modern times regarding the divine right of kings. The idea that kings were divinely anointed had a long history in human thought, and not just in the West; Chinese emperors, too, needed "the mandate of heaven." The idea was highly functional, providing a sturdy basis for political stability—as many astute observers recognized. However, the chronic gap between kingly ideals and realities was a source of severe ideological strain.

The doctrine of "The King's Two Bodies" (Kantorowicz 1957) provided useful leeway for understanding and accommodating the fact that mortal rulers were often manifestly less than divine in bearing and behavior. On this view, the king always intended to rule well and justly, but he was sometimes misled. As Edmund Morgan (1988, 30) described the situation in 17th-century England, "A host of ambitious schemers, according to the Commons' view, continually caught the king's natural ear and misinformed him in order to procure benefits to themselves. But the king in his body politic always wanted what was best for his subjects, all his subjects, and surely no subject could know better what that was than the combined representatives of all his subjects. 'If anything fall out unhappily,' said Sir Robert Phelips, 'it is not King Charles that advised himself, but King Charles misadvised by others and misled by misordered counsel.'" In their time, these ideas were widely credited among thoughtful people and important scholars. But of course, genuine political progress depended on abandoning this entire way of thinking.

In our view, the ideal of popular sovereignty plays much the same role in contemporary democratic ideology that the divine right of kings played in the monarchical era. It is "a quasi-religious commitment," in Stimson's terms, a fiction providing legitimacy and stability to political systems whose actual workings are manifestly—and inevitably—rather less than divine. The fiction feels natural within the Enlightenment mind-set of rationality and human perfectibility. Thoughtful people and important scholars believe it. And its credibility is bolstered by the undeniable practical successes of many of the political systems that invoke it.

The fiction of popular sovereignty is so much the sturdier—and more useful to our own ambitious schemers and powerful interests who profit from its fallacies—for being notoriously hard to pin down. As Henry Maine (1885, 185) wrote long ago, "the devotee of Democracy is much in the same position as the Greeks with their oracles. All agreed that the voice of an oracle was the voice of a god; but everybody allowed that when he spoke he was not as intelligible as might be desired." Thus, policies and practices that are unjust or simply unsuccessful can always be attributed to some mistranslation or temporary deflection of the people's will, with "special interests" trotted out to play the role played by "ambitious schemers" in 17th-century England. We even have our own "two bodies" doctrine: when majorities go seriously astray, it is not the people that "advised themselves," but rather the people misadvised by others and misled by misordered counsel. "The people are never corrupted," said Rousseau, "but sometimes deceived."

In all these ways, conventional thought has avoided the painful task of grappling seriously with all the evidence undermining the standard versions of democratic theory. "Well, yes, there are problems," we say, and then we turn back to the impossible dream. In consequence, cheerful illusions and wish fulfillment have dominated both popular and scholarly thought about democracy for two centuries. Democratic theory has sailed along as if no iceberg had struck and the engine room were not taking on water. But the damage to the intellectual structure is very real.

Both the allure and the cost of romanticism in this domain were eloquently described by political philosopher John Dunn (1999, 342–343) in an essay on democratic political accountability:

> To be ruled is both necessary and inherently discomfiting (as well as dangerous). For our rulers to be accountable to us softens its intrinsic humiliations, probably sets some hazy limits to the harms that they will voluntarily choose to do to us collectively, and thus diminishes some of the dangers to which their rule may expose us. To suggest that we can ever hope to have the power to make them act just as we would wish them to suggests that it is really we, not they, who are ruling. This is an illusion, and probably a somewhat malign illusion: either a self-deception, or an instance of being deceived by others, or very probably both.

Dunn went on to say that "a political science that did justice to democracy (in all its ambiguity) would have to be one in which the presence of these per-

ceptions and sentiments was recognized and explained, and their consequences accurately assessed, not one in which their existence was denied or
dismissed as irrational in the first instance."

The history of democratic thought—including much contemporary political
science—is marked by an addiction to romantic theories. As with any addiction, the first step toward recovery is to admit that we have a problem.

NOTES

1. We thank Jane Mansbridge for emphasizing the centrality of this concept in our
argument.

2. These two models by no means exhaust the variety of meanings of democracy
around the world, or even within the United States. For example, the (overlapping)
traditions of *participatory democracy, face-to-face democracy,* and *deliberative democracy* have received a great deal of attention from academic theorists (Pateman 1970;
Barber 1984; Habermas 1994; Fishkin 1995; Benhabib 1996; Gutmann and Thompson
1996; Sanders 1997; Macedo 1999; Cohen 2003), and they have been implemented with
more or less success in a variety of settings, especially in small groups and local communities (Mansbridge 1980; Mendelberg and Oleske 2000; Fung 2004; Karpowitz 2006).
However, notwithstanding some creative attempts to employ small-scale deliberative
exercises as simulations of how mass publics *would* decide controversial issues in a
deliberative fashion (Fishkin 1991; 2009), these models seem to us to be less relevant for
understanding democratic politics on a national scale than those we consider here.

3. Pateman (1970, 3–5, 16–20) correctly pointed out that no such "classical theorists"
exist; but she acknowledged that "one could extract something which bears a family
resemblance to Schumpeter's definition of the "classical theory" from the 19th-century
works of Jeremy Bentham and James Mill, among others. Some popular writers in the
Progressive Era, such as William Allen White (1910), nicely exemplify the viewpoint
that Schumpeter criticized. The high hopes for public opinion surveys as a guiding
force for democratic policy-making reflect the same Progressive logic (Gallup 1940/1968).

4. The authors of *The American Voter* adopted this view (Campbell et al. 1960, 545).
An updated version of Churchill's argument is that democracy promotes freedom,
human development, and material well-being (Dahl 1989; Mueller 1999; Przeworski
et al. 2000). Demonstrating causal effects in this domain is very hard, but even if they
exist, this line of argument generally does not speak to *how* democracy matters and
how it should be organized to work better.

REFERENCES

Barber, Benjamin R. 1984. *Strong Democracy: Participatory Politics for a New Age.*
   Berkeley: University of California Press.
Benhabib, Seyla. 1996. "Toward a Deliberative Model of Democratic Legitimacy." In
   Democracy and Difference: Contesting the Boundaries of the Political, edited by
   Seyla Benhabib, 67–94. Princeton, NJ: Princeton University Press.
Berelson, Bernard R., Paul F. Lazarsfeld, and William N. McPhee. 1954. *Voting: A
   Study of Opinion Formation in a Presidential Campaign.* Chicago: University of
   Chicago Press.
Bryce, James. 1894. *The American Commonwealth.* 3rd ed., vol. 2. New York: Macmillan.

Campbell, Angus, Philip E. Converse, Warren E. Miller, and Donald E. Stokes. 1960. *The American Voter*. New York: John Wiley.

Cohen, Joshua. 2003. "Deliberation and Democratic Legitimacy." In *Debates in Contemporary Political Philosophy: An Anthology*, Derek Matravers and Jon Pike, edited by Derek Matravers and Jon Pike, 342–60. London: Routledge.

Converse, Philip E. 1964. "The Nature of Belief Systems in Mass Publics." In *Ideology and Discontent*, edited by David E. Apter, 206–61. Glencoe, IL: Free Press.

Dahl, Robert A. 1961. *Who Governs? Democracy and Power in an American City*. New Haven, CT: Yale University Press.

———. 1989. *Democracy and Its Critics*. New Haven, CT: Yale University Press.

———. 1998. *On Democracy*. New Haven, CT: Yale University Press.

Dickinson, John. 1930. "Democratic Realities and Democratic Dogma." *American Political Science Review* 24: 283–309.

Dunn, John. 1999. "Situating Democratic Political Accountability." In *Democracy, Accountability, and Representation*, edited by Adam Przeworski, Susan C. Stokes, and Bernard Manin, 329–44. New York: Cambridge University Press.

Fishkin, James S. 1991. *Democracy and Deliberation: New Directions for Democratic Reform*. New Haven, CT: Yale University Press.

———. 1995. *The Voice of the People: Public Opinion and Democracy*. New Haven, CT: Yale University Press.

———. 2009. *When the People Speak: Deliberative Democracy and Public Consultation*. New York: Oxford University Press.

Fung, Archon. 2004. *Empowered Participation: Reinventing Urban Democracy*. Princeton, NJ: Princeton University Press.

Gallup, George. 1940/1968. *The Pulse of Democracy: The Public Opinion Poll and How It Works*. New York: Greenwood.

Gutmann, Amy, and Dennis Thompson. 1996. *Democracy and Disagreement: Why Moral Conflict Cannot Be Avoided in Politics, and What Should Be Done about It*. Cambridge, MA: Belknap.

Habermas, Jürgen. 1994. "Three Normative Models of Democracy." *Constellations* 1: 1–10.

Kantorowicz, Ernst H. 1957. *The King's Two Bodies: A Study in Mediaeval Political Theology*. Princeton, NJ: Princeton University Press.

Karpowitz, Christopher. 2006. "Having a Say: Public Hearings, Deliberation, and American Democracy." PhD dissertation, Department of Politics, Princeton University.

Key, V. O., Jr. 1966. *The Responsible Electorate: Rationality in Presidential Voting 1936–1960*. Cambridge, MA: Harvard University Press.

Kinder, Donald R. 1983. "Diversity and Complexity in American Public Opinion." In *Political Science: The State of the Discipline*, edited by Ada Finifter, 389–425. Washington, DC: American Political Science Association.

Lazarsfeld, Paul F., Bernard Berelson, and Hazel Gaudet. 1948. *The People's Choice: How the Voter Makes Up His Mind in a Presidential Campaign*. 2nd ed. New York: Columbia University Press.

Lippmann, Walter. 1914. *A Preface to Politics*. New York: Mitchell Kennerley.

———. 1922/1946. *Public Opinion*. New York: Penguin.

———. 1925. *The Phantom Public*. New York: Harcourt, Brace.

Lowell, A. Lawrence. 1913. *Public Opinion and Popular Government*. New York: Longmans, Green.

Macedo, Stephen, ed. 1999. *Deliberative Politics: Essays on Democracy and Disagreement*. New York: Oxford University Press.

Maine, Henry Sumner. 1885. *Popular Government: Four Essays*. London: John Murray.

Mansbridge, Jane J. 1980. *Beyond Adversary Democracy*. New York: Basic Books.

Mendelberg, Tali, and John Oleske. 2000. "Race and Public Deliberation." *Political Communication* 17: 169–91.

Morgan, Edmund S. 1988. *Inventing the People: The Rise of Popular Sovereignty in England and America*. New York: Norton.

Mueller, John E. 1999. *Capitalism, Democracy, and Ralph's Pretty Good Grocery*. Princeton, NJ: Princeton University Press.

Niebuhr, Reinhold. 1932. *Moral Man and Immoral Society*. New York: Scribner's.

———. 1944. *The Children of Light and the Children of Darkness*. New York: Scribner's.

Pateman, Carole. 1970. *Participation and Democratic Theory*. Cambridge: Cambridge University Press.

Przeworski, Adam, Michael E. Alvarez, José Antonio Cheibub, and Fernando Limongi. 2000. *Democracy and Development: Political Institutions and Well-Being in the World, 1950–1990*. New York: Cambridge University Press.

Sandburg, Carl. 1936. *The People, Yes*. New York: Harcourt, Brace.

Sanders, Lynn M. 1997. "Against Deliberation." *Political Theory* 25: 347–76.

Schumpeter, Joseph A. 1942. *Capitalism, Socialism and Democracy*. New York: Harper & Brothers.

Stimson, James A. 2004. *Tides of Consent: How Public Opinion Shapes American Politics*. New York: Cambridge University Press.

White, William Allen. 1910. *The Old Order Changeth: A View of American Democracy*. New York: Macmillan.

13.5

JAMES A. STIMSON

From *Tides of Consent: How Public Opinion Shapes American Politics*

Stimson helps us make sense of the confusing patterns of polls and campaign ups and downs for presidential candidates. By combining data from many election surveys conducted throughout presidential election years, he examines broad trends for winning and losing candidates. The overall trends lead to several key findings: nearly all voting Americans make up their minds about whom they will vote for over the summer; there is some movement in late summer after the party conventions; and debates occurring in the fall hardly move people in either direction. Stimson concludes that in most presidential election years, media attention on day-to-day campaigning is good for television and social media, but meaningful shifts in voter support are uncommon and, when they occur, tend to be gradual.

Much of what goes on in presidential campaigns that might matter is idiosyncratic. . . . However much they might matter, there is no systematic way to observe their influence. But every campaign has nominating conventions, and most have candidate debates. Those repeatable phenomena can be observed.

PARTY NOMINATING CONVENTIONS

At the dawn of the television age in the early 1950s, which is pretty much the dawn of serious political polling as well, presidential nominating conventions were raucous affairs, uncontrolled and unpredictable. Americans could tune in[to] their snowy black-and-white TVs and see history happening in front of them. And they did tune in. An electorate normally tuned out and uninterested found the conventions pretty interesting and exciting, the Olympic Games of politics. There were memorable calls of the states as the conventions fought over rules, platforms, and candidates.

That kind of citizen interest is so strikingly out of normal that you would expect the experience to carry influence. Just the time spent matters. Citizen attention to politics varies across the full scale from political junky to nothing. But for some, the three or four evenings in front of the TV set represent as many

From James A. Stimson, *Tides of Consent: How Public Opinion Shapes American Politics* (New York, NY: Cambridge University Press, 2004).

hours thinking about politics as occur in the four-year span between conventions. We expect change of attitude to occur when people are actually focused on politics, and this is the focal event.

Nominating conventions by the end of the twentieth century were anything but raucous. Convention managers had learned that the conventions, if run smoothly, could have big positive effects on the campaign. In the case of the Democrats, the 1968 convention riots also illustrated the harm that could come from out-of-control expression. Hubert Humphrey's campaign for the presidency never recovered from the events of four days of street battles between antiwar protesters and police.[1]

Coupled with the multiplication and progressively earlier staging of state presidential primaries, the element of unpredictability was lost. In 2000, for example, both George W. Bush and Al Gore had solid majorities of committed delegates in early March, four to five months before the conventions were staged. For many years the conventions were still a good show, as fights over the party platform or the vice presidential nominee replaced selecting the presidential nominee as the main events. Those too are now gone. Unfortunately for TV viewers, convention managers have learned that control makes for good TV impression. The impulse to have a good fight is now effectively suppressed by managers who want no interruptions of the unplanned into their scripted shows. Boring works.

As the conventions become ever more boring and predictable, TV coverage has fallen off and viewership has declined. The opportunity to see history being made is gone. The conventions merely ratify what has long been known, long ago decided. Nonetheless, the practices that have emerged over how the conventions are staged, how the attention is focused on one party in its special week, how the opposition goes quiet (convention week is normally scheduled as a vacation break for the other party's campaign), and how the media commentators limit their skepticism while the show is going on continue. So even as the public loses interest, it is possible that a party's convention could still produce a "bounce" for its candidate's team.

The net effect of the two conventions must, on average, be zero. Since both parties hold conventions, whatever their typical effects, the effects should be offsetting. Perhaps that accounts for the scarcity of analysis of their effects. But that is true only on average. In a particular campaign, the possibility exists that one side may get a bigger bounce than the other and hence a prospect that the convention bounce might matter for the outcome.

Because the two conventions in each campaign are at least partially offsetting, it is hard to see a clean picture of the effects. Party A holds its convention and gains a few points. Then two or three weeks later, B stages a convention and wins back the momentum that A had earlier gained. To get a sense of how much the conventions matter, I am going to assess only the second one for each campaign, the one case where we can see effects over several weeks that do not get cancelled.

Timing of the nominating conventions is not arbitrary. By convention, the "out" party always goes first. The party that currently holds the White House then follows some weeks later. The span between the two varies from almost nothing (1956), to the more typical two or three weeks, to six weeks (1972). It doesn't appear to matter which goes first. The sixteen elections divide into seven first convention winners, eight second convention winners, and, for harmony, the sixteenth case, a virtual tie in which the first convention party won the electoral vote and the second won the popular vote.

To assess the convention impact on the party that holds it, I estimated the gain in the party's share of the horse race polls for each of twenty-eight days following the opening of the convention.[2] The four-week period is chosen to provide the lengthiest period post-convention that does not entangle the summer convention effects with fall campaigning and debates. That effect is displayed in Figure [1] along with a smooth estimate of the convention effect that summarizes the twenty-eight independent estimates.

Two things are notable about the effect. One is that it is very large. The almost four-points impact of the convention is almost as much net movement as we have seen for a whole campaign. Second, it is permanent. A full four weeks after the convention, the effect has not decayed at all. Often called the convention bounce, this effect is clearly misnamed. Things that bounce go up and then come back down. The convention effect goes up and, the evidence says, stays up.

The idea of a bounce no doubt comes from observing both conventions. The effect of the first never lasts because it is promptly offset by the second. But what these data say is that the temporary appearance of the first is an illusion.

FIGURE [1] The Effect of the Second Party Convention Over Twenty-Eight Days: Daily Estimates and Smoothed Effect (in Bold)

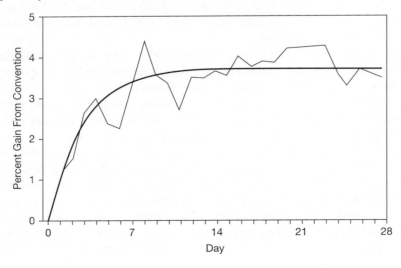

It is really a permanent gain for the first party that is later offset by a permanent loss of about the same magnitude when the second party holds its convention. This distinction matters. A true bounce would be transient, an effect in polls for a few days that would have been long gone by Election Day. A permanent effect means that the party that gets the better bounce, and things are never exactly equal, will carry that advantage into the election.

Consider an illustration, the Obama versus Romney contest of 2012. The Republicans were the party out of office and therefore held the earlier convention, August 27 through August 30, in Tampa.[3] In a race shaping up to be very close, but with Romney persistently trailing, a convention bounce was much needed. It didn't happen. In the six-day period when the bounce effect could have been observed (before the Democratic gathering in Charlotte a week later stole its spotlight), Mitt Romney actually suffered a fraction of a point decline in the polls.

Perhaps the growing polarization of American politics led voters to earlier decisions in 2012, with Democrats and independents leaning toward the Democratic Party already solidly opposed to Romney by the late August convention time. We can't say with confidence what is responsible. But it is quite clear that there was no Romney bounce.

The bounce from the Democratic National Convention, also smaller than normal, is at least observable. Following the first day of the Democratic convention, Barack Obama gained about half a point, a gain that grew steadily larger to about a full point over the ensuing month. Obama entered the convention leading by about 51 to 49%—a two-point lead that had held steady for much of the campaign—and gained a point to about 52 to 48% by late September. So the one-point bounce was only about one-fourth of the normal effect. But with the contest holding so steady, a one-point gain moved Obama to the safer lead he would hold through Election Day.

The Obama bounce can be seen in Figure [2], where the bars in the graph show the gain or loss from the beginning date of the convention and the smoothed line shows the predicted summary shape of the bounce effect. Interpreting the bounce can be difficult and subjective. Witness the infrequent days when the effect looked negative. It is important to focus on the signal—the smooth line— and ignore the noise of daily fluctuations. It is the cumulative effect that matters.

The convention effect in 2012 is one of the smallest ever. In 1992, in contrast, Bill Clinton and Al Gore put on an upbeat feel-good show that energized the Democratic Party for a sprint to the finish. The Republican Convention that year featured angry speeches about family values that did not play well at all. The result was a decisive edge to the Democrats, by my estimate the biggest differential ever, accounting for ten points of Bill Clinton's final margin. That is a good deal larger than Clinton's win (53.4% to 46.6%).

Only slightly smaller is the historic 1968 campaign, where the contrast between a united Republican show nominating Richard Nixon produced a better-than-average bounce while the Democrats featured the most closely

FIGURE [2]   The Obama Bounce in 2012

covered street riots of all times. The mob of press and TV in Chicago for the Democratic convention quickly refocused on the angry confrontations between demonstrators and Chicago police. The demonstrators featured the angriest and most unkempt, to whom the TV cameras naturally migrated. The Chicago police and their boss, Mayor Richard J. Daley, were a low point in modern law enforcement, appearing more intent on doing bodily damage to demonstrators than on keeping order. Hubert Humphrey, the "Happy Warrior," was left to try to run a campaign while an angry nation debated which side of the street riots it liked least. Humphrey had to try to explain how the Democrats, who couldn't organize a peaceful gathering to nominate a candidate, would be able to run the country. He didn't succeed. The convention effect I estimate was worth 7.8 points to Richard Nixon, which is about 6.8 more than needed to win the election.

Nixon also benefited from the contrast in 1972 but didn't need the edge in that contest. The Democrats put on the last of the anything goes, uncontrolled conventions in that year, managing to start late and fill prime time with lengthy speeches and floor fights while George McGovern's acceptance speech, the key opportunity to get attention from voters, was pushed backed to 3 AM, virtually early morning the day after. The size of his audience must have rivaled the numbers who heard acceptance speeches before the dawn of mass communications.

The other case of really decisive convention influence is 1988. This time there is no such obvious culprit on the Democratic side. Perhaps the party just lacked enthusiasm. The contrast was important. Running a close race going into the convention, Michael Dukakis got a typical bounce from the Democratic convention. George Bush got more than twice as much from the Republican convention, moving him into a lead that he held through Election Day.

The conclusion that emerges from this analysis is simple. Party nominating conventions are very important, a key influence on winning and losing. Compared to other things, which are small, scattered, and often offsetting, conventions are the key thing. But what is it exactly about a nominating convention that has such influence?

The Causality of the Bounce

What we know for sure, all we know for sure, about the convention effects is when they occur. We call them convention bounces because systematic movements in the polls tend to happen during and shortly after the conventions meet. If something else is happening at about the same time, then perhaps the conventions get too much credit. But there are no good candidates for that "something else" role.

The data are clear. In every contest since 1972 (with the exception of Romney in 2012) (which is to say, in every contest for which we have good data), the winner gained ground when his own party met and lost ground when the opposition met. All the way back to 1960, indeed, that pattern is broken by only one exception. In 1972, Richard Nixon, on his way to a landslide win, gained ground while the Democrats met to nominate McGovern. Something is going on. But what?

Why do the conventions have such big effects? The reasons are numerous. One is that they energize the faithful. Most partisans in the United States are willing to stray, to find the other party's candidates engaging or their programs attractive. What the conventions can do is remind them why they are on one side and not the other and reinforce emotional and symbolic ties. Democrats in 1980 who were Poles or Lithuanians and union members found Ronald Reagan, with his he-man image, optimism, and engaging smile, an attractive figure. But if they tuned in the Democratic convention of that year, they saw delegates who had Polish and Lithuanian names and union members wearing bowling shirts with the union local written on the back. Firming up the party base is easier to do than convincing the other side, or even neutrals, and usually pays bigger dividends in votes. Hence conventions prominently feature appeals to pure partisanship, reminders of common values, and memories of past candidates and campaigns. Four days of that symbolic appeal exert a powerful pull on those who tune in.

Conventions also unite the party factions. Many conventions occur after bruising intra-party battles over the nomination, where the losing side has reason not to like the nominee and not to be engaged in or supportive of the campaign. Conventions are an opportunity for winners, enlisting their beaten opponents as allies, to reach out to the losing side and say, "We are all Republicans" (or Democrats). The 1980 Republican convention was particularly crucial in that regard. Ronald Reagan, although a fixture in Republican politics since the 1960s, was an outsider, his campaign an insurgency against Republican regulars with whom he had jousted four years earlier when trying to unseat Gerald Ford. Had he not successfully healed the rift, starting with the choice of George Bush for the vice presidency, he could not have been successful in November.

We don't know very well who moves when the polls move. My surmise is that much of the convention bounce is from partisans of these sorts, the uninvolved who might have strayed and the involved on the losing side of primary campaigns. Both have reason to say they will not support the party's candidate before the convention, and both have reason to change, to come home to the comfortable associations of the past. We tend to think of campaigns and polls as a struggle for the undecided and the independents. But given how little interest those groups show in politics, they are not particularly likely to respond to conventions.

For the undecided, if they tune in—a very big if these days—they will be exposed to about twelve hours of unpaid political advertising. Increasingly scripted by advertising professionals, the conventions are the party's best opportunity to get out a wholly one-sided message. Some of this is the building or rebuilding of image. Voters who tuned into the Democratic convention in 2000 might have believed that Al Gore was born wearing a blue suit with his finger pointing in the air debating public issues. The convention was an opportunity to humanize Gore, to show that indeed he had a childhood and youth, had served in Vietnam, was a person. George Bush (the elder) accomplished the same thing, more successfully the data say. The rap on Bush was that he was a "wimp," a meaningless but nonetheless pejorative term. The real George Bush, anything but wimplike, had been an athlete in his youth and a courageous fighter pilot in the Pacific War against Japan. Little was heard of the "wimp factor" after the Republican convention.

Things that the parties do are not the whole story. Even if their show were uninspired and ineffective, they would still benefit from two customs. One of these is that the press changes its usual behavior during the conventions. Acting as if they were household guests, not the usual curmudgeons, they aren't quite as critical as normal. Not wholly uncritical, they still are somewhat restrained about calling the party message a pack of lies. We know that whether or not the press is a neutral arbiter, the public counts on it to play that role, to tell voters which interpretation is more plausible when the parties disagree. To the extent that criticism is restrained, the party holding the convention gains a temporary advantage.

The parties benefit also from the absence of opposition. Following custom, the other party does not schedule important campaign events during the convention. Often the other party convention is the occasion for a vacation from the hectic pace of the year-long campaign. These four-day periods, and perhaps a day or two before and after, represent the only one-sided campaigning we see. One party puts out its message without the usual counter message. This too should produce a bounce, although only a temporary one.

Some Long-Term Patterns

Some general conclusions emerge when one looks at over sixty years of data. First, it appears to be the case that maximum convention bounces occur for candidates who are not well known. For them the convention is the opportunity to fill an empty image with positive content. Image, we know, can be built for a candidate who is unknown but is very hard to change for someone the public knows well. For candidates who ran twice, for example, the convention bounce for their first run is more than twice that of the second, even though they were more likely to win the reelection bid and by bigger numbers. Look for conventions to matter most when an unknown challenger—for example, Bill Clinton in 1992—takes on a well-known opponent. In these cases the challenger is likely to come from behind and to gain the advantage at convention time.

Republicans have done about 30% better on average than Democrats. That probably is not an enduring advantage but just a reflection of the two Democratic disaster conventions of 1968 and 1972, in 1972 when all the action was after midnight and 1968 when the Democrats wished it had been. Excluding those two cases, the party bounces are near identical on average.

My bottom line on the conventions is that they are times of intense political learning. A public that is nearly always tuned out tunes in for a few days, and those are opportunities to learn about people and programs, times to change views. The more there is to learn, when candidates are unknown or suffer from inaccurate images as with vice presidents, the more important the occasion. Nothing else in campaigning compares.

When we look back at campaigns, and particularly when we do so through the lens of television, we are most apt to remember the candidates standing together on stage in the TV debate. The famous barbs and gaffes make good thirty-second recreations of the feel of an election. But do they matter for the outcome? Are they the moments that turned history? Or are they merely convenient stock footage for story telling?

CANDIDATE DEBATES

Next Tuesday is Election Day. Next Tuesday all of you will go to the polls; you will stand there and make a decision. I think when you make that decision, it might be well if you would ask yourself: Are you better off than you were four years ago? Is it easier for you to go and buy things in the stores than it was four years ago? Is there more or less unemployment in the country than there was four years ago? Is America as respected throughout the world as it was? Do you feel that our security is as safe, that we are as strong as we were four years ago? And if you answer all those questions, "Yes," why then I think your choice is very obvious as to who you will vote for [nods toward Jimmy Carter]. If you don't agree, if you don't think that this course that we have been on for the last four years is what you would like to see us follow for the next four, then I can suggest another choice that you have. (Ronald Reagan, October 29, 1980, from his closing summary)

One of the classic moments of televised presidential debates, Ronald Reagan's challenge to voters to evaluate the last four years, hit home. It became a defining characteristic of 1980. Great debates are the source of campaign legend. It was Richard Nixon's bad makeup job in the historic matchup with John F. Kennedy that made him look sweaty, tense, and untrustworthy. Jerry Ford lost the presidency over a silly claim about Eastern Europe, deflecting a Carter jab that didn't score anyhow. Ronald Reagan's joke about opponent Mondale's age was the key moment of the 1984 contest. These have become the standard fare of explaining election outcomes for the presidency. Do they really explain? Do the debates decide outcomes?

We know the typical scenario, and what we know should give us pause about strong interpretations. In the usual case, the polls of debate watchers ask "Who won?" and return a mixed verdict that is about proportional to the candidate's standing in the polls. Morning after newspaper accounts complain of boredom, bemoan the lack of real action, and deny that there could have been a winner. To read them again, years later, is to see how legends are created, for the decisive stories that come to be told don't seem to have been noticed by those writing fresh from just having witnessed the real thing. But some commentator, under the guise of neutrality, declares a winner. Then the polls change. Those who watched the debate didn't agree on a winner. But after the commentator "call," new polls, now including many who did not witness the event, say by larger numbers that the "winner" won. Eventually the win becomes fact; it acquires an "everybody knows" status as political legend.

Somebody does win the presidential contest. And once the person wins, we ask why. Why did the winner win? Why did the loser lose? It is tempting to use the debate to settle both questions, to find high moments that were good for the winner and lows that were bad for the loser. The horse race polls are a useful corrective to all this. They, unlike the stories we tell after the fact, are not a social construction. They are what they are. If the debates are as decisive as claimed, we should see the debate winner rise in the polls. To be truly decisive, the rise should be enough to account for the victory margin.

To get a feel for what's going on, we need to see beneath the surface of the polls. The surface is the roiling waves of sampling fluctuation, the ups and downs of daily movement that mean exactly nothing. The polls rise or fall by a point or two because today's sample of 1,000 citizens is a different 1,000 than yesterday's. We need to know what's happening beneath the waves, whether candidates are gaining or losing momentum.

How Much Influence?

Thomas Holbrook (1996), in his careful analysis of the effect of debates in three contests, makes the point that the debates can hardly be as influential as often claimed because they occur so late in the process that most voters have already decided on their candidate. That makes the voters rooters in the debates, cheering for their side, not dispassionate observers neutrally scoring points. And we also know that not a lot of change occurs in the time span between debates and voting, which can be as short as one week at the extreme. If the eventual winner is already well ahead when the debate is held, claims for debate influence on the outcome are not credible.

We can get a big picture view of the issue by looking at when change occurs in candidate standing and when debates are held. For a summary first view, Figure [3] combines the polls of the eight winners in the closely contested elections of 1976, 1980, 1988, 1992, 2000, 2004, 2008, and 2012. As if they were five versions of one campaign, the polls from each date are averaged together, and then the whole thing is smoothed to purge it of sampling variation.

This puts the Holbrook timing argument in even stronger light. The figure clearly shows that important things do happen: most eventual winners com-

FIGURE [3]   Winner Percent of the Two-Party Intended Vote for Eight Contested Campaigns, Smoothed: 1976, 1980, 1988, 1992, 2000, 2004, 2008, and 2012 ing from behind. But those important movements have already happened before the first debate is ever aired. The period in which the debates are going on is actually the flattest in the entire year, the time when change is least apparent.

We know something about why this should be so. Recall the fundamental argument that observed that change over the campaign is not people switching from one candidate to another; it is switching by the uninvolved between having no preference at all (but nonetheless answering when pressed to do so in a survey) into having a real preference. When people first think about the contest, first view it on TV, first have conversations about it with friends or family, then they come down on one side or the other, where most will stay through Election Day. When the numbers are showing systematic movement (the point of smoothing being to highlight systematic movement), then people are making decisions. When the movement stops, they have already decided. What the figure clearly shows is that, at least averaged over eight campaigns, systematic movement has stopped before the debates are held.

On average, the audience for a presidential candidate debate is about half the number of people who will go to the polls. What we know of decisions to participate in politics generally permits a surmise about who that half will be. They are much more likely, in the first instance, to be partisans—those who think of themselves as belonging to one of the two major parties—than independents. Either because having chosen sides makes one more interested or because those who are more interested are more likely to take sides, interest in matters political is highly associated with being committed to one side of the party debate. And then, even if one is not partisan, having decided for whom to vote makes the contest more interesting, as rooting is more engaging than neutral observation. So, even though we think of the debates as a struggle to influence the undecided, the numbers of undecided viewers should be small.

What we know about late deciders reinforces this view. Far from the editorial page heroes who calmly absorb facts and put off a decision until all the facts are in, real late deciders are instead people so totally uninvolved in politics, so little interested, so little informed, that they are barely aware that a presidential campaign is occurring.[4] It is highly improbable that they will tune in to the candidate debates when most citizens with greater interest in politics do not.

The debates occur so late in the process that most voters have already decided, and the audience they attract will consist in the main of loyalists to the two sides. That doesn't leave much room for influence. But a fair test requires looking at individual contests, where it is possible that some of the effects that are lost in averaging emerge where they matter.

The successful reelection campaigns can be set aside at the outset. With year-long large leads, debate effects are too late and too small to play a role in these contests. The 1984 campaign is an interesting case that is part exception and part confirmation of the general point. Ronald Reagan's performance in the first debate against Walter Mondale was poor. He didn't seem alert or on top of his game and seemed at moments confused and dazed. For a man later diagnosed with Alzheimer's disease, it seems possible that we were seeing early symptoms. His big lead did slip in the polls, and it seems possible that a second such performance would have shaken it. The American electorate was prepared to give him another four years, but a whiff of suspicion that he could not do the job might have changed that. In any case the second performance was strong, doubts were erased, and 1984 ended up being another case where debates didn't figure in the outcome.

We look to the closely contested races for the key evidence that debates might matter. That begins in Figure [4], which pictures the first three campaigns in which televised debates were held, 1960, 1976, and 1980.[5] The first of these is the 1960 squeaker, of which, like the later 2000 campaign, it can be said that *anything* could have altered the outcome. So if we ask if the debates might have mattered, the answer can only be yes. But so too it might have mattered if the elections were held on Monday or Wednesday instead of Tuesday. The smoothed horse race polls do show, however, that Kennedy's winning margin did not come from the debates with Nixon. Kennedy was by a trivial amount further ahead on the eve of the famous first debate than in his Election Day margin. And these data suggest that the trend that carried him to the finish line originated in late July, two months before the first debate.

Observers of the 1976 debates between Jimmy Carter and Gerald Ford generally gave the nod to Carter. Ford was hurt by his gaffe in claiming at an awkward

FIGURE [4] Debate Timing and Opinion Movement for the 1960, 1976, and 1980 Campaigns. (Smoothed Horse Race Data with Diamond Symbols Indicating Debates)

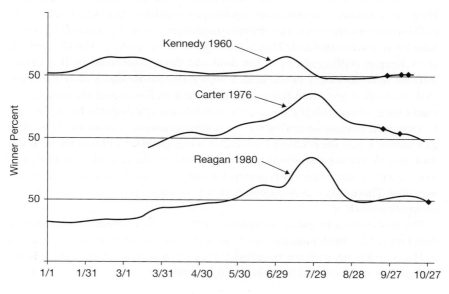

FIGURE [5]   Debate Timing and Opinion Movement for the 1988, 1992, and 2000 Campaigns. (Smoothed Horse Race Data with Diamond Symbols Indicating Debates)

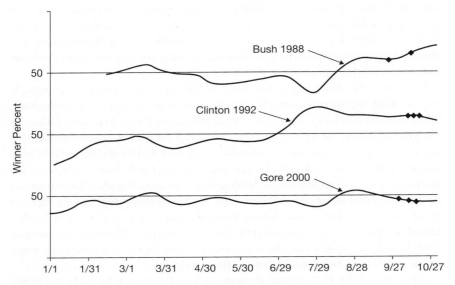

moment no Soviet influence in Eastern Europe. But if that was the case—that is, if Carter really was the winner—then the debates could have played no role because Carter lost some of his lead following the debates.

The 1980 campaign is one that might have turned on the last-minute debate. Here the data lead us astray, showing Reagan slipping at the end (in the public polls) when we know from the outcome (and from Carter's polls) that he had to have been moving upward. This is partly a matter of timing. The Carter polls show Reagan pulling ahead in the final two days, after most polling organizations were no longer in the field. Could it be that Reagan's effective line— "Ask yourself if you were better off four years ago"—turned the election? It might have, along with the hostage crisis, changed minds at the final moment. But we need to remember that the stagnating economy was an everyday Reagan theme; it was the problem for which his proposed tax cut was the solution. And, too, this is not just a well-turned debate line. The remark was made in a year in which consumer expectations for the economic future reached an all-time low. There was a real economy, real personal experience, that made the debate line work.

The Bush versus Dukakis campaign of 1988 was never close after Labor Day. (See Figure [5].) Bush took a steady lead in the July convention season and held it. His two debates with the colorless Dukakis might have added a point to his margin but aren't needed to explain why he won.

Much the same can be said of the 1992 Clinton campaign. Clinton's lead in the (sometimes) three-candidate race was built during the conventions and never seriously challenged after that. If the debates mattered for the 1992 outcome, then we must declare George Bush their winner because Bush gained a little ground after the debates.

In the Bush versus Gore 2000 race, like the 1960 race, anything could have changed this outcome, including trivial things. But this campaign is probably the best case for debate influence. Observers of the debates thought Gore soured voters by his aggressive behavior in [the] first debate, going for a knockout punch that he failed to achieve. These judgments are hard to confirm, but this one at least was true enough that Gore changed his style dramatically in subsequent debates. Recalling that Gore's horse race numbers were artificially low because millions of voters told pollsters that they would vote for Ralph Nader but then voted for Gore, we can surmise that Gore was probably actually ahead on the eve of the debates and perhaps by a big enough margin that his popular vote win would also have carried the Electoral College vote that mattered. Although Gore slipped following the debates, his downward trend was in place before the debates were held. This isn't a decisive call for the influence of TV debates, but influence certainly cannot be ruled out either.[6]

We examine the most recent three presidential contests in Figure [6], showing the campaigns of George W. Bush in 2004, and Barack Obama both in 2008 and again in 2012. What characterizes all three contests is that voters seemed

FIGURE [6]   Debate Timing and Opinion Movement for the 2004, 2008, and 2012 Campaigns. (Smoothed Horse Race Data with Diamond Symbols Indicating Debates)

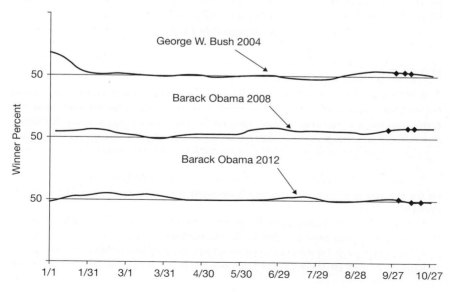

to make up their minds early in the contests and then never change. The three sets of trial heats, that is, show very little systematic change over the full election year.

And again we see a pattern of presidential debates staged so late in the contests that the elections had taken virtually their final shape before the debates started. Although it is very hard to see in Figure [6], 2012 is something of an exception. The first debate between Barack Obama and Mitt Romney showed a clear winner, Romney. Perhaps exhibiting the worst performance of his political career, President Obama was just not sharp, which was apparent both to polls of uncommitted voters and most of all to Obama himself and his campaign staff. The morning after brought visible disappointment and concern to the Obama camp—much as what had happened to another incumbent, Ronald Reagan, twenty-eight years earlier—and elation to the Romney forces. And the polls showed the expected effect, showing the steady Obama lead eroding into a virtual tie.[7] In the end Obama stopped the slide with strong performances in debates two and three and eventually claimed a larger-than-expected victory. So that first debate was not decisive. Its loser won the election. But it did matter, altering the dynamics in the final weeks of the campaign to the point that Mitt Romney believed that he was winning on Election Day.

What can we conclude then about the debates? What we have seen is perhaps some influence. The evidence is inconclusive to say that debates either matter or do not. But if they do matter at all, their influence is vastly smaller than that of, say, the conventions. The reelection landslides show that once voters have decided, debates will not change the outcome.

There is no case where we can trace a substantial shift to the debates. But in elections that were close at debate times, there are cases (1960, 1980, and 2000) where the debates might have been the final nudge. As to why they are so often featured as the central storyline of a presidential election campaign, I lean to the idea that they are conveniently available TV footage.

NOTES

1. My earlier speculation that conventions are particularly important for a "coming out" of former vice presidents into a new public image is richly consistent with the 1968 result. Instead of Hubert Humphrey, what 1968 convention viewers saw was Richard J. Daley, mayor of Chicago, the Chicago police at their low point, and antiwar demonstrators. There was a lot of action packed into those four days, but none of it was any good for Humphrey.

2. Because most survey respondents would be interviewed before the opening gavel on the evening of day one, the impact is assessed beginning on the first day after the opening.

3. Because Hurricane Isaac arrived on the same day as most of the GOP delegates, the convention was recessed on August 26, the planned starting date.

4. This should not be misconstrued as an argument about political independents. Independents, like partisans, come from across the span of political knowledge and

involvement. The late deciders, in contrast, are distinctly those of least knowledge, interest, and awareness of politics. It takes a powerful amount of noninvolvement not to have chosen sides so late in the game.

5. There were no debates in 1964, 1968, or 1972.

6. Mayer (2002) reports a fact that bears on the issue. Isolating "swing voters," those who are essentially neutral in the evaluations they offer in the National Election Studies preelection surveys of September and October (all or virtually all conducted before the debates), he finds that these voters came out slightly (52%) in Gore's camp. Since they were neutral before the debates and slightly pro-Gore after, there is no debate effect to be found that is pro-Bush, the consensus winner among the pundits.

7. This was true only of the national polls. State polls and the Obama internal polling showed a still steady, though slightly diminished, lead.

DISCUSSION QUESTIONS

1. What elements of the Constitution did the majority use to arrive at its decision in *Citizens United v. Federal Election Commission*? Do you agree with this decision? Why or why not?

2. What elements of the Constitution did the majority use to arrive at its decision in *Shelby County, Alabama v. Holder*? Do you agree with this decision? Why or why not?

3. Fox and Lawless place emphasis on efficacy as an important concept in explaining differences between men and women in politics. What do they find about efficacy and its role in helping understand different levels of political ambition?

4. Compare Achen and Bartels' "critical" theory of elections to the traditional theories that they describe. What kinds of evidence do they use to support their theory?

5. Describe the *typical* pattern of polling results for the winning presidential candidate throughout the summer and fall of an election year, focusing especially on what happens after the party conventions and what happens after the debates. How does Stimson explain these patterns?

6. What changes to the conduct of American elections do you think would be valuable in order to improve the functioning of democracy?

14

THE MEDIA

14.1

MATTHEW A. BAUM

From *Soft News Goes to War: Public Opinion and American Foreign Policy in the New Media Age*

Soft news refers to mass media programming that is primarily intended to entertain rather than provide news, but that also includes—as a by-product of the entertainment—information about politics and international events. Baum analyzes the degree to which people who are relatively uninterested in politics receive information about politics from soft news sources. He finds that international crises especially find their way into "water cooler" conversations—and thus the public's broader consciousness—because people learn about these events from soft news.

SUMMARY AND HYPOTHESES

Driven by market competition and the relatively low cost of producing soft news, broadcasters are finding human interest and other entertainment value in places where their predecessors saw only dry news. One implication is that soft news, as opposed to traditional news programming, may actually increase the likelihood that typical individuals—particularly those not normally interested in politics—will be exposed to information about at least *some* of the major issues of the day, especially those that become water-cooler events, albeit in a format that is less public-policy-oriented and less apt to provide a context for understanding an issue.

From Matthew A. Baum, *Soft News Goes to War: Public Opinion and American Foreign Policy in the New Media Age* (Princeton, NJ: Princeton University Press, 2003).

Under normal, everyday circumstances, these developments might not result in a public more attuned to political issues than were earlier generations. Given well-documented increases in political apathy and cynicism about politics, it is not surprising to find that typical individuals are no more interested in politics than their parents or grandparents were. This suggests that individuals have reacted to the explosion of available information by becoming increasingly selective regarding what information warrants their attention. Most of the time, the highly segmented modern television marketplace presumably allows individuals to *escape* news and information more effectively than in prior decades. Soft news programs, for instance, generally avoid such "mundane" political topics as foreign affairs, in favor of more salacious issues like celebrity sex scandals, murder trials, and fashion shows. Hence, with minimal effort, television viewers can remain blissfully uninformed about the day-to-day political issues facing the nation, including foreign policy.

When, however, potential water-cooler events emerge—and cross over from network evening newscasts to the soft news media—a far broader audience will likely confront such issues, albeit perhaps as the subject of an entertainment-oriented talk show or entertainment newsmagazine show. Moreover, unlike the relatively arcane or complex presentation of political information offered by traditional news outlets, soft news programs will focus on aspects of such issues of interest to their particular niche of the viewing audience.

For instance, during the Persian Gulf War, while CNN and the major networks filled the airwaves with graphic images of precision bombs and interviews with military experts, the daytime talk shows hosted by Oprah Winfrey, Geraldo Rivera, and Sally Jesse Raphael, as well as the original tabloid TV newsmagazine, *A Current Affair*, focused on episodic stories of the personal hardships faced by spouses of soldiers serving in the Gulf and on the psychological trauma suffered by families of Americans being held prisoner in Iraq as "human shields." In this context, learning about the war was an incidental byproduct of seeking entertainment (e.g., human drama or a fight between good and evil). War-related information was effectively piggybacked to entertainment-oriented information, and thereby made available to viewers at virtually no additional cost. In other words, when *The Oprah Winfrey Show* presented a program dealing with the Gulf War, substantive information about the war was "piggybacked," via cheap framing (e.g., human impact and injustice), to information presented primarily for its entertainment value. In choosing to watch Oprah, viewers also, at no additional cost, received substantive information about the Persian Gulf War.[1]

The incidental nature of soft news coverage of foreign crises is illustrated in the following comment by Barry Berk of *Access Hollywood*, regarding that program's rationale for covering some foreign crisis issues, despite the program's primary mission of providing their audience with information about movies and celebrities:

I think rather than just say [to a celebrity], "Why did you like that script?" or "Why do you want to make this movie?" . . . it's a way to get to know the celebrities better. And let [the audience] know there's another level there; that they [celebrities] do have opinions; that they're citizens and they're parents, and they have concerns. And they get very upset about the prospect that we're bombing Iraq. Or "good for them, I'm glad we're going in there." You know, they have opinions. I think people find that interesting.[2]

Hence, when a foreign crisis emerges, the numerous programming formats that comprise the modern television marketplace may focus their diverse lenses upon a single issue, albeit varying aspects of that issue. When the mass media unify their focus, I expect the contemporary public, in the aggregate, to be significantly more attentive to such an issue, compared to the publics of prior decades. In today's news environment, when an issue crosses over from traditional news outlets to the soft news media, politically uninterested citizens are far more likely to be exposed and pay attention to the issue—as an incidental by-product of seeking entertainment—relative to most typical political issues, which rarely reach beyond traditional news programming.

Most importantly, this mechanism does not depend on any overall increase in the public's interest in or knowledge about politics or foreign affairs.[3] Indeed, the basis for predicting increased attentiveness is entirely independent of the expected benefit for typical individuals of political information in general or information about foreign affairs in particular. Once someone is exposed to an issue in her preferred programming format, her cost-benefit calculus for paying attention to additional information about the issue is altered. For such an individual, this issue is no longer a typical mundane, and perhaps baffling, political news item.

■ ■ ■

WHAT ARE CRISES AND WHEN DO THEY BECOME WATER-COOLER EVENTS?

■ ■ ■

[D]ue in part to the increasing prevalence of soft news outlets, foreign military crises—as well as some other issues which are decidedly not "high politics"— are increasingly likely to attract the attention of typical individuals. In general, issues that can be readily framed in stark and dramatic terms, thereby priming widely accessible frames, without generating significant cognitive conflict between simultaneously accessible yet contradictory causal narratives, are most likely to be covered by the soft news media. Such issues are thereby most likely to attract the attention of even politically uninterested individuals. These are the issues that occasionally become water-cooler events.

A direct marketing revolution in television has systematically altered the cost-benefit calculus for a large segment of the public, which is not predisposed to follow politics. By transforming mundane political coverage into entertainment, the soft news media have successfully employed piggybacking and cheap framing strategies in order to capture a substantial segment, or niche, of the television audience. This has the perhaps unintended effect of increasing the likelihood that politically uninterested individuals will be exposed to information about those political issues that cross over from hard to soft news outlets.

. . . [T]he class of issues most likely to become water-cooler events [are] "dramatic crises" because these events typically possess the several characteristics necessary to appeal to the soft news media. Nonetheless, not all crises, nor even all dramatic crises, are covered by the soft news media or become water-cooler events. Indeed, it seems unlikely that there exists any foolproof formula for determining ex ante which issues will pass this attentiveness threshold. Rather, given the extraordinary complexity of the modern political, media, and public opinion environments, perhaps the best we can hope for in the near term is an improved understanding of the various factors that raise or lower the probability that a given issue or event will capture the public's imagination.

NOTES

1. The contrast between war coverage on *The Oprah Winfrey Show* and the emphasis of traditional news programming on military tactics and precision bombing campaigns also illustrates the increasing niche orientation of the traditional and soft news media. The former orientation may be intended, in part, to have a greater appeal for the largely female audience that typically watches *The Oprah Winfrey Show*, while the latter type of coverage has traditionally held greater appeal for a male audience.

2. Barry Berk, interview with author, Los Angeles, Calif., June 20, 2000.

3. I do, however, present some evidence in the concluding chapter [not included] that exposure to soft news outlets can enhance some individuals' knowledge about particular foreign crisis events.

14.2

MARISA A. ABRAJANO

From *Campaigning to the New American Electorate: Advertising to Latino Voters*

It has become increasingly important for candidates for federal office—Congress or the presidency—to make explicit appeals to the interests of Latino voters to win elections. Campaign advertisements in Spanish and appeals made in media tailored toward Latinos have become common even in locations with relatively few Latinos. As Abrajano argues, these behaviors of direct appeal to immigrant groups with new citizenship status follow a long tradition in American politics.

CAMPAIGNING TO ETHNIC AND RACIAL MINORITIES IN THE UNITED STATES
■ ■ ■

Candidates, particularly at the local level, have competed for the votes of immigrants since the 1800s (Erie 1990; Dahl 1961; Katznelson 1981). Perhaps the most infamous political machine of all, Tammany Hall, led by William Marcy "Boss" Tweed, pioneered numerous efforts aimed at persuading immigrants to join the powerful Irish machine. These newcomers arrived in droves to the port city of New York, and by 1930, Jews and Italians made up 36 percent of the population of New York City. Party bosses appealed to these groups by offering them party posts and providing "coal, food and rent money to needy Jews and Italians on the Lower East Side" (Erie 1990, 102). Other actions were less substantive in nature; for example, Tammany's "Big Tim" Sullivan "shamelessly 'recognized' the new immigrants with symbolic gestures and donned a yarmulke to solicit Jewish votes" (103). Tammany bosses were also known to eat "corned beef and kosher meat with equal nonchalance" (McNickle 1993, 17) and to advertise in the Yiddish press to reach out to these new immigrants. To gain the support of Italian immigrants, the Irish sponsored legislation to honor Columbus Day as a holiday. Substantively, Congressman James Michael Curley of Boston advocated against literacy tests as one of the requirements for U.S. citizenship and also fought for less-restrictive immigration laws.

From Marisa A. Abrajano, *Campaigning to the New American Electorate: Advertising to Latino Voters* (Palo Alto, CA: Stanford University Press, 2010), Chapter 3.

Not all immigrants were bowled over by these efforts. Instead of joining the Irish-led political machines, many offered their support to Tammany challengers. Jews became increasingly involved with the Socialist Party, particularly because of their concerns over labor and reform politics. Italian immigrants, though, lent their support to the Republicans.

As the earliest accounts on minority campaigning demonstrate, candidates have long believed that appealing to voters based on ethnic group membership is an effective and powerful strategy in gaining their support. The rationale for this behavior could be attributed to the perception that group membership is salient to the political decisions that individuals make. But as the responses from immigrant Jews and Italians indicate, such campaign appeals did not necessarily lead to unconditional support. Some immigrant groups were concerned about substantive matters, especially those that affected their community. Thus, although efforts to target ethnic minorities date back to the late nineteenth century, it is unclear what consequences these efforts may have had on the political well-being of the immigrant or minority group in question.

Historical Efforts at Latino Outreach

Latinos have been a presence on the American landscape for hundreds of years. In 1848, following the Mexican-American War, the northern portion of Mexico was annexed to the United States and, thus, many individuals of Mexican descent became part of the American fabric. The first documented effort aimed at the Latino electorate can be traced back to the 1960 presidential election. John F. Kennedy, the Democratic contender, established Latino outreach efforts by way of his Viva Kennedy clubs. Concentrated primarily in the Southwest and Midwest, these grassroots associations focused on organizing Mexican Americans to support Kennedy. The clubs also indirectly served to incorporate and familiarize them with the electoral process. According to community leader Rodolfo Ramos, "The best thing we did with Viva Kennedy Clubs was that we organized independent local Democratic institutions" (Pycior 1997, 117). And although these clubs were officially part of the Kennedy presidential campaign, they operated independently from the state party Democratic committees (Garcia 2000). Moreover, much like presidential candidates do today, Kennedy sought endorsements from Latino elected officials, such as State Senator Henry Gonzalez of Texas and Los Angeles City Councilman Edward Roybal.

The fact that Kennedy was a Roman Catholic gave him a considerable advantage with this ethnic group, as most Mexican Americans are also of the Catholic faith (Pew Hispanic Center 2007). According to Garcia (2000), Kennedy's religious affiliation "represented a cultural bridge to the Mexican American community . . . it meant that he valued family and tradition" (59). Without a doubt, this shared faith was something that Kennedy and the Democrats intended to capitalize on. Moreover, because "[Kennedy's] wife Jacqueline understood and spoke Spanish, [it] meant that Kennedy could communicate with Mexican Americans and understand their needs" (Garcia 2000, 59).

The Kennedy campaign took advantage of Jacqueline Kennedy's Spanish-language proficiency to create the first-ever televised Spanish-language ad. In a commercial that lasted slightly longer than a minute, she expressed the following sentiments:

> Dear friends, the wife of senator John Kennedy, candidate for the U.S. presidency, is talking to you. In these very dangerous times, when the world peace is threatened by communism, it is necessary to have in the White House a leader able to guide our destinies with a firm hand. My husband has always cared for the interests of all the portions of our society who need the protection of a humanitarian government. For the future of our children and to reach a world where true peace shall exist, vote for the Democratic Party on the eighth of November. Long live Kennedy![1]

The primary emphasis in this landmark political ad is on the personal qualities and traits of the candidate; there is also a subtle reference to Kennedy's commitment to underrepresented groups such as Latinos. Aside from the issue of communism, no mention is made about the policies that concerned Latinos during this time (for example, civil rights). His decision to target the Latino electorate turned out to be a prudent one; Kennedy captured 85 percent of the Latino vote, and some political analysts [have] attributed Kennedy's victory in the close election to the support he received from Latinos (Schmal 2004).

Kennedy's outreach efforts are noteworthy for one main reason. The Viva Kennedy campaign brought Latinos, primarily Mexican Americans at that time, to the national spotlight. Latinos were thus recognized as a constituency that presidential candidates needed to court. In the 1968 Democratic presidential primaries, Eugene McCarthy and Robert F. Kennedy battled for the support of Latinos in the key states of Texas and California. Kennedy's campaign enlisted the aid of the Mexican American Political Association (MAPA) and its president, Bert Corona, to target thousands of potential supporters in East Los Angeles. Kennedy also made a series of campaign appearances in San Antonio, Chicago, and Los Angeles. Another key endorsement came from César Chávez, civil rights advocate and founder of the United Farm Workers, who used his extensive network to mobilize Latino voters. The concerted outreach efforts resulted in Kennedy's victory in California; according to media reports, "Mexican Americans contributed most of the slender margin by which Kennedy beat McCarthy in California" (Pycior 1997, 225). The organizational and political skills exhibited by Latinos through the Viva Kennedy clubs secured their position as an important part of the Democratic base; these clubs also enabled many Latinos to familiarize themselves with the electoral process.

By 1980, Democrats were not the only ones who had established Latino outreach efforts. Along with incumbent Democratic president Jimmy Carter, Republican challenger Ronald Reagan developed a specific campaign for the Latino electorate (Subervi-Velez and Connaughton 2008; Segal 2003). Because Reagan was then the governor of California, he likely recognized the importance of the Latino electorate. Latino rates of electoral participation, however, were quite low, with only 29.9 percent of Latinos turning out to vote in the 1980 presidential election. It is estimated that 60.1 percent of Latinos nationwide supported Carter, but among Hispanic voters in Florida, who are mostly Cuban American, 80 percent voted for Reagan (Schmal 2004). Thus, although both candidates made efforts to reach out to Latinos, Reagan's decisive victory over Carter (50.9 versus 41.1 percent) meant that the Latino vote was not as pivotal as it was in the 1960 presidential race.

Four years later, Reagan stepped up his Latino outreach efforts even more and, with the help of the Republican National Committee (RNC), crafted the "Hispanic Victory Initiative '84: A Proposed Strategy for the Reagan-Bush '84 Hispanic Campaign" (Subervi-Velez and Connaughton 2008). One of the highlights from this sixty-six-page document is a statement indicating that although campaigns may be able "to reach [Latinos] in English . . . you have to convince them in Spanish." Lionel Sosa, the political consultant that spearheaded Reagan's Latino outreach efforts, was confident that Latinos would be willing to support the Republican party—it was just a matter of reaching out to them and convincing them to do so. The two Spanish-language ads developed by Reagan and the RNC, "Democrat All the Way" and "New Tradition," reflected these sentiments. The theme of these ads focused on the notion that although Latinos traditionally have been aligned with the Democrats, they should consider supporting Reagan because of his leadership skills. No specific mention is made, however, about the types of policies enacted or supported by Reagan that would benefit Latinos. Given his success with Cuban Americans in the previous election, Reagan also paid special attention to this community by emphasizing his tough anticommunist position toward Cuba. Moreover, Vice President George H. W. Bush assisted in these campaign efforts by speaking Spanish at various events to attack Mondale.[2]

The Democratic candidate in this election, Walter Mondale, also targeted Latino voters. Adopting Kennedy's campaign slogan, Mondale courted Latinos in both the primary and general elections through his Viva Mondale campaign. He made great efforts in the primary season to reach out to Latinos in California, because they were considered to be a critical swing group in the state. During the general election campaign, Mondale continued these efforts by promising Latinos in Texas that he would appoint coethnics to his cabinet.[3] A surge in the number of national network television news stories covering Latino voters was also evident in this election season, up from seven stories in 1980 to twelve in 1984.[4] As in the previous presidential race, Reagan defeated his opponent by a considerable margin (18.3 percent); he also continued to win the support of the Cuban population in Florida, capturing

82 percent of their votes. But the Latino electorate as a whole continued to cast their ballots in favor of the Democratic candidate, 66 percent versus 32.6 percent.

In the 1988 presidential election, both candidates, George H. W. Bush and Michael Dukakis, made even greater efforts to gain the support and allegiance of Latino voters. The Bush campaign developed a grassroots organization, Hispanics for Bush, in order to target specific campaign messages to Latinos. Altogether, the campaign created four Spanish-language ads that were broadcast on Spanish-language media; some were also dubbed into English and aired on shows with large Latino audiences. The Dukakis campaign created five Spanish-language ads for the general election, a strategy many considered advantageous because the candidate was fluent in Spanish (Subervi-Velez and Connaughton 2008). But, somewhat surprisingly, the campaign spent less than $1 million broadcasting these ads (Segal 2003, 7). The explanation for this low figure was attributed to the well-accepted belief at the time that Latinos were already strong Democratic voters who were unlikely to defect and vote for Bush. Despite these efforts, however, Bush soundly defeated Dukakis by a margin of 7.8 percentage points. Latinos remained supportive of the Democratic candidate, with 70.2 percent of the Latino vote going to Dukakis.

Part of Bush's re-election campaign in 1992 involved targeting the Latino electorate. His challenger in the general election, Bill Clinton, also recognized the importance of the Latino vote. Clinton mostly relied on English-language media to communicate to Latinos and created only one Spanish-language ad, which was aired in the New York media market as a response to a negative ad broadcast by Bush. In contrast, Bush allocated millions to Spanish-language media, mostly in the markets of Illinois, Colorado, New Mexico, and Texas. Both candidates relied on endorsements from either Latino relatives or prominent Latino elected officials; Bush received endorsements from his Latino family members (his daughter-in-law and grandson), whereas Clinton turned to Henry Cisneros, then mayor of San Antonio. It was Clinton who received the lion's share of the Latino vote (71 percent). And although he was similar to his Republican predecessors, Bush captured just 70 percent of the Latino vote in Florida.

The 1996 presidential race also witnessed both the incumbent and the challenger, Republican Bob Dole, developing outreach efforts toward the Latino electorate. Clinton's campaign allocated more than $1 million to Spanish-language ad buys in New Mexico, Nevada, and Arizona. Clinton's political ads focused on jobs and national unity; he also created several attack ads focusing on Dole's positions on immigration and bilingual education. Although Dole targeted Latino voters in Florida, his record on immigration and bilingual education hampered these efforts. As a result, Dole's share of the Latino vote (21 percent) was the smallest of any Republican presidential candidate in the past twenty-five years. Approximately 10 percent of Latino voters supported the third-party candidate, Ross Perot.

Media coverage on Latinos was low in the 1996 election—only one television news story focused on the Latino electorate during that campaign season.[5] Perhaps the decrease was due to the dynamics of this presidential election, because Clinton had a good relationship with the Latino electorate. In fact, this was a landmark election for the Democrats, as it marked the first time since 1976 that a Democrat captured Florida. One reason for this shift has been attributed to the inroads that Clinton made with Cuban Americans. He received 35 percent of their votes, a 15 percent increase from his 1992 share of the Cuban vote. Latinos also proved to be pivotal in Clinton's historic victory in Arizona. He captured 90 percent of the Latino vote there, and the last time Democrats had won that state was [in] 1948.

▪　▪　▪

Spanish-Language Campaigns in House Races, 2000–2004

During the 2000–2004 election cycles, twenty-one House races saw at least one candidate using Spanish-language ads. In total, twenty-six candidates advertised in Spanish, with only one candidate advertising in all three election cycles that I examine (see the next section, on New Mexico's 1st congressional district, for a more detailed discussion). Table [1] lists those House races with candidates that advertised in Spanish, along with the same information presented in Table 3.1 [not included]. As in the statewide races, House candidates that used Spanish-language ads competed in a district with a considerable number of Latino voters; in fact, many of these districts were majority and even super-majority Latino districts. At the low end of the population scale were California's 9th and Florida's 8th congressional districts—in each district, Latinos constituted approximately 17 percent of the population. At the high end, 77.5 percent of the 28th congressional district in Texas are Latino, and in the 4th district of Illinois, Latinos make up 74.5 percent of the population. The content of the ads targeting the House districts reflects the same general pattern as those used in the statewide races—the majority of the ads featured images of Latinos, as well as simple policy and character statements.

Forty percent of the elections were considered to be competitive, whereas the number of statewide races deemed competitive was considerably higher (75 percent). This difference could perhaps be attributed to the nature of House elections, because House members have smaller constituencies than do senators, and many representatives are long-time incumbents. As such, they may advertise in Spanish as a gesture of goodwill to their Latino constituents more than as a bid for votes. Of the twelve noncompetitive elections in which at least one candidate advertised in Spanish, five were incumbents. They were Luis Gutierrez (IL-4), Ed Pastor (AZ-2), Ileana Ros-Lehtinen (FL-18), Silvestre Reyes (TX-16), and Xavier Becerra (CA-30). Also note that in these five elections, the challengers did not create a Spanish-language advertising campaign. And with the exception of Ileana Ros-Lehtinen, all the incumbents are Democrats. Yet, Republican incumbents, such as Henry Bonilla (TX-23), Steve Pearce (NM-2), and Joe Skeen (NM-1), did not advertise in Spanish, even when their Democratic challengers chose to do so. Thus, there appears to be some partisan bias, because Democrats, at least in these three election cycles, were more apt to use this media outlet than were Republicans. This difference can perhaps be attributed to the long-standing relationship that Democrats have had with the Latino electorate. It is also interesting to note that of the sixteen Latino candidates competing in these elections, only one— former congressman Henry Bonilla (TX-23)—did not target his Latino electorate through Spanish-language ads.

Case Study: New Mexico's 1st Congressional District

During the 2000–2004 election cycles, Heather Wilson of New Mexico's 1st congressional district was the lone candidate who consistently developed a Spanish-language advertising campaign. Some characteristics of her district offer insight on why Wilson used such a campaign in each of these election cycles. Her district is 42.6 percent Latino, 25.5 percent of whom are Spanish speaking (U.S. Census Bureau 2000a). Moreover, only 1.2 percent of the population consists of foreign-born individuals (U.S. Census Bureau 2000a). Thus, more than half of the Latinos in her district could be exposed to her Spanish-language ads, and, more importantly, they are likely to be eligible voters (given that virtually all Latinos in this district are U.S. born). Finally, that Wilson faced a formidable competitor in all of her reelection bids, as evidenced by a margin of victory of 10 percent or less in each election, can also help explain why she regularly employed a targeted Latino campaign. The one recurring theme in her Spanish-language ads was a mention of the personal qualities of either Wilson or her opponent, and although Latinos were not featured in her 2000 commercials, she did include them in her subsequent campaign ads. Wilson also discussed policy in her Spanish-language ads, with a preference for simple and explained policy messages over complex policy statements.

This case study offers a number of insights about candidates' Latino-specific campaigns, and it helps support the theory of information-based advertising. Wilson's concerted efforts to campaign to Latinos, despite the fact that she is a Republican, reinforces the conventional wisdom that Latinos are considered a valuable swing group. And although Latinos have traditionally been aligned with the Democratic party, Wilson exemplifies the efforts made by the Republican party to appeal to this group of voters. She made her appeal by communicating messages that primarily focused on her or her opponent's personal characteristics and on easily understood policy statements. Specifically recognizing Latinos in her Spanish-language ads, either by featuring them or by having them speak in the ad, is another regular component of her campaign strategy. That the content of these Spanish-language ads focused more on character and cultural appeals, with less of an emphasis on substantively

TABLE [1] House Races Using Spanish-Language Advertising (2000–2004)

State and District	Year	Candidate	Types of Ads Advertised	Competitive Election?	Percent Latino in District
AZ-2	2000	E. Pastor (D)	Simple, Character	No	62.5
CA-9	2004	C. Bermudez (R)	Simple, Latino	No	17.3
CA-20	2000	C. Dooley (D)	Simple, Latino	Yes	63.7
		R. Rodriguez (R)	Latino		
	2004	J. Costa (D)	Simple, Latino, Character	No	
		L. Quigley (D)	Complex		
CA-30	2000	X. Becerra (D)	Simple, Character	No	64.3
CA-39	2002	L. Sanchez (D)	Latino	No	61.2
		T. Escobar (R)	Simple, Latino		
FL-8	2002	M. Diaz-Balart (R)	Latino, Explained, Simple, Character	Yes	17.6
		E. Diaz (D)	Explained, Latino		
FL-18	2004	I. Ros-Lehtinen (R)	Simple	No	70.5
IL-4	2000	L. Gutierrez (D)	n/a	No	74.5
NM-1	2000	H. Wilson (R)	Explained, Simple, Character	Yes	42.6
		J. Kelly (D)	n/a		
	2002	H. Wilson (R)	Character, Latino	Yes	
	2004	H. Wilson (R)	Explained, Simple, Latino, Character	Yes	

State and District	Year	Candidate	Types of Ads Advertised	Competitive Election?	Percent Latino in District
NM-2	2000	M. Montoya (D)	Latino	Yes	47.3
	2002	S. Pearce (R)	Latino, Complex, Explained, Simple, Character	No	
	2004	J. Smith (D)	Character, Explained, Latino	No	
		G. King (D)	Character, Latino		
NM-3	2000	T. Udall (D)	Latino	Yes	36.3
TX-16	2004	S. Reyes (D)	Character, Latino	No	78
TX-23	2000	W. Garza (D)	Character, Simple, Latino	No	65.1
TX-28	2004	H. Cuellar (D)	Explained, Latino	Yes	77.5
		C. Rodriguez (D)	Latino		
TX-32	2004	M. Frost (D)	Complex, Latino	No	36.2
		P. Sessions (R)	Character, Latino		

SOURCE: *The American Almanac of American Politics* (2000–2004) for competitive election information; U.S. Census for the percentage of Latinos in a district; ad content was discerned using data from the Wisconsin Advertising Project dataset, 2000–2004 motivated policy messages, lends some initial support for the theory of information-based advertising. Of course, this case study is not conclusive evidence, because the focus is only on the content of Wilson's Spanish-language ads. Nonetheless, it offers a glimpse into the campaign strategies used by the same candidate in three different races.

Summary

Clearly, politicians competing for both national and statewide races realize the importance of developing a specific campaign strategy directed toward Latinos. In a growing number of states across our nation, a successful bid for most elected offices requires that some effort be made to win the support of the Latino electorate. Particularly in states in which Latinos make up more than a third of the population, and therefore a sizeable part of the electorate, it is almost a given that candidates competing in statewide offices need to secure their allegiance. Just as California's Latinos were pivotal to Robert Kennedy's bid for the Democratic presidential nomination, Latinos play an equally, if not more, prominent role in today's elections. . . .

Those seeking elected office have long understood the importance of targeting specific groups within the electorate whom they believe may behave in a politically homogeneous manner. Although appeals to our nation's newest arrivals have resulted in candidates swapping corned beef for tamales, the motivations for such behavior appear to remain the same—candidates believe that campaigning to immigrants based on their ethnicity or culture is effective. That is, politicians believe that such efforts signal to these ethnic groups that politicians understand them and care about them. Candidates hope that, in turn, these groups will respond positively to the campaigns and will cast their ballots in favor of the candidate who appeals to them in this way.

This conventional wisdom appears to have carried over to the campaigns developed for the country's largest immigrant and minority group today. Given the technological advances in communication and the access that Latinos have to myriad Spanish-language media outlets, aspiring politicians can use these media sources to target ethnic messages to Latinos. Just as candidates have allocated the bulk of their campaign resources to televised political advertising for the general public, candidates have also turned to this medium in reaching out to Latino voters.

NOTES

1. This ad is titled "Mrs. JFK" and is available at http://www.livingroomcandidate .org/commercials/1960.

2. ABC Evening News, November 5, 1984.

3. CBS Evening News, November 4, 1984.

4. Television News Archive, Vanderbilt University.

5. ABC Evening News devoted 2 minutes and 10 seconds to discussing the Latino vote on June 29, 1996.

REFERENCES

Dahl, Robert. 1961. *Who Governs?* New Haven, CT: Yale University Press.

Erie, Steven P. 1990. *Rainbow's End: Irish-Americans and the Dilemmas of Urban Machine Politics, 1840–1985.* Berkeley, University of California Press.

Garcia, Ignacio M. 2000. *Viva Kennedy: Mexican Americans in Search of Camelot.* College Station, Texas A&M University Press.

Katznelson, Ira. 1981. *City Trenches: Urban Politics and the Patterning of Class in the United States.* New York, Pantheon Press.

McNickle, Chris. 1993. *To Be Mayor of New York: Ethnic Politics in the City.* New York, Columbia University Press.

Pew Hispanic Center. 2007. "Changing Faiths: Latinos and the Transformation of American Religion." Report. Washington, DC, Pew Hispanic Center and Pew Forum on Religion & Public Life.

Pycior, Julie L. 1997. *LBJ and Mexican Americans: The Paradox of Power.* Austin, The University of Texas Press.

Schmal, John P. 2004. "Electing the President. The Latino Electorate (1960–2000)." *La Prensa*, April 30. http://www.laprensa-sandiego.org/archive/april30-04/elect.htm.

Segal, Adam J. 2003. "The Hispanic Priority: The Spanish-Language Television Battle for the Hispanic Vote in the 2000 U.S. Presidential Election." Report. Hispanic Voter Project, Washington Center for the Study of American Government. Washington, DC, Johns Hopkins University,

Subervi-Velez, Federico A., and Stacey L. Connaughton. 2008. "Democratic and Republican Mass Communication Campaign Strategies: A Historical Overview." In *The Mass Media and Latino Politics: Studies of U.S. Media Content, Campaign Strategies and Survey Research: 1984–2004*, edited by Federico Subervi-Velez, 273–90. New York, Routledge.

U.S. Census Bureau. 2000a. "United States Foreign-Born Population." Population Division. March. http://www.census.gov/population/www/socdemo/foreign/cps2000.html.

14.3

HUNT ALLCOTT AND MATTHEW GENTZKOW

From "Social Media and Fake News in the 2016 Election"

This study of the impact of fake news in social media from the 2016 presidential election provides answers to key questions. Who was exposed to fake news about politics on social media in 2016? Who believed the fake news posts? Did the fake news affect people's voting decisions? Hunt and Gentzkow find that fake news generally targeted and was consumed by Republicans more than Democrats in 2016, but that both believe fake news that aligns with their beliefs more than fake news that does not. The people most believing in fake news are those who are generally exposed only to one-sided political news.

Following the 2016 election, a specific concern has been the effect of false stories—"fake news," as it has been dubbed—circulated on social media. Recent evidence shows that: 1) 62 percent of U.S. adults get news on social media (Gottfried and Shearer 2016); 2) the most popular fake news stories were more widely shared on Facebook than the most popular mainstream news stories (Silverman 2016); 3) many people who see fake news stories report that they believe them (Silverman and Singer-Vine 2016); and 4) the most discussed fake news stories tended to favor Donald Trump over Hillary Clinton (Silverman 2016). Putting these facts together, a number of commentators have suggested that Donald Trump would not have been elected president were it not for the influence of fake news (for examples, see Parkinson 2016; Read 2016; Dewey 2016).

Our goal is to offer theoretical and empirical background to frame this debate.

■　■　■

We present new data on the consumption of fake news prior to the election. We draw on web browsing data, a new 1,200-person post-election online survey, and a database of 156 election-related news stories that were categorized as false by leading fact-checking websites in the three months before the election.

■　■　■

From Hunt Allcott and Matthew Gentzkow, "Social Media and Fake News in the 2016 Election," *The Journal of Economic Perspectives* 31, no. 2 (2017): 211–235.

[W]e confirm that fake news was both widely shared and heavily tilted in favor of Donald Trump. Our database contains 115 pro-Trump fake stories that were shared on Facebook a total of 30 million times, and 41 pro-Clinton fake stories shared a total of 7.6 million times.

[We also] provide several benchmarks of the rate at which voters were exposed to fake news. The upper end of previously reported statistics for the ratio of page visits to shares of stories on social media would suggest that the 38 million shares of fake news in our database translates into 760 million instances of a user clicking through and reading a fake news story, or about three stories read per American adult. A list of fake news websites, on which just over half of articles appear to be false, received 159 million visits during the month of the election, or 0.64 per US adult. In our post-election survey, about 15 percent of respondents recalled seeing each of 14 major pre-election fake news headlines, but about 14 percent also recalled seeing a set of placebo fake news headlines—untrue headlines that we invented and that never actually circulated. Using the difference between fake news headlines and placebo headlines as a measure of true recall and projecting this to the universe of fake news articles in our database, we estimate that the average adult saw and remembered 1.14 fake stories. Taken together, these estimates suggest that the average U.S. adult might have seen perhaps one or several news stories in the months before the election.

▪　▪　▪

BACKGROUND: THE MARKET FOR FAKE NEWS

Definition and History

We define "fake news" to be news articles that are intentionally and verifiably false, and could mislead readers. We focus on fake news articles that have political implications, with special attention to the 2016 U.S. presidential elections. Our definition includes intentionally fabricated news articles, such as a widely shared article from the now-defunct website denverguardian.com with the headline, "FBI agent suspected in Hillary email leaks found dead in apparent murder-suicide." It also includes many articles that originate on satirical websites but could be misunderstood as factual, especially when viewed in isolation on Twitter or Facebook feeds. For example, in July 2016, the now-defunct website wtoe5news.com reported that Pope Francis had endorsed Donald Trump's presidential candidacy. The WTOE 5 News "About" page disclosed that it is "a fantasy news website. Most articles on wtoe5news.com are satire or pure fantasy," but this disclaimer was not included in the article. The story was shared more than one million times on Facebook, and some people in our survey described below reported believing the headline.

Our definition rules out several close cousins of fake news: 1) unintentional reporting mistakes, such as a recent incorrect report that Donald Trump had removed a bust of Martin Luther King Jr. from the Oval Office in the White

FIGURE [1]   Share of Americans Believing Historical Partisan Conspiracy Theories

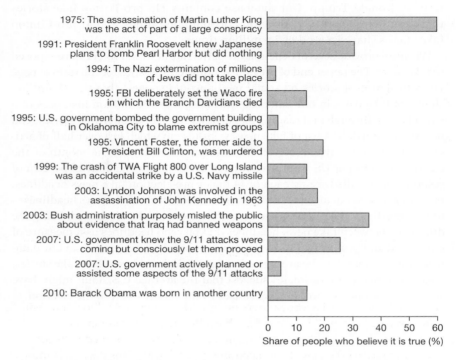

NOTE: From polling data compiled by the American Enterprise Institute (2013), we selected all conspiracy theories with political implications. This figure plots the share of people who report believing the statement listed, using opinion polls from the date listed.

House; 2) rumors that do not originate from a particular news article;[1] 3) conspiracy theories (these are, by definition, difficult to verify as true or false, and they are typically originated by people who believe them to be true [see Figure [1]]);[2] 4) satire that is unlikely to be misconstrued as factual; 5) false statements by politicians; and 6) reports that are slanted or misleading but not outright false (in the language of Gentzkow, Shapiro, and Stone 2016, fake news is "distortion," not "filtering").

▪   ▪   ▪

[T]here are several reasons to think that fake news is of growing importance. First, barriers to entry in the media industry have dropped precipitously, both because it is now easy to set up websites and because it is easy to monetize web content through advertising platforms. Because reputational concerns discourage mass media outlets from knowingly reporting false stories, higher entry barriers limit false reporting. Second, as we discuss below, social media are well-suited for fake news dissemination, and social media use has risen

FIGURE [2] Trust in Mainstream Media

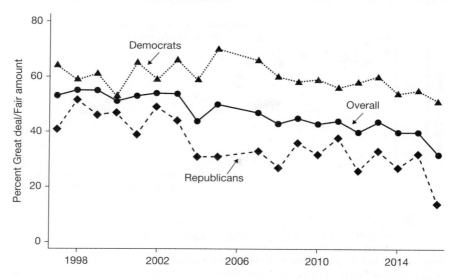

sharply: in 2016, active Facebook users per month reached 1.8 billion and Twitter's approached 400 million. Third, as shown in Figure [2], Gallup polls reveal a continuing decline of "trust and confidence" in the mass media "when it comes to reporting the news fully, accurately, and fairly." This decline is more marked among Republicans than Democrats, and there is a particularly sharp drop among Republicans in 2016. The declining trust in mainstream media could be both a cause and a consequence of fake news gaining more traction. Fourth, Figure [3] shows one measure of the rise of political polarization: the increasingly negative feelings each side of the political spectrum holds toward the other.[3] As we discuss below, this could affect how likely each side is to believe negative fake news stories about the other.

Who Produces Fake News?

Fake news articles originate on several types of websites. For example, some sites are established entirely to print intentionally fabricated and misleading articles, such as the above example of denverguardian.com. The names of these sites are often chosen to resemble those of legitimate news organizations. Other satirical sites contain articles that might be interpreted as factual when seen out of context, such as the above example of wtoe5news.com. Still other sites, such as endingthefed.com, print a mix between factual articles, often with a partisan slant, along with some false articles. Websites supplying fake news tend to be short-lived, and many that were important in the run-up to the 2016 election no longer exist.

Anecdotal reports that have emerged following the 2016 election provide a partial picture of the providers behind these sites. Separate investigations by

FIGURE [3] Feeling Thermometer toward Other Political Party

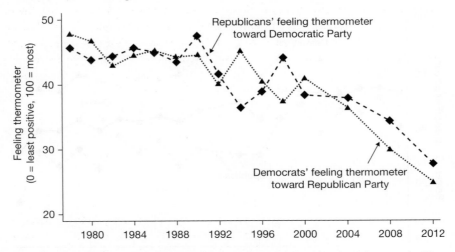

NOTE: Panel A shows the percent of Americans who say that they have "a great deal" or "a fair amount" of "trust and confidence" in the mass media "when it comes to reporting the news fully, accurately, and fairly," using Gallup poll data reported in Swift (2016). Panel B shows the average "feeling thermometer" (with 100 meaning "very warm or favorable feeling" and 0 meaning "very cold or unfavorable feeling") of Republicans toward the Democratic Party and of Democrats toward the Republican Party, using data from the American National Election Studies (2012).

BuzzFeed and the *Guardian* revealed that more than 100 sites posting fake news were run by teenagers in the small town of Veles, Macedonia (Subramanian 2017). Endingthefed.com, a site that was responsible for four of the ten most popular fake news stories on Facebook, was run by a 24-year-old Romanian man (Townsend 2016). A U.S. company called Disinfomedia owns many fake news sites, including NationalReport.net, USAToday.com.co, and WashingtonPost.com.co, and its owner claims to employ between 20 and 25 writers (Sydell 2016). Another U.S.-based producer, Paul Horner, ran a successful fake news site called National Report for years prior to the election (Dewey 2014). Among his most-circulated stories was a 2013 report that President Obama used his own money to keep open a Muslim museum during the federal government shutdown. During the election, Horner produced a large number of mainly pro-Trump stories (Dewey 2016).

There appear to be two main motivations for providing fake news. The first is pecuniary: news articles that go viral on social media can draw significant advertising revenue when users click to the original site. This appears to have been the main motivation for most of the producers whose identities have been revealed. The teenagers in Veles, for example, produced stories favoring both Trump and Clinton that earned them tens of thousands of dollars (Subramanian 2017). Paul Horner produced pro-Trump stories for profit, despite claiming to be personally opposed to Trump (Dewey 2016). The second motivation is ideological. Some fake news providers seek to advance candidates they favor. The Romanian man who ran endingthefed.com, for example, claims that he started the site mainly to help Donald Trump's campaign (Townsend 2016). Other providers of right-wing fake news actually say they identify as left-wing and wanted to embarrass those on the right by showing that they would credulously circulate false stories (Dewey 2016; Sydell 2016).

■ ■ ■

REAL DATA ON FAKE NEWS

Fake News Database

We gathered a database of fake news articles that circulated in the three months before the 2016 election, using lists from three independent third parties. First, we scraped all stories from the Donald Trump and Hillary Clinton tags on Snopes (snopes.com), which calls itself "the definitive Internet reference source for urban legends, folklore, myths, rumors, and misinformation." Second, we scraped all stories from the 2016 presidential election tag from PolitiFact (politifact.com), another major fact-checking site. Third, we use a list of 21 fake news articles that had received significant engagement on Facebook, as compiled by the news outlet BuzzFeed (Silverman 2016).[4] Combining these three lists, we have a database of 156 fake news articles. We then gathered the total number of times each article was shared on Facebook as of early December 2016, using an online content database called BuzzSumo (buzzsumo.com). We code each article's content as either pro-Clinton (including anti-Trump) or pro-Trump (including anti-Clinton).

■ ■ ■

Post-Election Survey

During the week of November 28, 2016, we conducted an online survey of 1,208 U.S. adults aged 18 and over using the SurveyMonkey platform. The sample was drawn from SurveyMonkey's Audience Panel, an opt-in panel recruited from more than 30 million people.

■ ■ ■

For the month before the 2016 election, our respondents report spending 66 minutes per day reading, watching, or listening to election news. (Again, these and all other survey results are weighted for national representativeness.) Of this, 25 minutes (38 percent) w[ere] on social media. Our survey then asked, "Which of these sources was your most important source of news and information about the 2016 election?" The word "important" was designed to elicit a combination of consumption frequency and trust in information. Figure [4] presents responses. In order, the four most common responses are cable TV, network TV, websites, and local TV. Social media is the fifth most common response, with 14 percent of U.S. adults listing social media as their most "important" news source.

Taken together, these results suggest that social media have become an important but not dominant source of political news and information. Television remains more important by a large margin.

PARTISANSHIP OF FAKE NEWS

In our fake news database, we record 41 pro-Clinton (or anti-Trump) and 115 pro-Trump (or anti-Clinton) articles, which were shared on Facebook a total of 7.6 million and 30.3 million times, respectively. Thus, there are about three times more fake pro-Trump articles than pro-Clinton articles, and the average pro-Trump article was shared more on Facebook than the average pro-Clinton article. To be clear, these statistics show that more of the fake news articles *on these three fact-checking sites* are right-leaning. This could be because more of the actual fake news is right-leaning, or because more right-leaning assertions are forwarded to and/or reported by fact-checking sites, or because the conclusions that fact-checking sites draw have a left-leaning bias, or some combina-

FIGURE [4]   Most Important Source of 2016 Election News

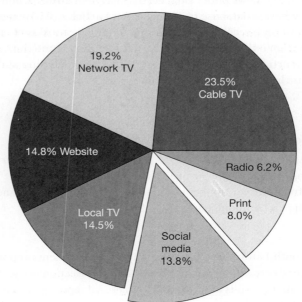

NOTE: Our post-election survey asked, "Which of these sources was your most important source of news and information about the 2016 election?" This figure plots responses. Observations are weighted for national representativeness.

tion. Some anecdotal reports support the idea that the majority of election-related fake news was pro-Trump: some fake news providers reportedly found higher demand for pro-Trump (or anti-Clinton) fake news, and responded by providing more of it (Sydell 2016).

There could be several possible explanations for a preponderance of pro-Trump fake news. The more marked decline of trust in the mainstream media among Republicans shown in Figure [2] could have increased their relative demand for news from nontraditional sources, as could a perception that the mainstream media tended to favor Clinton. Pro-Trump (and anti-Clinton) story-lines may have simply been more compelling than pro-Clinton (and anti-Trump) storylines due to particulars of these candidates, perhaps related to the high levels of media attention that Trump received throughout the campaign. Or, it could theoretically be that Republicans are for some reason more likely to enjoy or believe fake news.

■　　■　　■

Figure [5] presents the share of respondents that recalled seeing (left bar) and seeing and believing (right bar) headlines, averaging responses across all the headlines within each of our main categories. Rates of both seeing and believing are much higher for true than fake stories, and they are substantially higher for the "Big True" headlines (the major headlines leading up to the election) than for the "Small True" headlines (the minor fact-checked headlines that we gathered from Snopes and PolitiFact). The Placebo fake news articles, which never actually circulated, are approximately equally likely to be recalled and believed as the Fake news articles which did actually circulate. This implies that there is a meaningful rate of false recall of articles that people never actually saw, which could cause the survey measure to significantly overstate true exposure. On the other hand, people likely forgot some of the Fake articles that they were actually exposed to, which causes the survey responses to understate true exposure.

In summary, one can think of recalled exposure as determined both by actual exposure and by the headline's perceived plausibility—people might think that if a headline is plausible, they probably saw it reported somewhere. Then, we show that if the Placebo headlines are equally plausible as the Fake headlines, the difference between recall of Fake and Placebo headlines represents the rate of true exposure that was remembered.

■　　■　　■

We can use these results to provide a separate estimate of fake news exposure. The average Fake article that we asked about in the post-election survey was shared 0.386 million times on Facebook. If the average article was seen and recalled by 1.2 percent of American adults, this gives (0.012 recalled exposure) / (0.386 million shares) ≈ 0.03 chance of a recalled exposure per million Facebook shares. Given that the Fake articles in our database had 38 million

FIGURE [5] Percent of U.S. Adult Population that Recall Seeing or that Believed Election News

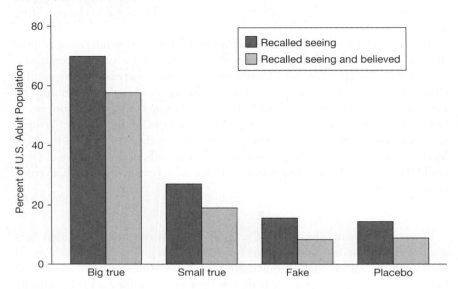

NOTE: In our post-election survey, we presented 15 headlines. For each headline, the survey asked whether respondents recall seeing the headline ("Do you recall seeing this reported or discussed before the election?") and whether they believed it ("At the time of the election, would your best guess have been that this statement was true?"). The left bars present the share of respondents who recall seeing the headlines in each category, and the right bars present the share of respondents who recall seeing and believed the headlines. "Big True" headlines are major headlines leading up to the election; "Small True" headlines are the minor fact-checked headlines that we gathered from Snopes and PolitiFact. The Placebo fake news headlines were made-up for the research and never actually circulated. Observations are weighted for national representativeness.

Facebook shares, this implies that the average adult saw and remembered 0.03/ million × 38 million ≈ 1.14 fake news articles from our fake news database.

All three approaches suggest that election-period fake news exposure was on the order of one or perhaps several articles read per adult. We emphasize several important caveats. First, each of these measures excludes some forms of exposure that could have been influential. All of them exclude stories or sites omitted from our database. Estimated page visits or impressions exclude cases in which users saw a story within their Facebook news feed but did not click through to read it. Our survey-based recall measure excludes stories that users saw but did not remember, and may be subject to other biases associated with survey-based estimates of media exposure (Bartels 1993; Prior 2009; Guess 2015).

▪   ▪   ▪

CONCLUSION

In the aftermath of the 2016 U.S. presidential election, it was alleged that fake news might have been pivotal in the election of President Trump. We do not provide an assessment of this claim one way or another.

That said, the new evidence we present clarifies the level of overall exposure to fake news, and it can give some sense of how persuasive fake news would need to have been to have been pivotal. We estimate that the average U.S. adult read and remembered on the order of one or perhaps several fake news articles during the election period, with higher exposure to pro-Trump articles than pro-Clinton articles. How much this affected the election results depends on the effectiveness of fake news exposure in changing the way people vote. As one benchmark, Spenkuch and Toniatti (2016) show that exposing voters to one additional television campaign ad changes vote shares by approximately 0.02 percentage points. This suggests that if one fake news article were about as persuasive as one TV campaign ad, the fake news in our database would have changed vote shares by an amount on the order of hundredths of a percentage point. This is much smaller than Trump's margin of victory in the pivotal states on which the outcome depended.

▪   ▪   ▪

[W]hat can and should be done? . . . [S]ocial media platforms and advertising networks have faced some pressure from consumers and civil society to reduce the prevalence of fake news on their systems. For example, both Facebook and Google are removing fake news sites from their advertising platforms on the grounds that they violate policies against misleading content (Wingfield, Isaac, and Benner 2016). Furthermore, Facebook has taken steps to identify fake news articles, flag false articles as "disputed by 3rd party fact-checkers," show fewer potentially false articles in users' news feeds, and help users avoid accidentally sharing false articles by notifying them that a story is "disputed by 3rd parties" before they share it (Mosseri 2016). [I]dentifying fake news sites and articles also raises important questions about who becomes the arbiter of truth.

NOTES

1. Sunstein (2007) defines rumors as "claims of fact—about people, groups, events, and institutions—that have not been shown to be true, but that move from one person to another, and hence have credibility not because direct evidence is available to support them, but because other people seem to believe them."

2. Keeley (1999) defines a conspiracy theory as "a proposed explanation of some historical event (or events) in terms of the significant causal agency of a relatively small group of persons—the conspirators—acting in secret."

3. The extent to which polarization of voters has increased, along with the extent to which it has been driven by shifts in attitudes on the right or the left or both, are widely

debated topics. See Abramowitz and Saunders (2008), Fiorina and Abrams (2008), Prior (2013), and Lelkes (2016) for reviews.

4. Of these 21 articles, 12 were fact-checked on Snopes. Nine were rated as "false," and the other three were rated "mixture," "unproven," and "mostly false."

REFERENCES

Abramowitz, Alan I., and Kyle L. Saunders. 2008. "Is Polarization a Myth?" *Journal of Politics* 70(2): 542–55.

American Enterprise Institute. 2013. "Public Opinion on Conspiracy Theories." AEI Public Opinion Study. Complied by Karlyn Bowman and Andrew Rugg. November, https://www.aei.org/publication/public-opinion-on-conspiracy-theories.

American National Election Studies. 2010. Times Series Cumulative Data File [dataset]. Produced and distributed by Stanford University and the University of Michigan. http://www.electionstudies.org/studypages/anes_timeseries_cdf/anes_time series_cdf.htm.

Bartels, Larry M. 1993. "Messages Received: The Political Impact of Media Exposure." *American Political Science Review* 87(2): 267–85.

Dewey, Caitlin. 2014. "This Is Not an Interview with Banksy." *Washington Post*, October 22. https://www.washingtonpost.com/news/the-intersect/wp/2014/10/21/this-is-not-an-interview-with-banksy/?tid=a_inl&utm_term=.8a9 5d83438e9.

Dewey, Caitlin. 2016. "Facebook Fake-News Writer: 'I Think Donald Trump is in the White House because of Me.'" *Washington Post*, November, 17. https://www.washingtonpost.com/news/the-intersect/wp/2016/11/17/facebook-fake-news-writer-i-think-donald-trump-is-in-the-white-house-because-of-me/.

Fiorina, Morris P., and Samuel J. Abrams. 2008. "Political Polarization in the American Public." *Annual Review of Political Science* 11: 563–88.

Gentzkow, Matthew, Jesse M. Shapiro, and Daniel F. Stone. 2016. "Media Bias in the Markiet-place: Theory." Chap. 14 in *Handbook of Media Economics*, vol. 1B, edited by Simon Anderson, Joel Waldofgel, and David Stromberg.

Gottfried, Jeffrey, and Elisa Shearer. 2016. "News Use across Social Media Platforms 2016." Pew Research Center, May 26. http://www.journalism.org/2016/05/26/news-use-across-social-media-platforms-2016.

Guess, Andrew M. 2015. "Measure for Measure: An Experimental Test of Online Political Media Exposure." *Political Analysis* 23(1): 59–75.

Keeley, Brian L. 1999. "Of Conspiracy Theories." *Journal of Philosophy* 96(3): 109–26.

Lelkes, Yphtach. 2016. "Mass Polarization: Manifestations and Measurements." *Public Opinion Quarterly* 80(S1): 392–410.

Mosseri Adam. 2016. "News Feed FYI: Addressing Hoaxes and Fake News." Newsroom, Facebook, December 15. http://newsroom.fb.com/news/2016/12/news-feed-fyi-addressing-hoaxes-and-fake-news/.

Parkinson, Hannah Jane. 2016. "Click and Elect: How Fake News Helped Donald Trump Win a Real Election." *Guardian*, November 14.

PolitiFact. No date. http://www.politifact.com/truth-o-meter/elections/2016/president-united-states/.

Prior, Markus. 2009. "The Immensely Inflated News Audience: Assessing Bias in Self-Reported News Exposure." *Public Opinion Quarterly* 73(1): 130–43.

Prior, Markus. 2013. "Media and Political Polarization." *Annual Review of Political Science* 16: 101–27.

Read, Max. 2016. "Donald Trump Won because of Facebook." *New York Magazine*, November 9.

Silverman, Craig. 2016. "This Analysis Shows how Fake Election News Stories Outperformed Real News on Facebook." *BuzzFeed News*, November 16.

Silverman, Craig and Jeremy Singer-Vine. 2016. "Most Americans Who See Fake News Believe It, New Survey Says." *BuzzFeed News*, December 6.

Spenkuch, Jörg L., and David Toniatti. 2016. "Political Advertising and Election Outcomes." CESifo Working Paper Series 5780.

Subramanian, Samanth. 2017. "Inside the Macedonian Fake-News Complex." *Wired*, February 15.

Sunstein, Cass R. 2007. *Republic.com 2.0.* Princeton University Press.

Swift, Art. 2016. "Americans' Trust in Mass Media Sinks to New Low." Gallup, September 14. http://www.gallup.com/poll/195542/americans-trust-mass-media-sinks-new -low.aspx.

Sydell, Laura. 2016. "We Tracked Down a Fake-News Creator in the Suburbs. Here's What We Learned." National Public Radio, November 23. http://www.npr.org/sections /alltechconsidered/2016/11/23/503146770/npr-finds-the-head-of-a-covert-fake-news -operation-in-the-suburbs.

Townsend, Tess. 2016. "Meet the Romanian Trump Fan behind a Major Fake News Site." *Inc.* http://www.inc.com/tess-townsend/ending-fed-trump-facebook.html.

Wingfield, Nick, Mike Isaac, and Katie Benner. 2016. "Google and Facebook Take Aim at Fake News Sites." *New York Times*, November 14.

DISCUSSION QUESTIONS

1. What is soft news? Describe how soft news can be important in making crises into "water cooler" events.

2. What specific tactics do candidates use to appeal to Latino voters? Are those tactics fundamentally different than candidate appeals to other groups of voters?

3. Describe the data Allcott and Gentzkow use to make their arguments and how they arrive at their conclusions about fake news.

4. Write an essay predicting how candidates and political parties will use social media and technology in 2028. Do you believe they will use it to improve the conduct of American democracy?

15

POLICY

15.1

SUZANNE METTLER

From *The Submerged State: How Invisible Government Policies Undermine American Democracy*

Many Americans are critical of government redistribution to help the poor. In her book, Mettler argues that the lack of support is caused by a basic disparity between perception and reality. A large proportion of middle-class Americans, according to surveys, do not recognize the degree to which their material well-being flows from government subsidies or payouts. Mettler writes about the "submerged state"—the large portion of the American economy that results from explicit government policy but is not openly acknowledged by the middle- and upper middle-class beneficiaries. This lack of understanding about government's role in their own lives can affect the degree to which they support candidates promoting governmental help for the poor. Relatively well-off Americans who benefit from government redistribution often criticize relief for the poor as undeserved handouts from government.

[T]he *submerged state*: existing policies that lay beneath the surface of U.S. market institutions and within the federal tax system. . . .

The "submerged state" includes a conglomeration of federal policies that function by providing incentives, subsidies, or payments to private organizations or households to encourage or reimburse them for conducting activities deemed to serve a public purpose. Over the past thirty years, American political

From Suzanne Mettler, *The Submerged State: How Invisible Government Policies Undermine American Democracy* (Chicago: University of Chicago Press, 2011).

discourse has been dominated by a conservative public philosophy, one that espouses the virtues of small government. Its values have been pursued in part through efforts to scale back traditional forms of social provision, meaning visible benefits administered fairly directly by government. In the case of some programs geared to the young or working-age people, the value of average benefits has withered and coverage has grown more restrictive.[1] Ironically, however, the more dramatic change over this period has been the flourishing of the policies of the submerged state, which operate through indirect means such as tax breaks to households or payments to private actors who provide services. Since 1980 these policies have proliferated in number, and the average size of their benefits has expanded dramatically.

Most of these ascendant policies function in a way that directly contradicts Americans' expectations of social welfare policies: they shower their largest benefits on the most affluent Americans. Take the Home Mortgage Interest Deduction (HMID), for example, which is currently the nation's most expensive social tax break aside from the tax-free status of employer-provided health coverage. Let us assume that a family buys a median-value home and to finance it borrows $230,000 at an interest rate of 6.25 percent for thirty years. The richer the household, the larger the benefit: in the first year, the average family, with an income between $16,751 and $68,000, would owe around $3,619 less in taxes; those in the next income group, with earnings up to $137,300, would reap an extra $5,146; and so forth, on up to the wealthiest 2 percent of families, with incomes over $373,650, who would enjoy a savings of $6,673. Of course, in reality, these differences are likely to be much greater. Low- to moderate-income Americans usually do not have enough deductions to itemize, so they would forgo this benefit and receive instead only the standard deduction. Meanwhile, the most affluent are likely to purchase far more expensive homes; if a family in the top income category opts for a more upscale home and borrows $500,000 for a mortgage, it will reap a benefit of $14,506 from the HMID; if this family purchases a truly exclusive property and borrows $1 million for a mortgage, it will qualify to keep a whopping $29,012! This pattern of upward redistribution is repeated in numerous other policies of the submerged state: federal largesse is allocated disproportionately to the nation's most well-off households. Such policies consume a sizable portion of revenues and leave scarce resources available for programs that genuinely aid low- and middle-income Americans.

Yet despite their growing size, scope, and tendency to channel government benefits toward the wealthy, the policies of the submerged state remain largely invisible to ordinary Americans: indeed, their hallmark is the way they obscure government's role from the view of the general public, including those who number among their beneficiaries. Even when people stare directly at these policies, many perceive only a freely functioning market system at work. They understand neither what is at stake in reform efforts nor the significance of their success. As a result, the charge leveled by opponents of reforms—that they amount to "government takeovers"—though blatantly inaccurate, makes many Americans at least uncomfortable with policy changes, if not openly hostile toward them.

Exacerbating these challenges, at the same time as the submerged state renders the electorate oblivious and passive, it actually promotes vested interests, and it has done so especially over the past two decades. The finance, real estate, and insurance industries all thrived (until the recent recession), and in turn they invested heavily in strengthening their political capacity, making them better poised to protect the policies that have favored them. As a result, reform has required public officials to engage in outright combat or deal making with powerful organizations. Such politics disgust most Americans and hardly epitomize the kind of change Obama's supporters expected when he won office.

▪   ▪   ▪

American politics today is ensnared in the paradox of the submerged state. Our government is integrally intertwined with everyday life from health care to housing, but in forms that often elude our vision: governance appears "stateless" because it operates indirectly, through subsidizing private actors. Thus, many Americans express disdain for government social spending, incognizant that they themselves benefit from it. Even if they do realize that benefits they utilize emanate from government, often they fail to recognize them as "social programs." People are therefore easily seduced by calls for smaller government—while taking for granted public programs on which they themselves rely. Meanwhile, economic inequality has soared in the United States over the past forty years, reaching levels not seen since 1929, yet over this same period, policymakers have adamantly protected submerged state policies that bestow their greatest rewards on the affluent.[2] Ordinary citizens fail to realize the upward bias of such policies. Political leaders who do seek to reform them, to make their benefits more accessible to Americans of low and moderate incomes, face charges of mounting a "government takeover." If against the odds they manage to succeed, the policies achieved, especially if they still cloak government's role, prove difficult to sustain.

▪   ▪   ▪

As long as the submerged state persists in its shrouded form, American democracy is imperiled. Contrary to popular claims, the threat to self-governance is not the size of government, but rather the hidden form so much of its growth has assumed, and the ways in which it channels public resources predominantly to wealthy Americans and privileged industries.

GOVERNANCE UNSEEN

■ ■ ■

The Origins of the Submerged State

How did so much of U.S. governance come to be so heavily obscured from view? Policymakers built the foundation of the submerged state as we know it today during the early and mid-twentieth century, first largely by happenstance and then as a means of brokering political agreements. During the last thirty years of conservative governance, the submerged state has flourished. The composition of its policies has appealed to conservatives and liberals alike, such that in an era of increasingly sharp partisan divisions, it has offered a rare format for agreement on new policy initiatives. Also, some of the aggressive growth of the submerged state occurred automatically, as policies established long ago offered increasingly larger benefits due to changes such as the rise in housing values or health care costs—while political leaders looked the other way. As a result of both trends, the submerged state has expanded—even while some visible policies that aid poor and middle-income Americans atrophied. Since the 1970s, programs geared mostly for seniors, such as Social Security and Medicare, have remained strong, but various of those for younger people—for example, Pell Grants, unemployment insurance, and welfare—feature benefits that have deteriorated in value or coverage that has grown more restrictive.[3] On balance, in the lives of most Americans other than seniors, the impact of visible governance has diminished while that of the submerged state has grown.

Some of the earliest provisions of the submerged state either predated group mobilization in relevant domains or occurred beyond its radar screen. For example, when the framers of the original income tax code in 1913 opted to exclude mortgage interest from taxable income, they were not responding to group pressure. Rather, in omitting consumer debt from taxation, they followed a tradition that dated back to the Civil War period, while also seeking administrative simplicity that would aid in effective implementation.[4] During the 1910s and 1920s, policymakers enacted several other major social tax breaks, including the deduction of state and local taxes and charitable contributions.[5] Ironically, these components—minor footnotes early on—have ballooned to become vast entitlements today, and they are fiercely defended by the industries that benefit from them.

During the post–World War II period, innovations in the submerged state epitomized the fruit of political compromise. On some issues, policy enactment appears to have been possible only when the demands of vested interests were met through policy designs that accommodated them and thus prompted key moderate Democrats or Republicans to vote in favor of legislation.[6] For example, when the Johnson administration encountered steadfast opposition to student loan policy from bankers—more than from any other group—it finally invited a group of them to the White House to discuss the terms on which they would be willing to accept such a policy. These negotiations broke the logjam, leading to a final bill that included several features favorable to the banks in exchange for their support.[7]

In recent decades of conservative dominance and political polarization, the submerged state entered into its new stage of aggressive growth. Increasingly, the design of its policies became not a last resort but rather the template of choice for new policy initiatives. In an era when direct visible social policies have been under attack, submerged policies contain several attributes that have enabled them to overcome partisan divisions and institutional gridlock. They have gained favor for four reasons: first, Republicans and conservative Democrats find them attractive; second, other Democrats have proven willing to go along; third, institutional features of Congress make them easier to enact than new direct spending programs; and fourth, over time they have cultivated the support of interest groups that defend them vigorously.

The submerged state has long fused well with conservatives' political values and priorities. While hallmark programs of the visible state originated at the hands of mainstream Democrats, from the very beginning Republicans and a few conservative Democrats took the lead in submerged state-building. Christopher Howard reports that southern Democrats and conservative Republicans helped enact the income tax back in 1913, complete with its early tax expenditures, and in 1926 pro-business Republican Senator George McLean (R-CT) nonchalantly introduced the amendment that henceforth excluded employer pensions from taxation. In the early 1970s, Senator Russell Long judged President Richard Nixon's welfare reform plan to be too generous. He devised an alternative policy—the Earned Income Tax Credit (EITC)—that aimed to help the working poor through tax relief, and it passed easily as part of a larger tax bill in 1975.[8]

Conservatives' leadership in the construction of the submerged state is not accidental. All elected officials, if they wish to stay in office, need to find ways to represent citizens, to respond to the needs of those who elected them and those whose votes they would like to attract. The challenge for conservatives is doing this without expanding the visible state. Conservative politicians favor submerged state policies primarily because they enable them to deliver goods and services to core constituencies while neither creating vast new direct spending programs nor enlarging the federal bureaucracy in the process.

Submerged policies appeal to some contemporary conservatives because they can appear to restrain government spending. Tax expenditures, at first blush, might seem consistent with this goal because they reduce the amount government collects in revenues. Of course, in fact they do not reduce government obligations—they only limit the funds available to it for spending on other programs. But some policymakers assume that curtailing revenues provides a means by which to reduce spending, an approach that became known as "starve the beast." As articulated by Reagan in 1981: "Over the past decade we've talked about curtailing spending so that we can lower the tax burden. . . . But there were always those who told us that taxes couldn't be cut until spending was reduced. Well, you know, we can lecture our children about extravagance until we run out of voice and breath. Or we can cure their extravagance simply by reducing their allowance."[9] Some policymakers also believe that submerged policies, by bestowing rewards on some people, may quell popular demands for more extensive visible social provision for all citizens. Republican Senator Robert Packwood, chair of the Senate Finance Committee, implied this in 1983 when he defended the tax-free status of employer health insurance: "I think the one reason we do not have any significant demand for national health insurance in this country among those who are employed is because their employers are paying for their benefits, by and large. And we will never go to the situation in Great Britain so long as that system exists, and I hate to see us nibble at it for fear you are going to have the demand that the Federal Government take over and provide the benefits that would otherwise be lost."[10] The submerged state is thus supported in part because it is thought to deter direct government spending, both by reducing revenues and by appeasing those who might otherwise be vocal proponents.

Submerged state policies can also appear to embody the principle of privatization, meaning the contracting out of government responsibilities to the private sector on the assumption that it can deliver goods and services more efficiently. As such, they seem to reflect the kinds of market-based approaches that Reagan championed and that have become commonplace in American politics ever since his presidency. It is the case that the officials on the front lines of service delivery for such policies are not government bureaucrats but, instead, representatives of institutions such as health insurance companies and banks. Yet, in fact, such policies function not through free-market principles of laissez-faire but rather through public subsidization of the private sector. Some submerged policies, such as tax breaks, subsidize individuals to participate in activities that promote the profitability of particular industries; others, such as student loans, function by delivering public funds directly to the private sector. In either case, they encourage people to act differently than if they were left to pure market forces; for example, consumers are more likely to purchase bigger houses than they would if home-owner tax advantages did not exist, and this fuels the real estate industry. Nonetheless, these features of the submerged state help explain why conservatives have not acted to restrain even its policies that have grown to be hugely expensive, and why they have continued to initiate new ones.

Another critical factor that has enabled the submerged state to flourish in recent decades is that over time, a wider array of Democrats became willing accomplices—and leaders—in its creation. During the New Deal and Great Society periods, Democrats initiated the creation of new direct spending programs. When in the 1980s that approach to governance began to seem politically infeasible, they looked to the submerged state instead to find ways to aid low- and middle-income people. They increasingly acquiesced and supported policies such as tax expenditures because, to quote one member of Congress, they became "the only game in town."[11] After Democratic candidate Walter Mondale lost his bid for the presidency in 1984, the Democratic Leadership Council (DLC) formed in an effort to take control of the party away from liberals. The DLC championed tax expenditures, and in 1988 its affiliates in Congress pushed successfully for large increases in the EITC and for other new tax credits for the working poor.[12] While Republicans had proposed tuition tax breaks as far back as the early 1960s, it was Democratic President Bill Clinton who finally called for their successful enactment in the form of the HOPE [Scholarship] and Lifetime Learning Tax Credits, which he signed into law. Once Democrats controlled both Congress and the White House in 2009, tax expenditures constituted their policy tool of choice, as numerous new and expanded tax breaks were tucked into bills intended to encourage particular activities and to stimulate the flagging economy.

With Congress so deeply and closely divided between the two major political parties in recent decades, submerged policies—particularly in the case of tax expenditures—have also proven easier to enact than other policies because the institutional hurdles are much lower. Direct new spending programs must overcome multiple hurdles in the budget process, gaining the approval of two separate committees in each chamber for authorization and appropriation. New tax breaks, by contrast, only need to pass muster with the tax committees, and they can be folded into large revenue bills, attracting little attention in floor votes.[13]

Over time, each well-established wing of the submerged state has been tended by the trade associations and other interest groups that represent its core industries—such as the National Association of Realtors and National Association of Home Builders in the case of the Home Mortgage Interest Deduction (HMID). Such groups have carefully cultivated and tended relationships with elected officials on both sides of the aisle. They have long made their positions known through lobbying in Washington, D.C., and by activating their constituencies; in recent decades, as the cost of campaigns has escalated, they have devoted substantial amounts to donations. Such influence serves as another important reason [for] why substantial components of the submerged state enjoy strong bipartisan support, resilient enough to withstand the sharp partisan divisions around most other issues.

In short, over the past thirty years, by nurturing and protecting the submerged state, conservatives did not downsize government; rather, they took the lead in restructuring and actually enlarging it, but in ways that elude the public. Liberals, with few alternatives, willingly followed suit. Meanwhile interest groups worked to maintain strong support for their favored policies from members of both parties.

The Size and Scope of the Submerged State

As a result of these attributes, submerged state policies of many varieties have proliferated in number and in scope during the conservative period of the

FIGURE [1]   Revenue Lost from All Social Tax Expenditures, 1981–2010 (2010 Dollars)

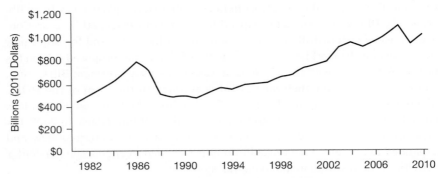

SOURCES: Joint Committee on Taxation, "Estimates of Federal Tax Expenditures for Fiscal Years" (various years), http://www.jct.gov/publications.html; Congressional Budget Office, "Tax Expenditures: Current Issues and Five-Year Budget Projections for Fiscal Years 1982–1986" (1981), http://www.cbo.gov/ftpdocs/51xx/doc5185/doc29-Entire.pdf.

past three decades. To illustrate such trends, this section will focus on social tax expenditures. When Reagan took office in 1981, 81 of these existed; by 2010, Obama's second year in office, the number had risen by 86 percent, to 151. The number of such policies increased steadily but slowly during the 1980s and 1990s, then grew more rapidly from 2000 to the present—both when Republicans controlled both chambers of Congress and the White House and more recently when Democrats did.[14]

The amount of total revenue lost to social tax expenditures soared between 1981 and 2010, in 2010 dollars, as shown in Figure [1]. The temporary decline in the late 1980s is attributable primarily to the effect of tax reform in 1986. It is important to note that even in this major legislation policymakers treated social tax expenditures as sacrosanct, leaving intact all of the most costly ones. The reason [for] why their overall value dipped was because tax reform lowered regular tax rates, and when households owe less, the worth of individual tax breaks is effectively reduced.[15] Nonetheless, after a few years of stasis, the actual cost of tax breaks began to grow steadily and rapidly again, increasing by more than 130 percent by 2008. In that year, just before the recession temporarily reduced their value, they cost the nation $1.086 trillion, and recently their cost has nearly returned to that level.

The three most expensive social tax expenditures were each created long ago—starting with the case of the Home Mortgage Interest Deduction in 1913—and have expanded tremendously in terms of their value in recent decades. Figure [2] shows the value, in 2010 dollars, of the HMID, and the nontaxable status of health insurance and retirement benefits. Notably, while

FIGURE [2]   Revenue Lost from Three Major Tax Expenditures, 1981–2010
(2010 Dollars)

─────── Home Mortgage Interest Deduction
─ ─ ─ Health Insurance Exemption
─ ─ ─ Retirement Benefits Exemption

Sources: Joint Committee on Taxation, "Estimates of Federal Tax Expenditures for Fiscal Years" (various years), http://www.jct.gov/publications.html; Congressional Budget Office, "Tax Expenditures: Current Issues and Five-Year Budget Projections for Fiscal Years 1982–1986" (1981), http://www.cbo.gov/ftpdocs/51xx/doc5185/doc29-Entire.pdf.

each diminished briefly in the late 1980s and early 1990s for the reasons mentioned above, they then once again resumed their growth, which was mitigated only briefly by the recession in 2008.

Their low profile notwithstanding, submerged state policies consume a large portion of federal resources relative to many social programs that are much more visible. Figure [3] shows the size of the three most expensive social tax expenditures compared to the value of a few well-known direct social programs. The HMID consumes four times the amount of the primary federal housing program for low-income Americans, called Section 8 Housing vouchers. Despite the amount of attention often given in public discourse to welfare (now called Temporary Assistance for Needy Families), it costs the nation less than one-fifth the amount of subsidizing employer-provided health insurance and less than one-seventh the expense of employer-provided retirement benefits. Neither the costs of food stamps, the most utilized program for low-income people, nor of unemployment insurance, which provides economic security for Americans of all income levels, amounts to as much as half the value of even the least expensive of these programs.

Fostering Economic Inequality

Because the submerged state typically distributes its rewards through more complex and circuitous processes than do more direct policies, its major

FIGURE [3]   Selected Visible and Submerged Social Expenditures, 2007 (2010 Dollars)

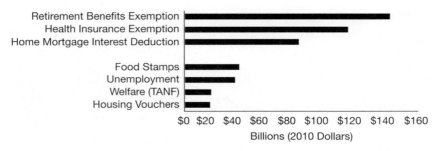

SOURCES: Joint Committee on Taxation, "Estimates of Federal Tax Expenditures, 2007–2011" (2007), http://www.jct.gov/publications.html?func=startdown&id=1198; Office of Management and Budget, *Analytical Perspectives: Budget of the United States Government FY 2009* (2008), tables 3.2, 8.5, www.whitehouse.gov/sites/whitehouse.gov/files/omb/assets/OMB/budget/fy2009; Congressional Budget Office, Budget Factsheets for TANF, Food Stamps, and Unemployment (March 2007).

beneficiaries are often not obvious. To the extent that lawmakers discuss the submerged state publicly, they usually imply that its policies facilitate widely held goals, such as the expansion of health care coverage or growth of retirement savings for average citizens. In some instances, such images are reasonably accurate depictions of policy effects, as exemplified by the Earned Income Tax Credit, which subsidizes the earnings of the working poor, or the tuition tax credits signed into law by Clinton, which aided middle-income Americans in paying for college. Most submerged policies, however, actually exacerbate inequality: they shower their most generous benefits on affluent people, and they generate detrimental side effects that adversely impact those who are less well-off. Some of the largest winnings, moreover, are accrued not by individuals and households but rather by the third-party organizations and businesses that benefit from the economic activities such policies promote.

Figure [4] illustrates how the three most costly tax expenditures distribute their benefits across income groups. Each bestows its bounty in an upwardly redistributive fashion, with the largest amounts going to those in the upper-income groups. The most skewed distribution accompanies the Home Mortgage Interest Deduction and the tax-free status of retirement benefits: in 2004, 69 percent and 55 percent of the benefits from each of these policies, respectively, were conferred on Americans with household incomes of $100,000 or more—the top 15 percent of the income distribution.[16] The tax-free nature of employer-sponsored health insurance is somewhat less biased, though still 30 percent of the benefit was allocated to families in the top 15 percent of the income distribution.

FIGURE [4]   Percent of Tax Subsidies Claimed by Households, by Income, 2004

Annual Cash Income Class (Thousands of Dollars)

■ Percent of Households in Income Category
▨ Exclusion for Employer-Sponsored Health Insurance
☐ Home Mortgage Interest Deduction
▥ Tax Benefits for Retirement Contributions (Defined Contribution and IRAs)

Sources: Leonard E. Burman et al., "Tax Code, Employer-Sponsored Insurance, and Tax Subsidies," in *Using Taxes to Reform Health Insurance*, edited by Leonard E. Burman and Henry J. Aaron (Washington, DC: Brookings Institution Press, 2008); Joint Committee on Taxation, "Estimates of Federal Tax Expenditures for Fiscal Years 2005–2009" (2005), http://www.jct.gov/publications.html?func=startdown&id=1200; Leonard E. Burman et al., "Distributional Effects of Defined Contribution Plans and Individual Retirement Accounts," Tax Policy Center Discussion paper No. 16 (2004), http://www.urban.org/uploadedPDF/311029TPC DP16.pdf.

On the rare occasions when policymakers ever talk about the Home Mortgage Interest Deduction, they typically convey the impression that it helps make home ownership possible for middle-income people. Scholars have not found evidence to support this effect, however; rather the policy merely offers an extra financial advantage to those who were already positioned to buy a home.[17] HMID offers particularly generous aid, as we have seen, to the wealthy. Whereas the median new home value in the nation has fluctuated between $200,000 and $260,000 since 2006, the HMID applies to mortgages up to $1,000,000; those who can afford to buy the most expensive homes and qualify for the largest mortgages reap by far the largest benefits from the policy.[18] Moreover, both the HMID and other benefits for home owners operate as artificial incentives that encourage people to purchase more expensive and larger homes than they would [otherwise]. As a result, such policies inflate prices, making home ownership more out of reach for non-owners. For those who are financially capable of buying a home, housing equity provides their primary source of wealth, and that further widens the economic gap between owners and renters. In addition, the lost government revenues leave lawmakers with insufficient funds to maintain or create policies that could more effectively enhance the social welfare of low- and moderate-income citizens.[19]

The employer-provided and government-subsidized benefits of the sub-merged state are also tilted to higher-income Americans and have become more so over time. During the 1940s, increasing numbers of jobs offered work-ers such benefits, and before long, the majority of Americans enjoyed coverage. As health care costs soared in recent years, however, fewer and fewer jobs granted health coverage to employees: the percentage of Americans possessing it diminished in every consecutive year from 2000 to 2009, falling from 68 to 59 percent over the period.[20] In addition, the extent of the plans that are still offered by employers has diminished.[21] While higher-income people have long been most likely to gain employment in positions that offer health insurance and have had the good fortune of being covered by more generous plans, the inequality fostered by such arrangements has become exacerbated recently. As of 2009, in the lowest income quintile, only 16 percent of Americans under age sixty-five had employer-sponsored health insurance—compared to 85 percent of those in the top quintile; while rates of coverage had declined among all quintiles, they had fallen most precipitously for those at and near the bottom.[22] In addition, even among those who do have such coverage, the value of the tax subsidies is sharply skewed to the wealthy: the average subsidy for households with incomes between $200,000 and $500,000 is over three times the average subsidy for those in the $10,000 to $20,000 range, $4,791 compared to $1,535.[23] As a result, this large portion of the submerged state, which not many Ameri-cans realize is subsidized by government, showers its benefits far more gener-ously on the haves than on the have-nots.

Well beyond its impact on individuals and families, the submerged state exacerbates economic inequality by promoting some entire sectors of the economy over others, at government expense. In delivering subsidies to par-ticular industries and creating incentives for people to participate in specific market activities, its policies protect and enhance profit-making capabilities in those areas. From 1980 until the [recent] recession, the core sectors that it nurtures—finance, insurance, and real estate—outpaced growth in other sectors of the American economy.[24] The fortunes of these industries ema-nated not from "market forces" alone but rather from their interplay with the hidden policies that promoted their growth and heaped extra benefits on them.

Such patterns are exemplified by the rise in profitability of the student loan sector. Americans' need for student aid escalated during the 1980s and 1990s as the rise in tuition rates exceeded inflation. Amid the growing partisan div-ide in Congress, policymakers could forge agreement more easily on terms for student loans, for which they needed to do little more than expand bor-rowing limits and loosen eligibility requirements, than they could on Pell Grants, the direct form of tuition assistance for low-income students, for which rate increases would have involved the highly conflictual and many-staged process of legislative approval for increased spending.[25] As a result of these trends, growing numbers of students borrowed, the average amount of their loans soared, and lending became increasingly lucrative. Student lender Sallie Mae, created by the federal government in 1973 and permitted to become a private company in 1996, saw the value of its stocks rise by nearly 2000 percent over the next decade, compared to the Standard and Poor 500's average gain of 228 percent. Its CEO became the most highly compensated in the nation, with approximately $37 million in salary, bonuses, and stock awards in 2006.[26]

Similarly, government subsidies for health insurance appeared more complicit in the development of the "winner take all" society than in providing for the health care of the nation's citizens. Health insurance companies enjoyed soaring profits that did not abate even with the recession: the five largest insurers reported $12.2 billion in profits in 2009, a 56 percent increase from 2008.[27] For the CEOs of the top seven health insurance companies, average total compensation, including stock options, soared to $10.6 million.[28] Meanwhile, among ordinary Americans, the ranks of the uninsured escalated, reaching 16.7 percent in 2010, and the insured faced mounting costs.[29]

Whereas most Americans assume social welfare policy exists in order to provide economic security to average people and to lessen inequality, the policies of the submerged state have aided and abetted the upward distribution of riches, with more and more of the largesse accrued to those at the very top. The sectors that it nurtures, in turn, have invested in strengthening their political capacity, fortifying their ability to defend existing arrangements.

NOTES

1. Suzanne Mettler and Andrew Milstein, "American Political Development from Citizens' Perspective: Tracking Federal Government's Presence in Individual Lives over Time," *Studies in American Political Development* 21 (Spring 2007): 110–30.

2. Thomas Piketty and Emmanuel Saez, "Income Inequality in the United States, 1913–1998," *Quarterly Journal of Economics* 118 (February 2003): 1–39.

3. Mettler and Milstein, "American Political Development from Citizens' Perspective."

4. Christopher Howard, *The Hidden Welfare State: Tax Expenditure and Social Policy in the United States* (Princeton, NJ: Princeton University Press, 1997), 48–54.

5. Ibid., 176–77.

6. Paul Starr and Gosta Esping-Andersen, "Passive Intervention," *Working Papers for a New Society*, July/August 1979, http://www.princeton.edu/~starr/articles/articles68-79/Starr_Esping-Andersen_Passive_Intervention.pdf (accessed October 19, 2010).

7. Muhammad Attaullah Chaudhry, "The Higher Education Act of 1965: An Historical Case Study" (PhD diss., Oklahoma State University, 1981), 97–99; Jose Chávez, "Presidential Influence on the Politics of Higher Education: The Higher Education Act of 1965" (PhD diss., University of Texas at Austin, 1975), 121–23.

8. Howard, *Hidden Welfare State*, 46, 61, 64–70.

9. Ronald Reagan, "Address to the Nation on the Economy," February 5, 1981, http://www.reagan.utexas.edu/archives/speeches/1981/20581c.htm (accessed February 29, 2011).

10. Quoted in Howard, *Hidden Welfare State*, 190–91.

11. Pete Stark (D-CA), referring to the Targeted Jobs Tax Credit, quoted in Christopher Howard, "Tax Expenditures," in *The Tools of Government: A Guide to the New Governance*, ed. Lester M. Salamon (New York: Oxford University Press, 2002), 428.

12. Howard, *Hidden Welfare State*, 151–52.

13. Ibid., 179–80.

14. Office of Management and Budget, *Analytical Perspectives: Budget of the United States Government*, FY 1997, 2002, 2007, 2011; Joint Committee on Taxation, "Estimates of Federal Tax Expenditures for Fiscal Years 1990–1994" (1989); Congressional Budget Office, "Tax Expenditures: Current Issues and Five-Year Budget Projections for Fiscal Years 1982–1986" (1981).

15. C. Eugene Steuerle, *Contemporary U.S. Tax Policy*, 2nd ed. (Washington, DC: Urban Institute Press, 2008), 128, 130, 132, 133, 248; Hacker, *Divided Welfare State*, 160–63. Tax reform also increased the standard deduction, so fewer people qualified to itemize deductions.

16. U.S. Census Bureau, "Annual Social and Economic (ASEC) Supplement" (2005), last modified August 28, 2007, http://pubdb3.census.gov/macro/032007/hhinc/new06_000.htm.

17. Edward L. Glaeser and Jesse M. Shapiro, "The Benefits of the Home Mortgage Interest Deduction," NBER Working Paper no. 9284 (October 2002), http://papers.nber.org/papers/w9284 (accessed October 24, 2010).

18. U.S. Census, "Median and Average Sale Prices of New Homes Sold in the United States," http://www.census.gov/const/uspricemon.pdf (accessed October 20, 2010).

19. Starr and Esping-Andersen, "Passive Intervention."

20. Elise Gould, "Employer-Sponsored Health Insurance Erosion Accelerates in the Recession: Public Safety Net Catches Kids but Fails to Adequately Insure Adults," *EPI Briefing Paper*, November 16, 2010, Briefing Paper #283, http://www.epi.org/publications/entry/bp283 (accessed December 2, 2010).

21. Jacob S. Hacker, *The Divided Welfare State: The Battle over Public and Private Social Benefits in the United States* (New York: Cambridge University Press, 2002), 36–39; Jacob S. Hacker, *The Great Risk Shift: The Assault on American Jobs, Families, Health Care, and Retirement, and How You Can Fight Back* (New York: Oxford University Press, 2006), 139.

22. Gould, "Employer-Sponsored Health Insurance Erosion Accelerates in the Recession."

23. Len Burman, Surachai Khitatrakun, and Sarah Goodell, "Tax Subsidies for Private Health Insurance: Who Benefits and at What Cost?" Robert Wood Johnson Foundation, Synthesis Project, Update, July 2009, http://www.rwjf.org/files/research/072209policysynthesis3update.brief.pdf (accessed January 15, 2011).

24. Frank Levy and Peter Temlin, "Inequality and Institutions in 20th Century America," Industrial Performance Center, MIT, Working Paper Series, MIT-IPC-07-002 (2007), 36–37, http://papers.ssrn.com/sol3/papers.cfm?abstract_id=984330.

25. National Center for Public Policy and Higher Education, *Losing Ground: A National Status Report on the Affordability of American Higher Education* (San Jose, CA: National Center for Public Policy and Higher Education, 2002), 8–9, 12, 22–30.

26. Bethany McLean, "Sallie Mae: A Hot Stock, A Tough Lender," CNNMoney.com, December 14, 2005, http://money.cnn.com/2005/12/14/news/fortune500/sallie_fortune_122605/index.htm (accessed January 29, 2011); "Top 100 Executives by Total Compensation," *Washington Post* (2006), http://projects.washingtonpost.com/post200/2006/executives-by-compensation/ (accessed January 29, 2011).

27. "Fortune 500: Health Care: Insurance and Managed Care, 2009," CNNMoney .com (2010), http://money.cnn.com/magazines/fortune/fortune500/2010/industries /223/index.html (accessed October 25, 2010).

28. Dan Bowman, "2009 Health Insurance CEO Compensation," *Fierce Health Payer*, May 11, 2010, http://www.fiercehealthpayer.com/special-reports/2009-health-insurance -ceo-compensation (accessed October 28, 2010).

29. Mike Lillis, "Census: Number of Uninsured Americans Skyrocketed Last Year," *The Hill*, September 16, 2010, http://thehill.com/blogs/healthwatch/health-reform -implementation/119271-census-number-of-uninsured-americans-skyrocketed-last -year (accessed October 26, 2010).

15.2

ANDREA LOUISE CAMPBELL

From *How Policies Make Citizens: Senior Political Activism and the American Welfare State*

Campbell makes the argument that government social programs change the political preferences of beneficiaries from those programs. She focuses on Social Security and Medicare, enacted in the 1930s and the 1960s, respectively, as examples of major social programs that provided senior citizens with resources that lifted many out of poverty but also allowed senior citizens as a group to become politically very powerful. A feedback cycle develops with a generous social program: the program provides resources to a group, those resources increase the political power of that group, that group can then use this power to protect and expand the social program. Campbell points to high voter turnout among the elderly as well as the powerful lobbying groups supported financially by the elderly as key means of political influence.

PARTICIPATION, POLICYMAKING, AND THE POLITICAL IMPLICATIONS OF PROGRAM DESIGN

The enactment and development of Social Security and Medicare have fundamentally altered the American democratic landscape. The programs helped transform seniors from the poorest, most beleaguered age group to the most comfortable. In supplying seniors with income, health, and free time, the programs have materially enhanced their participatory capacity. The programs' cognitive effects have heightened senior constituents' interest in and vigilance over the political process, a watchfulness of which elected officials are keenly aware. Interest groups arose to fill service niches created by the programs, and as a by-product, the groups serve as informational networks for seniors, alerting them of policy actions. Political parties clamor to mobilize seniors, and elected officials concentrate their casework efforts on them. Seniors learn that they matter politically and that policymakers are receptive. Seniors' political efficacy rises over time as they draw positive lessons about government responsiveness and about themselves as citizens.

. . . [I]n its early years, Social Security expanded through the urgings of the Social Security Administration; as these program expansions enhanced

From Andrea Louise Campbell, *How Policies Make Citizens: Senior Political Activism and the American Welfare State* (Princeton, NJ: Princeton University Press, 2003).

seniors' participatory capacity, seniors began to exert political pressure themselves to achieve further expansions. Finally, when Social Security and Medicare were threatened in the 1980s, seniors' participatory capacity, thanks largely to the programs themselves, had grown to such a formidable degree that seniors were able to beat back the threats. Crucially, the design of Social Security meant that seniors had no moral qualms about defending the program. That Social Security is both universal and self-contributory is a major factor in seniors' individual sense of entitlement. As one elderly woman said, "We supported these programs, we paid for these programs, and now it's time to collect."[1] Hence government policy enhanced senior participation levels over time, and seniors, through this participation, have been able to shape policy outcomes.

One observer, writing in 1942, warned, "The demands of the old are rapidly increasing. . . . They are beginning to expect much more of life because of the expansion of programs designed to give them a more enjoyable old age." He predicted that "these growing desires" coupled with "the likelihood of their becoming an increasingly effective pressure group" would create tensions between their needs and those of children, youth, and the middle-aged. Indeed, he even warned that there might be "movements put on foot during this generation to dis[en]franchise those who reach retirement age, in order to protect the interest of other age groups in the population."[2]

It hasn't come to that. There is no credible movement to disenfranchise senior citizens. Even the debate among elites about generational equity—whether the elderly get more than their fair share of society's resources—has never become a focus for the greater public.[3] But other aspects of this early warning have come to fruition. Seniors' participation shapes government outputs. Their programs have largely escaped retrenchment efforts and continue to grow both in terms of spending per recipient and as a share of the federal budget. Through seniors' participation, their aging-policy preferences are fulfilled.

One other aspect of that sixty-year-old prediction has come true: because seniors are a politically dominant group, their preferences on other issues also matter. Policy effects spill over: if seniors' participatory capacity is enhanced by their programs, and if politicians and parties work to mobilize seniors rather than other groups, then issue areas beyond Social Security are affected. Analysis by the economist James Poterba shows that per student education spending is lower in states with a greater proportion of senior citizens.[4] In her history of retirement, Dora Costa argues that seniors lower the price of recreation for themselves by congregating geographically and substituting senior centers and golf courses for playgrounds and public schools.[5] The demographer Samuel Preston noted in 1984 that starting in the late 1950s there had been a sharp decline in the child population and [a] large increase in the elderly population. Demographers would probably predict that such a change would have "favorable consequences for children and troubling ones for the elderly," as fewer children competed for benefits earmarked for them and more elderly competed for resources directed at their group.[6] But as we know, the opposite occurred, perhaps best encapsulated by the divergent trends in poverty rates. Thus, while age-related programs have had laudable effects like the reduction in senior poverty, they have also significantly redistributed public sector resources to the elderly, at all levels of government, crowding out other expenditures.[7]

In addition to these concerns about the allocation of societal goods, we must consider the nature of expenditures as well. Spending on children represents both consumption and investment, while spending on the elderly is primarily consumption.[8] Arguably it is in the collective interest to invest in the future, but American democracy is more responsive to organized interests like the elderly. Some might counter that large programs for the elderly are in the interest of the nonelderly, since they relieve younger people of financial burden. But whether that benefit trumps other interests or not, there is little prospect for meaningful debate on the subject, given the political dominance of the organized and highly participatory senior citizen constituency.[9]

. . . [O]ther groups gain or lose from governmental action depending upon the force of their participation. That some groups participate less and suffer policy disappointments as a result is problematic for political equality and democratic governance. Robert Dahl concludes that "if a group is inactive, whether by free choice, violence, intimidation, or law, the normal American system does not necessarily provide it with a checkpoint anywhere in the process."[10] Participatory quiescence can lead to policy disaster.

Indeed, we can add government policy to Dahl's causes of group inactivity. The design of social welfare programs can enhance recipient participation, as with Social Security, or hinder it, as with welfare. Government policy magnifies groups' participatory advantages or disadvantages, affecting the ability of groups to voice their preferences, therefore influencing subsequent policymaking. Groups get on upward or downward policy trajectories, and advantages or disadvantages accrue.

Democratic theory is predicated on the equal proximity of citizens to government. But public policy itself can undermine this foundation. . . . American history is marked by extensions of political equality but not of economic equality.[11] In the latter realm, Americans have traditionally let market outcomes prevail, preferring individualism and self-determination to redistribution. But the lack of economic equality undermines our nominal political equality, muting the voice of the poor. And government programs can make matters worse by elevating some groups over others in the political arena.

Indeed, the effects of policy on recipients and their political participation provide yet another argument for universal social welfare programs. . . . [T]argeted, income-tested programs like welfare lack public support because members of the middle class see themselves only as taxpayers, not as potential beneficiaries.[12] Added to this taxpayer consciousness is an association in the United States between such programs and race.[13] Wilson advocates replacing means-tested programs with universal programs to which "the more advantaged groups of all races can positively relate." Skocpol argues for "targeting within universalism," giving extra benefits and services to the poor within larger, publicly supported programs, just as Social Security redistributes income to poor seniors in a relatively hidden, non-stigmatizing way. In either case, including the poor in universal programs is touted as the key to winning the battle for public approval.

[T]he merits of universal programs extend beyond the public support they enjoy. These programs incorporate low-income recipients, minorities, women, and other disadvantaged groups into democratic citizenship on an equal footing with the more affluent. Rather than subject prospective beneficiaries to the stigma and bureaucratic red tape associated with means-tested programs, universal programs treat their recipients with dignity and respect. The programs are set up to ease the way for recipients to secure the benefits they have "earned," rather than face a demeaning process of proving eligibility. The programs have institutionalized appeals processes to dispute benefits decisions. The interactions between government and beneficiary are marked by professionalism and the equal application of well-publicized standards. The result is increased individual efficacy vis-à-vis the government, which enhances participation levels. The degree to which universal programs would enhance the participation rates of the disadvantaged depends on many factors, including benefit levels, but at a minimum the citizenship lessons learned would not actively decrease participation as is the case under welfare's current means-tested design.

▪ ▪ ▪

CONCLUSION

[There are] a number of fundamental political questions summarized by Lasswell's famous query: "Who gets what, when, how?"[14] First, high-participation groups do prevail in the policy arena; this study supports the assumption behind decades of participation research—that participatory inputs influence policy outputs. Second, existing policies do structure subsequent political processes. And these feedback effects are pronounced for the mass public and are certainly not limited to state or interest group capacities. Finally, self-interest is an impetus to political activity, when the stakes are high, the informational barriers low, and moral or social reservations absent. [T]his [occurs] particularly in the activity of low-income seniors with regard to Social Security. But the cross-program comparison showed that interest is not enough; individuals must have at least minimal resources for participation. In the case of senior citizens, these means come in part from government programs. Welfare state programs laudably mobilize a low-income group—poor seniors—which is a rarity in American politics. But senior programs also serve to elevate the participation of seniors in general over that of other groups. . . .

Policy studies typically evaluate policy instruments in terms of their "efficiency, effectiveness and feasibility of adoption and implementation."[15] [T]he design of social programs has significant implications for politics as well. Politically relevant aspects of program design include the size and characteristics of the beneficiary group, the level of benefits, the funding mechanism, and the method of conferring benefits. These program characteristics influence electoral politics, the politics of distribution, and the politics of retrenchment. Over time, Social Security itself has enhanced the participation rates of a large group of people. Benefits are high enough to have tangible effects on senior participatory capacity and to heighten their interest in a program that provides such a large share of their income. Because the program is self-contributory, seniors confront no welfare stigma in receiving benefits, feel no moral compunction exercising their self-interest in defending their benefits, and have faced little backlash from the rest of the public. Social Security is a highly regarded and effective program that seniors rationally and unequivocally defend. It is also a program that because of its very design has led to disproportionate senior influence on electoral politics and on policymaking. Seniors get more out of the government than less-participatory groups, in part because of the structure of their welfare state programs. This presumably unintended consequence shows that both economic *and* political implications must be considered when designing social programs.

NOTES

1. Quoted in Saul Friedman, "Greedy Geezers: These Folks Say No," *Newsday*, 20 March 2001, p. B12.

2. P. H. Landis, "Emerging Problems of the Aged," *Social Forces*, May 1942, reprinted in *Readings in Social Security*, ed. William Haber and Wilbur J. Cohen (New York: Prentice Hall, 1948), pp. 228–38.

3. For an overview of the generational equity debate, see Jill Quadagno, "Generational Equity and the Politics of the Welfare State," *Politics and Society* 17 (1989): 253–76.

4. James M. Poterba, "Demographic Structure and the Political Economy of Public Education," *Journal of Policy Analysis and Management* 16 (1997): 48–66. See also James W. Button, "A Sign of Generational Conflict: The Impact of Florida's Aging Voters on Local School and Tax Referenda," *Social Science Quarterly* 73 (1992): 786–97.

5. Dora L. Costa, *The Evolution of Retirement: An American Economic History, 1880–1990* (Chicago: University of Chicago Press, 1998).

6. Samuel Preston, "Children and the Elderly: Divergent Paths for America's Dependents," *Demography* 21 (1984): 435–57.

7. Costa, *The Evolution of Retirement*, p. 160.

8. Preston, "Children and the Elderly."

9. The political scientist Paul E. Peterson has suggested one remedy: give children the vote. "An Immodest Proposal," *Daedalus* 121 (1992): 151–74.

10. Robert Dahl, *A Preface to Democratic Theory* (Chicago: University of Chicago Press, 1956), p. 138.

11. Sidney Verba and Gary Orren, *Equality in America: The View from the Top* (Cambridge: Harvard University Press, 1985), chap. 2

12. William Julius Wilson, *The Truly Disadvantaged: The Inner City, the Underclass, and Public Policy* (Chicago: University of Chicago Press, 1987); Theda Skocpol, "Targeting within Universalism: Politically Viable Policies to Combat Poverty in the United States," in *The Urban Underclass*, ed. Christopher Jencks and Paul E. Peterson (Washington, D.C.: Brookings, 1991).

13. Wilson, *The Truly Disadvantaged*. See also Martin Gilens, *Why Americans Hate Welfare* (Chicago: University of Chicago Press, 1999).

14. Harold D. Lasswell, *Politics: Who Gets What, When, How* (New York: McGraw-Hill, 1936).

15. Janet A. Weiss, "Policy Design for Democracy: A Look at Public Information Campaigns," in *Public Policy for Democracy*, ed. Helen Ingram and Steven Rathgeb Smith (Washington, D.C.: Brookings, 1993), p. 99.

15.3

MATT GUARDINO AND DANNY HAYES

From "Foreign Voices, Party Cues, and U.S. Public Opinion about Military Action"

Do Americans pay attention to foreign leaders when formulating opinions about foreign policy matters? Using experiments in an opinion survey, Hayes and Guardino show that statements from foreign leaders can influence public opinion about whether U.S. military intervention is warranted. Democrats generally support a greater role for multi-lateral, international institutions such as the United Nations (U.N.), while Republicans generally are more skeptical of the value of such institutions. The experiments show, somewhat surprisingly, that a sizable proportion of people from both parties are influenced by statements from a U.N. representative about a U.S. foreign policy involving potential military action.

[A] growing body of work indicates that international institutions and foreign officials can significantly shape Americans' attitudes. For example, presidents appear to get a boost in approval ratings when the United Nations Security Council supports their calls for military intervention (Chapman, 2011; Chapman & Reiter, 2004). Americans may look abroad for a "second opinion" about military endeavors, perceiving U.N. or North Atlantic Treaty Organization views as strong signals about the desirability of a proposed intervention. These effects are especially likely when the U.S. news media devote significant attention to foreign elite perspectives, as has been the case since the end of the Cold War. Moreover, research shows that American political leaders and public diplomacy efforts can shape public opinion in foreign countries. In an increasingly interconnected world, policy perspectives from beyond international borders appear increasingly influential in shaping public attitudes.

. . . [R]esearch has not clearly determined whether Americans are likely to respond to messages from the international community when they are simultaneously exposed to messages from prominent domestic political leaders. Because of the sheer frequency and political resonance of partisan voices in media coverage, the lack of precise comparisons between the effects of party elite and foreign elite messages represents an important gap in our knowledge.

[W]e report the results of a survey-experiment about possible U.S. air strikes on Iranian nuclear installations that was constructed to expand our under-

From Matt Guardino and Danny Hayes, "Foreign Voices, Party Cues, and U.S. Public Opinion about Military Action," *International Journal of Public Opinion Research* 30, no. 3 (2018): 504–516.

standing of the influence of foreign voices on domestic public opinion. . . . [S]ubjects were presented with combinations of messages from the U.N. Security Council as well as Republican and Democratic party elites. We find that people will sometimes resist signals from party leaders in favor of messages from a foreign actor, even when presented with a domestic bipartisan elite consensus in favor of military action. . . . Messages from [foreign] actors can indeed move U.S. public opinion in opposition to messages from party leaders. Our findings suggest that when news media outlets consistently incorporate messages from foreign elites, mass public opinion on foreign policy will be less likely to reflect the positions of Republican and Democratic leaders.

Our study focuses on the United States, but its results are relevant for analogous effects in other countries. . . .

LIMITATIONS OF EXISTING EMPIRICAL WORK

▪ ▪ ▪

[P]revious research demonstrates that Republicans and Democrats in the U.S. public differ significantly in their general foreign policy predispositions. Most significantly for our study, Democrats tend to be more favorable toward multilateral approaches, defined simply as a preference for cooperating with other countries and international institutions. This may make them more likely than Republicans both to seek cooperation with non-U.S. actors and to see foreign voices as credible sources of policy views when encountering such actors in media coverage. These predispositional factors suggest that Democrats' opinions might be influenced by views expressed by foreign actors when those views are consistent with Democrats' predispositions, and when the messages conflict with the positions staked out by their own domestic party elites. Despite the theoretical plausibility of these effects, however, we lack precise and explicit empirical evidence for the influence of foreign elite messages in the presence of party cues.

▪ ▪ ▪

In actual policy debates, Americans almost always have access to domestic partisan messages. . . . In the next section, we describe an experiment that improves empirical confidence in the influence of foreign voices by randomly exposing people to realistic treatments that test the possible effects of U.N. messages in the presence of domestic party cues.

EXPERIMENTAL DESIGN AND RESULTS

Our experiment centered on the debate in 2012 about whether the United States should undertake military action in response to Iran's nuclear program. We study Americans' support for military intervention because that has been the focus of most research on foreign actors and U.S. public opinion, and because the U.S. news media's frequent inclusion of foreign voices during these debates suggests that non-U.S. actors are most likely to be influential in such contexts. Our experiment was embedded in George Washington University's module of the 2012 Cooperative Congressional Election Study (CCES), a nationally representative survey of American adults.

In the postelection wave of the CCES, 815 respondents were assigned to one of four treatments in which they read a vignette about the debate over the Iranian nuclear program. In every treatment, subjects were told that President Barack Obama suggested that the United States should consider launching air strikes, a plausible scenario given the administration's rhetoric at the time.[1] In the first treatment—in which all elites, including members of the U.N. Security Council, were united in support—the vignette read:

> There has been a lot of debate recently about Iran's nuclear program. This month, President Obama suggested that the United States should consider launching air strikes against suspected Iranian weapons facilities. Republican Speaker of the House John Boehner has said he supports the air strikes. Members of the United Nations Security Council also have said they support the air strikes.

We refer to this as the elite consensus condition. The remaining three treatments varied whether Boehner and Security Council members supported or opposed military action. In Figure [1], we refer to these as "Obama Pro, Boehner Pro, UN Con"; "Obama Pro, Boehner Con, UN Pro"; and "Obama Pro, Boehner Con, UN Con." After seeing the vignette, subjects answered the following question: "Would you say that you support or oppose U.S. military strikes on Iranian nuclear facilities?" Subjects could answer that they "strongly" or "somewhat" supported or opposed action. We dichotomize responses into support or opposition, which eases interpretation of the treatment effects. After dropping those who said "don't know," we were left with 695 respondents.[2] Aggregate support for military intervention ranged from 40% to 65% across the treatments.

The left side of Figure [1] displays the predicted effects of the treatments on the likelihood of supporting military action, compared with the elite consensus condition. . . . We find that messages from foreign voices can move public opinion, even in the face of bipartisan domestic elite support for a policy proposal.

In the top row, changing the vignette so that subjects are told that Security Council members oppose air strikes reduces the likelihood of support among all subjects by a statistically significant 0.16. Messages from the international community can affect support for military intervention, even when domestic elites are united behind the proposal. Switching Boehner from pro to con (an admittedly unlikely scenario in the case of the Iranian nuclear program) reduces that support half as much (0.08, $p = .07$). Turning to the bottom data

FIGURE [1] Effect of Variations in Elite Support for Air Strikes Against Iran.

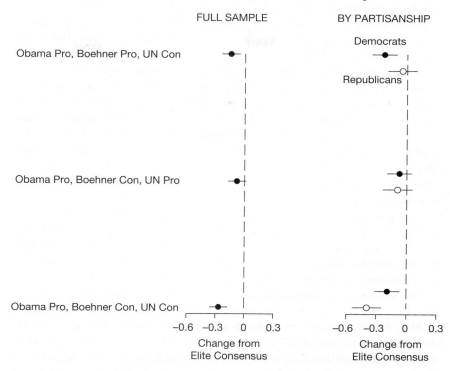

NOTE: Figure shows the change in the likelihood of a respondent supporting air strikes against Iranian nuclear facilities compared with the elite consensus condition (Obama Pro, Boehner Pro, UN Pro). Negative numbers indicate lower odds of support. In the left-hand graph, predicted probabilities are estimated from the Baseline model. In the right-hand graph, predicted probabilities are estimated from the Interaction with Partisanship model. Lines around the estimates are 95% confidence intervals. Subjects were part of the 2012 Cooperative Congressional Election Study.

point, we find more evidence consistent with a foreign voices effect. Opposition from Security Council members, paired with Boehner opposition, depresses the odds of overall support by 0.27.

The estimates for Democrats and Republicans on the right side of Figure [1] show results from a model in which we interact the treatments with a respondent's partisanship.[3] A Democratic subject told that U.N. Security Council members opposed air strikes against Iran is 0.24 less likely to support military action than a Democrat in the elite consensus condition. This suggests that if a president—even one basking in the glow of re-election, as Obama was at the time of our study—proposes a policy action at odds with fellow partisans' underlying values, many of them will be reluctant to follow him when they are offered a message from the international community that is more resonant with their predispositions.

In the second row, the effect of Boehner opposition among Democrats is about one-third the size of the effect of U.N. opposition, and is not statistically different from zero. This is consistent with the notion that cue-givers must meet some minimum credibility threshold, as Boehner was unlikely to be viewed as a trusted voice by most Democrats. That interpretation is supported by the last treatment, in which the odds of Democratic support for military action decline by about 0.19, roughly the same as when only Security Council members were opposed. GOP elite opposition to military action does not amplify Democratic opposition in the mass public, but a cue from foreign voices does.

As we consider Republican opinion, it is important to note that the proposal by a Democratic president in this instance—a hawkish, national security-focused action—is consistent with most Republicans' predispositions. It is no surprise, then, that U.N. opposition (in the first row) has no effect on GOP support. Nor do we find that Republicans move against their predispositions when Boehner opposes intervention: here is yet more evidence for the limits of partisan heuristics and the power of substantive political messages. It could also be that the absence of movement in response to Boehner's opposition is owing to the strong signal that U.N. support for military action sends. If Republicans view the Security Council as typically disposed to oppose a preemptive strike like the one described in our experiment, then a U.N. endorsement might be seen as a costly, and thus, especially credible, signal, keeping GOP support relatively high even in the face of Boehner's opposition. Our experimental design is not suited to distinguish between these mechanisms, but both are consistent with the importance of substantive predispositions as they interact with specific policy signals and messengers.

We do find, however, that the likelihood of Republican support decreases by 0.39 when U.N. opposition is paired with Boehner's opposition. In this scenario, we would not have expected U.N. opposition to matter, as most Republicans do not think highly of the organization and have generally hawkish predispositions. But it is plausible that this unusual Boehner–U.N. alliance merely confirms for GOP identifiers that what President Obama is proposing must be a bad idea. If even the U.N. Security Council is defying Obama and opposing military action against Iran, Republicans may be thinking, then it really must be foolhardy. We cannot say for sure what is happening here. But given the absence of any movement toward opposition among Republicans in the "Obama Pro, Boehner Pro, UN Con" treatment, we are reluctant to attribute the effects in the final condition to GOP identifiers being won over by U.N. Security Council members' substantive positions.

Altogether, however, our results suggest that many Americans will respond to policy messages from foreign elites, especially if those messages are consistent with their general predispositions. These influences can be considerable even when people are exposed to a competing message from their own party leader. Taken as a whole, our experiment provides significant evidence confirming that foreign elites have substantial real-world causal effects on U.S. public opinion.

CONCLUSION

Our study of public support for military action against Iran shows that cues from foreign elites can move U.S. public opinion, even when domestic elites are unified. Democrats responded to opposition from the United Nations when those messages were consistent with their substantive predispositions. Remarkably, this was true even when a popular president of their own party argued in favor of a preemptive strike against Iran. These findings highlight important limits on domestic leaders' ability to shape mass opinion, even among fellow partisans. Partisanship is a powerful force in American political discourse and behavior, but its effects are not automatic, unconditional, or wholly determinative.

Our findings are likely to be generalizable outside the context of our experiment in part because American media audiences are increasingly exposed to non-U.S. voices during policy debates. For example, foreign elites comprised as much as one-third of the voices on network TV news during debates over the Persian Gulf War and military action in Iraq in 2002 and 2003. Our results from a preliminary study during debates over the Iranian nuclear program in 2011 and 2012 show that about 15% of all quoted actors in *USA Today* were foreign officials. Despite increasing media consumption choices, foreign voices appear frequently in the news outlets that garner the most public exposure: Broadcast television remains the main source of political and public policy news for the greatest percentage of Americans, major traditional U.S. media organizations like TV networks and national newspapers operate a majority of the most popular Web sites, and *USA Today* is the largest circulation daily newspaper in the United States.[4]

■　■　■

Our findings also illuminate important political dimensions of high-stakes debates over military action. Even if other domestic and international factors exert more immediate causal influences on U.S. elites' decisions about using force against a nation like Iran, public sentiments can still play important constraining or enabling roles, shaping the political conditions under which military action takes place, and affecting subsequent dynamics of elite accountability for policy outcomes. In particular, our results indicate that presidents have a strong political incentive to win over U.S. allies and international organizations in an effort to build public support for military action. And because the media is the primary vehicle through which ordinary Americans are exposed to the positions of foreign elites, our findings highlight the crucial role of news outlets in shaping the domestic political conditions under which policy debates with major international implications will unfold.

NOTES

1. Obama said multiple times that "all options are on the table" in dealing with Iran's nuclear program (see http://www.theatlantic.com/international/archive/2012/03/obama -to-iran-and-israel-as-president-of-the-united-states-i-dont-bluff/253875/), indicating a willingness to consider preemptive military action. Thus, his stated position in the experiment likely would not have seemed unrealistic to our subjects, all of whom were debriefed after the study.

2. The likelihood of saying "don't know" was not different—substantively or statistically—across the treatment groups. Consistent with previous work on the distribution of political knowledge (Delli Carpini & Keeter, 1996), we found that respondents who answered "don't know" were more likely to be independent, female, and non-White.

3. Lacking large numbers of independents (75), we restrict the analysis in this model to partisans (including independents who said they "leaned" toward one of the parties [Keith et al., 1992]).

4. See http://www.poynter.org/2014/usa-today-wsj-nyt-top-u-s-newspapers-by-circul ation/277337/.

REFERENCES

Chapman, T. L. (2011). *Securing approval: Domestic politics and multilateral authorization for war.* Chicago and London: University of Chicago Press.
Chapman, T. L., & Reiter, D. (2004). The United Nations Security Council and the rally 'round the flag effect. *Journal of Conflict Resolution, 48,* 886–909. doi: 10.1177 /0022002704269353.
Delli Carpini, M. X., & Keeter, S. (1996). *What Americans know about politics and why it matters.* New Haven: Yale University Press.
Keith, B, E., Magleby, D. B., Nelson, C. J., Orr, E., Westlye, M. C., & Wolfinger, R. E. (1992). *The myth of the independent voter.* Berkeley, CA: University of California Press.

DISCUSSION QUESTIONS

1. What is the submerged state? How did it come about and how does it continue to exist?
2. Policies make political constituencies. Describe how Campbell illustrates this idea using Social Security and Medicare.
3. Describe the data Hayes and Guardino use to make their arguments and how they arrive at their conclusions about the influence of foreign leaders on public opinion.
4. In these readings, what evidence is presented to support the argument that public pressure plays a very large role in determining what policies governments adopt, even in areas of taxation and foreign policy?

ACKNOWLEDGMENTS

Marisa Abrajano: Excerpts from *Campaigning to the New American Electorate: Advertising to Latino Voters* Marisa Abrajano. Copyright © 2010 by the Board of Trustees of the Leland Stanford Jr. University. All rights reserved. Used with the permission of Stanford University Press, www.sup.org.

Christopher Achen and Larry Bartels: Republished with permission of Princeton University Press, from *Democracy for Realists: Why Elections Do Not Produce Responsive Government*, © 2016 Princeton University Press; permission conveyed through Copyright Clearance Center, Inc.

John Aldrich: *Why Parties: A Second Look* by John Aldrich. Copyright © 1995, 2011 by The University of Chicago. Reprinted by permission of The University of Chicago Press.

Hunt Allcott and Matthew Gentzkow: From "Social Media and Fake News in the 2016 Election," *Journal of Economic Perspectives* 31:2, 211–236 (2017). Copyright American Economic Association; reproduced with permission of the *Journal of Economic Perspectives American Economic Review*.

Larry M. Bartels: Republished with permission of Princeton University Press, from *Unequal Democracy: The Political Economy of the New Gilded Age*, © 2008 by Russell Sage Foundation; permission conveyed through Copyright Clearance Center, Inc.

Matthew Baum: Republished with permission of Princeton University Press, from *Soft News Goes to War*, © 2003 Princeton University Press; permission conveyed through Copyright Clearance Center, Inc.

William Bernhard and Tracy Sulkin: *Legislative Style*. Copyright © 2018 by The University of Chicago. Reprinted by permission of The University of Chicago Press.

Charles M. Cameron: From *Veto Bargaining: Presidents and the Politics of Negative Power* (Cambridge University Press, 2000). Reprinted by permission of Cambridge University Press.

Andrea Louise Campbell: Republished with permission of Princeton University press, from "Participation, Policymaking, and the Political Implications of Program Design," in *How Policies Make Citizens: Senior Political Activism and the American Welfare State*, © 2003 Princeton University Press; permission conveyed through Copyright Clearance Center, Inc.

Angus Campbell: "The Impact of Party Identification" from *The American Voter: An Abridgement* by Angus Campbell, Phillip E. Converse, Warren Edward Miller, Donald E. Stokes. Reprinted by permission of Jean Campbell.

James Campbell: From *POLARIZED: Making Sense of a Divided America* by James E. Campbell. Copyright © 2016 by Princeton University Press. Reprinted by permission.

Brandice Canes-Wrone: *Who Leads Whom? Presidents, Policy, and the Public.* Copyright © 2006 by The University of Chicago. Reprinted by permission of The University of Chicago Press.

Daniel Carpenter: *The Forging of Bureaucratic Autonomy.* Princeton University Press. Reprinted by permission of Princeton University Press.

Marty Cohen: *The Party Decides: Presidential Nominations Before and After Reform* by Marty Cohen, et al. Copyright © 2008 by The University of Chicago. Reprinted by permission of The University of Chicago Press.

Gary W. Cox and Mathew D. McCubbins: From *Setting the Agenda: Responsible Party Government in the U.S. House of Representatives.* Copyright © 2005 Gary W. Cox and Mathew D. McCubbins. Reprinted with the permission of Cambridge University Press.

Katherine Cramer: From *The Politics of Resentment: Rural Consciousness in Wisconsin and the Rise of Scott Walker.* Copyright © 2016 The University of Chicago. Reprinted by permission of the University of Chicago Press.

Robert A. Dahl: *How Democratic Is the American Constitution?* Copyright © 2002 by Yale University. Reprinted by permission of Yale University Press. *Polyarchy: Participation and Opposition.* Copyright © 1971 by Yale University. Reprinted by permission of Yale University Press.

Richard F. Fenno: *Home Style: House Members in Their Districts, 1ˢᵗ Edition,* © 2003, pp. 1–2, 8–10, 18, 24, 27–28. Reprinted by permission of Pearson Education, Inc., Upper Saddle River, NJ.

Richard Fox and Jennifer Lawless: Republished with permission of John Wiley and Sons, from "Gendered Perceptions and Political Candidacies: A Central Barrier to Women's Equality in Electoral Politics." *American Journal of Political Science*, 55: 59–73. Copyright © 2011; permission conveyed through Copyright Clearance Center, Inc.

Tracey E. George and Lee Epstein: "On the Nature of Supreme Court Decision Making," *American Political Science Review*, Vol. 86, No. 2, 1992. © American Political Science Association 1992. Reprinted by permission of Cambridge University Press.

Matt Guardino and Danny Hayes: "Foreign Voices, Party Cues, and U.S. Public Opinion about Military Action," *International Journal of Public Opinion Research*, 2017, Vol. 30, No. 3, pp. 1–11, by permission of World Association for Public Opinion Research.

Christopher Hammons: From "State Constitutions, Religious Protection, and Federalism," *University of St. Thomas Journal of Law and Public Policy*, Volume 7, Issue 2, Spring 2013. Reprinted by permission of the author.

Garrett Hardin: From "The Tragedy of the Commons" by Garrett Hardin, *Science*, Vol. 162, No. 3859 (December 13, 1968). Reprinted with permission from American Association for the Advancement of Science.

Eitan D. Hersh: From *Hacking the Electorate: How Campaigns Perceive Voters* (Cambridge University Press, 2015). Reprinted by permission of Cambridge University Press.

William G. Howell: Republished with permission of Princeton University Press, from *Power without Persuasion*, Copyright © 2003 Princeton University Press; permission conveyed through Copyright Clearance Center, Inc.

Donald Kinder and Cindy Kam: *Us Against Them: Ethnocentric Foundations of American Opinion* by Donald Kinder and Cindy Kam. Copyright © 2010 by The University of Chicago. Reprinted by permission of The University of Chicago Press.

Ken Kollman: *Outside Lobbying.* © 1998 Princeton University Press. Reprinted by permission of Princeton University Press.

Frances E. Lee: *Insecure Majorities: Congress and the Perpetual Campaign.* Copyright © 2016 by The University of Chicago. Reprinted by permission of The University of Chicago Press.

Jan E. Leighley and Jonathan Nagler: Republished with permission of Princeton University press, from "On the Representativeness of Voters" in *Who Votes Now?: Demographics Issues, Inequality, and Turnout in the United States,* © 2014 Princeton University Press; permission conveyed through Copyright Clearance Center, Inc.

Arthur Lupia and Mathew D. McCubbins: From *The Democratic Dilemma: Can Citizens Learn What They Need to Know?* Copyright © 1998 Cambridge University Press. Reprinted with the permission of Cambridge University Press.

Lilliana Mason: *Uncivil Agreement: How Politics Became Our Identity.* Copyright © 2018 by The University of Chicago. Reprinted by permission of The University of Chicago Press.

David Mayhew: *Congress: The Electoral Connection* by David Mayhew. Copyright © 1974 by Yale University. Reprinted by permission of Yale University Press.

Pamela J. Clouser McCann, Charles R. Shipan, and Craig Volden: "Top-Down Federalism: State Policy Responses to National Government Discussions," *Publius: The Journal of Federalism*, 2015, Vol. 45, No. 4, pp. 495–525, by permission of Oxford University Press.

Mathew D. McCubbins and Thomas Schwartz: Republished with permission of John Wiley and Sons, from "Congressional Oversight Overlooked: Police Patrols versus Fire Alarms," *The American Journal of Political Science*, Vol. 28, No. 1, 1984; permission conveyed through Copyright Clearance Center, Inc.

Suzanne Mettler: *The Submerged State: How Invisible Government Policies Undermine American Democracy* by Suzanne Mettler. Copyright © 2011 by The University of Chicago. Reprinted by permission of The University of Chicago Press.

Susan Moffitt: *Making Public Policy: Participatory Bureaucracy in American Democracy* by Susan Moffitt. Copyright © 2014 Cambridge University Press. Reprinted with the permission of Cambridge University Press.

Richard E. Neustadt: From PRESIDENTIAL POWER AND THE MODERN PRESIDENTS: The Politics of Leadership from Roosevelt to Reagan by Richard E. Neustadt. Copyright © 1990 by Richard E. Neustadt. Reprinted with the permission of The Free Press, a division of Simon & Schuster, Inc. All rights reserved.

Mancur Olson, Jr.: "A Theory of Groups and Organizations" reprinted by permission of the publisher from *The Logic of Collective Action: Public Goods and the Theory of Groups* by Mancur Olson, pp. 5–48, Cambridge, Mass.: Harvard University Press, Copyright © 1965, 1971 by the President and Fellows of Harvard College.

Benjamin I. Page and Martin Gilens: *Democracy in America?: What Has Gone Wrong and What We Can Do About It.* Copyright © 2017 by The University of Chicago. Reprinted by permission of The University of Chicago Press.

Hanna F. Pitkin: From *The Concept of Representation*, by Hanna F. Pitkin, © 1972 by the Regents of the University of California. Published by the University of California Press.

William Riker: "Chapter 6: Is the Federal Bargain Worth Keeping?" from *Federalism: Origin, Operation, Significance*. Reprinted by permission of the Estate of William Riker.

Corey Robin: THE REACTIONARY MIND: CONSERVATISM FROM EDMUND BURKE TO DONALD TRUMP 2ND EDITION by Robin (2017) pp. 239–245, 253–254, 258–260, 265, 306–313. By permission of Oxford University Press, USA.

Gerald N. Rosenberg: *The Hollow Hope: Can Courts Bring about Social Change?* by Gerald N. Rosenberg. Copyright © 1991, 2008 by The University of Chicago. Reprinted by permission of The University of Chicago Press.

Eric Schickler: Republished with permission of Princeton University Press, from "Introduction" in *Racial Realignment: The Transformation of American Liberalism, 1932–1965*, © 2016 Princeton University Press; permission conveyed through Copyright Clearance Center, Inc.

James A. Stimson: From *Tides of Consent: How Public Opinion Shapes American Politics*, Second Edition (Cambridge University Press, 2015). Reprinted by permission of Cambridge University Press.

Michael Tesler: *Post-Racial or Most-Racial: Race and Politics in the Obama Era*. Copyright © 2016 by The University of Chicago. Reprinted by permission of the University of Chicago Press.

James Q. Wilson: *Bureaucracy: What Government Agencies Do and Why They Do It* by Wilson, James Q. Reproduced with permission of BASIC BOOKS via Copyright Clearance Center.

Janelle S. Wong, Karthick Ramakrishnan, Taeku Lee, and Jane Junn: Republished with permission of Russell Sage Foundation Press, from *Asian American Political Participation: Emerging Constituents and Their Political Identities*. Pp. 152, 161–166, 177–179. © 2011 Russell Sage Foundation; permission conveyed through Copyright Clearance Center, Inc.

John R. Zaller: From *The Nature and Origins of Mass Opinion*. Copyright © 1992 Cambridge University Press. Reprinted with the permission of Cambridge University Press.